ENCYCLOPEDIA OF
RACE
and
CRIME

Editorial Board

ENCYCLOPEDIA OF
RACE
and
CRIME

Editors
HELEN TAYLOR GREENE
Texas Southern University

SHAUN L. GABBIDON
Pennsylvania State University, Harrisburg

1

SAGE

Los Angeles | London | New Delhi
Singapore | Washington DC

A SAGE Reference Publication

For information:

 SAGE Publications, Inc.
2455 Teller Road
Thousand Oaks, California 91320
E-mail: order@sagepub.com

SAGE Publications Ltd.
1 Oliver's Yard
55 City Road
London EC1Y 1SP
United Kingdom

SAGE Publications India Pvt. Ltd.
B 1/I 1 Mohan Cooperative Industrial Area
Mathura Road, New Delhi 110 044
India

SAGE Publications Asia-Pacific Pte. Ltd.
33 Pekin Street #02-01
Far East Square
Singapore 048763

Printed in the United States of America.

Library of Congress Cataloging-in-Publication Data

Encyclopedia of race and crime / editors, Helen Taylor Greene, Shaun L. Gabbidon.
    p. cm.
Includes bibliographical references and index.
ISBN 978-1-4129-5085-5 (cloth)
1. Crime and race—United States—Encyclopedias. 2. Criminal justice, Administration of—United States—Encyclopedias. 3. Discrimination in criminal justice administration—United States—Encyclopedias. 4. Minorities—United States—Encyclopedias. I. Greene, Helen Taylor, 1949– II. Gabbidon, Shaun L., 1967–

HV6789.E43 2009
364.973089—dc22   2008045849

This book is printed on acid-free paper.

09 10 11 12 13 10 9 8 7 6 5 4 3 2 1

Publisher:	Rolf A. Janke
Assistant to the Publisher:	Michele Thompson
Acquisitions Editor:	Jim Brace-Thompson
Developmental Editor:	Diana E. Axelsen
Reference Systems Manager:	Leticia Gutierrez
Reference Systems Coordinator:	Laura Notton
Production Editor:	Tracy Buyan
Copy Editors:	Colleen B. Brennan, Pam Suwinsky
Typesetter:	C&M Digitals (P) Ltd.
Proofreaders:	Kevin Gleason, Andrea Martin
Indexer:	Joan Shapiro
Cover Designer:	Bryan Fishman
Marketing Manager:	Amberlyn McKay

Contents

Volume 1

Volume 2

List of Entries

Reader's Guide

The Reader's Guide is provided to assist readers in locating entries on related topics. It classifies entries into 14 general topical categories: (1) Biographies, (2) Cases, (3) Concepts and Theories, (4) Corrections, (5) Courts, (6) Drugs, (7) Juvenile Justice, (8) Media, (9) Organizations, (10) Police, (11) Public Policy, (12) Race Riots, (13) Specific Populations, and (14) Violence and Crime.

Biographies

Abu-Jamal, Mumia
Bonger, Willem Adriaan
Brown, Lee P.
Bully-Cummings, Ella
Byrd, James, Jr.
Cochran, Johnnie
Davis, Angela
Du Bois, W. E. B.
Ferguson, Colin
Frazier, E. Franklin
Goetz, Bernard
Harvard, Beverly
Higginbotham, A. Leon, Jr.
Houston, Charles Hamilton
Jackson, George
King, Rodney
Mann, Coramae
McVeigh, Timothy
Peltier, Leonard
Pictou-Aquash, Anna Mae
Thomas, Clarence
Till, Emmett
Walker, Zachariah
Ward, Benjamin
Wells-Barnett, Ida B.
Wilson, Genarlow
Work, Monroe Nathan

Cases

Batson v. Kentucky
Brown v. City of Oneonta
Brown v. Mississippi
Castaneda v. Partida
Coker v. Georgia
Dred Scott Case
Duke University Assault Case
Escobedo v. Illinois
Furman v. Georgia
Gregg v. Georgia
Illinois v. Wardlow
In re Gault
Jena 6
Johnson v. California
Kennedy v. Louisiana
Kimbrough v. United States
Mapp v. Ohio
Martinsville Seven
Maryland v. Wilson
McCleskey v. Kemp
Miranda v. Arizona
Missouri v. Celia, a Slave
Moore v. Dempsey
Norris v. Alabama
O. J. Simpson Case
Oliphant v. Suquamish Indian Tribe
Powell v. Alabama
Roper v. Simmons
State v. Soto
Tennessee v. Garner
Terry v. Ohio
Till, Emmett
United States v. Antelope
United States v. Armstrong
United States v. Booker

Black Panther Party
Brown Berets
Bureau of Indian Affairs
Guardians, The (Police Associations)
Historically Black Colleges and Universities
John Jay College Center on Race, Crime and
    Justice
Ku Klux Klan
LatinoJustice PRLDEF
League of United Latin American Citizens
NAACP Legal Defense Fund
National African American Drug Policy Coalition
National American Indian Court Judges
    Association
National Association for the Advancement of
    Colored People (NAACP)
National Association of Blacks in Criminal
    Justice
National Commission on Law Observance and
    Enforcement
National Council of La Raza
National Criminal Justice Association
National Native American Law Enforcement
    Association
National Organization of Black Law
    Enforcement Executives
National Tribal Justice Resource Center
National Urban League
Nation of Islam
Northeastern University Institute on Race and
    Justice
100 Blacks in Law Enforcement Who Care
Sentencing Project, The
Southern Poverty Law Center
Universal Negro Improvement Association
U.S. Department of Justice, Office of Civil Rights
Vera Institute of Justice
W. Haywood Burns Institute for Juvenile Justice
    Fairness and Equity

Police

Boston Gun Project
COINTELPRO and Covert Operations
Disproportionate Arrests
DNA Profiling
Police Accountability
Police Action, Citizens' Preferences
Police Corruption
Police Use of Force

Profiling, Ethnic: Use by Police and Homeland
    Security
Profiling, Mass Murderer
Profiling, Racial: Historical and Contemporary
    Perspectives
Profiling, Serial Killer
Rampart Investigation
Slave Patrols
Statistics and Race and Crime: Accessing Data
    Online (Appendix B)
Tasers
Tribal Police

Public Policy

Anti–Drug Abuse Acts
Chinese Exclusion Act
Christopher Commission
Dyer Bill
Gang Injunctions
Hate Crimes Statistics Act
Immigration Legislation
Immigration Policy
Indian Civil Rights Act
Indian Self-Determination Act
Ku Klux Klan Act
Mandatory Minimums
Mediation in Criminal Justice
Mollen Commission
National Commission on Law Observation and
    Enforcement
No-Fly Lists
Omnibus Crime Control and Safe Streets Act
Operation Wetback
President's Commission on Law Enforcement and
    Administration of Justice
President's Initiative on Race
Racial Justice Act
Three Strikes Laws
Tuskegee Syphilis Study
War on Terror
Willie Bosket Law

Race Riots

Chicago Race Riot of 1919
Detroit Riot of 1967
Elaine Massacre of 1919 (Phillips County,
    Arkansas)
Harlem Race Riot of 1935

Los Angeles Race Riot of 1965
Los Angeles Race Riots of 1992
Miami Riot of 1980
Race Riots
Rosewood, Florida, Race Riot of 1923
Tulsa, Oklahoma, Race Riot of 1921
Zoot Suit Riots

Specific Populations

African American Gangs
African Americans
Arab Americans
Asian American Gangs
Asian Americans
Consumer Racial Profiling
Dehumanization of Blacks
European Americans
Female Gangs
Human Trafficking
Immigrants and Crime
Jamaican Posse
Japanese Internment
Latina/o/s
Latino Gangs
Mara Salvatrucha (MS-13)
Mariel Cubans
Militias
Minutemen
Model Minorities
Native Americans
Native Americans: Culture, Identity, and the
   Criminal Justice System
Native Americans and Substance Abuse
Prison Gangs
Rastafarians
Religious Minorities
Statistics and Race and Crime: Accessing Data
   Online (Appendix B)
Violent Females
White Gangs
White Supremacists
Wilmington Ten

Violence and Crime

Anti-Semitism
Central Park Jogger
Child Abuse
D.C. Sniper
Domestic Violence
Domestic Violence, African Americans
Domestic Violence, Latina/o/s
Domestic Violence, Native Americans
Elder Abuse
Gambling
Gringo Justice
Hate Crimes
HIV/AIDS
Homicide Seriousness Dyad
Immigrants and Crime
Interracial Crime
Intraracial Crime
Lynching
Native American Massacres
Opium Wars
Organized Crime
Racial Conflict
Sixteenth Street Baptist Church Bombing
Skinheads
Slave Rebellions
Slavery and Violence
Statistics and Race and Crime: Accessing Data
   Online (Appendix B)
Stop Snitching Campaign
Victim and Witness Intimidation
Victimization, African American
Victimization, Asian American
Victimization, Latina/o
Victimization, Native American
Victimization, White
Victim Services
Vigilantism
Violence Against Girls
Violence Against Women
Violent Crime
Wilding
Zoot Suit Riots

About the Editors

Helen Taylor Greene is Professor and Interim Chair of the Administration of Justice Department in the Barbara Jordan–Mickey Leland School of Public Affairs at Texas Southern University in Houston, Texas. She authored two of the earliest compilations of contributions by Black authors to the study of criminology and criminal justice. Dr. Greene has also authored and coauthored peer-reviewed articles and book chapters on Black perspectives on crime and criminal justice, delinquency prevention, police brutality, police use of deadly force, community policing, and women in policing. She has coauthored and coedited several books, including *African American Classics in Criminology and Criminal Justice* (2002), *Race and Crime* (2005, 2009), and *Race, Crime, and Justice: A Reader* (2005). Dr. Greene was the corecipient of the Coramae Richey Mann Award for outstanding scholarship in the area of race, ethnicity, and crime in 2005 and recipient of the Coramae Richey Mann Leadership Award in 2007.

Shaun L. Gabbidon is Professor of Criminal Justice in the School of Public Affairs at Penn State Harrisburg. In addition to having authored numerous peer-reviewed articles, he is the author or editor of seven books. His most recent books are *Criminological Perspectives on Race and Crime* (2007), *W. E. B. Du Bois on Crime and Justice: Laying the Foundations of Sociological Criminology* (2007), and the newly published *Race, Ethnicity, Crime, and Justice: An International Dilemma* (2010). Dr. Gabbidon also serves as editor of the State University of New York (SUNY) Press's *Race, Ethnicity, Crime, and Justice* book series and as coeditor of Routledge's *Criminology and Justice Studies* series. In 2005, he was the corecipient of the Coramae Richey Mann Award for outstanding scholarship in the area of race, ethnicity, and crime, and in 2007 he was the recipient of Penn State Harrisburg's Faculty Award for Excellence in Research and Scholarly Activity.

Contributors

Dwight Aarons
University of Tennessee

Reem Ali Abu-Lughod
California State University, Bakersfield

Terri M. Adams
Howard University

Efua Akoma
Virginia Polytechnic Institute

Heather Alaniz
University of Houston, Clear Lake

Frankie Y. Bailey
State University of New York at Albany

Maldine Bailey
Nova Southeastern University

Tiffiney Y. Barfield-Cottledge
University of North Texas–Dallas Campus

Dawn Beichner
Illinois State University

Ellen H. Belcher
John Jay College of Criminal Justice

Joanne Belknap
University of Colorado

Scott Belshaw
Prairie View A&M University

Mark T. Berg
University of Missouri–St. Louis

Ronald J. Berger
University of Wisconsin–Whitewater

Lindsey Bergeron
North Dakota State University

Robert L. Bing III
University of Texas at Arlington

Donna M. Bishop
Northeastern University

Ashley G. Blackburn
University of North Texas

Robert M. Bohm
University of Central Florida

Kendra Bowen
Indiana University of Pennsylvania

Lorenzo M. Howell
Fayetteville State University

Andrew Bradford
Indiana University of Pennsylvania

Michele P. Bratina
Indiana University of Pennsylvania

Todd E. Bricker
Shippensburg University

Avi Brisman
Emory University

Willie Brooks, Jr.
University of Houston, Victoria

Patricia L. Brougham
Salem International University

Michael P. Brown
Ball State University

Gloria J. Browne-Marshall
John Jay College of Criminal Justice

Christopher Bruell
Northeastern University

Alison S. Burke
Indiana University of Pennsylvania

Catherine E. Burton
The Citadel

Frank Butler
La Salle University

Sophia Buxton
Hampton University

Lisa M. Carter
Indiana University of Pennsylvania

Abraham Castillo
University of Houston, Clear Lake

David R. Champion
Slippery Rock University

Elsa Y. Chen
Santa Clara University

Liza Chowdhury
*Rutgers, The State University
of New Jersey*

Jennifer Christian
*Indiana University,
Bloomington*

Diane Cismowski
*Rutgers, The State University
of New Jersey*

Shelly Clevenger
*Indiana University of
Pennsylvania*

Michael T. Coates
*Institute for the Study of
Violent Groups*

John K. Cochran
University of South Florida

Tyrell Connor
Hampton University

Charles Corley
Michigan State University

George Coroian
*Indiana University of
Pennsylvania*

Allison M. Cotton
*Metropolitan State College of
Denver*

Amanda K. Cox
*Indiana University of
Pennsylvania*

Ronald O. Craig
Troy University

Tommy Curry
Southern Illinois University

Douglas J. Dallier
Florida State University

Alejandro del Carmen
University of Texas at Arlington

Jo-Ann Della Giustina
Bridgewater State College

Michael DeValve
Fayetteville State University

Cherie Dawson Edwards
Eastern Kentucky University

Helen Eigenberg
*University of Tennessee at
Chattanooga*

Christine Eith
Towson University

Traqina Quarles Emeka
*University of Houston,
Downtown*

Peggy A. Engram
*University of Houston,
Downtown*

Monica Erling
University of Wisconsin

Doug Evans
*Indiana University,
Bloomington*

Amy Farrell
Northeastern University

Elizabeth M. Fathman
Saint Louis University

Raúl Fernández-Calienes
*St. Thomas University School
of Law*

Marianne Fisher-Giorlando
Grambling State University

Benjamin Fleury-Steiner
University of Delaware

Allison J. Foley
*University of Colorado at
Boulder*

Antonio Ford
*University of Houston, Clear
Lake*

Rebecca D. Foster
University of North Texas

Kelli Frakes
ITT Technical Institute

Teresa Francis
Central Washington University

Nadine Frederique
University of Maryland

Marvin D. Free, Jr.
*University of Wisconsin–
Whitewater*

Brent Funderburk
*Indiana University,
Bloomington*

Huan Gao
*California State University,
Stanislaus*

Tammy S. Garland
*University of Tennessee at
Chattanooga*

Philip Gasper
*Madison Area Technical
College*

Gilbert Geis
*University of California,
Irvine*

Daniel E. Georges-Abeyie
Texas Southern University

Adrianne Gilbert
Hampton University

Cynthia Golembeski
University of Wisconsin

Sean Goodison
*University of Maryland–College
Park*

Jennifer L. Gossett
*Indiana University of
Pennsylvania*

Gilton Christopher Grange
Bridgebuilder Consortium

Megan L. Gray
Sam Houston State University

Shani P. Gray
Valdosta State University

Tanya Greathouse
University of Colorado

Alfonzo Greenidge
Mountain View College

Sean Patrick Griffin
Penn State Abington

Timothy Griffin
University of Nevada, Reno

Georgen Guerrero
Sam Houston State University

Vikas Gumbhir
Gonzaga University

Hong-Le Ha
University of Houston, Clear Lake

Kimetta R. Hairston
Penn State Harrisburg

Anne-Marie Hakstian
Salem State College

Ralph A. Hamlett
Brevard College

Phillip J. Hammons
University of Arkansas at Little Rock

Nicole Hardy
University of Houston, Clear Lake

Kylo-Patrick R. Hart
Plymouth State University

Jennifer Hartsfield
University of Oklahoma

Rebecca Hayes
University of Florida

Ella Henderson
University of Houston, Clear Lake

Geraldine R. Henderson
Northwestern University

Howard Henderson
Sam Houston State University

Martha L. Henderson
The Citadel

Kendrick Henley
Hampton University

George E. Higgins
University of Louisville

Carly M. Hilinski
Grand Valley State University

Elizabeth Hines
University of North Carolina–Wilmington

Marigny Hluza
University of Houston, Clear Lake

Rebecca J. Howell
University of Alabama

Jennifer L. Huck
Indiana University of Pennsylvania

Don Hummer
Penn State Harrisburg

Li-Ching Hung
Mississippi State University

Scott Ingram
Indiana University, Bloomington

Robert Irving
University of Houston, Clear Lake

Jessica James
Wesley College

Richard Janikowski
University of Memphis

Michael J. Jenkins
Police Institute

Charles E. Jones
Georgia State University

Marlyn J. Jones
California State University, Sacramento

Nikki Jones
University of California, Santa Barbara

Ebone' Joseph
Hampton University

Lindsey Kane
University of Houston, Clear Lake

David Kcys
New Mexico State University

Jonathan Kramer
Kutztown University of Pennsylvania

Kenneth A. Lachlan
Boston College

Jennifer L. Lanterman
Rutgers, The State University of New Jersey

Misha S. Lars
John Jay College of Criminal Justice

Jennifer Lasswell
Indiana University of Pennsylvania

Tiffany Latham
Hampton University

Kristin Lavin
Villanova University

John Lemmon
Shippensburg University

Eric Yang Liu
Baylor University

Keith Gregory Logan
Kutztown University

Melissa A. Logue
Saint Joseph's University

Lucien X. Lombardo
Old Dominion University

Billy Long
Indiana University, Southeast

Marilyn D. Lovett
South Carolina State University

Arthur J. Lurigio
Loyola University Chicago

Joan Luxenburg
*University of Central
    Oklahoma*

Michael J. Lynch
University of South Florida

David A. Mackcy
Plymouth State University

Alison Marganski
*Rutgers, The State University
    of New Jersey*

Favian Alejandro Martín
Penn State Harrisburg

Damian J. Martinez
*Rutgers, The State University
    of New Jersey*

Ramiro Martinez, Jr.
Florida International University

Ryan B. Martz
Michigan State University

Kristy N. Matsuda
University of California, Irvine

James P. Mayes
North Carolina A&T

Darrell McCloud
*University of Houston, Clear
    Lake*

Elizabeth H. McConnell
*University of Houston, Clear
    Lake*

John A. McConnell
*University of Houston, Clear
    Lake*

Jack McDevitt
Northeastern University

Zina McGee
Hampton University

Karen McGuffee
*University of Tennessee at
    Chattanooga*

Kenethia L. McIntosh
Fayetteville State University

Jerome McKean
Ball State University

Joseph B. McSherry
*University of Arkansas at Little
    Rock*

Stephen E. Medvec
Holy Family University

Jon'a F. Meyer
*Rutgers, The State University
    of New Jersey*

Vincent E. Miles
Thaddeus Stevens College

Carla Miller
*Virginia Polytechnic Institute
    and State University*

J. Mitchell Miller
*University of Texas at San
    Antonio*

Debbie Mills
*University of Houston,
    Clear Lake*

David R. Montague
*University of Arkansas at Little
    Rock*

Patrice K. Morris
*Rutgers, The State University
    of New Jersey*

Lisa R. Muftić
University of North Texas

Bahiyyah M. Muhammad
*Rutgers, The State University
    of New Jersey*

Robert Muhammad
The Nation of Islam

Ed A. Muñoz
University of Wyoming

Denise D. Nation
Winston-Salem State University

Lorenda A. Naylor
University of Baltimore

Alisa Neilan
*University of Houston, Clear
    Lake*

Matthew F. Nichter
*University of Wisconsin–
    Madison*

Gwendelyn S. Nisbett
University of Oklahoma

Krystal E. Noga
*Central Washington
    University*

Rhonda Y. Ntepp
*Metropolitan State College of
    Denver*

Stephanie M. Oakley
*Institute for the Study of
    Violent Groups*

Evaristus Obinyan
Albany State University

Dan Okada
Sacramento State University

J. Michael Olivero
Central Washington University

Chibueze W. Onwudiwe
University of Teesside

Ihekwoaba D. Onwudiwe
Texas Southern University

Leanne Owen
Holy Family University

Vivian Pacheco
*Rutgers, The State University
of New Jersey*

Wilson R. Palacios
University of South Florida

Diana Papademas
*State University of New York
College at Old Westbury*

Rhonda Pavlu
*University of Houston, Clear
Lake*

Brian K. Payne
Georgia State University

Terrylynn Pearlman
*Indiana University of
Pennsylvania*

Tracy S. Penn
Gardere Law Firm

Wendy Perkins
*AMP Center for Crime Prevention
& Community Wellness*

Rachel Philofsky
University of Maryland

Monica B. Pinalez
*University of Houston, Clear
Lake*

Danny Pirtle
Holy Family University

Alexander W. Pisciotta
Kutztown University

William C. Plouffe, Jr.
Kutztown University

Katherine Polzer
Texas Christian University

Margarita Poteyeva
University of Delaware

Hillary Potter
*University of Colorado at
Boulder*

Pamela Preston
Penn State Schuylkill

Byron E. Price
Texas Southern University

Todd F. Prough
Northeastern University

Doris Marie Provine
Arizona State University

Charles E. Reasons
Central Washington University

Sharon RedHawk Love
Ball State University

David A. Rembert
Sam Houston State University

Callie Marie Rennison
*University of Missouri–St.
Louis*

Eran Reya
KMBA Enterprises, LLC

Stephen K. Rice
Seattle University

Kaylene A. Richards-Ekeh
*California State University,
Sacramento*

Jeffrey Ian Ross
University of Baltimore

Lee E. Ross
University of Central Florida

Tawandra L. Rowell
University of Pennsylvania

Mitch Ruesink
*Waukesha County Technical
College*

Jim Ruiz
Penn State Harrisburg

Leila Sadeghi
*Rutgers, The State University
of New Jersey*

Laurie J. Samuel
*Metropolitan (DC) Police
Department*

Kathryn Scarborough
Eastern Kentucky University

Amie R. Scheidegger
Brevard College

Dorothy Moses Schulz
*John Jay College of Criminal
Justice*

Julia E. Selman-Ayetey
King's College London

Martha L. Shockey-Eckles
Saint Louis University

Elithet Silva-Martínez
University of Iowa

Phillippia Simmons
*University of Houston, Clear
Lake*

Barbara Sims
Penn State Harrisburg

Yvonne Sims
Penn State Harrisburg

Sherry Lynn Skaggs
University of Delaware

Cary Stacy Smith
Mississippi State University

Jaclyn Smith
National Institute of Justice

Jacqueline Smith-Mason
Virginia Commonwealth University

Catherine Stern
LaGuardia Community College

Daniel P. Stevens
The Citadel

Eric A. Stewart
Florida State University

Philip Matthew Stinson
Indiana University of Pennsylvania

Jacob I. Stowell
University of Massachusetts Lowell

Ivan Y. Sun
University of Delaware

Sam Swindell
Sam Houston State University

Shenique S. Thomas
Rutgers, The State University of New Jersey

Aaron Thompson
Eastern Kentucky University

Sherrise Y. Truesdale-Moore
Minnesota State University, Mankato

Heather R. Tubman-Carbone
Rutgers, The State University of New Jersey

Deonna S. Turner
University of Houston, Clear Lake

Craig D. Uchida
Justice and Security Strategies

Alana Van Gundy-Yoder
Miami University

PJ Verrecchia
York College of Pennsylvania

Maria R. Volpe
John Jay College of Criminal Justice

Courtney A. Wade
North Dakota State University

Randy Wagner
Portland Community College

Jeffery T. Walker
University of Arkansas at Little Rock

Isis N. Walton
Virginia State University

Geoff Ward
University of California, Irvine

Judith Ann Warner
Texas A&M International University

Casey C. Watkins
University of Wyoming

Kelly Welch
Villanova University

Michael Welch
Rutgers, The State University of New Jersey

Jamie L. Weldon
Indiana University of Pennsylvania

Elvira White
Fayetteville State University

Kideste M. Wilder-Bonner
John Jay College of Criminal Justice

Patricia Wilkerson
University of Arkansas at Little Rock

Jennifer Williams
University of Houston, Clear Lake

Jerome D. Williams
University of Texas at Austin

L. Susan Williams
Kansas State University

Michael Williams
Indiana University of Pennsylvania

Robert W. Williams
Bennett College

Tonya Y. Willingham
Federal Defender Office

Keith A. Wilmot
Florida Atlantic University

Alese C. Wooditch
Penn State Harrisburg

Benjamin S. Wright
University of Baltimore

Yuning Wu
University of Delaware

LaSheila S. Yates
Southern Illinois University

Julie Yingling
Villanova University

Lisa Anne Zilney
Montclair State University

Introduction

The Field

Criminology and criminal justice involve the scientific study of crime, criminals, and the criminal justice system. Interest in the problem of crime began centuries ago, and in the 18th century, after several European countries experienced social unrest, writings about crime began to appear. During the 19th century, social scientists studied social problems, including crime and responses to it. Interest in criminology in the United States began in the late 19th century and flourished in the 20th century. Initially there were two major areas in the study of criminology: theoretical and applied criminology. Theoretical criminology included the etiology of crime, theories of criminality, typologies of crime and criminals, and the extent of crime. Applied criminology included the study of justice agencies and processes, often referred to as criminal justice, as well as the law. Today, the terms *criminology* and *criminal justice* are often used interchangeably, and the dichotomy between the two is less clear. For example, some of the subject matter in many criminology and criminal justice textbooks often overlaps although the original foci of each remain.

During the late 20th and early 21st centuries, the field of criminology has grown nationally and internationally. Today there are hundreds of undergraduate and graduate programs in the United States. Criminology is an interdisciplinary field of study with contributions to the body of knowledge by economists, historians, political scientists, psychologists, sociologists, and other scholars. The study of criminology and criminal justice has expanded considerably and includes administration of justice, comparative studies, convict criminology, critical analyses, feminist criminology, prisoner reentry, homeland security, juvenile justice, policy analyses, race and crime, and terrorism.

Rationale for the Encyclopedia

The study of race and crime has a long history in the discipline of criminology and the study of criminal justice. In the 19th century Cesare Lombroso, an Italian positivist considered by many to be the father of criminology, suggested that crime was a product of biological factors, including race (Lombroso, 1876/1911). In the early 20th century, some American scholars, including Kellor (1901), Du Bois (1904), Work (1913), Sellin (1928), Moses (1936), Shaw and McKay (1942), and Frazier (1949), countered the biological perspective by noting how social, economic, and political conditions contribute to crime, regardless of race. Early criminology texts devoted whole chapters to race and crime that not only presented crime figures but also sought to explain the trends related to race and crime (Gabbidon & Greene, 2001). At that time, race was a much broader concept that focused on minorities, especially Blacks, and took into consideration the ethnicity of White immigrants. Even so, there was not a significant emphasis on the topic (Bonger, 1943/1969) until the last quarter of the 20th century, when race and crime became a recognized specialty area of study within the field (Gabbidon, 2007; Gabbidon & Greene, 2009; Walker, Spohn, & DeLone, 2007). In fact, many criminology and criminal justice programs now either require or offer a course on race and crime as an elective.

Race has historically featured, and continues to feature, prominently in reporting on crime and justice within the United States. Incidents like the alleged rape of a Black female North Carolina

Central University student by (White male) members of the Duke University Lacrosse Team in Durham, North Carolina; the Jena 6 incident in Jena, Louisiana; the Tulia, Texas, drug arrests; the Rodney King beating; the O. J. Simpson trials in the 1990s and in 2008; and more recent racial profiling incidents remind us of the race and crime nexus.

These historical and contemporary issues signaled the need for a comprehensive compilation of relevant facts and information on topics related to race and crime and the crime and justice experiences of racial/ethnic groups in the United States. Also needed was an alternative source of information other than the media that can better explain and objectively analyze complex issues related to race and crime.

The encyclopedia is designed to provide reference material and an introduction to historical and contemporary race and crime topics. It supports study, research, and instruction by presenting brief overviews and references to more in-depth presentations in other published sources. This volume will give undergraduate and graduate students, laypersons, professionals, researchers, and scholars access to information on race and crime topics that heretofore has been difficult to find in one place. Such a volume will provide users with state-of-the-art knowledge on the topic.

Content and Organization

The encyclopedia includes entries related to race and crime that are organized in the Reader's Guide as follows:

Biographies

Cases

Concepts and Theories

Corrections

Courts

Drugs

Juvenile Justice

Media

Organizations

Police

Public Policy

Race Riots

Specific Populations

Violence and Crime

Each entry includes a definition of the term and explains how it is related to race and crime. The entries also provide cross-references to other entries that likely provide additional information on the topic. Each entry closes with a Further Readings section that provides references to additional scholarly sources on the topic.

It should be noted that the encyclopedia uses a variety of terms to describe racial and ethnic minorities. For example, it is well established that the term *race* refers to the classification of distinctive groups. In the United States, the major racial groups are Whites (also referred to as Caucasians), African Americans (also referred to as Blacks), Native Americans (also referred to as American Indians), and Asian Americans. The term *ethnicity* refers to ethnic groups that are believed to be identifiable less by race and more by culture and place of origin. For example, the largest ethnic group in America is Latinos (also referred to as Hispanics). Latinos come from the Caribbean and Latin American countries. Arab Americans represent another ethnic group that is well established in the United States.

We have followed the American Psychological Association's policy of capitalizing the terms *Black* and *White* when used to refer to race/ethnicity. We have used the term *Latina/o/s* as the plural form in entry titles; however, in the text of entries themselves, we have used the shorter form *Latinos* for typographical simplicity.

It is important to pause here to remind readers that both race and ethnicity are social constructs or terms that were created to note the differences among human groups. At the moment, scientists have found that all racial and ethnic groups have the same general biological makeup, with only 1% variation among groups. As such, the classification of humans based on race and ethnicity is severely flawed. For example, how would we classify a naturalized citizen who immigrated to the United States from another country? Should we classify him or her as African American just because his or her skin is black?

By doing so, we would not be adequately accounting for his or her unique experience. The point here is that not only the classification but also the perceptions that attach to the classifications are problematic. Therefore, someone dark-skinned from Africa might evoke a different response from someone dark-skinned from India. Why? Because even a social construct has the power to influence the way people are perceived. In sum, although this encyclopedia uses these terms, readers should consider the limitations and dangers of doing so.

Appendixes: Statistics on Race and Crime

Many of the entries in the encyclopedia include statistical data on race and crime. We have included two appendixes to help readers locate and understand this information.

Locating and Interpreting Statistical Data on Race and Crime

Two programs administered by the U.S. Department of Justice are the major sources of federal data on crime, including statistical data by racial/ethnic groups: the Uniform Crime Reporting (UCR) Program and the National Crime Victimization Survey (NCVS). Because the UCR and NCVS programs are conducted for different purposes, use different methods, and focus on somewhat different aspects of crime, the information they produce together provides a more comprehensive panorama of the nation's crime problem than either could produce alone. Appendix A provides a brief history and overview of these programs and describes the kind of information available on race and crime.

Websites With Data on Race and Crime

Appendix B contains URLs and detailed instructions on accessing statistical data from both governmental sources and various nongovernmental organizations. Users of the electronic version of the encyclopedia will be able to click on these links to go directly to the relevant websites in order to obtain the most recent data available online. This information will enable readers to explore and evaluate empirical evidence on a variety of topics related to race and crime, including the following:

Arrests
Contacts between police and the public
Death penalty
Drugs and crime
Gang membership
Hate crimes
Homicide trends in the United States
Juvenile justice
Prison populations
Racial profiling
Victimization

How the Encyclopedia Was Created

Creation of the encyclopedia involved several stages, including identifying topics, choosing headwords/entries, recruiting authors, and reviewing and editing. The preliminary list of headwords was developed by the volume editors with the assistance of Diana Axelsen, the developmental editor. Review Board members were asked to review the initial list and make revisions and suggestions via e-mail and at a meeting with the editors at the 2006 annual meeting of the American Society of Criminology. Additional headwords were suggested by contributors and as a result of emerging issues like the Jena 6 and the Supreme Court's ruling in *Kennedy v. Louisiana*.

The methods used for identifying authors included requests for contributors sent to listservs for the Division of People of Color and Crime and the Division of Women and Crime of the American Society of Criminology, the Minorities and Women's Section, regional organizations of the Academy of Criminal Justice Sciences, and the Association of Doctoral Programs in Criminology and Criminal Justice. Review Board members were also asked to identify contributors and to distribute information about the encyclopedia at their institution and among their colleagues elsewhere. The *2007 Directory of Minority Criminologists* was also a valuable resource for identifying contributors. Contributors also were identified during attendance at the annual meetings of the American Society of Criminology and the Academy of Criminal Justice Sciences and by perusing the conference programs.

Reviewing and editing of the entries began with assigning a reviewer to read, edit, and provide feedback to the author of each entry. Entries were assigned to editors and Editorial Board members according to their expertise in criminology and criminal justice. After the initial review and editing, the entry was processed through Sage's developmental editor.

Acknowledgments

The authors would like to thank the Review Board members, Marvin D. Free, Delores Jones-Brown, Ramiro Martinez, Jr., Everette B. Penn, and Vernetta D. Young, for their assistance in both locating and reviewing entries. Countless members of the American Society of Criminology, the Academy of Criminal Justice Sciences, and the Association of Doctoral Programs in Criminology and Criminal Justice were also instrumental in helping us secure the contributors. We are especially thankful for Hillary Potter (DPCC Listserv) and Lorenzo Boyd (Minorities and Women Listserv) for repeatedly posting our messages concerning the encyclopedia. Many of our colleagues coauthored entries with graduate students, providing those students with an opportunity to experience both research and publishing. We especially thank Everette Penn and Zina McGee for working with so many of their graduate students on several entries. Elycia Daniel, our managing editor, is thanked for helping us to manage numerous tasks that the project entailed. Of course, we are grateful for the knowledgeable contributors who took time away from their busy academic (and personal) lives to write entries. We have learned so much from your work!

At Sage, we want to thank Jerry Westby for suggesting that we consider doing an encyclopedia on race and crime. Jerry put us in touch with Jim Brace-Thompson, who was supportive of the project from the beginning. Along the way, his continued positive encouragement kept us going. We also thank Laura Notton and Leticia Gutierrez for their technical assistance. A special acknowledgment is reserved for Diana Axelsen, for her invaluable assistance and for keeping us motivated to complete the final stages of the project. Thanks, Diana!

Helen would like to thank her family and colleagues for inspiration during this project. I also thank Ms. Monica Freelon, Ms. Crystal Hadnott, and Ms. Lakesha Jones for their assistance. I am grateful for the privilege and experience of working with Dr. Gabbidon on this project.

Shaun would like to thank his family for putting up with him at the computer for long hours working on another book project! I also thank Dr. Greene for her leadership on this project. There is no doubt in my mind that this project would not have been completed without her devotion. Thanks, Helen! At Penn State Harrisburg, I continue to be grateful for the outstanding research support. I thank my graduate assistant Ms. Lisa Kim for her assistance with the appendixes.

Helen Taylor Greene and Shaun L. Gabbidon

References

Bonger, W. (1969). *Race and crime*. Montclair, NJ: Patterson Smith. (Original work published 1943)

Du Bois, W. E. B. (Ed.). (1904). *Some notes on Negro crime, particularly in Georgia*. Atlanta, GA: Atlanta University Press.

Frazier, E. F. (1949). *The Negro in the United States*. New York: Macmillan.

Gabbidon, S. L. (2007). *Criminological perspectives on race and crime*. New York: Routledge.

Gabbidon, S. L., & Greene, H. T. (2001). The presence of African American scholarship in early American criminology textbooks (1918–1960). *Journal of Criminal Justice Education, 12*, 301–310.

Gabbidon, S. L., & Greene, H. T. (2009). *Race and crime* (2nd ed.). Thousand Oaks, CA: Sage.

Kellor, F. A. (1901). The criminal Negro: I. A sociological study. *The Arena, 25*, 59–68.

Lombroso, C. (1911). *Criminal man*. New York: G. P. Putnam's Sons. (Original work published 1876)

Moses, E. R. (1936). Community factors in Negro delinquency. *Journal of Negro Education, 5*, 220–227.

Sellin, T. (1928). The Negro criminal: A statistical note. *Annals of the American Academy of Political and Social Sciences, 140*, 52–64.

Shaw, C., & McKay, H. D. (1942). *Juvenile delinquency in urban areas*. Chicago: University of Chicago Press.

Walker, S., Spohn, C., & DeLone, M. (2007). *The color of justice: Race, ethnicity, crime and justice in America* (4th ed.). Belmont, CA: Wadsworth.

Work, M. N. (1913). Negro criminality in the South. *Annals of the American Academy of Political and Social Sciences, 49*, 74–80.

ABU-JAMAL, MUMIA (1954–)

Mumia Abu-Jamal was born Wesley Cook on April 24, 1954, in Philadelphia, Pennsylvania. An award-winning African American journalist and political activist who has contributed to dozens of newspapers, written several books, and hosted his own radio show, Abu-Jamal is currently a prisoner serving a life sentence at Pennsylvania State Correctional Institution–Greene for the 1981 murder of a police officer, Daniel Faulkner. At the time of his arrest, Abu-Jamal was the president of the Philadelphia chapter of the Association of Black Journalists and was known as "the voice of the voiceless" as a result of his news broadcasts on numerous radio stations. Dubbed a political prisoner by some, including many activists and scholars, Abu-Jamal maintains his innocence of the crime for which he was convicted and has supporters across the nation and in many foreign countries. However, there are many who claim that justice was served and that Abu-Jamal is guilty of the crime and admitted to his guilt long ago. This entry briefly reviews the political life of Mumia Abu-Jamal as well as the crime for which he has been convicted and the current status of his case.

Abu-Jamal established his status as a political activist at an early age. At the age of 14, he took part in a protest against a rally for presidential candidate George Wallace and was subsequently arrested by Philadelphia police. The arrest did not deter him from further political activism, as he became one of the founding members of the Philadelphia chapter of the Black Panther Party, an African American organization founded with the goals of promoting civil rights and self-defense, in 1968. He furthered his work with the Black Panther Party in 1970, working at the Black Panther newspaper in Oakland, California, and returning to Philadelphia a short time later. Also during the 1970s, Abu-Jamal published a piece in which he openly criticized the Philadelphia police department as well as the administration of Mayor Frank Rizzo, the former police commissioner. These criticisms increased the hostility between Abu-Jamal and the Philadelphia police department. Abu-Jamal was fired from his broadcasting job in the late 1970s as a result of his activism and began working as a night-shift cab driver to support his family.

According to his own account, in the early morning hours of December 9, 1981, Abu-Jamal was driving his cab when he saw that his younger brother, William Cook, had been pulled over by Philadelphia police. There are conflicting claims about what happened when Abu-Jamal got out of his cab; however, the following sequence of events was accepted by the jury at Abu-Jamal's trial: Cook assaulted Officer Faulkner during the traffic stop and, consequently, Faulkner attempted to control Cook, at which point Abu-Jamal got out of his cab and shot Faulkner in the back. Though wounded, Faulkner was able to return fire, leaving Abu-Jamal seriously wounded. Abu-Jamal then shot Faulkner four more times at close range, fatally wounding the officer. Because of his injuries, Abu-Jamal was unable to leave the scene of the crime and was taken into custody by Philadelphia police. He was immediately taken to the hospital in order to receive treatment for his wounds. Several witnesses claimed that, while he was being treated, Abu-Jamal confessed to shooting Officer Faulkner. Police also claimed that the bullets found in Faulkner's brain were fired from Abu-Jamal's .38-caliber revolver.

Abu-Jamal, however, continues to claim that this sequence of events is incorrect. According to Abu-Jamal, he was sitting in his cab on December 9 when he heard gunshots and saw his brother standing in the street, staggering and dizzy. He claims that he was shot and beaten by a police officer and that someone else was responsible for the shooting death of Officer Faulkner. Abu-Jamal also maintains that he was beaten and tortured by police officers prior to receiving medical attention for his wounds.

Abu-Jamal was charged with first-degree murder and was represented by public defender Anthony Jackson at his June 1982 trial. The prosecution called a number of eyewitnesses who claimed that Abu-Jamal was the individual who shot Officer Faulkner. However, one eyewitness, who was never called to testify in the original trial, has since claimed that Abu-Jamal was not the gunman. The witness testified at a later date that police had torn up his original statement and forced him to sign another statement that implicated Abu-Jamal. Three additional witnesses claimed that, while being treated for his injuries at the hospital, Abu-Jamal admitted to shooting Officer Faulkner and expressed hope that the officer would die. Despite this, the original police report by Officer Gary Wakshul, who was with Abu-Jamal during his arrest and medical treatment, indicated that Abu-Jamal made no statement regarding Officer Faulkner and the shooting. At a later time, however, Officer Wakshul claimed that he had heard Abu-Jamal confess to the murder of Officer Faulkner on December 9. Wakshul stated that he did not think that the confession was important at the time the original police report was written. Other witnesses at the hospital have claimed that their statements regarding Abu-Jamal have been misconstrued by police and the media.

There are also a number of disagreements regarding the physical evidence in the case. While the coroner who did the autopsy on Officer Faulkner stated in his notes that the bullet he extracted was a .44-caliber, he later stated that he was simply making a rough estimate about the caliber of the bullet and claimed that the bullet that killed Faulkner had actually been a .38-caliber. It has been claimed, however, that ballistics tests have not shown that a bullet from Abu-Jamal's .38-caliber gun caused the death of Officer Faulkner.

Abu-Jamal was found guilty of first-degree murder and was sentenced to death by Judge Albert F. Sabo on May 25, 1983. In 2001, District Judge William Yohn overturned his death sentence, citing inconsistencies in the original sentencing process. On March 17, 2006, the Commonwealth of Pennsylvania filed an appeal seeking to reinstate the order for the execution of Abu-Jamal. On May 17, 2007, the U.S. Court of Appeals for the Third Circuit heard oral arguments in Abu-Jamal's appeal, with his attorneys attempting to obtain a new trial and the government seeking the reversal of Judge Yohn's overturning of Abu-Jamal's original death sentence. On March 27, 2008, the three-judge panel upheld Judge Yohn's 2001 opinion but rejected Abu-Jamal's attorneys' claims of racial bias on the part of the jury. On July 22, 2008, Abu-Jamal's petition seeking reconsideration of the decision by the full Third Circuit panel of 12 judges was denied.

Amanda K. Cox

See also Black Panther Party; Police Use of Force; Political Prisoners

Further Readings

Abu-Jamal, M. (1996). *Live from Death Row*. New York: Perennial.

Bisson, T. (2000). *On a move*. Farmington, PA: Litmus Books.

Edginton, J. (Producer/Director). (1996). *Mumia: A case for reasonable doubt?* [Motion Picture]. United States: Home Box Office.

Weinglass, L. (1995). *Race for justice: Mumia Abu-Jamal's fight against the death penalty*. Monroe, ME: Common Courage.

ABUSE, CHILD

See Child Abuse

ABUSE, ELDER

See Elder Abuse

AFRICAN AMERICAN GANGS

As society changes, so do the perception and defining characteristics of what constitutes a gang. In 1971, Klein defined a gang as an identifiable group of youngsters who are generally perceived as a distinct aggregation by others within their neighborhoods and who recognize themselves as a denotable group that has been involved in enough delinquent incidents to call forth a consistently negative response from neighborhood residents and/or law enforcement agencies. Triplett (2004) notes that some law enforcement agencies define a gang simply as three or more youth ages 14 to 24 who associate with each other primarily to commit crimes. The media have contributed to perceptions of African American gang members and their involvement in urban violence. This entry presents historical and contemporary information on African American gangs in America, focusing in particular on the Crips and Bloods, two of the most prominent African American gangs today. Although they originated in Los Angeles, today they have a significant presence in Chicago, New York, and other large metropolitan areas. Other large African American gangs include the Chicago-based El Rukns (formed in the 1960s as the Blackstone Rangers) and the Black Gangster Disciples.

History

Early African American Gangs

The history of African American youth gangs extends as far back as the early 1900s. At that time, and until very recently, gangs were characterized by young people hanging out on street corners in certain locales. This pattern of association existed throughout the 20th century, especially in urban centers of migration including Chicago, New York City, and Los Angeles. It is thought that these early groups formed to protect their localities from other groups of youths, including immigrants from other countries. Early gangs in South Los Angeles served as an outlet for many Black youth who fought against local White youth who did not approve of Black southern immigrants in their neighborhood. These gangs often fought over parties and hangout spots that revolved around high school rivalries. Most gangs used baseball bats, bumper jacks, or an occasional knife.

During the 1960s, 50% of gangs in Los Angeles were African American. One of the first black gangs was known as Baby Cribs, later termed "Cribs" and referred to as "Crips" today. During the late 1970s and 1980s, gun use increased as gang violence escalated. The Piru Crips Street Boys (AKA Piru Street Crips) banded together against the Crips in Los Angeles and formed a gang called the Bloods. By the mid-1970s, battles between the Bloods and the Crips were common on the streets as well as in jails and prisons.

Expansion of the Crips and Bloods

Around 1970, the Crips were dressing in a fashion so as to become recognized within society; they wore black leather jackets and walked with canes. The leather jackets became a symbol of Crips membership. The Crips began to commit robberies and assaults and were involved in extortion of merchandise, mugging the elderly, and ripping off weak youth.

By the 1980s, the Bloods' gang membership had expanded. Members wore red as a sign of their gang identity. Their involvement in selling drugs increased. Selling narcotics was a major part of the gangster lifestyle, bringing in large sums of money and more powerful weapons.

With the expansion of the Bloods and Crips, violence increased within the inner cities. Gangs and the war on drugs became a federal concern. In 1992, a coalition of gang leaders from 28 cities participated in a National Gang Peace Summit in Chicago to call for a truce in gang violence.

Media Portrayals of Gang Life

During the 1990s, rap music became a way of promoting the gangster lifestyle. This genre of music was the voice for many unprivileged minority youth within the inner-city ghettos. Through rap music, many gang members now had a way of expressing their voice on their personal world of values, culture, and general gangster life. The gangster life was no longer just an inner-city street problem. Many gangsters now had a way to make money from their lyrics, and record sales enabled them to launder illegal drug money through record sales. Much of the gangster life expounded from the underground rap world to mainstream society. For example, the Black Entertainment Television (BET) network created shows that mimicked the life of street gangsters. Although the rap music industry became a trivial market for gangs, it exposed the world to images of young men and women who glorified drug use, dealing, robberies, assaults, drive-by shootings, alcohol abuse, and violence directed at their perceived enemies.

Contemporary African American Gangs

According to the U.S. Department of Justice's National Youth Gang Survey for 2006, approximately 785,000 gang members and 26,500 gangs were active in the United States. The great majority of the nation's street gang members are male, and about a third are African American. One prominent feature of African American gangs today is that they tend to be concentrated in disenfranchised neighborhoods with high levels of poverty and drugs. Gangs have spread to rural and suburban areas as well. African American gangs have had a profound influence on street gang culture.

The term O. G. (Original Gangster) refers to an older gang member who has been a member of a gang since it began. These members may have jobs and families, so they typically are less involved in day-to-day gang life. Nevertheless, they still take part in some gang activities; for example, they may attend the funeral of another gang member to pay respect. Although data on the age of gang members are limited, the Department of Justice noted that during the period from 1996 to 1998, the percentage of gang members ages 18 and older increased from 50% to 60%.

Today the Bloods and Crips both are involved in illegal immigration trafficking, drug trafficking, intergang conflicts, robbery, burglary, and assaults, as well as nondelinquent acts such as partying. According to the 2006 National Youth Gang Survey, the majority of gangs in rural areas and smaller cities reported no gang-related homicides (86% and 89%, respectively; however, most cities with populations greater than 100,000 reported one or more gang-related homicides (i.e., homicides in which the perpetrator and/or the victim was a gang member). The crimes that increased the most in 2006 (compared to 2004 and 2005) were assault and drug sales, followed by robbery, larceny/theft, burglary, and auto theft.

African American gangs like the Bloods and the Crips remain very stable today and continue to be a challenge to the rest of society. Moving from illegal drugs to auto theft, extortion, property crimes, and home invasion, some East Coast gangs have begun trafficking in fraudulent identification papers that could be used by terrorists.

Heather Alaniz

See also Asian American Gangs; Female Gangs; Hip Hop, Rap, and Delinquency; Latino Gangs; Media Portrayals of African Americans

Further Readings

Egley, A., Jr., & O'Donnell, C. E. (2008, August). Highlights of the 2006 National Youth Gang Survey. *OJJDP Fact Sheet* (FS-200805). Retrieved from http://www.ncjrs.gov/pdffiles1/ojjdp/fs200805.pdf

Klein, M. W. (1971). *Street gangs and street workers.* Englewood Cliffs, NJ: Prentice Hall.

Morris, D., & Williams, T. (2008). *War of the Bloods in my veins: A street soldier's march toward redemption.* New York: Scribner/Simon & Schuster.

Triplett, W. (2004). Gang crisis. *Congressional Quarterly Researcher, 14*(18), 421–444.

Websites

National Youth Gang Center: http://www.iir.com/nygc

AFRICAN AMERICANS

The fundamental contradiction in American socio-political and economic history is race. Race theory has been used to perpetuate a caste system in America. An integral postulate of this theory asserts that there is a direct correlation between African American identity and criminal behavior. This entry presents a brief historical look at the issue of race and crime as it relates to African Americans, examines some of the erroneous and pejorative opinions on African American identity, and reviews African American experience and the historical evolution of African American identity. The entry concludes with a discussion of African Americans as perpetrators and victims of crime and contemporary views of African American criminology.

Historical Perspective

There are two primary considerations in any discussion of African Americans and crime: (1) African American identity and (2) the depiction of African Americans as criminals and as victims. Historic racial attitudes in the United States have characterized African Americans as being predisposed to criminal activity because of culture, immorality, psychological and genetic inferiority, and religious theology and ideology; for example, the mark of Cain and the curse of Ham. One of the results of these attitudes has been the disparate treatment of African Americans by judicial and/or extrajudicial processes. The rights heralded by the Declaration of Independence and the privileges and immunities provided for by the U.S. Constitution were not originally intended for African Americans. Richard Bardolph, in his work *The Civil Rights Record: Black Americans and the Law, 1849–1970* (1970), carefully chronicled, as have many other scholars, the relegation of African Americans to an inferior legal and social status in American society. The American legal system operates as two systems, one for White citizens and another for African Americans as exemplified in the *State v. Celia* (1855), *Dred Scott v. Sanford* (1858), and the *Plessy v. Ferguson* (1896) decisions. The disproportionate presence of African Americans in the criminal justice system is partially attributable to the racial legacy in the legal system. There are some, however, who believe that the correlation between African Americans and crime is the result not of a "White conspiracy" or racist criminal justice system, but of the socioeconomic condition and/or cultural behavior of African Americans. Other academics and policy analysts simply conclude that African Americans appear in crime statistics more often than others because they commit more of the crimes that are documented.

The debate over African American criminology is centuries old. Dispelling the pejorative notions of Black crime was an important part of the "uplift the race" advocacy in the 19th and 20th centuries. African American religious leaders, reformers, and academics used every medium and opportunity to argue against a direct correlation between race and crime, and more specifically, between their race and crime. Among these advocates were prominent African American sociologists W. E. B. Du Bois, Charles Spurgeon Johnson, Kelly Miller, and Ira de Augustine Reid. In response to a dominant society that believed otherwise, they asserted that the alleged correlation between race and criminal behavior was spurious.

African American Identity

For the greater part of African American history, African American identity was created and controlled by non–African Americans. As a condition of their servitude and suppression, the majority of African Americans were kept illiterate. Thus for many years they were either unable or prohibited from asserting their identity within the dominant society. It is not that African Americans lacked awareness of their history and personality beyond what White people thought; it is simply that Whites controlled the intellectual products, be they government records, literature, sermons, or scientific treatises. The portrayal of African Americans in these items was through the eyes of a domineering and hostile society.

Contemporary African American identity is complex. It begins with the Africans, free and slave, who helped the Spaniards and Portuguese explore the Americas. Africans and their descendants also participated in the clash and synthesis of cultures that unfolded in the Americas—indigenous, European, and African. In the 19th and 20th centuries, the African American population in the United States diversified, experiencing significant growth from African immigration and migration from other Blacks in the Diaspora. The 2006 American Community Survey of the U.S. Census Bureau reported that among the Black population in the United States, there were more than 1.2 million Africans of foreign birth. Of the 35 million Blacks in the United States in 2006, nearly 2.3 million listed their ancestry as sub-Saharan Africa, and 2.2 million listed their ancestry as West Indian (non-Hispanic). Contemporary American Blacks are a diverse group who do not necessarily identify with one another.

The Encounter: Origins of a New Identity

African American identity is a derivative of the African historical experience. The Africans' encounter with Europeans, both in their indigenous lands and in European indigenous lands, resulted in the reconstruction of African identity. Africans have had a historic presence in the Mediterranean region, the Near East, and what is now Europe. Ancient texts from a variety of sources document the presence of Africans without making the geographic distinction between Northern Africa and sub-Saharan Africa. A new identity for Africans did not begin to develop until the 15th century C.E., when Europe had emerged as a distinct entity, Northern Africa had succumbed to several invasions and become principally Arab, and the Portuguese had begun their slave trade in Africans. The development of a new identity for the African facilitated European imperialism, religious evangelism, and scientific quest. European imperialism reduced millions of Africans to forced laborers in "New World" colonies. Africans were transformed into commodities and valued for their commercial utility rather than their humanity. In both Christian and Islamic evangelism, the African was declared a heathen and thus eligible for enslavement, exploitation, and "redemption."

Science as a means for understanding the natural world was adapted to explaining and organizing human society. "Scientific" race theory postulates that distinguishing physiological traits among humans, such as skin color, defined racial groups and determined the innate abilities of each racial group. This theory supported the classification of Africans as subhuman, thus justifying exploitation of, experimentation on, and the expendability of Africans.

Transformation: From African to African American

The reconstruction of the African identity into African American identity is based on four historic experiences: (1) the Middle Passage, (2) seasoning or slave breaking, (3) slavery, and (4) class oppression. The African Diaspora in the Americas shares these four historic experiences. The following discussion, however, focuses primarily on the experience of African Americans in the United States.

The process of capture and sale of African *humans* to slave traders began the transformation from African to African American. The collection of various Africans at slave ports merely represented the diversity of African ethnicity. The Middle Passage, however, forged diverse ethnic groups of Africans into a new "tribe." The passage across the Atlantic Ocean marked a traumatic departure from "Mother Africa" and created a class of people united by this journey. Other than the thousands of Africans spirited away by Arabs to work on salt plantations in the Fertile Crescent centuries earlier, the Middle Passage was an unprecedented initiation. These Africans entered the holds of ships with memories of their native communities; they emerged as a new people.

Upon arriving in the New World, Africans had to be transformed into a single labor force. The objective of seasoning/breaking the African was to create a slave, a subservient laborer. This process required force and violence. It required the suppression of native language, values, family structures, religious practices, and so on. These were replaced by the social usage created by the masters of the slave society to perpetuate the condition and mentality of servitude and subservience. After many generations, the memories of Africa faded and the African became an African American.

Slavery and subservient caste status were both de jure and de facto. While there are several prominent exceptions, slavery was the primary condition of the majority of African Americans. All

African Americans, however, whether slave or free, suffered the status of a subservient caste. The exploitation of African American labor survived the legal demise of slavery. The litany of exploitative and demeaning acts experienced by African Americans included, but was not limited to, chain gangs and other forced labor schemes, forced rape and prostitution, pay disparity, lynching and other forms of summary judgment, deprivation, property seizures, substandard education facilities, and workplace segregation. In 1896, the U.S. Supreme Court in its *Plessy v. Ferguson* decision lent the force of law to the American caste system.

As a class of people, African Americans were not only deprived but also despised. Many Whites who had fought in the Civil War and supported Reconstruction believed that there was little government could do to change customs and racial attitudes in American society. Nineteenth-century science and social science convinced many Whites that racial differences made political and economic equality impossible. Thus a culture of prejudice and violence permeated the American experience of African Americans. For example, in the 2-year period from 1892 to 1893 an estimated 150 blacks were lynched and mutilated each year. Justifications for the caste structure were reinforced by scientific, sexual, and religious myths. One such myth promoted the notion that African Americans were predisposed to criminal behavior.

Diversity in the Face of Adversity

African Americans are not a monolithic group. It is true that enslavement, slavery, and racial oppression forged a new identity for captured Africans. It is equally true, however, that African Americans, despite their common experience, retained and developed elements of diversity. The African American population is diverse ethnically, racially, and by class.

Ethnic diversity among African Americans stems from a number of factors. First, vestiges of African culture survived the seasoning process, and the transformation did not always produce the same results. For example, the sea coast islands of the Carolinas and Georgia, the tidewater regions of the Atlantic Coast, and the bayous of Louisiana and Mississippi all contain African Americans with peculiar customs and vernaculars. Urban and rural environments also contributed to diversity. The plantation life of African Americans often contrasted with that of slaves living in towns and cities. African Americans were profoundly affected by the language and culture of their masters. As a result they spoke several European languages, properly and in the vernacular. American societies, both domestic and foreign, were dynamic, and people, especially African Americans, moved frequently. The myriad of cultural inputs into their identity caused continual change in their self-awareness and self-expression.

Race is not a natural attribute but a theoretical construct invented to distinguish humans politically, economically, and socially. The concept of race was once construed as a scientific certainty, but in contemporary discourse it is understood as a social construct. In the United States, racial constructs delineated social caste and thus determined the American experience of individuals and groups of individuals. Privilege was reserved for Whites. To varying degrees, Asians, Hispanics, and Native Americans were less privileged and were subject to prejudice and racial violence. African Americans occupied the lowest caste in American society. Skin color and other physical features emerged as an obsession in social interaction. Complicating the operation of the racial caste system was the inevitable and sometimes unwelcome intermingling of the races. While the quantum of blood varied for all other castes, one drop of "Black" blood made a person Black. The blood quantum for racial classification was established as a de jure standard by many states in their statutes. The one-drop rule replaced many of the older race identification statutes, and between 1910 and 1931 as many as 20 states codified the one-drop rule. In 1967, the U.S. Supreme Court ruled Virginia's Racial Integrity Act unconstitutional in *Loving v. Virginia,* thus invalidating the one-drop rule. Many "one droppers" were White enough to "pass" the color bar. Those who could not pass remained within the African American community, making it racially diverse. Thus, in contemporary American society, Blacks come in all shades of complexion, eye color, and hair texture.

Crime and African Americans

While attending a conference on crime and police, the late mayor of Atlanta, Maynard Jackson, stated that "race should not raise the presumption of criminality." However, it is still common for many Americans to interpret the criminal behavior of African Americans as a function of their race. African Americans are more often seen as criminals than the victims of crime. Recent studies have challenged each of these views.

African Americans as Criminals

African Americans are disproportionately represented in the criminal justice system. Historically, in the past 50 years they have represented 11% to 12% of the general population of the United States (12.3% according to the 2000 census). Their percentage of arrests, convictions, and persons under state and federal correctional supervision exceeds their representation in the general population. For example, the *Uniform Crime Report* in 2006 reported that Blacks accounted for 28.0% of total arrests; Whites accounted for 69.7%. In 2003 the Bureau of Justice Statistics (BJS) reported that Blacks accounted for 27.7% of new court commitments to state prison for violent offenses; Whites accounted for 26.1%. BJS reported in June 2007 that there were 4,618 Black men in prison for every 100,000 Black males in the U.S. population. Whites had only 773 men in prison per 100,000 White males and Hispanics had 1,747 men in prison per 100,000 Hispanic males. In its 2004 bulletin reporting on prison populations, BJS stated that 8.4% of Black males between the ages of 25 and 29 were incarcerated. For the same period and age demographic, only 1.2% of Whites and 2.5% of Hispanics were incarcerated in state and federal prisons. BJS also reported that, in 1986, 5.7% of African Americans were under correctional supervision, and by 1997 that number had increased to 9.0%. By comparison, the percentage of Whites under correctional supervision was 1.4% in 1986 and 2.0% in 1997. It is reasonable to infer that African Americans have a greater encounter with the criminal justice system than do other segments of the population. The statistics do not, however, support race-based criminological explanations. Pronounced poverty and discrimination have played major roles in criminological explanations of African Americans and crime.

African Americans as Victims

African American victims of crime are nearly invisible. The typical image of the offender is African American, and the typical victim of crime is depicted as White. The data, however, suggest otherwise. BJS, in its report on criminal victimization for 2005 (National Crime Victim Survey), reported that "males, blacks and persons age 25 or younger continued to be victimized at higher rates than females, whites and persons age 25 and older." In addition, Blacks accounted for 47.6% of murder victims and Whites accounted for 49.8%. In 1993 the violent victimization rate for Blacks was 67.4 per 1,000 persons age 12 or older, and it was 47.9 per 1,000 for Whites. By 2005 the violent victimization rates had declined for both groups: 20.1 per 1,000 for Whites and 27.0 per 1,000 for Blacks. The rates of violent victimization for crimes such as rape, robbery, and assault were reported greater for African Americans than Whites in 2005. Reported victim perceptions of offenders also contradict popular notions of offender identity. Again, according to statistics reported by BJS, *Criminal Victimization in the United States* (1996), 63.1% of victims perceived the race of the violent offenders as White and 27.3% as Black. Other data suggest that most victims are offended by persons of their own race.

African Americans report two other types of victimization: lynching and police brutality. Lynching was a prevalent form of violence used by Whites against African Americans for many years, and as a crime it often was unreported, underreported, and unpunished. Police brutality is a contemporary and controversial subject. Many African Americans believe that excessive use of force by police has been and continues to be brutal and lethal. The acquittal of officers in cases litigating their accountability for excessive use of force has led to demonstrations, boycotts, and riots.

Conclusion

In contemporary culture, the very stereotypes and idioms early generations fought to dispel have become normative behavior in some segments of the African American community. Deviant criminal behavior operates as a community value system and commercial enterprise. At the same time that authors Richard Herrnstein and Charles Murray published their research on the correlation between intelligence, class structure, and criminal behavior in American society, young African Americans were embracing criminal and prison values. The "gangsta" culture helps perpetuate the historic myth of Black criminality. At best, it is difficult in the present context to argue that the criminal justice system is racist. The disproportionate presence of African Americans in the criminal justice system may be attributable to racial disparity in American justice, but it may also be due to an increase in African American criminal behavior.

James P. Mayes

See also Chain Gangs; Hip Hop, Rap, and Delinquency; Slavery and Violence; Victimization, African American

Further Readings

Ajayi, J. F. A., & Crowder, M. (Eds.). (1972). *History of West Africa*. New York: Columbia University Press.

Bardolph, R. (Ed.). (1970). *The civil rights record: Black Americans and the law, 1849–1970*. New York: T. Y. Crowell.

Blassingame, J. W. (1979). *The slave community: Plantation life in the Antebellum South*. New York: Oxford University Press.

Chambers, B. (Ed.). (1968). *Chronicles of Black protest*. Denver: Mentor Books.

Dain, B. R. (2002). *A hideous monster of the mind: American race theory in the early republic*. Cambridge, MA: Harvard University Press.

Delgado, R., & Stefancic, J. (2001). *Critical race theory: An introduction*. New York: New York University Press.

Franklin, J. H. (Ed.). (1968). *Color and race*. Boston: Beacon Press.

Gabbidon, S. L., & Greene, H. T. (2001). *African American classics in criminology and criminal justice*. Thousand Oaks, CA: Sage.

Higginbotham, A. L. (1973). Racism and the early American legal process, 1619–1896. *Annals of the American Academy of Political and Social Science, 407*(1), 1–17.

Higginbotham, A. L. (1996). *Shades of freedom: Racial politics and presumptions of the American legal process*. New York: Oxford University Press.

Nash, G. B. (1974). *Red, White and Black: The peoples of early America*. Englewood Cliffs, NJ: Prentice Hall.

White, W. L. (1948). *Lost boundaries*. New York: Harcourt, Brace & Company.

ALIENATION

Alienation is the separation of an individual from another human being or group of people. The act of alienation is unfriendly and hurtful and causes the individual who is alienated to become excluded from a particular societal unit (i.e., family, community, school, state, government, etc.). The theory of alienation as presented by Karl Marx linked alienation to human experience and relationships in various domains of society. When individuals are alienated, they are taken away from themselves and from human possibilities that create and define their experiences. The implications and effects of alienation often result in humiliation and degradation of character, which can lead to retaliation, murder, suicide, and/or some other tragic incident on the part of the alienated individual.

Alienation can take several forms, including cultural and political, educational, and societal. Individuals who are alienated experience dehumanization and lack of compassion from others who dwell in the same society. Often these alienated individuals retaliate with harmful acts toward themselves and/or others in the societal setting in which they were alienated. Acts of violence by such individuals may result in their being placed in jails or other restricted institutions, further alienating them from society. When an individual's family, peers, state, government, or other societal component displaces him or her, the individual is forced out of the normal growth and experiences that can occur in his or her life.

Cultural and Political Alienation

Cultural and political alienation can be linked together because the laws of a state or country can contribute to cultural alienation. An immigrant—a person who migrates to another country for permanent residence—may be classified as an alien and excluded from certain benefits and rights reserved for citizens. Race, ethnicity, and immigrant status are key factors for cultural and political alienation. The term *alien* itself suggests difference from societal laws and norms.

In the United States, immigrants who abide by the laws of the United States and meet certain requirements can achieve U.S. citizenship. However, some immigrants who did not comply with U.S. immigration laws when they entered the United States are referred to as "illegal aliens" and often experience more difficulty obtaining U.S. citizenship. Thus, they are alienated from laws and rights that U.S. citizens possess and are excluded from voting and other political activities.

Controversy regarding cultural and political alienation exists because some cultural and ethnic groups have a more difficult time obtaining citizenship than others. For example, of the estimated 8.5 million illegal aliens in the United States, 4.5 million of those individuals are Mexican. Negative stereotypes have developed around this cultural group, and many Mexicans living in the United States often experience ridicule and become targets of discrimination, even after they become citizens. As Mexicans and other immigrants and minorities filter into American society, they may fall victim to other forms of alienation as well, such as educational alienation.

Educational Alienation

There are several examples of alienation in education that link to culture and politics. Racism and lack of social assimilation play key roles in educational alienation. Social assimilation occurs when a person is accepted into a particular group because he or she conforms to certain rules and practices. In a school setting, these groups are referred to as "cliques." Students who are English as a second language (ESL) speakers, minorities, and/or social outcasts from peers may be alienated by teachers and other students. As the number of immigrants to America continues to increase, the number of ESL students also grows. Some of these students are placed in ESL classes because they need extra help in certain subject areas. However, sometimes these students are placed in ESL classes simply because of their ethnic identity. When schools alienate certain students due to ethnicity and dialect differences, these students are isolated from their fellow classmates and may be deprived of an equal education. Alienation can lead to inadequate education and an achievement gap not only for ESL students but for other groups as well, such as African American students.

The achievement gap can be linked to the lack of multicultural education curriculum in their schools.

Multicultural education integrates critical and social pedagogies and ideas that focus on diverse cultural beliefs, attitudes, and behaviors in schools and other educational settings. The concept is built upon freedom, equality, justice, equity, and human dignity—philosophical ideals that were written in the U.S. Constitution and Declaration of Independence. Students affected by this type of educational alienation often have low self-esteem and score low on standardized tests. Race and culture are the key components for minorities in education with regard to alienation. Students who are not socially assimilated, considered unpopular or different, and made to feel dehumanized often experience another form of alienation, referred to as "social alienation."

Social Alienation

Alienation in social relations has increased worldwide. One indication of such alienation is the increasing number of school shootings by teens and adults in the United States during the past 9 years. From February 1996 to November 2007, there were 51 documented incidents of school shootings worldwide; 38 occurred in America. The majority of the teens committing these school shootings were described by the media as "teens alienated" from society. Their adult assailants were described as "isolated" and "alienated" as well. The final outcomes of the school shootings were murder-suicides. The alienation of the shooters from friends, families, and other social norms led to retaliation, cruel and devastating injuries to the victims, and death.

Another example of societal alienation is parental alienation. In this form of alienation, a parent alienates an estranged partner from their children. The alienation extends to the person being alienated from his or her family. Often this occurs in custody battles, when one parent may tell untruths to children to keep the other parent at a disadvantage. Fathers are more likely than mothers to experience parental alienation. The children, although not the intended target, may feel alienated as a result of being disconnected from their father and/or other family members. The parental alienation often leads to depression, remorse, and hatred.

Kimetta R. Hairston

See also Colonial Model; Dehumanization of Blacks; School Shootings

Further Readings

May, S. (1999). *Critical multiculturalism: Rethinking multicultural and antiracist education.* New York: RoutledgeFalmer.

Schacht, R. (1994). *The future of alienation.* Chicago: University of Illinois Press.

Smith, D. G., & Wolf-Wendel, L. E. (2005). The challenge of diversity: Involvement or alienation in the academy? *ASHE Higher Education Report, 31*(1). Hoboken, NJ: Jossey-Bass.

A timeline of recent school shootings. (2007, December). *Daily Almanac.* Available at http://www.infoplease.com

ALLIANCE FOR JUSTICE

The Alliance for Justice (AFJ) is one of several organizations dedicated to the pursuit of justice for all Americans, which includes the provision of legal representation and advocacy in areas such as consumer rights, civil rights, and human rights. The AFJ was founded by Nan Aron in 1979 with 20 advocacy groups. Twenty-eight years later, the AFJ comprises 78 advocacy groups on the national, local, and regional levels that are associated with a variety of related causes (e.g., women's rights, environmental protection, civil rights, children's rights, and mental health). Since its founding, the AFJ has worked to influence public policy through lobbying, court cases, partnering with nonprofits, and student groups. In the United States, historically race and ethnicity have been significant in the ways in which justice is administered, especially in regard to the equitable application of justice (e.g., equal prosecution and disposition of similar crimes regardless of race) and the provision of judicial protection (e.g., prohibition of civil rights violations). This entry discusses ways in which the AFJ has historically advocated for equal justice for all Americans and how it is currently fulfilling its mission. It also describes the various waysthe advocacy agenda of the AFJ directly and indirectly relates to racial and ethnic issues of justice.

Several conditions must be met to ensure the equitable application of justice and judicial protection regardless of race. Two of the most important factors are the existence of a fair and independent judiciary and open access to the courts. It would be impossible to define, restore, and preserve human and civil rights and liberties without the existence of these factors. The AFJ advocates a fair and independent judiciary, open access to the courts, and the protection of human and civil rights and liberties primarily through the support for education; political lobbying; and immediate public responses to related court cases (e.g., the revocation of parents' voluntary school desegregation rights and racial discrimination in the workplace), legislation (e.g., Habeas Corpus Restoration Act of 2007), and judicial selection, especially at the federal level (e.g., U.S. Supreme Court nominees).

AFJ Projects

In addition to advocating for unimpeded access to the courts and human and civil rights and liberties, the AFJ provides information about current issues related to the administration of justice in the United States, such as the free speech rights of nonprofits, ways to counteract attempts to expand executive power, and the location of fair judges and independent courts. The AFJ has undertaken several projects to accomplish **its** organizational objectives and fulfill the organizational mission.

The Nonprofit Advocacy Project and the Foundation Advocacy Initiative

Nonprofit organizations have always been actively involved in community issues. The AFJ recognized that nonprofit organizations could also become actively involved in political issues (e.g., public policy debates) on the national level. In 1983 the AFJ launched the Nonprofit Advocacy Project to educate nonprofit organizations on the laws that regulate the extent to which nonprofit organizations can participate in national political issues. Ten years later, to further support the efforts of the Nonprofit Advocacy Project, the Foundation Advocacy Initiative was launched to encourage foundations to support the advocacy efforts (e.g., lobbying) of organizations.

The Judicial Selection Project

In 1984, numerous federal judgeship vacancies desperately needed to be filled in order to respond to rapidly increasing caseloads (civil and criminal). Understanding the importance of the selection of federal judges who were committed to the administration of equitable justice and judicial protection, the AFJ launched the Judicial Selection Project. Since its inception, the Judicial Selection Project has monitored the nominations of all judges at the federal level, including nominations to the U.S. Supreme Court. The AFJ continues to provide federal judicial nomination information to the public, and it encourages members of the public to become involved in the selection and confirmation of federal judiciary. It has been successful in influencing the defeat of judicial nominations to the U.S. Supreme Court (e.g., that of Robert Bork, nominated by President Ronald Reagan in 1987) and has actively supported the nomination of African American and women judges to various judgeships in the federal judiciary (including the U.S. Supreme Court).

Access to Justice Project

The AFJ continues to advocate for the equitable provision of rights to all Americans regardless of their demographics (e.g., race, ethnicity, gender, age, or income). Not only is it important to ensure that all people have continued open access to the courts; it is also paramount that those parties responsible for wrongdoing—including individuals, government entities, corporations—be brought to justice. In 2003, in order to continue to advocate for these rights in the 21st century, the AFJ launched the Access to Justice Project. This project is designed to pursue the AFJ's progressive agenda through the involvement of a network of various organizations and individuals, including nonprofits, corporations, unions, environmental groups, student organizations, academia, and bar associations.

Shani P. Gray

See also National Urban League; Racial Justice Act; Vera Institute of Justice

Further Readings

Alliance for Justice. (1995). *Being a player.* Washington, DC: Author.

Alliance for Justice. (2006). *Strategies for creating and operating 501(c)(3)s, 501(c)(4)s, and political organizations.* Washington, DC: Author.

Aron, N. (1989). *Liberty and justice for all: Public interest law in the 1980s and beyond.* Boulder, CO: Westview.

Websites

Alliance for Justice: http://afj.org

AMERICAN INDIANS

See Native American Courts; Native American Massacres; Native Americans; Native Americans: Culture, Identity, and the Criminal Justice System; Native Americans and Substance Abuse

ANTI-DEFAMATION LEAGUE

The Anti-Defamation League (ADL) is an advocacy organization established in New York in 1913 to stop, by appeals to reason and conscience, and if necessary, by appeals to law, the defamation of the Jewish people; to secure justice and fair treatment to all citizens; and to put an end forever to unjust and unfair discrimination against and ridicule of any sect or body of citizens. The ADL has 30 regional offices in the United States and three overseas offices in Israel, Russia, and Italy and an annual budget of more than $50 million. Local efforts include assisting law enforcement agencies to investigate and prosecute extremists, rallying support for Israel, advocating for the separation of church and state, organizing outreach efforts between diverse ethnic and religious groups, providing anti-bias and diversity training, monitoring extremist activity, and publishing Holocaust and tolerance curricula. The ADL meets with U.S. and foreign leaders, assesses hate crimes and anti-Semitism in various countries, disseminates pro-Israel information, and addresses anti-Semitism in media. The entry examines the history of the ADL's efforts and successes in challenging anti-Semitism, religious and racial intolerance, advocacy on behalf of the state of Israel, as well as some of the institutional changes, controversies, and criticisms.

ADL: 1900–1940s

In 1913, Leo Frank, a Jewish factory executive and president of the B'nai B'rith lodge in Atlanta, was wrongly convicted of murdering a 13-year-old girl and was then lynched by an angry mob shortly after the judge commuted his death sentence. The trial and related incidents of injustice and prejudice gave impetus to the revival of the Ku Klux Klan, as well as the formation of the ADL as the first organization to explicitly address anti-Semitism. Sigmund Livingston, a young Chicago lawyer, started the ADL with $200 and the sponsorship of the Independent Order of B'nai B'rith, a Jewish service organization established in 1843.

At the onset of the 20th century, the United States was home to approximately 1 million Jews and the third largest Jewish population center in the world. Substantial anti-Semitic hostility and discrimination contributed to resorts featuring signs warning "No dogs! No Jews!" and magazines publishing derogatory caricatures of Jewish people. The ADL promoted and ensured fair, accurate, and inclusive representations on stage, in film, and in print media as a means of eliminating anti-Semitism and discrimination. Adolph Ochs, *New York Times* publisher and an ADL executive committee member, contributed toward a vast reduction in defamatory cultural representations by sending letters to newspaper editors throughout the United States discouraging the use of objectionable and vulgar references to Jews in the media.

Throughout the 1920s, the ADL sought to address the public bigotry and anti-Semitism of the Ku Klux Klan, whose membership numbered in the millions. Henry Ford's distribution of the anti-Semitic and literary forgery, *The Protocols of the Elders of Zion,* alleging a Jewish and Masonic plot to achieve world domination, became another focus of attention for the ADL, which was able to debunk the widely circulated text as a hoax. Livingston circulated pamphlets, and the ADL solicited the aid of President Woodrow Wilson and others to denounce Ford's anti-Semitism. After years of censure, Ford publicly apologized and expressed hope that hatred of the Jews, commonly known as anti-Semitism, and hatred against any other racial or religious groups shall cease for all times.

The Great Depression was followed by Hitler's ascendance to power, which ushered in support and funds for an array of fascist groups in the United States, including such leaders as Fritz Kuhn of the German-American Bund and Charles Coughlin of the pro-fascist Christian Front. The ADL embarked on public education campaigns and jointly produced a monograph countering Coughlin's anti-Semitic claims and proving that he plagiarized a speech by Joseph Goebbels. The ADL expanded its staff during the 1930s and established its fact-finding and information-gathering operation centering on extremist individuals and organizations.

Throughout the 1940s and 1950s, the ADL continued to raise public awareness and to investigate fascist groups in the United States. Postwar aftermath found the ADL working on behalf of civil rights legislation enactment and campaigning against Jewish quotas in college and university admissions as well as discrimination in housing, employment, and education. In 1948, the U.S. Supreme Court case of *Shelly v. Kraemer* resulted in the declaration of restrictive covenants as unenforceable. The ADL focused its efforts toward reforming restrictive immigration laws and filed an amicus brief in the 1948 landmark Supreme Court case *McCollum v. Board of Education* in order to question the constitutionality of "released time" for religious instruction held in tax-supported public school classrooms.

ADL: 1950–1970s

The ADL continued its crusade against prejudice and bigotry by joining forces with a sympathetic southern journalist who infiltrated the Klan and retrieved information that was delivered to law enforcement authorities and the press. Following President Dwight Eisenhower's signing of the first civil rights bill approved by Congress since Reconstruction, the ADL filed an amicus curiae brief in the 1954 landmark case of *Brown v. Board of Education.* The ADL launched a large-scale educational effort to eliminate intolerance, bigotry, and anti-Semitism and developed tools to teach democracy and to challenge right-wing extremism and McCarthyism.

The ADL actively worked for the passage of the Civil Rights Acts of 1964 and 1968 and the Voting Rights Act of 1965. The ADL publications exposed ideas disseminated by the radical right and countered the anti-Catholic bias levied against John F. Kennedy's presidential campaign. Moreover, the ADL commissioned University of California sociologists to investigate anti-Semitism and prejudice in U.S. life, which resulted in a series of publications. The ADL presented study findings at the Vatican II Council and sponsored interfaith conferences and educational programs, which resulted in the Vatican Council's public statement on the Jews, repudiating Jewish guilt in the death of Jesus and denouncing hatred, persecutions, and displays of anti-Semitism directed against Jews at any time by any one. The ADL also assisted with the U.S. Supreme Court case *Engel v. Vitale* in 1962, resulting in a decision that the recitation of prayers in public schools is unconstitutional.

Following the Yom Kippur War of 1973, the ADL attempted to foster support for the state of Israel, which was established in 1948, and condemned the 1975 UN resolution that equated Zionism with racism. Several ADL publications asserted that the Palestinian Liberation Organization (PLO) was involved in terrorist activity. In addition, ADL leaders played a key role in the passage of the 1977 Anti-Boycott Bill, banning U.S. participation in the Arab blacklist against firms doing business in Israel. The ADL also launched a missions program to Israel and expanded an exchange program in Germany.

Although the ADL became a leading civil rights organization and a key actor in the Black-Jewish alliance, the advent of the Black power movement contributed to a shift in the league's priorities toward focusing on extremism. In 1974, an ADL study titled *The New Anti-Semitism* reflected perceptions of insensitivity and indifference toward Jews on the part of various individuals and organizations in the United

States and abroad, which prompted books with similar arguments to be published in 1982 and 2003. Scholars such as Walter Laqueur and Norman Finkelstein have criticized such claims and posited that there is little evidence of new anti-Semitism in North American society, although there may be disapproval of some Israeli policies. Moreover, Noam Chomsky and Rabbi Michael Lerner contend that the ADL categorizes any criticism of Israel, even by Jews, as anti-Semitic, while more traditional forms of anti-Semitism may be neglected.

ADL: 1980s–Present

By the late 1970s, the ADL established the Braun Center for Holocaust Studies and founded regional offices throughout the United States and offices in Israel and Europe. Initiating a media campaign in the 1980s, the ADL denounced Soviet human rights violations and urged the U.S.S.R. to allow Jews to emigrate. The ADL's annual *Audit of Anti-Semitic Incidents,* which includes all hate crimes, was first published in 1979 and pioneered the development of the penalty enhancement approach for bias-related crimes. A growing religious right movement prompted the ADL to further advocate for a separation of church and state and to file amicus briefs in cases related to Christmas observances in public schools, publicly sponsored sectarian displays, and federal aid to parochial schools.

The ADL contributed to diversity awareness, anti-bias training, and Holocaust education in the mid-1980s for classrooms, college campuses, corporate settings, and law enforcement professionals. The ADL worked toward creating the 1990 Hate Crimes Statistics Act (HCSA), which requires states to determine whether crimes including physical acts of racial violence as well as statements that might lead to violence are committed because of the victim's race, ethnicity, religion, or sexual orientation. States are required to relay such information to a federal anti-hate data bank, which is shared with law enforcement officials nationwide.

Throughout the 1990s, the ADL closely monitored extremists and provided expert testimony to Congress and urged states to enact anti-paramilitary training laws. An ADL survey of antigovernment extremists suggested that armed militias posed a significant threat of violence, disorder, and vigilante justice. During the 1990s, some of the ADL's militia-monitoring activities became controversial because aspects of the information did not relate to "extremist" groups and may have been gathered via illegal or unconstitutional means. The ADL has issued numerous reports and launched a website to counter hate propaganda on the Internet. A 1993 U.S. Supreme Court decision upheld the constitutionality of a Wisconsin statute informed by the penalty enhancement hate crime legislation guidelines developed by the ADL.

The ADL witnessed the historic signing of the 1993 Israel-PLO treaty, continued to be a vocal supporter of the peace process, worked to solidify U.S. backing of Israel, and voiced concern about what it perceived to be terrorism on the part of the Palestinians. The assassination of Israeli Prime Minister Yitzhak Rabin and subsequent suicide bombings prompted the ADL to establish a task force to develop and distribute educational material about Israel's capital. Abe Foxman, who has been ADL's director since former director Nathan Perlmutter's death in 1987, has been criticized for his conservative leadership style amidst a less intense climate of anti-Semitism. Some have criticized the ADL for reacting negatively to Nazi comparisons made on the left, such as a MoveOn.org advertisement comparing George W. Bush to Adolf Hitler, while the ADL has remained silent when right-wing figures such as Bill O'Reilly have compared liberals to Nazis. During the 1990s, Foxman welcomed Christian conservatives with pro-Israel tendencies and exacerbated Black-Jewish tensions through negative public exchanges with Jesse Jackson and Louis Farrakhan. Although the ADL has sought to work with some elements of the Islamic community to promote interfaith dialogue and to condemn bigotry against Arabs, Muslims, and Blacks, such groups are often at odds with the ADL on issues related to Israel and anti-Semitism.

In 2006, the ADL spoke out against the U.S. Senate's attempts to ban same-sex marriage and cautioned that illegal immigration debates drew in neo-Nazis and anti-Semites. The ADL has worked to counter Holocaust denialism and revisionism and to urge action to stop contemporary ethnic cleansing and genocide. Recent controversy surrounds Foxman's 2007 opposition to the recognition of the death of Armenians at the hand of Turks during World War I as genocide. After a staff member publicly dissented, the ADL changed its position to acknowledge the genocide but maintained its opposition to congressional resolutions aimed at recognizing it as such. The ADL continues to develop materials, programs, and services in order to fight anti-Semitism and other forms of bigotry in the United States and abroad by serving as a resource for government, media, law enforcement, educators, and the public in assisting with information, education, legislation, and advocacy-related efforts.

Cynthia Golembeski

See also Anti-Semitism; Hate Crimes; Hate Crimes Statistics Act; Ku Klux Klan; Militias; Race Relations; Religious Minorities; Skinheads; U.S. Department of Justice, Office of Civil Rights; White Supremacists

Further Readings

Finkelstein, N. (2005). *Beyond chutzpah: On the misuse of anti-Semitism and the abuse of history*. Berkeley: University of California Press.

Foxman, A. (2003). *Never again? The threat of the new anti-Semitism*. San Francisco: Harper.

Kaufman, D., et al. (2007). *From the protocols of the Elders of Zion to Holocaust denial trials: Challenging the media, the law and the academy*. London: Vallentine Mitchell.

Laqueur, W. (2006). *The changing face of anti-Semitism: From ancient times to the present day*. Oxford, UK: Oxford University Press.

Websites

Anti-Defamation League: http://www.adl.org

ANTI–DRUG ABUSE ACTS

The first anti–drug abuse acts were enacted with the purpose of controlling drugs such as cocaine and opium. These drugs were used by Whites and minorities for both medical and recreational purposes. The racial influence of anti–drug abuse acts is evident in early and contemporary legislation.

During the Great Depression, the Marijuana Tax Act of 1937 was enacted partially to force Hispanics out of the country because of the shortage of jobs.

In the 1950s and 1960s, concern over drugs continued to increase, prompting passage of more anti–drug abuse acts. The Vietnam War in the 1970s caused more attention to be directed toward the use of drugs by returning veterans. More racial disparities arose in the 1980s with the introduction of crack cocaine in the slums of New York. During the 1980s, President Ronald Reagan declared a so-called War on Drugs that brought the passage of a number of anti–drug abuse acts focused on stopping the spread of crack cocaine. These acts led to increased law enforcement presence in poor, lower-class areas that were populated mainly by minorities, thus leading to a number of arrests and an overrepresentation of minorities in prisons. This entry chronicles the assorted pieces of legislation enacted during the 20th century to control drugs. Throughout this period, the impact of such legislation on minorities has been a concern. This is also considered in this entry.

Anti–Drug Abuse Acts of the 1900s

The Pure Food and Drug Act of 1906 was one of the first acts for preventing the manufacture, sale, or transportation of adulterated or misbranded drugs or medicines. This act required that the U.S. Department of Agriculture be responsible for determining if any drug had been adulterated or misbranded within the meaning of the act. The Pure Food and Drug Act of 1906 was little more than a "quality control" measure; it ensured that drugs had the proper labels, strength, and purity.

Around the same time as passage of the Pure Food and Drug Act, Congress passed the Opium Exclusion Act of 1909, which restricted the importation of opium from the Philippines. The Opium Exclusion Act of 1909 was the first antinarcotics law created with the idea of restricting use of a drug. The anti–drug abuse acts that soon followed were aimed more at taxing drugs and controlling who could distribute them rather than preventing the use of them.

The Harrison Narcotics Tax Act of 1914 imposed a special tax on all persons who produced, imported, or manufactured opium or coca leaves or derivatives. The act required persons who qualified within the description of the act to register and pay a special tax at the rate of $1 per annum. Moreover, the act made it illegal for any person not registered under the provisions of the act to be in possession or in control of any drug named within the act. With the Harrison Act, the government started a more formal system of tracking drugs such as opium and coca.

Like the Harrison Act, the Marijuana Tax Act of 1937 imposed a small tax on all persons who dealt in the manufacture, sale, or distribution of marijuana. Furthermore, the Marijuana Act made it unlawful for any person who was not registered to possess, sell, or distribute marijuana. Unlike the Harrison Act, the Marijuana Act carried large fines and prison sentences for violation of the act. Moreover, physicians who prescribed marijuana were required to report all patient information to the federal government. If a physician failed to report patient information, then the physician and the patient would be subject to prosecution under the Marijuana Act.

According to John Helmer, the Harrison and Marijuana acts caused a steady decline in the number of drug users until the late 1940s. During the late 1950s and early 1960s, concern over the use of illicit drugs started to rise once again; however, it was not until the Abuse Prevention and Control Act of 1970 that legislation began to control these drugs.

The Abuse Prevention and Control Act of 1970 created five schedules of drugs, with the first schedule containing the most addictive and dangerous drugs. For example, heroin and lysergic acid diethylamide (LSD) have a high risk for abuse and no accepted medical use; therefore, these two drugs are included in the first schedule. The second, third, and fourth schedules contain drugs having a high to low risk of abuse but also provide some medical use. The final schedule contains drugs with low dependency and abuse that are used mainly for medical treatment.

In the 1980s, Congress passed the Comprehensive Crime Control Act of 1984 and Anti-Drug Abuse Act of 1986 and 1988. These acts began the so-called War on Drugs by imposing enhanced penalties and strengthening federal efforts to slow international drug trafficking. The 1990s saw the creation of the Crime Control Act of 1990 and the Violent Crime Control and Law Enforcement Act of 1994. Collectively, these acts were responsible for the large growth in prison populations and a disproportionate representation of minority groups in arrests, convictions, and incarceration.

Anti–Drug Abuse Acts and Race

There is some evidence that the first three major pieces of legislation of the 20th century had negative affects on minority groups. For example, John Helmer opined that the Pure Food and Drug Act of 1906, the Opium Exclusion Act of 1909, and the Harrison Act of 1914 directly targeted African Americans and lower-class Whites, among whom cocaine and opium were widely used for medicinal purposes. For example, Tucker's Asthma Cure, Agnew's Powder, and Anglo-American Catarrh Powder were medications containing cocaine used by African Americans and lower-class Whites. Because of the impoverished conditions of these groups, doctors and hospitals were not always an option for the treatment of illness. Helmer concluded that because of this limited access to professional medical treatment, these groups were sometimes limited only to patent medicine that contained cocaine; therefore, the Pure Food and Drug Act of 1906, the Opium Exclusion Act of 1909, and the Harrison Act of 1914 had negative effects on them by placing new regulations on medications they relied on.

Helmer also argued that the Marijuana Tax Act of 1937 had negative effects on Mexican nationals living in the Southwest. The reason that marijuana was not addressed in the earlier acts was that at that time marijuana was primarily used by a relatively small number of Hispanics living in the Southwest. Helmer concluded that in response to the effect of the Great Depression on employment in the United States, the Marijuana Tax Act of 1937 was passed to move Mexicans back into Mexico.

The negative influence of these laws began to become evident after the 1940s. Helmer stated that after World War II, the number of narcotic arrests among African Americans and Hispanics grew to more than 3 times that of Whites. He suggested that the increased number of African Americans and Hispanics arrested could be attributed to racial bias in policing.

Ruth Peterson and John Hagan noted that the late 1960s and early 1970s marked a more intense period of legislation, culminating with the Abuse Prevention and Control Act of 1970. In the 1980s, however, a new derivative of cocaine, "crack," together with President Reagan's War on Drugs, led to a greater law enforcement focus on minority groups. John Helmer pointed out the popular opinion that the manufacture and distribution of cocaine and crack cocaine were primarily a result of activity by African American and Hispanic drug rings. This generalization placed minority offenders in a negative light, which produced a call for stiffer anti–drug abuse acts providing harsher punishments. Even though the passage of this legislation was prompted by high levels of addiction and violence related to drug use, the unintended side effect was the negative influence on minority groups. The generalization that minorities were responsible for the manufacture and distribution of cocaine and crack, combined with the anti–drug abuse acts of the 1980s and 1990s, resulted in minority groups beginning to receive harsher punishments than White offenders.

The War on Drugs was a response to the growing fear of cocaine and crack. The low cost and easy availability of crack made it the drug of choice over the more expensive cocaine. The legislative response to crack in the 1980s and 1990s included the Crime Control Act of 1984, Anti-Drug Abuse Act of 1986, Anti-Drug Act of 1988, Crime Control Act of 1990, and Violent Crime Control and Law Enforcement Act of 1994.

A study conducted by Steven Belenko, Jeffrey Fagan, and Ko-Lin Chin found that law enforcement's efforts to stop the spread of crack cocaine led to race disparities. They stated that because of the widespread fear that crack was responsible for other serious crimes, legislation was passed to target areas responsible for the distribution of crack. Unfortunately, most of the areas responsible for the distribution of crack were low-income areas primarily populated with minorities. When examining arrest records from the New York City Police Department in 1986, John Helmer found 50.8% of crack arrests were of African American suspects, 44.4% of Hispanic suspects, and 4.8% of White suspects.

Christopher Hebert found that African American and Hispanic drug offenders were more likely to go to prison and receive longer prison sentences than were White drug offenders. Hebert also found that African Americans were more likely to be sentenced to prison for even small amounts of cocaine; however, it was noted that Hispanics were not at an increased risk of being sentenced to prison any more than White offenders for cocaine offenses. When comparing Whites with Hispanics, Hebert found that Hispanics were at higher risk of being sent to prison for marijuana offenses. He concluded that African Americans convicted of cocaine offenses and Hispanics convicted of marijuana offenses were more likely than White offenders to be sent to prison. The findings of John Helmer and Christopher Hebert indicate that the early anti–drug abuse acts and the anti–drug acts of the 1980s and 1990s affected the same groups. Helmer and Hebert both found that with respect to cocaine, African Americans were affected more than Whites by anti–drug abuse acts; when examining marijuana, they found that Hispanics seemed to be affected more than African Americans and Whites. It could be argued that if anti–drug abuse acts began with the noble purpose of protecting people from dangerous drugs, that purpose was somehow lost with such disparities among the different races.

The anti–drug abuse acts of the 1900s have affected minority groups in many negative ways, from restricting availability of patient medicine to overrepresentation in prison. The War on Drugs and stiffer anti–drug abuse acts may have seemed like the answer to heroin problems in the 1970s and crack problems in the 1980s and 1990s; however, these acts led to increased numbers of minorities in prisons and prison overcrowding.

Jeffery T. Walker and Phillip J. Hammons

See also Drug Cartels; Drug Sentencing; Sentencing Disparities, African Americans; Sentencing Disparities, Latina/o/s; Sentencing Disparities, Native Americans

Further Readings

Belenko, S., Fagan, J., & Chin, K.-L. (1991). Criminal justice response to crack. *Journal of Research in Crime and Delinquency, 28,* 55–74.

Hawkins, D. F. (1986). Race, crime type and imprisonment. *Justice Quarterly, 3,* 251–270.

Hebert, C. G. (1997). Sentencing outcomes of Black, Hispanic, and White males convicted under federal sentencing guidelines. *Criminal Justice Review, 22,* 133–156.

Parker, K. F., & Maggard, S. R. (2005). Structural theories and race-specific drug arrests: What structural factors account for the rise in race-specific drug arrests over time? *Crime & Delinquency, 51,* 521–547.

Peterson, R. D., & Hagan, J. (1984). Changing conceptions of race: Towards an account of anomalous findings of sentencing research. *American Sociological Review, 49,* 56–70.

ANTI-IMMIGRANT NATIVISM

Anti-immigrant nativism is related to a complex set of attitudes and behavior dating to the late 19th century. A nativist is a person who fears or resents immigrants to the United States and wants to take action. These actions include violence, restrictive immigration policy, and limiting the rights of legal immigrants already present. Nativism refers to ideologies, groups, and social movements that support restrictions on immigration. Currently, undocumented migrants who entered clandestinely and legal permanent resident immigrants are often featured in the media as lawbreakers who take jobs from the native born or in other negative ways. In the absence of reasoned discussion and research, this is called "immigrant bashing."

Some negative publicity is aimed at legal immigrants, who may become scapegoats for social troubles and blamed for taking jobs or for the rising cost of public education. In the United States, however, the greatest anger is directed at an estimated 12 million undocumented immigrants who are represented as criminals in the media. In the 21st century, many hostile media stories about immigration have involved speculation about criminality and, after the attacks of September 11, 2001, fear of terrorism. Immigrant bashing involves the stereotyping of specific ethnic immigrant groups, undocumented immigrants, or all immigrants as an entity. Historically, the public stereotyping of immigrants as criminals has occurred with each large passage of newcomers into American society and then faded. This entry examines the history of hostility toward immigrants, the expanded criminalization of immigrants, the current state of immigrants in a post–9/11 context, and the consequences of immigrant bashing.

History of Interethnic and Racial Hostility Toward Immigrants

The Colonial and Postcolonial Immigration Stream

During the early colonial era, the English, French, Dutch, and Spanish engaged in conflict over territory and tried to keep other religious or ethnic groups from entering their colonies. In the 13 English colonies and after independence, two groups joined the English Protestant settlers: the Protestant Scotch-Irish and Protestant Germans. Scotch-Irish were viewed as drinkers and brawlers, while both the Scotch-Irish and the Germans were accused of illegally squatting on land. Hostile incidents occurred between these groups, but both groups were incorporated into what would become American society. Subsequently, three more waves of immigration, each marked by inter-ethno/racial conflict, have occurred.

The First Wave (1821–1890)

During the first wave, approximately 4 million northwestern European immigrants from Ireland, Germany, the United Kingdom, Scandinavia, and some areas of southern and eastern Europe arrived via the eastern United States. The Irish were still stereotyped as drinkers and brawlers. Yet nativistic responses focused on Irish and German Roman Catholicism. During this period, Anglo and German Protestants stereotyped the Catholic clergy as capable of lurid sexual acts and regarded the political influence of the pope with suspicion.

In California and elsewhere in the western United States, hostility developed toward Chinese immigrants. Workers blamed the Chinese for taking jobs and then accepting low wages and poor working conditions. They also connected them to organized crime ("triads"), opium use, and prostitution. The end result was the Chinese Exclusion Act of 1882. Subsequently, hostility toward the Japanese over economic issues ensued. In 1907, the United States signed the Gentleman's Agreement with Japan, ending Japanese immigration to America during the second great wave of immigration.

The Second Wave (1891–1924)

The cultural origins of the second wave of immigration were very different from those of the northwestern Europeans who had settled the United States. The primary sending regions were southern and eastern Europe. More ethnic stereotyping and friction occurred. In this stream, the Italians became stereotyped as criminals because of public fascination with organized crime. The Mafia was originally a Sicilian organization. There is considerable debate about whether an organization of the complexity of the Mafia could have developed during the 19th century or if the organized crime groups that did develop had any distinct Italian cultural character. Sociologist Richard Alba does not believe that groups like the Mafia evolved until Prohibition. The first-generation Italian crime rate was similar to that of other immigrant ethnic groups and lower than the native-born crime rate. Organized crime groups developed among various ethnic groups to bring bootleg liquor.

In the early 20th century, nativistic hostility toward second-wave immigrants resulted in passage of a series of restrictive immigration laws culminating in the Johnson-Reed Act of 1924. This legislation established quotas restricting immigration from all but the northwestern European countries of the first wave of immigration. This was done because of racism toward these groups and a fear that their cultural diversity would undermine the core American culture. In the aftermath of this legislation, immigration dropped to low levels until the criminalization of entrance without paperwork, which began with the Immigration Act of 1917, was challenged by Mexican border crossers in the 1950s.

Criminalization of Immigrants

The Immigration Act of 1917 banned and criminalized immigrant entrants who were illiterate in English or their native language, excluded felony offenders or those who had committed a misdemeanor crime of "moral turpitude," and required payment of a fee. Thus began a tradition of Mexican entry without inspection through a relatively unpoliced border. The social problem of undocumented immigration developed after World War II. During this global conflict, the bracero program (1941–1964) began an agreement between the United States and Mexico to bring Mexican guest workers into the United States. Migrants participating in this program learned about sources of employment and routes to enter the United States and came without formal paperwork—the first act of which is a civil offense and the second and subsequent were criminal felonies. At this time, the derogatory term *wetback* was used to describe Mexican migrants, as some entered by swimming over the Rio Grande. The border patrol launched "Operation Wetback" to control Mexican entry, returning individuals without paperwork to Mexico. Nevertheless, enforcement efforts to keep potential immigrants from entering without inspection have never been completely successful, and the buildup of undocumented immigrant population has occurred repeatedly. Each buildup of so-called illegal aliens has prompted public outcry about U.S.–Mexico border control.

The Third Wave (1965–Present)

In 1965, the Immigration and Nationality Act ended racist quotas and established a system of immigration open to all countries with which the United States had diplomatic relations. As a result, immigrants began to be legally admitted from the developing countries of Latin America, Asia, and Africa. Opportunities were given to Europeans, but relatively few responded as compared to the demand from developing world regions.

The third-wave immigrants are ethnoracially and culturally divergent. As with earlier waves of immigration, there has been hostility toward the practice of admitting large numbers of immigrants of diverse backgrounds as well as pressure for immigration reform. In particular, hostility has been directed toward immigrants from Mexico and Central America, who are perceived as less educated, less likely to culturally assimilate than earlier groups, and more likely to need government and taxpayer benefits and entitlements such as welfare or education. To compound the situation, because of the proximity of Mexico to the United States, more than 50% of those who entered without inspection come from Mexico, and the great majority of the undocumented are from Mexico and Central America.

Social Concerns Related to Immigrant Bashing

The 1970s recession and 1980s economic problems brought the first concentrated negative reaction to the "new immigration." The specific social concerns mirrored reactions to second-wave immigrants and, with an increasing undocumented population, led to the passage of the Immigration Reform and Control Act of 1986, which failed to control undocumented entry. During the 1990s, immigration law expert Stephen H. Legomsky identified several themes in nativistic public reaction to immigrants:

1. Beliefs that immigrants take jobs, increase the number of children and the costs of receiving a public education, or that some receive government benefits such as welfare

2. Racism or lack of cultural acceptance of the diversity of the third wave

3. Fear that the cultural diversity will rip apart what holds American society together

4. Fear of immigrants committing crime

5. A continual high level of immigration

6. Anger about high undocumented immigration and a frustration about border control

7. Ignorance about the degree of restriction already embedded in immigration law

Many of these concerns lack a solid basis, while others demonstrate either outright or implicit racism.

Expanded Criminalization of Immigrants

A major reason that criminality is a major theme in immigrant bashing is the convergence of immigration law and the criminal law. There are three ways in which immigration has been subject to increased criminalization. First, there has been an expansion of the grounds on which immigrants can be excluded and deported. At present, there are many categories of crime for which legal permanent residents can be retroactively deported. These crimes are referred to as "aggravated felonies." The creation of aggravated felonies began with the War on Crime, when violent and drug- and weapons-related crime was made grounds for deportation. This trend has expanded with repeated passage of immigration law and now includes a misdemeanor offense of shoplifting. Second, many immigration violations were civil offenses but now are deemed criminal offenses or carry heightened penalties. For example, the penalty for unlawful reentry has increased from 2 years. Now, 10 to 20 years is the prison term, with increased enforcement. Third, immigrants can be detained and deported if they are deemed *likely* to be a threat to national security. Immigration law does not have the constitutional protections of criminal law, and it has been used to expel noncitizens on the basis of suspicion.

The expansion of immigration enforcement into a professional policing organization has made border control similar to crime fighting. Border patrol agents can conduct surveillance, chase suspected undocumented entrants, stop persons or vehicles, and make arrests. At present, the number of federal immigration cases is greater than other types of prosecution, greater even than those for drugs and weapons violations. The Department of Homeland Security initiative to collect information on immigrants has blurred the boundary that made immigration solely the object of federal enforcement, because state and local police have access to this database.

Further, public perception of how immigration is handled is affected by parallels between criminal law and immigration law. Although immigrants have the protection of due process, their cases are heard by immigration judges who rule on their cases on the basis of witness testimony and other evidence. The immigrant has the right to hire counsel as well. Detention for a hearing is similar to incarceration, and the Department of Homeland Security now detains permanent residents, women, and even children in addition to unauthorized entrants.

These progressively more severe laws have changed how immigrants were perceived in the past. The public has tended to view even undocumented immigrants as hard workers who want to live the American dream. Currently, undocumented immigrants are increasingly viewed as criminals, because they came unlawfully, or as connected to terrorism. This view obtains despite the fact that the 9/11 terrorists all entered the country legally (albeit in some cases using fraudulent documentation).

Terrorism and Arab or Muslim Immigrants

After 9/11, some Americans developed a xenophobic reaction to individuals of Arab or Muslim appearance. *Xenophobia* is a fear of foreigners. It is known that air passengers requested "Muslim-looking" passengers to be taken off of aircrafts. In response to the World Trade Center catastrophe, the federal government initiated the National Security Entry/Exit Registration System (NSEERS) in September 2002, which required men who were citizens and nationals of certain countries to register. In conjunction with the Department of Homeland Security Absconder Apprehension initiative, many noncitizen Arab or Muslim men were detained and deported for commission of "aggravated felony offenses," which carry the additional penalty of deportation or criminal violations of immigration law. The government, by its actions, treated Arab and Muslim immigrants as outsiders. The failure to locate immigrants connected to the 9/11 attacks has been described by criminologist Michael Welch as an instance of immigrant scapegoating.

Undocumented Entry and Latina/o Immigrants

The size of the Latina/o population and its substantial undocumented component has caused anti-immigrant sentiment to be focused on this group. Politicians have campaigned with immigration as a central issue and often concentrated on the U.S.–Mexico border as a site of controversy. Yet in the 21st century, the label of "nativist" has been avoided by many politicians and academicians advocating immigration restriction or criticizing the undocumented immigration or legal entry of Latinos. Anti-Latina/o immigration restrictionists such as Samuel Huntington often identify as mainstream Americans and represent themselves as patriots who are trying to protect American culture and society from low-income, less-educated minorities whom they fear will not culturally assimilate and consequently will increase crime. They disavow the use of the term *nativist* in a society that has become concerned about social acceptance of cultural diversity following the civil rights era. The generation of the term *immigrant bashing* is a response to the claims of immigration restrictionists that they are not nativists.

Social Consequences of Immigrant Bashing

Immigrant bashing promotes interethnic hatred and conflict. In the post–civil rights era, the criminal and civil law has begun to provide protections for individuals who are attacked on the basis of racial, ethnic, religious, and other sources of difference. One counteractive type of law has been the criminalization of aggressive acts of bigotry. Any act of property damage, assault, rape, or homicide carries an additional penalty if it is committed as the result of antagonism toward a group. The action, which gets a penalty add-on, is called a "hate crime." Another result of attitudinal and legislative change promoting civil rights is that groups formerly labeled as nativistic are called "hate groups." One consequence of immigrant bashing is that nativists and nativist groups can now be divided into non-hate and hate categories. Organizations like the Federation for Immigration Reform (FAIR) may advocate immigration restriction and generate negative publicity about immigration, but they are different from hate groups like the Ku Klux Klan.

Increase in Hate Group Membership

Immigrant-bashing news and politics is associated with increased activity of hate groups linked to the Ku Klux Klan, skinheads, and neo-Nazis. Deborah Lauter, National Civil Rights Director of the Anti-Defamation League, reported that between 2000 and 2005, White supremacist factions grew by 33% and that Ku Klux Klan chapters grew by 63% (Associated Press, 2007). Street protests against unfavorable immigration bills put forward in Congress created immigrant visibility and led to increased nativist hostility. New Klan groups have formed in the South and in states such as Michigan, Iowa, and New Jersey.

Hate Crimes

According to Mark Potok with the Southern Poverty Law Center, White supremacists blame immigrants, particularly Hispanics, for crime, problems with public school funding, and loss of jobs. In reaction, some Americans have committed hate crimes. In Kentucky in September 2006, a Salvadorean family found a cross burning on their lawn. In 2006, a Latino teenager was sodomized and beaten in Houston while "White power" was yelled. One of the attackers has received life in prison.

Lisa Navarette, vice president of La Raza, indicated that negative reactions to Latinos were at a much higher level than previously. As a result of continual negative publicity about U.S.–Mexico border crossers, the FBI has reported a 34% increase in hate crimes against Latinos from 2003 to 2008 (Mock, 2007).

Conclusion

Today, those who vilify and would make immigrants into faceless enemies are becoming polarized from citizens with more complex views about immigration reform. Citizens need to make a reasoned judgment about how immigrants came to commit crimes—whether they are traditional crimes or immigration crimes related to undocumented entry. In addition, one should consider whether legal permanent residents were retroactively deported and separated from families for crimes for which they had served time and had been released from jail or prison. The criminalization of immigration has fostered nativism, hate groups, and hate crimes. In turn, the government is using immigration law—which lacks many constitutional protections afforded to citizens—as a tool to empty the society of undocumented and even legal permanent resident immigrants. Citizens need to come to terms with fear of crime and terrorism in a humane manner and advocate responsible immigration reform.

Judith Ann Warner

See also Immigrants and Crime; Immigration Legislation

Further Readings

Alba, R. (1985). *Italian Americans: Into the twilight of ethnicity*. Englewood Cliffs, NJ: Prentice Hall.

Anbinder, T. (2006). Nativism and prejudice against immigrants. In R. Ueda (Ed.), *A companion to American immigration* (pp. 177–201). New York: Blackwell.

Associated Press. (2007, February 5). *Report: Supremacist activity flourishes*. Retrieved from http://www.msnbc.msn.com/id/16995297

Buchanan, S., & Kim, T. (2005, Winter). The nativists. *Intelligence Report*. Retrieved from http://www.splcenter.org/intel/intelreport/article.jsp?aid=576

Burner, D., Fox-Genovese, E., & Bernhard, V. (1991). *A college history of the United States* (Vol. 1). St. James, NY: Brandywine.

Hoeffer, M., Rytina, N., & Campbell, C. (2007). *Estimates of the unauthorized immigrant population residing in the United States: January, 2006.* Washington, DC: Department of Homeland Security, Office of Immigration Statistics Policy Directorate. Retrieved from http://www.dhs.gov/xlibrary/assets/statistics/publications/ill_pe_2006.pdf

Huntington, S. (2004). Who are we? The challenges to America's national identity. New York: Simon & Schuster.

Legomsky, S. H. (1996). *E Pluribus Unum*: Immigration, race and other deep divides. *Southern Illinois University Law Journal, 101*, 106–111.

Miller, T. (2003). Citizenship and severity: Recent immigration reforms and the new penology. *Georgetown Immigration Law Journal, 17*, 611–666.

Mock, B. (2007, Winter). Immigration backlash: Hate crimes against Latinos flourish. *Intelligence Report*. Retrieved from http://www.splcenter.org/intel/intelreport/article.jsp?aid=845

Pew Hispanic Center. (2006). *Modes of entry for the unauthorized migrant population fact sheet.* Washington, DC: Pew Hispanic Center.

Potok, M. (2004, Winter). The immigration backlash. *Intelligence Report*. Retrieved from http://www.splcenter.org/intel/intelreport/article.jsp?aid=504

Schermerhorn, R. A. (1949). *These our people*. Boston: D. C. Heath.

Southern Poverty Law Center. (2008, March 9). Hate group numbers up by 48% since 2000. *Intelligence Report*. Retrieved from http://www.splcenter.org/news/item.jsp?aid=300

Stumpf, J. (2006). The crimmigration crisis: Immigrants, crime and sovereign power. *American University Law Review, 56*(2), 367–419.

Welch, M. (2006). *Scapegoats of September 11th: Hate crimes and state crimes in the War on Terror*. New Brunswick, NJ: Rutgers University Press.

ANTI-SEMITISM

Anti-Semitism is prejudice toward Jewish people as a religious, racial, and/or ethnic group. Although the term *anti-Semitism* was not coined until the late 1800s by a German writer and political activist, hatred of Jews covers nearly 4 millennia. Jewish people were viewed as alien in the Graeco-Roman world. Hatred of Jews intensified with the emergence of Christianity; Jews were characterized as lawless and dissolute people who were responsible for the killing of Christ. During the Middle Ages, Jews were viewed as Satanic and were subject to massacre. Negative stereotypes of Jews became a central feature of western European cultures in the postmedieval period, including the Enlightenment through the 19th and 20th centuries. The new "science" of racial classification would further be used to castigate and demonize Jewish people, providing a basis for the rise of Nazism and the Holocaust. The establishment of Israel has led to a resurgence of anti-Semitism.

Early History

Pagan anti-Semitism was largely cultural rather than religious, though it provided the basis for Christian anti-Semitism. It appears to have arisen in Alexandria, the most advanced city of the Hellenized world outside of Greece, where Jews constituted 40% of the population and competed with Egyptians for power and privilege. An organized massacre of Jews (pogrom) took place in 38 C.E. in Alexandria with the justification that Jews were unpatriotic and did not worship the same gods as others. Jews refused to acknowledge the gods of others, did not engage in sacrifices or send gifts to their temples, and practiced marriage and kept to themselves. These cultural practices provided justification for anti-Semitism during the pagan period. Examples of antipathy to Jews and Judaism during ancient times include the story in the biblical Book of Exodus of the Egyptian pharaoh ordering all newborn Hebrew boys to be drowned in the Nile. Greek rulers desecrated the Temple and banned Jewish religious practices, such as circumcision, Sabbath observance, study of Jewish religious books, and so on. Many pagan Greek and Roman writers exhibited prejudice toward Jews and their religion in their works.

The Rise of Christianity

Jews have lived as a religious minority in Christian and Muslim lands since the Roman Empire became Christian. Christianity and Islam have both portrayed Jews as those who rejected God's truth. Christians and Muslims have, over the centuries, alternately lived in peace with Jews and persecuted them.

With the emergence of Christianity, both Christians and Jews vied for followers. However, after the Roman Empire became Christian, Jews were increasingly persecuted. Prejudice against Jews in the Roman Empire was formalized in 438, when the *Code of Theodosius II* established Roman Catholic Christianity as the only legal religion in the Roman Empire. The Justinian Code a century later stripped Jews of many of their rights, and church councils throughout the sixth and seventh centuries, including the Council of Orleans, further enforced anti-Jewish provisions. These restrictions began as early as 305, when, in Elvira (now Granada), a Spanish town in Andalusia, the first known laws against Jews of any church council appeared. Christian women were forbidden to marry Jews unless the Jews first converted to Catholicism. Jews were forbidden to extend hospitality to Catholics. Jews could not keep Catholic Christian concubines and were forbidden to bless the fields of Catholics. In 589, in Catholic Spain, the Third Council of Toledo ordered that children born of marriage between Jews and Catholics be baptized by force. By the Twelfth Council of Toledo (682), a policy of forced conversion of all Jews was initiated. Thousands fled, and thousands of others converted to Roman Catholicism.

Influential early Christian writing was strongly anti-Semitic. A cornerstone of such anti-Semitism is the belief that Jewish people should be collectively held responsible for the killing of Jesus. A number of passages in the New Testament have been used to promote anti-Semitism by suggesting Jews committed deicide, the murder of a god. After Jesus' death, the New Testament portrays the Jewish religious authorities in Jerusalem as hostile to Jesus' followers and as occasionally using force against them.

During the Middle Ages in Europe, there was full-scale persecution of Jews in many places, with blood libels, expulsions, forced conversions, and massacres. A main justification of prejudice against Jews in Europe was religious. Jews were frequently massacred and exiled from various European countries. The persecution hit its first peak during the Crusades. In the First Crusade (1096), flourishing Jewish communities on the Rhine and the Danube were utterly destroyed. In the Second Crusade (1147), the Jews in France were subject to frequent massacres. The Jews were also subjected to attacks by the Shepherd's Crusades of 1251 and 1320. The Crusades were followed by expulsions, including the banishing of all English Jews in 1290; in 1396, 100,000 Jews were expelled from France; and in 1421, thousands were expelled from Austria. Many of the expelled Jews fled to Poland.

As the Black Death epidemics devastated Europe in the mid-14th century, annihilating more than half of the population, Jews were taken as scapegoats. Rumors spread that they caused the disease by deliberately poisoning wells. Hundreds of Jewish communities were destroyed by violence. Although Pope Clement VI tried to protect them by the papal bull of July 6, 1348, and another 1348 bull, several months later, 900 Jews were burned alive in Strasbourg, where the plague hadn't yet affected the city.

During the Middle Ages, Jews were often accused of blood libel, the supposed drinking of blood of Christian children in mockery of the Christian Eucharist. Jews were subject to a wide range of legal restrictions throughout the Middle Ages, some of which lasted until the end of the 19th century. Jews were excluded from many trades, the occupations varying with place and time and determined by the influence of various non-Jewish competing interests. Often Jews were barred from all occupations except money lending and peddling, with even these at times forbidden.

In the Muslim world, Jews, as were Christians, were allowed to practice their religion and administer their internal laws subject to a tax and inferior status under Islamic rule. They could not bear arms or testify in court regarding Muslims, and they were required to wear distinctive clothing. Jewish people were also subject to periodic segregation and mob violence. A Muslim mob massacred nearly 4,000 Jews in 1066 in Granada in one of the most violent pogroms.

The Enlightenment

While the Protestant Reformation destroyed medieval Christendom and its extreme anti-Semitism, it did not free Jewish people from prejudice and discrimination. The Enlightenment of the 18th century helped reduce anti-Semitism, particularly in Europe. Based on science, rationality, and the belief in unalienable rights, the Enlightenment rejected the church as the provider of all truth. Humans could, through scientific inquiry, understand the world around them and thus improve the world. With the English Revolution and the emergence of the notion of basic human rights, tolerance, understanding, and progress became the new pillars of society. Since the notion that only those who accepted Christ could be saved was rejected by Enlightenment thinkers, Jews were viewed as human beings who had the inalienable rights. Throughout Europe, most Jews were no longer segregated and discriminated against. They were assimilated into the schools, workplace, military, and other social institutions. Enlightenment thinkers believed this would be the end of prejudice and the triumph of reason. However, anti-Semitism in a new pseudo-scientific form arose with the development of racial classifications. Thus, the old anti-Semitism could be presented not in a religious form, but a "scientific" one. This gave rise to Social Darwinism and the belief that certain racial groups were superior to others and justified colonization and subjugations of "inferior" peoples.

Race

Racist thinkers argued that races differ not only physically but also morally, spiritually, and intellectually. This was often expressed in terms of the "White Man's Burden," which entailed "superior" Aryan races and civilizations needing to conquer and civilize other cultures and races throughout the world. In new pseudo-scientific writing, Jews were viewed as socially inferior. Houston Stewart Chamberlain, an Englishman who became a German citizen, led the way in his book, *The Foundations of the 19th Century* (1899), in which he purportedly "scientifically" showed that Germans were true Aryans and superior to others, particularly Jews. This book was very influential in Germany and became the foundation of the Nazi regime.

Increasing anti-Semitism arose in the 19th century not only in Germany but also in France,

Austria-Hungary, England, Russia, and Muslim countries. This increased anti-Semitism, now founded on pseudo-science, laid the foundation for massive and violent anti-Jewish racism in the 20th century.

While anti-Semitism was evident in early American history, in the first half of the 20th century, American Jews were discriminated against in employment, access to residential and resort areas, membership in clubs and organizations, and in tightened quotas on Jewish enrollment and teaching positions in colleges and universities. The lynching of a Jew, Leo Frank, by a mob of prominent citizens in Marietta, Georgia, in 1915 turned the spotlight on anti-Semitism in the United States and led to the founding of the Anti-Defamation League. In an opposite direction, the case was also used to build support for the renewal of the Ku Klux Klan (KKK), which had been inactive since the 1870s. The KKK was violently opposed to Jews, Blacks, and Catholics. In Germany, increasing hatred of Jews and Jewish assimilation arose. After defeat in World War I (WWI), many Germans saw the Jews as the major benefactors of separation and the Treaty of Versailles. Following WWI, Germany became a federal republic and after a brief period of prosperity fell into a Great Depression. In 1933, Adolf Hitler was appointed chancellor of Germany. He held strong racist beliefs that the Jews were inferior and that they polluted the German state. He had authored *Mein Kampf* in the 1920s while in prison for anti-state activities. It laid out his vision of Germany's future, with Jews blamed as the cause of all of Germany's problems. Given a position of power as chancellor, he saw the most effective method of gaining power through propaganda.

Through propaganda against Communists, Socialist trade unions, and Jews, plus the alleged burning of the Reichstag (the German capitol building) by a Communist, the German Constitution was dissolved and the Nazi Party gained more power in the 1933 elections. Subsequently, the German cabinet gave the government dictatorial powers. The Nazi Party and Hitler now could pass legislation discriminating against Jews in employment, housing, business, and all areas of life. This culminated in the Nuremburg Laws in 1933, which redefined German citizenship, prohibited the pollution of the race, and required couples to undergo medical examinations before marriage. In 1938, Hitler expelled 18,000 Jews who had been born in former Polish provinces. Subsequently, there were bonfires of Jewish sacred books in towns and villages in Germany, Jewish shops were destroyed, and new laws excluding Jews from German economic life were enacted. With the Nazi invasion of Poland in 1939, 2 million Jews were encaptured. Their money and valuables were taken and they were forced into labor. As the Germans invaded Russia and other European countries, the stage was set for the Holocaust.

Holocaust

Although the word *Holocaust* can be traced back to the 17th century as the violent death of a number of people, contemporary usage refers to the systematic slaughter of Jews in all areas of Nazi-occupied territory during World War II (WWII), in what are now 35 separate European countries. It was at its worst in central and eastern Europe, which had more than 7 million Jews in 1939. About 5 million Jews were killed there, including 3 million in occupied Poland, and more than 1 million in the Soviet Union. Hundreds of thousands also died in the Netherlands, France, Belgium, Yugoslavia, and Greece. Nazi documents make it clear that the Nazis also intended to carry out their "final solution of the Jewish question" in England and Ireland upon their victory in these countries.

Anyone with three or four Jewish grandparents was to be exterminated without exception. Historically, in other genocides, people were able to escape death by converting to another religion or in some other way assimilating. This option was not available to the Jews of occupied Europe. All persons of recent Jewish ancestry were to be exterminated in lands controlled by Germany.

The systematic elimination of Jews by the Nazis was based upon the racist ideology that Jews were inferior and the belief that they were responsible for Germany's ills and that there was an international Jewish conspiracy to control the world. Never before has a Holocaust of such magnitude been based largely on upon ideology and myths. The process of extermination included medical experiments, ghettos, concentration and labor camps, death camps, and gassing. According to the lengthy

records kept by the Germans, plus other documents and evidence, at least 6 million Jews were exterminated, as were other Russian and Roman groups, other Poles, other Slavs, the physically and mentally disabled, religious dissidents (e.g., Jehovah's Witnesses), and political enemies (e.g., Communists). The total number of people exterminated is estimated at 9 million to 11 million.

United States

During the first half of the 20th century, anti-Semitism greatly increased in the United States. Between 1881 and 1924, 3 million Jews immigrated from Tsarist Russia to the United States. The White Anglo-Saxon Protestant (WASP) establishment viewed them as alien and un-American. Segregation and discrimination arose quickly in employment, housing, education, and other institutions. Racial theories were popular in the United States, with the Aryans/Whites on top, and Asians, Blacks, and now Jews on the bottom. The belief in racial purity was fueled by purported scientific differences in races. This led to the eugenics movement, the sterilization of so-called inferiors in Canada and the United States. The KKK was able to greatly increase its political and social power in the first 3 decades of the 20th century by leading attacks on this "inferior" Jewish race, plus other inferior races.

The leader of U.S. anti-Semitism was Henry Ford, the auto tycoon. With his newspaper, *The Dearborn Weekly,* he wrote about the international Jewish conspiracy and the threat of Jews. It was widely read in Nazi Germany, and Ford was admired by Adolf Hitler. Ford said Jews were responsible for all the evils of progress (e.g., liberalism, unionism, bolshevism). Hitler was admired by Ford and by many others in the United States. In 1939, thousands attended a Nazi rally at Madison Square Garden in New York City.

After World War II

Following their victory in World War II, the Allies outlawed the Nazi Party. The Nuremburg Trials were held, and several criminals were convicted of war crimes in the wake of WWII. International laws were established covering crimes against humanity and establishing human and social rights, and there was the emergence of the United Nations as a body to address such issues.

Israel

With the creation of Israel after WWII, anti-Semitism increased in the Middle East and Arab worlds. Although anti-Semitism greatly diminished in the United States in the second half of the 20th century, it has changed its nature and form. Racial anti-Semitism now has no credibility since the changing nature of racial classifications no longer includes Semites. However, religious and cultural hatred remains. The establishment of a Jewish state surrounded by Arab (largely Muslim) states has led to numerous wars and continued terrorism against the state of Israel. In fact, several scholars have identified the opposition to the existence of the state of Israel as a new form of anti-Semitism. However, the "traditional" forms of anti-Semitism remain.

A 2005 U.S. State Department Report on Global Anti-Semitism found anti-Semitism in Europe has increased in recent years. Beginning in 2000, oral attacks directed against Jews increased, while incidents of vandalism (e.g., graffiti, fire bombings of Jewish schools, desecration of synagogues and cemeteries) surged. Physical assaults, including beatings, stabbings, and other violence against Jews in Europe increased markedly, in a number of cases resulting in serious injury and death.

France is home to Europe's largest population of Muslims (6 million) as well as the continent's largest community of Jews (600,000). Jewish leaders perceive an intensifying anti-Semitism in France, mainly among Muslims of Arab or African heritage, but also growing among Caribbean Islanders from former colonies. The British Parliament set up an all-parliamentary inquiry into anti-Semitism in 2004, which published its findings in 2006. The inquiry found that since 2000, anti-Semitism has increased.

Since September 11, 2001, anti-Semitism in the United States has arisen in violence against Jews, Jewish institutions, and Jewish symbols due to the alliance between the United States and Israel. Anti-Semitic acts include beatings and shootings of Jews, vandalism and destruction of synagogues,

and spreading of Nazi symbols. The rise of many hate groups, some neo-Nazi, has produced increased anti-Semitism and Holocaust denial.

Charles E. Reasons

See also Anti-Defamation League; Hate Crimes; Immigrants and Crime; Racialization of Crime; Racism; Skinheads

Further Readings

Brustein, W. I. (2003). *Roots of hate: Anti-Semitism in Europe before the Holocaust.* Cambridge, UK: Cambridge University Press.

Cohn-Sherbok, D. (2002). *Anti-Semitism: A history.* Gloucestershire, UK: Sutton.

Katz, J. (1980). *From prejudice to destruction: Anti-Semitism, 1700–1933.* Cambridge, MA: Harvard University Press.

Laqueur, W. (2006). *The changing face of anti-Semitism: From ancient times to the present day.* Oxford, UK: Oxford University Press.

Lee, A. (1980). *Henry Ford and the Jews.* New York: Stein & Day.

Perry, M., & Schweitzer, F. M. (2002). *Anti-Semitism: Myth and hate from antiquity to the present.* New York: Palgrave Macmillan.

ARAB AMERICANS

Arab Americans are citizens or permanent residents of the United States who trace their origin to countries in the Middle East or northern Africa (Algeria, Bahrain, Djibouti, Egypt, Iraq, Jordan, Kuwait, Lebanon, Libya, Mauritania, Morocco, Oman, Palestine, Qatar, Saudi Arabia, Somalia, Sudan, Syria, Tunisia, United Arab Emirates, or Yemen). This entry provides a brief overview of the sociocultural background of Arab Americans and then describes their experiences of hostility and discrimination following the attacks of September 11, 2001.

History

The first influx of Arab immigrants to the United States took place between the late 1880s and the

1920s. A second wave began in the late 1940s, particularly after the 1948 Arab-Israeli war. Between 1925 and 1948, political restrictions were placed on Arab immigration to the United States, and it was further limited by the Depression and by World War II. Most of the recent immigration took place following the 1967 Arab-Israeli war, the civil war in Lebanon, the Kurdi-Iraqi conflict of the 1960s, the Iraq-Iran war from 1980 to 1988, and the Gulf War of 1990. These conflicts have contributed to a large influx of Arab Americans who have come to the United States in search of refuge from war, education, better health care, and an opportunity to establish their own businesses. Many of the Arab Americans in this immigration flow were Muslim, with higher educational backgrounds and incomes than their predecessors.

Demographics

Counting the number of Arab Americans in the United States is challenging in many respects, mainly because of misrepresentation or misidentification of their ancestry. Prior to the 1920s, census data counted Arabs along with Turks, Armenians, and other ethnic groups who were not of Arab origin; non-Syrian Asian Arabs were counted as "other Asians"; and Palestinians were counted as refugees, as Israelis, or according to their last country of residence. While the 1990 census data reported 870,000 Americans identifying themselves as having Arab ancestry, by 2000 this number had grown to 1.2 million. Assuming that census data are adjusted for its race/ethnicity category and that Arab Americans fill out census forms, it is estimated that by 2010 their number will increase to approximately 3 million.

One of the limitations of the census is that, to some extent, it does not overcome the problem of geographic location when taking "Arab" ancestry into consideration. For example, Egypt may be considered by many as an Arab country (particularly because its nationals speak Arabic as their official language); however, some Egyptians consider themselves Africans rather than Arabs. Another limitation is that people may identify themselves by the color of their skin rather than their ethnic origin. The U.S. Bureau of the Census categorizes Arab Americans as Whites, although some of them are Black.

Arab Americans live throughout the 50 United States, but the greatest percentage are in California, New York, New Jersey, Michigan, Ohio, Texas, Illinois, Massachusetts, Maryland, and Virginia. Dearborn, Michigan, has been identified by the U.S. Census Bureau as the city with the highest percentage of Arab Americans. A number of Arab Americans were exposed to multilingual education in their home country before immigrating to the United States and are bilingual, primarily in English and Arabic (the official language of Arab countries). However, they have different dialects, depending on their country of origin.

The majority of Arab American immigrants before 1960 were Christians (Maronites, Coptics, Chaldeans), while the most recent immigrants are mostly Muslim. According to the Arab American Institute, in 2002, 63% of Arab Americans were Christian (Roman Catholics, 35%; Eastern Orthodox, 18%; Protestant, 10%); 24% were Muslim; and the remaining 13% had another affiliation or no affiliation.

About 54% of Arab Americans are male, compared with 49% of the total U.S. population. Approximately 82% of Arab Americans have at least a high school diploma, while 36% have earned a bachelor's degree or higher, and 15% have earned graduate degrees. On average, Arab Americans' earnings are 22% more than the U.S. national average.

Impact of the September 11 Attacks

Prior to the September 11, 2001, attacks, Arab Americans assimilated fairly well with the American community as a whole in terms of dealing with trade, business, education, and other aspects of community living. While to some extent, they were subject to some level of stereotyping, scapegoating, hostility, prejudice, and discrimination prior to 9/11, the September 11, 2001, attacks were followed by increased hostility toward Arab Americans on the part of members of other racial and ethnic groups. One of the misconceptions created toward Arab Americans following the attacks was that they are all Muslim. Religion was therefore confused with cultural background, heritage, and race. Ironically, Arab Americans belong to many different religions, and the greatest number of those residing in the United States are Catholics. This labeling and generalization about Arab Americans, particularly post-9/11, created hostile environments in Arab communities, instilled fear among them, and contributed to an array of incidents occurring against Arab Americans, with hate crimes being the most evident and most reported following the attacks.

The racial/ethnic identification of Arab Americans became even more problematic following 9/11. Hostility and acts of violence were directed against Sikhs, Pakistanis, Indians, and others because they were mistaken for Arabs. Part of this misidentification stems from the misconception that all Arab Americans are Muslim and from misperceptions about multiracial groups.

Hate Crimes and Arab Americans

Hate crimes are crimes motivated by religious, racial, ethnic, national origin, gender, disability, and sexual orientation bias. Although criminal acts motivated by hatred and prejudice have occurred throughout U.S. history, the term *hate crime* did not enter the nation's vocabulary until the 1980s. The FBI has investigated what are known today as "hate crimes" as far back as the 1920s; however, it was only after the passage of the Hate Crime Statistics Act of 1990 and a recommendation to the Attorney General that the FBI's Uniform Crime Reporting program began gathering hate crime statistics. Since 1992, it has published reports on hate crimes annually. From 1992 until 2000, crimes motivated by racial bias comprised the largest portion of "reported" hate crimes, followed by religious and sexual orientation bias. The fewest were crimes motivated by ethnic and national origin bias. (When the disability component was added in 1997, it comprised the smallest number of reported incidents and generally has remained the category with the fewest crimes, particularly since hate crimes based on ethnic and racial bias are combined.)

The distribution of hate crimes based on racial/ethnic bias changed following the 9/11 attacks, with a significant increase in the number of hate crimes against Arab Americans. While the largest number of hate crimes remained those motivated by racial bias, crimes motivated by ethnic bias and national origin bias became the second most frequently reported in 2001. The other significant increase in hate crimes in 2001 was in the category of religious affiliation. Prior to 9/11, the second least reported religion-based hate crimes were anti-Islamic incidents; however, such crimes were the second highest reported following 9/11. (According to data from the *Uniform Crime Reports,* anti-Jewish hate crimes represented the largest number of religion-based hate crimes.)

Both official and community-based organization tabulations—derived from self-reported incidents and newspaper accounts—clearly demonstrate the severity of the September 11 backlash. According to Human Rights Watch, the FBI reported that the number of anti-Muslim hate crimes rose from 28 in 2000 to 481 in 2001, a seventeen-fold increase; the American-Arab Anti-Discrimination Committee reported more hate crimes committed against Arabs, Muslims, and those perceived to be Arab or Muslim, such as Sikhs and South Asians; and the Council on American-Islamic Relations, which tabulated backlash incidents ranging from verbal taunts to employment discrimination to airport profiling to hate crimes, reported 1,717 incidents of backlash discrimination between September 11, 2001, and February 2002 (Human Rights Watch, 2002, Section V, "The Human Rights Backlash").

These hate crimes occurred throughout the United States. Some involved threatening phone calls and other forms of verbal harassment; others were violent crimes, including even murder. The victims included both adults and children, and the attacks targeted Arab American businesses, schools, and mosques as well as individuals. The majority of these acts were against Arab Americans, but some were directed at people who were *perceived* to be of Arab descent or Muslim. For instance, attacks were directed against Sikhs, Iranians, Indians, and other people of different nations who met the racial classification and features of an Arab. Such incidents reflected a widespread misconception of what an Arab American really *looked* like. The persons attacked, whether they were Arab Americans or not, were arbitrarily targeted primarily on the basis of physical appearance or dress.

Law Enforcement and Arab Americans

There is no doubt that the September 11 attacks affected the relationship between Arab American communities and law enforcement officials. One such impact were increases in government scrutiny of Arab American communities and in patrol. An important issue with which Arab Americans were concerned was an increase in immigration enforcement, surveillance, and racial profiling directed at Arab Americans. These actions, along with language barriers and a lack of understanding of cultural and racial differences on the part of the police, contributed to Arab American mistrust of law enforcement personnel. Arab American fears of deportation are another factor in relationships with police and immigration officers.

One strategy that law enforcement officials are using to rebuild trust and stronger ties with Arab Americans is community policing, with a particular focus on issues of public safety and security. Although feelings of distrust and discomfort between Arab Americans and police arguably stemmed from the September 11 attacks, Arab immigrants who have experienced an authoritative, dictatorial regime in their original home countries may have preconceived negative ideas about police and government. Organizations such as the Vera Institute's Center on Immigration and Justice have worked to improve relations between law enforcement and Arab Americans. The Arab-American Law Enforcement Association—a coalition of law enforcement personnel based in Dearborn, Michigan—has partnered with the Vera Institute to identify ways in which the needs of law enforcement can be balanced with the needs of Arab Americans.

Reem Ali Abu-Lughod

See also Community Policing; Media, Print; Hate Crimes; Immigration Legislation, Race Relations; Profiling, Ethnic: Use by Police and Homeland Security; Profiling, Racial: Historical and Contemporary Perspectives

Further Readings

de la Cruz, P., & Brittingham, A. (2003). *The Arab population: 2000. Census 2000 brief*. Washington, DC: U.S. Census Bureau.

Elliott, A. (2006, June 12). After 9/11, Arab-Americans fear police acts, study finds. *The New York Times*. Retrieved November 11, 2008, from http://www .nytimes.com/2006/06/12/us/12arabs.html

Haddad, Y. (2004). *Not quite American? The shaping of Arab and Muslim identity in the United States*. Waco, TX: Baylor University Press.

Human Rights Watch. (2002). The September 11 backlash. *Human Rights Watch, 14*(6). Retrieved October 31, 2008, from http://hrw.org/reports/2002/ usahate/usa1102-04.htm#P310_48768

Jamal, A., & Naber, N. (2008). *Race and Arab Americans before and after 9/11: From invisible citizens to visible subjects*. Syracuse, NY: Syracuse University Press.

Kayyali, R. (2005). *The Arab Americans (The new Americans)*. Westport, CT: Greenwood.

Londner, R., & Hunter, E. (2001, November). Lutheran Arab Americans fear hate crimes. *The Lutheran*. Retrieved November 6, 2008, from http://findarticles.com/p/articles/mi_qa3942/ is_200111/ai_n9017631

Paulson, A. (2003, April 10). Rise in hate crimes worries Arab-Americans. *Christian Science Monitor*. Retrieved November 6, 2008, from http://www .aaiusa.org/press-room/1984/mustread041003

The Prejudice Institute. (n.d.). *Factsheet 5: Arab Americans*. Retrieved October 31, 2008, from http:// www.prejudiceinstitute.org/Factsheets5-ArabAmericans.html

Samuel, W., Cassia, S., & DeLone, M. (2004). *The color of justice: Race, ethnicity, and crime in America* (3rd ed.). Belmont, CA: Wadsworth.

Shakir, E. (1997). *Bint Arab: Arab and Arab American women in the United States*. Westport, CT: Praeger.

Suleiman, M. (1999). *Arabs in America: Building a new future*. Philadelphia: Temple University Press.

Suleiman, M. (2004). Image making and invisible minorities: A case of Arab American students. In G. Goodman & K. Carey, *Critical multicultural conversations* (pp. 79–91). Cresskill, NY: Hampton Press.

U.S. Department of Justice. (2008). *Policing in Arab American communities after September 11*. Retrieved November 11, 2008, from http://www.ncjrs.gov/ pdffiles1/nij/221706.pdf

Websites

National Arab American Journalists Association: http://www.themediaoasis.com/NAAJA-US

ASIAN AMERICAN GANGS

Asian American gangs, operating in U.S. cities since at least the 1960s, attracted police and media attention in the late 1970s and early 1980s when their members were involved in violent, headline-grabbing incidents in New York City and San Francisco. In the 1990s, sociologists began contributing insights into gang-related activities of young Asians in North America. This entry examines explanations that academics, law enforcement authorities, and the media have offered for Asian gang activity since the 1960s, including their connection to adult criminal organizations; social and cultural factors leading to Asian gang formation and participation; and similarities and contrasts between Asian American gangs and gangs from other ethnic groups, and between gangs within different Asian subcultures.

Rise and Proliferation of Asian American Gangs

Asian American gangs formed and began to operate in the Chinatown neighborhoods of New York City and San Francisco in the mid-1960s. The timing makes sense: Prior to 1965, U.S. policy restricted immigration of youths and women from Asian nations. The population of Chinese permitted to enter the United States when immigration policy was reformed supplied the youths who formed the first gangs. Through the 1970s, the Chinatown gangs were composed of immigrants. By the 1980s, American-born Chinese were becoming members.

A large increase in the number of crimes committed by these gangs was recorded through the 1990s. Ko-Lin Chin has pointed out that this increase is likely due to more than just the sheer number of crimes being committed. As Chinatown became a tourist destination, crimes committed there against non–gang members and against non-Asians caught the attention of law enforcement authorities and journalists. At the same time, Chinese gangs began to operate outside Chinatown, another factor widening the circle of victims and making crimes more visible. And the crimes themselves, because they were becoming more serious, were more likely to be reported by victims.

Gangs also formed in Japanese, Korean, and Filipino communities in the 1960s, and later among Southeast Asians. Immigrants from Vietnam and Cambodia came to the United States in great numbers just prior to the fall of Saigon in 1975. A second surge of Vietnamese and Cambodian refugees arrived in the late 1970s and early 1980s. Both waves of immigration included youths who would form and join gangs. Though especially evident in southern California, Vietnamese and Cambodian gangs operate in other locales too. Southeast Asian gang members have been reported in San Francisco, points east, and Chicago, Houston, and cities on the East Coast.

That Asian American gangs proliferated from the mid-1960s until the present is clear, though no precise measurement of activity exists. By the mid-1990s, one quarter of American cities reported problems involving Asian American gangs or gang members who were Asian. A decade later, Canadian authorities reported activity by Asian American gangs in the cities of Vancouver, Edmonton, Calgary, and Toronto. In 2002, police department sources put the number of Asian American gangs during the past 15 years in the West San Gabriel Valley (in Los Angeles County) at 100. It has been claimed that Los Angeles County is home to as many as 20,000 Asian gang members.

Increases in Asian gang membership and activity in the past 4 decades must be put in perspective: overall, a very small percentage of Asian youths who immigrated to or were born in the United States have become members of gangs. As well, the number of Asian American gangs and the number of Asians who are members of gangs are small relative to the same numbers for African Americans, Latinos, and Whites.

Links Between Asian American Gangs and Adult Crime Organizations

With Chinese immigration to the United States in the 1880s came the importation of tongs and triads, social clubs and secret societies that served (and still serve) many functions in Asian communities. While they have acted as legitimate social organizations, performing as political alliances and business associations, they have also participated in organized criminal activities like gambling and prostitution. Inevitably, where these groups engaged in illegal activities, links developed between adult crime organizations and Asian American gangs.

The nature of that linkage is subject to debate. When law enforcement authorities and media discover connections between tongs and Asian American gangs, they often portray a well-organized network of underworld activity, an Asian or Chinese mafia, perhaps of international dimensions, in which youth gangs play the role of junior partners under tong direction. But two scholars—Ko-Lin Chin, who studied Asian American gangs in New York City, and Calvin Toy, who studied Asian American gangs in San Francisco—paint a more nuanced picture. Youth gangs active in Asian communities attract the attention of adult crime organizations. Tongs see advantages in relying on youth gangs for "street-level" assistance in their illegitimate affairs. Gang members, in addition to performing tasks of their own design, take on roles that assist the adult organization. The relationship expands the criminal activities that gang members undertake and provides financial resources to the gangs. On this view, youth gangs are neither organized nor supervised by tongs. Rather, gangs form mutually beneficial relationships with tongs.

Explaining Asian American Gang Involvement

Discussion of Asian American gang etiology and what attracts some Asian American youths to gangs typically takes one of two tacks: the first emphasizing that Asian American gangs form in response to the same factors fostering gang activity among other societal groups, the second emphasizing factors unique to the Asian experience in the United States. Both explanations are accurate.

In the Chinatown areas of San Francisco and New York City, the sudden immigration of a large number of youths in the mid-1960s overmatched the capacity of those communities to meet the newcomers' needs—for education, for jobs, for housing, and so on. Within Chinatown, and outside of Chinatown in neighborhoods where other races predominated, these youths often met a hostile reception. Delinquency rates rose as some youths turned to crime. To bolster their own sense of community, and to protect themselves against attacks from gangs from other neighborhoods, these youths organized themselves, modeling their efforts on the other gangs they encountered. Thus, the story of Asian American gangs mirrors that of other ethnic groups whose youths meet and respond to difficult conditions: alienation and hostile encounters lead to criminal activity. Self-help and self-defense are primary motivations to form gangs. Individuals forming and joining gangs are those who, not welcome or provided for in their environment, find a home, material support, and a sense of identity in gangs.

There are also factors and qualities unique to the Asian American experience that lead to gang formation and membership. As noted previously, tongs have contributed to the development of Asian American gangs. Perhaps this society's characterization of Asian Americans as the "model minority" has played a role in the development of alienation leading to gang involvement, where poor performance in school, a reliable correlate of gang participation in all cultures, may affect Asian American youths with particular force. Also relevant is the tendency for young immigrants attracted to gangs to have more quickly adapted to and taken cues from their new culture than have their parents. Parents of these gang members, some accounts show, are often unaware their children are involved in gangs.

The experience of Southeast Asians who entered the United States from 1975 through the early 1980s is, to researchers and authorities, a special case even within the set of Asian American gangs. It has been hypothesized that trauma refugees suffered fleeing Vietnam, and the stress they experienced when resettling in the United States, had a profound negative effect on the capacity of family relationships to discourage youth involvement in crime and gangs.

Nature and Activities of Asian American Gangs

Descriptions of Asian American gangs from academics, law enforcement authorities, and the media agree on many characteristics describing Asian American gangs. Members represent a wide age range, from early teens to late thirties. Members are almost exclusively male; female participation in

Asian American gangs is very rare. There is apparently little stigma in leaving an Asian gang, or even in joining, leaving, and rejoining. While Chinatown gangs have been concerned with defending their territory, the more recently formed Vietnamese gangs operate with great mobility. It is not uncommon for their members to commit a crime in one city and immediately leave for another location.

Other traits describing Asian American gangs are not accepted by all commentators. Many believe that crimes Asian American gangs commit are almost always for financial ends. Extortion and providing protection to businesses are common examples. Vietnamese gangs are portrayed as relying heavily on "home invasions," where gang members barge into a private residence, often brutalizing the inhabitants, and make off with money and valuables. Asian American gang members, many believe, are less likely than members of non–Asian American gangs to mark their membership with tattoos and scars, preferring to maintain public anonymity.

Randy Wagner

See also Asian Americans; Immigrants and Crime; Juvenile Crime; Model Minorities; Youth Gangs

Further Readings

Chin, K. (1996). *Chinatown gangs.* New York: Oxford University Press.

Kodluby, D. W. (1996). *Asian youth gangs: Basic issues for educators.* Publication of National Alliance of Gang Investigators' Associations. Retrieved from http://www.nagia.org/Gang%20Articles/Asian%20 Youth%20Gangs.htm

Spencer, J. H., & Le, T. N. (2006). Parent refugee status, immigration stressors, and Southeast Asian youth violence. *Journal of Immigrant Health, 8,* 359–368.

Toy, C. (1992). A short history of Asian gangs in San Francisco. *Justice Quarterly, 9*(4), 647–665.

Zhang, S. X. (2002). Chinese gangs: Familial and cultural dynamics. In C. R. Huff (Ed.), *Gangs in America: III* (pp. 219–236). Thousand Oaks, CA: Sage.

Asian Americans

Although they have physical similarities and their ancestral origins are in continental Asia, individuals who identify themselves as Asian come from a broad range of cultures, ethnicities, and societies. With the 2000 U.S. Census, the category of Asian American was expanded to include immigrants from various island nations: Sri Lanka, Indonesia, Micronesia, Melanesia, Polynesia, and Hawai'i. In most demographic reports, these latter locales have given rise to the identifiable reporting category of Asian and Pacific Islander American (APIA). Each immigrant identifies with a particular group, and these groups share many unique and distinct social and sometimes physical characteristics. Over the course of immigration history, Asians have been depicted as a "model minority" who keep to themselves, are industrious, and rarely engage in antisocial behavior. This entry summarizes the way the term *Asian American* is defined, provides an overview of Asian American immigration, and describes crime in the Asian American community, including both crimes against Asian Americans and crimes committed by Asian Americans.

Definition

Knowing who is an Asian American requires knowledge of a map of Asia and an appreciation of global geopolitics and economics, history, cultural anthropology, and the consequences of war. Asians, at one time, were known as Orientals and were described broadly as those whose origins could be traced to the largest continent on Earth. Asia stretches from the Mediterranean Sea in the west to the Pacific Ocean in the east, from the Indian Ocean in the south to the Arctic Ocean in the north. Those who live within these boundaries have been, at times, nomadic and urbane, civil and barbaric; they have been tribal as well as isolationist and possess some of the oldest known civilizations and cultures ever uncovered. The ethnic groups that have immigrated to the United States are as broad and diverse as the land that spawned them. They have rarely shared the same language, although confusion arises because some share the same alphabet. They are unique, and while they share a number of similar characteristics, they cannot be considered the same. To identify any one member of any of these dissimilar groups by an ethnicity not his or her own can be and has been perceived as an insult and can lead and has led to physical conflict.

In general, Asian Americans who migrated to the United States come from Central, South, and East Asia. They can be identified by their specific Asian nationalities, ethnicities, and cultural heritages. In many cases the specific historical epoch in which they left their native lands and established residence as they evolved into Americans is also significant. Each of these groups has its own unique history, culture, and language. Some have had the experience of having a written alphabet created for them after they arrived in the United States, as their history and language did not include literature and was orally or visually based. Another historical curiosity is that West and North Asians are typically excluded from the Asian American designation. Those who have been included have ancestors who migrated from China, Japan, Korea, the Philippine Islands, India, Pakistan, Mongolia, Nepal, Bhutan, Bangladesh, Thailand, Vietnam, Cambodia, Laos, and Burma/ Myanmar. Ethnic groups such as the Hmongs, the Miens, the Kampucheans, and the Taiwanese are also included.

History

Asians came to the United States in identifiable waves of immigration. The first wave was exclusively Chinese immigrants who arrived in the United States in the 1840s. The second wave began in the late 19th century and included primarily Japanese immigrants. The third wave was prompted by the exigencies of the Korean War in the 1950s. The cold war, exemplified by the conflict in Southeast Asia, the Vietnam War, led to the most recent Asian immigration epoch. As each Asian immigrant began the dynamic process inherent in displacement, settlement, and assimilation, he or she faced an American culture and society that was simultaneously and perplexingly resistant and accepting, hostile and friendly, aloof and inviting. World history and the ancillary sociological phenomena that accompany immigration, social movements, and contemporary culture are critical to understanding the effect that time, place, and sociopolitical decision making had on these groups.

The First Wave

In the 1840s, stoop labor was needed to harvest sugar cane in Hawai'i and to lay track for the Trans-Continental Railroad. The first Asian immigrants were virtually exclusively the Chinese who provided service for these industries. A growing body of evidence suggests that immigrant Chinese women were brought to the United States to serve as prostitutes. The completion of the railroad and a national economic downturn led to the enactment of the Chinese Exclusion Act of 1882, which forbade the immigration of subsequent Chinese workers or the family members of those immigrants already in residence.

The Second Wave

The Alaskan Gold Rush of the 1890s and the 1882 Exclusion Act conspired to create a demand for additional stoop and cheap labor to fill the gap necessitated by the masses of laborers who sought their fortunes in the Yukon gold fields. With an invitation extended by President Theodore Roosevelt, the United States requested that the emperor of Japan allow the immigration of more workers to fill this void. This second wave of immigration brought the first immigration of Japanese around the turn-of-the-century 1900s. These "sojourners," as compared to settlers, were young men looking for adventure and opportunity but not necessarily a home. They found the opportunities and lifestyle afforded in the United States to be both challenging and appealing; however, they faced similar discriminatory attitudes and xenophobic laws, such as the so-called Gentleman's Agreement, as those experienced by the Chinese.

Because of various exclusionary laws specifically enacted to monitor rates of immigration for these two groups, over the years, new immigration was limited. In the late 20th century, global economics and history succeeded in decreasing the numbers of new Japanese immigrants while increasing Chinese migration.

The Third Wave

After two world wars and another armed conflict, the door was opened to the next wave of Asian immigration. The 1950s Korean War allowed for economic opportunities and a broadening recognition of life on the Korean Peninsula that had previously received little attention. The tribulations of war created displacement, leading to movement that contributed to another Asian ethnic group seeking a new life in the United States.

The Fourth Wave

The period between the 1950s and 1970s was highlighted by a cold war in Europe that was complemented by a shooting war in Southeast Asia that introduced Americans to a new vocabulary of Asian cultures, countries, and ethnicities. Because of the tribal nature of Southeast Asian populations and the area's history of staving off invasions as well as incorporating from various colonizers—Mongols, the Chinese, the Japanese, the French, and ultimately the Americans—displacement generated migration within the entire region that led to the flow of other landed immigrants to the United States during the 1970s and 1980s. War and displacement opened the door to another wave of immigration, highlighted by Vietnamese, Cambodian, Laotian, and Hmong pilgrims.

Asian Americans in the U.S. Population Today

Figures from the 2000 U.S. Census show that APIAs constitute 4.6% of the total U.S. population. Hawai'i is an anomaly to this discussion, as 49.1% of its total population falls into the APIA category. California (12.8% of its total population), Washington (7.1%), New York (7%), Nevada (6.5%), Alaska (5.2%), and Maryland (5.0%) constitute the largest proportion of Asian residents. Virginia (4.9%) and Illinois (4.3%) likewise have significant Asian populations. However, in the late 20th and early 21st centuries, North Dakota, Nevada, New Hampshire, Arizona, and Florida have all been affected by the dramatic Asian diaspora as the number and variety of Asians establishing residence have settled in the Midwest and East.

Crime and Asian Americans

First-wave immigrants of all stripes, in spite of the historical epoch identifying their migration, have experienced fear and excitement, exploitation and oppression, success and failure. Often compelled to live in specifically defined geographical ethnic enclaves housing others with similar language and cultural awareness, many of these immigrants lacked the economic and employment resources necessary to establish a comfortable and reasonable evolution into the American mainstream. Many became victims of exploitation, despair, crime, frustration, and but a very few experienced prosperity. Much like the prototypical rural resident who seeks a new life and riches in the city but instead finds conflict and anomie, many first-generation Asian immigrants were rural in background and lacked the cosmopolitan sophistication necessary to fend off those who would attempt to victimize them. Over time, most made the cultural adjustments necessary to establish domiciles and integrated communities, establish extended kinship groups, raise their families, and succeed. Their children, those born in the United States as second-generation citizens, like many other immigrant groups, eschew the "model minority" label and ironically turn to those opportunities that would lead them from being victims to becoming victimizers.

Recent hate crime reports depict the victimization of APIAs. Reported incidents in the 2005 FBI *Uniform Crime Report* indicate that law enforcement agencies reported 8,804 victims of hate crimes. Of these, 55.7% were identified as racial bias offenses, and of this number, 4.9% identified victims as Asian/Pacific Islander. One of the most celebrated hate crime cases in the Asian American community was the infamous Vincent Chin slaying outside Detroit in 1982. Chin was beaten by two out-of-work White auto workers who preceded their attack by yelling racial epithets and complaining how the Japanese automotive industry was responsible for the economic plight of the U.S. automobile industry and their own employment status. Chin became their scapegoat.

One of the cultural realities of Asian American crime specifically and ethnic crime in general is that it is adamantly intraracial. Research on victimization rates finds that most ethnic and racial crime victim and offender relationships are committed specifically within class. In this case, most Asian victims can identify their victimizer as an Asian from his or her particular ethnic category.

The history of Asian American crime is steeped in the legend of organizational crime syndicates, for example, the Chinese and their triads and the Japanese *yakuza;* however, these criminal organizations have had little reported influence on U.S. crime. Aside from the rare criminal of Asian descent who finds him- or herself subject to popular cultural scrutiny, such as the tragedy at Virginia Technological Institute in 2007, current reports of Asian American crime are widely attributed to a different sort of criminal organization, the street gang.

Where there is a significant concentration of ethnic Asians in any location—for example, Hmongs in Minnesota and California and Vietnamese in Virginia, Texas, and California—incidents involving "Asian gangs" have gained public notoriety. Ethnic enclaves have long been the focus of immigration and cultural awareness in many metropolitan areas, as Chinatown, Little Tokyo, Little Saigon, Koreatown, and others became ubiquitous. Many Chinatown-organized crime affiliations—that is, tongs—do exist and have been known to utilize newly landed Southeast Asian youths to staff their street enforcers. In New York, these enforcers carry monikers such as the Ghost Shadows or Green Dragons. From about 2002 on, California and Minnesota in particular have seen dramatic increases in the level of violent crime in the Hmong community. Hmongs, a nomadic population originally from Northern Laos and Burma/Myanmar, provide an interesting case study as there are now more Hmongs, per capita, in two U.S. states—California and Minnesota—than there are anywhere else in the world. Homicides, home invasions, assaults, and robberies have increased among self-identified Hmong gangs to the point that sheriffs' offices and police departments in those jurisdictions having Hmong concentrations have created gang task forces, similar to the 1970s–1980s "Jade Squad Detective Unit" of the New York City Police Department that dealt exclusively with crime in Manhattan's Chinatown, to investigate crimes committed by Hmongs. These gangs have taken on the popular culture accoutrement and tactics of tagging, violence, gang inclusion, and community notoriety found in other ethnic gangs throughout the United States.

Official statistics on rates of Asian American crime and victimization are only suggestive and not definitive. Of the total number of inmates in the United States, barely 1% are APIAs and are more often classified as "Other" in official reports.

In Hawai'i, where APIAs are a significant number of the total population, and thus are the exception to the rule, APIAs contribute 65.5% to the total prison population. In Washington, 6.2% of all inmates are APIAs; in Nevada, 5.2%; in California, 4.9%; and in Minnesota, 3.6%. This is to suggest that where APIA populations are densest, they also contribute to the overall crime rate. States without significant Asian populations (less than a percentage point) have only traces of APIAs in their prisons. Of the more than 3,300 inmates on American death rows, six are Asian.

Research Directions

Why Asians commit criminal acts can only be answered through speculation, as not much scientific inquiry has been directed at them. It can be speculated that a combination of economics, conflict, popular culture, and social ecology intersect to create social dissonance among those youths engaged in gang activity. Because many of the current generation of immigrants came from underdeveloped homelands, their economic and workplace wherewithal typically relegates them to lower-income residences and jobs. The environment and population surrounding them, even though they may include those from similar countries and arenas, is often interstitial and inhospitable as all residents compete for limited resources. Schools for the children of these immigrants are often those associated with American inner cities, as economics and popular culture depictions force those less academically gifted students to seek innovative means of social advancement. Added to this is the potential victimization they may face from other similarly disadvantaged ethnic gang members; these Asian Americans seek safety and collegiality with their own gang. Given this reality, those whose desires outweigh their prosocial strengths are destined to find their rewards through alternative sources. The cycle of crime thus becomes perpetuated as antisocial experiences reduce prosocial success.

Because Asians are not uniform in their perspective, thought, or practice, intimate knowledge of one group does not always translate to similar knowledge of a subsequent group. The cliquish nature of the various groups within the Asian communities makes research access challenging.

Language is also a barrier because primary research may require direct contacts with non-English speakers. In some cases, distrust of those who are unfamiliar with cultural customs and mores may result in less than candid interactions and may hamper critical examination and inquiry.

A historical reality is that most Asian Americans have fallen into the category of "model minority," actively engaging in prosocial activity and quietly adding to the mosaic of Americana. Yet seen through the prism of criminological thought, many recent immigrants appear to have more eagerly embraced the antisocial opportunities afforded and have been influenced by the popular culture to engage in criminal activities. Theory construction and testing that examines economics, culture conflict, critical race, and critical criminology hold the richest areas from which to explore these groups.

Dan Okada

See also Asian American Gangs; Immigrants and Crime; Immigration Legislation

Further Readings

Chang, R. S. (1999). *Disoriented: Asian Americans, law, and the nation-state.* New York: New York University Press.

Chin, K.-L. (1996). *Chinatown gangs: Extortion, enterprise, and ethnicity.* New York: Oxford University Press.

Flowers, R. B. (1988). *Minorities and criminality.* New York: Greenwood.

Hamilton-Merritt, J. (1993). *Tragic mountains: The Hmong, the Americans, and the secret wars for Laos, 1942–1992.* Bloomington: Indiana University Press.

Hobson, B. (1987). *Uneasy virtue: The politics of prostitution and American reform tradition.* New York: Basic Books.

Kaplan, D. E., & Dubro, A. (1986). *Yakuza: The explosive account of Japan's criminal underworld.* Reading, MA: Addison-Wesley.

Takaki, R. (1989). *Strangers from a different shore: A history of Asian Americans.* New York: Penguin.

ATLANTA UNIVERSITY SCHOOL OF SOCIOLOGICAL RESEARCH

The Atlanta University School of Sociological Research (AUSSR) is a term of recent vintage intended to highlight the historical importance of work conducted under the auspices of the university in the late 19th and early 20th centuries. The accomplished scholar and social justice advocate W. E. B. Du Bois (1868–1963) became the principal researcher and coordinator of the AUSSR. The Atlanta University School was notable for its general mission—to discover social scientific truth about African Americans as the basis for racial uplift—and also for its incorporation of students, scholars, and community members into a multifaceted and long-term research agenda. Increasingly, Atlanta University is acknowledged as having pursued one of the first U.S. research programs in sociology. This entry sketches the founding of the AUSSR and its research activities, especially the Atlanta University Conferences (AUCs). Also examined are the findings related to African American crime as well as the strengths and limitations of the AUSSR's overall research.

The AUSSR: Its Founding and Activities

Atlanta University was a suitable place to create a research organization, or what Du Bois called a "laboratory in sociology": its goals, location, and institutional norms encouraged critical scholarship. Chartered in 1867, the mission of the university devoted itself to educating newly freed African Americans in a range of skills and courses that spanned high school and college levels of instruction in the industrial and liberal arts. Du Bois himself considered that Atlanta was near the "geographical center" of African Americans in the southern states, an advantageous proximity for the studies to be undertaken. In addition, Atlanta University challenged the norms of the city by the nonsegregated relations of the African American students with the White members of the faculty and their families.

The goal of the AUSSR was similar to those of organizations like the American Social Science Association: following established scientific procedures would enable one to discern the information needed to craft reasonable public policy on societal problems. Typically, the AUSSR conducted research using multiple methodologies (mail-in surveys, personal interviews, personal observations, and archival work with the U.S. Census and other official reports). The use of multiple methodologies helped to overcome the weaknesses of relying on only one method. Given the geographic scope of the research, the AUSSR utilized the services of a range of persons with differing levels of social science training. Some were current students or alumnae of Atlanta University, while others were college-educated or African American professionals in cities around the country.

The annual Atlanta University Conferences (AUCs) were initiated by Atlanta University President Horace Bumstead with the important assistance of George Bradford, a trustee of the university. The AUCs' focus lay in African American urban life and conditions and as initially envisioned was to be the start of many future conferences. The urban focus complemented the annual conferences sponsored by Hampton Institute and Tuskegee Institute, which concentrated mainly on rural issues via promoting how-to information and moral reform. President Bumstead hired Du Bois to teach at Atlanta University and to continue the AUCs. Du Bois greatly expanded the quest for scientific credibility by emphasizing the social sciences and their crucial foundation for social policy or even personal uplift. The goal of the AUCs was to establish a set of 10 research topics, each of which was to be studied every 10 years for a total of 10 cycles. Thus, over the course of a century Du Bois hoped to build a comprehensive knowledge base of African American life, experiences, and institutions—a project never before attempted. Various topics were chosen, involving economics (businesses, property holdings; skilled trades, occupations), religion (churches as social institutions), "morals and manners," and education (institutions and educational attainment), among others. The plan of work of a typical AUC involved commissioning investigators to study a topic in a particular locale using surveys and/or available data sources and convening a conference at Atlanta University at which the data gathered were introduced and other presentations were made by those knowledgeable about the topic. An edited volume, an Atlanta University Publication (AUP), resulted some months later.

Under the auspices of the AUSSR, research projects other than the AUCs and their associated publications were conducted. The U.S. Department of Labor published a few pieces on the conditions of African American life in rural and urban settings. Also, Du Bois presented his findings from a summer research trip in Dougherty County, Georgia, to the congressionally authorized U.S. Industrial Commission. In addition, Du Bois coordinated and set up the "Georgia Negro Exhibit" at the Exposition Universelle held in Paris in 1900, for which he received a gold medal for "Collaborator as Compiler of Georgia Negro Exhibit." Not to be overlooked were Du Bois' many publications in the popular press and his well-known book, *The Souls of Black Folk*.

Critiques of the Atlanta University Publications

The Atlanta University Publications (AUPs) often received favorable reviews from their contemporaries. However, scholars also have highlighted problems with the AUPs, some of which Du Bois himself had previously acknowledged. In many instances, attempts were made to be as comprehensive as possible (e.g., trying to locate all African American college graduates or to survey criminal justice officials in all Georgia counties), thereby obviating the need for sampling procedures. However, in practice the response rate often was low or the answers were deemed unusable. That problem and others, such as ascertaining the veracity of the mail-in self-responses to surveys, remain even today as limitations for survey research. Accordingly, the AUPs repeatedly cautioned that some of the data provided only modest support for the contentions made. Several AUPs were exemplary and fulfilled the mission of the AUCs (for example, in the studies of the African American artisans—that is, skilled workers—one could easily compare official data in similar categories over time). But other AUPs were somewhat problematic.

Although later AUPs often cross-referenced related ideas or findings with earlier ones, the AUPs often did not compare data from a later study with the previous ones in any explicit way. Thus, diachronic analysis—one of the long-term goals of the AUSSR—would not be possible in the strictest sense. This was compounded by changes in the questions or wording of the survey instruments, a point that Du Bois suggested might occur if practical considerations warranted it. Moreover, many of the survey responses were simply quoted in the text, but were not coded and quantified. While certainly important in a qualitative sense, this did not fulfill the quantitative mission of conventional social science.

Du Bois' Departure and Return to Atlanta University

In 1910, Du Bois left Atlanta University to take a position as editor of *The Crisis*, the periodical of the newly organized National Association for the Advancement of Colored People (NAACP). Sufficient money to finance the AUCs had been a recurring concern, although the conferences did receive funding over time from philanthropic organizations. Du Bois believed that his personal politics on race, including his disagreements with Booker T. Washington's strategies for racial progress, had made it difficult for Atlanta University to secure funding. Another reason for Du Bois' departure was that he wished personally to expand the scope of his activities in pursuit of racial and social justice. The AUCs continued for several years after Du Bois' move to *The Crisis*. He provided support and editorial input, coediting four more AUPs with Augustus Granville Dill, who had been a student at Atlanta University. Nevertheless, the AUCs ultimately ceased many decades short of their projected long-range plans.

During his years at the NAACP, Du Bois' ideas for racial justice reached a national and international audience, but his views increasingly clashed with many in the NAACP's leadership. By 1934, Du Bois had returned to Atlanta University and the opportunity to further pursue his academic scholarship. At the school, Du Bois directed some of his energy toward research that was more historical than sociological; yet he never abandoned social science. During the 1940s Du Bois sought to rekindle the social scientific research begun decades earlier, but on a much larger scope. He began editing and publishing *Phylon: The Atlanta University Review of Race and Culture*, an academic journal that showcased social science research. In addition, Du Bois coordinated plans with representatives from various land-grant colleges across the country, designing an extensive program of state-centered research on African Americans. Several

conferences were held and their findings published as AUPs, but Du Bois' unexpected and forced retirement from Atlanta University in 1944 ended those efforts.

Findings on Crime in Specific Works of the AUPs

Two publications of the AUSSR analyzed in some detail the issue of African American crime and criminals: *Some Notes on Negro Crime, Particularly in Georgia* in 1904, and to a lesser extent, *Morals and Manners Among Negro Americans* in 1914. *Some Notes on Negro Crime* accepted the U.S. Census data that depicted African Americans as committing more crimes relative to their numbers in the overall population. However, in the critical spirit that animated the AUSSR, this study questioned the official reports and the conclusions drawn from them, raising the following issues:

1. The amount of African American crime was exaggerated by the enumeration method used by the U.S. Census and by the sentencing disparities between White and Black defendants for the same crime.

2. African American crime was not trending upward as reflected in reinterpreted official data and by qualitative responses from mail-in surveys sent to Georgia local government officials.

3. Education was not directly associated with African American criminality because official census data indicated that illiterate African Americans committed more crime in both northern and southern states than did literate African Americans.

4. African Americans were not innately (not biologically) more criminal than other races because the behaviors associated with criminals (e.g., illiteracy, poverty, low self-esteem, intemperance, and lack of thrift), it was argued, were the result of slavery and the ongoing discrimination and inequities of the U.S. social system.

To strengthen the case that those historical factors—a mix of social-structural and cultural causes—were major influences on African American crime, more data would have been useful than was available in this work. Pertinent data to present would have included data on Whites and Blacks in similar demographic categories, data on Whites in different demographic categories, and data on Blacks in other countries.

The AUCs did not follow *Some Notes on Negro Crime* with a paired study 10 years later. A footnote in a 1917 AUP indicated that a follow-up study on crime was indefinitely delayed. Nevertheless, *Morals and Manners Among Negro Americans* did provide one section specifically focused on African American crime. New data were not collected, but it did present comparative data on Whites that would strengthen support for the contention that sociohistorical conditions, rather than innate, immutable racial traits, explained African American criminal actions. In addition to suggesting ways for African Americans to morally uplift themselves, *Morals and Manners* recommended various societal ways to mitigate Black crime, including the end of discrimination in jobs, housing, and the criminal justice system, as well as the promotion of political and civil rights.

The Lasting Significance of the AUSSR

The AUCs did not span the 100 years envisioned by Du Bois. Yet for many reasons the AUSSR was a significant endeavor. It was the first attempt at a detailed social scientific research program that studied African American lives, conditions, and progress and that publicized the findings in different venues. It entailed a network of Black professionals collaborating on a research process that directly challenged prevailing theories based on the idea of unchangeable, inheritable racial traits. The research into social scientific explanations of African American actions did not repudiate personal responsibility. But the sociohistorical explanations examined by the AUSSR did spotlight the glaring inequities and discriminatory practices experienced by African Americans in a country commonly accepted as an exemplar of democratic freedom and equality.

Robert W. Williams

See also Biological Theories; Crime Statistics and Reporting; Du Bois, W. E. B.; Historically Black Colleges and Universities; National Association for the Advancement of Colored People (NAACP)

Further Readings

Du Bois, W. E. B. (1968). *The autobiography of W. E. B. Du Bois*. New York: International.

Gabbidon, S. L. (1999). W. E. B. Du Bois and the "Atlanta School" of Social Scientific Research, 1897–1913. *Journal of Criminal Justice Education, 10*, 21–38.

Gabbidon, S. L. (2007). *W. E. B. Du Bois on crime and justice: Laying the foundations of sociological criminology*. Aldershot, UK: Ashgate.

Lewis, D. L. (1993). *W. E. B. Du Bois: Biography of a race, 1868–1919*. New York: Holt.

Lewis, D. L. (2000). *W. E. B. Du Bois: The fight for equality and the American century, 1919–1963*. New York: Holt.

Wright, E., II. (2002). The Atlanta Sociological Laboratory 1896–1924: A historical account of the first American school of sociology. *Western Journal of Black Studies, 26*, 165–174.

AT-RISK YOUTH

At-risk youth is a concept that emerged in education literature in the early 1980s to denote an individual's probability of failure to complete high school and/or actively participate in the labor market. In 2008, the term is used to identify, label, and classify adolescents who are vulnerable to adverse economic and social conditions.

The ever-increasing classification of at-risk youths continues to be one of the most significant predictors of antisocial and risky behavior, delinquency, and criminal offending. Extant literature suggests that the concept has evolved over time from a labor market–focused conceptualization of risk to one centered on more broad implications. More specifically, the conceptualization of risk has shifted from one associated with an array of individual costs to one associated with the greater social costs to society. The increased labeling of at-risk youth coupled with the shift in the conceptualization of this population has resulted in the disproportionate classification of minority youth in general, and Black and Hispanic youth in particular. While this concept has predominated in educational research, social scientists have become intrigued with the associated attitudes and behaviors attributable to antisocial behavior and the onset of criminal offending. Although *risk*, broadly defined, encompasses a broad range of factors that have implications for the individual as well as society, social scientists have tended to focus on those factors that disproportionately affect communities characterized by physical decay and social disorder. As such, discussions centered on at-risk youth tend to be focused on particular segments of a larger population.

Education, the High School Dropout, and the Creation of the At-Risk Youth

The failure to complete high school, more commonly referred to as "dropping out" in education literature, has been and continues to be a fundamental educational and social phenomenon plaguing the American public school system. In the early 1980s, the system came under scrutiny due to students' inability to meet the minimum course requirements in fulfillment of graduation and resultant retention issues. The heightened awareness and increased concern about this growing problem resulted in numerous reports on education and state reforms to raise the current academic standards.

A Nation at Risk

In 1983, the National Commission on Excellence in Education published *A Nation at Risk,* a report addressing the risk that less than full participation in the labor market posed to the individual, society, and the nation. Predicated on the belief that all children were equipped with the tools to secure gainful employment in an effort to be self-sufficient, productive citizens of society, the commission concluded that one's inability to fulfill this role would have grave individual, social, and societal costs. The failure to complete high school was considered both detrimental to the individual and a risk to society and the nation as a whole. The commission concluded that individuals ill prepared for the "information age" would inevitably be disenfranchised and unable to participate fully in national life. The commission's characterization of dropping out as an academic failure and a risk to the nation dramatically shifted the way in which the phenomenon of dropping out was both viewed and addressed by academicians, state officials, and the general public.

At-Risk Youth: History, Definition, and Consequences

Research addressing issues related to failure of high school completion and the associated consequences began to predominate in fields outside of education and economics. As individual and social consequences associated with dropping out continued to be identified, a new conceptualization of risk emerged.

The predominance of research coupled with the growing popularity in nontraditional fields has resulted in the reconceptualization of the concept predicated on the assumption that youth are at risk not because they engage in behavior that has been deemed risky, but rather because they reside in environments that pose a severe threat to their quality of life and well-being. The reconceptualization of risk, as predicted by socially situated factors, inevitably widens the net and increases the probability of classification. Moreover, the vagueness of the concept results in the likelihood that practically any youth could be considered *at risk* by the very accident of birth. One of the critical concerns related to employing this advanced, albeit conventional, definition has to do with the disproportionate number of Black and Hispanic youths who are increasingly being classified as at risk or risk prone.

Individual, Social, and Societal Consequences

Implicit in the language of *A Nation at Risk* are the consequences that directly affect society and the nation as a whole. The failure to complete high school has traditionally served as the most significant predictor of risk—individual, social, and societal. The failure of individuals to be self-sufficient, productive citizens able to participate fully in national life results in a significant burden on the society. The reduced national income and tax revenues for the support of government services and increased demand for social services result from a lack of full participation in the labor market.

The consequences are not limited to one's relationship to the labor market and economic realization. Rather, an added consequence of limited educational attainment is the risk of antisocial behavior and criminal involvement. Social scientists, in an effort to investigate crime and antisocial behavior, have been particularly intrigued by the utility of the concept, as it allows for a prediction to be made without the presence of direct support.

An ever-increasing number of children, adolescents, and youth are labeled *at risk* based on a countless number of economic and social factors. The term has become a codeword to identify, label, and classify the ever-increasing number of youth, especially Black and Hispanic youth, that are represented in the foster care, juvenile justice, and social service systems.

Misha S. Lars

See also Delinquency and Victimization; Juvenile Crime; Labeling Theory; Profiling, Racial: Historical and Contemporary Perspectives

Further Readings

Fischer, M. L., & Kmec, J. A. (2004). Neighborhood socioeconomic conditions as moderators of family resource transmission: High school completion among at-risk youth. *Sociological Perspectives, 47*(4), 507–527.

Fishbein, D. H., & Perez, D. M. (2000). A regional study of risk factors for drug abuse and delinquency: Sex and racial differences. *Journal of Child and Family Studies, 9*(4), 461–479.

Kolberg, W. H. (1987). Employment, the private sector, and at-risk youth. *Annals of the American Academy of Political and Social Science, 494*, 94–100.

McDill, E. L., Natriello, G., & Pallas, A. M. (1986). A population at risk: Potential consequences of tougher school standards for student dropouts. *American Journal of Education, 94*(2), 135–181.

National Commission on Excellence in Education. (1983). *A nation at risk: The imperative for educational reform.* Retrieved from http://www.ed.gov/pubs/NatAtRisk/title.html

Patchin, J. W., Huebner, B. M., McCluskey, J. D., Varano, S. P., & Bynum, T. S. (2006). Exposure to community violence and childhood delinquency. *Crime & Delinquency, 52*(2), 307–332.

Resnick, D., & Burt, M. R. (1996). Youth at risk: Definitions and implications for service delivery. *American Journal of Orthopsychiatry, 66*(2), 172–188.

Rumberger, R. W. (1987). High school dropouts: A review of issues and evidence. *Review of Educational Research, 57*(2), 101–121.

Stroup, A. L., & Robins, L. N. (1972). Elementary school predictors of high school dropout among Black males. *Sociology of Education, 45*, 212–222.

VandenBos, G. R. (Ed.). (2007). *American Psychological Association Dictionary of Psychology.* Washington, DC: American Psychological Association.

ATTICA PRISON REVOLT

From September 9 to September 13, 1971, prisoners in New York State's Attica Correctional Facility held control of this maximum-security prison. Forty-three people died during that time; state police and correctional officers killed 29 prisoners and 10 correctional staff members and wounded 80 people during the quarter of an hour that it took for officials to retake the prison. The McKay Commission, which provided the official report on the events at Attica, called it the "bloodiest one day encounter between Americans since the Civil War." When these events occurred, nearly 60% of Attica's population was Black and 100% of the correctional officers were White.

The prisoner revolt at Attica took place during 5 days. However, the event is best understood within three contexts that span decades both before and after the Attica revolt: (1) historical contexts of protest and state repression preceding the revolt; (2) the period during the revolt: initial taking of the prison, the negotiations, and the retaking of the prison; and (3) the years of litigation after the revolt that have affected prisoners, correctional staff, and the families of both.

Historical Context of Attica

The historical context of the revolt at Attica provided the formative years for the prisoners and correctional staff and government officials involved in the events. During the 1960s, the civil rights and other rights movements (including prisoner rights), protests against the Vietnam War, violent disturbances in America's urban centers and prison riots in New York and other states prior to the events at Attica, and police action against protest and activist organizations (including the Black Panthers and Black Muslims) provided a model for violence for prisoners and for the state. Other instances of violence during this period included the assassinations of Malcolm X,

Martin Luther King, Jr., and Robert Kennedy, as well as the killings of Black Panther members George Jackson (one of the Soledad Brothers) and Fred Hampton (a Black Panther leader in Chicago). Criminal justice reforms that occurred in the decade before the 5 days of the revolt are also part of the historical context. In addition, a new emphasis on research on all aspects of criminal justice during the decision-making processes from arrest decisions to parole during the 1960s was finding race to be an important factor throughout. Through these events and the understanding of the politics of criminal justice it produced, prisoners were redefining themselves as "political prisoners."

In New York State, prisoner disturbances and takeovers of correctional facilities in New York City's House of Detention (Tombs) in August 1970 and Auburn Correctional Facility (November 1970) preceded the events at Attica. While these two events did not result in the violent retaking of the institutions seen at Attica, they did add to the tensions and expectations of both prisoners and correctional officials in New York regarding the potential for further prison revolts. Prisoners from Auburn were transferred to Attica and placed in segregation (contrary to correctional officials' promises of no reprisals for those involved in the Auburn protest over the handling of a Black Solidarity Day event).

The Attica Revolt

On September 8, 1971, confusion over the handling of an inmate interaction was one spark for what was to come on September 9; there was a question whether the interaction had been a fight or horseplay. Other precipitating factors included the striking of a lieutenant by a prisoner, the taking of the prisoners to a special housing block, and inmate expectations concerning the treatment of the prisoners. On September 9, when a lieutenant involved in the September 8 incident asked a group of prisoners to return to their cells after breakfast, he was attacked. In the chaotic violence that followed, prisoners eventually gained control of the institution after a failed weld on a gate allowed them access to a central control area called "Times Square." The McKay Commission that investigated the events at Attica reported that

the inmates had control of all four cellblocks and all of the tunnels and yards in the Attica complex and that more than 1,200 inmates had gathered in "D" yard with more than 40 hostages.

The Negotiations

While the prison revolt at Attica was part of a larger pattern of prison disturbances and protests during the late 1960s and early 1970s, for a number of reasons the negotiations that occurred in an attempt to obtain a peaceful settlement made the event much more significant and visible. First, that the negotiations took place at all is unique since negotiating with prisoners is not common practice. Second, an agreement was made to utilize an "observers committee" containing prominent African American and Hispanic political leaders from New York, activist lawyers, journalists, activists from the Black Panthers and Young Lords, and others representing more conservative perspectives. Members of the committee were used to mediate the negotiations and provided diverse perspectives and advice to Russell Oswald, Commissioner of Corrections. Third, the decision to allow TV reporters to enter the prison and film negotiations and comments of prisoners and hostages brought the events inside the prison to national attention. During the 5 days of negotiations, tensions within groups of correctional personnel and their families, prisoners and their families, and state police officials continued to build. On the evening of Sunday, September 12, negotiations finally ended; the assault of the prison took place the next day.

The Retaking of the Prison

On the morning of September 13, 1971, after a final ultimatum from Commissioner Oswald was read to prisoners, they took eight hostages to catwalks and held knives to their throats or bodies. Fifteen minutes after inmates' rejection of the ultimatum, a helicopter dropped tear gas into the yard and shotgun and rifle fire from state police and correctional officers commenced. When the firing stopped, 10 hostages and 29 inmates were dead or dying. From a state police helicopter, inmates were told to place their hands on their heads and surrender. They were told to sit or lie down and that they would not be harmed. Within an hour the prison had been secured. State police and correctional officers then started the process of dealing with the dead and wounded correctional personnel and prisoners and having the surrendered prisoners stripped, searched, and moved back to the cell blocks. In December 1971, a Federal Court of Appeals found that the harassment and reprisals directed at prisoners by correctional officers in the days after the riot entitled prisoners to protections against any recurrence.

One of the most infamous incidents of the revolt at Attica occurred shortly after the main yard had been secured. Gerald Houlihan, Public Information Officer for the Department of Corrections, told the press that several hostages had died as a result of inmates having slashed the officers' throats. The interviews with state police officers who reported being eyewitnesses to such inmate brutality generated headline stories describing inmate brutality. Less than 24 hours later, however, autopsy reports of the dead hostages found that all had died from gunshot wounds.

The Years Following Attica

Throughout the years after the events at Attica, criminal prosecutions of inmates, court hearings, and lawsuits seeking to hold prison and government officials in New York State responsible for the deaths continued. In all, 62 inmates were indicted for more than 1,200 criminal acts, while during that time one trooper was charged for one crime. In 1974, then–New York Governor Hugh Carey sought to end inquiries into the Attica uprising when he pardoned seven inmates and commuted the sentence of a prisoner convicted of killing a correctional officer. In addition, Governor Carey ruled that no disciplinary action should be taken against 19 police officers and one civilian whom investigators had suggested should be disciplined for their actions in the retaking and aftermath of the disturbance. While criminal prosecutions had ended, civil suits by prisoners seeking monetary damages for the use of excessive force continued for years. It was not until 2000, nearly 30 years after the events, that the state of New York settled a civil suit brought by inmates for $12 million. In 2005, Governor George Pataki created a $12 million fund as a settlement with the "Forgotten Victims of Attica," families of hostages and other correctional officers killed and injured during the retaking of the prison.

Lucien X. Lombardo

See also Black Panther Party; Police Use of Force; Prison, Judicial Ghetto; Race Riots; Social Justice

Further Readings

Badillo, H., & Haynes, M. (1972). *A bill of no rights: Attica and the American prison system.* New York: Outerbridge & Lazard.

Bell, M. (1985). *Turkey shoot: Tracking the Attica cover-up.* New York: Grove.

Chen, D. W. (2000, January 5). $8 million offered to end Attica inmates' suit. *The New York Times,* pp. A1, 23.

Clark, R. X., & Levitt, L. (1973). *The brothers of Attica.* New York: Links.

Featherstone, R. A., & Paschen, S. (2005). *Narratives from the 1971 Attica prison riot.* Lewiston, NY: Edwin Mellin.

Jackson, G. (1970). *Soledad Brother: The prison letters of George Jackson.* New York: Bantam.

Kerner Commission. (1968). *Report of the National Commission on Civil Disorders.* New York: Bantam.

McKay Commission. (1972). *New York State Special Commission on Attica.* Attica, NY: Basic Books.

National Lawyers Guild/New York City Chapter. (1992, March 6). *The sound before the fury: An evening commemorating the 20th anniversary of the Attica uprising and the continuing struggle.* New York: Author.

Oswald, R. (1972). *Attica: My story.* Garden City, NY: Doubleday.

Wicker, T. (1975). *Attica: A time to die.* New York: Quadrangle/New York Times Books.

Websites

Attica Revisited: A Talking History Project: http://www .talkinghistory.org/attica/pacifica-1.html

BALDUS STUDY

The Baldus study, designed and conducted by David C. Baldus, George C. Woodworth, and Charles A. Pulaski, Jr., is a study of "equal justice" in death sentencing during a period of judicial conflict and controversy over capital punishment. This landmark study focused on levels of arbitrariness and racial discrimination in capital sentencing in Georgia during the period 1969–1979.

Three principal reasons led the authors of the study to concentrate on the state of Georgia. First, Georgia led the nation from 1930 to 1980 in the total number of offenders executed. Second, the U.S. Supreme Court's decisions in both *Furman v. Georgia* (1972), which invalidated all capital sentencing statutes, and *Gregg v. Georgia* (1976), which upheld the constitutionality of the death penalty for murder, focused on Georgia's capital sentencing system. Third, the study was designed to challenge Georgia's post-*Furman* capital sentencing system on issues of arbitrariness and racial discrimination. As a consequence, the Baldus study was created to contest the effects of several key factors in the post-*Furman* era: the trial court sentencing reforms adopted by state legislatures, the expanded appellate oversight by state supreme courts, and the strict oversight of death penalty sentencing systems by state courts to ensure that they operate in a nondiscriminatory fashion.

The Baldus study consists of two empirical studies known as the Procedural Reform Study (PRS), which compares pre- and post-*Furman* results as a basis to estimate fairness in Georgia's capital sentencing in the post-*Furman* period, and the Charging and Sentencing Study (CSS), which was designed to study racial discrimination patterns for defendants indicted for murder or voluntary manslaughter between 1973 and 1979. Although the two studies differ in design, they both challenge the effects of the death sentence process in Georgia.

The impact of the Baldus study culminated in the U.S. Supreme Court case of *McCleskey v. Kemp* (1987) as an unsuccessful attempt to dispute the effectiveness of Georgia's death penalty statute. The petitioner in the *McCleskey* case argued that the Georgia death penalty statute under post-*Furman* law purposefully discriminated against defendants who were Black and against defendants whose victims were White, which subsequently violated the Fourteenth Amendment's equal protection clause. In addition, *McCleskey* argued that this discriminatory application of the death penalty violated the Eighth Amendment as a result of the arbitrary, capricious, and irrational nature in which the death sentence had been invoked. The question would follow as to what magnitude the Court would give empirical data and statistical analysis as evidence in proving discrimination in a post-*Furman* death sentencing system.

Research Design, Sample, and Data

The PRS

The PRS focused on decision making by the prosecutor and the jury in the final two stages of

Georgia's charging and sentencing process. More specifically, it examined the prosecutor's decision to seek the death penalty based on a capital murder conviction at trial and the jury's decision to declare a life or death sentence after a penalty trial. Therefore, only defendants convicted of murder after a jury trial were included for analysis. The primary purpose of the PRS was to compare the extent of arbitrariness and racial discrimination for those offenders convicted of murder at trial before and after the statutory reforms established as a result of the *Furman* decision.

In response to *Gregg v. Georgia*, another objective for the PRS was to evaluate the Georgia Supreme Court's system of comparative sentence review of murder trials. The comparative sentence review is mandated by Georgia statute and establishes a method in which to compare sentencing decisions in similar cases as a means to circumvent excessive or disproportionate penalties for defendants who receive a death sentence.

The pre-*Furman* data set consisted of 156 defendants tried and convicted of murder before the *Furman* decision, from 1969 to 1972. The post-*Furman* data set included 594 offenders who were apprehended, charged, prosecuted, and convicted for murder under the post-*Furman* law between 1973 and 1978. These offenders either received a life or death sentence as a consequence of a jury trial or received a death sentence as a result of pleading guilty to murder. The defendants in both data sets were selected from the Georgia Department of Offender Rehabilitation files and from the official reports of the Georgia Supreme Court and the Georgia Department of Pardons and Parole. In addition, more than 150 aggravating and mitigating factors were collected and developed for both the pre- and post-*Furman* data sets.

The CSS

The CSS was initiated at the request of the NAACP Legal Defense and Educational Fund to challenge the constitutionality of Georgia's death sentencing as it had been applied as a result of the *Gregg v. Georgia* decision. The primary purpose of the CSS was to expose which racial and other illegitimate case characteristics might influence the criminal justice process from indictment up to and including the penalty trial for a death sentencing

decision. Five decision points in the Georgia charging and sentencing process allowed analysis of the multistage case review. The multistage decision points include the grand jury indictment stage, prosecutorial plea bargaining and the plea of guilt, jury conviction decisions, prosecutorial decision to seek the death penalty after a capital murder conviction at the trial phase, and jury sentencing decisions at the trial's penalty phase.

The CSS data set consisted of a stratified random sample of 1,066 cases selected from the offenders listed in the records of Georgia's Department of Offender Rehabilitation between 1973 and 1979. These offenders had been arrested and convicted of homicide and were subsequently convicted of murder or involuntary manslaughter. For each case, a file of more than 230 variables was created from the files of the Georgia Board of Pardons and Paroles as a foundation for multivariate statistical analysis.

Methodology

The PRS

For the PRS, the authors created a sophisticated statistical construct formulated on a regression-based culpability index that was used in conjunction with both ordinary least squares and logistic multiple regression models designed to detect the effects of which legal factors (i.e., prior record, aggravating or mitigating circumstances) or extra-legal factors (i.e., race of defendant and victim, offender-victim relationship) were statistically significant when predicting which defendants received the death penalty. Furthermore, two additional indexes were developed to measure excessiveness and discrimination for each of the following outcomes: (a) pre-*Furman* death sentence decisions among defendants convicted of murder at trial; (b) post-*Furman* death sentence decisions for defendants convicted of murder at trial; (c) post-*Furman* decisions by prosecutors to pursue a death sentence for defendants convicted of murder at trial; and (d) post-*Furman* jury decisions to impose a death sentence in a penalty trial. The primary objectives of the statistical analyses were to identify the likelihood of arbitrariness and discrimination in death sentences and to identify which case characteristics affect death sentence decisions for prosecutors and juries for defendants convicted of murder at trial for both pre- and post-*Furman* periods.

A subsequent objective of the PRS was to determine whether death sentences in Georgia were either excessive or disproportionate under the 1973 statute, which required the Georgia Supreme Court to conduct a comparative review of similar cases for every capital felony case that was imposed after January 1, 1970. The purpose of comparative sentence review by the court was to determine whether it was imposed by reason of "passion" or "prejudice." To accomplish this analysis, the authors conducted an extensive assessment of 68 death sentence cases that the Georgia Supreme Court reviewed and affirmed between 1973 and 1979 using three different measures of case culpability in which to identify similar cases (Baldus et al., 1990).

The CSS

The CSS incorporated a principal culpability index to explain which defendants in the multi-stage analysis were ultimately selected to receive a death sentence by prosecutors and juries. Utilizing their culpability index, the authors applied a variety of linear and logistic regression procedures to determine which variables accounted for racial effects. The two primary models used 39 and 230+ variables respectively in conjunction with racial variables to identify factors that showed a statistically significant relationship with the dependent variables (multiple stage outcomes from indictment to the jury penalty trial decision).

Findings

The PRS

In the pre-*Furman* era studied by the authors, death sentencing was observed to be infrequent. In addition, the study found no meaningful basis on which to distinguish a large portion of pre-*Furman* death sentences from cases that ended in life sentences during the same period. For example, even when penalty trials did occur, juries generally imposed death sentences in only about one half of the cases, and only a fraction of the death sentences occurred in extremely aggravated cases. In part, the authors found pre-*Furman* death sentencing

excessive, partly attributable to geographic disparities (statewide), and partly because of the implication of racial discrimination among moderately aggravated cases (the most prominent finding). It is within these moderately aggravated cases that racial factors have the most influence in the pre-*Furman* period—defendants who were Black or whose victims were White received more harsh sentences than other defendants equally blameworthy. Therefore, even though excessiveness could be shown within the range of moderately aggravated cases in all pre-*Furman* death sentence cases in Georgia, racial factors were not always determinative.

The authors' assessment of Georgia's proportionality review system of 68 death sentence cases that were affirmed by the court on appeal between 1973 and 1979 suggested that about one fourth were presumptively excessive. Many of the excessive death sentences fall into the mid-aggravation range of culpability where race effects are concentrated. From this perspective, the Georgia Supreme Court appeared more likely to be evenhanded and non-excessive when it affirmed death sentences based on similar cases for comparative purposes of the Court's findings. However, the caveat is, as the authors observed, when the court selects "similar" cases, it generally overselects cases that resulted in death sentences and underselects life sentence cases. In fact, the Georgia Supreme Court had never vacated a death sentence as racially discriminatory or comparatively excessive. As a result, this selection process made it difficult to determine the overall magnitude of racial factors. Although the Georgia court had not vacated a death sentence based on proportionality review, it had reversed more than 20% of the death sentence cases that it had reviewed based on procedural reasons.

When racial factors in the post-*Furman* logistic multiple regression analysis were considered, a higher percentage of accuracy was obtained when predicting who received a death sentence. Race of the victim was the most significant racial variable. For example, the authors found that for offenders convicted of murder at trial, the odds of a defendant whose victim was White receiving a death sentence was 4.3 times greater than a defendant whose victim was Black. Only the legal variable, number of aggravating circumstances, had more explanatory power than race of the victim. In contrast, race of the defendant had no effect except when cases from urban and rural areas were separately critiqued. Also included in the analysis were other ethically questionable case characteristics that had a statistically significant impact in determining who was sentenced to death. These case characteristics included the defendant's socioeconomicstatus, the victim's socioeconomic status, the defendant's out-of-state residence, the presence of a race motive for the crime, defendants with a court-appointed attorney, and bloody circumstances of a murder. The authors found within these factors that the presence of a racially "antagonistic" motive increases the likelihood of a death sentence in Black defendant/White victim cases. In contrast, in White defendant/Black victim cases, the racial motive is a statistically significant mitigating circumstance.

Post-*Furman* results show that the impact of the defendant's race changed dramatically from the pre-*Furman* period. In post-*Furman* cases, Black defendants suffered more in rural areas as a result of prosecutorial decisions. In contrast, White rather than Black defendants were more likely to receive a death sentence in Georgia's urban areas as a result of both jury and prosecutorial decisions. In addition, defendants with low socioeconomic status were at a disadvantage in rural areas as a consequence of jury decisions, whereas high-socioeconomic-status defendants were more disadvantaged as a consequence of urban prosecutors. Thus, the interactive effects of racial factors, socioeconomic status of the defendant and victim, and the residence of the defendant (urban or rural) all had a significant impact on post-*Furman* death sentence decisions; most notable, though, was the race of the victim. Therefore, from their analyses, the authors found that the offender's culpability and the strength of the evidence were not the only factors being considered for death sentences after the *Gregg v. Georgia* decision.

The CSS

The results of the statewide CSS study presented during the *McCleskey v. Kemp* case were quite similar to the PRS findings. The major difference was that while there was a race of defendant-victim relationship in the PRS, only the victim's race was significant in the CSS study. The authors found that in both post-*Furman* studies, the odds multiplier calculated from the race-of-the-victim coefficientin their respective analyses was 4.3 for defendants found guilty of murder at trial. As in the PRS study, the CSS analysis shows a distinct association between the aggravation range of culpability and the magnitude of the race-of-the-victim effects. Specifically, the greatest race-of-the-victim effects occur in the mid-aggravation range of culpability, where the death sentencing rates are quite high. When compared with other legal variables in the 39-variable model, the race-of-the-victim variable was similar in the magnitude of effect to factors such as "multiple stabbing," "serious prior record," and "armed robbery involved."

Prosecutorial decisions to seek a death sentence following a murder conviction at trial and the jury penalty trial decision were two additional areas of focus for the authors. The results of both the linear and logistic multiple regression analyses of racial discrimination in jury decisions were mixed; however, the race-of-the-victim effects in death sentencing among defendants indicted for murder were linked principally to prosecutorial pretrial and posttrial decisions. As a result, the analyses show that within the decision-making stages after indictment in murder trials, it is the prosecutor who is the main source of race-of-the-victim discrimination, especially within the midrange level of aggravation.

McCleskey v. Kemp

The Baldus study had its most prominent exposure during the U.S. Supreme Court case *McCleskey v. Kemp* (1987). Prior to the *McCleskey* case reaching the Supreme Court, the results of the Baldus study had already gone through an extensive evaluation in Atlanta by Judge J. Owen Forrester during a postconviction evidentiary hearing of the case involving Warren McCleskey. Judge Forrester rejected McCleskey's discrimination and arbitrariness claim because he felt the database used in the Baldus study was not trustworthy, that the statistical procedures used were flawed, and the data and statistical procedures were not sufficient to support a claim of deliberate discrimination under the Fourteenth Amendment or a purposeful claim of arbitrariness under the Eighth Amendment.

Subsequently, the Eleventh Circuit Court of Appeals also found that the petitioner had failed to prove his claim of arbitrariness and discrimination. Although the court acknowledged the validity of the Baldus study, it essentially found that the statistical evidence rendered by the statistical analyses did not expose the level of disparity that could justify intent or motivation.

In 1987, the U.S. Supreme Court, by a 5–4 vote, affirmed the Eleventh Circuit's rejection of McCleskey's claim. The majority (led by Justice Powell) also acknowledged the validity of the Baldus study; however, they rejected the use of statistics to prove an equal protection violation in the context of the death penalty. Furthermore, Justice Powell held, with regard to McCleskey's Eighth Amendment claim, that although the statistical evidence "at most" indicates "a discrepancy that appears to correlate" with race, "[it] does not demonstrate a constitutionally significant risk of racial bias affecting the Georgia capital-sentencing process" (*McCleskey v. Kemp*, 1987). In sum, although the Baldus study did not prevail in the *McCleskey* case, it brought to light the importance of empirical studies on issues of discrimination and arbitrariness within the court system.

Keith A. Wilmot

See also Death Penalty; *Furman v. Georgia*; *Gregg v. Georgia*; *McCleskey v. Kemp*; NAACP Legal Defense Fund

Further Readings

Baldus, D. C., Woodworth, G. C., & Pulaski, C. A. (1990). *Equal justice and the death penalty: A legal and empirical analysis*. Boston: Northeastern University Press.

BATSON V. KENTUCKY

This entry discusses the impact of the U.S. Supreme Court's ruling in *Batson v. Kentucky* (1986) on the use of peremptory challenges during the jury selection process of the American justice system. The case brought attention to the role of race as reason for dismissal from jury participation and highlighted the importance of a defendant's right to trial by an impartial jury.

Synopsis of the Case

James Batson, an African American man, was convicted of burglary and receiving stolen property in a Kentucky circuit court. Controversy arose from the verdict because it was handed down by an all-White jury. Attorneys for Batson appealed on the basis that the voir dire (the jury selection process) had been unfair.

During voir dire, potential jurors are often selected on the basis of how their attitudes, opinions, and experiences may be related to the case being tried. Depending on these attributes, the prosecution and defense may utilize a limited number of peremptory challenges. Peremptory challenges can be used to excuse a potential juror member if one side feels that the juror may side with the opposition. Traditionally, attorneys were able to excuse a member from voir dire without a stated reason.

The prosecuting attorney for the case, Joe Gutmann, used his challenges to excuse all four African American people who could have potentially served as jurors for the case. This led defense attorneys to appeal to the U.S. Supreme Court, stating that Batson's rights under the Sixth and Fourteenth Amendments were violated during jury selection.

Significance of *Batson* for Peremptory Challenges

The U.S. Supreme Court has stated that peremptory challenges should not be exercised in any way that would violate the rights of the defendant. When used in a discriminatory manner, these challenges have the potential to violate the equal protection clause granted under the Fourteenth Amendment. In addition to this, the challenges may violate the Sixth Amendment, which guarantees a person the right to a speedy and public trial by an impartial jury of the state and district where the crime had been committed. This means that a jury selected for trial should be representative of the community to which the defendant belongs. The selection of a representative and impartial jury protects the defendant from any arbitrary and unfair actions by the prosecution.

Peremptory challenges not only protect the rights of defendants but also protect those members of the venire (i.e., potential jurors). If venire members are excused solely on the basis of their race, they are not given a fair chance to serve the courts of their community. These members may be able and qualified to serve and may be an asset to the defendant by helping to ensure that the trial is fair and impartial. That chance is destroyed when race alone is a determining factor in jury selection.

Supreme Court Decision

The *Batson* side appealed the case to the U.S. Supreme Court, citing the case of *Swain v. Alabama*, 380 U.S. 202 (1965). This case set the precedent that applied the equal protection clause to peremptory challenges. The Court recognized that denying African Americans participation as jurors violated this clause of the Fourteenth Amendment of the Constitution. Certiorari (an order for lower courts to send documentation for the higher courts to review the lower court's decision) was granted to determine if Batson was indeed tried under an impartial jury and an unfair representation of the community.

In its final decision, the U.S. Supreme Court lowered the burden of proof for prima facie case of discrimination during the selection of a jury. The Court also held that a state denies African American defendants equal protection when it puts that person on trial before a petit jury excluding members of that person's race. Also, persons cannot be excluded from the venire based on the belief that members of his or her race are not qualified to serve as jurors.

Criticisms of *Batson* Challenges

Criticisms surrounding the *Batson* case and peremptory challenge regulations have arisen since the U.S. Supreme Court's decision. Some critics contend that unlawful racial discrimination is still a concern within the criminal justice system and that peremptory challenges should be closely regulated and monitored more often in courtroom situations. The second viewpoint is that because of increasing number of restrictions being placed on the use of peremptory challenges protections they are slowly being eliminated.

Others argue that *Batson* challenges are ineffective in the fight against discrimination during the jury selection process. Proving that a person was excused based solely on race can be a difficult matter to prove to the court.

Critics also suggest that a lottery system or the use of surveys and questionnaires may offer an alternative to face-to-face interaction between attorneys and potential jurors. Some suggest that these methods would keep the race factor hidden, so that a person could not be excused because of his or her race. The opposing side claims that such systems would be inferior ways to select a jury because they deprive attorneys of the opportunity for personal interaction with potential jurors.

The issues raised by *Batson* continue to be a subject of debate. Some argue that the guidelines for peremptory challenges established in *Batson* are an obstacle to the choice of the most qualified jurors. Others suggest that potential jurors are being dismissed in a discriminatory manner. In any case, the *Batson* case raised important questions about the role of race in the U.S. judicial system and calls attention to the central role of equal protection as guaranteed by the U.S. Constitution.

Lisa M. Carter

See also Capital Jury Project; Jury Nullification; Jury Selection

Further Readings

Batson v. Kentucky, 476 U.S. 79 (1986).

Goldwasser, K. (1989). Limiting a criminal defendant's use of peremptory challenges: On symmetry and the jury in a criminal trial. *Harvard Law Review, 102*(4), 808–840.

Stoltz, B. W. (2007). Rethinking the peremptory challenge: Letting lawyers enforce the principles of Batson. *Texas Law Review, 85*(4), 1031–1056.

Swain v. Alabama, 380 U.S. 202 (1965).

BIOLOGICAL THEORIES

Biological explanations of crime emphasize physiological and neurological factors that may predispose a person to commit crime. Biological theories are outgrowths of the positivist school of criminology. The advent of the scientific method during the 19th century spurred an increasing interest in aggravating and mitigating factors to criminal behavior. Positivism succeeded classical criminology's free will and choice model, positing instead that criminal behavior is the result of an innate, involuntary biological force beyond individuals' control.

The earliest biological theories searched for the "criminal man"; they were intent on pinpointing a criminal gene or telling physical feature. Later biological theories are more sophisticated in their inclusion of social or environmental factors. These explanations of criminal behavior posit that biological factors contribute to traits that are conducive to crime, and that such developments may be mediated by social environments. This entry traces the development of biological theory as it is developed, tested, and implicated in policy. Earlier theories, which focus on innate individual characteristics rather than environmental factors, are described chronologically. Modern evolutionary, biosocial, and biochemical theories are described, along with contemporary claims concerning biological risk factors and environmental toxins. The policy implications of both early and modern biological theories are also reviewed.

The First Biological Theories

Claims that there is a link between biology and crime were made in Europe as early as the 1700s as positivist theory. The chronologically ordered works of major contributors to the theory detail its progression.

In the 1760s in Germany, Johann Lavater reported a relationship between facial features and behavior. F. J. Gall, 4 decades later, studied phrenology; he believed skull shape determined criminality. Cesare Lombroso, the "father of modern criminology," developed the notion that ailments and diseases contributed to mental and physical deficiencies that could result in violence. As his career progressed, he paid greater mind to environmental explanations, believing there were hereditary, social, economic, and cultural variables to criminality, but he never relinquished the notion of a born criminal type. One of his students, Enrico

Ferri, emphasized those latter elements, focusing on the interrelatedness of factors that contributed to crime. He presented five criminal types; their common thread was a lack of individual rationalization or choice. Similar to Ferri's work is Raffaele Garafalo's; both were representative of the times and of Mussolini's regime, based on ideas of racial purity, national strength, and authoritarian leadership. The publication of Garafalo's major works coincided with the height of the Darwinian era, when suggestions from biology, psychology, and the social sciences related how criminal law and penal practice could guarantee the survival of the fittest.

Overall, these biological theories were too simplistic; comparisons provided little support for such theories. The works mentioned previously were not advanced by statistical evidence. Distinctions made between criminals and noncriminals were speculative, a problem for biological theories that was not short lived. In 1913, Charles Goring's statistical computations regarding physical differences between criminals and noncriminals confirmed his hypothesis of criminals' physical inferiority but fell short of illuminating a physical criminal type. In 1930, G. J. Mohr and R. H. Gundlach associated some of those same body types with specific criminal behaviors; yet they did not demonstrate a relationship to any psychic elements. Earnest Hooten found criminals inferior to civilians in nearly all of their body measurements in 1939; however, his work had clear racial overtones and lacked a proper sample. In 1949, William Sheldon found that the factors that produce delinquency are inherited; his physical findings were supported one year later by Sheldon and Eleanor Gleuk. Despite the ability of the positivist theories to be tested based on their scientific modeling, replication in testing and in turn validity was scant. However, the influence of biological theories on policy was not.

Policy Implications of Early Theories

Biological theories, on the foundation of positivism, turned the goals of penology from abstract metaphysical and legal explanations to scientific studies of the individual actor and the conditions under which acts are committed. The following two policy examples illustrate the danger this vein of theory threatens in both passively or explicitly promoting racism.

According to earlier biological theories, government-sponsored social change is an improper interference with nature. Social welfare policies were considered defective because they perpetuated the survival of the less able while interfering with the natural abilities and resources of those most able. This concept was extended by crime control policies enacted to prevent the introduction of criminals to society by not permitting those deemed defective to reproduce. Lombroso's concept of "born criminal" and Garafalo's "policy of elimination" were based on the assumption that the only remedy for criminality was to eliminate affected individuals from society and provided a basis for penal philosophy based on incapacitation. As well, rehabilitation policies based on biological theories operationalized medical reasoning that individuals, as biological objects, need treatment; it can be argued that these policies were among the most repressive policies in U.S. history. More than 30 states passed eugenics laws requiring sterilization for behavioral traits thought to genetically affect criminality.

Modern Biological Theories

By the 1960s, biology's influence in criminology had lessened. This could be attributed partly to the uses of such theories by the Nazis in the Holocaust. The scientific prominence of natural sciences and the influence of the rapidly growing social sciences were increasing. In 1975, E. O. Wilson published *Sociobiology,* which proposed to interpret all new discoveries of social and behavioral sciences in essentially biological terms. Neurological research began citing potential links between "brain damage" and "neurological defects" and criminality. Several research efforts were approved to map the human genome and to study DNA fingerprinting. An increase in medical treatment of behavior disorders was indicative of a biological focus as well. Thus, the search for the criminal man as a biologically distinctive offender continued.

Currently at issue is whether this search will contribute to the view that criminals are a distinctive,

dangerous class of people who are inherently depraved and beyond redemption. Most current theories are more nuanced than this, rejecting the idea that biology translates into predestined fate, suggesting instead that biological traits interact with social environments to shape human behavior. These approaches are called "biosocial theories." J. R. Lilly, F. T. Cullen, and R. A. Ball's *Criminological Theory* provides an etiology for these theories.

Evolutionary Theories

Efforts have been made to formulate theories based on evolutionary principles. Evolutionary theories are generally "biosocial" although they tend to emphasize nature over nurture. Often considered evolutionary-ecological theories, some stress the impact of environmental (ecological) forces. Though empirical support is negligible, evolutionary theories, such as the following examples, are important because they carry a value judgment that the behaviors they cite are "useful," "valuable," "effective," and "desirable" in terms of human survival. Cheater theory argues that whereas "dads" obtain reproductive opportunities by fulfilling female desires for a mate who can support offspring, "cads" use force or deception to impregnate a female. Persistent criminals fall into the cads category. r/K theory cites two approaches to reproduction. Rapidly producing organisms follow an "r strategy," emphasizing more reproduction and spending less time caring for each. "K strategy" involves slower reproduction and careful care of each offspring. Criminals would be more prone to the r strategy. Based in Darwinian thought, conditional adaptation theory maintains that children who live in unstable or hostile environments engage in sexual activity early as an adaptive response to ensure reproduction. Evolutionary expropriative theory assumes all humans are genetically driven to acquire resources with the ultimate goal of reproduction. Some do this through creation and development of resources, others expropriate resources through victimization.

Biosocial Theories

Biosocial approaches acknowledge the importance of learning but emphasize the extent to which learning and conditioning of behavior occur differently for different individuals because of neurological variations. An individual does not inherit a specific behavior but tends to respond to environmental factors through general predispositions. Newer theories have attempted to locate genetic factors by examining behavioral similarities among family members. They stress behavioral characteristics such as hyperactivity and attention deficit disorder. Literature has noted biochemical differences between controls and individuals with psychopathy, antisocial personality, violent behavior, or conduct disorder, including levels of certain neurotransmitters and metabolic processes as well as psychophysicological correlates of psychopathy.

Biochemical Theories

Recent biochemical theories focus on sex hormones and neurotransmitters. For males, sex hormone theory has concentrated on connections between testosterone and aggression. Biosocial theorists who favor a testosterone-based theory of criminality use it to explain relatively higher rates of male criminality. Similarly, theories have suggested females are affected by hormonal shifts before menstruation, leading to a syndrome characterized by seriously distorted judgment and tendencies toward violence; along with postpartum depression, these theories have been used as defenses in infanticide and other cases.

Effects of neurotransmitters (chemicals mediating signals between brain neurons) have been examined as well. Association between biochemical factors and antisocial behavior falls prey to the-chicken-or-the-egg conundrum: Which came first? Of the various environmental factors influencing physiology, biological theorists have focused on diet, allergies, vitamin deficiencies, exposure to lead or cadmium, and consumption of certain substances found in foods.

Biological Risk Factors

The more sophisticated biosocial approaches trace antisocial behavior to many biological risk factors that increase the odds of delinquency and criminal behavior, especially if combined with any negative environmental conditions. One example of this is an alleged link between low IQ or learning disability and criminal behavior. However, there is no direct link between low IQ and crime.

Rather, low IQ can result in poor performance in school, which in turn can lead to lack of resources (employment), which can lead to crime.

Biosocial factors work in two directions. They contribute to criminality and they insulate against it. For example, "kin altruism" is considered a protective factor. Some statistics show that the rate of fatal child abuse against a stepchild by a stepparent runs 40 to 100 times greater than that against a biological child by a biological parent. This suggests that biological kin have a greater affinity for one another that serves to reduce the violence that might otherwise be higher.

Environmental Toxins

Biosocial criminologists are joined by radical theorists in arguing that environmental damage is among the most serious contributors to criminality today. Research indicates that frontal lobe deficits associated with antisocial behavior can often be traced to common environmental neurotoxins such as lead. If biosocial theorists are correct, these pose a serious criminogenic problem. Environmental toxins are significant risk factors to hyperactivity, learning disabilities, and IQ deficits, all of which are then risk factors for antisocial behavior identified by biosocial theory.

Policy Implications of Modern Biological Theories

As biological theorizing gained prominence during the 1980s and 1990s, concern turned to policy consequences. Richard Herrnstein and Charles Murray's *The Bell Curve* spawned great discussion of the disparate effect such theories can have on particular groups in society, especially with regard to race.

The Bell Curve reports significant correlations between intelligence and ethnic categories, including that Blacks have lower IQ scores than Whites. Simultaneously, it argues that IQ is hereditary and one of the greatest predictors of criminality, thus arguing for a public understanding of this nature of intelligence and its social correlates to guide policy decisions. However evidence-based and logically stepwise the conclusions, the implications of such policies possess inherent potential for disparate effect on minority populations (according to the book's reported IQ scores).

Overall, biosocial theorists report that whether a genetic predisposition toward criminal activity is encouraged or discouraged depends on the environment. Rather than race as a direct predictor of criminality, particular groups may be more likely to live in criminogenic environments and, as such, commit more crime. No criminal gene has been discovered, and history lingers as a reminder of the negative potential of policies informed by biological theory. Perhaps it was this concern that led D. H. Fishbein to establish four forms of evaluation to be performed upon biological perspectives before they may inform policy; these include estimation of the incidence of biological disorders among antisocial populations and identification of etiological or causal mechanisms.

Heather R. Tubman-Carbone

See also Conservative Criminology; r/K Theory; Social Disorganization Theory; Strain Theory

Further Readings

Fishbein, D. (2001). *Biobehavioral perspectives in criminology.* Belmont, CA: Wadsworth/Thomson Learning.

Gabbidon, S. L. (2007). *Criminological perspectives on race and crime.* New York: Routledge.

Herrnstein, R., & Murray, C. (1994). *The bell curve: Intelligence and class structure in American life.* New York: Free Press.

Lilly, J. R., Cullen, F. T., & Ball, R. A. (2007). *Criminological theory: Context and consequences* (4th ed.). Thousand Oaks, CA: Sage.

BIRTH OF A NATION, THE

The year 1915 marked the premiere of the film *The Birth of a Nation.* The film was unprecedented for its time and represented a new milestone in filmmaking and presentation, replete with an orchestral score. The movie not only ushered in a new theatergoing experience but also set the mark for many silent films to come. Though theatergoers were charged an unheard-of $2 to see the film, the admission fee was quite minimal compared to the production cost of the film, which was estimated at $110,000—the highest of its time and for many years to come. The response to this film was parallel only to its production cost. In addition to the cost and epic proportions of the film, a storm of criticism and violence ensued, and drums were beating for the return of the Ku Klux Klan. This entry describes the basis for the film, positive and negative criticisms, political and community reactions to the film, and the process leading up to the revival of the Ku Klux Klan.

The film, directed by D. W. Griffith, was based on Thomas Dixon's novel *The Clansman.* Dixon's novel was based on the Civil War, the ensuing Reconstruction period, and the redemption of the defeated South through the hands of the Ku Klux Klan. Dixon, after having studied at John Hopkins and serving in the North Carolina legislature, served as a minister in North Carolina, New York, and Boston. During his time as a minister in the North, Dixon's fiery sermons found a receptive audience. These sermons, often targeting Black Americans, were replete with racism and bigotry, and the receptiveness of audiences sparked the writing of *The Clansman.*

Given the political atmosphere and sociocultural mores of the times, Dixon's novel was met with much success. In particular, the success of the novel was strengthened by northern fears of Black migration, President Woodrow Wilson's federal segregation policies and cutbacks of Blacks from civil service, and renewed interest in deportation and colonization of Blacks.

Although Griffith was fully aware of the sensationalistic attacks on Black Americans, he felt that he could use a combination of history and fact to mold Dixon's novel into a successful film. Griffith's interest in directing the film was drawn by Dixon's romanticized story of southern defeat and its rise to redemption during Reconstruction. Dixon's own distaste of interracial relations also came through during the movie.

The film opened in Los Angeles to positive acclaim and was soon scheduled for showing in New York City. Although the Los Angeles premiere was met with success, the newly created National Association for the Advancement of Colored People (NAACP) soon challenged the merits of the film. The NAACP was emerging as a vocal interest group preserving the rights of Black citizens. As

W. E. B. Du Bois and other early members of the organization began to challenge the basis of the film, Dixon began to mount his defense of the film by calling on figures of prominence and national recognition who might help to buttress the film.

On February 13, 1915, Dixon called on President Wilson, a former friend and student at Johns Hopkins, to arrange for a private screening of the movie. Dixon called on President Wilson because of the president's scholarly background in history and sociology. Prior to the screening, Dixon asserted to President Wilson that the film would serve as a new medium for presenting information to a wide audience and for collecting public support. Five days after having spoken to President Wilson, Dixon was entertained at the White House and presented the movie to Wilson and several colleagues. After viewing the film, President Wilson claimed it was like "writing history with lighting" and advanced his view that, unfortunately, the story was true.

Following the positive response from President Wilson, Dixon continued to gather support by asking U.S. Supreme Court Chief Justice Edward D. White to view the film. Dixon was able to persuade Chief Justice White to see the film by drawing on White's southern heritage and sympathy. Having gathered the support of President Wilson and the Chief Justice of the Supreme Court, Dixon arranged for a showing with the National Board of Censorship. Dixon and Griffith, having received the support of the National Board of Censorship, amassed a substantial amount of support from the political elite of Washington and were then ready to promote the premiere of the film in New York.

Having become aware that the National Board of Censorship approved the film, the NAACP sent members to the board and presented a list of demands. They demanded the names of the board members who had approved the film, a list of cities showing the movie, and a private screening of the film. All the NAACP's demands were denied. On appeal, Chairman Frederic Howe, who had voted against the film, provided a list of all board members and arranged for a private screening. The NAACP felt that the movie depicted Black Americans as dangerous sexual predators and played into the worst fears of Whites.

On the day the film was to premiere, the NAACP called Griffith and Spottiswoode Aitken, the producer of the film, to report to a New York police court on complaints that the film presented a "public nuisance" and was a threat to basic public welfare. Attorneys for Aitken and Griffith argued that the film was not a risk to public welfare and cited the support of President Wilson. After their successful argument, the lay judge presiding over the case ruled that he could not prohibit the premiere of the film since there was no evidence of public endangerment.

Although Dixon had gathered substantial support for the film and Griffith remained untouched by the criticism of the film, the storm created by the film continued. Oswald Villard, owner of the *New York Evening Post* and a staunch opponent of President's Wilson segregation policies, attacked the film as a vessel of racism, bigotry, and prejudice. Villard extended his attack by requesting that New York Mayor John P. Mitchell cancel showings of the film. Following this request and increasing pressure by the NAACP, the National Board of Censorship, after viewing the movie, ordered that select scenes in the movie be removed.

Upon completion of the film edits, the NAACP viewed the film and was still displeased. After repeated requests were made to Mayor Mitchell, the mayor viewed the film and deemed it capable of breaching the peace. The producers of the film were made aware of the mayor's position, and they removed additional scenes from the film, although the NAACP was still displeased with the second revisions.

One month later, after the second revision of the film, a Boston theater showing the film witnessed the first case of public disruption when an audience member threw refuse at the movie screen. Within the same month, a violent altercation occurred when a group of Black customers was denied access to tickets to view the film. A large crowd formed, and police officers were called to quell the demonstration. Massachusetts Governor David Walsh seized the opportunity to put forth a bill in the legislature that would prohibit racially inflammatory films. Ultimately, the bill failed when the state judiciary committee ruled it to be unconstitutional but was eventually solicited in the U.S. Congress.

Reactions like the one in Boston began to occur across the country. Du Bois realized that the increasing criticism coming from the NAACP was only increasing interest in the film and limited the negative position of the organization.

Following the events in Boston, Dixon was asked the purpose of the film. Dixon's response was interpreted to mean that he wanted the country to learn the true story of Reconstruction and that the film portrayed the story with accuracy. Specifically, the film was intended to create hate in White males and females toward Black males.

President Wilson, having previously voiced support of the film, disliked the negative publicity that it had garnered. His chief of staff, Joseph Tumulty, advised the president that his support of the film would cost him votes in the 1916 presidential election. A steady flow of criticism came from the New York headquarters from the National Colored League, and national newspapers reported outbreaks of violence in cities where the movie had premiered.

Despite the film's historical inaccuracies, numerous attempts to censor the film, and the repeated criticisms and attacks by the NAACP, all of which were aimed at discrediting the film, the appeal of the film remained strong and widespread. As a result of the film's success, a large number of White Americans fell victim to the film's romantic and inaccurate story of the dramatic redemption of the South by the Ku Klux Klan. Support for the film ignited a renewed interest in the Ku Klux Klan and the country's secret societies, fueling organizations to revive the fraternal order.

Griffith received a great deal of criticism for his making of the film. Despite the criticism, he maintained that the film was an accurate portrayal of history based in large part on the use of scholarly sources to construct the story of the film. Though the film is widely criticized due to its purported historical inaccuracies, it is important to note that the sources and scholarly texts Griffith relied on as a basis for the film were claimed to be the most thorough and accurate at the time.

Andrew Bradford

See also Du Bois, W. E. B.; Ku Klux Klan; Ku Klux Klan Act; Lynching; NAACP Legal Defense Fund

Further Readings

A hundred years of terror. Retrieved from http://vlib.iue .it/history/USA/ERAS/klukluxklan.html

Jackson, K. T. (1967). *The Ku Klux Klan in the city.* New York: Oxford University Press.

O'Reilly, K. (1997). The Jim Crow policies of Woodrow Wilson. *The Journal of Blacks in Higher Education, 17,* 117–121.

BLACK CODES

Following the Civil War, southern legislatures created the Black Codes to regulate the civil and legal rights and responsibilities of former slaves and free Blacks. In the face of the devastation caused by the Civil War and the ensuing economic depression in the agriculturally based economy, severe restrictions were imposed on Black people so that they would not gain legal, political, economic, and social rights. Indeed, the Black Codes were designed to maintain White control over the Black population. While the Black Codes were different from restrictions during slavery, they placed the states in a position similar to that of the former slave masters.

Black Codes not only controlled the lives of Black people but also were the source of free labor, which was needed to replace the abolished slave labor. Since the Thirteenth Amendment allows slavery as a punishment for a criminal conviction, several states enacted vagrancy and other racially based laws to alleviate the South's labor shortage. Since Blacks were often snagged by these vagrancy laws, and were unable to pay fines, they increasingly became enmeshed in the criminal justice system. This led to an increase in the Black prison population and provided a legal foundation for forced labor as a punishment.

This entry provides an overview of the Black Codes by explaining the various forms of the racialized laws and their effects, including their use as the basis for a changing prison system. The differences among the Black Codes, antebellum Slave Codes, and Jim Crow segregation laws are also examined.

Examples of Black Codes

The Black Codes varied from state to state but most regulated employment. In addition to requiring Black people to work, the codes dictated the type of work to be performed, work hours, duties, and prescribed behavior. For instance, in South Carolina, the Black Codes restricted former slaves from any occupation other than as agricultural workers or household servants unless they obtained a special license and paid an annual tax. In addition, Black people were often restricted from renting or leasing land outside a town or city, which meant that they could not raise their own crops. As a result, Blacks were often forced to work on agricultural lands owned by Whites.

In addition to restricting the type of work Black people could perform, residency within towns and cities was often discouraged. For example, local Louisiana ordinances prohibited urban residency unless a White employer agreed to be responsible for his employee's conduct.

Freedom to travel was also restricted. To enter the town of Opelousas, Louisiana, for instance, Blacks needed written permission from their employer. A Black person without such a note could be arrested and imprisoned if found in the town after 10 p.m.

In addition to employment and residency restrictions, the Black Codes prohibited the right to vote, required poll taxes and literacy tests to vote, forbade being on juries, limited the right to testify against White men, outlawed interracial marriage, restricted carrying weapons in public places, prohibited preaching the gospel without a license, banned the use of insult gestures or language directed toward a White person, and forbade doing "malicious mischief," which was broadly defined. Conviction for any of these could result in a fine or forced labor, including on plantations.

An example of how the lives of Black people were controlled and used to provide free labor for Whites can be found in the Black Codes of Mississippi. In Mississippi, anyone who was guilty of theft, was absent from work, had left a job in breach of a job contract, was intoxicated, used insulting language or conduct, had neglected a job or family, had handled money carelessly, and all other idle and disorderly persons were convicted of vagrancy, which could result in forced labor. Other vagrancy laws required every former slave to have written evidence of a legal home. Moreover, failure to pay a yearly tax was prima facie evidence of vagrancy. The sanction for vagrancy was being hired out by a justice of the peace. Further, any former slave under the age of 18 could be apprenticed against his will, with the former slave owner having preference to the apprentice.

Another example is Florida, where the Black Code of 1865 provided that anyone who did not pay a fine resulting from a conviction of assault, vagrancy, misdemeanors, malicious mischief, and offenses against religion, chastity, morality, and decency, could be sentenced to up to 6 months.

Black Codes were not limited to southern states. Vagrancy and convict leasing laws existed in the North. For instance, Ohio enacted Black Codes that regulated residency and employment of Black people.

Black Codes as the Basis for Changing Prison Systems

Faced with the challenge of the increase in the prison population and lack of money to fund new prisons, the prison system developed penal farms, chain gangs, and the convict lease system. As the inmate population shifted from predominantly White inmates to predominantly Black inmates, the new prison systems became extensions of the slave system.

Convict labor was a very efficient and rational strategy to quickly achieve industrialization of the South. For example, the Georgia railroads were built by convicts, and Alabama used convict labor in the coal mines. By 1888, all of Alabama's able male prisoners were leased to two mining companies.

Eventually, the convict lease system was abolished, but its structures of exploitation have reemerged in the patterns of privatization and wide-ranging corporatization of punishment that has produced a prison industrial complex.

Jim Crow Laws

Black Codes were not the same as the Slave Codes or the Jim Crow laws. The Slave Codes were passed in colonial America to regulate the lives of slaves, whereas Jim Crow laws, adopted after the fall of Reconstruction, enforced racial segregation by mandating separate but equal status for Black people. They required that public accommodations, including schools, public places, and public transportation, have separate facilities for Whites and Blacks. Jim Crow laws remained in existence until the 1960s.

Jo-Ann Della Giustina

See also Chain Gangs; Convict Lease System

Further Readings

Carper, N. G. (1976). Slavery revisited: Peonage in the South. *Phylon, 37*(1), 85–99.

Currie, J. T. (1980). From slavery to freedom in Mississippi's legal system. *The Journal of Negro History, 65*(2), 112–124.

Foner, E. (1988). *Reconstruction: America's unfinished revolution 1863–1877.* New York: HarperCollins.

Wilson, T. B. (1965). *The Black Codes of the South.* Birmingham: University of Alabama Press.

Black Criminology

Katheryn K. Russell-Brown coined the term *Black criminology* in a seminal 1992 article that appeared in *Justice Quarterly*. Black criminology entails the development of an integrated theoretical construction and an empirical research analysis that focus on race as an essential variable in the study of crime committed by Blacks. While Black criminology remains a subfield of mainstream criminology, it addresses and explains the race–crime relationship as it relates to the involvement of Blacks in the criminal justice system. This approach goes beyond the spotlight on the impact of the criminal justice system on Blacks by emphasizing the expansion of criminological perspectives that elucidate Black criminality and the formulation of new assumptions to explicate the race–crime connection. Additionally, the study of Black criminology involves an understanding of the historical experiences of Blacks and how they are perceived by the majority population, the historical use of American legal instruments against Blacks, the role of Black threats, fertilization of Black criminality, and the continued significance of race in the study of crime and justice.

For nearly 2 decades, academic criminology has witnessed a proliferation of the literature on the connection between race and crime, focusing on a variety of topics. Some criminologists have called for the development of a Black criminological perspective. Others have examined holistically the major theoretical paradigms as they relate to minority issues in criminology; the effects of racial threat in the criminological enterprise; and African American attitudes and the effects of economic inequality. Researchers have scrutinized the issue of race and ethnicity, the impacts of racial stereotypes in the American justice systems, and the imperative concept of jury nullification. There is important and still emerging literature on petit apartheid realities or microaggressions in the criminal justice system, as well as diverse literature on racial classifications and the question of skin color as they relate to adjudicatory practices.

While a plethora of existing works examine the race–crime association in criminology, Russell has called for development of the Black subfield, which will synthesize the connection of race and crime in a collective whole. Some scholars argue that a Black criminological perspective is needed to counter the false assumption that Blacks are more prone to criminal behavior and to provide an adequate explanation of Black participation in crime. Others hold that criminological perspectives have failed to explain the relationship between race and crime.

As originally conceptualized, Black criminology simply calls for a novel model in criminological theorizing that will explain Black criminality. This nucleus of a new paradigmatic perspective will reintroduce essential variables and concepts in criminological research that have been generally ignored or categorically dismissed by mainstream study of the phenomenon of crime. Additionally, Black criminology seeks to provide a historical context for the changing relationship between race and crime that may integrate innovative theoretical approaches (domain assumptions) in the understanding of crime. A Black criminological perspective is also needed to explain the differences in White and Black crime rates in a way that does not rely on mainstream approaches to the study of minority involvement in crime. A detached and distinct approach within the confines of the discipline is needed to address such issues as historical experiences of Blacks in America, cultural variations, and ethnic or racial drives, as well as tribal responses and tolerance. The parameters of this subfield should not be restricted to a simple analysis of what constitutes the meaning of race or Blackness; rather, it should also consider issues such as decarceration of the Black population under total surveillance, Black coding, and social distance, while also emphasizing the articulation of new theoretical paradigms that explain Black criminality.

Black Criminology and the Black Prison Population

Jeremy Bentham's concept of the Panopticon (a prison structure that allowed guards to monitor the every move of the prisoners without them being aware that they were being monitored) in the 18th century involves an architectural plan for penitentiaries that became a focal point in Michel Foucault's prison theory of surveillance. What Foucault calls the "capillary method of the social organism," the minutiae of everyday life routines, is penetrated by the new surveillance of industrialist establishment in America. Blacks make up the single largest ethnic group in prison, even though they make up about 13% of the total population. Black criminology must focus on developing models that will help to reclaim the Black population under total electronic surveillance. A recent report released by the Pew Public Safety Performance Project indicates that 1 in every 100 adults is currently held in American detentions or prisons. For Blacks in particular, the Pew finding is upsetting. While 1 in 30 male adults between the ages of 20 and 34 is in prison or jail, for Black men in the same age category the figure is 1 in 9. For White men ages 18 and older, the figure is 1 in 106, and for Hispanic male adults, the figure is 1 in 15. This is compared to 1 in 265 for all women and 1 in 297 for Hispanic women. For Black women in their mid- to late 30s, the incarceration rate is 1 in 100. In total, the report shows that the total adult prison population at the beginning of 2008 in both state federal prison centers stood at 2,319,258.

The Pew study finds that policy changes, such as the three strikes laws, longer sentences, and policy changes in parole and probation, have contributed to the massive prison population. Most Black male and female inmates are sentenced for selling marijuana and other drugs. In many cases, they are imprisoned as a result of petit apartheid realities such as the inability to make high bails, discrimination in sentencing and in the use of sentence guidelines, and other instances of discrimination in the criminal justice system.

Black criminology is essential to an articulation of the ontological and etiological antecedents—rooted in history—that are important to understanding and addressing the overincarceration of Blacks in American total institutions. A coherent subfield will continue to examine scientifically the problems and the motives that have resulted in the overrepresentation and marginalization of Blacks in prisons. Racial coding is one example of such a problem that is worthy of more research. *Race coding* refers to biased opinions and attitudes of some Whites toward minorities. One criminological example of this is the previous disparity in federal sentencing against violators of crack cocaine and powdered cocaine usage, in which the penalties for crack cocaine were 100 times more punitive than those for powder cocaine. The racial divide identified by scholars in election laws and housing and welfare policies affects racial coding as well. Welfare policy changes in this country are rooted in negative majority attitudes toward Blacks: a racial coding that implies that Blacks are obviously poorer than Whites. A covert implication that emerged from changing the welfare rule was to stop supporting Black women who may have relied on welfare policies for minimum existence. Another example of race coding is the myth that Blacks are dangerous, as is evidenced in the Willie Horton presidential campaign advertisements aired during the Bush–Dukakis presidential election of 1988. The videotaped beating of Rodney King in 1991 also characterizes this covert agenda.

Black criminology can also increase our understanding of the concept of social distance and its impact on the sentencing of minorities. *Social distance* depicts the detachment between different groups in the community, including the differences or the degree of contacts among races, ethnic groups, social class, gender relations, and sexual relationships. The early conceptualization of social distance scale was designed to assess individual keenness to partake in societal events of changeable degrees of closeness. While the concept originally relates to cities, criminologists have applied it to the study of race and crime, with special emphasis on the disproportionate representation of Blacks in the criminal justice system based on skin color. In the sphere of criminology, social distance is characterized by several factors, including physical characteristics, individual accomplishments to society, perceived dangerousness of racial groups, accepted values of individuals, and perceptions of minority threat.

Historical evidence shows that other oppressed groups in America were viewed as uncultured, while Blacks were analyzed as unsophisticated and regarded as less than human.

The Concept of Black Threat in Black Criminology

The concept of Black threat can help elucidate the argument for and relevance of a Black criminological perspective in mainstream theoretical explanation of crime and justice as it pertains to ethnic minorities. While rational choice perspective insists that urban resources are shared in order to achieve the goals of social control, the conflict approach holds that societal resources are distributed with the aim of controlling ethnic and racial minorities. On this view, the majority fear minority power in terms of economic, political, social, educational advancement, and population explosion, especially in times of economic retardation. The police, as the primary gatekeepers of the criminal justice system, are utilized for social control mechanisms. Basically, changes in immigration policies, increases in minority population, and stereotypes of minority groups may amplify the chances that minorities will be labeled as threats to society. This means that the concept of minority threat, and in this case, Black threat, is important as a part of Black criminology theorizing, since there is historical evidence to demonstrate that Blacks have been viewed as a threat by the majority policymakers and judicial precedent leaders.

The concept of minority threat describes a process of inflicting penalties and injuries onto a minority group through overt or covert policies of social control due to perceived increases in population, distribution of political and economic rewards, and perceptions of dangerousness.

New Directions for Black Criminology

While Russell's conceptualization of Black criminology is novel in its emphasis on the development of new paradigms in criminology that will explain Black criminality, advances in Black criminology must continue to focus on the plight of Blacks in the criminal justice system. Articulating and explaining the race–crime relationship requires study of the impact of the justice system on all Black people, including the differential treatment of Blacks by the criminal justice system. Black criminology ought to include explanations of issues affecting all Black people of African descent, whether they are in the United States, on the African continent, the West Indies, the United Kingdom, or elsewhere in the African Diaspora. The focus of Black criminology must be inclusive without confining itself to explanations of the criminality of African Americans. It may even include the explanation of crimes committed by Hispanics and other neglected ethnic minorities by mainstream criminology.

This means that this subfield as articulated originally must also continue to examine the definitional issues relating to race and ethnicity in the study of crime and justice in order to minimize the definitional dilemma of these concepts. An acceptable typology of the race variable will enable Black criminology to provide objective characteristics of the lawbreakers and the victims of crime and will help to build and construct plausible theoretical assumptions. Since criminology can be described as the study of crime and criminals, which involves causes and consequences as well as state regulations and reactions to rule violations, Black criminology must pay attention to the crimes associated with Blacks, male and female participants in criminality, and the treatment of Black people in criminal justice practice while still focusing on theoretical explanations of the causes of Black criminality by incorporating new concepts and variables and other ideas that have not yet been fittingly examined.

Ihekwoaba D. Onwudiwe and
Chibueze W. Onwudiwe

See also Disproportionate Incarceration; Disproportionate Minority Contact and Confinement; Minority Group Threat; Prison, Judicial Ghetto

Further Readings

Covington, J. (1995). Racial classification in criminology: The reproduction of racialized crime. *Sociological Forum, 10,* 547–568.

Franks, S. E., & Garand, J. C. (2002, November). *Race coding and White support for crime spending: Subjective evaluations, objective conditions, and media influences.* Paper presented at the annual meeting of the Southern Political Science Association, Savannah, GA.

Gabbidon, S. L. (2007). *Criminological perspectives on race and crime.* New York: Routledge.

Gabbidon, S. L., Greene, H. T., & Wilder, K. (2004). Still excluded? An update on the status of African American scholars in the discipline of criminology and criminal justice. *Journal of Research in Crime and Delinquency, 41,* 384–406.

Georges-Abeyie, D. (1989). Race, ethnicity, and the spatial dynamic: Toward a realistic study of Black crime, crime victimization, and criminal justice processing. *Social Justice, 16,* 35–64.

Gilens, M. (1996). Race coding and White opposition to welfare. *American Political Science Review, 90,* 593–604.

Harer, M. D., & Steffensmeier, D. (1992). The differing effects of economic inequality on Black and White rates of violence. *Social Forces, 70,* 1035–1054.

Herrnstein, R. J., & Murray, C. (1994). *The bell curve: Intelligence and class structure in American life.* New York: The Free Press.

Holmes, M. D., Smith, B. W., & Freng, A. B. (2008). Minority threat, crime control, and police resource allocation in the southern United States. *Crime & Delinquency, 54,* 128–152.

Hurwitz, J., & Peffley, M. (1997). Public perceptions of race and crime: The role of racial stereotypes. *American Journal of Political Science, 41,* 375–401.

Mendelberg, T. (1997). Executing Hortons: Racial crime in the 1988 presidential campaign. *Public Opinion Quarterly, 61,* 134–157.

Myers, M. A. (1990). Black threat and incarceration in postbellum Georgia. *Social Forces, 69,* 373–393.

Myrdal, G. (1944). *An American dilemma.* New York: Harper & Row.

Onwudiwe, I. D. (1994, November). *Black criminology: A sub-field of mainstream criminology.* Paper presented at the 46th annual meeting of the American Society of Criminology, Miami, FL.

Onwudiwe, I. D., & Lynch, M. J. (2000). Reopening the debate: A reexamination of the need for a Black criminology. *Social Pathology: A Journal of Reviews, 6,* 182–198.

Parker, K. D., Onyekwuluje, A. B., & Murty, K. S. (1995). African Americans' attitudes toward the local police: A multivariate analysis. *Journal of Black Studies, 25,* 396–409.

Peffley, M., Hurwitz, J., & Sniderman, P. M. (1997). Racial stereotypes and Whites' political views of Blacks in the context of welfare and crime. *American Journal of Political Science, 41,* 30–60.

Russell, K. K. (1992). Development of a Black criminology. *Justice Quarterly, 9,* 667–683.

Tatum, B. L. (2000). Deconstructing the association of race and crime: The silence of skin color. In M. W. Markowitz & D. D. Jones-Brown (Eds.), *The system in Black and White: Exploring the connections between race, crime, and justice* (pp. 31–46). Westport, CT: Praeger.

BLACK ETHNIC MONOLITH

The disproportionality of so-called Negroid, or Black, criminality in North America is documented in numerous federal, state, and local data sources. Unfortunately, Negroid criminality is usually discussed as if persons of Negroid racial ancestry in North America constitute a "Black ethnic monolith," which is blatantly incorrect. Thus, the studies of the causative or associative factors in Negroid criminality are at best suspect. This entry reviews the assumptions underlying this concept and examines implications for the analysis of disproportionate criminality.

The Concepts of Race and Ethnicity

Criminologist and social-cultural-political geographer Daniel E. Georges-Abeyie in 1989 challenged the concept of a "Black ethnic monolith" that equates the social reality of alleged Negroid racial identity with ethnic identity. He noted that a realistic study of Black/Negroid crime, Black/Negroid crime victimization, and the criminal justice processing of Blacks/Negroids must be cognizant of the ethnic diversity that exists within the African Diaspora of North America (i.e., the result of enslavement and forced immigration of Africans to the Americas). An additional consideration is that the African Diaspora of North America included numerous cultural groups with shared cultural experiences, varied social interaction patterns, and distinct spatial locations and identities. Thus, race is a false biological delineator. In fact, the false biological delineator of race also frequently alleges mental characteristics associated with intelligence, temperament, morality, predisposition, and mood. Hence, it can be concluded that the false biological delineator of race for Negroid North Americans has become the equivalent of ethnicity in the minds of Whites and of non-Whites, including so-called Blacks, or Negroids, thereby resulting in the concept of a "Black ethnic monolith." Georges-Abeyie also concluded that Negroid North Americans frequently exhibited the multidimensional value space of dominant cultural mores and norms, subcultural mores and norms, and contracultural mores and norms first noted by Lynn A. Curtis in 1975. Similar to Curtis, Georges-Abeyie believed that the representatives of the dominant culture criminalized some of the Negroid North American subcultural and contracultural norms.

The concept of a Black ethnic monolith at its very core is faulty in that the social-cultural delineations of race and ethnicity are not equivalent. Although there is no single widely accepted, much less universally accepted, definition of race, race is theoretically a biological delineator—a false one that the American Anthropological Association has rejected since 1998. It is also a questionable biological concept that geographers critique and tend to replace with the spatial concept of "geographic races" (i.e., persons in close residential proximity with similar, not identical, genetic-based physical characteristics). Similar to race, there is no single accepted, much less universally accepted, definition of ethnicity. However, social scientist Milton Gordon's classic 1964 study of assimilation in North American life coined one of the most enduring definitions of ethnicity. Gordon's work focused on European Americans. Gordon noted that ethnicity was the intersection of race, religion, and national origin. Gordon's concept of ethnicity included a questionable biological component as well as a spatial component and a cultural component (i.e., learned behavior and beliefs [norms and mores]). The problem with the European-oriented ethnic delineator typically utilized by European-oriented social scientists or those influenced by them is threefold when discussing the disproportionality of Negroid North American criminality.

1. The *spatial component—nation of origin—*is of little utility when discussing Negroid North American national origin, in that most Negroid North Americans have little to no knowledge of their African (nation-state) origin. Thus, of greater utility in discussing the spatial component of Negroid North American origin is the concept of "place of origin" in North America, introduced by Georges-Abeyie in 1989.

2. The *study of religion* in reference to the Negroid North American is questionable in that the institution of intergenerational enslavement truncates historical study of religion as a component of an indigenous culture. Slave masters and postbellum practices during and after the Jim Crow era in the United States intentionally obliterated much of the indigenous African culture. Nonetheless, it is logical and prudent to study the mores and norms that developed during and after the initial African Diaspora and the subsequent spatial reality in rural and urban North America.

3. The *study of race,* as noted previously, is at best suspect in that the social construction of racial delineation typically focuses on specific phenotypic characteristics such as somatotype, phrenology, physiognomy, and skin color while ignoring others. Anyone with the most rudimentary acquaintanceship or interaction with Negroid North Americans knows that Negroid North Americans are phenotypically dissimilar: some are tall, others short; some are dark complexioned, others light complexioned; some are ectomorphic (slender), others endomorphic (plump/heavyset) or mesomorphic (muscular).

Implications for Criminology

The significance of the Black ethnic monolith in reference to the apparent disproportionality of so-called Negroid or Black criminality in North America relates to crime and/or criminal victimization etiology. *Etiology* is the cause or the study of the causes of a phenomenon or phenomena. The core problem with regard to the study of Negroid North American criminality is that the Black ethnic monolith is a mass media and social science delusion like that of race. Psychology defines a *delusion* as a false fixed belief. The Negroid North American

Black ethnic monolith is heterogeneous in terms of ethnicity, if ethnicity is defined as identity based upon race, culture, and place of origin. Different self-identifying persons as well as externally identified persons of Negroid North American racial identity have experienced different interaction patterns as individuals and as collectives with persons culturally similar or dissimilar to themselves.

The Black ethnic monolith includes individuals whose first languages are English, French, French Patois, Spanish, Portuguese, Garifuna, Gullah, Ibo, Yoruba, Zulu, Xhosa, Fanti/Fante, Amharic, and, literally, hundreds of other languages currently spoken on the African continent by indigenous people. Millions of Negroid North Americans are of antebellum origin (existing before the U.S. Civil War), while millions of others are of Caribbean and Afro-Latino origin from Central America and South America. Hundreds of thousands of Negroid North Americans are postbellum African immigrants or the offspring of postbellum African immigrants. Each Black ethnic community has unique experiences in North America, and each community brings a unique complex of norms and mores, including those concerning family, education, religion, morality, amorality, immorality, and adherence to and respect for the law and law enforcement agents and agencies. Each ethnic community has its own unique role sets, that is, complex of mores and related norms and folkways.

In turn, each Negroid North American community—ethnic group—manifests social distance toward its own ethnic group as well as toward other Negroid North American communities and non-Blacks. Each Negroid North American community in turn manifests social distance from the perspective of others who know of their existence or who interact with them, if *social distance* is defined as the type and amount of desirable interaction with members of one's own identity grouping or those of another identity grouping.

The concept of honor varies among and between Negroid North American identity groupings, as do hygiene, religion, attire, jewelry, eye contact, scarification and body adornment, the carrying of weapons, what constitutes an insult, appropriate interaction by persons of the same sex or by persons of different sexes and sexual orientations, concepts of gender (masculinity and femininity), body spacing, dialect, syntax, intelligence, intrafamilial

respect, loudness of speech, and a host of other verbal and nonverbal indicators of subservience, passivity, submissiveness, politeness, deception, and aggression.

The problem of the etiology of criminality and criminal victimization as denoted in Part I index crimes (e.g., FBI's Part I Index Offenses; more serious offenses) by Negroid North Americans identified as the Black ethnic monolith is, in part, a misunderstanding of the concepts of race and ethnicity, especially when discussing the social-cultural-spatial reality of the African Diaspora of North America. The manifestation of culture is, in large part, the consequence of actual and perceived shared experiences. Thus, an individual need not directly experience an overt act to share in the cultural space or consequence of that act. Experiences are passed, in part, from generation to generation as well as among the membership of each generation via music and other performance art, body language, imagery on paper and in the electronic media, and by the spoken word, including rumors and facts. Language is nonverbal as well as verbal.

Group identity and individual experience filter, focus, and modify culture including what a member of a specific ethnic or racial identity grouping perceives as appropriate or inappropriate or even criminal. Although there are few data disaggregated for different Black ethnic groups, the cultural heterogeneity of these groups should and probably does result in differential crime rates among different ethnic identity groups within the African Diaspora in North America. Thus, a realistic study of the etiology of the disproportionality of Black criminality requires an understanding of the unique experiences shared by members of each Black ethnic identity group.

Daniel E. Georges-Abeyie

See also Chicago School of Sociology; Prison, Judicial Ghetto; Social Disorganization Theory

Further Readings

Curtis, L. A. (1975). *Violence, race, and culture.* Lexington, MA: Lexington Books.

Georges-Abeyie, D. E. (1989, Winter). Race, ethnicity, and the spatial dynamic: Toward a realistic study of Black crime, crime victimization, and criminal justice processing of Blacks. *Social Justice, 16,* 35–54.

Gordon, M. M. (1964). *Assimilation in American life: The role of race, religion, and national origin.* New York: Oxford University Press.

Parrillo, V. N. (2000). *Strangers to these shores: Race and ethnic relations in the United States.* Boston: Allyn & Bacon.

BLACK FEMINIST CRIMINOLOGY

Black feminist thought is collective knowledge used to empower African American women. Such knowledge empowers women by making them conscious of how change can occur in their everyday lives. This entry first reviews the status of African American women and describes key themes in Black feminist thought. It then considers ways in which an understanding of the values emphasized by Black feminism might decrease the rates of criminal behavior among African American women.

African American Women in the United States

Research suggests that African American women in the United States share a variety of common experiences, such as family and work within the African American culture, that are not experienced by non–African Americans or by males. Though there are commonalties in the experiences among African American women, this does not suggest every experience or its significance is the same.

Some sociologists suggest that African American women have been thought to be oppressed; however, Black feminist thought challenges that idea. Research by Patricia Hill Collins, for example, has shown that members of subordinate groups identify with the powerful and do not have powerful interpretations of their own oppression. In this case, the powerful can be viewed as non–African American men and women along with African American males. Black feminist thought reveals that African American women are becoming increasingly knowledgeable about their past experiences and continuously looking for ways to uplift each other.

Themes in Black Feminist Thought

African American women have had noticeable effects on the functioning of each generation of African Americans. Black feminist thought focuses on such topics as the objectification of African American women, the oppression of African American women and the controlling images that surround them, the self-image of the African American woman (hair color, texture, and standards of beauty), and finally the reaction of African American women to the various controlling images. African American women have been portrayed as mammies, jezebels, matriarchs, and welfare recipients, all of which help to promote the idea of oppression. Releasing African American women from these stereotypes has been a goal of Black feminist thought. Supporters believe that the power of self-definition and a rejection of society's negative views of the African American woman can promote the ideas behind Black feminist thought. African American women have the power to promote unity and encouragement through interaction with each other, the community, and most important, through the mother-daughter relationship. Black feminist thought is built around the following themes:

- Self-valuation
- Respect
- Independence
- Self-reliance
- Change
- Empowerment

The values that most African American women place on education, sex, love, marriage, motherhood, work, and womanhood in general are shaped by the ideas set forth by the dominant society. Black feminists are working to change the negative view of African American women both within the African American community and in the broader society. Current self-perceptions of African American women are saturated with ideas of oppression and struggle, and many of these women turn to crime and violence in response to previous victimization and alienation within their families and communities. These negative self-perceptions and a lack of encouragement or uplift within a community leave an absence of the idea of a "safety net," often viewed as friends, family, and the community.

Black feminist theorists suggest that increasing crime rates among African American women are related to the negative characteristics of their self-image, social environment, and status. Currently, the rate of female incarceration is increasing, and the number of non-White women incarcerated is disproportionately high compared to their numbers within the general population. In light of this increase in incarceration, Black feminists seek to show ways in which the value system embodied in Black feminist thought can decrease criminal offending by African American women.

Black Feminist Thought and Crime Among African American Women

African Americans in general have disproportionately higher incarceration rates within the United States than do other groups in America. Research shows that according to the Department of Justice, from 1997 to 2006 the number of crimes committed by African Americans declined; however, there continues to be a steady increase in the number of incarcerations every year. The number of incarcerated women has more than doubled, growing 11.2% annually, and women accounted for more than 7% of the prison population in 2007. The majority of women who are incarcerated are minorities, with two thirds of the women confined in jail being Black, Hispanic, or of another non-White ethnic group. According to Dallaire, the demographic characteristics of the incarcerated women often include those 25 years of age or older. The majority of the women are from low-income communities in which rates of homelessness (often described as "contemporary urban poverty") continue to increase substantially. The majority of crimes committed by African American women are nonviolent crimes such as drug offenses, theft, and prostitution, which can be labeled as "low-self-esteem" or instrumental crimes. Black feminist theorists note that such crimes can result from low self-esteem or may result from attempts to maintain relationships within the family. These crimes are normally "repeat offender crimes" among African American women. If a lack of self-awareness and self-esteem makes African American women more likely to participate in such harmful activities, the values emphasized by Black feminist thought might lead to a decrease in these nonviolent crimes, as the women view themselves in a more positive manner and develop greater self-respect.

Research Suggestions

Scholars have pointed out a variety of initiatives that could implement the values of Black feminist thought within the African American community. Community outreach programs that specifically target those who would be most affected by Black feminist thought would be valuable. Mentoring programs for African American women would also be beneficial. Specifically, programs that strengthen mutual understanding and support among African American women are necessary, as are those that help to dismantle views of hate and discrimination that often constrain self-esteem and self-confidence.

Additionally, counseling would be an effective measure for implementing the values underlying Black feminist thought. Counselors are valuable resources for those in need of guidance or those who need to be empowered, uplifted, or enlightened. Moreover, to increase understanding and knowledge of Black feminist thought, accessibility to educational courses that include it would also be beneficial.

Zina McGee, Sophia Buxton, and Tyrell Connor

See also Drug Sentencing; Female Gangs; Mentoring Programs

Further Readings

Collins, P. H. (2000). *Black feminist thought: Knowledge, consciousness, and the politics of empowerment.* New York: Routledge.

Dallaire, D. (2006). Children with incarcerated mothers: Developmental outcomes, special challenges and recommendations. *Journal of Applied Developmental Psychology, 28,* 15–24.

Greene, H. T., & Gabbidon, S. L. (2000). *African American criminological thought.* Albany: SUNY Press.

Huebner, B., & Gustafson, R. (2007). The effect of maternal incarceration on adult offspring involvement in the criminal justice system. *Journal of Criminal Justice, 35,* 283–296.

Potter, H. (2006). An argument for Black feminist criminology: Understanding African American women's experiences with intimate partner abuse using an integrated approach. *Feminist Criminology, 1,* 106–124.

Richie, B. E. (2001). Challenges incarcerated women face as they return to their communities: Findings from life history interviews. *Crime & Delinquency, 47,* 386–389.

Siegel, L. (2000). Prison life: Females. In *Criminology* (7th ed., pp. 599–600). Belmont, CA: Wadsworth/ Thomson.

Black Panther Party

The Black Panther Party (BPP), a revolutionary Black Nationalist organization, was cofounded in 1966 in Oakland, California, by two college students, Huey P. Newton and Bobby Seale. They created the Black Panther Party because recently passed civil rights legislation seemed to have had little impact on the multitude of dismal circumstances facing Black communities in the United States. To this end, Newton and Seale composed their Ten Point Platform and Program, in which they outlined critical issues that were facing Black communities, among them substandard housing, police brutality, inadequate education, and a racially discriminatory legal system. Although its platform emphasized practical "bread and butter" issues, the BPP considered itself to be a revolutionary organization, one whose ultimate goal remained the total political and economic transformation of the United States. The party's cofounders drew from the works of a broad range of revolutionary theory, including Franz Fanon's *Wretched of the Earth,* Che Guevara's *Guerrilla Warfare,* and the writings of Mao Tse-tung. Newton and Seale adopted the symbol of a black panther for their fledgling organization, borrowed from the Lowndes County Freedom Organization, a branch of the Student Nonviolent Coordinating Committee (SNCC) established to secure Black voting rights in Alabama.

The Black Panther Party rapidly morphed from an Oakland-based group with fewer than 50 individual members into a national organization with more than 5,000 members in 29 states and in Washington, D.C., as well as an international chapter in Algeria. Panther chapters existed in other locations, including Seattle, Des Moines, Omaha, and Denver; they also appeared in numerous southern cities, including New Orleans, Memphis, and Winston-Salem, North Carolina.

During its 16-year life span, 1966 to 1982, the BPP went through five distinct stages. In the first stage, from October 1966 to December 1967, the party was a revolutionary California-based organization engaged in grassroots activism in the Oakland/San Francisco Bay Area and Los Angeles. The second phase, January 1968 to April 1971, represents the heyday of the Black Panther Party, during which the overwhelming majority of the BPP chapters across the United States were formed. This rapid expansion led to intense political repression by the U.S. government and intrafactional conflict. In the third phase, May 1971 to July 1974, the party's leadership stressed community outreach programs and electoral politics rather than armed confrontations against the government. This deradicalization era was highlighted by the Bobby Seale–Elaine Brown campaign for political office in Oakland. This shift toward electoral politics was deemed so important that Minister of Defense Huey P. Newton decided to close all Black Panther Party chapters outside of Oakland and ordered party members to relocate to Oakland to support the campaign. This phase concluded with the departure of Chairman Bobby Seale, who resigned from the organization due to irreconcilable differences with Newton. The party's fourth stage, August 1974 to June 1977, was characterized by Newton's exile in Cuba. The official explanation put forth by the BPP was that Newton fled to Cuba to escape a contract placed on his life by the city's drug dealers. However, it is more likely that Newton left the country to avoid pending criminal charges. In his absence, Elaine Brown, a member of the central committee who had served as a minister of information to the organization, assumed leadership of the Black Panther Party, which successfully wielded its influence in Oakland politics. In the final phase, July 1977 to June 1982, the party's membership dwindled to fewer than 50 members, and the organization lacked the resources to implement many of its survival programs. The closing of the Oakland Community School in June 1982 marked the end of the Black Panther Party.

Throughout the course of their relatively short existence, the Black Panthers electrified the nation with their dynamic image—berets, black leather jackets, weapons—and their revolutionary zeal. Panther comrades galvanized communities and regularly participated in coalitions with the White Left and other radical minority groups. Their community outreach activities, later named "survival programs," fed, clothed, educated, and provided health care to thousands. The party's socialist orientation, advocacy or armed resistance, effective community organizing, and inflammatory rhetoric triggered intensive governmental surveillance and political repression. More than a dozen members died in gun altercations with the police. Panthers were frequently arrested and were often the target of the FBI counterintelligence program, COINTELPRO, whose actions had been levied against the Black Panther Party.

Among the acts of repression levied against the BPP was the 1969 arrest of 21 New York Panthers on a host of conspiracy charges to bomb department stores, the Bronx Botanical Gardens, police precincts, and a commuter train. Those arrested included Afeni Shakur, the mother of the late hip hop icon Tupac Shakur. The fabricated charges lodged against the New York 21 resulted in an excessive $100,000 bail for each individual. Two years later, the Panther 21 were exonerated by a jury who deliberated for a mere 4 hours before rendering a not guilty verdict.

The organization's bravado, community service, and uncompromising leadership captivated the imagination of oppressed people across the nation and throughout the world. Panther solidarity committees were formed in England, Denmark, Sweden, Germany, and France. Similarly, aborigines in Australia formed the Australia Black Panther Party, and there was a branch of the Black Panther Party in Israel. For many people, the Panthers became an icon of Black militancy.

Shortly before daybreak on October 28, 1967, Oakland police officer John Frey stopped a car driven by Newton and his passenger Gene McKinney, Newton's longtime friend. After Frey identified Newton's automobile as a Panther vehicle, he radioed for assistance. Soon after Patrolman Herbert Heanes arrived at the scene, gunfire erupted. An unarmed Newton was rendered unconscious by two bullets in his stomach, Officer Frey was shot to death, and Patrolman Heanes suffered serious gunshot wounds. Newton was later arrested at Kaiser Hospital on multiple criminal charges, including first-degree murder of a police officer, attempted murder, and kidnapping.

Under the leadership of Eldridge Cleaver, the party's minister of information, the Panthers launched a massive legal defense campaign to win Newton's freedom, transforming the Oakland shooting incident into a cause célèbre. Rallies were organized on the Oakland courthouse grounds during the trial and across the nation. International sympathizers held rallies abroad, in Europe and Dar Es Salaam, Tanzania. He was convicted of voluntary manslaughter in 1968. He appealed the conviction, which resulted in two mistrials. The case was later dropped by the State of California.

The Free Huey campaign was the precursor to scores of BPP legal defense campaigns to secure the freedom of imprisoned Panthers, and coalition politics was a critical component in these efforts. Unlike other Black power organizations, the Black Panther Party, which is often perceived to have been anti-White, willingly engaged in coalitions with the White Left. Alliances were formed with the Peace and Freedom Party, the Students for a Democratic Society, antiwar groups, and various other radical organizations. The Chicago BPP chapter's Rainbow Coalition—organized by Fred Hampton, the legendary Panther leader killed with Mark Clark in the infamous December 4, 1969, raid by the Chicago police—included the Black Panther Party, the Young Patriots, the Students for a Democratic Society, and the Young Lords, a Puerto Rican protest group.

The BPP operated extensive community outreach projects to address the immediate material needs of the Black urban poor. In November 1969, the party's outreach efforts were formalized into the nationwide Serve the People Program and later reconceptualized, in 1971, by Newton as "survival programs." The most well-known of the survival programs was the Free Breakfast for Children Program, which was sponsored by the majority of Panther affiliates, who solicited food donations and funds from local businesses and community residents. Panthers often used the kitchens of sympathetic churches to prepare a typical meal of juice, eggs, grits, bacon, and toast. It is estimated that they fed more than 20,000 schoolchildren by the close of 1969.

Several party chapters followed the lead of the Kansas City, Missouri, chapter, which initiated the organization's first free health clinic when it opened the Bobby Hutton Community Clinic on August 20, 1969. Subsequently, chapters in Chicago, Seattle, Baltimore, Oakland, Boston, Cleveland, and Philadelphia created free health clinics. In 1974, Panthers in North Carolina established the Joseph Waddell People's Free Ambulance Service in Winston-Salem with funding from a grant sponsored by the National Episcopal Church. The party's preventive efforts for the treatment of sickle-cell anemia, a rare blood disease that largely affects people of African descent, represent another prominent example of its health outreach services. Members tested thousands of individuals for the blood disease at Panther health clinics and political rallies. The party also sponsored the Seniors Against a Fearful Environment (SAFE) program, which provided transportation for the elderly.

Education was central to the Panthers' community outreach, and the Intercommunal Youth Institute, based on earlier Panther liberation schools, was established in January 1971. During the second year of its existence, the party named the school in honor of Samuel L. Napier, a party member killed during a conflict within the organization. In 1975, the Napier Intercommunal Youth Institute was renamed the Oakland Community School (OCS) to broaden its community appeal, and this alternative school existed 11 years, from 1971 to 1982.

Women had prominent leadership positions throughout the existence of the organization—Ericka Huggins, the longtime director of the Oakland Community School, and Audrea Jones, head of the Boston BPP chapter, are but a few examples of party leadership. Indeed, Elaine Brown, the party's chair from August 1974 to July 1977, is the sole woman to head a protest organization during the Black power era.

In 1973, the BPP mounted a campaign to elect Bobby Seale as Oakland's mayor and Elaine Brown to the city's council. The Seale-Brown campaign reflected the organization's multifaceted strategy, which is often obscured by a preoccupation with the party's advocacy of armed resistance. Under the direction of Herman Smith, a Philadelphia Panther, the BPP devised and implemented a grassroots campaign strategy that relied heavily upon personal appearances by Bobby Seale. The BPP mobilized and registered thousands of potential voters via door-to-door organizing and through political rallies. During one event, the party distributed 10,000 bags of groceries, with a chicken in every bag. However, both Seale and Brown lost their respective bids for political office. Although the BPP failed to capture political power in 1973, its efforts provided groundwork for the historic 1977 election of Lionel Wilson as the city of Oakland's first Black mayor.

Among the multiple factors that contributed to the demise of the Black Panther Party, government repression is first and foremost. The systematic political repression not only took a toll on the membership but also diverted critical resources from community organizing to legal defense campaigns. However, there were internal problems as well. Newton's substance abuse and erratic dictatorial tendencies severely crippled the organization, contributing to its downfall. A cult of personality around Newton permitted his unprincipled behavior to go unchallenged. In addition, intrafactional conflict over tactics—urban guerilla warfare versus an emphasis on survival programs—resulted in deaths of two Panther comrades in 1971 and prompted the exodus of other members, including several key players who had the stature to challenge Newton's leadership dominance. Finally, the organization eventually ceased to exist due to membership burnout. Black Panther Party membership required a full-time commitment. After years of tireless service, communal living, and constant government harassment, many Panthers eventually left the organization to regain a sense of normalcy.

Charles E. Jones

See also COINTELPRO and Covert Operations

Further Readings

Alkebulan, P. (2007). *Survival pending revolution: The history of the Black Panther Party.* Tuscaloosa: University of Alabama Press.

Cleaver, K., & Katsiaficas, G. (Eds.). (2001). *Liberation, imagination, and the Black Panther Party: A new look at the Panthers and their legacy.* New York: Routledge.

Jeffries, J. L. (Ed.). (2007). *Comrades: A local history of the Black Panther Party*. Bloomington: Indiana University Press.

Jones, C. (Ed.). (1998). *The Black Panther Party reconsidered*. Baltimore: Black Classic Press.

Seale, B. (1991). *Seize the time: The story of the Black Panther Party and Huey P. Newton*. Baltimore: Black Classic Press. (Originally published 1970)

BLAXPLOITATION MOVIES

Frank Beaver, author of *Dictionary of Film Terms*, defines *blaxploitation* as "commercially minded films made to appeal specifically to the interests of black audiences" (p. 37). The origin of the term is credited to then-President of the National Association for the Advancement of Colored People's Beverly Hills chapter, Junius Griffin, who deemed the genre of movies geared toward African Americans as blaxploitation—that is, exploitative toward Black Americans. Melvin Van Peebles' *Sweet Sweetback's Baadasssss Song* (1971) is credited with opening the door for many Black-themed movies that would later become known as blaxploitation.

From the period of 1970 to 1975, more than 200 blaxploitation movies were made, in genres ranging from horror, westerns, comedy, drama, and by far the most popular subgenre, action. In discussing blaxploitation, African American cultural critics aptly point to stereotyping as the most pervasive and damaging effects of the movies as well as the lack of a Black cultural aesthetic in making these movies. Studios received much criticism for their role, but the most stinging indictment was reserved for the actors and actresses for portraying characters that treated crime solely as one of race restricted to urban areas. While there is significant scholarship linking crime and socioeconomic conditions, many critics of the genre argue that, in playing pimps, prostitutes, street hustlers, and other unsavory types, blaxploitation actors in particular contributed to the portrait of African American men as menacing, shadowy crime figures.

Three prominent actors of the early 1970s who did little to sway the court of public opinion of the genre as anything other than one-dimensional caricatures of African Americans were Fred Williamson; Jim Brown, who after retiring from professional football sought a career in acting; and the late Ron O'Neal. These actors were regularly lambasted for their roles as drug kingpins in the inner city. Many urban youths looked up to the actors as heroes and were unable to separate the actors from their parts. This led many prominent African Americans, such as Harvard psychiatrist Alvin Pouissant, Jesse Jackson, and others, to question the responsibilities of actors involved in blaxploitation movies to abandon Stephin Fetchit depictions and roles that in their collective judgment further cemented the onscreen images of African Americans and crime as detrimental to the community.

Of the three actors, it was O'Neal, in the role of drug kingpin "Priest" in Gordon Parks, Jr.'s highly successful *Superfly* (1973), who came under heavy scrutiny for depicting the character as a cool, sophisticated, always stylish person who was popular with women, lived in plush comfort, drove the very latest car, and as his signature trademark donned a cocaine spoon as fashion attire. In the December 1972 issue of *Ebony* magazine, writer B. J. Mason explores this criticism in his article "The New Films: Culture or Con Game? Rash of 'Black' Movies Draws Both Condemnation and Praise." In pointed remarks made about *Superfly*, Griffin described the film "as an insidious film which portrays the black community at its worst. It glorifies the use of cocaine and casts blacks in roles which glorify dope-pushers, pimps and grand theft" (p. 62).

Throughout the movie, "Priest" snorts cocaine at every opportunity, but this apparently does not affect his ability to control his drug empire. Shortly after the movie was released, many African American youths began wearing cocaine spoons around their necks as fashion statements and also tried earnestly to look like Ron O'Neal's character. Critics of the movie "insisted that Priest must be seen as nothing more than a well-dressed Cadillac-driving murderer of young blacks" (p. 64). And while Parks, Jr., vehemently defended his movie by focusing on the net returns in stating "studios make films to get people to see them on whatever basis they're on. And if someone is going to put their money in a project, they expect a return" (p. 62). It is undeniable that this movie and similar Black action movies had an impact on young African Americans looking for heroes. Further adding to Parks, Jr.'s woes for making a film that glorified drug dealers as the only viable option for those living in the urban area was his depiction of "three civil rights organizers as money-grubbing extortionists" (p. 64).

In *Black Caesar* (1972), Fred Williamson portrayed a crime lord who gets his comeuppance in the end but returns for revenge in the sequel. Jim Brown rarely played a crime figure, but his character in *Slaughter* (1972) often acted outside the bounds of what would have resulted in a jail sentence if impressionable youths tried similar tactics, such as when his character "collars a white policeman" (p. 64).

In response to civil rights activists' concerns about the depictions of crime in blaxploitation movies, the studios and directors stated they "only give audiences what they want" (p. 64). One would be pressed to find hard statistics to support the idea that blaxploitation movies were linked to crime in the African American community, but portraying characters with no redeemable attributes and to which African American youths could not have looked up to as role models certainly did not help the stigma in the minds of many that African Americans and crime were inextricably linked.

Much of the remarks made about blaxploitation movies put the blame on the actors themselves for perpetuating stereotypes of African American men as hustlers and drug dealers and African American women as prostitutes, but the biggest culprits were movie studios that saw the success of Van Peebles' film and decided to target a new market: African Americans. Despite highly weak storylines, one-dimensional characters, and budget constraints, movie studios, particularly American International Pictures, produced many blaxploitation movies with little regard to the stereotypical representations they reinforced. Prior to blaxploitation movies, actors such as Williamson, Brown (who was the only one of the three consistently acting in major studio roles), and O'Neal had difficulty making inroads into the Hollywood system. With the arrival of the genre, they could pick and choose their roles, and often the storylines were built around their respective characters.

The genre remains a heavily contested point of debate even some 38 years after the initial run of Van Peebles' *Sweet Sweetback's Baadasssss Song.* Unfortunately, the movies created stereotypical crime-involved characters that many impressionable young African American youths found appealing. But they also sparked healthy dialogue in not simply addressing depictions of African Americans in film, but underscoring the need for civil rights organizations to address *why* youths found these particular characters appealing and the need to address the hopelessness, despair, and sense of no-way-out many in the inner city felt then and now.

Yvonne Sims

See also Media Portrayals of African Americans; Social Construction of Reality

Further Readings

Beaver, F. (1983). *Dictionary of film terms.* New York: McGraw-Hill.

Leab, D. J. (1975). *From Sambo to Superspade: The Black experience in motion pictures.* Boston: Houghton Mifflin.

Mason, B. J. (1972, December). The new films: Culture or con game? Rash of "Black" movies draws both condemnation and praise. *Ebony,* pp. 61–70.

Sims, Y. D. (2006). *Women of blaxploitation: How the action heroine changed American popular culture.* Jefferson, NC: McFarland.

BONGER, WILLEM ADRIAAN (1876–1940)

Willem Adriaan Bonger was a preeminent Dutch criminologist and scholar whose pioneering research transcended the landscape of criminological thought at a historical juncture when biologically based explanations of crime predominated. His work was rooted in economic determinism, as a lens through which he believed that examinations of the etiology of crime were best explored.

The Marxist Influence

Bonger was characterized as a staunch anti-Lombrosian or someone who was adamantly against biological positivism and an advocate of Marxist historical materialism. His research emerged as a critique of extant criminological theory in general and of the capitalistic economic structure that was a dominant feature in Europe in the late 19th and early 20th centuries. A revival of Marxist thought, Bonger's work provides the earliest systematic application of Marxian concepts to explore the etiology of crime as a manifestation of capitalism.

Advancing the work of Karl Marx, Bonger viewed capitalism as a vehicle whereby economic and social conditions induced criminality. Bonger's critique of biological determinism and capitalistic ideology distinguished him from other scholars of his era. A strong proponent of theoretically and empirically sound methods, he challenged American and British scholars to defy conventional wisdom by investigating crime as a by-product of the complexity of capitalistic ideology rather than relying on what he considered to be simplistic, disingenuous assertions rooted in deficiency and pathology. It is with Bonger's utility of economic determinism to explore the etiology of crime that a more sociological criminology emerged, illustrating his most significant contribution to the criminological body of knowledge.

Crime and Economic Conditions

Prior to the early 20th century, the criminological landscape had been dominated by scholars who were committed to exploring crime through a singular lens of biological deficiency. Critical of the theoretical and empirical soundness of such assertions, Bonger's research emerged as a critique of biologically based explanations of crime and its prevailing dominance. His doctoral dissertation—*Criminalité et Conditions Économique*—was published in 1905. It was translated into English in 1916 (*Criminality and Economic Conditions*) as a volume in the Modern Criminal Sciences Series of the Association of American Law Schools.

In this work, a critique of Lombrosian thought in general and capitalism in particular, Bonger opined that it was neither biological nor racial traits that led to a greater proclivity toward criminality and immorality, but rather economic and social conditions as manifestations of a dominant capitalistic economic structure. Existing criminological

thought, according to Bonger, was flawed in its assumption that crime was a consequence of biological and/or racial defects. He argued that these claims lacked empirical support and failed to acknowledge the influence of the social environment. Bonger held that the capitalist mode of production was the fundamental mechanism whereby unlimited egoism emerged and led to immorality and criminal behavior.

Race and Crime

In 1943, Bonger published *Race and Crime*, his final and most contentious book. Advancing his earlier premise that crime was a manifestation of socioeconomic conditions in a capitalistic society, Bonger is credited with being the first criminologist to explore how capitalism adversely affects racial/ethnic groups. More specifically, the text serves as a critique of race relations in the United States, employing a historical analysis and official statistics.

Seeking to dispel criminological explanations based on race as a cause of criminal behavior, Bonger argued that claims asserting a causal relationship between race and crime were devoid of theoretical and empirical support and instead were evidence of prejudice and pettiness. Influenced by Marx, Bonger held that crime, a manifestation of capitalism, would be best remedied by improving the economic and social conditions of the poor. Attracted to both the ideology and promise of Marxism in addressing all social ills plaguing the poor by improving their economic and social realities, Bonger believed that consequences of these realities were best addressed through the employment of socialist-based theory.

Negro Criminality

Intrigued by the complexity of race relations in the United States and its influence on criminological thought, Bonger dedicated a chapter examining criminality among "Negroes," among other racial/ethnic groups. Bonger argued that during slavery and the post–Civil War era, Blacks in the United States were subjected to a social caste system that adversely affected their social situation relative to Whites. While acknowledging some progress among Blacks, Bonger argued that they had been subjected to deplorable economic and social conditions that inevitably diminished their quality of life. The higher rates of crime among Blacks compared to Whites could be explained, Bonger held, by their continued inferior and oppressed status rather than by racial or cultural predisposition. Bonger's examination of race and crime was, in part, a critique of race relations in the United States and the accepted prejudice among criminologists.

Academic Scholarship

Bonger's work exemplifies a transformative force that significantly shifted the trajectory of American criminological thought, and he was one of the few Dutch criminologists to be recognized among American scholars. His scholarship represents his commitment to combating dilettantism, hypocrisy, and untruths and to employing theoretically and empirically sound methods. Amid his research, books, and numerous articles, Bonger's most significant contribution is the usefulness of economic determinism in exploring the etiology of crime.

Misha S. Lars

See also African Americans; Biological Theories; Ethnicity; Racism; Slavery and Violence

Further Readings

Bonger, W. A. (1916). *Criminality and economic conditions*. Boston: Little, Brown.
Bonger, W. A. (1943). *Race and crime* (M. M. Hordyk, Trans.). New York: Columbia University Press.
Bonger, W. A. (1972). Criminality and economic conditions. In S. F. Sylvester (Ed.), *The heritage of modern criminology*. Cambridge, MA: Schenkman.
Gabbidon, S. L. (2007). *Criminological perspectives on race and crime*. New York: Routledge.
Sylvester, S. F. (Ed.). (1972). *The heritage of modern criminology*. Cambridge, MA: Schenkman.
Taylor, I., Walton, P., & Young, J. (2008). Marx, Engels, and Bonger on crime and social control. In A. Walsh & C. Hemmens (Eds.), *Introduction to criminology: A text/reader*. Thousand Oaks, CA: Sage.
van Bemmelen, J. M. (1960). Willem Adriaan Bonger. In H. Mannheim (Ed.), *Pioneers in criminology* (pp. 349–363). Chicago: Quadrangle.
van Swaaningen, R. (2006). Criminology in the Netherlands. *European Journal of Criminology, 3*(4), 463–501.
Wigmore, J. H. (1941). Willem Adriaan Bonger. *Journal of Criminal Law and Criminology, 31*(5), 657.

BOOT CAMPS, ADULT

Adult boot camps, also known as "shock incarceration" programs, were first implemented in Georgia and in Oklahoma in late 1983. Boot camps are a form of intermediate sanction that emphasize a military-style atmosphere with hard physical labor, strict physical training, exercise, and an intensive focus on self-discipline. Boot camps have traditionally targeted young, first-time offenders convicted of nonviolent and less serious crimes. Boot camps are aimed at scaring or shocking an individual away from criminal behavior by providing a tough physical atmosphere.

Program goals and objectives vary from one facility to another. Most target goals such as diverting offenders from incarceration, instilling confidence and self-respect, and promoting self-discipline through military-style treatment.

The length of stay in each boot camp varies, with an average length of stay of approximately 3 to 6 months. During this time frame, boot camp cadets are under the guidance and supervision of a military-style drill instructor and are expected to adhere to all commands given by the instructor and to all program rules and expectations. Upon completion of the boot camp program, the cadets participate in a formal graduation ceremony to acknowledge their accomplishments.

All boot camps incorporate various activities in their programs, such as physical exercise, a structured daily schedule, physical work, community service, academic and vocational education, and various forms of treatment such as drugs and alcohol treatment. The programs vary in accordance to the style of boot camp. First-generation boot camps, which came into existence in 1983, encompassed rigorous physical training, which included extensive jogging, push-ups, and sit-ups. First-generation boot camps are generally what individuals think of when they think of boot camps. Very few facilities still operate under this style or approach.

In the late 1980s and early 1990s, second-generation boot camps emerged. Like their predecessors, these camps followed a strict military regimen, but they also required their participants to complete a drug or alcohol treatment program while at the boot camp. In addition, second-generation boot camps also include an educational component through which participants attend either academic or vocational courses.

In the late 1990s, third-generation boot camps began to flourish and continue today. These camps incorporate the same drug and alcohol treatment programs as the second-generation boot camps. However, third-generation boot camps emphasize an aftercare component when individuals are released back into society. Individuals are required to attend various drug and alcohol treatment programs once they are released from the boot camp.

Shortly after the emergence of the third-generation boot camp, the fourth-generation boot camp came into existence. The fourth-generation boot camp focuses on housing and employment issues for its participants upon their release from the boot camp, in the same manner as parole boards address the issue once an inmate is released from prison.

Correctional boot camps have enjoyed a great deal of support from both conservatives and liberals as an alternative to traditional incarceration. Among the reasons for such broad support is the ability of the boot camp to save taxpayers thousands of dollars in incarceration costs while at the same time ensuring that offenders are held accountable for their criminal behavior. Additionally, boot camps allow politicians to address the issue of prison overcrowding and sky-rocketing incarceration rates without appearing soft on crime.

Boot camps have also received a great deal of support from the American public. The media's portrayal of drill instructors shouting in an offender's face and commanding the offender to complete numerous sets of rigorous exercises or engage in physical labor has resulted in the general public favoring the use of boot camps in lieu of correctional treatment. In general, the public has been very supportive of having offenders work and sweat for their offenses as opposed to sitting in a jail cell waiting for their time to expire.

The impact boot camps have had has been the subject of a great deal of controversy. Generally, boot camps are credited with providing an alternative to incarceration and thus reducing incarceration cost and overcrowding. They have also been credited for having short-term effects on the participants' prosocial attitudes; however, since most participants volunteer, research warns that changes in participants' attitudes need to be evaluated with caution. Proponents have argued that individuals who complete boot camp programs have lower rates of recidivism than nonparticipants. However, research has found that recidivism rates are reduced only for short periods after release, generally for less than 6 months. Recidivism rates in some cases have risen and have matched the rates of nonparticipants in evaluation periods from 6 to 12 months after release.

Finally, after 20 years the popularity of boot camps has continued to grow. Since their inception in 1983, boot camps that initially targeted only adults now target juveniles in the public and private sectors. Many inner-city minorities have been able to benefit from the strict discipline and rehabilitative programs that boot camps have to offer. Boot camps have been credited with building self-esteem, self-discipline, and physical fitness levels and helping address family problems, drug and alcohol abuse, and even anger management issues for many inner-city minorities who are often the most targeted in the criminal and juvenile justice systems.

Georgen Guerrero

See also Boot Camps, Juvenile

Further Readings

MacKenzie, D. L. (2004). *Correctional boot camps: Military basic training or a model for corrections?* Thousand Oaks, CA: Sage.

MacKenzie, D. L., Brame, R., McDowall, D., & Souryal, C. (1995). Boot camp prisons and recidivism in eight states. *Criminology, 33*(3), 327–357.

MacKenzie, D. L., & Souryal, C. (1994). *Multisite evaluation of shock incarceration.* Washington, DC: U.S. Department of Justice, Office of Justice Programs, National Institute of Justice.

BOOT CAMPS, JUVENILE

Juvenile boot camps are residential facilities for adolescents who have broken the law or who have been labeled delinquent. The model for juvenile boot camps is taken from military training camps where the emphasis is on socialization for military life. The first juvenile boot camp was established in Orleans Parish, Louisiana, in 1985 following the establishment of the first adult boot camp in the state of Georgia in 1983. The goals of adult and juvenile boot camps are similar in that both are structured as a residential intermediate sanction employing the strategies of shock incarceration. Residency within most boot camps is intended for a brief period of time followed by a period of supervised probation. Although this may vary from program to program, some boot camps include a therapeutic component that may encompass counseling in the areas of anger management and drug and alcohol abuse as well as opportunities for academic and vocational training. The underlying philosophy of the boot camp is that the military style of strong discipline, rigorous exercise, and rigid program structure will serve to rehabilitate young nonviolent offenders. Boot camps are designed to be a deterrent to further participation in criminal activity.

Data on race and ethnicity extracted from the *Census of Juveniles in Residential Placement* reveal that during the period from 1997 to 2003 the racial makeup of all juveniles in residential placement in the United States, including but not limited to boot camps, was between 38% and 40% White; between 38% and 40% Black; between 17% and 19% Hispanic; 2% Asian; and 1% Other. Based on these statistics, it appears that the racial makeup of juveniles in residential placement mirrors that of juveniles under other forms of supervision within the juvenile justice system.

The term *juvenile boot camp* has been used interchangeably with reference to two different types of facilities: those that are under the supervision of the formal criminal justice system and those that are privately run by organizations such as nonprofits or religious groups. The common thread in both types of boot camps is that the offenders have been involved in some form of antisocial, nonviolent behavior. Usually, they are not repeat offenders at the time of sentencing.

The administrative personnel and the organizational structure of privately run juvenile boot camps determine what the exact structure of those facilities will be, but they are generally fashioned with a military structure focusing on discipline, behavior modification, and some therapeutic format. Private boot camps vary greatly from camp to camp depending on the philosophy of the organization. The juvenile's participation and or involvement in privately run camps is usually at the discretion of the parent or guardian, and in most cases there is a cost associated with participation. Parents and guardians have often chosen private boot camps as a preventative measure to amend behavior that they believe will be problematic if continued. Both the parent and the camp administration see participation as preventive. The major criticism of private boot camps is the issue of oversight. These camps are separate and apart from those that are administered by the criminal justice system.

The term *juvenile boot camp* most frequently refers to a residential facility run by the criminal justice system in which inhabitants have been adjudicated and sentenced through the court system. Structure of juvenile boot camps and the sentencing structure can vary from state to state, depending on the laws that govern that state.

Boot camp sentences usually range from 3 to 6 months, and juvenile boot camps represent an alternative to long-term incarceration, thus decreasing costs to the juvenile justice system.

Although juvenile boot camps have served as a method of juvenile correction for nearly 25 years, the effectiveness of this method of punishment is still under question. Research has focused on comparing recidivism rates of those who have been exposed to a boot camp program and those who have not. Generally, the research has concluded that juvenile boot camps are no more effective than other methods of punishment in terms of recidivism rates.

In a study published by the National Institute of Justice in 2001, researchers Doris Layton MacKenzie, Angela R. Gover, Gaylene Styve Armstrong, and Ojmarrh Mitchell attribute the finding that boot camps have not been effective in reducing recidivism to the fact that few of the boot camps or traditional facilities examined in their study had information about what happens to these juveniles after they are released. The implication here is that in order to determine the effectiveness of juvenile boot camps, programs should include a component of close follow-up after release to determine whether there has actually been a positive change in behavior. Comparing recidivism rates discloses which juveniles are rearrested but does not give an indication whether or not there has been a significant change in the initial offending behavior.

Similarly, in a study that compared long-term arrest data for young offenders who had served time in boot camps along with a follow-up intensive parole program to data on juveniles who had been in standard custody and parole, Jean Bottcher and Michael Ezell (2005) found that there were no significant differences between individuals who had served time in boot camps and those who had not in terms of rearrest records. Thus over time, empirical research has shown that juvenile boot camps are about as effective in reducing recidivism as other traditional forms of juvenile punishment.

Conclusion

A review of the empirical research on juvenile boot camps does not lead to a clear indication that juvenile boot camps are totally effective or ineffective. The major criticism of opponents of juvenile boot camps surrounds the appropriateness of the military style of discipline for adolescents, while the major proponents of juvenile boot camps focus on the financial aspects and argue that juvenile boot camps lessen the financial strain on the juvenile justice system.

Although there has been no determination that juvenile boot camps are any more effective than other forms of traditional punishment, they are still operational under the juvenile justice system in many states. It is also important to note that even though there has been some debate surrounding their effectiveness, private boot camps are still operational and thriving.

Peggy A. Engram

See also Boot Camps, Adult; Delinquency Prevention, Juvenile Crime

Further Readings

Bottcher, J., & Ezell, M. (2005). Examining the effectiveness of boot camps: A randomized experiment with a long-term follow-up. *Journal of Research in Crime and Delinquency, 42*(3), 309–332.

MacKenzie, D. L., Gover, A. R., Styve Armstrong, G., & Mitchell, O. (2001). A national study comparing the environments of boot camps with traditional facilities for juvenile offenders. *National Institute of Justice Research in Brief.* Retrieved from http://www.ncjrs.gov/pdffiles1/nij/187680.pdf

BOSTON GUN PROJECT

The Boston Gun Project, also known as "Operation Ceasefire," is a deterrence-based, problem-oriented criminal justice intervention that occurred in 1996 and 1997. The project was intended to reduce youth homicide and youth firearms violence in Boston, Massachusetts. The Boston Gun Project was characterized by an innovative partnership among researchers, practitioners, community leaders, and clergy to assess Boston's youth homicide problem and implement an intervention designed to have a substantial near-term impact on the problem. The Boston Gun Project was based on the "pulling levers" deterrence strategy that focused criminal justice attention on a small number of Boston's youth who were chronic offenders, involved in gang-related activities, and responsible for much of the city's youth homicide problem. Many of these youths were minorities. The Boston Gun Project working group held communications meetings with at-risk members of the community, warning them that further violence and criminality would not be tolerated and would be met with the full complement of the law.

Research suggested that the Boston Gun Project/Ceasefire intervention was associated with significant reductions in youth homicide victimization, shots-fired calls for service, and gun assault incidents in Boston. A comparative analysis of youth homicide trends in Boston relative to youth homicide trends in other major U.S. cities also supports a unique program effect associated with the Ceasefire intervention. This communications-based intervention was coupled with a police crackdown on violent crimes. Homicide rates in Boston fell by two thirds after the strategy was implemented.

The Boston Gun Project is a type of problem-oriented intervention strategy. Problem-oriented interventions work to identify specific problems and to frame responses using a wide variety of often-untraditional approaches. Using a basic repetitive approach of problem identification, analysis, response, evaluation, and adjustment of the response, this strategy has been effective against a wide variety of crime.

The Boston Gun Project was designed to proceed by

1. assembling an interagency working group of largely line-level criminal justice and other practitioners;

2. applying quantitative and qualitative research techniques to create an assessment of the nature of, and dynamics driving, youth violence in Boston;

3. developing an intervention designed to have a substantial, near-term impact on youth homicide;

4. implementing and adapting the intervention; and

5. evaluating the intervention's impact.

The driving force behind the success of the Boston Gun Project was the corporation of an interagency working group consisting primarily of front-line criminal justice practitioners and community leaders. The agencies that were involved included the Boston Police Department; the Massachusetts departments of probation and parole; the office of the Suffolk County district attorney; the office of the U.S. attorney; the Boston Field Office of the Federal Bureau of Alcohol, Tobacco, and Firearms (ATF); the Massachusetts Department of Youth Services (juvenile corrections); Boston School Police; gang outreach and prevention "street-workers"; the TenPoint Coalition of activist Black clergy; the Drug Enforcement Administration; the Massachusetts State Police; and the office of the Massachusetts attorney general.

The basic premise underlying the Boston Gun Project included two strategic elements. The first element was a direct law enforcement attack on illicit firearms traffickers supplying Boston's youth with guns. The second element was an attempt to generate a strong deterrent to gang violence. The systematic attack on illegal firearms traffickers

included the expanded focus of local, state, and federal authorities to include firearms trafficking in Massachusetts in addition to interstate trafficking. ATF set up an in-house tracking system that flagged guns that had been confiscated by the police within 18 months of being sold. They also focused attention on the city's most violent gangs and their gun suppliers. ATF attempted to restore obliterated serial numbers of confiscated guns and investigated trafficking based on the restored serial numbers.

The second element came to be known as the "pulling levers" strategy by working-group members. The intent was to deter violent behavior (especially gun violence) by chronic gang offenders by reaching out directly to gangs, explicitly telling them that violence would no longer be tolerated, and backing that message by pulling every lever legally available when violence occurred. Pulling levers included applying appropriately severe sanctions from all possible criminal justice agencies.

Simultaneously, street workers, probation and parole officers, and later church leaders (Boston's TenPoint Coalition) as well as other community groups offered gang members services and other kinds of help. The working group delivered their message in formal meetings with gang members, through individual police and probation contacts with gang members, through meetings with inmates in secure juvenile facilities, and through gang outreach workers. The deterrence message was not a deal with gang members to stop violence. Instead, it was a promise to gang members that violent behavior would evoke an immediate and intense response from the criminal justice system. If gangs committed crimes but refrained from violence, the normal workings of the criminal justice system would deal with them. But if gang members committed violent crimes, the working group focused all of its enforcement actions on them.

Studies show that the Boston Gun Project was likely responsible for a substantial reduction in youth homicide and youth gun violence in the city of Boston. In a time series analysis (1991–1998), youth homicide rates were examined before and after the implementation of the Boston Gun Project and found that monthly homicide rates in Boston fell by 63%.

Research shows that actively engaging at-risk offenders is an important first step toward altering their perception of sanctions and sanction risks. These sanctions were implemented and supported by a multiagency working group. The police were the cornerstone of this working group, but including many other front-line practitioners and agency workers was paramount in the successful implementation of the Boston Gun Project and the Operation Ceasefire intervention plan.

Lorenzo M. Boyd

See also At-Risk Youth; Youth Gangs

Further Readings

Braga, A., Kennedy, D. M., Waring, E. J., & Piehl, A. M. (2001). Problem-oriented policing, deterrence, and youth violence: An evaluation of Boston's Operation Ceasefire. *Journal of Research in Crime and Delinquency, 38,* 195–226.

Kennedy, D. (1998, July). Pulling levers: Getting deterrence right. *National Institute of Justice Journal,* pp. 2–8.

McDevitt, J., Braga, A. A., Nurse, D., & Buerger, M. (2003). Boston's youth violence prevention program: A comprehensive community wide approach. In S. Decker (Ed.), *Policing gangs and youth violence* (pp. 77–101). Belmont, CA: Wadsworth.

McGarrell, E. F., Chermak, S., Wilson, J. M., & Corsaro, N. (2006). Reducing homicide through a "lever-pulling" strategy. *Justice Quarterly, 23,* 214–231.

BROWN, LEE P. (1937–)

From humble origins as the son of farmers, Lee Patrick Brown, whose birth certificate read "Baby Brown," rose to leadership positions in local, county, and federal law enforcement before becoming the first African American mayor of Houston, the fourth largest city in the United States, in 1998. Brown served three terms as mayor, until 2004, when term limits prohibited him from running a fourth time.

Born October 4, 1937, in Wewoka, Oklahoma, Brown was one of six sons and a daughter whose family moved to rural Fowler, California, when he was 5. He recalled living in a one-bedroom house and his family working the fields "like migrant workers," but his mother valued education and encouraged her children to do the same. Brown, more than 6 feet tall and solidly built, won a football scholarship to Fresno State University, earning a bachelor's degree in criminology in 1960. Among the first group of highly educated African American police leaders, Brown went on to obtain two master's degrees (1964 and 1968) and a doctorate in criminology in 1970 from the University of California, Berkeley.

Brown's career has been unusual due to his career mobility, the number of departments he has led, and also, as one of few police executives to have earned a doctorate, his ability to shift seamlessly between law enforcement and academe. He began work as a police officer in San Jose, California, in 1960, but in 1968 moved to Portland, Oregon, to establish Portland State University's administration of justice department. In 1972 he became a professor of public administration and the associate director of the Institute for Urban Affairs and Research at Howard University, a historically Black institution in Washington, D.C.

In January 1975, he returned to law enforcement in Portland when he was appointed sheriff of Multnomah County; unlike most sheriffs' offices, the Multnomah office had in 1964 been named Division of Public Safety (Sheriff's Office) and was an appointed rather than elected position. Here, Brown instituted team policing and developed and put into practice early elements of community policing with which he would be closely associated throughout his career. He also directed publication of *Neighborhood Team Policing: The Multnomah County Experience,* articles by him and others on the implementation of his ideas, another indication of his ability to combine practitioner and academic careers. Eighteen months later, in June 1976, he was named the county's director of justice services, making him coordinator of all county criminal justice agencies.

Brown was in 1978 selected by Atlanta, Georgia, Mayor Maynard Jackson as commissioner of public safety, in charge of the city's police, fire, corrections, and civil defense departments. He managed the police department's arrest of Wayne B. Williams for the Atlanta child murders, in which nearly 30 mostly African American teenage boys were killed between 1979 and 1981. Williams was found guilty of two murders in February 1982, ending the investigation, but in 2006 the DeKalb County (in which Atlanta is located) Police Department reopened and then closed some of the cases; in 2007 Williams, maintaining his innocence, was still attempting to win a new trial. The case received worldwide attention for Brown and for the Atlanta Police Department's public information officer, Beverly Harvard, who would in 1994 be named chief, becoming the first African American woman to lead a major city police department and one of a number of law enforcement leaders—male and female, Black and White—whom Brown mentored.

In 1982, Mayor Kathy Whitmore selected Brown as Houston's first African American police chief. His departmentwide use of community policing strategies in Houston earned him the designation of "father of community policing" in recognition of his efforts to increase police involvement not only with citizens but with other government agencies to mount a concerted effort to fight crime.

Brown's 8 years in Houston was the longest chief's position he held; when he left, he was replaced by another female protégée, Elizabeth (Betsy) Watson, who became the first woman to lead a department in a city of more than 1 million people.

Brown departed from Houston in January 1990, after he was persuaded by New York City's first African American mayor, David Dinkins, to run the nation's largest police department, the New York City Police Department (NYCPD), then about 30,000 officers. In New York, Brown faced some of the same issues as in Houston and had a more difficult task reorienting the more bureaucratic and tradition-bound NYCPD. Rank and file officers disliked him because he was an outsider and because of his emphasis on community policing, which sought to involve all ranks of police officers more closely with the neighborhoods they patrolled through foot patrol and frequent community get-togethers. Although New York City's drop in crime accelerated during his tenure, he was criticized for an inadequate police response to the 1991 riots in Crown Heights, Brooklyn, involving Blacks and Hasidic Jews.

Brown left the NYCPD in September 1992 and briefly returned to Houston before President William J. Clinton named him director of the cabinet-level Office of National Drug Control Policy (ONDCP) that had been established by Congress in 1988 to coordinate the nation's drug control program. Confirmed by the Senate unanimously on June 21, 1993, Brown supported creation of High Intensity Drug Trafficking Area (HIDTA) teams and investigation of the Colombian Cali drug cartel, but budget and staff cuts and demands from Congress that the White House develop a stiffer anti-drug message led to his resignation on December 12, 1996, when he voiced frustration with the bureaucratic and political nature of Washington, D.C.

He returned to Houston to teach at Rice University and in 1997 was elected mayor. He served three two-year terms, during which downtown Houston was revitalized. Brown expanded his concept of community policing into a broader philosophy he called "neighborhood-oriented government." Since retiring, he has been a motivational speaker and a security consultant whose firm, the Brown Group International, among other assignments, worked with the New Orleans Police Department (NOPD) in the wake of Hurricane Katrina. His 188-page NOPD reform plan, released in July 2007, included more than 70 recommendations, most of which relied on his belief in community involvement rather than on reliance on crime and arrest statistics as productivity measurements. True to Brown's beliefs that patrol officers were the key to a department's success, the report was based on interviews with hundreds of New Orleans officers and numerous questionnaires completed by all ranks, not only senior-level administrators.

Throughout his career, Brown has been active in professional associations. In addition to being the first African American president of the 18,000-member International Association of Chiefs of Police (IACP) in 1990, he was a founding member in 1976 of the National Organization of Black Law Enforcement Executives (NOBLE), through which Black police executives have addressed police community relations and raised issues of fairness in the administration of justice, and he has served on the advisory board of the U.S. Conference of Mayors.

In addition to putting community policing into practice, Brown has edited or co-authored numerous works on it, including a textbook (with Thomas

Alfred Johnson and Gordon C. Misner), *The Police and Society: An Environment for Collaboration and Confrontation*. Others include *The Death of Police Community Relations* and *The Administration of Criminal Justice: A View from Black America* (1973 and 1974); *Community Policing: A Practical Guide for Police Officers* (1989); and *Problem-Solving Strategies for Community Policing: A Practical Guide* (1992). While he chaired the National Minority Advisory Council on Criminal Justice to LEAA (Law Enforcement Assistance Administration), the council published *The Inequality of Justice: A Report on Crime and the Administration of Justice in the Minority Community* (1982), which, based on four years of research, portrayed the adverse impact of the criminal justice system on minorities with chapters on Blacks, Hispanics, Native Americans, and Asians.

Brown has been awarded honorary degrees from six American universities, has taught at universities in China, has been honored by University of California, Berkeley, and has been inducted into both the Gallup and Black Public Administrators halls of fame. Brown, the father of four adult children, often mentions his selection as father of the year in 1991 from the National Father's Day Committee.

In addition to being the first African American to hold many of the positions he did, Brown was selected as police chief in three major American cities (Atlanta, Houston, and New York), through his mentoring efforts was able to expand the philosophy of community policing to departments throughout the United States, and as mayor of Houston was able to expand the tenets of community policing into an overall philosophy of urban government. His academic credentials have given him credibility outside policing that has rarely been achieved by any police administrator.

Dorothy Moses Schulz

See also Community Policing; Harvard, Beverly; National Organization of Black Law Enforcement Executives; War on Drugs

Further Readings

Brown, L. P. (Ed.). (1976). *Neighborhood team policing: The Multnomah County experience*. Portland, OR: Multnomah County Sheriff's Office.

Dulaney, W. M. (1996). *Black police in America*. Bloomington: Indiana University Press.

Harry Walker Agency. (2005). *Lee P. Brown*. Retrieved from http://www.harrywalker.com/speakers_template_printer.cfm?Spea_ID=704

Johnson, T. A., Misner, G. C., & Brown, L. P. (1981). *The police and society: An environment for collaboration and confrontation*. Englewood Cliffs, NJ: Prentice Hall.

McCarthy, B. (2007, July 18). N.O. chief welcomes plan for reform. *The Times-Picayune*. Retrieved from http://blog.nola.com/times-picayune/2007/07/no_chief_welcomes_plan_for_ref.html

Office of National Drug Control Policy. (n.d.). *Dr. Lee P. Brown*. Retrieved November 11, 2008, from http://clinton1.nara.gov/White_House/EOP/ondcp/html/Lee_Brown.html

Office of National Drug Control Policy. (1996). *Drug czar Lee Brown resigns*. Retrieved from http://www.ndsn.org/jan96/drugczar.html

BROWN BERETS

The Brown Berets were the most prominent youth organization addressing issues in Chicano communities during the late 1960s and early 1970s. During their brief existence (1967 to 1972), the Brown Berets were involved in numerous protests and organized around aspects of Chicano life that would positively impact the lives of Chicano people. This entry reviews the development of the organization, the assorted activities of the organization, and its eventual dissolution.

As the population of Mexicans increased in the 1960s, a sense of cultural identity and a need to address inequitable treatment of this group fostered the development of several organizations. The Brown Berets, formed by David Sanchez in Los Angeles, was one such group. Sanchez's initial involvement with the Young Citizens for Community Action spurred the development of the Brown Berets to serve as an alert patrol, with defending the Chicano neighborhoods as their primary objective. The membership of the Brown Berets reached 5,000, with 90 chapters throughout the United States; it included neighborhood youth who were mostly from lower socioeconomic backgrounds. Many members were formerly involved in gangs but came together to protect their *barrios* (neighborhoods). The creation of this organization was part of the Chicano Youth Movement (CYM), which included students and neighborhood youth; however, the Brown Berets differed from other organizations being created during the Chicano movement because they were a paramilitary group composed primarily of neighborhood youth. While there were female members of the organization, all leadership positions were held by men.

The members of the organization were advocates of Chicanismo, the vehicle to express Chicano nationalism. Chicano nationalism encompassed the new realities, values, and meanings that come out of being Mexican in America and confronting the inequalities that resulted from this. The organization grew in popularity by challenging an inequitable situation in the public school system. Protesting the treatment of students in the public school system in east Los Angeles (L.A.), students, parents, and members of various organizations gathered to express their discontent. The east L.A. sheriffs chose to use force to end the boycotts and walkouts, but the Brown Berets intervened. They defended and protected the students by placing themselves between the students and officers, which often resulted in their arrests. As a result of these actions, the group gained favor within the Chicano communities, especially when several Brown Berets faced a possible 45 years in prison on charges of engaging in conspiracies to disrupt the public schools. After 2 years of litigation, the charges were dropped.

In addition to the east L.A. school walkouts, the Brown Berets protested and organized against involvement in the Vietnam War and were involved with some of the work in conjunction with the Southern Christian Leadership Conference. They developed a free medical clinic in 1969, offering social, psychological, and medical services. Sustaining itself through donations, the clinic was open from 10 a.m. to 10 p.m. and the only requirement for an entrance was a need to see a doctor. The organization also published their own newspaper, *La Causa,* and some members were instrumental in forging bonds among the Chicano, the Black Power, and American Indian movements.

The members of the organization united around a self-defense platform and a nationalistic 10-point program that drew attention from law enforcement agencies. These agencies committed themselves to discrediting the Brown Berets in the eyes of both White and Chicano communities. The Los Angeles Police Department infiltrated the organization, resulting in arrests of members but not the destruction of the group or its work.

The "Ten Point Program" the organization put forth demanded changes such as an $8,000 minimum annual salary, the right to bilingual education, and to be tried by juries of only Mexican Americans, among other things. The program was meant to hold the United States accountable for providing an equitable life for Mexican Americans, so the organization based its demands on the U.S. Constitution, the Bill of Rights, and the Treaty of Guadalupe Hidalgo. In line with their desire for self-determination, the Brown Berets were advocates of Aztlan, the recognition of a separate Chicano nation.

They wore militaristic uniforms consisting of khaki clothing and brown berets with an emblem of a yellow pentagon and two bayoneted rifles behind a cross. The words *La Causa* ("The Cause") appeared above the emblem. Presenting themselves in this kind of clothing projected an image of discipline, readiness, and willingness to engage on behalf of the people if necessary. According to the creator of the emblem, Johnny Parsons, the name of the organization was adopted because east L.A. sheriffs often referred to members as the "Brown Berets."

The Chicano movement began its decline around 1971, and the Brown Berets attempted to reinvigorate the movement by organizing *La Marcha de la Reconquista* ("The March of the Reconquest"). This march was designed to tour Chicano neighborhoods, hold rallies, and talk to people in an attempt to give them a voice and address key issues like farm workers' rights, education, welfare rights, prison reform, and police interaction.

The year 1972 proved to be the last for the organization. Despite their attempts at renewing the energy of the Chicano movement, their final endeavor was invading Catalina Island (an island they believed still belonged to Mexico). The action ended peacefully. Shortly thereafter, Sanchez held a press conference announcing the disbanding of the organization.

Efua Akoma

See also Gringo Justice; Latina/o/s; League of United
Latin American Citizens

Further Readings

Chavez, E. (2002). *"¡Mi Raza Primero!" Nationalism,
identity, and insurgency in the Chicano movement in
Los Angeles, 1966–1978.* Berkeley: University of
California Press.

Navarro, A. (1995). *Mexican American Youth
Organization: Avant-Garde of the Chicano movement
in Texas.* Austin: University of Texas Press.

Rodriguez, R. (2000). The origins and history of the
Chicano movement. In R. I. Rochin & D. N. Valdes,
Voices of a New Chicana/o history (pp. 295–307).
East Lansing: Michigan State University Press.

BROWN V. CITY OF ONEONTA

Brown v. City of Oneonta was a federal civil
rights lawsuit filed after nearly all the African
American men in Onconta, New York, were questioned by local law enforcement officials. Some of
the notoriety of the case is due to opinions issued
by the U.S. Court of Appeals for the Second
Circuit, which decides federal appellate cases from
New York, Connecticut, and Vermont. Those
opinions reveal different sensitivities about the use
of race as part of a description of suspects wanted
by law enforcement officials.

Early on September 4, 1992, an elderly woman
was raped and robbed in Oneonta, New York. The
victim informed the police that during the attack
she stabbed the assailant with the assailant's knife.
She also told police that she believed the assailant
was an African American man and that she
believed he was young based on how quickly she
heard him move across the floor. The police used a
canine to track the assailant's scent, but lost it near
the State University of New York College at
Oneonta (SUCO).

A state police officer informed an SUCO officer
that the perpetrator's trail led to a wooded area on
the edge of the campus. At the state police's
request, campus safety officials produced a list of
Black male students with their addresses. This list
was distributed to law enforcement officers, who
used the information to locate and question the

listed students. Some officers, when conducting a
general sweep of the Oneonta campus during the
next several days, stopped and questioned several
non-White persons. No suspect was arrested.

In 1993, SUCO students whose names were
on the list and non-White students who had been
stopped and questioned by the police filed a class
action lawsuit in the U.S. District Court for the
Northern District of New York. The suit named as
defendants the officers who had participated in the
investigation or conducted the sweeps, supervisory
officials and the City of Oneonta, its police department, and the local sheriffs' department.

The defendants eventually filed pretrial motions
to dismiss the suit. The trial judge granted the
motions and dismissed claims that were based on
an alleged violation of the educational privacy
laws. The Second Circuit upheld that ruling on
appeal. After additional pretrial proceedings, the
trial court dismissed the remainder of the suit. It
rejected claims based on the Fourth Amendment,
ruling that the encounters were not seizures within
the meaning of that provision, and rejected claims
based on the Fourteenth Amendment because
there was no allegation that nonminority individuals were treated differently than the plaintiffs.

On appeal, a panel of three Second Circuit
judges noted the implications of the issues before
it, as it stated, "This case bears on the question of
the extent to which law enforcement officials may
utilize race in their investigation of a crime." The
court affirmed the Fourteenth Amendment ruling.
According to the court, those claims failed because
the plaintiffs did not identify any law or policy
used by the state officials to conduct the investigation. The plaintiffs "were questioned on the altogether legitimate basis of a physical description
given by the victim of a crime. . . . This description
contained not only race, but also gender and age,
as well as the possibility of a cut on the hand." The
court panel did reverse the trial court on some of
the Fourth Amendment claims.

In response to a motion for a rehearing, the
panel of judges amended portions of its opinion.
Language added expressed sympathy for the
plaintiffs' experience, and the court changed its
disposition of most of the Fourth Amendment
claims, allowing those plaintiffs to continue to
litigate them in the trial court. The plaintiffs then
moved for reconsideration and a suggestion for a

rehearing en banc, that is, before all of the judges of the Second Circuit. The entire Second Circuit ultimately denied the request. Such motions are usually denied without comment. However, in this case there were opinions issued both for and against en banc consideration. The two most pertinent opinions are described as follows.

In support of the denial, Chief Judge John M. Walker, Jr., the author of the panel and the amended opinions, wrote that the proposals in the dissenting opinions would hamper law enforcement efforts when a suspect's race was part of the description used in the search. He stated that the restrictions provided by the Fourth Amendment's prohibition on unreasonable searches and seizures were sufficient to limit law enforcement officials from stopping persons based only on their race.

Judge Guido Calabresi, who dissented from the denial of rehearing en banc, saw the case as involving what liability, if any, attached when state officials ignored every part of a suspect's description except the racial element and stopped and questioned every member of that race, even if those persons otherwise failed to fit the physical features of the suspect's description. According to him, the equal protection clause of the Fourteenth Amendment applied instead of the Fourth Amendment. He cautioned that since courts were largely incompetent to fashion more than general rules in the area, legislatures, executive branch officials, and those patrolled by the law enforcement agencies should establish guidelines on the permissible conduct of law enforcement officials.

Brown v. Oneonta is a modern version of an old practice—the rounding up of African American men in the locale—when a victim or witness to a crime provides a general but race-based description of the suspect. The roundup practice perpetuates stereotypes and fears about African American men and criminal activity. The ruling in *Brown v. Oneonta* joins a growing list of federal court decisions that apply the Fourth Amendment instead of the Fourteenth Amendment when reviewing law enforcement officials' conduct. In doing so, the courts typically either declare that a search or seizure has not occurred or focus on the propriety of the search or seizure; in most instances, the conclusion is the same—the Fourth Amendment has not been violated. These decisions have the impact of essentially insulating the investigatory practices of law enforcement officials. Assessing the practices under the Fourteenth Amendment—and asking whether the law enforcement official's actions were motivated by race—might occasionally result in legal disapproval of the activities.

Dwight Aarons

See also Criminalblackman; Profiling, Ethnic: Use by Police and Homeland Security; Profiling, Racial: Historical and Contemporary Perspectives; Racialization of Crime

Further Readings

Brown v. City of Oneonta, N.Y., Police Dep't, 106 F.3d 1125 (2nd Cir. 1997).

Brown v. City of Oneonta, N.Y., Police Dep't, 221 F.3d 329 (2nd Cir. 2000), vacating 195 F.3d 111 (2nd Cir. 1999).

Brown v. City of Oneonta, N.Y., Police Dep't, 235 F.3d 769 (2nd Cir. 2000) (denial of en banc petition).

Carter, W. M., Jr. (2004). A Thirteenth Amendment framework for combating racial profiling. *Harvard Civil Rights and Civil Liberties Law Review, 39*, 17.

Johnson, E. L. (1995). "A menace to society": The use of criminal profiles and its effects on Black males. *Howard Law Journal, 38*, 629.

Thompson, A. C. (1999). Stopping the usual suspects: Race and the Fourth Amendment. *New York University Law Review, 74*, 956.

BROWN V. MISSISSIPPI

The United States has long been a proponent of fair and equitable justice for all citizens. The Constitution of the United States declares that "all citizens are created equal" and shall be given equal protection under the law. *Brown v. Mississippi* (1936) is a pivotal case in U.S. history that demonstrates various procedural faults and erroneous judgments of the criminal justice system. Additionally, it speaks about the racial overtones of that era and what that meant for African Americans facing the criminal justice system.

Following a murder but prior to a court hearing, residents of Giles, Mississippi, prompted by law enforcement officers, including the sheriff, determined the guilt of the accused. The defendants, also known as the "Kemper County Trio," were subjected to a trial, conviction, and attempted execution before they were arrested or indicted for the alleged crime of murder. The question that is central in this case is whether the convictions, which were based solely on coerced confessions—the only evidence of guilt—were obtained in a manner that was consistent with the due process clause of the Fourteenth Amendment of the U.S. Constitution.

Facts of the Case

Raymond Stuart of Giles, Mississippi, was murdered on March 30, 1934. His body was discovered at his home at 1:00 p.m. Stuart, a White farmer, had been brutally butchered with an axe. The then-deputy sheriff, Dial, was determined that he would find the killer(s). Eventually the investigation centered on Ed Brown, Henry Shields, and Arthur Ellington. Deputy Sheriff Dial went to the home of Arthur Ellington and then took the suspect to the scene of the crime. Upon their arrival, a mob of angry White men congregated and began to accuse Ellington. These individuals initiated the torment and torture of Ellington and insisted that Deputy Dial make Ellington confess. The mob, along with the law enforcement officers, tied a noose around Ellington's neck and hung him to get a confession. After releasing the suspect from the tree and hearing Ellington's protests of innocence, they hung him again. Ellington kept professing his innocence. This angered the mob, and they tied him to a tree and severely beat him. Despite his obvious pain, Ellington did not confess, and he was allowed to return home. However, on March 31, Deputy Dial and the mob returned, and Dial arrested Ellington, who still bore the strangulation marks of the execution attempted on the previous day. In returning to the county jail, Dial took Ellington through Alabama, where Dial whipped and tortured Ellington until he confessed to the murder of Stuart.

On April 1, 1934, Deputy Dial returned to the county jail where Ellington, Ed Brown, and Henry Shields were being held. Dial, along with a number of White men, made Brown and Shields remove their clothing and bend over a chair, where they were brutally beaten with metal buckles of leather straps until they confessed to the murder of Stuart, including exact details. During this beating, both Brown and Shields were told that the whippings would continue if they did not confess. Shortly afterward, Dial convened with another officer of the law and several witnesses to hear the confessions of the trio, and Brown and Shields were indicted.

On April 4, the three defendants—Ed Brown, Henry Shields, and Arthur Ellington—were charged for the murder of Raymond Stuart. Since the defendants had not spoken with counsel, counsel were appointed and the trial was set to begin the next day, April 5, 1934. The trial ended on April 6, 1934, with a guilty verdict and a sentence of death. The trio appealed their case to the Supreme Court of the State of Mississippi, which upheld the convictions and sentences imposed by the local court despite the knowledge of the torture, coerced confessions, and the lack of evidence apart from the so-called confessions.

The defendants appealed their case to the U.S. Supreme Court, which heard the case on January 10, 1936. The Kemper County Trio was defended by Earl Brewer (former governor of Mississippi) and J. Morgan Stevens, with monetary support from the National Association for the Advancement of Colored People (NAACP) and other organizations. The Court unanimously reversed the lower courts' decisions on February 17, 1936.

Historical Context of *Brown*

The *Brown* case serves as a reminder of how the justice system has evolved and has come to acknowledge the importance of civil liberties for individuals either accused or convicted of a crime. Much of the literature on the *Brown* decision discusses the historical context of the case. The South has historically been a place of widespread racial discrimination. For many years, African Americans were subject to a very different type of jurisprudence than were their White counterparts. Often, accused African Americans never received a criminal trial but rather were tried by either the general public or the media, with their sentences being death by lynching. At the time of the *Brown* trial, Kemper County, Mississippi, was referred to as "Bloody Kemper" because its rate of lynching was nearly twice that of the rest of the state.

One of the most disturbing aspects of the *Brown* case is that the entire ordeal took place during only 6 days from the time Stuart's body was found. Modern criminal procedure would likely not consider a trial conducted in such haste to be consistent with the due process clause of the Fourteenth Amendment. The 1930s reflected a societal temperament that displayed a burgeoning intolerance for the brutal practice of lynching. The moral compass was moving in a direction that made such acts deplorable, so the solution was to ensure a "fair and speedy trial" in order to prevent the lynch mob from taking a state matter into the hands of private citizens. To avoid lynching, trials were conducted in haste and thus, in this case, resulted in wrongful convictions. After the original trial, in 1934 a Mississippi newspaper, *The Meridian Star,* reported that the defendants "enjoyed" a fair and impartial trial. The media's determination of fairness came from the community view that the trial was better than the lynching that would have normally occurred. Ironically, after the U.S. Supreme Court reversed and remanded the case, the local newspapers neglected to report on the monumental ruling.

The Birth of Modern Criminal Procedure

The *Brown* decision, along with *Powell v. Alabama,* represented a philosophical shift in the manner that the U.S. Supreme Court interpreted the protection of individual rights in criminal proceedings as dictated by the U.S. Constitution. Some scholars suggest that these cases mark the beginning of contemporary criminal procedure; as such they are often discussed in tandem since both have been attributed as the bases for the landmark *Miranda v. Arizona* decision (Cortner, 1986; Klarman, 2000). *Miranda* is commonly known as the source of the "bright line rule" invoking Fifth and Sixth Amendment protections in state criminal cases and mandating that police inform an individual of these rights prior to conducting a custodial interrogation. A violation of *Miranda* should lead to the suppression of the confession.

The relationship between *Brown* and *Miranda* lies in the fact that the *Brown* decision prohibited tortured confessions in a similar vein as the *Miranda* ruling finally extinguished all coerced confessions. The ruling in *Brown* was instrumental in establishing the "voluntariness test" used to determine whether or not an individual's confession was coerced. *Brown* has been viewed as one of the first cases in which the U.S. Supreme Court intervened in a state criminal case based on the method of obtaining a confession. As Swanson, Chamelin, and Territo (2003) note, prior to Brown, the determination of whether or not a confession was voluntary was based on a loosely defined concept of voluntariness. The elimination of the use of torture as a method for securing a confession was a drastic shift from the vagueness of the voluntariness test. Subsequent to *Brown,* the voluntariness test underwent further interpretation and eventually led to the application of the federal privilege against compulsory self-incrimination to the states.

As a proclaimed precursor for *Miranda,* one would assume that the constitutional basis for the *Brown* decision would lie in Fifth or Sixth Amendment jurisprudence. However, the rationale for the *Brown* decision was fair trial rule under the due process clause of the Fourteenth Amendment. Similar to the High Court's rationale in *Powell,* the *Brown* decision was based on the defendants' inability to receive a fair trial because of the nature of their confessions. More specifically, since the coerced confessions were the principal evidence in the case, the fact that they were obtained through torture made the trial unfair.

Though the *Brown* Court created a semblance of Fifth Amendment protection in state criminal proceedings, they were not yet committed to "nationalizing" the U.S. Constitution. The Court did not extend Fifth Amendment protection to the states in all respects, or as later extended. For example, the Court did not overturn the standing *Twining v. New Jersey* decision, where they had previously ruled that the Fifth Amendment privilege against self-incrimination did not apply to states. That would not come for another 30 years, in *Malloy v. Hogan.*

Brown v. Mississippi is significant for various reasons. First, it helped to set a precedent that the U.S. Supreme Court can regulate state courts when violations of constitutional amendments occurred, particularly in cases involving due process. Second, *Brown v. Mississippi* helped established rules for the "test of voluntariness," by which the court determines whether confessions were truly given freely and not coerced. Last, the case helped lay the foundation for the landmark decision of *Miranda v. Arizona*, which resulted in the ruling that police must make detainees aware of the rights before police questioning begins.

Isis N. Walton and Cherie Dawson Edwards

See also *Miranda v. Arizona*; National Association for the Advancement of Colored People (NAACP); Police Use of Force; *Powell v. Alabama*

Further Readings

Brown v. Mississippi, 297 U.S. 278 (1936).

Cortner, R. C. (1986). *A "Scottsboro" case in Mississippi: The Supreme Court and* Brown v. Mississippi. Jackson: University Press of Mississippi.

Klarman, M. J. (2000). The racial origins of modern criminal procedure. *Michigan Law Review, 99,* 48–97.

Malloy v. Hogan, 378 U.S. 1 (1964).

Miranda v. Arizona, 384 U.S. 436 (1966).

Powell v. Alabama, 287 U.S. 45 (1932).

Swanson, C. R., Chamelin, N. C., & Territo, L. (2003). *Criminal investigation* (8th ed.). Boston: McGraw-Hill.

Twinning v. New Jersey, 211 U.S. 78 (1908).

BULLY-CUMMINGS, ELLA (1958–)

Ella May Bully was working in the ticket booth of a Detroit theater in the mid-1970s when she saw an unusual sight: a woman police officer patrolling Detroit's streets. Three years later, the 19-year-old high school graduate decided to try walking the same beat; 23 years later she became only the second African American female named chief of one of the 10 largest police departments in the nation.

When Bully entered the Detroit Police Department (DPD) Academy in July 1977, she faced hostility from the mostly White male officers who resented the city's affirmative efforts to integrate the department. But she persevered, serving in every rank until, on November 3, 2003 (now

Bully-Cummings), she was named interim chief of the 4,200-member DPD by Mayor Kwame Kilpatrick, who on December 4 of that year removed the interim from her title. Although Kilpatrick described Bully-Cummings's rise through the ranks as "meteoric," her career is typical of large-city police executives; she worked only in one police department, served in many ranks and assignments, and continued her education while working. This resulted in strong internal support for her, the opposite of what she faced as a rookie officer.

Bully-Cummings was born in Japan in 1958, the second daughter of an African American U.S. Army serviceman and a Japanese mother. Before she turned 2 years old, the family moved to Detroit, where her Mississippi-born father worked as a television repairman and struggled to support the family, which grew to six daughters and one son, all of whom at one time lived in a one-bedroom apartment. She graduated from Cass Technical, Detroit's top academic high school. As the second-oldest child, she worked to increase the family's income and to help pay for her siblings' education, but she did not continue her education until after joining the police department. She received a bachelor's degree with honors in public administration from Detroit's Madonna University in 1993 and a juris doctorate cum laude from the Detroit College of Law at Michigan State University in 1998, passing the state bar exam the same year.

Like most officers, Bully-Cummings was given a first assignment of walking a foot post. She recalled that few men wanted to work with women; some men would feign illness or give other reasons to avoid working with women, in part because they believed women would be unable to assist in dangerous situations on the high-crime Detroit streets. Even the few men who would work with her showed their distrust by using their portable radios to call for backup before they arrived at a scene. Her first arrest involved a drunk-driving stop during which her partner was kicked in the groin. Bully-Cummings, at 5 foot, 8 inches and only 110 pounds, jumped on the 6-foot, 5-inch suspect's back so she would not be hit and so that he would not flee; she knew that if he did, her reputation would be ruined. Just as she was establishing credibility, Detroit, like many cities, was faced with a fiscal crisis, and Bully-Cummings was laid off in the mid-1980s, and began work for the *Detroit Free Press* in a clerical position.

Rehired, Bully-Cummings was promoted to sergeant in 1987 and to lieutenant in 1993, managing a precinct investigative unit. Within 2 years she was appointed an inspector in charge of the public information and crime prevention sections, where she created community outreach and awareness programs before being named administrative services bureau commander. In 1998, she was promoted to commander and placed in charge of a precinct, and later such high-profile units as the special response team, traffic, mounted, and aviation, as well as officers assigned to the city's housing developments. In 1999, she retired to become an associate at Miller, Canfield, Paddock & Stone, at Foley & Lardner, and again at Miller, Canfield, where she represented companies in labor and employment discrimination cases.

In May 2002, Bully-Cummings was urged to return to the DPD as its first female assistant chief by newly appointed chief Jerry Oliver and became the department's highest-ranking woman. In October 2003, Oliver, an unpopular outsider, was charged in Wayne County (in which Detroit is located) with possession of an unlicensed handgun at Detroit Metro Airport while traveling to a police conference. Although he had purchased it in 1973 while a police officer in Phoenix and said he was unaware he had to register it in Michigan, Oliver resigned and Bully-Cummings, 46, was named his successor.

Bully-Cummings is active in local and national police and legal organizations, including the International Association of Chiefs of Police (IACP), the National Organization of Black Law Enforcement Executives (NOBLE), and the state chiefs' association and is on the board of the Police Executive Research Forum (PERF) and the National and Wolverine bar associations. Bully-Cummings has been a role model and mentor to many. She leads a department that is nearly 25% female, one of the highest percentages of women—including minority women—in the nation. She is only the second woman to lead one of the country's 10 largest departments (the first was Houston's Elizabeth Watson from 1990 to 1992), and the second African American woman major city chief (the first was Atlanta's Beverly Harvard, from 1994 to 2002).

Bully-Cummings has said that women have to push harder than men to get ahead, and that men and women officers may have different styles that on the street may translate into a verbal rather than a physical response and in the executive suite may translate into a more collaborative style. Both her style and her legal training have assisted Detroit in addressing consent decrees signed with the U.S. Department of Justice in 2003 that required reforming lethal force policies and treatment of prisoners and that in late 2007 were extended to July 2011 in recognition of her successes in professionalizing the department and changing its institutional culture. She has also addressed the city's gun violence, including the deaths of two officers in February 2004 during a traffic stop, by creating a task force to reduce violence, while remaining a vocal and visible police leader independent of her race and sex.

Dorothy Moses Schulz

See also Harvard, Beverly; National Organization of Black Law Enforcement Executives

Further Readings

Ashenfelter, D. (2007, September 22). Cops get break on reform: More time given for changes in use of force, other issues. *Detroit Free Press*. Retrieved from http://www.accessmylibrary.com/coms2/summary_0286-32947075_ITM

Hackney, S., & Schmitt, B. (2003, November 8). New chief lays down the law: Preferring progress over praise, she has changes planned. *Detroit Free Press*, p. 1A.

Leinwand, D. (2004, April 26). Lawsuits of '70s shape police leadership now. *USA Today*, p. 13A.

Schulz, D. M. (2004). *Breaking the brass ceiling: Women police chiefs and their paths to the top*. Westport, CT: Praeger.

BUREAU OF INDIAN AFFAIRS

The Bureau of Indian Affairs (BIA), also known as the Office of Indian Affairs, provides an array of services to the 561 Native American tribes that are federally recognized in the United

States. These services include developing forests, overseeing and directing agricultural programs, developing and maintaining the infrastructures of Indian reservations, and economic development. The agency also provides to Native Americans who live on or near reservations housing, health care, and educational services to nearly 48,000 students in 60 schools. It manages 55.7 million acres of land entrusted to Native American tribes, including Native Alaskans. This entry reviews the formation and the history of the BIA as well as the controversies that surround the agency.

History

Before the establishment of the BIA, the United States had made efforts to provide services to Native Americans. In 1775, the Continental Congress created three departments of Indian affairs—Northern, Central, and Southern— that were under the supervision of Benjamin Franklin and Patrick Henry. These departments were responsible for negotiating treaties between the Native Americans and U.S. colonists to ensure that the Native Americans remained neutral during the American Revolutionary War. In 1798, the three departments merged into the War Department, which continued to maintain Native American relations. Earlier, in 1790, the U.S. Congress passed the first of several Trade Acts and Intercourse Acts to deal with Native American relations. The Trade Act regulated commerce between the Native Americans and White settlers and prohibited the purchasing of Native American lands other than by federal treaties. It also set guidelines prescribing punishment for crimes against Native Americans. The Intercourse Acts restricted non–Native Americans from traveling onto Native American lands and established trading posts, which were referred to as "factories." These acts provided the basis for the War Department to protect Native Americans from exploitation.

In 1824, the secretary of war, John C. Calhoun, officially created the BIA, which was under the supervision of the War Department, to oversee relations between Native Americans and the U.S. government. The agency was to oversee existing treaties, negotiate new treaties, and appropriate funds to facilitate Native American assimilation into White culture. As more Native American tribes came under control of the U.S. government, the agency barred Native American languages and religious customs.

Because of Native American dissatisfaction with the War Department's handling of Native American affairs, the BIA was transferred to the Department of the Interior (DOI) in 1849, where it remains today. The agency assigned Native American agents to oversee operations on the reservations. Many of these agents were Christian missionaries who tried to impose Christianity on the Native Americans. However, several Indian agents were involved in illegal activities, such as selling supplies that were intended for Native Americans to the general population. The Indian agents also unlawfully allowed corporations to cut timber and mine for minerals on reservations for profit. Native Americans were unable to air grievances regarding Indian agent activities, enabling the exploitation of their culture to continue.

In order to address this mismanagement, Congress commissioned the Peace Commission in 1867. The agency soon appointed honest and effective Indian agents. The commission also recommended that the BIA be removed from the DOI, but this recommendation was never implemented. By the late 1800s, the agency's presence on the reservation increased heavily. Indian agents bore the responsibility of managing schools, supplies, and contracts and serving as law enforcement authority. In essence, the Indian agent became the tribal government. While these were noted successes of the BIA, the agency was ineffective in preventing the Indian wars of the late 1800s and in protecting the rights of Native Americans.

In 1928, the Meriam Report detailed the mismanagement of services on Indian reservations. The administration of President Theodore Roosevelt and Congress responded to this report by implementing the Indian Reorganization Act (IRA), also known as the Wheeler-Howard Act of 1934, to expand the agency's services to forestry and agricultural development. The act ended the sale of surplus Native American land to Whites, reestablished tribal autonomy, and promoted cultural pluralism. This act caused the BIA to become a trustee of Native American lands and funds. The BIA was viewed as a figurehead and was making decisions on behalf of Native Americans. But the decisions that were being made were in the best interests of the U.S. government, and most of these decisions deprived the Native Americans of their freedoms. In fact, during the 1930s, only a few Native Americans were allowed to serve as reservation police officers. As of today, more than 95% of the agency's employees are Native American.

During the 1970s, the Bureau of Indian Affairs granted Native American tribes more control over their culture and tribal governments. Congress passed the Indian Self-Determination Act, Health Care Improvement Act, and the Indian Child Welfare Act to improve the quality of life on the reservations. Despite these acts, Native American groups such as the American Indian Movement (AIM) began to protest the dissatisfaction with the agency. In November 1972, more than 500 members of AIM took over the offices of the BIA in Washington, D.C., to force BIA to address social issues such as housing and health for Native Americans. The protests lasted a week and caused more than $700,000 in damages to the BIA building.

Controversy

The role of the BIA has been controversial. The agency has the ability to determine who is Native American by evaluating an individual's bloodline to determine its authenticity. The agency also creates guidelines determining what constitutes a tribe by assessing the history of the tribe and the authenticity of tribal members. There is a program run by the agency dealing with groups requesting federal recognition. As of 1978, more than 200 groups have petitioned the agency for federal recognition, which enables tribes to be eligible for health, education, and housing services. If approved, this could increase the present number of federally recognized tribes from 561 to over 860. An increasing number of Native Americans have petitioned to shut down the BIA, and some tribes have asked to be viewed as sovereign nations. The Indian Self-Determination and Education Assistance Acts have been amended to allow tribes to plan for self-governance.

Present-Day BIA

Presently, the BIA has worked toward changing its goals from land management to being advisory in nature. The agency advocates that Native Americans should manage their own affairs: "The Bureau of Indian Affairs is responsible for administering Federal Indian policy; fulfilling its Federal trust responsibilities to American Indians, Tribal Governments, and Alaska Natives; and promoting tribal self-determination and self-governance." The agency is an advocate for public and private assistance for the advancement of Native Americans. In 1997, the DOI auditors accused the agency of mismanaging money owed to Native Americans; as a result, the BIA became the focus of a class action lawsuit. The suit is believed to be the largest one ever against the United States. The potential number of Native Americans involved in the lawsuit is estimated between 250,000 and 500,000. If the judgment of civil action is in favor of the defendant, the federal government may have to pay $176 billion in damages. As of 2008, the trial is still ongoing.

Native Americans believe that the BIA has outlived its usefulness and that corruption plagues the agency's ability to provide for Native Americans. They also feel that the agency needs to be more diligent when it comes to providing health care, educational programs, and other social services for Native Americans. The BIA has undergone many transitions and still struggles with meeting the needs of Native Americans.

Favian Alejandro Martín

See also Indian Civil Rights Act; Indian Self-Determination Act; National Native American Law Enforcement Association; National Tribal Justice Resource Center; Native American Courts

Further Readings

Bakken, G. M., & Kindell, A. (Eds.). (2006). *Encyclopedia of immigration and migration in the American West* (2 vols.). Thousand Oaks, CA: Sage.

Barker, C. (2003). *Cultural studies: Theory and practice.* Thousand Oaks, CA: Sage.

Gabbidon, S. L., & Greene, H. T. (2009). *Race and crime* (2nd ed.). Thousand Oaks, CA: Sage.

Griswold, W. (2008). *Cultures and societies in a changing world.* Thousand Oaks, CA: Sage.

Monette, R. P. (2009). *Bureau of Indian Affairs: From broken treaties to casinos.* Westport, CT: Greenwood.

Websites

Bureau of Indian Affairs: http://www.doi.gov/bia

BYRD, JAMES, JR. (1949–1998)

James Byrd, Jr., was an African American man who, on June 7, 1998, in the small segregated east Texas town of Jasper, was brutally dragged to his death after being chained by the ankles to the back of a pickup truck by three White men (John William King, Lawrence Russell Brewer, and Shawn Allen Berry).

Byrd, the third of seven children born to James and Stella Byrd, was born and raised in Jasper. In 1967 Byrd was in the last segregated class to graduate from Jasper's Rowe High School before it was consolidated with Jasper High as part of a desegregation plan. He was a gifted musician and played the trumpet and piano. Byrd married in 1970 and had three children before divorcing in 1993. Between 1969 and 1996, Byrd was incarcerated several times for various offenses, including theft, forgery, and violation of parole. Byrd was well known around Jasper, and could frequently be seen walking about town, as he did not own a car.

The Killers

Shawn Allen Berry, 23, Lawrence Russell Brewer, 31, and John William King, 24, all had spent time in prison for various convictions. Berry and King had been buddies since high school and remained close. While in prison, King met Brewer, who had been in and out of prison since 1987. Just weeks before Byrd's slaying, Brewer had come to Jasper and moved into King's apartment. Nobody in town knew much about Brewer. He had no other connection to Jasper except for King and Berry and was seldom seen without them.

Brewer and King were both associated with a White supremacy group while in prison and came home covered with many blatantly racist tattoos. King had a tattoo of a cross with a Black man hanging from it. He had swastikas and Nazi-like "SS" symbols. On one arm was an evil-looking woodpecker peeking from beneath a Ku Klux Klan hood. In King's apartment, investigators found a copy of the White supremacists' manifesto "The Turner Diaries" and other literature indicating his connection with Klan-like groups. King also had a tattoo of the words *Aryan Pride*, and the patch for the Confederate Knights of America, a gang of White supremacist inmates.

The Murder

On Saturday, June 7, 1998, Byrd spent the day drinking and socializing with friends and family in Jasper, across town from his apartment. As he was walking home that Saturday, Berry, Brewer, and King offered him a ride, and he accepted. The three men had been driving around Jasper in Berry's grey pickup truck for much of the evening, drinking beer and looking for young women. Witnesses report seeing Byrd riding in the bed of a gray pickup with two or three men in the cab between 2:30 and 2:45 a.m. Berry later testified that he had stopped and given Byrd a ride. He said he didn't know Byrd but had recognized him as somebody who walked around Jasper a lot.

Instead of taking Byrd home, Berry, Brewer, and King drove east out of Jasper and stopped at a small clearing in the woods, a secluded spot for locals to drink beer without having to fear the police. Investigators believe there was a fight in the clearing because of the upturned grass, disturbed dirt, and a broken beer bottle, which were consistent with signs of a struggle. In the clearing, the investigators also found several items that could have fallen out of a truck while someone was being pulled out or that could have been left during a struggle.

In the clearing, the three men beat Byrd, and Brewer sprayed Byrd's face with Black paint. After the beating, Byrd was chained by the ankles to the back of Berry's pickup. The truck traveled along the dirt trail and turned onto the pavement of Huff Creek Road. Byrd was dragged roughly 3 miles.

Investigators found Byrd's shoes, wallet, shirt, and other personal items along the dirt trail. His dentures and keys were found on the pavement. The trail of blood and flesh wove from one side of the road to the other and back again. Then, coming around a curve to the left, Byrd's body apparently bounced into a ditch on the right side of the road, hitting the ragged edge of a concrete culvert (a roadside drainage ditch) just below the right arm. The impact severed the arm, shoulder, neck, and head from the rest of the body, which continued to be dragged for another mile. King, Berry, and Brewer dumped James Byrd's mutilated remains in the town's segregated Black cemetery and then went to a barbecue. Byrd's body was found just west of the county line about 8 a.m. on Sunday, June 8, 1998.

It is not known how long he was alive during the dragging, but Brewer claimed that Byrd's throat had been slashed before he was dragged. Forensic evidence suggests that Byrd had been attempting to keep his head up, and an autopsy suggested that Byrd was alive for much of the dragging and died only after his head, shoulder, and right arm were severed when his body hit the culvert.

State law enforcement officials and Jasper's district attorney determined that since King and Brewer were well-known White supremacists, the murder was classified as a hate crime, and the FBI was brought in less than 24 hours after the discovery of Byrd's brutalized remains. After three separate trials, all three men were found guilty of capital murder. Brewer and King were sentenced to death. Berry received life in prison.

Lorenzo M. Boyd

See also Lynching; Racial Conflict; White Crime

Further Readings

Ainslie, R. C. (2004). *Long dark road: Bill King and murder in Jasper, Texas.* Austin: University of Texas Press.

King, J. (2003). *Hate crime: The story of a dragging death in Jasper, Texas.* New York: Anchor.

Temple-Raston, D. (2003). *Death in Texas: A story of race, murder, and a small town's struggle for redemption.* New York: Holt.

Capital Jury Project

The Capital Jury Project (CJP) is a national study of jury discretion in death penalty cases that began in 1991. In order to conduct interviews with former capital trials in all major regions of the country, the CJP brought together a broad consortium of legal and social science scholars. Typically, four jurors were administered a 2- to 3-hour interview about their entire trial and posttrial experience—from jury selection to sentencing decision to how the experience has influenced their present views on capital punishment. In order to provide a detailed comparison of the sentencing process, equal numbers of cases ending in life sentences and in death penalty sentences were sampled. Over the past 17 years, more than 1,200 juror interviews from some 350 capital trials have been conducted in 14 states.

This entry describes some of the CJP's major findings, highlighting four of the most detailed lines of empirical inquiry undertaken thus far: jurors' sentencing dispositions, jurors' evaluations of a life sentence, the impact of the defendant's youthfulness, and the influence of jurors' race on the capital sentencing process. The entry concludes with reflections on how the CJP contributes to a broader understanding of race and crime in America today. Understanding how jurors see themselves and how they see capital defendants sheds light on jurors' decisions to impose the death sentence. In particular, detailed research on jurors' narratives of their sentencing decisions elucidates the centrality of racial identity in jurors' sense making. More broadly, these stories can be seen as windows into the prevalence of racial ideology in taken-for-granted understandings of the crime problem in the United States today.

Major Findings of the CJP

Jurors' Sentencing Dispositions

One of the main purposes of jury selection in death penalty cases is to ensure that citizens selected to serve can keep an open mind on punishment. The capital trial is bifurcated into guilt and sentencing hearings. The selection process in theory is meant to ferret out those jurors who are likely to prejudge the defendant without adequate consideration of *both* the facts of the case and, in the sentencing phase, the aggravating factors (i.e., factors that make the crime worse, such as multiple victims) and mitigating factors (i.e., factors that make the crime less severe, such as the defendant was abused as a child) in determining whether or not the defendant will live or die.

The CJP data demonstrate failures in the selection process in a number of important respects. First, a majority of jurors in the sample were found to have their minds made up on punishment before the sentencing phase of the trial had begun. Indeed, a significant number of jurors were "absolutely convinced" that the defendant deserved a death sentence at this point, unsurprisingly holding to that position and sentencing the defendant to death. One such juror described this early death decision "automatic." In some cases, jurors who were undecided on the issue of guilt agreed to convict the defendant of capital murder on the condition that jurors predisposed to give the death penalty did not vote to impose it—a kind of "trade-off" that undermines the requirement that jurors are supposed to keep their punishment and guilt decisions separate.

Jurors' Evaluations of a Life Sentence

The CJP data document that an overwhelming number of jurors did not believe that a life sentence actually means that the defendant will remain in prison the rest of his or her life. Such a belief has toxic effects on jurors' sentencing discretion. Specifically, many capital jurors in the CJP sample sentenced the defendant to death not because of retribution but because they were afraid that the defendant would be released from prison and kill again. Some jurors cited this knowledge as coming straight from the news media. In Georgia, more than half of the jurors believed that a life sentence meant release in exactly 7 years. In subsequent analysis of this phenomenon, it was discovered that the "myth of release in 7 years" was widespread in the Georgia media, even though capital murderers not sentenced to death are rarely ever released in the state.

The Death Penalty for Juveniles

In the months just prior to the U.S. Supreme Court's 2005 decision in *Roper v. Simmons* to abolish the death penalty for defendants under 18 years of age, an analysis of all cases involving juvenile offenders in the CJP data was undertaken (e.g., Bowers et al., 2004). This analysis demonstrated that jurors were extremely reluctant to impose the death sentence in such cases. Indeed, an overwhelming majority cited the defendant's age as the "most important" reason for imposing a life sentence instead of death.

The Impact of Jury Racial Composition and Jurors' Race in Combination With the Defendant's and Victim's Race on Sentencing

The CJP is the first systematic investigation of the influence of both individual juror race and jury racial composition on the capital sentencing process. Perhaps not surprisingly, the CJP data show that the fewer non-Whites on the jury, the greater the likelihood of a death sentence being imposed, especially in Black defendant–White victim (BW) cases. Moreover, in BW cases a strong majority of White jurors as compared to Black jurors are more likely to be predisposed to the death sentence even before the sentencing trial begins. Second, the CJP explored the role of race in jurors' application of sentencing guidelines. The weighing of aggravating and mitigating factors was the essential way the U.S. Supreme Court, when it lifted the moratorium on capital cases in 1976 (*Gregg v. Georgia*), believed that capital jurors' sentencing discretion could be insulated from arbitrary factors such as the race of defendants or victims. However, CJP data systematically document jurors' failure to consider clearly presented mitigating evidence, especially in BW cases.

Concluding Reflections: Race and Crime as a Story of "Us" and "Them"

The CJP data provide insights into the role of race in jurors' beliefs about crime that go beyond the formality of a capital trial. Detailed analyses of jurors' narrative accounts of their sentencing decision reveal the pervasive influence of racial ideology, especially in cases in which the defendant is Black and the victim is White and cases in which the disproportionately White juries can find greater empathy for victims of their own race and often similar social status. Specifically, jurors' narratives from Black defendant–White victim (BW) cases reveal their taken-for-granted, media-driven beliefs in the patent immorality and irresponsibility of Black and Latino/a defendants. Drawing on dehumanizing archetypes of *inferior* others, capital jurors in BW cases deny non-White defendants the complexity of their own lives.

Benjamin Fleury-Steiner

See also Baldus Study; Criminalblackman; Dehumanization of Blacks; Racialization of Crime

Further Readings

Bowers, W. J., Fleury-Steiner, B., Hans, V. P., & Antonio, M. E. (2004). Too young for the death penalty: An empirical examination of community conscience and the juvenile death penalty from the perspective of capital jurors. *Boston University Law Review, 84,* 609.

Bowers, W. J., Sandys, M., & Brewer, T. W. (2004). Crossing racial boundaries: A closer look at the roots of racial bias in capital sentencing when the defendant is Black and the victim is White. *DePaul Law Review, 53,* 1497.

Bowers, W. J., Sandys, M., & Steiner, B. D. (1998). Foreclosed impartiality capital sentencing: Jurors' predispositions, guilt trial experience, and premature decision making. *Cornell Law Review, 83,* 1474.

Bowers, W. J., & Steiner, B. D. (1999). Death by default: An empirical demonstration of false and forced choices in capital sentencing. *Texas Law Review, 77,* 605.

Bowers, W. J., Steiner, B. D., & Sandys, M. (2001). Death sentencing in Black and White: An empirical analysis of the role of jurors' race and jury racial composition. *University of Pennsylvania Journal of Constitutional Law, 3,* 171.

Brewer, T. W. (2004). Race and jurors' receptivity to mitigation in capital cases: The effect of jurors,' defendants' and victims' race in combination. *Law and Human Behavior, 28,* 529.

Fleury-Steiner, B. D. (2002). Narratives of the death sentence: Toward a theory of legal narrativity. *Law & Society Review, 36,* 549.

Fleury-Steiner, B. D. (2004). *Jurors' stories of death: How America's death penalty invests in inequality.* Ann Arbor: University of Michigan Press.

Fleury-Steiner, B., & Argothy, V. (2004). Lethal "borders": Elucidating jurors' racialized discipline to punish in Latino defendant death cases. *Punishment & Society, 6,* 67.

Steiner, B. D., Bowers, W. J., & Sarat, A. (1999). Folk knowledge as legal action: Death penalty judgments and the tenet of early release in a culture of mistrust and punitiveness. *Law & Society Review, 33,* 461.

Websites

Capital Jury Project: http://www.albany.edu/scj/CJPhome .htm

CAPITAL PUNISHMENT

See Death Penalty

CASTANEDA V. PARTIDA

The question confronting the U.S. Supreme Court in its 1976 review of the criminal conviction of Rodrigo Partida was whether the grand jury that had indicted him had unconstitutionally been composed of an inadequate representation of Hispanics on the panel, in violation of the Fourteenth Amendment's equal protection clause prohibiting discrimination based on race and ethnicity. More generally, the issue concerned the adequate representation of citizens of racial and ethnic minorities in the determination of criminal guilt or innocence.

Function of Grand Juries

Grand juries perform two functions. The first is to judge the strength of the prosecutor's case by examining the indictment and questioning witnesses about the alleged criminal action of the accused person. The second is to investigate wrongdoing based on its members' concerns or in regard to matters put before the grand jury by the judge who appointed it.

Grand juries were a cornerstone of the criminal justice system in England. Their origin commonly is traced to the Assize of Clarendon in 1166. It was required that criminal accusations thereafter be "presented" to grand juries composed of 12 "good and lawful men" selected from the locale. The tradition was incorporated into American law in colonial times and thereafter enshrined in the Fifth Amendment of the Bill of Rights. It initially was presumed that in the tightly knit communities from which grand jury members were recruited, they would personally be aware of illegal behavior and the character of persons who were said to be responsible for it. Today, there is much debate about the need for grand juries, since they often rubber stamp the wishes of the prosecutor who presents cases to them. Nonetheless, grand jury panels, whose work is secret (though news of their proceedings sometimes is leaked), have the ability to protect persons who are innocent or whose guilt is unlikely to be proven before a petit or trial jury from the expense and personal distress of a public hearing.

In Texas, grand juries were chosen by what was known as the "key-man" system, whereby three to five jury commissioners were appointed by district judges and charged with putting together a list of 15 to 20 candidates for service on the grand jury. The judge then picked the panel from the list compiled by the commissioners.

Judicial Rulings in *Castaneda v. Partida*

Partida had been convicted in 1972 in Hildalgo County, an area in south Texas on the Rio Grande, for the crime of burglary of a private residence in the nighttime with the intent to commit rape. He was sentenced to a minimum of 5 years and a maximum of 8 years of imprisonment.

The first federal court to consider Partida's appeal declared that the key-man system was highly subjective and archaic and inefficient. Nonetheless, it ruled against Partida on the ground that Mexican Americans constituted a governing majority in the county and that it therefore could not be presumed that they would intentionally discriminate against themselves.

The U.S. Court of Appeal for the Fifth Circuit disagreed with the lower court's "governing majority" emphasis but held that the state had not satisfactorily demonstrated that Partida was not a victim of discrimination that resulted from the selection of members of the grand jury.

By a vote of 5–4, the U.S. Supreme Court in *Castaneda v. Partida* (430 U.S. 482) disagreed with that view, pointing out that the 1970 census had found that 79.1% of the country's population of 181,535 persons were Mexican American but only 39% of those summoned for grand jury service between 1962 and 1972 shared that ethnic identity. In terms of population, 688 Mexican Americans should have been summoned for grand jury duty during this 11-year period; only 339 were. Writing for the majority, Justice Harry Blackmun concluded that Mexican Americans represented an identifiable group whose total population and its satisfactory representation on Hildalgo County's grand juries could be confidently calculated. Blackmun argued that if a racial or ethnic disparity is sufficiently large, then it is unlikely that it is due solely to chance or accident; therefore, in the absence of evidence to the contrary, it had to be concluded that racial or class-related factors had entered into the selection process.

In a concurring opinion, Justice Thurgood Marshall dismissed the idea of a "governing majority" as a determinate consideration. Marshall noted that social scientists agreed that members of minority groups frequently respond to discrimination and prejudice by attempting to dissociate themselves from their group, even to the point of adopting the majority's negative attitudes toward the minority.

Taking note of the Supreme Court's opinion, the Texas legislature in 1979 specifically required counties continuing to employ the key-man selection system for grand juries (in contrast to random selection) to be race conscious and to ensure that the choice of panel members resulted in a satisfactory cross-section of the community in regard to race, gender, and age.

By mid-2007, the Supreme Court opinion in *Castaneda v. Partida* had been cited 1,155 times in published court opinions in the United States and referenced in 630 law review articles. The most recent U.S. Supreme Court opinion referring to *Castaneda* came in 1998 when Terry Campbell, a White man convicted of murder in Louisiana by an Evangeline parish grand jury prevailed on his claim that the jury had excluded African Americans. "Regardless of his or her skin color, the accused suffers a significant injury in fact when the composition of the grand jury is tainted by racial discrimination," the 1998 opinion in *Campbell v. Louisiana* (522 U.S. 392, 398) declared, adding, "Discrimination on the basis of race . . . strikes at the fundamental values of our judicial system because the grand jury is a central component of the criminal justice process."

Gilbert Geis

See also Jury Selection; Latina/o/s

Further Readings

Albritton, E. M. (2003). Race-conscious grand jury selection: The equal protection clause and strict scrutiny. *American Journal of Criminal Law, 31,* 175–214.

Fukurai, H. (2001). Hispanic participation on the grand jury: Key-man selection, jurymandering, language, and representative quotas. *Texas Hispanic Journal of Law & Policy, 5,* 7–39.

CENTER FOR THE STUDY AND PREVENTION OF VIOLENCE

In 1992, scholars at the University of Colorado at Boulder formed the Center for the Study and Prevention of Violence (CSPV). Under the direction of Dr. Delbert Elliott, this multidisciplinary organization works to compile and disseminate information on youth violence and the policies and programs related to its prevention. In the 1990s, when the CSPV was founded, youth violence had become an increasing concern. Rates of youth violence appeared to be rising faster than ever before. In the 1980s, gang and drug-related violence in urban, high-poverty areas became increasingly visible. These high-crime, high-poverty areas were largely populated by racial minorities, especially African Americans, linking race and crime together in the minds of many. Many scholars began work designed to better understand the purported relationship between race and crime. The CSPV began a number of research projects aimed at developing a general understanding of the various forms of youth violence, with and without regard to race, and the approaches taken to curb it. These projects provide some insight on the race-crime relationship but overall provide a foundation for the CSPV's ongoing research aimed at determining "what works" in preventing youth violence.

Today, the CSPV conducts research, provides training and technical assistance for those developing, implementing, and evaluating violence prevention programs, and operates an "Information House" to synthesize and organize violence-related literature into a number of publicly accessible online databases. Individuals can then customize a search for violence prevention programs and related books, academic journal articles, professional reports, media and instruction manuals, and surveys to aid the measurement of violence. Currently, the group works toward development of an additional database that will allow users to search for intervention programs specifically useful for youth of different genders and various ethnicities.

The Problem of Youth Violence

The CSPV initially set out to research violence among American youth through publication of a series of "center papers." In 1994, the center began the Violence in American Schools project. Funded by the W. T. Grant Foundation, the project integrated past research on the causes and nature of youth violence with current research on the relationship between adolescent violence and the school system. Colorado Trust then funded the Violence Prevention Initiative, designed to help Colorado-based organizations plan and implement effective prevention programs. The Youth Handgun Violence Prevention Project was later implemented when those involved in the Violence Prevention Initiative expressed concern over the increasing use of handguns by youth in their areas. This research continues today under the Safe Communities-Safe Schools initiative.

Other early projects investigated the relationship between violence and race, class, gang involvement, drugs and alcohol, hate-motivated crimes, and sexual aggression. These studies revealed that violence victimization and perpetration occurred more often during adolescence and young adulthood than during other years of life. African American men ages 15–24 were at particularly high risk for homicide victimization, followed by Hispanic males and Native American males; White males of the same age were of much lower risk. Economic variables were important in understanding homicide rates, however, as rates were (and still are) higher among economically marginalized populations of all races and ethnicities, relative to more economically privileged groups.

These initial studies also revealed inaccuracies in media depictions of youth violence. Though America experienced increases in youth violence from 1980 through the 1990s, there is more to the story. Many more adolescents, especially those ages 12–15, became victims of violence, but there were no dramatic changes in self-reported violent offending. After 1988, however, the rates of juvenile homicide substantially increased. This suggests that, while youth violence did not become a more frequent occurrence, it became more lethal in its consequences, largely because of the increasing availability of guns. The presence of guns in schools also became an increasing concern after a number of high-profile, fatal school shootings, such as the shootings at Columbine High School in nearby Littleton, Colorado. Society's attempts to deal with handguns, as well as violence more generally, both within and outside of the school system became issues of central focus for the CSPV.

What Works in Preventing Youth Violence

A variety of approaches were implemented in the 1990s to address youth violence. New legislation was passed to enact tougher punishments for convicted offenders, in the form of longer sentences and/or "boot camp" programs for young offenders. Other legislation allowed for juveniles as young as 10 years of age to be "waived" or transferred to adult court for violence offense. New gun control policies came into effect, and schools and communities began to implement a number of prevention programs.

The CSPV took on the challenge of researching a number of these strategies and, in doing so, made significant contributions to our knowledge of "what works" in dealing with youth violence. Many programs, including neighborhood watches, gun buy-backs, boot camps, and the widely implemented D.A.R.E. (Drug Abuse Resistance Education) program, were found to be ineffective, while shock and scare approaches like the Scared Straight program appeared to increase a juvenile offender's likelihood of reoffending. In response to gun violence within schools, many districts chose to install metal detectors or implement locker searches. These approaches have not been proven effective either.

Various organizations conducted evaluations of school- and community-based prevention programs and concluded that many were effective in reducing violence and other related behaviors, such as drug use and childhood aggression. CSPV-based scholars, however, believed that the

standards for judging the scientific quality of the program evaluations were too low. In response, the CSPV proposed a new method for evaluating such evidence and, with funding from the Centers for Disease Control and Prevention, the Colorado Division of Criminal Justice, and the Pennsylvania Commission on Crime and Delinquency, began the Blueprints for Violence Prevention initiative in 1996.

Blueprints for Violence Prevention

The initiative continues today. The CSPV has, to date, reviewed evaluations of more than 600 programs, critically examining both the methods used to evaluate each program and the evidence of the program's effect on outcomes such as drug use, delinquency, and violence. Exemplary programs are rated as either "Model" or "Promising." To qualify as a Model, a program must demonstrate deterrent effects through a scientifically sound evaluation design. Strong designs are those that either randomly assign individuals or schools to a treatment or a no-treatment condition or utilize a no-treatment comparison group that is "matched" to the treatment group on a range of variables, especially the drug, delinquency, and/or violence-related outcome measures. Statistical analysis should also control for any differences between the two groups before the program is implemented, even when random assignment is used.

The studies should also include a large sample size and should retain a large amount of the sample throughout the study period. Loss of study participants can result in nonequivalent comparison groups. Effects should be replicated by at least one other evaluation and should be sustained at least 1 year after the program ends. Programs without replicated, sustained effects may instead qualify for "Promising" status. (See Table 1.)

Now that effective programs have been identified, the task is to successfully disseminate information about the programs and assist sites in implementing them with fidelity. To achieve this, the CSPV developed the Blueprints Replication Initiative, which examined implementation of a number of violence prevention programs in 42 sites and the Life Skills Training program in 70 sites across the country. To be most successful, those interested in developing a program must take

Table I   Model and Promising Programs

Model	Promising
• Midwestern Prevention Project • Big Brothers Big Sisters of America • Functional Family Therapy • Life Skills Training • Multisystemic Therapy • Nurse-Family Partnership • Multidimensional Treatment Foster Care • Olweus Bullying Prevention Program • Promoting Alternative Thinking Strategies • The Incredible Years: Parent, Teacher and Child Training Series • Project Towards No Drug Abuse	• Athletes Training and Learning to Avoid Steroids • Behavioral Monitoring and Reinforcement Program • Brief Alcohol Screening and Intervention of College Students • Brief Strategic Family Therapy • CASASTART • FAST Track • Good Behavior Game • Guiding Good Choices • I Can Problem Solve • Linking the Interests of Families and Teachers • Perry School Project • Preventative Treatment Program • Project ALERT • Project Northland • School Transitional Environmental Program • Seattle Social Development Project • Strong African American Families Program

time in developing the capacity to implement it in any one particular location. Quality training and technical assistance are also important if the program is to achieve its goals.

The CSPV now hosts a Blueprints Conference, with hopes of better disseminating information about these programs and providing technical assistance directly from the program designers to those who are interested in implementing such programs. Today, the center continues to study implementation of various Blueprints Model programs. It continuously updates its database of prevention and treatment programs, looking specifically at how well each program works for youths of different genders and racial backgrounds.

Allison J. Foley

See also Boot Camps, Juvenile; Delinquency and Victimization; Delinquency Prevention; Violent Juvenile Offenders

Further Readings

Elliott, D. (1998). *Prevention programs that work for youth: Violence prevention.* Boulder: University of Colorado, Center for the Study and Prevention of Violence.

Elliott, D., Hamburg, B., & Williams, K. (Eds.). (1998). *Violence in American schools: A new perspective.* New York: Cambridge University Press.

Mihalic, S., Irwin, K., Elliott, D., Fagan, A., & Hansen, D. (2001). *Blueprints for violence prevention.* Washington, DC: U.S. Department of Justice, Office of Justice Programs, Office of Juvenile Justice and Delinquency Prevention.

Websites

Center for the Study and Prevention of Violence: http://www.colorado.edu/cspv

CENTER ON RACE, CRIME AND JUSTICE

See John Jay College Center on Race, Crime and Justice

Central Park Jogger

Central Park jogger refers to a female rape victim who was attacked while jogging in New York's Central Park in 1989. The particularly brutal nature of the attack and the young ages of the suspects led to extensive national attention for the crime and sparked a media frenzy over youth violence in New York. As the case proceeded, it became a symbolic battleground for race, class, and gender issues in the late 1980s and early 1990s.

The jogger, a 28-year-old White investment banker was beaten, raped, and left for dead in a ravine in Central Park on April 19, 1989. Several other joggers and bicyclists had been assaulted the same evening, and police rounded up about 30 teenage boys for questioning. Ultimately, five African American and Latino youths, ages 14 to 16, were charged with the rape. Their arrests and subsequent convictions were based largely on the videotaped confessions of four of the boys. There was no physical evidence connecting them to the crime scene, none of the other assault victims could identify any of the boys, and the rape victim, who awoke from a coma after 12 days with no memory of the attack, was unable to identify her attacker. Media outlets reported that one of the boys had said they had been out "wilding," a new term that supposedly referred to random sexual violence committed by groups of urban teenagers for amusement. Supporters of the boys claimed that police, who had held the boys in custody for 2 days before videotaping them, had coerced the confessions, while prosecutors argued that the confessions were too detailed to be made up. All five boys served prison sentences of 5 to 10 years. In 2002, a man serving a prison sentence for several other violent crimes confessed to the Central Park jogger rape and insisted that he had acted alone. DNA testing, which was not available in 1989, matched the semen from the crime scene to the man. Although the police and prosecutors of the original case insisted that the five boys had still been involved, their convictions were ultimately vacated.

Race, Class, and Gender

The attack occurred in the context of peaking homicide rates in New York City, fueled by the crack cocaine epidemic, increasing gentrification of the areas around Central Park, growing gaps between those who had benefited and those who had suffered under President Ronald Reagan's economic policies, and increasing gender and racial tension resulting from several other divisive court cases. With these trends as the background, the Central Park Jogger case became a field upon which these conflicts could play out. With the help of the media and several high-profile public figures, the case resulted in what some have called a "moral panic," a vastly disproportionate response to a real or imagined public threat. Public fear of so-called wilding, or out-of-control minority youth committing racially motivated random violence, skyrocketed.

Media reporting of the case contributed significantly to its framing in terms of racial conflict. The races of both the defendants and victim were mentioned frequently. Although the defendants were minors, the police released their names, addresses, and pictures for publication because of the seriousness of the crime. The defendants were frequently described in news articles as a gang, a term with distinct racial connotation, even though they were not members of any street gang. Media accounts also frequently described the defendants as "animals," "feral beasts," "savages," a "wolf pack," and a "roving gang," invoking negative racial stereotypes and fueling racial conflict. The term *wilding* became a buzzword for any violence or disorder committed by minority youth against Whites. The case also contributed to the myth of the rise of the juvenile superpredator: brutal, amoral, minority adolescent criminals who were beyond the reach of social and rehabilitative programs. The superpredator myth was frequently used to justify harsher criminal justice policies in the face of falling crime rates in the 1990s.

The Central Park jogger case also sparked debates over class issues in the media. Initially, the defendants were described as troubled youths from the ghetto, despite the fact that most hailed from stable families in a middle-class housing development. Though the victim's identity was withheld, her background was widely reported: undergraduate degree from Wellesley, graduate degrees from Yale, an up-and-coming investment banker at Salomon Brothers. For many, the attack came to represent the extreme resentment of working-class minority youth against successful young urban professionals. The backlash against the youth was fueled when several prominent New Yorkers called for the death penalty in the case.

The public debate over the case also caused a split between African American activists and feminists. African American activists believed the defendants were targeted because of their race and were coerced by police into falsely confessing the crime. They argued that the main issue in the case was violation of the rights of the defendants. Feminists, on the other hand, were eager for a conviction and argued that the real issue was violence against women. Many feminists criticized the African American community for failing to support the victim and drawing attention away from the brutality of the attack itself.

When the convicted youths were exonerated in 2002, the earlier debates were revisited. The case then brought increased attention to the problems of false confessions by adolescent suspects, police coercion, and criminal racial stereotyping.

Monica Erling

See also Moral Panics; Wilding; Wrongful Convictions

Further Readings

Chancer, L. (2005). Before and after the Central Park jogger: When legal cases become social causes. *Contexts, 4*(3), 38–42.

Hancock, L. (2003). Wolf pack: The press and the Central Park jogger. *Columbia Journalism Review, 41*(5), 38–42.

Johnson, M. B. (2005). The Central Park jogger case—police coercion and secrecy in interrogation: The 14th annual Frantz Fanon MD memorial lecture. *Journal of Ethnicity in Criminal Justice, 3*(1/2), 131–143.

Meili, T. (2003). *I am the Central Park jogger: A story of hope and possibility.* New York: Scribner.

Sullivan, T. (1992). *Unequal verdicts: The Central Park jogger trials.* New York: American Lawyer Books/Simon & Schuster.

CHAIN GANGS

This entry examines the history of chain gangs in the United States. The use of chain gangs in America is analyzed against a backdrop of changing social and economic conditions. The eventual disdain for and reemergence of this form of punishment are also briefly addressed.

The Progressive Movement

Chain gangs as an American penal institution can be traced back to the late 19th century and are borne of ideas not new in the history of practices related to punishment. As early as 1697, convicts were transported from the British Isles to serve in the American colonies as slaves and indentured servants. Convict labor was also used in 1718 to clear the land that would eventually become the city of New Orleans. In 1786, Pennsylvania law declared convicts should "publicly and disgracefully labor" and were put to work maintaining the streets of Philadelphia.

Despite this history, the use of chain gangs did not become widespread penal policy until the late 1800s; it is most commonly associated with the Progressive movement of reforms instituted at the time. Progressives were concerned with the excesses and abuses of the convict leasing system, which was legislatively enacted to supply convicts to private enterprise as a cheap source of unskilled workers thought necessary to fill the vacuum in labor created by the enactment of antislavery laws. The convict leasing system also served as both a source of revenue for penal institutions and a means to reduce expenditures related to housing and caring for inmate populations. Businesses eligible to lease convicts profited from an inexpensive, strike-free source of labor.

Living Conditions Under Convict Leasing

Unfortunately, the efforts of capitalists to increase profits came at the expense of human rights for convicts. Leased convicts were typically housed in long plank houses with low, two-story bunks and were under constant watch by shotgun-toting guards; they were punished for the slightest of provocations despite laws prohibiting Draconian disciplinary measures such as impromptu whipping and shooting. Adequate food and health care were minimal at best, in order to keep costs low and profits high. Consequently, the average life span for inmates working within the convict leasing system was approximately 7 years, a death rate considerably higher than that for inmates confined within the walls of a conventional prison cell.

Emergence of the "Good Roads" Movement

Despite demands for retributive forms of justice, the convict leasing system was viewed as functionally equivalent to the repressive Russian prison system known as *gulags*. In 1890, a Mississippi constitutional convention called for an end to convict leasing, and by 1903 the system was openly critiqued in the press as a form of human slavery. Among those who protested the system were a surprising number of capitalists who were neither able to procure convicts as laborers nor able to compete effectively in the free marketplace with those who were employing inmate workers. Corresponding legislation sought to restrict the sale of goods produced through convict labor in the open market. In addition, those who did employ convict labor found their profits declining as states increased the cost of individual convict leases.

A growing consensus of interest groups sought an end to convict leasing and demanded that convicts instead be employed in developing the public roadways. This group consisted of the aforementioned organized labor, penal reformers, the media, Progressive legislators, and supporters of the "good roads" movement. Aside from critiquing the unfair market advantages given to those employing convicts, organized labor trumpeted the benefits that could be derived from developing roads that linked agriculture and industry with burgeoning urban markets. Penal reformers detailed the brutality of the leasing system as they expounded the reformative benefits that working in the "fresh air and sunshine" would entail. The press acted as early muckrakers in exposing how private enterprise profited at the expense of human rights and dignity under the leasing system, and they proposed a system of convict road work as an alternative. Progressive legislators of the time saw the institutionalization of convict road work as a means to further what is best described as a paternalistic system of race relations founded on notions of a need to control newly freed African Americans seen as inherently "childlike" and criminogenic.

Perhaps the most vocal of the interest groups were proponents of the "good roads" movement. The existing antiquated system of road development held that citizens of each county were conscripted to serve a number of days each year in maintaining and improving public roadways. The system was inefficient, primarily for social reasons, as worksite overseers and foremen were often unwilling to demand much from their neighbors in the physically demanding enterprise. Using conscripted labor was also unpopular, and aside from unpopularity stemming from the grueling nature of the work, farmers and employers were not enthusiastic about relinquishing employees for public projects. Taxation was not seen as a viable alternative to using conscripted labor, as it would alienate taxpayers and be too financially burdensome on state and county fiscal resources. Proponents of the "good roads" movement suggested convict labor as the solution to this and many other problems.

Initiated in 1892 as a means to connect major population centers and develop the national economy, the "good roads" movement was vocal in trumpeting the benefits of employing convict labor. The movement coexisted with the attack on the convict leasing system and was composed of a variety of different groups. Among its most published supporters were members of the North Carolina State Geological Survey, who also served as leaders of the national "good roads" movement. They promoted convict labor as a means to improve the economic infrastructure of the South through improving the available system of transportation. Furthermore, they forwarded the idea that convict labor on public roadways would provide simultaneous benefits for the state as well as convicts.

As late as 1913, convict labor was promoted as a penal policy that would better convert the convict into a respectable citizen in comparison with the brutalizing effects of the leasing system. "In the fresh air and out of the prison cells and coal mines" was the mantra of penal reformers associated with this movement. Other proponents of the "good roads" movement promoted it as a means to forestall migration from rural areas, improve access to education, provide compulsory work for tramps and vagrants (often a euphemism for newly freed African Americans), and decrease isolationism in rural areas. Railroad owners also naively promoted the movement as a means to increase freight on their lines, supposing a developed system of roads would serve as connectors between rail lines.

Chain Gangs in the South

However, compulsory convict labor on public roads was already in use during the era of convict leasing in southern states, where the two practices coexisted, according to a U.S. Department of Labor study published in 1886. By that year, most southern states had legislative provisions enabling the use of convict labor on public streets. But the practice did not achieve widespread implementation until the convict leasing system had been thoroughly undermined as a legitimate penal practice, and consequently it was abolished in 1908. Whether laboring on public roadways, state-owned farms, or toiling amid the deadly chemicals of the turpentine mills, "chain gangs" (a colloquial reference to the form of physical control used to hinder escape from the worksite) became one of the hallmark penal institutions in the South. Nearly all states in the union had legal provisions to implement chain gangs; their widespread use in southern states has been attributed to climactic conditions favorable to outdoor work, a lack of competing uses for unskilled labor, and a population that did not concertedly object to seeing predominantly African American convicts publicly brutalized and humiliated.

Despite its conception as a Progressive and humanitarian penal policy aimed at the reformation of convicts as well as the economic development of a flailing southern infrastructure, in practice chain gangs were a vicious retributive practice that served to reinforce existing racial stereotypes and hierarchies. Only those convicts deemed physically able for the exhausting work were permitted on the chain gangs, the others left to serve their time in conventional prison cells. Early proponents of chain gangs recognized the potentially stigmatizing effect convicts might experience through being forced to wear striped uniforms publicly marking them as convicted criminals. They subsequently declared that African Americans would be more suitable for the chain gangs, as their "childlike" dispositions were less affected by the negative consequences of being labeled "criminal." Following from this misguided rationale, chain gangs were

composed primarily of African Americans and, in the spirit of race relations of the time, were nearly always beaten into submission.

Unfortunately, concern over the effects of stigmatization on Whites was not coincident with concern over the atrocious working conditions to which chain gang laborers were subjected. Similar to the convict leasing system, laborers in the chain gangs were scattered across many road work camps, with little state oversight, resulting in comparably horrible working conditions for the convicts themselves. After excruciatingly laboring in the heat and humidity characteristic of the southern United States, chain gang workers could expect to receive little to eat, and what was provided was poor in quality. In the parlance of the time, they were often "beat like dogs" to keep pace with the impossible demands of their armed overseers; corporal punishment and sadistic forms of torture were employed to ensure compliance. Although originally employing the labor of misdemeanants, chain gangs developed to include more serious felons and often chained the two classes of offenders together in work crews. Early chain gang inmates typically slept chained together under the constant watch of armed guards. Journalists of the time likened the conditions to a modern form of slavery.

Chain gangs were originally implemented in the "plantation belt," where a high percentage of former African American slaves resided. In terms of developing the transportation infrastructure, the use of chain gangs was an unmitigated success, and its implementation as a penal institution-*cum*-economic stimulus consequently spread to neighboring regions in the South. However, much like the architectural works of antiquity that were also constructed through the use of slave labor, development of the transportation infrastructure was achieved at the expense of recognizing the detrimental effects on human life and dignity.

The Dissolution and Reemergence of Chain Gangs

Chain gangs fell out of favor as a penal practice for a variety of reasons. The publication of a book highlighting the excesses and brutality of the system challenged the notion that "fresh air and sunshine" were equivalent to rehabilitation. Along with the need to reposition workers to support the war effort during World War II, road building technology had also changed to render unskilled manual labor superfluous. Prisoners working in tightly chained groups were inefficient and incompatible with the new technological developments. In addition, existing racial stereotypes were being challenged in ways that undermined the legitimacy of a penal policy functionally aimed at controlling African Americans.

The mid-1990s saw a resurgence of chain gangs as a penal practice, and it was first reinstituted in Alabama in 1996. Aside from a desire to reduce prison expenditures, chain gangs were reimplemented by legislators eager to appease voting constituencies that demanded their representatives appear "tough on crime." While politicians trumpeted the potential deterrent effects chain gangs may produce, they failed to address the historic rationales that underpinned its original institutionalization, namely the need to develop a fledgling transportation infrastructure and provide an alternative to an even more barbaric penal practice. They also downplayed the role that racist ideology played in the implementation of chain gangs as a penal practice, much to the dismay of civil rights groups. Researchers evaluating the impact of chain gangs must measure its effectiveness as a penal practice aimed at reducing recidivism against its impact on the fundamental value of human life and dignity.

Douglas J. Dallier, Lindsey Bergeron,
and Courtney A. Waid

See also Convict Lease System; Private Prisons; Racialization of Crime; Racism

Further Readings

Allen, H. E., & Abril, J. C. (1997). The new chain gang: Corrections in the next century. *American Journal of Criminal Justice, 22,* 1–12.

Lichtenstein, A. (1996). *Twice the work of free labor: The political economy of convict labor in the New South.* Brooklyn, NY: Verso.

Potts, C. S. (1903). Convict labor system of Texas. *Annals of the American Academy of Political and Social Science, 21,* 84–95.

Pratt, J. H. (1913). Convict labor in highway construction. *Annals of the American Academy of Social and Political Science, 46,* 78–87.

Steiner, J. F., & Brown, R. M. (1969). *The North Carolina chain gang: A study of county convict road work.* Glen Ridge, NJ: Patterson Smith.

Zimmerman, J. (1951). The penal reform movement in the South during the Progressive era 1890–1917. *The Journal of Southern History, 17,* 462–492.

CHICAGO RACE RIOT OF 1919

The Chicago Race Riot of 1919 occurred during the "Red Summer," a 6-month period when race riots occurred in 25 cities in the United States. This entry describes the Chicago Race Riot, which was one of the most violent and deadly during that time. The Chicago Race Riot is important to the study of race and crime because it provides a temporal perspective on race riots and race relations.

Precursor to the Events

Following World War I, Black veterans believed that they should be given employment and better wages since they had fought in the war, but many Whites opposed efforts to bring about racial equality in the workplace. Unionization of factories and plants was in progress in an effort to secure higher wages at the same time that Blacks were migrating to the North in search of jobs. Many Blacks filled in as strike breakers and refused to join unions. These actions led to racial tension among the Blacks and Whites. White immigrant workers also immigrated to Chicago to get work, and this contributed to the tension. Housing costs for Blacks were double those of Whites, and Blacks were paid considerably less. Food and clothing costs also rose, which also contributed to poor living conditions for Blacks in the worst part of Chicago, the Black Belt. Two Black men were murdered on June 21 by the Ragen's Colts, a White gang, and the Chicago police refused to investigate the matter. As a result, Blacks had even less faith in law enforcement in Chicago, and these events fueled what followed during the 5 days beginning on July 27, 1919.

The Events of July 27, 1919

On July 27, 1919, in the middle of a very hot, tense summer in Chicago, a young Black boy named Eugene Williams inadvertently swam into an informally segregated area in Lake Michigan with his friends when they were attacked by a White man. A rock was thrown at the young boys, striking Eugene Williams on the head and causing him to drown.

At the same time, a few blocks away at the 29th Street beach, several Black men and women attempted to enter the White-only beach. After being threatened by the Whites with rocks and verbal threats, the Blacks left, only to return with backup. This time, the Blacks threw rocks at the Whites. The White bathers fled the beach but returned with their entourage, and there was more rock throwing.

Friends of Eugene Williams identified to the police the White man who threw the rock that killed their friend. Originally a Black police officer took the report but was denied authority to make an arrest by a White police officer. Instead, the White police officer arrested a Black man. The boys spread the word about what had happened at the beach, and coinciding with what was happening at 29th Street, a bloody warfare began.

Rumors began to spread as to what happened at the beach. The story was told among the Whites that it was a White boy that had drowned at the hands of a Black man. Another rumor suggested that the Black boy's death could have been prevented but the White officer would not allow anyone to jump in and save him. Hundreds of angry Whites and Blacks went to the beach. Violence escalated when a patrol wagon arrived to transport the arrested Black man. A Black man named James Crawford drew a revolver and fired into a group of policemen, wounding one of them. A Black officer returned the fire, killing Crawford. It was this gunfire that started the race riot.

The race riot lasted for 5 days. Whites and Blacks carried guns and clubs to protect themselves. More rumors spread throughout the city among both races, leading to still more tension and anger. Members of Ragen's Colts drove their vehicles into the Black Belt, shooting at everyone in their sight as they passed by them, and Black snipers fired back. Mobs of Whites roamed around looking for Black people to attack by stoning, stabbing, and shooting them. Blacks' houses were burned down, with families inside barely escaping. Although most of the violence occurred in the Black Belt, violence occurred in areas throughout the city, including the Chicago Loop.

Timeline

The calm on the evening of July 27, with the streets empty and abandoned, led Governor Frank Lowden to believe the police force could handle the situation. The next day, Monday, July 28, White gangs and workmen waited near the gates of the stockyards with wooden clubs, iron pipes, and hammers. They attacked the Black workers as they attempted to pass through the gates. Some escaped by running and boarding street cars. Eventually the street cars were also attacked. White mobs canvassed the city looking for prey and attacking Black men on sight. By Tuesday, trains had ceased operation, forcing Blacks to walk. Only a few Black workers reported to the stockyards and other agencies to work. By this time, the violence had spread to the Chicago Loop. On this day, a mob of 100 young White males, many of whom were soldiers and sailors, hunted for Blacks in the downtown district. Black men and boys were dragged into the streets, beaten, and shot.

The Illinois State Militia was called up by the city's mayor, William Hale Thompson, but the order was not implemented until Wednesday night at 10 p.m., after much bloodshed. At that time, 6,200 troops in the militia moved out of the armories to control the city. They were told that both Black and White rioters were dangerous and that both should be arrested. Disciplined and even impartial, the militia did crack down on the White gangs affiliated with the athletic clubs. After the involvement of the militia, rioting and violence became sporadic and sparse, especially after rain began that night. It is not known why Mayor Thompson waited so long to enlist the militia; one explanation is that he saw the inability of the Chicago police to deal with the situation as a reflection upon himself.

On Thursday, July 30, many Black workers attempted to go to work, but it quickly became evident that the hostility was not over. White workers attacked the Black workers with hammers and clubs. A mob attacked a Black man who was already dazed by a previous barrage of hits by a hammer, striking him with shovels and brooms. The stockyards were safe only for White workers. On Friday, July 31, meat packers established emergency pay stations, traction workers voted to end the strike, and Black men and women were able to go outside their homes. On Saturday, August 1, the use of street cars and elevated train service resumed. The meat packers, head of the militia, and the deputy chief of police made arrangements for everyone to return to work safely and under the guard of the police and militia. Flyers and signs were posted, instructing everyone to come back to work on Monday at 7:00 a.m. sharp. Whites attempted to revive the riot by setting a fire to the ramshackle dwellings of Polish and Lithuanian laborers who resided in a neighborhood located behind the stockyards. The perpetrators painted their faces Black so the Blacks would be blamed. The grand jury charged the athletic clubs with setting the fires. Sunday and Monday, August 1 and 2, were uneventful for Chicago. On August 8, the militia marched out of Chicago, and the rioting was officially over.

In the end, police officers had killed seven Black men during the riot. Mobs and gang members had killed 16 Blacks and 15 Whites. More than 500 Chicagoans of both races had sustained injuries. Across the city, more than 1,000 Black families were burned out of their homes.

Causes of the Riot

Competition in the Job Market

Many factors, including housing and politics, precipitated the riot, but a long-standing discord between both races competing in the same job market is perhaps the most important reason for the riot. The Blacks arriving from the South were seen as less sophisticated and less educated than Blacks who had lived in Chicago since before World War I; longtime residents felt that the new migrants spoiled things and disturbed the balance that the Blacks had with the Whites. Laborers in Chicago also had an intense sense of class consciousness. Blacks were getting along with Whites

as long as they were doing jobs that Whites did not want. However, Whites felt threatened when Blacks became competitive with Whites in the job market. Blacks' acceptance of low wages, refusal to join unions, and strikebreaking activities increased racist responses by Whites. Between 1910 and 1920, the Black population in Chicago had grown from 44,103 to 109,594, a gain of 150%. This put a strain on the Black neighborhoods and frightened White blue-collar workers.

Most new Blacks from the South were recruited by the stockyards and the meat packers and were a part of what is known as the "Great Migration" from 1916 to 1930. Blacks seeking to escape the South provided the packinghouses with new workers, especially when current employees were drafted for service in World War I. *The Defender,* a Black newspaper, encouraged the migration to the North by advertising jobs and housing. It also explained the do's and don'ts to new arrivals in Chicago so as not to embarrass the settled Blacks. Black Chicagoans realized that in the event of a depression they would be easily expendable, and many did not want to jeopardize their employment by joining White unions. Those who did not join unions were seen as enemies of the union, and White workers referred to nonunionized Blacks as "scabs." Laborers in Chicago also had an intense sense of class consciousness.

Housing

From July 1917 to July 1919, approximately 26 bombs exploded at Black residences and at the homes of White real estate agents' homes who sold homes to Blacks. Bombs were used to chase Blacks out of what had once been all-White neighborhoods and regain control over the neighborhoods. More than half of the bombs were exploded 6 months prior to the riot. Blacks would choose to leave after being intimidated by threats of violence. The Black Belt was the only place Blacks could live without being harassed by Whites.

Politics

During the mayoral election, Blacks had supported Mayor Thompson, whom they considered another Abraham Lincoln and whom they wanted to run for president. Whites felt that Mayor

Thompson was a "lover of Blacks" who kissed Black babies. Blacks' voting record reinforced the anger, hostility, and racial hatred of numerous groups, which in turn precipitated violence. The migrants saw the ballot box as a symbol of their freedom, and they wanted to vote to demonstrate they could with the utmost honesty and dignity. The White resented the powers of the Black vote and the way in which Blacks had put Mayor Thompson in office. All of these factors are important to understanding race relations in Chicago during the Red Summer of 1919.

Rhonda Pavlu

See also Race Relations; Race Riots; Racial Conflict; White Gangs

Further Readings

Fusfeld, D. R., & Bates, T. (1984). *The political economy of the urban ghetto*. Carbondale: Southern Illinois University Press. Retrieved from http://www.questia.com/PM.qst?a=o&d=6139061

Gilje, P. A. (1996). *Rioting in America*. Bloomington: Indiana University Press. Retrieved from http://www.questia.com/PM.qst?a=o&d=101540458

Marable, M. (1991). *Race reform and rebellion* (2nd ed.). Jackson: University Press of Mississippi.

Street, P. (1996). The logic and limits of "plant loyalty": Black workers, White labor, and corporate racial paternalism in Chicago's stockyards, 1916–1940. *Journal of Social History, 29*(3), 659–681. Retrieved from http://www.questia.com/PM.qst?a=o&d=5000374620

Tuttle, M. (1970). *Race riot: Chicago in the Red Summer of 1919*. New York: Athenaeum.

CHICAGO SCHOOL OF SOCIOLOGY

In the late 1800s, the sociologist Émile Durkheim theorized that areas experiencing rapid social change would experience few, if any, informal social controls, which would result in an increase in crime and delinquency. This framework was utilized by sociologists working at the University of Chicago during the years of the early 20th century in efforts to understand which environmental factors contributed to increased rates of crime and delinquency in specific neighborhoods. In determining correlations between neighborhood location and higher crime and delinquency rates, it was hypothesized that social-structural determinants of crime could be identified. Through the work of George Herbert Mead, Robert Park, Ernest Burgess, Frederic Thrasher, and Florian Znaniecki, the Chicago School of Sociology was founded, thus beginning a rich tradition in the sociological inquiry into the dynamics of the urban environment and its relationship to crime and delinquency. Eventually, through the work of Clifford Shaw and Henry McKay, the Chicago School became integral in the study of the causes of crime and delinquency in urban environments. The theory of social disorganization was a prominent theory to come from the foundations of the Chicago School. This theory has been a key explanation of crime and delinquency since its formulation in the mid-20th century, and it continues to influence criminological theory and urban policy today.

General Concepts

Several concepts are central in understanding the development of the Chicago School and the work of sociologists attempting to understand crime in urban areas in the early to mid-20th century. The Chicago School sociologists placed an emphasis on influences outside of the individual, specifically the structural conditions of neighborhoods and the social influences of these areas. The Chicago School sociologists proposed that crime is a normal response by persons not suffering from biological or psychological impairments to abnormal social conditions. The Chicago School emphasized empiricism through ethnographic data collection, the use of demographic and population data, and systematic observation.

Because crime was viewed as originating outside the individual, criminal activity was hypothesized as a normal response by normal people to conditions viewed by society as abnormal. Because of this, communities were viewed as a critical focus of study, as the mix of cultures in growing urban areas led to culture conflict among residents. As such, the theory of social disorganization, the most prominent theory to come from the Chicago School, emphasized the social-structural determinants of residential mobility, poverty, and racial heterogeneity as the prime conditions for culture conflict in urban communities.

Early Chicago School Work

Many urban centers were experiencing rapid population growth at the turn of the 20th century. The city of Chicago saw not only a marked increase in population, but an increase in the numbers of European immigrants and African Americans migrating from the rural southern states in search of work in one of the city's vast number of developing industries. Progressive thinkers of the time were against rapid industrialization, as the costs to the quality of human life were viewed as too great. The promise of the American dream did not extend to all groups within society, especially individuals living in slum neighborhoods. From this came a movement to provide persons from disadvantaged backgrounds, especially youth, with services that would lessen the frustrations presented by poverty-level living conditions. It was at the same time that the University of Chicago began a Department of Sociology with the primary focus of helping individuals living in areas of social unrest. The department's mission was the improvement of slum areas close to the center of the city.

In the early years of the 20th century, Robert Ezra Park, a newspaper writer who investigated the social conditions of Chicago's densely populated urban neighborhoods, was appointed as a faculty member in the Department of Sociology at the University of Chicago. Park's work examined how communities, especially those characterized by poverty, developed within the city of Chicago. Park, along with his colleague Ernest Burgess, proposed that Chicago tended to grow and expand in a pattern of concentric circles from the center of the city. They hypothesized that the city was similar to the natural ecological communities of plants in that plant life tends to grow outward from a point of initial vegetation. Park and Burgess also noted the development of "natural areas" where different immigrant and racial groups developed their own communities. Physical barriers (i.e., train tracks or bodies of water) formed some natural areas, whereas other natural areas were dominated by specific labor needs (i.e.,

factories). Furthermore, people invaded and dominated certain neighborhoods in search of work or suitable housing, which led the previous inhabitants to move away from the city's center. Clifford Shaw and Henry McKay later used these concepts of invasion, dominance, and succession within this framework to locate and determine characteristics of delinquency areas within the city of Chicago.

The theory of social disorganization, which places an emphasis on the geographical patterns of urban areas marked by high crime and delinquency and the structural components of such areas, has been regarded as a leading explanation of crime in the United States for more than 70 years. Although 19th-century European studies by Adolphe Quételet, Andre Michel Guerry, and Cesare Lombroso examined the geographic distribution of crime and delinquency, researchers who worked at the University of Chicago within the Chicago School tradition initially developed social disorganization theory. These sociologists studied urban crime and delinquency, utilizing the foundation laid by Park and Burgess in the city of Chicago during the 1920s and 1930s. Clifford Shaw and Henry McKay, the initial proponents of social disorganization theory, conducted intensive studies to locate areas of delinquency within the city of Chicago. Furthermore, they examined the environmental and social structures of these delinquency areas. Through their investigations, emerging patterns were delineated; areas prone to high rates of delinquency were characterized by ethnic heterogeneity, high residential mobility, dilapidated homes, weak informal social control, and a high number of residents classified as living at poverty level. In addition, high rates of delinquency could be found near the center of the city, and incidences of delinquency dissipated as the distance from the city's nucleus increased.

The first zone, located at—and directly around—the central point of the city, housed much of the business and industrial activity. Directly adjacent to the first zone was the zone of transition, characterized by dilapidated housing and the ever-present threat of invasion and domination by expanding commercial and industrial establishments. The proximity of this area to the city's established industry made it undesirable for living, causing property to be inexpensive and, therefore, attractive to persons of low socioeconomic status. In Chicago, during the early 1900s, many poor migrants and immigrants settled within this second zone. Zone three was designated as the area in which working-men resided. The fourth and fifth zones, known as the residential and commuters' zones, respectively, were populated with mostly White, middle- to upper-class persons.

As Chicago's population continued to grow, each zone continued to expand as well through the process of invasion, dominance, and succession. Sociologists at the University of Chicago, however, were not only interested in city development and growth; they were also concerned with locating areas of the city prone to delinquency and crime. Shaw and McKay, students of Park and Burgess, expanded the concentric zone theory by conducting studies in Chicago to determine in which zone male delinquency was most prevalent. Results of Shaw and McKay's investigations showed that male delinquency was concentrated within the zone of transition. This area was described in detail by Shaw and McKay as a community marked by an abundance of homes suffering physical decay, broken homes, a high rate of illegitimate births, and a heterogeneous population that was characterized by instability. A large majority of the residents were paid low wages and were undereducated. In addition to high rates of juvenile delinquency, this area experienced high rates of adult crime, drug addiction, alcoholism, prostitution, and mental illness. All of these indicators were interpreted as the result of social disorganization within the urban area. Thus, it was deduced that delinquency was caused by the processes operating within the disorganized social structure of communities close to the inner city. Examples of such processes include culture conflict and lack of informal social control. Regardless of the findings, it is important to examine the methods and analysis utilized by Shaw and McKay in order to fully comprehend the assumptions of the social disorganization theory.

Juvenile Delinquency in Urban Areas: The Studies of Shaw and McKay

Shaw and McKay were interested in utilizing the framework of urban growth developed at the University of Chicago to locate areas of male delinquent activity within the city of Chicago. Additionally, they sought to determine whether areas of high and low rates of delinquency maintained their respective rates over a period of many years. If certain areas depicted high delinquency rates through longitudinal inquiry, it could then be deduced that characteristics of the delinquent area, and not the individuals residing in the area, could be attributed as the cause of delinquent behavior.

Methodology

Since Shaw and McKay were trying to establish an accurate depiction of delinquency patterns, they chose to use official records for the purposes of analysis. Data utilized included alleged delinquents brought before the Juvenile Court on delinquency petitions, delinquents committed to residential correctional institutions, and alleged delinquents who came into contact with probation officers regardless of prior court appearance.

The three types of data were used to obtain a sample size large enough to be representative of the large population of Chicago. Moreover, Shaw and McKay supplemented their data analysis with several case histories obtained through interviews with selected offenders from high-delinquency areas.

Data were obtained for three 7-year increments: (1) 1900–1906, (2) 1917–1923, and (3) 1927–1933. This longitudinal analysis afforded the researchers an opportunity for a comparison of time periods and for analysis of long-term trends and processes that could not be possible if a cross-sectional research design was employed. The residence of each male delinquent was plotted on a map of Chicago, and emerging patterns indicated that delinquency tended to be concentrated in the zone of transition. This zone was marked by its proximity to industrial areas, low-rent housing, and areas of racial heterogeneity.

Correlation With Other Community Problems in Chicago

It is interesting to note that delinquency areas also experienced high levels of other activities indicative of a disorderly environment. The areas reporting high rates of delinquent activity also reported high rates of school truancy and young adult offenders. Additionally, rates of infant mortality, tuberculosis, and mental disorder prevailed in delinquency areas. Shaw and McKay concluded that other problems highly correlated with rates of delinquency could be associated with neighborhood conditions.

Conclusions Drawn From the Chicago Studies

Shaw and McKay inferred that the prevalence of delinquency in certain areas, as well as the stability of these rates for a period of years, indicated a socially disorganized environment. This environment, in turn, led to the occurrence of delinquency and other community problems. The next step for Shaw and McKay was determining exactly what factors cause a socially disorganized environment.

A socially disorganized environment, it was concluded, had three main characteristics: (1) a high incidence of poverty, (2) racial heterogeneity, and (3) high rates of residential mobility. Residential areas located in the zone of transition consisted of dilapidated housing; industry threatened constant takeover. Poor, uneducated migrants and immigrants settled in this zone, where the ensuing ethnic heterogeneity caused culture conflict since different groups did not share the same norms and values. Furthermore, as immigrants and migrants moved in, the current residents fled to outlying areas of the city. High rates of residential mobility created conditions unfavorable to community cohesion because people were reluctant to interact with neighbors and become involved in community organizations if the social networks were to be short-lived. Also, community organizations were virtually nonexistent in disorganized neighborhoods.

The social disorganization fostered by such weak control and competing values in turn caused unconventional activity such as delinquency. Residents in areas classified as socially disorganized are incapable of settling on common values and solving common problems. It is also important to note that it was hypothesized that communities maintained their dynamic characteristics over a period of years, thus maintaining a stable ecological pattern. This was exemplified in the stable rates of high and low delinquency in respective areas, unheeding of the changes occurring within such areas.

The development of social disorganization theory appealed to criminological inquiry because it was one of the first macrosocial theories of crime.

In other words, the theory was able to explain crime in terms of its relationship to social structures and social systems at large. Also, the theory emphasized that irregular social conditions, not abnormal individuals, were central in crime causation. This was important to many criminologists working during the early to mid-20th century, as sociology was beginning to influence the growing field of criminology, and much of this work traced its roots to the Chicago School.

As social disorganization theory gained recognition and began influencing other theories of crime, Shaw and McKay began several replication studies to validate their previous findings. The delinquency area studies were not limited to the city of Chicago. They also examined delinquency patterns in other cities in the United States: Philadelphia, Pennsylvania; Boston, Massachusetts; Cincinnati, Ohio; Cleveland, Ohio; Richmond, Virginia; and Birmingham, Alabama. Similar results to those found in Chicago were found in these cities, although several studies were limited to cross-sectional research designs.

Limitations and Modifications of Shaw and McKay's Social Disorganization Model

The tenets of Shaw and McKay's model, as well as the methodology employed, have not gone without criticism. Some scholars feel that the theory failed to explain exactly how characteristics of social disorganization caused amplified rates of delinquency. As stated earlier, Shaw and McKay postulated that conditions in the long-term processes of urbanization encouraged situations conducive to delinquency, yet due to the difficulty, time commitment, and extreme costs of longitudinal analyses, studies testing the theory were, and often still are, limited to cross-sectional research designs. Although the use of longitudinal methods was a considerable strength of Shaw and McKay's studies, questions have been raised regarding whether cities still operate under the same structure and processes as they did in the earlier part of the 20th century.

Another limitation of Shaw and McKay's model concerns their use of official court and police records. The sole use of official data still tends to be an invalid measure of crime and delinquency. The police and court records used by Shaw and McKay, as well as subsequent researchers, indicated only cases of delinquent activity that were detected and processed by the criminal justice system. The detection of criminal activity may be the result of increased police surveillance in certain neighborhoods. Also, in areas of close proximity, such as the zone of transition, people may have more opportunities to detect suspicious behavior. As a result, more reports to the police may be made in socially disorganized neighborhoods. Hence, delinquent activity may not be more prevalent in socially disorganized areas, just detected by the community, reported to the police, and processed through the juvenile justice system more frequently than in other areas. Alternative measures of social disorganization that have been employed in recent years include victimization data and calls to the police. It has been argued that calls to the police reduce police biases; however, it is important to note that citizen and victim response is critical when using this measure.

Possibly the most debilitating criticism of early social disorganization models is the lack of attention paid to processes that intervene between the structural determinants of communities (such as racial heterogeneity, mobility, and poverty) and crime; thus, the variables that mediate between neighborhood structure and criminal behavior, as well as delinquency, have been neglected in social disorganization research. This is necessary in order to test the theory adequately. Early criticism in this vein cited the theory's lack of attention to the factors involved in the cultural transmission of delinquent and criminal values. A landmark study conducted by Sampson and Groves in the late 1980s attempted to directly measure neighborhood social disorganization. In this investigation, a neighborhood's organization was measured by examining friendship networks, social control of teenage delinquent activity, and the degree of participation in structured community activities. It was hypothesized that communities exhibiting the classic description of social disorganization (ethnic heterogeneity, low socioeconomic status, and residential mobility) would exhibit deteriorated social controls, a lack of friendship networks, and little participation in organizational activities. Using the British Crime Survey, Sampson and Groves were able to obtain self-report data on criminal offending, criminal victimization, and community activities for more than 200 British neighborhoods. The instrument consisted of measures to empirically test specific characteristics of both formal and informal neighborhood social organization. The data obtained were consistent with conclusions drawn by Shaw and McKay and other researchers utilizing the basic social disorganization model. Crime was higher in areas with a large number of unsupervised teens and areas lacking friendship networks and organizational participation.

Although the concepts and propositions of the early Chicago School theorists have been greatly modified, the legacy of the work continues today in contemporary social disorganization research. Some modifications have been strictly at the empirical level, as described previously, whereas other modifications have greatly restructured the focus of the theory and how it can explain contemporary urban crime and delinquency. In the late 1980s, William Julius Wilson proposed that the failed liberal policies of the mid-20th century have created an urban underclass that is marked by low residential mobility, racial homogeneity, and poverty. With the shift to a service economy and the flight of White and middle-class African American residents to suburban neighborhoods, African Americans of low-income status were left with few role models. The result was an emerging underclass that was unskilled, with few employment opportunities and family ties. In considering the structure of communities at the end of the 20th century, Wilson concluded that the organization of society was hindering the personal and professional advancement of African American residents of urban areas throughout the United States; thus, Wilson argued that the likelihood that African American residents of disadvantaged communities will engage in crime and delinquency is greater given the blocked opportunities in urban communities.

Courtney A. Waid

See also Code of the Streets; Ethnicity; European Americans; Social Disorganization Theory; "Truly Disadvantaged"

Further Readings

Bursik, R. J., Jr. (1986). Ecological stability and the dynamics of delinquency. In A. Reiss & M. Tonry (Eds.), *Communities and crime* (pp. 35–66). Chicago: University of Chicago Press.

Kornhauser, R. R. (1978). *Social sources of delinquency.* Chicago: University of Chicago Press.

Sampson, R. J., & Groves, W. B. (1989). Community structure and crime: Testing social-disorganization theory. *American Journal of Sociology, 94*(4), 774–802.

Shaw, C. R., & McKay, H. D. (1942). *Juvenile delinquency and urban areas.* Chicago: University of Chicago Press.

Warner, B. D., & Pierce, G. L. (1993). Reexamining social disorganization theory using calls to the police as a measure of crime. *Criminology, 31*(4), 493–517.

Wilson, W. J. (1987). *The truly disadvantaged: The inner city, the underclass, and public policy.* Chicago: University of Chicago Press.

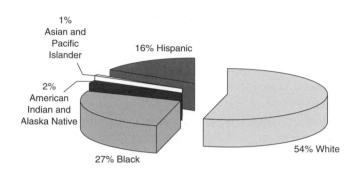

Figure 1   U.S. Foster Care Population by Race, 2001

Source: U.S. Department of Health and Human Services (2003).

Child Abuse

Child abuse is any conduct or failure to act by an adult resulting in sexual, physical, and emotional abuse and neglect of a child under the age of 18. *Race* is used to distinguish persons from others based on either physical characteristics or ethnicity. Each year, disproportionately high numbers of abused Black children are removed from their families and placed into the U.S. child welfare system. Overrepresentation exists when a racial group of children are represented in foster care at a higher rate than they are represented in the general population. For example, Black children constitute 27% of the U.S. foster care population (Figure 1), but 13% of the total U.S. child population (Figure 2). In contrast, White, American Indian, and Alaska Native children are underrepresented in foster care compared to their representation in the U.S. child population.

Differences in the relationships between race and child abuse occur in the substantiation of child abuse, placement in out-of-home care, length of stay in foster care, and reentry into foster care after attempts at family reunification by child protection agencies. Researchers have sought to identify, examine, and understand the issues related to race, child abuse, and child protection.

In the literature, explanations of child abuse are inconclusive regarding the incidences of child abuse and neglect by race. There is an ongoing debate about whether or not the disproportionality

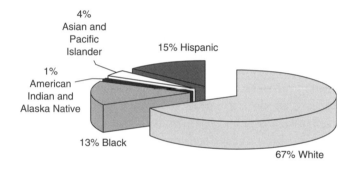

Figure 2   U.S. Child Population by Race, 2001

Source: U.S. Census Bureau (2001).

by race in foster care reflects racial differences in the incidence of risk factors associated with child abuse. These risk factors may include domestic violence, social isolation, alcohol and drug abuse, parental incarceration, and poverty. For example, studies have shown that the effect of poverty interacts with domestic violence and substance abuse, which can increase the likelihood of child abuse. Thus, if minority populations are disproportionately poor, a disproportionate number of minority children will enter foster care.

It is the responsibility of child protection agencies to ensure the protection and safety of children who are victims of abuse and neglect. Routinely, child protection agencies are criticized for being racist and biased toward minority children. As a result, child protection agencies, along with state and local leaders, have made racial equity a priority in the best interest of families. Relatedly, inconsistency in the treatment of Black and other minority youth has prompted agencies and organizations to become more proactive by creating or improving cultural sensitivity and diversity training.

Although protecting children developed out of the efforts of religious and charitable groups, child protection services are the primary function of state governments. Historically, child welfare provisions were based upon English and patriarchal traditions. Both women and children were the property of their husband or father. This guaranteed the right of men to discipline their families any way they saw fit, inclusive of severe beating, as well as sexual and mental abuse of close relatives. During early colonial times, children were required to work in factories, workhouses, and apprenticeships under hazardous conditions as young as 5 years of age in order to support their families. It was not until 1874, with the case of Mary Ellen Wilson, the first child abuse case in America, that reformers began to recognize that children needed protection against abuse. This started the House of Refuge movement, a strict educational home, where children did not have to deal with harsh labor, poverty, or the corruption that came with city life. Conversely, this early form of child protection provision was exclusively for White abused children.

During this same period, Blacks were not represented or were underrepresented in the child welfare provision. Until 1865, the institution of slavery was the child protection provision for Black children. As a result, indenture and almshouses typically overlooked or denied Black children social services. Whites would never allow a dependent poor White child to receive less support than an enslaved Black child or immigrant. Therefore, the only options for Black and immigrant children were churches, social organizations, and schools advocating improvement of services on behalf of abused and neglected minority children. Black children as well as other minority racial groups continued to be treated as inferior and were underrepresented in child welfare provisions throughout the 20th century.

In 1935, the creation of Title IV-A of the Social Security Act established Aid to Dependent Children. States received federal funding to determine eligibility requirements and provide public assistance to needy families. Some states adopted arbitrary welfare clauses that increasingly denied assistance to Black families, which subsequently labeled their children neglected without follow-up services. These clauses forbade assistance to families with an unmarried man in the house, children of unwed mothers, and parental behaviors deemed immoral by state child welfare workers.

As a result, the Flemming Rule was established in 1961 to rectify this situation. It required states to provide services to make unsuitable homes suitable and remove children from homes while providing funding and services to the families on behalf of children. Unfortunately, these mandated services gave culturally insensitive foster care workers the excuse to remove abused and neglected Black children from their homes at alarming rates. Thus, for the first time child protection workers began to see abused and neglected minorities in their foster care caseloads.

The extent of incidents of child abuse and neglect among racial groups remain inconclusive, partly due to underreporting. The U.S. child welfare system continues to be involved by recognizing and addressing the problem of overrepresentation of minority children. Despite the fact that studies demonstrate that Black families are not more likely to abuse or neglect their children than are other racial groups, the complexities of child protection continue to challenge families, agencies, and organizations. Recently, efforts to address race and child abuse have resulted in legislative initiatives, class action lawsuits, training, technical assistance, better data, and media attention.

David A. Rembert and Howard Henderson

See also Child Savers; Ethnicity; Racism; Reformatories; Status Offenses; "Truly Disadvantaged"; Victimization, Youth

Further Readings

Billingsley, A., & Giovannoni, J. M. (1972). *Children of the storm: Black children and American child welfare.* New York: Harcourt Brace Jovanovich.
Roberts, D. (2002). *Shattered bonds: The color of child welfare.* New York: Basic Civitas Books.
U.S. Census Bureau. (2001). *Survey of income and program participation, 2001 panel, wave 2.* Washington, DC: U.S. Government Printing Office.

U.S. Department of Health and Human Services. (2003). *Administration on children, youth and families, child maltreatment 2001.* Washington, DC: U.S. Government Printing Office.

CHILDREN OF FEMALE OFFENDERS

Race and sex have long been recognized as significant correlates of crime and criminality in U.S. society. In a similar vein, incarceration rates have served as a yardstick, albeit an imperfect one, for measuring changes in crime and criminality over time. As a result, scholars, criminal justice practitioners, and the media have focused much of their attention on the male offender, particularly the Black man who is grossly overrepresented in the U.S. prison population. Since the early 1980s, attention has turned toward a different group of offenders: women. During the past 2 decades, female incarceration rates have dramatically outpaced those of their male counterparts, thus opening up a new line of research as academicians, practitioners, and theorists alike attempt to explain the unprecedented rise in women's criminality. Only recently have these same scholars and practitioners shown an interest in, and concern about, the children of female offenders—the group that has been called the "collateral damage" associated with a burgeoning female prison population. This entry examines what is currently known about this highly specialized and rapidly growing group referred to as the "children of female offenders."

The Female Offender

Although female prisoners continue to represent a small percentage (approximately 7%) of all who are incarcerated, their numbers have increased dramatically since the 1980s. Researchers consistently document close to a fivefold increase in women's incarceration rates during the last 2 decades of the 20th century, with the numbers of female inmates rising from 11 per 100,000 in 1980 to more than 51 per 100,000 by the start of the new millennium. While male inmates continue to outnumber females, women's rates of incarceration rose at a pace twice

that of their male counterparts during the time period identified. As with the general prison population, race becomes an important issue when considering the incarcerated female. Recent data indicate the incarceration rate for African American women is 8 times greater than that for White women, while Hispanics and Latinas face imprisonment at a rate nearly 4 times that of White females. The implications associated with these data affect not only the adults in question but also their children, as African American youth are nearly 9 times more likely than White children to have at least one incarcerated parent.

Although offenders of both sexes share many background characteristics, three distinct differences appear between the men and women behind bars. First, females tend to be incarcerated more often than men for property and nonviolent crimes, while men are more likely to commit violent offenses. Second, women prisoners are more likely than men to have experienced abuse, either physical or sexual, prior to their incarceration. Finally, women prisoners are much more likely than men to be responsible for family caregiving at the time of their incarceration, with data indicating two thirds of these females leave behind minor children (under the age of 18) at the time of their incarceration. Approximately 90% of men leave offspring in the care of the mother when entering prison, while only 23% of female offenders indicate the children's father assumed custody upon her incarceration. While many factors account for this difference, it is undoubtedly due in large part to the fact that women more often than men serve as single heads of households prior to their arrests. It is also the case that women often give birth while in prison, adding yet more children to the mix. Immediate child care and the future of these children are fast becoming issues of concern for both the mothers who find themselves behind bars and society at large.

The Children Left Behind

Researchers have only recently turned their attention to the plight of the children left behind when female offenders enter the prison environment. Much of what has been written to date represents inference—projections of what "will be"—based on past psychological and sociological research focusing on issues of parent-child bonding, separation, and child development. In spite of this paucity of research, early findings suggest that children of female offenders share many common characteristics, experiences, and behavioral outcomes as a result of their mother's imprisonment.

Researchers have consistently documented a negative correlation between parental incarceration and children's well-being, with states reporting the highest incarceration rates also sharing increased rates of infant mortality, child abuse, and neglect, as well as juvenile arrests. Intuitively, it would seem that children raised in crime-oriented families would benefit from the removal of the offending parent. Contrary to this popular belief, little benefit is realized by the displaced children of incarcerated parents. Rather than mitigating family problems, parental imprisonment compounds the dysfunctions already present in the home.

When the offending mother goes to prison, the first issue to be addressed is that of providing a stable, nurturing environment for her children. As mothers face incarceration, many fear losing custody of their offspring, a concern that contributes to the caregiving decisions made at the time of the arrest. Here, too, differences appear according to race. Whereas White children are more likely to be placed with their father or in foster care following the mother's arrest, extended family members more often assume custody of non-White youth. Neither outcome is ideal.

When children are placed in a relative's care, it is often the case that they remain in the same physical environment and/or social milieu that contributed to the mother's offending behaviors in the first place. Approximately 60% of female offenders suffered abuse in the home prior to engaging in crime. The risk of the child suffering the same abuse leads some child welfare advocates to view placement with relatives as merely setting the stage for disaster. In addition, at least some theorists maintain family placement brings with it an added risk—the generational transmission of crime—as children are taught the same lessons of crime and deviance once learned by the mother.

The alternative to family care is state custody, resulting in either foster care or group home placement. Studies show foster placement to be more beneficial for the child than family placement, with research indicating children receive a higher quality of both material and emotional care in the former. Yet state custody is not without its problems.

When placed in state custody, children find themselves in unknown and unfamiliar environments. The abrupt changes and lack of familiar surroundings exacerbate feelings of separation and anxiety, thus compounding the psychological damage brought about by the mother's arrest.

Problems are also experienced by those children born in prison. When the female offender gives birth in prison, rarely is she given adequate time with her newborn to fully develop the parent-child bond necessary for optimal psychological and emotional development. Only a handful of prisons accommodate the new mother and her infant in a way that allows the time and contact necessary for this bonding to occur. Research is mixed on this issue, with some claiming the prison environment is, in and of itself, unhealthy and unsafe for newborns. Those who disagree cite evidence that mother-infant programs such as the one initiated at Bedford Hills, New York, contribute to the developmental well-being of the infant and reduce recidivism rates among female offenders.

The psychological problems experienced by the children of female offenders are often rooted in events occurring well before the mother's incarceration. Studies indicate many youth suffer from posttraumatic stress disorder (PTSD) as a result of being privy to the mother's crimes and/or witnessing her arrest. Child psychologists report many children suffer from a sense of abandonment, along with other, more classic, symptoms of PTSD that include depression, anxiety, and feelings of guilt and rage. Flashbacks are not uncommon long after the mother's arrest, nor are the experiences of hearing the mother's voice even though she is physically absent from the child's life. As with many individuals who suffer from PTSD, the children of female offenders are troubled for many years following the initial traumatizing event.

Although the findings are both tentative and sometimes contradictory in nature, research indicates children of both sexes experience psychological and behavioral problems following their mothers' incarceration. Separation from the maternal parent under any circumstances is a disruptive event for the child, one that interferes with individual and social development. This is especially true for the child whose mother is arrested and placed behind bars.

Children of incarcerated mothers tend to display difficulty in mastering what are considered to be "normal" developmental tasks. As they mature, they exhibit school-related difficulties, increased aggression and emotional dysfunction, lowered self-esteem, and diminished emotional functioning. Research conducted in 1999 by Hagan and Dinovitzer examined the children of incarcerated mothers. Forty percent of the males ages 12 to 17 included in this study were identified as delinquent, with a teen pregnancy rate of 60% reported among the adolescent females. Additional findings led the authors to conclude that children of incarcerated parents may, themselves, be 6 times more likely than the general youth population to face incarceration at some point in their lives.

Not all researchers agree with these conclusions. A 2004 study conducted by Lawrence-Wills examined delinquency and antisocial behavior among adolescent daughters of incarcerated mothers. Using self-reported survey data from 101 incarcerated women, Lawrence-Wills tested four hypotheses related to the mother–daughter relationship and mother–child supervision to examine their effects on daughters' behaviors. No significant effect of mother's incarceration on daughter's behavior was found; the daughters included in this study were reported to have low levels of both delinquent and antisocial behaviors. In response to admitted study limitations, including lack of input from daughters and reliance upon mothers' perceptions, Lawrence-Wills suggests two possible conclusions. First, it is possible that female offenders promote prosocial behaviors in their daughters, as do many in the noncriminal population. Second, it may be the case that daughters use their mothers' experiences as a deterrent, thus making the conscious decision to avoid crime and criminality.

To date, few studies have examined the children of female offenders. Even fewer policies and programs are in place to address the specialized needs of this unique population. This is undoubtedly due, in large part, to the fact that the mothers themselves have only recently garnered the attention of scholars and practitioners. As women's incarceration rates continue to rise and more youth are identified as the children of female offenders, future research will be necessary in order to bring forth a comprehensive, theoretically driven understanding of these youth.

The Future of Research

Criminologists offer a plethora of explanations for criminality. Explanatory factors vary according to each theorist's training, personal ontology, and theoretical grounding. Some rely on poverty and inequality to explain criminal behavior. Others turn to factors such as learning, social support, the environment, labeling, or control. When considering the children of female offenders, the limited findings reported to date suggest all these factors may be salient in the lives of children raised by an offending mother. While the findings from this early research offer some contradictions, most suggest life with an offending mother results in negative, perhaps even deleterious, consequences for the offspring. All agree on the need for an enhanced understanding of this unique group. This requires additional research.

Future research will undoubtedly, and must, integrate the work of many fields and many researchers. Within the field of criminology, both structural and individual explanations for crime and criminality abound. Research conducted to date clearly suggests the children of female offenders are, at the very least, *at risk* for becoming criminal; criminological explanations may help in understanding that aspect of their lives. A thorough understanding of these youth, their experiences, and their needs will require researchers to move beyond that narrow perspective. Veracity and comprehensiveness will be achieved through the collaboration of numerous professionals representing varied disciplines. Already we have witnessed the work of professionals from the fields of criminal justice, psychology, sociology, and social work. Each has added something to the overall, albeit limited and fragmented, understanding of these youth. The next wave of research must move beyond the colored lens of one discipline and work toward a more complete understanding of these children if we are to improve their lives via social policies and programs designed to address the totality of who they are and what they need.

Martha L. Shockey-Eckles

See also Delinquency Prevention; Family and Delinquency

Further Readings

Bruns, D. A. (2006). Promoting mother-child relationships for incarcerated women and their children. *Infants & Young Children, 19*(4), 308–322.

Crawford, J. (2003, June). Alternative sentencing necessary for female inmates with children. *Corrections Today, 65*(3), 8–11.

Gonnerman, J. (2004). *Life on the outside: The prison odyssey of Elaine Bartlett.* New York: Farrar, Straus & Giroux.

Hagan, J., & Dinovitzer, R. (1999). Collateral consequences and imprisonment for children, communities, and prisoners. In M. Tonry & J. Petersilia (Eds.), *Prisons: Crime and justice* (pp. 125–147). Chicago: University of Chicago Press.

Lawrence-Wills, S. (2004). Incarcerated mothers' reports of their daughters' antisocial behaviors, maternal supervision, and mother-daughter relationship. *Journal of Family Social Work, 8*(3), 55–73.

Loper, A. B. (2005, February). How do mothers in prison differ from non-mothers? *Journal of Child and Family Studies, 15*(1), 83–95.

Poehlmann, J. (2005, December). Children's family environments and intellectual outcomes during maternal incarceration. *Journal of Marriage and Family, 67,* 1275–1285.

Sharp, S. F., & Erikson, M. E. (2003). Imprisoned mothers and their children. In B. H. Zaitzow & J. Thomas (Eds.), *Women in prison: Gender and social control* (pp. 119–136). Boulder, CO: Lynne Rienner.

Zaitzow, B. H. (2003). "Doing gender" in a women's prison. In B. H. Zaitzow & J. Thomas (Eds.), *Women in prison: Gender and social control* (pp. 21–38). Boulder, CO: Lynne Rienner.

CHILD SAVERS

Social movements during the 19th and 20th centuries led to the establishment and development of autonomous juvenile justice systems and other child welfare reform in the United States and elsewhere. These movements, led by civic actors who would come to be called "child savers," resulted in numerous reforms and institutions that collectively extended greater state authority over families and youth, on the premise of rescuing or protecting young people from "deviant" socialization and thus, by extension, regulating societal development. These were especially pressing concerns in 19th- and early-20th-century United States, where industrialization, rapid urbanization, emancipation and reconstruction, mass immigration, and internal migrations, among other developments, were reconfiguring the face of the nation.

To a significant extent, "child saving" was conceived and carried out as a nation-building movement, focused on the tributaries of child welfare, socialization into adulthood, and ultimately civil society. The child saving movement actually involved numerous civic actors, drawing upon as many inspirations, and should therefore be understood as a reference to several, and in some ways, competing civic initiatives. These reformers had much in common, such as their shared interests in addressing what came to be called "delinquency" and "dependency," their belief in the rehabilitative potential youth, and tendencies to attribute problems in young people's lives to family dysfunction, urbanization, faith, and other factors. However, child savers also varied significantly in their social identities, outlooks, and interests and developed movements that were often quite distinct and at times at odds with each other, as initiatives expressing the aspirations of a nation divided.

This entry provides a brief review of scholarship on the historical development of juvenile justice, focusing on the common accounts of who were these reformers, what motivated them, and how we should understand their historic significance. After highlighting several major arguments and limitations of the existing research literature, the review considers emerging research on child saving in the Black American experience, a movement that challenges and expands our perspective on the protagonists, their agendas, and the significance of child saving initiatives in U.S. history.

The Child Saving Movement: Critical Perspectives and Reconsiderations

What scholarship later termed "child saving" in American criminal justice seems to have gotten underway around 1819, when the 2-year-old New York Society for the Prevention of Pauperism launched a companion Society for the Reformation of Juvenile Delinquents. Six years later, the groups opened the New York House of Refuge, the first institution expressly geared to serve the young among those accused and condemned of crime, delinquency, and dependency. This distinct system of juvenile justice, many promised and believed, signaled an enlightened strategy of juvenile social control—a more modern, scientific, and liberal democratic approach to the regulation of young deviants and dependents, and by extension their families, communities, and, most important, civil society itself. The economy, polity, culture, and more were at stake in what came of troubled youth. With this rallying cry, a series of favorable court rulings and the passage of legislation, the movement by 1900 yielded a proliferation of juvenile "rehabilitative" strategies and institutions promising delinquency and dependency services and the development of the first juvenile court. By 1927, there were juvenile courts in all but a few states, and juvenile justice was clearly established as a distinct national strategy and institution of social control.

The term *child savers* was never apparently used by these reformers but was coined in a still influential early study of the movement to establish specialized courts for youth, and what is now commonly known as the juvenile justice system. In *The Child Savers: The Invention of Juvenile Delinquency* (1969, 1977), Anthony Platt studies the development of the juvenile court in Progressive-era Chicago, one of the first "specialized courts" of the sort in the United States, and what leading advocates and their efforts reveal of the culture, politics, and history of juvenile justice reform. Several studies have since reconsidered Platt's analysis and otherwise delved further into the history of American juvenile justice, albeit along generally similar lines of inquiry.

Existing research on child saving focuses on the identities, status characteristics, social networks, and experiences of the primarily women leaders and their reflection in the work to develop the juvenile court. By most published accounts, the child saving movement was led by prominent White moral entrepreneurs and civic leaders, who along with their allies and through particular social networks drew on the growing ranks of White middle-class counterparts in American cities at the turn of the century to transform the approach to juvenile social control. The prototypical child saver was a White woman not only tied to influential men (i.e., fathers and husbands), but fast becoming detached from a restrictive and sexist culture of domesticity

in her own right, gaining new access to influence within the public sphere. While genuinely interested in improving the lives of poor youth and families in emerging cities, some argue, these reformers also seized opportunity to bolster their own social status and advance their political interests through this limited but unprecedented access to the professions, philanthropy, and civic leadership. Platt and others point out that child saving was a measured break from existing boundaries of access and influence, only moderately departing from gendered social roles, including notions of child-raising responsibility. Through the child saving movement and invention of juvenile justice, women could rise to new ranks of authority and influence, albeit within an institution defined in theory and law as the "parental state," whose role and promise President Theodore Roosevelt once characterized as "manufacturing citizens." With these grand ambitions and agendas, child saving work gave birth to juvenile justice systems, through which women gained new entrée to government circles, professional roles, and philanthropic realms long dominated by men, yet with familiar duties in the delivery and rearing of yet another brood, this time defined as "embryonic citizens."

On a rapidly changing social landscape, especially in growing northern and eastern seacoast cities, but also throughout the South, as we shall see, child savers responded to what they saw as a number of old and new American problems— involving poverty, morality, education, health, public safety, and inequality—and attempting to fashion solutions. These problems were thought to be exacerbated or threatened by all sorts of factors, including rapid urbanization and industrialization, the breakdown of the nuclear family, mass immigration of poor European ethnic minorities to emerging cities, and racial oppression and domination. In theory, the juvenile court and its services would facilitate removal of youth from these "unhealthful" home environments, neighborhoods, and other situations. Moreover, many maintained, intelligent use of "rehabilitative" institutions and various and sundry programming furnished a means of installing the moral codes, skills, habits, character, and discipline alleged to be missing, and required for, lives of labor, domesticity, industriousness, and perhaps prosperity upon return to society.

In many accounts, these child savers are characterized less as compassionate or progressive agents of change than as coercive agents of control who imposed their own norms and interests upon the marginal and powerless among them. Noting the overrepresentation of first-generation European ethnic minorities among those classified as delinquent, for example, Platt and others have suggested that child saving involved the selective regulation of immigrant families and their children, to facilitate their forced acculturation and thus integration into the American economy, culture, and polity on someone else's terms. Thus, Platt says child savers "invented" the concept of delinquency to cast a net of "social control" over another class of people and their children, whose development they sought to influence, especially for economic reasons. The motive was not only to create socioeconomic opportunity for themselves, Platt and others have argued, but to socialize the obedient laboring class required of a rapidly growing manufacturing economy.

Other critical histories of child saving develop somewhat different "control" theses, stressing the moralizing elements of these reforms. For example, several authors note the religious agendas of the largely Protestant child savers, noting the prominence of religious instruction in early juvenile institutions, under auspices of rehabilitation. Others stress the gender politics of child saving initiatives, stressing the intense surveillance and disparate standards of "policing" young women's and girls' bodies and souls, which was often rationalized by the expectation of their future domestic role (i.e., to make healthful homes). Finally, more recent work has looked more closely at the institutions and organizational networks that took shape through child saving initiatives, drawing attention to the bureaucratic, legal, and political challenges these reformers and reforms faced. These and other studies challenge and complement earlier research on the child savers, uncovering more of the motivations, strategies, constraints, and opportunities bound up in the history and legacy of the child saving movement.

There still remains a need for further research on this movement's origins, organization, and significance. Revisionist histories have been criticized for simplifying the organizational complexity of civil society and the logics and systems of punishment and social control that form amid these dynamic and contested relations. The main problem with the revisionist literature on American criminal and juvenile justice, critics seem to agree, is its failure to capture the full range of social forces shaping the idea and practice of social control. Control, they argue, is too often reduced to a rational or functional scenario of typically class-based domination administered by the penal state. These accounts neglect not only how other dynamics of conflict, and politics of difference, influence the organization of social control but also the ways in which "control" may be co-opted by nonstate actors, even in ways that suggest a communitarian outlook on the development of social control. In fact, as we shall see in the discussion of the Black child saving movement, the child saving movement has always included elements of group conflict and cooperation.

There has been especially limited attention to the racial and ethnic diversity of child saving operatives and their initiatives and what this reveals of the liberal democratic politics of the child saving movement, more generally. Emerging research on the Black child saving movement is beginning to fill that void.

The Black Child Savers

Numerous 19th- and 20th-century factors brought juvenile justice reform to the early and lasting attention of generations of Black civic actors traveling the long path of the Black freedom movement. Generally, of course, the end of Reconstruction and rise of Jim Crow brought dramatic reversals in the civil rights, and civic prospects, of Black Americans in the U.S. South and throughout the United States. This retraction of democratic freedoms ironically coincided with such Progressive era reforms as the establishment of the juvenile court, and the denial of Black access to opportunity and influence in modern juvenile justice did not go uncontested. From its beginning around 1898, and long thereafter, the movement introduced important changes in the understanding of racial stratification within juvenile justice, and in the very race relations of juvenile justice systems.

Few freedoms have been more valued by Black or other Americans than access to education and equal protection under law, and juvenile justice was an idea and institution embodying both. In its attention to moral, vocational, and other areas of child and youth development, and general identification as a "citizen-building" endeavor, the modern idea and practice of juvenile justice signified much of what freedom seemingly offered, and required, especially for a subpopulation striving to break the chains of generational, intentional, human, and community underdevelopment. Yet, assaults on Black character (i.e., morality and intelligence) and denials of equal citizenship, which grew rampant in the Progressive era, essentially disqualified Black Americans in what first emerged as a White citizen- and state-building institution, not only marginalizing Black children in child welfare endeavors, but excluding Black communities from participating in the development and administration of juvenile justice. Black youth, families, and communities found early juvenile court services closed to them, especially in the rigidly segregated South, but also in the North and West, where Black youth enjoyed relatively greater access to often inferior and segregated juvenile justice resources, and Black adults were as likely to be denied any authority in the court community.

Fundamentally, then, Black child saving was a contemporaneous oppositional movement, a counter to what was developing, explicitly and implicitly, as a White child saving movement and juvenile justice system, organized in the image of, and to advance, a White-dominated liberal democracy.

Framing Black child welfare and Black liberation as inseparable social causes, the Black child saving movement gradually co-opted, and eventually succeeded in transforming, institutions of juvenile social control by struggling for Black youth *and* adult inclusion.

The Black child saving movement proceeded in two somewhat distinct phases. An initial phase involved reformers working primarily under the auspices of local, state, and regional Black women's civic associations, affiliates of the National Council of Colored Women's Clubs, which as its first national meeting in 1898 established juvenile justice reform as a leading item on the agenda. These women leaders leveraged their social networks to establish largely voluntary, self-help initiatives, and particularly modest reformatories across the South, lobbying White government and court officials to support and make use of these institutions, with generally mixed results. By World

War I, these self-help strategies were giving way to a more confrontational and integrationist agenda, driven by pressure group politics and employing the new skill sets and networks of a growing Black professional class, and civil rights establishment. While self-help initiatives continued, Black child savers increasingly shifted to protest in the streets, courts, and halls of government, demanding equal youth and community access to opportunity and influence in the arms of the parental state.

Change came gradually, and haltingly, as the Black child saving movement stretched into the mid-20th century. By the 1940s, many southern states had begun to make greater provision for court-involved Black youth; several northern states had formally integrated their juvenile institutions (though segregation persisted); and it was becoming more common to find Black decision makers in juvenile courts, albeit limited to the role of probation and supervising Black youth. These changes were especially common in the various destinations of the great Black migration from the South to the cities north, east, and west, where growing Black communities, problems of Black delinquency, and demands for equal rights compelled juvenile courts to act. The most important legal victory of the Black child saving movement came in the decision of *Brown v. Board of Education,* declaring segregation inherently unequal. National Association for the Advancement of Colored People (NAACP) lawyers would later use *Brown* to force the desegregation of juvenile court communities.

Ironically, and rather tragically, the disproportionate confinement of Black youth in juvenile institutions today would not exist but for the achievements of the Black child saving movement; it is important to note, however, that Black child savers were not interested in the equal proportional representation of Black youth in institutions, but securing youth and community access to citizen-building ambitions and by extension the American dream. Its many limits, failures, and ironies notwithstanding, the Black child saving movement was effective in reconfiguring prevailing "color lines" of juvenile social control, not by making race insignificant, but by pushing Black youth and community stakeholders into child welfare networks of juvenile social control, uplifting the deliberative racial democracy of American juvenile justice.

In closing, there is a long history of research on child saving initiatives, and much of this research constitutes the best historiography in American criminology and justice studies. However, there is still much that is misunderstood and unknown about the child saving movement. Child savers have often been characterized as powerful and coercive agents of control, imposing social norms, authority, and discipline upon the marginal and powerless among them, but new research is revealing many other streams of civic engagement, ambition, and influence that defy reduction to any particular logic and illustrate that progressive politics also informed juvenile justice reform efforts. What is clear is that child saving brought various social actors into a protracted democratic experiment, where they worked in cooperation with some, and struggled against others, to build their more "ideal" nation through juvenile social control. Further research is still needed to fully grasp the complex and varied sociological origins, organization, politics, and historical significance of the "child savers" and their movements. If the Black child savers are any indication, the more this research incorporates the neglected voices of "other" Americans, and their American dreams, the more it will likely discover and usefully reveal about the true history, and present significance, of this fascinating and transformative movement.

Geoff Ward

See also Delinquency Prevention; Family and Delinquency; Houses of Refuge; Reformatories

Further Readings

Bailey, V. (1987). *Delinquency and citizenship: Reclaiming the young offender, 1914–1948.* New York: Oxford University Press.

Billingsley, A., & Giovannoni, J. (1972). *Children of the storm: Black children and American child welfare.* New York: Harcourt.

Odem, M. (1995). *Delinquent daughters: Protecting and policing adolescent female sexuality in the United States, 1885–1920.* Chapel Hill: University of North Carolina Press.

Platt, A. (1969). *The child savers: The invention of delinquency.* Chicago: University of Chicago Press.

Schlossman, S. (1977). *Love and the American delinquent.* Chicago: University of Chicago Press.

Tanenhaus, D. (2005). *Juvenile justice in the making.* New York: Oxford University Press.

CHINESE EXCLUSION ACT

The Immigration Act of 1882, popularly known as the Chinese Exclusion Act, was the first major and the only federal legislation that banned immigrants explicitly based on a specific nationality. It represented one of the darkest moments in the history of U.S. race policy, set the precedent for later restriction against immigration of other races and nationalities, and started a new era in which the country became a gate-keeping nation.

The Act

The Chinese Exclusion Act was passed by Congress and signed by President Chester A. Arthur in 1882. The act lasted for 10 years and was extended for another 10 years by the 1892 Geary Act. The basic exclusion law prohibited Chinese laborers, who were defined excludable as "both skilled and unskilled laborers and Chinese employed in mining" (Chinese Exclusion Act), from entering the United States; subsequent amendments to the law prevented Chinese laborers who left the United States from returning. Later measures limited the access of the Chinese to bail bonds, required that they carry identification certificates or face deportation, and restricted the categories of persons who could enter to teachers, students, diplomats, and tourists. In 1902, Congress closed the gate to Chinese immigrants entirely by making the Geary Act extension permanent.

The Chinese Exclusion Act was repealed in 1943 with the passage of the Magnuson Act, which permitted a quota of 105 Chinese immigrants annually. Various factors contributed to the repeal, such as the quieted anti-Chinese sentiment, the establishment of quota systems for immigrants of other nationalities who had rapidly increased in the United States, and the political consideration that the United States and China were allies in World War II.

Causes and Effects

Many scholars explain the exclusion laws as a product of the widespread anti-Chinese movement in California in the second half of the 19th century. The Chinese had constituted a significant minority on the West Coast since the mid-19th century. Initially, they labored in the gold mines, where they were more adept than White American miners at finding gold. As a result, the Chinese encountered hostility and were gradually forced to leave the field and move to urban areas such as San Francisco, where they continued to perform some of the dirtiest and hardest work. Americans in the West persisted in their stereotyping the Chinese as degraded, exotic, dangerous, and, outrageously, competitors of jobs and wages. California Senator John F. Miller, who introduced the bill to bar Chinese immigrants, argued that the Chinese workers were "machine-like…of obtuse nerve, but little affected by heat or cold, wiry, sinewy, with muscles of iron." Therefore, restricting the influx of Chinese into the United States through federal legislation became one of the goals of organized labor in the West. In other words, the exclusion was the result of a grassroots anti-Chinese sentiment. Other scholars argued that the exclusion should be blamed by top-down politics rather than bottom-up movement, explaining that national politicians manipulated the White workers to gain electoral advantage. Still others adopted a "national racism thesis" that focused on anti-Chinese racism in early American national culture.

The exclusion laws had dramatic impacts on Chinese immigrants and communities. They significantly decreased the number of Chinese immigrants into the United States and forbade those who left to return. According to the census in 1880, there were 105,465 Chinese in the United States, compared to 89,863 by 1900 and 61,639 by 1920. Immigrants were placed under a tremendous amount of government scrutiny and were often unfairly excluded from the country. In 1910, the Angel Island Immigration Station was established, where upon arrival a Chinese immigrant could be detained from weeks to years before being granted or denied entry. Chinese communities underwent dramatic changes too. Families were forced apart and businesses were closed down. There emerged a largely bachelor society that lacked the capacity to reproduce due to the severe restrictions on female immigrants and the pattern of young men migrating alone. Under the continuing anti-Chinese pressure, Chinatowns were established in urban cities where the Chinese could retreat into their own cultural and social colonies.

The excluded Chinese, however, did not passively accept these laws and unfair treatments but rather used all types of tools to challenge these laws or to circumvent these laws. One such tool was the U.S. judicial system. Despite coming from a nation without a litigious tradition, Chinese immigrants learned quickly to use courts as a venue to fight for their rights and won many cases in which ordinances that aimed against the Chinese were declared unconstitutional by either the state or federal courts. They also protested against racial discrimination through other venues, such as the media and petition.

Some Chinese simply evaded the laws altogether by illegal immigration. In fact, illegal immigration became one of the most significant consequences of the Chinese exclusion era. Despite the disproportionate time and resources spent by U.S. immigration officials to control Chinese immigration, many Chinese migrated across the borders from Canada and Mexico or used fraudulent identities to enter the nation. The "paper son" system was a common strategy, through which young Chinese males attempted to enter the United States on identity papers that claimed they were sons of U.S. citizens but that had in fact been bought for them. Thus, the Chinese exclusion is not only an institution that produced and reinforced a system of racial hierarchy in immigration law, but also a process that both immigration officials and immigrants shaped and a site of power dominance, struggle, and resistance.

The impact of the exclusion laws went beyond restricting, marginalizing, and, ironically, activating the Chinese. For the first time in its history, the United States changed its open immigration policy and started exerting federal control over immigrants and gradually setting criteria in terms of race, gender, and class to determine who could be admitted into this country. Immigration patterns, immigration communities, and racial identities and categories were significantly affected. The very definition of what it meant to be an "American" became more exclusionary. Meanwhile, Chinese exclusion practices shaped immigration law during that time period. Believing that courts gave too much advantage to the immigrants, the government succeeded in cutting off Chinese access to the courts and gradually transferred administration of Chinese exclusion laws completely to the Bureau of Immigration, an agency operating free from court scrutiny. By 1910, the enforcement of the exclusion laws had become centralized, systematic, and bureaucratic.

Yuning Wu

See also Deportation; Immigration Legislation; Japanese Internment; Race Relations

Further Readings

Chan, S. (Ed.). (1991). *Entry denied: Exclusion and the Chinese community in America, 1882–1947.* Philadelphia: Temple University Press.

Gyory, A. (1998). *Closing the gate: Race, politics, and the Chinese Exclusion Act.* Chapel Hill: University of North Carolina Press.

McClain, C. (1994). *In search of equality: The Chinese struggle against discrimination in nineteenth-century America.* Berkeley: University of California Press.

Salyer, L. (1995). *Laws harsh as tiger: Chinese immigrants and the shaping of modern immigration law.* Chapel Hill: University of North Carolina Press.

CHRISTOPHER COMMISSION

The Independent Commission on the Los Angeles Police Department, informally named the Christopher Commission after its chair, Warren Christopher, was a panel charged by Los Angeles Mayor Tom Bradley to give a comprehensive report on the use of excessive force by members of the Los Angeles Police Department (LAPD) during police–citizen encounters. The commission was formed in response to the beating of Rodney King on March 3, 1991. King was brutally beaten by four members of the LAPD who had stopped him after he led them on a high-speed chase. Three of the officers were charged with excessive use of police force, and a fourth was charged with failure to prevent the assault; all were acquitted. This entry examines the context and purpose of the Christopher Commission, its findings, and the subsequent response.

The race of the LAPD officers and King and his passengers played a significant role in the post–vehicle pursuit incident. The four police officers who were directly involved in the brutal beating of King were White; King and his two passengers were African American. At the time of the incident, questions were raised about the harsh treatment that racial and ethnic minorities received from LAPD officers. Also, it was thought that African Americans and Latinos were treated much more harshly than other racial/ethnic groups in their encounters with police officers. Many critics believe that the prevalence of such practices (and the underlying attitudes) partly explain why none of the other LAPD officers present attempted to prevent or minimize the harsh treatment of King and his passengers.

King and his passengers, Bryant Allen and Freddie Helms, were ordered to get out of the car at the conclusion of the pursuit. At first, King refused to comply with the order, but Allen and Helms immediately got out of the car and followed the officers' orders to lie flat on the ground in the "prone-out" position. They were handcuffed and ordered to keep their heads on the ground. Helms indicated that when he lifted his head to get it out of the dirt, he was kicked in the side of the head and hit with a baton until his head was bleeding. Allen stated that he was kicked several times when he lifted his head to see why King was screaming. After King's beating, the officers handcuffed him, and they pulled Allen and Helms to their feet. They took Allen and Helms to one of the California Highway Patrol (CHP) squad cars and checked their identification; when it was verified by computer the two of them were released at the scene.

In its July 1991 report, the Christopher Commission reported that they had found a culture of racial bias and intolerance among a large percentage of LAPD officers. That perceived culture of racial intolerance makes the study of the Christopher Commission of significant relevance to the study of issues associated with race and crime. The Christopher Commission was given the responsibility of investigating and making recommendations about the specific operating structure of the LAPD. In his charge to the commission, Mayor Bradley made it clear that their work would not entail examining individual complaints against the LAPD. Instead they were to investigate the level of responsiveness and accountability of the LAPD to community concerns and to provide a better understanding of what impact, if any, LAPD practices may have on the investigation and prosecution of alleged use of excessive force and other related departmental procedural issues.

Christopher, the commission's chair, was a former deputy attorney general of the United States and secretary of state in the Clinton administration. Other members of the commission included John Arguellas, the vice chair and a retired Justice of the

Supreme Court of California, and other prominent members of the business and legal professions.

Need for the Christopher Commission

The Christopher Commission was created in response to the brutal beating of Rodney King. The behavior of the LAPD and other public safety officers called into question police use of force, in general, and particularly the excessive use of force against racial and ethnic minorities. The public observed behavior displayed by the LAPD in that incident that did not instill a great deal of confidence in the ability of law enforcement officers to treat criminal suspects with dignity and respect.

What the public saw was that Rodney King was brutally beaten by three LAPD officers in the presence of a White LAPD sergeant of supervisory rank and representatives from other California law enforcement agencies who were a racially and ethnically diverse group of police officers. All of these law enforcement officers stood by and did nothing to prevent the continued beating of Rodney King. Therefore, it was not only the actions of the three White officers who directly participated in the beating, but also the inaction of the bystanding officers that caused a public outcry. Rodney King's race and the race/ethnicity of the police officers who battered him were closely examined by the commission in an attempt to determine if they were the primary precipitating factors in the incident. In the next section, the race and ethnicity of the police officers and of Rodney King and his companions are scrutinized a bit more closely to determine their role in what happened on that night in March 1991.

The Commission's Examination of the Relevance of Race

The Christopher Commission found evidence that race did matter when considering how the LAPD responded to various segments of the community. Citizens who testified before the commission stated that African Americans and Latinos were consistently treated in a disrespectful manner; they were harassed and police dogs were used more frequently in their neighborhoods than in White neighborhoods. The commission investigated these issues extensively and found that a great deal of the

testimony could be corroborated. In their investigation, the commission found that the South and Central LAPD bureaus used police canine units for more searches and apprehension of suspects and had a large percentage of criminal suspects who were bitten by the dogs. Upon closer examination, it was found that the South and Central Police bureaus provided law enforcement assistance to neighborhoods that were predominantly African American and Latino. Throughout the LAPD, police dogs were used to threaten and intimidate suspects. But, in most instances, the race of the suspect was a key factor in requesting that a police dog be sent to the scene of an investigation. There were also minority citizens who testified before the commission that they were frequently treated with disrespect and verbally abused on a regular basis by LAPD officers. Numerous minority citizens reported a particularly degrading way that they were treated, many times during informal contacts with police officers.

According to the Commission Report, the citizens found it very demeaning when they were ordered into the "prone-out" position. The prone-out position was described as a control technique used by LAPD officers, where they order the person to lie flat on the ground on their stomach, with their arms stretched out to the side. The commission reported that they received numerous accounts from African American and Latino males indicating that they were ordered into the prone-out position after being stopped for minor traffic violations. What the commission found was that African American or Latino males had a greater chance of being a victim of excessive use of force by police than any other group of people living in Los Angeles at that time.

The Post–Christopher Commission LAPD

The Christopher Commission made several recommendations, but none of them as crucial as the one about excessive use of force. A major finding in the Commission Report was that LAPD officers consistently used excessive force against members of the public, in direct violation of the department's written policy on the use of force. Therefore, the commission stated that the problem of excessive use of force was directly related to poor management and oversight of subordinates. The officers had no fear of punishment or disciplinary action from their direct supervisors. The report went further and stated that citizen trust and confidence in the LAPD could not be restored until management moved beyond making excuses for bad police officer behavior and began terminating those who consistently used excessive force and abused their position of authority in police–citizen encounters.

Another significant recommendation by the commission was that the problem of excessive use of force was deeply intermixed with racial and ethnic discrimination against the very people that the police agency was supposed to protect and serve. It was found that the officer's transmitted radio communications were full of racial prejudice and hatred. These messages were transmitted in violation of the LAPD policy against such messages and they were conveyed without any concern about possible punishment. It was evident that police supervisors either did not monitor the communications or were active participants. Relative to this problem, the commission recommended that the LAPD chief take an active leadership role in creating and disseminating policy that makes it clear that racial and ethnic discrimination, internal and external to the department, would not only not be tolerated but would be severely punished.

Human Rights Watch conducted an investigation of the commission's finding in 1997, a full 6 years after the final report was submitted to the Los Angeles mayor, and found that many of the most critical recommendations had not been fully implemented. On the issue of officer use of excessive force, especially against minority citizens, they found limited improvements. According to Human Rights Watch, the LAPD still lacked a comprehensive system designed to effectively manage officer use of force.

Progress on implementing many of the pivotal Christopher Commission recommendations was slow and in some instances nonexistent. Such slow progress caused community and government officials to question Los Angeles's commitment to righting the wrongs detailed in the Commission Report. As the Rodney King and similar types of abusive incidents faded into the past, the desire for quick action that was specified in the commission's recommendations also faded and was not a high priority for a new mayor and new police chief.

Benjamin S. Wright

See also King, Rodney; Police Accountability; Police Use of Force

Further Readings

Gates, D. F., & Shah, D. (1992). *Chief: My life in the LAPD*. New York: Bantam.
Human Rights Watch. (1998). *Shielded from justice: Police brutality and accountability in the United States*. New York: Human Rights Watch.
Williams, W. L., & Henderson, B. (1996). *Taking back our streets: Fighting crime in America*. New York: Scribner.

CIA Drug Scandal

During the cold war, the Central Intelligence Agency (CIA) cooperated with drug traffickers who assisted the United States in military and covert operations against Communist-aligned insurgents and governments around the world. This alliance with drug criminals immunized traffickers from law enforcement investigation and prosecution and contributed to the contraband that was imported into the United States, with devastating consequences for minority communities.

CIA complicity in the global drug trade seems to have begun in the 1950s, when the agency collaborated with Corsican criminal syndicates in Marseilles, France, to curtail Communist influence on the city's docks at a time when the Corsicans were becoming the United States' leading supplier of heroin. During that decade, the CIA also supplied anti-Communist forces in Burma with arms and air logistics that they used to build a burgeoning trade in opium.

One of the most well known cases of CIA complicity occurred during the Vietnam War when the agency enlisted the support of General Vang Pao, the leader of an army of Hmong tribesmen in Laos whose primary cash crop was opium. Vang Pao operated a laboratory for the conversion of opium to heroin at CIA headquarters in Long Cheng, in northern Laos, and the agency permitted him to use its airline, Air America, to transport drugs. Some of the profits from the Southeast Asian drug trade were allegedly laundered through the Nugan Hand Bank, an Australian institution that had a branch in

Thailand. Several CIA officials, including former CIA Director William Colby, had close ties with this bank, and Drug Enforcement Administration (DEA) agents reported that their investigation into this drug network was blocked by the CIA.

During the 1980s, the same pattern of complicity and interference in DEA investigations was a by-product of the CIA's support of Afghan guerrillas who were resisting the Soviet Union's invasion of their country, as well as the agency's involvement with contra insurgents who were working with the United States to overthrow the Sandinista government of Nicaragua. In the latter case, CIA cargo planes and airstrips that were used for the illegal transport of arms to the contras were exploited by traffickers to smuggle drugs from Latin America into the United States. Proceeds from the drug trade also were used by the contras to fund the anti-Sandinista military campaign. This CIA complicity, which was investigated in the mid-1980s by a Senate subcommittee on Terrorism, Narcotics, and International Operations headed by John Kerry, included tolerance of drug trafficking by Panamanian dictator Manuel Noriega and the notorious Colombian Medellín cartel. One drug trafficker, John Hull, a rancher from the United States living in Costa Rica, was a CIA agent or asset who operated a half-dozen airstrips protected by the agency that were off limits to local police and customs officials.

Perhaps the most controversial allegation of CIA involvement in the Latin American drug trade was advanced by reporter Gary Webb in an investigative series published in the *San Jose Mercury News* in 1996. Webb exposed a connection between the contra drug network and Danilo Blandon, a former Nicaraguan official who lived in California. Webb claimed that the contra-Blandon connection was a significant part of the low-cost crack cocaine market that emerged in some African American communities in the 1980s. Blandon allegedly supplied "Freeway Rick" Ross, an African American drug dealer in Los Angeles, with tons of cocaine that Ross converted to crack to build a burgeoning drug business that spread throughout California and the Midwest. Webb further alleged that the CIA had provided the Blandon-Ross network with immunity from investigation and prosecution by local law enforcement, the DEA, and U.S. customs during the time of the anti-Sandinista operation. In

the late 1980s, after the operation had ended, Blandon and Ross lost their protection and were prosecuted. While Ross received a 10-year prison sentence, the U.S. Justice Department arranged to free Blandon and repatriate him to Central America.

Webb's exposé outraged African Americans, some of whom accused the CIA of willfully attempting to inundate their communities with drugs. When then-CIA Director John Deutch denied any CIA complicity, more than 2,000 protestors marched in the streets of Los Angeles demanding an official investigation. Maxine Waters, a Los Angeles congresswoman and leader of the Congressional Black Caucus, wrote a letter to the U.S. attorney general charging that the city she represented may have been introduced to crack cocaine because of the actions of U.S. government officials. At this point, President Bill Clinton instructed Deutch to attend a public meeting in Los Angeles where he faced some 800 angry African Americans and promised a full investigation of the story that had appeared in the *Mercury News*.

Subsequently, a CIA investigation was launched under the direction of Inspector General Frederick Hitz. Seventeen investigators conducted 365 interviews and examined 250,000 pages of documents over a period of about one-and-a-half years and published a two-volume report. When Hitz formally presented the report to Congress in 1998, he said he had found no evidence that the CIA as an organization or anyone in its employ had been involved in trafficking that brought drugs into the United States. Hitz was parsing words, however, because he admitted that there were in fact instances in which the CIA had not terminated relationships with individuals who were alleged to be involved in drug trafficking, nor had the agency made any effort to investigate such allegations. Hitz also told Congress that at the start of the contra operation in 1982, the CIA had reached an understanding with U.S. Attorney General William French Smith that it would not report drug trafficking violations by "nonemployee" assets to law enforcement authorities.

Ronald J. Berger

See also Asian American Gangs; Asian Americans;
   Crack Epidemic; Drug Trafficking

Further Readings

Chambliss, W. J. (1988). *On the take: From petty crooks to presidents* (2nd ed.). Bloomington: Indiana University Press.

McCoy, A. W. (2003). *The politics of heroin: CIA complicity in the global drug trade* (Rev. ed.). Chicago: Lawrence Hill.

Scott, P. D., & Marshall, J. (1991). *Cocaine politics: Drugs, armies, and the CIA in Central America.* Berkeley: University of California Press.

CIVIL RIGHTS

See Black Codes; *Brown v. City of Oneonta*; *Brown v. Mississippi*; Death Penalty; *Escobedo v. Illinois*; *Illinois v. Wardlow*; *Mapp v. Ohio*; *Maryland v. Wilson*; *Miranda v. Arizona*; *Moore v. Dempsey*; *Norris v. Alabama*; Petit Apartheid; Profiling, Ethnic: Use by Police and Homeland Security; *Terry v. Ohio*; *United States v. Armstrong*; *United States v. Booker*; *United States v. Brignoni-Ponce*; *United States v. Wheeler*

COCAINE LAWS

Sentence disparities between powder and crack cocaine were enacted in 1986 under the Anti-Drug Abuse Act. This act imposed strict penalties for simple possession and/or trafficking of crack cocaine as a result of the crack epidemic of the early 1980s. A federal mandatory minimum sentence structure with very different penalties for crack and powder cocaine was enacted as part of the War on Drugs, which was based on the deterrence model of punishment that prevailed during the 1980s. This entry reviews the nature of the problem related to cocaine laws, their impact on African Americans, and attempts to equalize the cocaine and crack cocaine penalties.

One aspect that is of concern, when examining the disproportionate sentencing of African Americans, is whether cocaine users are more likely to be White than African American. Data from the National Survey on Drug Use and Health in the United States in 2004 showed that 1,508,000 White Americans and 347,000 African Americans had used powder cocaine in the previous month. Thus, many more White Americans use cocaine, yet fewer White Americans have been tried and sentenced under federal mandatory minimum drug laws. According to the survey, 66% of cocaine users were White Americans, while only 15% of cocaine users were African Americans. In 2004, the National Survey on Drug Use and Health reported that 281,000 White Americans and 246,000 African Americans had used crack cocaine in the previous month. However, in 2000, 85% of offenders sentenced by the federal government for mandatory minimum crack cocaine sentences were African American.

Mandatory minimum prison sentences have increased the number of individuals incarcerated for drug offenses. Because African Americans are overrepresented in the prison system, their removal from the family or community structure has a significant negative effect on their families and communities. Imprisonment often imposes great financial and emotional strain on families. The direct financial costs associated with incarceration can encompass bail, attorney fees, charges for pretrial confinement at the county jail, and loss of income during pretrial confinement and incarceration. The high incarceration rate for African American men and women also negatively affects the children of incarcerated parents. A large majority of these children live with their grandparents; however, 9.6% of state inmates' children are placed in foster care, and 3.2% of the children of federal inmates are placed in foster care. Thus, a disproportionate number of African American children are placed outside the home in the child welfare system.

Research has revealed that African Americans are arrested more frequently and punished more harshly than are White Americans. White Americans are often more affluent, and therefore they may use and possess drugs in their homes or in areas that are not in the "policing spotlight" of urban inner cities. Policing policies that put more officers in urban inner cities for special operations like drug stings account for some of the disproportionate arrest and incarceration rates of African Americans.

Federal mandatory minimum sentences for cocaine originated as a result of what has been termed the "crack epidemic"—what could be considered a "moral panic" created by the news media about the sudden increase in crack cocaine use in urban areas. As a result of the media hype and widespread citizen support, Congress adopted federal mandatory minimums for the possession of crack and powder cocaine. The adopted sentences exhibited discrepancies in sentence length of individuals arrested for possessing crack cocaine compared to those possessing powder cocaine. The ratio of crack and powder cocaine was set at a 100-to-1 level. Thus, for example, an individual caught possessing 5 grams of crack cocaine would receive the same 5-year mandatory minimum sentence as a defendant in possession of 500 grams of powder cocaine.

Most researchers have reached the consensus that crack cocaine and powder cocaine are pharmacologically identical. The main difference between crack cocaine and powder cocaine lies in the methods of production and consumption. A document compiled by the Sentencing Project identifies two reasons that addiction to crack cocaine is often viewed as more severe and/or dangerous than addiction to powder cocaine. First, crack cocaine is considered to be more dangerous and to have more potential for abuse because it produces very rapid, intense highs that last for only a short time. This experience can create a "want" or perceived "need" for more of the drug. The second reason that crack cocaine may have a higher potential for abuse and addiction is that crack is relatively cheap and more readily available than powder cocaine.

Another reason given to justify the sentence disparities between crack and powder cocaine is related to how and where the drug is sold. Because crack cocaine is cheap and easily available, it can be sold in many types of locations. The Sentencing Project mentions that crack is often sold in "volatile" open-air settings. Most of the violence associated with crack cocaine occurs while persons are attempting to obtain crack, as opposed to the effects of consuming it. Although powder cocaine can be sold in similar locations, sales of powder cocaine more often take place behind closed doors, due to the larger proportion and quantities that powder cocaine is often sold. Because crack is sold in lesser quantities, by lower-level dealers, to lower-income individuals desiring the drug, there seems to be "extra" violence associated with crack. Because powder cocaine is more expensive and most likely sold by individuals in larger organizations, with better protection, it seems logical for violence in the drug trade to be focused on crack as opposed to powder cocaine.

The U.S. Department of Justice makes the argument that crack cocaine is more harmful and dangerous than powder cocaine. However, they have only limited research to support this claim. Additional research is needed to refute or validate this claim. One argument is that in order to continue the mandatory minimum sentences, the dangerousness of crack must be supported through empirical evidence. If research established the imminent dangers of crack cocaine and showed that these dangers were greater with crack than with powder cocaine, such evidence would provide justification and quell some of the controversy regarding crack cocaine mandatory minimums.

Numerous research studies show the disproportionate number of African Americans incarcerated by mandatory minimum prison sentences because of crack cocaine legislation. Legislators and other politicians have been made aware of the racial disparity of crack cocaine mandatory minimums for quite some time. Data from the early 1990s revealed that nearly 90% of crack cocaine federal mandatory minimum sentences were applied to African Americans. More recent research indicates that nearly 100% of federal crack cocaine mandatory minimum sentences are applied to minorities. Little to nothing was done to change the mandatory minimum sentences for crack cocaine convictions until *United States v. Booker* (2005). The *Booker* case created an opportunity for the U.S. Sentencing Commission to recommend that Congress change the federal sentencing guidelines concerning crack cocaine. The ruling in *Booker* gives judges the ability to sentence outside of the sentencing guidelines as long as they can adequately justify their decision.

In two separate and unrelated federal crack cocaine cases after *Booker,* sentences that were lighter than those mandated by the federal sentencing guidelines were overturned on appeal. The appeals court ruled that judges could disregard the current 100-to-1 crack to powder cocaine sentencing guideline only when individual circumstances justified leniency toward the defendant. In these two cases, Judge Ernest Torres did not make his decision based on individual circumstances but stated that he disagreed in principle with the sentencing ratio.

A lack of research concerning the effects of crack and powder cocaine has forced legislators and politicians to continue to support the disparate sentences. In June 2005, Connecticut Governor Jodi Rell vetoed a bill to reduce crack cocaine sentences. In a press conference, Governor Rell acknowledged the concerns of the African American and Latina/o community and the disproportionate sentences imposed upon those communities, but that she would not reduce the crack cocaine possession penalties. Governor Rell called the proposed law that would decrease the crack cocaine sentence "a dramatic shift in our public policy regarding illegal possession, use, and sale of drugs" (Schain, 2005). This sentiment has also been expressed at the federal level, with the Justice Department expressing apprehension about any change to the laws (U.S. Department of Justice, 2002).

Even though the *Booker* case provided an opportunity to revisit the federal mandatory crack cocaine sentence guidelines, it does not mean that anything will change. In a very recent study of 24 cases of crack cocaine mandatory sentences after *Booker*, it was found that courts were likely to give harsh penalties for serious offenses and more likely to depart from the sentencing guidelines (mandatory minimums) if the defendant does not pose a great risk to society. Most of the courts in this particular study looked past the current mandatory minimums and sentenced according to the newest U.S. Sentencing Commission (USSC) recommendations. The USSC recommends a reform of the current 100-to-1 crack to powder cocaine ratio to a 20-to-1 or 10-to-1 ratio.

Numerous deviations and misclassifications of the federal mandatory minimum sentence policies have occurred. Originally, only midlevel and high-level crack cocaine and powder cocaine defendants were eligible for federal mandatory minimum sentences. However, the legislation has set the possession amounts much lower than what would be normal for a mid- to high-level dealer. Because of this error, most of the individuals who are incarcerated under mandatory minimum sentences (more than 60% of these inmates) are street-level dealers. The majority of offenders arrested and sentenced for possession of crack cocaine had a median of 52 grams, while midlevel drug dealers would be expected to possess at least 250 grams of crack cocaine (King & Mauer, 2006).

Prior research suggests that mandatory minimum sentences may not be most effective when fighting illegal drugs within the United States. According to the former director of the Office of the National Drug Control Policy, the focus and/or purpose is "reducing illicit drug use and its consequences" (RAND, 1997). According to a study completed by the RAND Organization, the policy of mandatory minimums for cocaine consumption and crime reduction is the least cost effective. If law enforcement agencies would focus more attention on arresting high-level dealers and provide treatment to heavy drug users, the results would be better. Just recently, as a result of the U.S. Supreme Court decision in *Kimbrough v. U.S.* (2007), the sentencing guidelines were adjusted and numerous inmates sentenced under the crack laws of the 1980s and 1990s became eligible for early release. In 2008, the releases began.

Michael Williams

See also Crack Babies; Crack Epidemic; Crack Mothers; Decriminalization of Drugs; Drug Dealers; Drug Sentencing; Drug Sentencing, Federal; Drug Trafficking

Further Readings

Benekos, P. J., & Merlo, A. V. (2006). *Crime control, politics, and policy* (2nd ed.). Cincinnati, OH: Anderson.

Betsey, C. (2005). Income and wealth transfer effects of discrimination in sentencing. *Review of Black Political Economy, 32*(3/4), 111–120.

Drug War Chronicle. (2002, March 29). Justice Department fights to maintain crack & powder cocaine sentencing disparities. Retrieved from http://stopthedrugwar.org/chronicle-old/230/sentencingcommission.shtml

Kimbrough v. United States, 522 U.S. __ (2007).

King, R., & Mauer, M. (2006). *Sentencing with discretion: Crack cocaine sentencing after* Booker. Retrieved from http://www.sentencingproject.org/Admin/Documents/publications/dp_sentencing_cc_afterbooker.pdf

Nadelmann, E. (2004). Criminologists and punitive drug prohibition: To serve or to challenge? *Criminology and Public Policy, 3*(3), 441–450.

RAND. (1997, May 12). *Study finds current sentencing laws undermine drug control goals.* Retrieved from http://www.rand.org/news/Press.97.98/mandatory .5.97.html

Schain, D. (2005). *Governor Rell vetoes crack cocaine sentencing bill: Asks for new bill, outlines proposals to address racial disparities.* Retrieved from http:// www.ct.gov/governorrell/cwp/view.asp?Q=293422& A=1761

The Sentencing Project. (n.d.). *Crack cocaine sentencing policy: Unjustified and unreasonable.* Retrieved November 11, 2008, from http://www .sentencingproject.org/pdfs/1003.pdf

U.S. Department of Justice. (2002, March 19). *Justice Department releases report analyzing crack and powder cocaine penalties.* Retrieved from http:// www.usdoj.gov/opa/pr/2002/March/02_olp_ 161.htm

U.S. Sentencing Commission. (2000). *Commission recommendations.* Retrieved from http://www.ussc .gov/hearings/test52202cht.pdf

U.S. v. Booker, 543 U.S. 160 (2005).

COCHRAN, JOHNNIE (1937–2005)

Johnnie Cochran was an African American lawyer and advocate of minority rights and equality of justice for everyone. He played an instrumental role in bringing attention to race and injustice in the criminal justice system in California as well as elsewhere in the United States. This entry examines the life of Johnnie Cochran and his contributions to the administration of justice as a prosecuting and defense attorney.

The Beginning

Born in 1937, Johnnie Cochran, Jr., earned his bachelor's degree from University of California, Los Angeles in 1959 and a law degree from Loyola Law School (part of Loyola Marymount University) in 1963. Inspired by Thurgood Marshall, Cochran thought he could make a difference through practicing law. In 1963, he passed the California bar and took a job with the city of Los Angeles, serving as a deputy city attorney in the criminal division. He worked as a prosecutor until 1965, and then he began private practice.

By handling civil and criminal cases, Cochran became a prominent advocate for victims of alleged police brutality. A very influential case for Cochran was that of Leonard Deadwyler, a Black man shot and killed by police as he tried to rush his pregnant wife to the hospital in 1966. Cochran represented the Deadwyler family, and although he lost that case, Cochran realized that accountability for police brutality was an important issue for minorities, and that these types of cases deserved more attention. His involvement in such cases made him a well-known attorney in Los Angeles.

In an interesting move, Cochran worked for the Los Angeles County district attorney's offices in 1978 as the assistant district attorney. Cochran took on this role to broaden his political contacts and to alter his image. In the early 1980s, he went back to private practice and began delivering crucial wins for the Black community in civil lawsuits against police brutality. As Cochran's fame grew, celebrities began hiring Cochran to take on their cases.

Becoming a Household Name

One of Cochran's first major celebrity clients was Michael Jackson, whom Cochran represented after child molestation allegations were leveled against Jackson. Cochran was able to arrange an out-of-court settlement with the boy's family, and Cochran also had the case retired in such a way that no criminal charges were ever filed against Jackson concerning the incident.

Cochran is perhaps most known for his lead role in the "Dream Team" defense in the 1995 O. J. Simpson trial. Simpson was accused of the 1994 murder of his wife, Nicole Brown Simpson, and Ron Goldman. Cochran prepared a strong defense from the beginning of the trial and continually weakened the prosecutors' case. One of the crucial ways Cochran delivered this was by challenging the evidence and paying special attention to the racist attitudes (known as "playing the race card") of the police officers, especially those of one of the investigating officers, Mark Fuhrman. In the Simpson trial's summation, Cochran's famous words were, "If it doesn't fit, you must acquit," when reminding the jurors that Mr. Simpson's hand could not fit in the bloody glove that was recovered at the scene of the killings. The acquittal of the Simpson case instantly made Johnnie Cochran a national household name.

Cochran also represented Elmer "Geronimo" Pratt, a former Black Panther who spent 27 years in prison for a murder that he didn't commit. In 1997, Cochran helped Pratt get the conviction overturned, and Pratt was freed from the charges. In 2000, Cochran represented Sean "Diddy" Combs when he was indicted on stolen weapons' charges and bribery and won him an acquittal. Thereafter, Cochran vowed that he would take no further criminal cases because of their exhausting nature.

Accomplishments

Johnnie Cochran is the only lawyer in Los Angeles to receive both the Civil Trial Lawyer of the Year award and the Criminal Trial Lawyer of the Year award. Also, in 1995, the *National Law Journal* named him America's Trial Lawyer of the Year. He was also named one of the top 50 trial attorneys in America in 1999 by the *Los Angeles Business Journal*. Cochran was inducted into the American College of Trial Lawyers, a prestigious position only given to the top 1% of trial lawyers in the United States, and was a member of the International Academy of Trial lawyers, which is reserved for only the best trial lawyers in the world. He also has served as a role model for lawyers across the nation.

The Legacy

Johnnie Cochran died on March 29, 2005, at the age of 67, of a brain tumor. Upon his death, the middle school he had attended as a child was renamed in his honor. Formerly known as Mount Vernon Middle School, the Los Angeles school changed its name in 2006 to Johnnie L. Cochran Jr. Middle School, in an attempt to keep his legacy alive.

Cochran established the Cochran Firm in 1981. The firm currently has 20 office locations in 15 states. It is one of the premier plaintiff litigation and criminal defense law firms in the United States. Just Cochran's presence on cases resulted in many settlements due to his dominating presence. As a result of his dominant profile in the courtroom and his celebrity status, Cochran has been enshrined and parodied not only in professional settings but also in American pop culture. Cochran made it clear that he believed that race played a crucial role throughout society. He is remembered as a prominent figure in bringing racism in the criminal justice system to the forefront and attention of the public.

Kendra Bowen

See also O. J. Simpson Case; Police Use of Force; Race Card, Playing the

Further Readings

Cochran, J. (1996). *Journey to justice.* New York: One World/Ballantine.
Cochran, J. (2002). *A lawyer's life.* New York: Thomas Dunne.

CODE OF THE STREETS

Explanations for racial disparities in violence are tailored to further an understanding of variation at both the individual and aggregate levels of analyses. Commonly, conceptual arguments refer to the social-structural arrangements of society as a key cause of unlawful behavior. Many in fact look to the neighborhood for the sources of violence. Even the most disadvantaged Whites likely do not reside in a neighborhood approximating the impoverished conditions of moderately poor Blacks. Some attribute high rates of violent crime by Blacks to these conditions. But few claim that the disproportionate level of lethal crime committed by Blacks is an absolute product of structural forces existing at the state, city, or neighborhood level. Theorists argue that abstract properties intervene in the causal pathway, linking conditions like poverty, joblessness, and family structure to the individual's likelihood of engaging in violence. Elijah Anderson's term, the "code of the streets," represents a variant of a cultural concept purported to intervene between broader structural forces and violent crime committed by young Black males in urban centers. His writing merges key conditions across levels of analyses into a coherent explanatory narrative. This entry examines the origins of subcultural theory, Anderson's theory, and the current level of empirical support for the theory.

Theoretical Origins

Criminology has a rich history of attempting to understand configurations of criminal behavior through a cultural lens. Early theoretical models attributed a subculture to segments of the population *purportedly* most involved in violence, including working-class adolescents, Italians, southerners, and urban dwellers. A separate body of literature emerged along these lines that imputed a subculture to Blacks. According to models of this variety, Black males—plagued by a recent history of systemic racism and periods of brutality at the hands of the White majority— abided closely to alternative conduct norms embodied in a "culture of violence." These norms stipulated that persons deploy serious and even lethal aggression to resolve interpersonal disputes. Marvin Wolfgang and Franco Ferracuti, for instance, speculated that adversity in the African American experience was responsible for this cultural substrate, but this was never specified concretely. Further, theorists gave little weight to structural conditions and therefore were virtually silent as to whether oppositional norms were linked—in any way—to broader forces. By the early to late 1960s, following the publication of several contentious works in urban policy and sociology, the idea that deviant conduct norms explain violence among Blacks and lower-class persons became increasingly unpopular. The scholarly orientation in criminology at the time mirrored this trend. Ruth Kornhauser's critical evaluation of cultural models contributed further to the waning status of subcultural theory. However, there was a resurgence of interest in cultural models in the last decade of the 20th century, perhaps due to the explanatory limitations of purely structural explanations.

Violent crime rates climbed in America's cities throughout the 1970s and again in the 1980s. By the early 1990s, rates of homicide involving Black youth peaked at an unprecedented level. While this was occurring, many cities were witnessing structural decline brought about by large-scale transformation in the industrial sector. William Julius Wilson noted that urban communities were becoming distinguished by a disproportionate concentration of impoverished, female-headed Black families. Middle-class flight ensued, dense person-institution networks evaporated, and, in the wake of this, the urban poor grew increasingly isolated from mainstream role models. Wilson suggested that alternative behavioral protocols emerged from this milieu; these were less apt to assign negative sanctions to deviant and violent behaviors. Within this intellectual context, Elijah Anderson researched the cultural mechanisms driving violence in contemporary urban America.

Anderson's Perspective

Elijah Anderson's research expands on the cultural tradition in criminology. It shares themes found in ethnographies originating during the middle portion of the 20th century, demonstrating the diversity of conduct norms among residents of urban centers. His book *Code of the Street* is essentially a continuation of his writing on the nature of urban existence among poor African Americans. Similar to his predecessors, he focuses on the normative aspects of violent actions and specifically among urban Blacks. Anderson's approach, however, explicates the social structural, historical, and political backdrop against which these values subsist. Broadly speaking, his work is a rich description of the symbolic and behavioral patterns characterizing social life in urban areas. Evidence is presented in noncausal language. Analysts have deduced ideas from these observations and translated them into testable theorems. Anderson's study of the cultural origins of violence is perhaps better referred to as a "scientific" perspective, an ethnographic study affording important conceptual insight into the complex reality of urban life.

Anderson's perspective is not unlike others at the time with regard to the way structural organization affects the values shaping behavioral protocols. The cultural substrate he defines purportedly sanctions the use of violence. In contrast, Wilson insisted that violent behavior is simply tolerated, but not directed. Anderson argues that Black men residing in disadvantaged urban areas construct their identities early in life according to the standards of the oppositional culture. He proposes that the social "alienation" brought about by economic transformation has spawned an oppositional "street culture" or "street code" in inner-city settings. It supplies the "rules" regarding the proper way to defend oneself, and, at the same time, it assigns the normative rationale for those seeking to provoke aggressive actions. The code serves as a shared relational script by which both victims and offenders must abide if they are to successfully navigate their precarious social world. In this sense it is useful in the ecological context in which it exists. The content of the code is composed foremost of the "rules" to achieve honor; Anderson posits that deference is a valuable commodity in the subculture. Someone who is respected is better equipped to avoid potential threats of violence and the unwanted situation of being "bothered" by others. But perhaps more important, respect is an end in itself that affords the luxury of self-worth. By displaying a confident demeanor and wearing the appropriate attire, actors communicate a "predisposition" to violence. The street code requires actors to express their willingness to engage in physical aggression if the situation demands it. When an attack occurs, the code dictates that it should be met with a retaliatory response of like proportion. Otherwise, respect is undermined and the victim invites future attacks. With regard to victimization, how persons respond illuminates the broad cultural disparities between the conventional and the oppositional system. In the case of the former, persons who are victimized will either contact formal authorities or move on without rectifying the situation despite the degradation they experienced. In contrast, persons whose existence is dominated by the imperatives of the street code actively pursue a strategy for revenge. The former groups' status does not hinge on whether or not they avenge their aggressor; rather, rank is determined by their merit in conventional avenues.

Anderson notes that not everyone accepts the oppositional culture as a legitimate value system. The urban symbolic landscape is occupied by two coexisting groups of people: those who hold a "decent" orientation and those whose lives conform more closely to standards of the code—a group he refers to as "street." Decent people socialize their children according to mainstream values. They believe that success is earned, in part, by working hard and maintaining a law-abiding lifestyle. Parents in decent families rely on strict methods of discipline in order to socialize their children according to mainstream values. Cognizant of the hazardous social environment they occupy, decent parents establish curfews and keep a watchful eye on their children's activities. As opposed to decent families, street families are more devoted to the oppositional orientation embodied in the code. Their interpretations of their reality as well as their interpersonal behaviors rigidly conform to its precepts. Street families' orientation approximates that held by youths in the subculture envisioned in early cultural theories of crime. The cluster of values street folks abide by are antithetical to the precepts of middle-class, conventional existence. Furthermore, they place less emphasis on work and education, which is underpinned by their deep distrust in the formal structure as a whole. Most are financially handicapped, and whatever income they earn is "misused," spent on other priorities like "cigarettes" and "alcohol." Children of street families witness numerous incidents suggesting that violent aggression versus verbal negotiation is a means to achieve a desired end. For youth reared in a street family, their unfavorable early life experiences and the inept, aggressive socialization they receive culminate to shape their strong proclivity toward an orientation consistent with the oppositional code.

According to Anderson's portrayal, the cultural standards that decent and street families adhere to are diametric opposites. Since both groups are immersed in the same contextual environment, their orientations are prone to clash, though the aggressive posture of the street orientation generally prevails. Because of this circumstance, Anderson argues that decent folks have an incentive to become intimately familiar with the behavioral imperatives of the code; moreover, they must be prepared to momentarily perform them. The code represents an ecologically situated property directing individuals' behavioral responses, independent of their own culturally defined inclinations. Anderson's depiction of the code as a spatially bounded objective property is perhaps his most unique theoretical contribution.

Empirical Support

Researchers have developed a latent construct meant to capture the attitudinal components of the street code. Findings from survey data show that youth who reside in disadvantaged neighborhoods and who feel discriminated against are likely to adopt this orientation. Results of other studies also indicate that the street code predicts violent delinquency and has a positive impact on individuals' odds of victimization. Kubrin and Weitzer reveal that retaliatory homicides—those reflecting subcultural imperatives regarding honor—are more likely to occur in disadvantaged neighborhoods. This finding closely coincides with the subcultural theory in general. Also, it supports Anderson's view that oppositional culture thrives in places lacking social-structural resources, where honor is an indispensable ideal. Much qualitative research also uncovers evidence in support of Anderson's claims regarding the nature of individuals' identification with the subcultural system. Echoing Anderson's observations, a prominent finding throughout the qualitative literature is offenders' desire for respect and status in their local context. The link between individuals' lack of faith in the justice system and adherence to the street code is also clearly illuminated in qualitative studies. In a paper by Rosenfeld, Jacobs, and Wright, informants report, for instance, that the cultural imperative opposing the criminal justice system is so salient within their neighborhoods that those who cooperate with the police risk their own lives.

To summarize, most empirical research is consistent with Anderson's perspective. Estimates tend to suggest that in disadvantaged urban areas—places disproportionately inhabited by Blacks—(a) behavior is shaped by an oppositional cultural orientation that assigns less credibility to conventional modes of conduct, and (b) such value systems are influenced by contextual factors. With respect to the question of whether values favoring violence predict violent behavior, a significant body of evidence indicates that oppositional values in fact vary closely with involvement in violence. Results also show that values measured in the aggregate affect individuals' behavior independent of their own commitment to these values; Anderson's observations regarding decent and street orientations seem to anticipate this finding.

Research Directions

The weight of the empirical evidence fails to disconfirm the idea that nonconventional culture plays a powerful role in stimulating violent behavior. Again, what appears untenable is the notion that Black violence is driven by an inherent subculture. Despite this, research focused on high rates of violence among the Black population has not abandoned cultural explanations entirely. Robert Sampson and William Julius Wilson link structural social organization to cultural organization to formulate a unified ecological model of violence. They propose that Black violence is the outcome of social disorganization as well as cultural social isolation and that both processes are produced from extreme structural disadvantage. Sampson and Wilson's logic assumes that since Black communities disproportionately experience structural disadvantage, they also disproportionately experience the processes that fuel violent crime. Under the same social structural conditions, Blacks and Whites should exhibit similar rates of involvement in violent offending.

Mark T. Berg and Eric A. Stewart

See also At-Risk Youth; Family and Delinquency; Social Disorganization Theory; Subculture of Violence Theory

Further Readings

Anderson, E. (1999). *Code of the street: Decency, violence, and the moral life of the inner city.* New York: Norton.

Hannerz, U. (1969). *Soulside: Inquiries into ghetto culture and community.* New York: Columbia University Press.

Kornhauser, R. (1978). *Social sources of delinquency.* Chicago: University of Chicago Press.

Sampson, R. J., & Wilson, W. J. (1995). Towards a theory of race, crime, and urban inequality. In J. Hagan & R. D. Peterson (Eds.), *Crime and inequality* (pp. 37–54). Stanford, CA: Stanford University Press.

Sellin, T. (1938). *Culture conflict and crime.* New York: Social Science Research Council.

Stewart, E., & Simons, R. (2006). Structure and culture in African-American adolescent violence. A partial test of the code of the street thesis. *Justice Quarterly, 23,* 1–33.

Wilson, W. J. (1987). *The truly disadvantaged: The inner city, the underclass, and public policy.* Chicago: University of Chicago Press.

Wolfgang, M. E., & Ferracuti, F. (1967). *The subculture of violence.* London: Tavistock.

COINTELPRO AND COVERT OPERATIONS

COINTELPRO is the acronym used to refer to counterintelligence programs conducted by the Federal Bureau of Investigation (FBI) to discredit and neutralize organizations considered subversive to U.S. political stability. These programs were covert and often used extralegal means to criminalize various forms of political struggle and derail several social movements in the United States. Contemporary race relations, political activism, and crime fighting are intimately intertwined in the context of these counterintelligence programs. The story of COINTELPRO is important to the study of race and crime because many Americans, including minorities, were the focus of COINTELPRO operations. This entry discusses early counterintelligence programs that target Puerto Ricans and African Americans involved with the Puerto Rican Independence movement and the Black Liberation movement.

The FBI has acknowledged conducting COINTELPRO operations between 1956 and 1971. These operations were allegedly abandoned after public and legislative scrutiny, though it remains unclear whether such activities have continued. COINTELPROs were initiated against various organizations, including the Communist Party, Socialist Workers Party (SWP), Puerto Rican Nationalists, Black Panther Party (BPP), and American Indian Movement (AIM). Their tactics included intense surveillance, organizational infiltration, anonymous mailings, and police harassment. These programs were exposed in 1971 when the Citizens Committee to Investigate the FBI burglarized an FBI office in Media, Pennsylvania, stole confidential files, and then released them to the press. More information regarding COINTELPRO was later obtained through the Freedom of Information Act, lawsuits lodged against the FBI by the BPP and the SWP, and statements by agents who came forward to confess their counterintelligence activities.

A major investigation was launched in 1976 by the Select Committee to Study Governmental Operations with Respect to Intelligence Activities of the U.S. Senate, commonly referred to as the "Church Committee," for its chairman, Senator Frank Church of Idaho. However, millions of pages of documents remain unreleased, and many released documents are heavily censored. In its final report, the committee sharply criticized COINTELPRO:

> Many of the techniques used would be intolerable in a democratic society even if all of the targets had been involved in violent activity, but COINTELPRO went far beyond that. . . . The Bureau conducted a sophisticated vigilante operation aimed squarely at preventing the exercise of First Amendment rights of speech and association, on the theory that preventing the growth of dangerous groups and the propagation of dangerous ideas would protect the national security and deter violence.

According to Ward Churchill and Jim Vander Wall in their 1990 book on the FBI papers, many COINTELPRO actions were not documented in writing and ex-operatives are now legally prohibited from disclosing them.

COINTELPRO and the Puerto Rican Independence Movement

The United States acquired Puerto Rico in 1899 after the Spanish-American War. In 1916, President Woodrow Wilson suspended voting until after the Jones Act was passed. This act conferred U.S. citizenship to Puerto Ricans, with all of its encumbered responsibilities, despite Puerto Rican sentiments.

In 1922 the Puerto Rican Nationalist Party (NPPR) was founded by Pedro Albizu Campos. He rejected the rule of the United States and called for a sovereign Puerto Rico. The island's police commander, Frank Riggs, with support from the FBI, launched a campaign to silence Puerto Rican nationalists like Campos. In response Campos declared that for every nationalist killed, a continental American would die. Thus, when police fired into a crowd of nationalists at the University of Puerto Rico on October 24, 1935, killing five of the demonstrators, the NPPR responded by assassinating Colonel Riggs. Campos and seven compatriots were arrested. After a mistrial, they were convicted and Campos spent the next 18 years in federal prison. Without Campos and hampered by FBI investigations, as well as the failure of assassination plots, the NPPR lost its momentum. However, the cause of Puerto Rican independence would continue to be a rallying call to Puerto Ricans.

COINTELPRO operations directed toward the Puerto Rican independence movement began in 1960 through a memorandum from FBI Director J. Edgar Hoover to the San Juan Senior Agent in Charge (SAC). According to Hoover, the SAC's goals were to disrupt, create doubt, and cause defections from the movement. The SAC was also directed to expose the Marxist leanings of nationalists and replace conservative pro-independence leaders with younger men who were more easily influenced by Marxism and agreeable to the use of violence.

Agents hired informants to raise criticisms of the leadership. Agents also investigated nationalists' weaknesses, specifically their morals, criminal records, spouses, children, family life, educational qualifications, and personal activities. According to Churchill and Vander Wall (1990), the FBI gave warnings to owners of local radio stations implying that their Federal Communication Commission (FCC licenses would be revoked if pro-independence material was aired. By spreading rumors, threatening radio stations with revocation of their FCC licenses, and branding nationalists as communist and pro-Cuba, the FBI was able to create factionalism among these groups.

In addition to the FBI's campaign to discredit nationalists, there are allegations that the FBI engaged in lethal violence against pro-independence organizers. According to Churchill and Vander Wall, there were 170 documented attacks—including beatings, shootings, and bombings of pro-independence activists and their organizations. One example is the Cerro Maravilla episode of July 25, 1978, which some historians consider a COINTELPRO operation despite official claims that the program had ended in 1971. Two activists, Arnaldo Rosado and Carlos Soto Arrivi, were killed. Official reports claimed they were planning to blow up a television tower. They reportedly fired on police and were killed when officers returned fire. However, a witness contradicted this story, stating that police officers executed the young men. His story was later corroborated by one officer, Julio Cesar Andrades, who testified that the assassination was planned by senior police officials with cooperation from the FBI. None of the police officers or other officials was ever tried or convicted for their role in the murders.

The FBI's COINTELPRO on Puerto Rican independence served to rein in the independence movement. In a referendum on July 23, 1967, Puerto Ricans voted to maintain commonwealth status. Though the FBI claimed to suspend COINTELPRO operations in 1971, several historians have provided evidence that operations persisted against Puerto Rican nationalists well into the 1980s.

COINTELPRO: The Black Liberation Movement and Black Panther Party

On the heels of FBI successes against the Communist Party, the Socialist Workers Party, and Puerto Rican nationalists, COINTELPRO Director William C. Sullivan sought to reallocate the Bureau's resources to fighting more mainstream revolutionaries within the country. He turned his attention to the Black liberation movement.

For years, the FBI had Martin Luther King, Jr., and his Southern Christian Leadership Conference (SCLC) under surveillance due to their association with the American Communist Party. Evidence suggests that as early as 1962, the FBI planted articles alleging that SCLC had communist connections. Despite efforts to discredit him, Dr. King was awarded the Nobel Peace Prize in 1964. Dr. King continued to be under FBI surveillance until his assassination in 1968.

With the assassination of King, Black Nationalism took on a more militant tone under leaders like Stokely Carmichael and H. Rap Brown of the Student Nonviolent Coordinating Committee (SNCC). Their cries of "Black Power!" were credited with inciting widespread riots between 1964 and 1968 in cities across the country. As a result, COINTELPRO–Black Nationalism Movement was initiated in a memo dated August 25, 1967. The goals of the COINTELPRO were (a) to prevent coalitions between groups; (b) to target key leaders; (c) to discredit them within the Black community, to other Black radicals, to the White community, and to any liberals who might sympathize with them; and (d) to prevent them from recruiting young people into the organization. The counterintelligence program targeted the activities of groups like SCLC, SNCC, Revolutionary Action Movement (RAM), Congress for Racial Equality (CORE), and the Nation of Islam. These groups were labeled violent hate groups in FBI papers.

The FBI was very effective in discrediting the Black Panther Party. The BPP was founded in Oakland, California, by students, including Huey P. Newton and Bobby Seale, in 1966. The organization was formed around a 10-point program for Black self-determination. Members exercised their constitutional right to bear arms for self-defense and formed patrols to deter both Ku Klux Klan attacks and police brutality. Newton and Seale were also social activists and created feeding programs for inner-city children as well as health care programs for poor residents. They promoted education while at the same time reaching out to street gangs and drug dealers to form a political base from the most oppressed and alienated sectors of the population. Their message resonated with inner-city Blacks. The BPP membership rose dramatically, from 5 in 1966 to more than 5,000 in 2 years. Hoover once said the Panthers were the greatest single threat to the internal security of the country.

The Bureau mounted a successful campaign against the BPP. According to Brandeis University professor Peniel Joseph, the FBI manipulated antagonisms between the BPP and United Slaves, which resulted in the deaths of several BPP members. They also targeted individuals in leadership positions. H. Rap Brown, BPP minister of justice, was arrested for inciting a riot in Maryland and later convicted of carrying a weapon across state lines. He was sentenced to 5 years in a federal prison. Stokely Carmichael's influence in the United States was minimized when agents planted documents making it appear that he was a CIA agent. A rumor was also circulated that a BPP hit team was looking for him and as a result he fled to Africa. In Los Angeles, another BPP leader, Eldridge Cleaver, was involved in a shoot-out with police. When Cleaver and his associates exited the building with their arms raised, police opened fire, killing Bobby Hutton and wounding Cleaver. Cleaver was charged with parole violations and attempted murder. He fled to Algeria to avoid prosecution. Fred Hampton and Mark Clark, BPP leaders in Chicago and Peoria respectively, were killed in a police raid. An FBI informant drew a map of the apartment where the men would be. Agents and police raided the apartment in the early morning hours. In the ensuing gun battle, Hampton and Clark were both killed. Similar raids occurred in Los Angeles, San Francisco, Chicago, Salt Lake City, Indianapolis, Denver, San Diego, and Sacramento with similar results. According to one FBI document, key Black activists were arrested repeatedly on any excuse until they could no longer make bail.

The FBI admits to conducting 233 separate COINTELPRO operations against the Black Panther Party between 1967 and 1971. As a result of the neutralization of key leaders, the success in creating factionalism within the BPP, the smear campaign to alienate supporters, and the use of the criminal justice system to threaten, harass, and intimidate members of the BPP, the organization faltered. Members either abandoned the party or joined other militant organizations such as the Black Liberation Army or the Weather Underground.

Nadine Frederique

See also Black Panther Party; Davis, Angela; LatinoJustice PRLDEF

Further Readings

Blackstock, N. (1975). *COINTELPRO: The FBI's secret war on political freedom.* New York: Vintage Books.

Churchill, W., & Vander Wall, J. (1988). *Agents of repression: The FBI's secret war against the Black Panther Party and the American Indian Movement.* Boston: South End Press.

Churchill, W., & Vander Wall, J. (1990). *The COINTELPRO papers: Documents from the FBI's secret wars against domestic dissent.* Boston: South End Press.

Joseph, P. E. (Ed.). (2006). *The Black Power movement.* New York: Taylor & Francis.

Joseph, P. E. (2006). *Waiting 'til the midnight hour.* New York: Holt.

Schmidt, O. (2005). *The intelligence files: Today's secrets, tomorrow's scandals.* Atlanta, GA: Clarity.

COKER V. GEORGIA

In the 1977 case of *Coker v. Georgia,* the U.S. Supreme Court case held that capital punishment, the death penalty, is grossly disproportionate to the crime of rape and is therefore prohibited by the Eighth Amendment as cruel and unusual punishment. This case is important to the study of race and crime because, before it was decided, African Americans were more likely to receive the death penalty for rape, especially in the southern states.

The facts, decision, and historical significance of the case are presented in this entry.

Ehrlich Anthony Coker was serving six separate sentences in the Ware Correctional Institution near Waycross, Georgia, including two terms of life imprisonment for assault, kidnapping, rape, and murder. Coker escaped from Ware Correctional Institution on September 2, 1974. At approximately 11:00 p.m. that same day, Coker entered through the unlocked kitchen door of the house occupied by Allen and Elnita Carver. Coker threatened the couple, tied up Mr. Carver in the bathroom, obtained a knife from the kitchen, and raped Mrs. Carver. Coker then took money and the keys to the Carver's car, forced Mrs. Carver to ride with him, and threatened her with death and serious bodily harm. Coker was apprehended by the police a short time later. He was charged and convicted on various counts, including rape. The jury's verdict regarding the rape count was death by electrocution. Coker appealed on the grounds that the death penalty for rape was cruel and unusual punishment under the Eighth Amendment. Most other death penalty cases at this time were racially based, revealing a disproportion toward African Americans. However, race was not an issue in this case, as Coker and his victims were White. Both the conviction and the sentence were affirmed by the Georgia Supreme Court. Coker was granted a writ of certiorari to the U.S. Supreme Court.

In *Coker*, the U.S. Supreme Court addressed the issue of the constitutionality of the death penalty when imposed for crimes other than murder, specifically, in this case, with respect to rape of an adult woman. The Court, in a split decision on June 29, 1977, ruled that capital punishment is grossly disproportionate to the crime of rape and is therefore prohibited by the Eighth Amendment as cruel and unusual punishment. Justice Byron White, joined by Justices Potter Stewart, Harry Blackmun, and John Paul Stevens, held in a plurality opinion that the death penalty, while not disproportionate in the case of murder, was "grossly disproportionate" and "excessive punishment" in the case of rape. Thus, Georgia's death penalty for rape was found unconstitutional.

In the proportionality analysis, comparing the type and severity of punishment to the crime committed, Justice White noted that although the crime of rape was serious and revealed "almost total contempt for the personal integrity and autonomy of the female victim," it did not compare with murder as it did not involve an unjustified taking of human life. Thus, the death penalty was held to be excessive.

As a result of the U.S. Supreme Court's holding in *Coker v. Georgia*, 20 inmates—3 White inmates and 17 Black inmates—who were awaiting execution on rape convictions around the country were removed from those death rows. The holding in *Coker v. Georgia* has been interpreted in some instances to state that the state and federal governments may not extend capital punishment to most nonmurder offenses. However, the Supreme Court has applied the proportionality rationale regarding capital punishment to later cases wherein it invalidated death penalty sentences for murders committed by mentally incapacitated individuals and youths and for the rape of a child.

The decision in *Coker* caused some dispute among the Supreme Court Justices hearing and deciding the case. Justices William Brennan and Thurgood Marshall filed separate concurring opinions, wherein they concluded the death penalty was cruel and unusual punishment in all cases, including intentional murder cases. While Justice Powell agreed that the death penalty was disproportionate punishment under the facts of the *Coker* case, because Mrs. Carver did not suffer what he considered to be serious or lasting injury, he dissented from the view that the death penalty would be unconstitutional in all rape cases. Specifically, he stated the death penalty could be imposed when the rape involved extreme brutality or caused serious lasting harm. Justice Warren Burger, with Justice William Rehnquist joining, dissenting, agreed that while the death penalty could not be imposed for "minor crimes," rape was not a minor crime, and consequently the death penalty in the case of rape did not in itself violate the Eighth Amendment's ban on cruel and unusual punishment. The Justices noted that the Supreme Court majority had not considered the total effect of the rape in terms of the suffering imposed on the victim as well as the victim's loved ones. Finally, Justice Burger noted that it should be left to the state to determine under what circumstances the death penalty constituted a proportionate sentence for rape.

Critics of the decision in *Coker v. Georgia* have argued that Justice White's statement that a rape victim's life "may not be nearly as happy as it was," but that the victim is still alive—unlike the victim of a murder—is a slighting of the harm incurred by the victim of rape. Critics also take offense at the wording by Justice Lewis Powell, wherein he states there was no indication that Coker committed the offense with excessive brutality or that Mrs. Carver sustained serious or permanent injury. Supporters of the decision agree that rape should carry a lesser sentence than intentional murder, arguing that the lesser punishment will provide some type of incentive for the rapists to not kill their victims. A counter-argument is made that if rape carried the death penalty as its punishment, rapists would have an incentive not to rape their victims in the first place.

On May 22, 2007, the Louisiana Supreme Court addressed the case of *State v. Kennedy*, in which the court imposed the death penalty on Patrick Kennedy, who had been convicted of raping his 8-year-old stepdaughter in Harvey, Louisiana. The Louisiana court held that it is constitutional to impose the death penalty for rape where the rape victim is a child. It should be noted here that the *Coker* decision by the U.S. Supreme Court left open the possibility that children constituted a protected class and did not rule out the Louisiana law. The Kennedy case was ultimately appealed to the U.S. Supreme Court. The Supreme Court held that the Eighth Amendment bars Louisiana from imposing the death penalty for the rape of a child where the crime did not result, and was not intended to result, in the victim's death.

George E. Coroian, Jr.

See also Death Penalty; Martinsville Seven; *Kennedy v. Louisiana*

Further Readings

Coker v. Georgia, 433 U.S. 584 (1977).

Kennedy v. Louisiana, 554 U.S. ____ (2008), 957 So. 2d 757, U.S. Supreme Court October Term 2007, Decided June 25, 2008.

Rise, E. W. (1995). *The Martinsville Seven: Race, rape, and capital punishment.* Charlottesville: University of Virginia Press.

COLONIAL MODEL

In an effort to explain high rates of crime and violence among African Americans, some criminologists have used the colonial model to analyze the effects of race and social class and their interactive effect on specific attitudes and behaviors.

The model has its foundations in the work of Frantz Fanon, who examined relations between majority and minority groups in colonial settings. According to this perspective, colonization occurs when one group forcibly takes over the country of another group. During this process, those who are colonized are then forced to adhere to the norms of the colonizer. As a result, the colonized are exposed to a different set of cultural standards that become the standard by which the native group will be measured. However, the colonized are then forced to exist within a colonial society with limited resources.

Scholars argue that Black crime can emerge as a result of the political and economic inequalities that propel many minorities into criminal lifestyles since their chances for equal justice under the law are minimized. From the perspective of the colonial model, racial disparities and inequality in the U.S. criminal justice system suggest that the colonizer (Whites) has targeted Blacks, resulting in higher arrest rates and lengthy prison sentences. Those who resist this colonial authority are seen as political prisoners. Robert Staples, who refers to the police as "internal military agents," has also noted the critical role the police play in maintaining order within the colonial society.

Colonialism and the Death Penalty

Throughout the history of the American justice system, Blacks and minorities have been overrepresented in criminal cases and prison sentences, particularly in cases involving the death penalty. Scholars have used colonial theory to analyze racial disproportionality in the prison population and in the application of the death penalty. Recent governmental and state-sponsored reports have found that Blacks and other minority defendants are more likely than White defendants to receive the death penalty for the same crime. Specifically, evidence has shown higher execution rates for Black defendant/White victim crimes compared to those in which the defendant is White and the victim is Black. The role of race and racism remains controversial, and it continues to be addressed by the U.S. Supreme Court and in other legal cases. According to some governmental reports, a majority of studies of racial discrimination in implementation of the death penalty show that the race of the victim correlates significantly with the death penalty (i.e., when a similar homicide under similar circumstances is committed by defendants with similar criminal histories, the defendant is several times more likely to receive the death penalty if the victim is White than if the victim is Black).

Several criminologists have noted that colonial theory is compatible with many conflict-theoretical analyses of American racism, emphasizing that Whites have systematically controlled and exploited racial minorities. Others have elaborated by pointing out that conflict theorists have tended either to ignore the role played by race in relation to criminal justice or to subordinate its significance to social class. As a result, these critics argue, conflict theorists have simply lumped all poor people together, regardless of their race/ethnicity, on that assumption that socioeconomic class is the major factor determining treatment in the criminal justice system. The evidence, however, remains consistent with the tenets of the colonial perspective.

A sense of threat emerges when Whites believe that Blacks' actions would loosen their controlling grip, and criminal behavior, particularly violent criminal behavior, can often produce that sense. Through the evaluation of the model, one can better see who, where, why, and how inconsistencies in the criminal justice system affect Blacks and other minorities.

Colonialism and Youth

The colonial model has furthered dialogue about the juvenile justice system in general and, specifically, about the transfer of juveniles to adult courts. Scholars have presented evidence that the primary purpose of the juvenile court, as well as the transfer of juveniles to adult court, is to control and punish minority youth rather than youth in general. Many politicians are forced to support such policies because of public pressure, resulting from perceptions and fear of crime shaped in large part by media coverage that contributes to a state of moral panic. Racial discrimination and bias in decision making then occur for various reasons throughout the processing of youths by juvenile justice officials and ultimately culminate in racially disparate rates of transfers to adult court. Scholars have noted that the causes of such discrimination making may include conscious and unconscious biases as well as differences in specific backgrounds. Compounding this injustice, current research suggests that treating juveniles as adults has no deterrent effect on serious juvenile crime and violence, and in fact is more likely to make things worse for the youths as well as the minority communities. The colonial model addresses the limitations of mainstream structural theories in explaining high rates of crime and violence among African American youth by speaking to the key precursor of these conditions: colonization. Making both inter- and intragroup comparisons, the perspective argues that lower-class African American youth, especially males, are at the greatest risk of selecting violent and criminal responses. The perspective is not without its criticisms. For example, Tatum notes that the model is often difficult to test empirically and often gives less attention to issues addressing class.

Further Research

Criminologists have suggested that one method of reducing the effects of colonialism would be to allow for greater community control of police. Proponents of the community policing proposal argue that in order to diminish negative views of police, the police should be required to live in their specific precincts. Others urge that greater emphasis be placed in ensuring that minority defendants are tried by a jury of their peers. Still others have noted that structural changes must occur to change economic conditions to reduce the impact of racism and discrimination within the administration of justice as it pertains to minorities who are most affected by the colonial power structure.

*Zina McGee, Tiffany Latham,
and Sophia Buxton*

See also Conflict Theory; Critical Race Theory; Dehumanization of Blacks; Minority Group Threat

Further Readings

Staples, R. (1975). White racism, Black crime, and American justice: An application of the colonial model to explain crime and race. *Phylon, 36,* 14–22.

Tatum, B. L. (1994). The colonial model as a theoretical explanation of crime and delinquency. In A. T. Sulton (Ed.), *African American perspectives: On crime causation, criminal justice administration and prevention* (pp. 33–52). Boston: Butterworth-Heinemann.

Tatum, B. L. (2000). *Crime, violence and minority youths.* Aldershot, UK: Ashgate.

Tatum, B. L. (2000). Toward a neocolonial model of adolescent crime and violence. *Journal of Contemporary Criminal Justice, 16,* 157–170.

Tatum, B. (2004). Trying juveniles as adults: A case of racial and ethnic bias? In M. D. Free, Jr. (Ed.), *Racial issues in criminal justice: The case of African Americans.* Monsey, NY: Criminal Justice Press.

COMMUNITY POLICING

Prefaced by an atmosphere of racial tension, activism, and civil unrest, community policing (COP) has emerged as one of the most profound police innovations of the 20th century. COP can be defined as a philosophy, strategies, tactics, or programs that seek to alter the traditional definition of policing from crime control to one of community problem solving and empowerment. Driven by the Crime Control Act of 1994, which provided federal funding for the hiring of COP officers, COP has flourished as an alternative to what many perceive as the inadequacy of professional policing to deal effectively with crime and resistance. Given the disparate impact of criminal justice processing on communities of color, the growth of COP provides a new opportunity to address the racialization of neighborhood crime and allows police greater resources to better assist communities in mobilizing against violence and disorder. This entry examines variations in the definition of COP, its historical development including the role of racial minorities and social science research, and an evaluation of COP programs.

Community Policing Defined

COP has been popularly defined by Robert Trojanowicz and Bonnie Bucqueroux as a new philosophy of policing based on police–citizen partnerships that work together in creative ways to solve community problems such as crime, fear of crime, disorder, and neighborhood decay. Fundamental to this philosophy is the ideal that citizens as active members of the community can be empowered to enhance the quality and safety of their neighborhoods rather than relying solely on police services. This broadened view of police recognizes that cooperation between police and the public will allow police greater access to information provided by the community, in turn fostering better police responses to community needs. While the actual definition of COP is highly debated, inherent to most COP models is the goal of establishing collaborative community–police partnerships, which address crime and disorder at the neighborhood level in a proactive, community-sensitive approach.

Still, COP exists in various forms in different environments, with models changing to meet the specific needs of the community involved. For some departments, this means a focus on activities that are designed to bring police officers closer to the communities they serve through increased foot and bicycle patrols, police decentralization through the use of substations, and the long-term assignment of officers to specific beats. In other departments, COP suggests more order maintenance and service delivery initiatives such as crime prevention programs and efforts that seek to revitalize disorganized neighborhoods.

History of COP

While early police practices illustrate many aspects of contemporary COP models, the call for police professionalism coupled with rapid innovations in technology led to increased distance between police and citizens. As police isolation, weakened community ties, and increased social and political protest offered evidence of the ineffectiveness of professional policing, criminologists and police administrators began to recognize the need for better community–police relations.

As with other reforms throughout history, the evolution of COP occurred within the historical context of American community–police relations. While many acknowledge the inherent difficulty of policing in a representative democracy, the historical role of American police has been to maintain the status quo by protecting politically powerful citizens. Thus, for communities with little or no access to political power, the road leading to COP was marred by injustice, over- and underenforcement, and fear.

Because the evolution of COP is indistinguishable from the development of American policing, George Kelling and Mark Moore's typology of policing eras serves as an adequate starting point. In the first period of policing, identified as the *political era,* the earliest functions of police were mainly crime control, prevention, and order maintenance, with foot patrol and rudimentary investigation being the primary police tactics. Police during the political era had close ties with the community they served, often residing in the same neighborhoods as their beats. While many contend that early forms of policing such as the watchmen system formed in the North prior to the political era, others note that the precursor to American policing occurred in the South with the creation of slave patrols in the 1700s. Akin to the watchmen system, slave patrols in the fashion of citizen obligation granted full power and authority to poor Whites in the apprehension of runaway slaves. In a critique of Kelling and Moore's work, Hubert Williams and Patrick Murphy contend that White owners combined foot and mounted patrol to prevent slaves from congregating and to repress any attacks upon the status quo.

While police were highly integrated into neighborhoods and provided services to communities with power, their closeness to political leaders and decentralized structure gave rise to police corruption and discrimination. In communities with no access to political power, the situation was very different. Early police officials and legal doctrine supported and sustained institutions, including slavery, segregation, and discrimination, that were injurious to Blacks and other minorities. Police were bound to uphold that order, which has served as a foundation for police behavioral patterns and attitudes toward minority communities that persist today. Williams and Murphy denote that as minorities have historically had fewer rights and freedoms, the task of police has been to control minorities, with little responsibility in protecting them from crime within their communities.

During the 1930s, the political era of policing yielded to a period of reform in which administrative control, police accountability, and professionalism guided public response. In hopes of combating corruption, officers became more distant from political and social communities and often had rotating shifts to prevent the formation of close bonds. The *reform era* also brought about police expansion of the military style of organization and administration modeled after Sir Robert Peel's efforts in England in the early 1800s. Still, for citizens without political clout, this shift in policing offered little reprieve from the injustice that had come to characterize the policing of minority groups.

Innovations in police technology also greatly affected community–police relations. In addition to motorized patrol, the creation of 911 dispatch systems allowed officers to respond quickly to crimes, which severely limited broad police interaction with communities. Moreover, as computers generated data on crime patterns and trends and increased the efficiency of dispatch and speed of police response, focus shifted away from community satisfaction with police services and furthered an "us versus them" mentality, elevated in communities with greater social distance separating citizens from police.

Beginning in the late 1950s and continuing into the following 2 decades, the police as a formal institution of government encountered perhaps its most alarming challenge as assaults on the legitimacy of police and the legal system gained nationwide attention. In the face of growing civil disobedience, national commissions were established throughout the mid-1960s and 1970s that documented widespread, systematic corruption among major policing departments and the use of aggressive tactics. Minorities played a key role in initiating the third era known as the *community era* as African Americans and middle-class Whites joined together to challenge police professionalism in the backdrop of the civil rights and antiwar movements. The political and social climate of this era, aggravated by historical injustices felt by minority citizens and widespread police corruption, provided the impetus for the transition in many police agencies from traditional to community oriented policing approaches.

The Role of Research

By the mid-1970s many police organizations were committed to improving policing methods through research, as federally funded victimization surveys for the first time documented the existence of unreported crime and resident fear of crime. Research throughout the 1970s paved the way for many contemporary COP programs by highlighting the success of COP tactics such as foot patrol, officer knowledge about beats, and fear reduction in improving citizen satisfaction and community–police relations. Early research studies, including the Kansas City Preventive Patrol, the Newark Foot Patrol Experiment, and the San Diego Police Department's Community-Oriented Policing project shed light on the limited ability of police to affect crime. Together, these efforts demonstrated that foot patrol and police interaction with the community could improve the attitudes of officers toward their jobs and communities as well as encourage them to develop creative solutions to complex problems and improve community attitudes of police. Thus, the 1980s ushered in a new era of community and problem-oriented policing that helped to reduce violent crime in several major cities. The introduction of the SARA (Scanning, Analysis, Responding, Assessment) model, CompStat, and other crime-mapping technologies has also refocused police attention on ecological approaches to crime prevention.

Evaluation of COP Programs

Early studies of COP focused on not only practices that enhance community–police relations but also those that reduce crime and disorder through the use of police crackdowns, strict code enforcement, and aggressive patrolling of quality-of-life offenses. One of the most well-known successes of this nature is that of Rudolph Giuliani and New York City. Variations of *broken windows policing* that address crime and disorder have also experienced crime reduction effects on the cities of Newark, New Jersey, and Denver, Colorado. Still, one of the most cited examples of COP was implemented in Chicago and studied by Wesley Skogan and Susan Hartnett. In an evaluation of the Chicago Alternative Policing Strategy (CAPS), researchers found residents in all five CAPS districts reported more favorable perceptions about police, including police responsiveness as a result of the CAPS effort. Residents' perceptions of police misconduct also declined, especially with respect to the African American population. However, Black and Latina/o residents were more doubtful than their White counterparts of the improvements in policing based on the CAPS efforts. Additionally, many of these districts, like most COP programs, suffered from a lack of citizen participation.

In a study of COP in Omaha, Nebraska, conducted by Vincent Webb and Charles Katz, residents ranked "preventative" COP activities lower than enforcement tactics that had a more direct effect on crime. Respondents with less education, however, rated "preventative" functions such as graffiti removal, trash cleanup, and youth programs as more important than did respondents with more education, suggesting residents' preferences for specific police functions often vary. This finding is complicated by evidence that many community members disagree with neighborhood police about which activities are the most beneficial.

In a more recent study that employed community data to assess residents' satisfaction with police, researchers concluded that residents who were familiar with neighborhood officers expressed higher levels of satisfaction than did other residents. This finding is specifically relevant, as numerous evaluations of COP suggest minority residents participate less in beat meetings and are generally less knowledgeable about the goals of COP. Other studies suggest COP produces only minimal and often transient effects on crime and fear of crime.

Despite the growth of COP programs, efforts to implement COP are often limited by a lack of commitment to longitudinal change and confusion and ambiguity associated with COP definitions. Hence, COP in practice may involve little philosophical or organizational change as popular COP tactics are simply added to existing police practices. One of the most important challenges facing COP is community mobilization. Given the history of minority–police relations and concerns of police legitimacy, as well as less satisfaction with police more generally, some minority residents simply chose not to become involved with police for any reason. Still, racial diversification within police departments may increase police sensitivity and encourage positive interactions between police and communities of color.

Recent examples of COP successes in communities of color include the case of Wichita, Kansas, and Austin and Fort Worth, Texas. Led by Chief Norman Williams, the first African American chief in the department's 129-year history, officers in Wichita through the implementation of COP tactics and "weed & seed" efforts (including monthly food programs and the development of a "community house") have greatly improved police–citizen interactions and lowered crime rates. COP efforts in both Austin and Fort Worth, Texas, have also credited increased citizen participation and closer community ties to significant drops in overall crime. Chief Gwendolyn V. Boyd, of North Miami, Florida, has also made significant strides in crime reduction in the city due in part to COP efforts, as the first Black and first female chief in the North Miami Police Department.

Altogether, the benefits of COP appear to be constrained by group status, as those on the bottom of the social ladder are largely unaffected by COP tactics while Whites, homeowners, and those better educated report the greatest results. The efficiency of COP is restricted in communities that are fragmented by race, class, and other lifestyle factors. As such, the effectiveness of COP in enhancing minority–police relations and mobilizing communities of color is not clear as implementation problems and limited citizen participation complicate questionable findings. While the implications of the new "war on terrorism" and growth of zero tolerance policing on COP efforts remain to be seen, routine negative experiences with police, cases of excessive force, and racial profiling continue to challenge the future of police–community relations.

Kideste M. Wilder-Bonner

See also Police Action, Citizens' Preferences; Profiling, Racial: Historical and Contemporary Perspectives; Violent Crime

Further Readings

Jones-Brown, D. (2000). Debunking the myth of officer friendly: How African American males experience community policing. *Journal of Contemporary Criminal Justice, 16,* 209–229.

Kelling, G., & Moore, M. (1988). The evolving strategy of policing. *National Institute of Justice, 4,* 3–27.

Morash, M., & Ford, K. J. (Eds.). (2002). *Community policing: Making change happen.* Thousand Oaks, CA: Sage.

Skogan, W. G., & Hartnett, S. M. (1997). *Community policing: Chicago style.* New York: Oxford University Press.

Trojanowicz, R. C., & Bucqueroux, B. (1990). *Community policing: A contemporary perspective.* East Lansing: Michigan State University.

Webb, V. J., & Katz, C. M. (1997). Citizen ratings of the importance of community policing activities. *American Journal of Police, 14,* 45–66.

Williams, H., & Murphy, P. (1990). The evolving strategy of police: A minority view. *National Institute of Justice, 13,* 29–51.

CONFLICT THEORY

Conflict theory is sometimes thought of as an alternative theory of crime and delinquency. In the 1960s and 1970s, conflict theorists such as George Vold, Austin Turk, and Richard Quinney began to call attention to the role of social structure and the distribution of political and economic resources in influencing who became enmeshed in the criminal justice system. Such theories were considered radical or outside the mainstream of well-established criminological theories (e.g., strain theory, social disorganization theory, differential association theory). It was radical to argue that theorists, researchers, and criminal justice public policymakers alike should turn their attention to the competition in society for sometimes scarce resources. It was even more radical to ask the question, "Who gets to say what is a crime and what the punishment will be for those who break the law?" Conflict theorists saw a plethora of evidence suggesting that those with the most power and money had the wherewithal to ensure that their group traditions, mores, and identified acceptable behaviors remained those to which all other groups must subscribe. Through the years, conflict theorists have been able to demonstrate, through scientific research, that early conflict theorists were correct in their assumptions. This entry reviews the contributions of Vold, Turk, Quinney, and others to an understanding of criminal behavior and discusses the relationship between the public policies and the conflict theory approach to criminology.

The basic underlying assumption of conflict theory is that every society is organized around tension among competing interest groups. At any given time, any one of these groups can gain control of the resources associated with the major political and economic institutions of society. The group that is able to garner a majority of these institutions' resources will decide under which laws the rest of society will live and what will be done to those individuals who break those laws.

In 1969, George Vold argued that groups form because of an underlying common interest that is in direct opposition to other groups. Vold argued further that the groups in power control institutions of control, such as the police, the courts, and other components of the justice system. This pendulum of control swings back and forth and has a major impact on those groups who continually find themselves at the bottom of the social order: the poor and those from historically disenfranchised populations.

In the 1960s and 1970s, Austin Turk wrote about the process through which crime is defined. Mirroring the arguments associated with labeling theories of crime, Turk argued strongly that crime is defined by those in power; these controlling groups are able to subjugate individuals who lack the resources of the majority in the political machinery of society. Turk suggested that through interactions with each other, people acquire either a superior or inferior status and, as a result, assume either a dominating or submissive role.

The evolution of conflict theories of criminology continued with Richard Quinney's 1970 book *The Social Reality of Crime*. Like Turk, Quinney saw criminal behavior as behavior that is defined by authorized agents in a politically organized society. Like his fellow conflict theorists, he believed that criminal behavior is that behavior that is in conflict with the interests of those groups with the power and the resources necessary to affect public policy. Further, Quinney argued that under capitalism, individuals engage in two types of crime: (1) crimes of accommodation, such as property or violent offenses, often directed at people within their own social or ethnic group, and (2) crimes of resistance, such as those acts committed by workers as a revolt against a system. For Quinney, crimes of accommodation are the result of false consciousness among individuals within a capitalist system. In other words, when brutalized by a capitalist economy, with more and more people having very little in material goods, individuals may turn to crime in order to survive or to become more like the ruling classes. Loss of opportunities to succeed often leads to psychological maladjustment coupled with actions that are destructive to themselves and the greater society in general.

Conflict Theory and Criminal Justice Policies

Conflict theory has been used to explain many public policies in the United States and other developed countries that seemingly target the poor and minority race and/or ethnic groups. For example, William Chambliss used conflict theory to explain the development of vagrancy laws as far back as the 14th century. In England, the Black Death killed nearly one half of that nation's work force. This critical occurrence drove up wages, much to the chagrin of the landowners. Chambliss argued strongly that these statutes were used as a means through which to force workers into accepting low-wage jobs for the ruling class. In other words, the Black Death had killed off all the workers such that in order to entice people back into the work force, a higher wage had to be paid. Laws against vagrancy were intended, according to Chambliss, to keep citizens from just hanging around doing nothing. Instead, they would be forced into work by those with control over the legislative body through the enacting of a law that would make just "hanging out" a criminal offense.

More recently, conflict theory has been used to explain repressive policies by the U.S. criminal justice system toward primarily minority and poor populations. In 2000, Pernille Baadsager and her colleagues used conflict theory to explain the overrepresentation of minorities in secure juvenile holding facilities. The fact that this disproportionality exists is not surprising given the fact that, according to Walter Miller, minority juveniles, primarily Black or African Americans, are arrested for drug violation at a rate 5 times that of their White counterparts. This is in direct conflict with self-reported data among young people that indicate that White youth are more likely to report using drugs than are their non-White counterparts. Further, conflict theorists point to the discrepancy in treatment between White and non-White youth in Operation Pressure Point in New York City. A crackdown by police on drug crimes led to the use of multiple resources in an attempt to rid the streets of drug dealers. Where conflict theory comes into play is that many young people of color in neighborhoods targeted by the police were detained and arrested, while White youth who were in the neighborhood to purchase drugs were not arrested.

One study used conflict theory, along with social disorganization theory, to examine the role that coercion by the dominant group, coupled with social decay, plays in determining who is, and who is not, arrested for a drug violation in U.S. cities. This study, using data from 187 U.S. cities, relied heavily on one basic argument that is associated with conflict theory. The more economically stratified a society becomes, with some having a lot and others having very little, it becomes increasingly important for those groups in power to create coercive control tactics, including laws and criminal justice policies, that bolster their conduct norms. For example, studies indicate that cities with larger minority populations have higher drug possession and trafficking arrest rates, a finding that is related to the fact that arrests are much easier to make in disorganized inner-city areas where many minority dealers operate than they are in middle- and upper-class neighborhoods where White dealers operate. From the perspective of conflict theory, this finding is problematic given the fact that national data indicate that most of the illegal drug users in the United States are White, and other data that indicate that at least half of crack cocaine users are White.

In one study on racial profiling, conflict theory was used to explain the term *hurdle effect*. Although race did not matter, empirically, in police stops of automobiles, it did have an effect on searches. Police were more likely to search Blacks and African Americans than they were Whites, especially when the stop occurred in a predominantly Black or African American neighborhood. This suggests that there could be empirical evidence to support the underlying assumption of conflict theory that less powerful people are more likely to be officially defined as criminal and put into the criminal justice system while having very little power or say-so in the legislation process.

One final example of how empirical investigations of hypotheses suggested by conflict theory can be used to confirm its basic underlying premise can be demonstrated by the disproportionate representation of minorities in death penalty statistics in the United States. Since the early 1900s and beyond, there is no doubt that the race/ethnicity of both the offender and victim matter when it comes to who will, and who will not, receive a death sentence. When the victim is White and the offender is of minority status, capital punishment is far more likely to be implemented than when the offender is White and the victim of minority status. Too, the U.S. Supreme Court has ruled that a showing of racial discrimination is the burden of each defendant in his or her individual case; defendants cannot show proof of discrimination overall relying on groups of cases. This is a much more difficult hurdle to clear.

Barbara Sims

See also Bonger, Willem Adriaan; Dehumanization of Blacks; Interracial Crime; Racial Conflict; Social Capital; White Privilege

Further Readings

Chambliss, W. J. (1964). A sociological analysis of the law of vagrancy. *Social Problems, 12*, 67–77.

Chambliss, W. J., & Seidman, R. (1971). *Law, order, and power*. Reading, MA: Addison-Wesley.

Lockwood, D., Pottieger, A., & Inciardi, J. (1995). Crack use, crime by crack users, and ethnicity. In D. Hawkins (Ed.), *Ethnicity, race, and crime: Perspectives across time and place* (pp. 212–234). Albany: SUNY Press.

Mosher, C. (2001). Predicting drug arrest rates: Conflict and social disorganization perspectives. *Crime & Delinquency, 47*(1), 84–104.

Petrocelli, M., Piquero, A. R., & Smith, M. R. (2002). Conflict theory and racial profiling: An empirical analysis of police traffic stop data. *Journal of Criminal Justice, 31*, 1–11.

Quinney, R. (1970). *The social reality of crime*. Boston: Little, Brown.

Turk, A. (1960). *Criminality and legal order*. Chicago: Rand McNally.

Vold, G. B. (1969). *Theoretical criminology*. New York: Oxford University Press.

CONSERVATIVE CRIMINOLOGY

The dissolution of the rehabilitation and deinstitutionalization era of the 1960s and early 1970s paved the way for the development of a new conservative wing of criminological theory and policy—one highly critical of many liberal sociologists and criminologists. Beginning with the presidential campaign of Barry Goldwater in the 1960s, the discussion of crime causation moved from social pathology (i.e., economics and injustice) to one of individual immorality and personal shortcomings. The surfacing of the conservative criminology movement was symptomatic of many changing opinions concerning crime and punishment in the United States since the 1970s. At its core, the conservative criminology doctrine rejects social welfare programs and suggests harsher punishments and extended imprisonments. The development of the conservative branch of criminology has accompanied many changes in crime control and penal policy since the idealistic "rehab era" of nearly 40 years ago. This entry reviews the evolution of conservative criminology's central claims, its focus on the social utility of incarceration, and its critique of contemporary culture.

History

The most prominent conservative thinkers in criminology, such as James Q. Wilson and George L. Kelling, have sparked a revival of certain "positivist" thinkers within the classical sphere of the field. Most notably, the 1876 writings of the Italian military doctor Cesare Lombroso provided a blueprint for the incapacitation of "evil" criminals from "moral individuals" in society; the use of specific punishments fit to the offender (not the offense) to separate the offender from the rest of society are central to the conservative criminology movement. Wilson in particular emphasized a marked nostalgia for the importance of 1950s-era family- and religious-centered values. He believed such a reversion would help galvanize better parenting and informal social controls, which he believed had fallen by the wayside since the "free-spirited" idealism of the 1960s. In addition, conservative criminologists display ideologically centered thinking often not based on valid empirical research of any kind with solutions coming by way of a flashy rhetoric as opposed to sound facts. For example, many of the social welfare programs that aided Americans from many social classes, such as the New Deal and the G.I. Bill, are dismissed by conservative criminologists as too expensive and overused by the poor and minorities. However, much evidence exists to the contrary, and those within the conservative movement tend to simply ignore facts invalidating or debunking their central tenets.

Many politicians now stake electoral campaigns on the omnipresent promise to reduce crime and protect the public. Politicians across the political spectrum have favored the infamous "three strikes" laws as well as measures that require prisoners to serve the majority of their prison time—these policies represent an emphasis on deterrence and incapacitation rather than rehabilitation or ameliorating social woes. Many of these policies fell under the banner of conservative criminology and the main tenets espoused by its followers.

Conservative Criminology and the Sociological Tradition

Structural Inequalities and Racial Issues

The key writings of the conservative criminology movement, beginning in the mid-1970s, reformulated societal responses to crime in a manner highly critical of many social welfare approaches of the time (i.e., reducing crime through reducing poverty). Some examples of key criticisms put forward in these liberal-minded sociological policies related to race, poverty, and other structural deficiencies as key causes of crime—conservative criminologists often balked at these explanations. While the conservative criminology movement did not deny the existence of these problems within society, many of them suggested that these deficiencies did not in and of themselves "cause" crimes to occur. Conditions of abject poverty throughout history have not always produced crime, the conservative criminologist would argue, and, therefore, striving for a more equal society would not necessarily have an impact on crime rates.

Critique of Sociological Theories of Delinquency

The conservative criminology movement further criticized many theories of delinquency based around noxious familial environments through careful analysis of practical policy implications. Moreover, although such circumstances can indeed be criminogenic, it was infeasible to expect the government to make deficient families adequately comply with a corrective policy that would, essentially, tell them how to "coexist" as a family. In addition, many conservative scholars argued that such repairs would simply be ineffective if a child had already undergone his or her formative years in a fractured family.

The Movement Away From Social Welfare

Finally, conservative criminology suggested that social welfare programs were not the remedy for crime because of the cost of such enactments and the potential lack of benefits. Thus education and poverty reduction programs favored by liberal sociologists and criminologists should be left behind in favor of increased punishments—sociological and/or structural causes of crime are not part of criminal justice policy. The resultant policies have contributed to the escalation of prison populations over the past 30 years (from roughly 250,000 in the mid-1970s to 1.45 million in 2005) (Irwin, 2005). Conservative criminology, moreover, argued that tougher crime control policies should focus on incapacitating offenders through prison time and completely taking chronic repeat offenders out of the equation.

The Renewed Emphasis on Imprisonment

The movement away from the view of prisons as cruel and criminogenic—one espoused by many sociologists and criminologists—marked conservative criminology as a distinct new movement in the mid-1970s. With a focus on incapacitation

and harsher punishments, this burgeoning branch of criminology proposed that the prison was a useful asset to be handled by those in government to reduce crime and put away dangerous offenders. By increasing the certainty and swiftness of punishment, the potential criminal would decide that the costs of committing a crime outweighed any potential benefits. Thus conservative criminology did not advocate simply locking up all who committed crimes but thought the consistent and timely use of imprisonment would deter other potential criminals from committing crimes, seeing as the majority of them are rational and calculating human beings.

Joan Petersilia and Shadd Maruna, two noted criminological and penological scholars, have lodged criticisms at the conservative criminology movement for ignoring the issue of the re-release of more than 1,600 inmates from jail and prison *each day* in the United States. As Petersilia and Maruna point out, the rising costs, both economic and social, of releasing many disenfranchised and diseased (both physically and mentally) inmates back into civil society are largely ignored by the conservative movement; the "commonsense" approach of this movement often suggests, without empirical support, that the costs of escalating imprisonment are worth keeping society safe and reflect problems of lenient policy in the criminal justice system.

Rational Choice Theory

The specific theoretical perspective often utilized by conservative criminologists is known as "rational choice theory." If offenders are rational they should be punished not only because they committed a criminal act but also because they need to learn that crime does not produce lasting benefits. Finally, an emphasis should be placed on chronic offenders who must not be released back into society; repeat offenders were those who should be locked up for good. Because many of these chronic offenders will be allowed back into society, strong efforts must be made to keep them incapacitated so as to stymie "preventable" crimes that they would likely commit. In sum, conservative criminology suggested crime was due to certain wayward and dangerous people that must be isolated, not structural inequalities or deficiencies in larger society. Although much conservative criminology focuses on inner-city crime, remedying these conditions is not particularly important in reducing crime. The conservative criminology movement is not, therefore, concerned with social inequality, hardscrabble conditions, and/or social disorganization as root causes of crime.

Degraded Morality and the Critique of the Counterculture

Moral Decline and a Culture of Permissiveness

The conservative criminology movement is highly critical of moral atrophy in society following the idealistic movements of the 1960s; this downturn can be linked to many social problems, not the least of which is crime. Moreover, the prominence of liberal politics and lifestyle choices during the 1960s caused a deterioration of the moral fabric of society. The 1960s "Cultural Revolution" saw an emphasis on promiscuity, self-gratification, and reckless behavior. A host of new behaviors previously viewed as immoral were now overtaking the nation's youth. The result was a society that allowed and—the tenets of conservative criminology argued—even encouraged deviance through lack of clear moral guidelines and welfare programs that created dependence on government assistance rather than gainful employment.

The cultural permissiveness of the 1960s further created households in which discipline is not adequately meted out, religious faith is eschewed, respect for authority is not taught, and self-discipline is not instilled. Because children are not being inculcated with adequate values and a clear moral compass, they may go down criminal paths. This moral depravation can also lead to drug use, disruptive relationships, poor job skills, and other adjustment issues throughout the life course. Thus according to conservative criminologists, both cultural and individual factors combine to create troubling moral problems and potential criminality.

Brent Funderburk

See also Family and Delinquency; General Theory of Crime; Inequality Theory; Juvenile Crime; Mandatory Minimums; Public Opinion, Punishment; Racialization of Crime; Recidivism; Social Control Theory; Strain Theory; Three Strikes Laws

Further Readings

Cullen, F. T., Pratt, T. C., Miceli, S. L., & Moon, M. M. (2002). Dangerous liaison? Rational choice theory as the basis for correctional intervention. In A. R. Piquero & S. G. Tibbetts (Eds.), *Rational choice and criminal behavior: Recent research and future challenges* (pp. 279–296). New York: Routledge.

Irwin, J. (2005). *The warehouse prison: Disposing of the new dangerous class.* Los Angeles: Roxbury.

Kelling, G. L., & Coles, C. M. (1996). *Fixing broken windows: Restoring order and reducing crime in our communities.* New York: Simon & Schuster.

Pratt, T. C., & Cullen, F. T. (2005). Assessing macro-level predictors and theories of crime: A meta analysis. In M. Tonry (Ed.), *Crime and justice: A review of research* (Vol. 32, pp. 373–450). Chicago: University of Chicago Press.

Skogan, W. G. (1990). *Disorder and decline: Crime and the spiral of decay in American neighborhoods.* Berkeley: University of California Press.

Wilson, J. Q. (2002). *The marriage problem: How our culture has weakened families.* New York: HarperCollins.

CONSUMER RACIAL PROFILING

Consumer racial profiling (CRP) is discrimination in which consumers are suspected of criminal activity because of their race/ethnicity. Racial profiling in general has long been a concern for members of racial and ethnic minority communities. It is estimated that one third of the U.S. population is at risk of being victimized because they belong to a racial, ethnic, or religious group whose members are commonly targeted by police for unlawful stops and searches. While most of the interest has focused on the profiling of motorists based on race, there has been a gradual shift in attention to the profiling of consumers in the marketplace. This entry first provides a general overview of CRP, followed by a brief comment on the prevalence and evidence of CRP. Then the entry provides a more detailed look at the individual components of the CRP definition, an overview of research and theory related to CRP, and a review of legislation applicable to CRP cases. The entry concludes with a brief comment on future directions.

Overview of CRP

CRP is one type of discrimination against consumers. It involves differential treatment of consumers that either denies or degrades products and/or services based on the customer's race or ethnicity. This differential treatment involves suspecting that a customer is engaging in criminal activity.

The colloquial expression "Shopping while Black or Brown" is derived from a similar expression—"Driving while Black or Brown" (DWB)—which typically refers to incidents in which law enforcement officers stop, question, investigate, detain, and/or arrest motorists based on their race or ethnicity rather than on probable cause or even a reasonable suspicion that they have engaged in criminal activity. Attempts to justify such behavior by law enforcement officials are often based on the assumption that minority motorists are more likely to engage in criminal activity while driving. Due to increased concern over DWB, many states are now engaged in ongoing data collection to assess the validity of traffic-related racial profiling claims. Results of some of these early studies call into question the assumption that minority drivers have a greater propensity to engage in criminal activity. For example, in one recent study of Rhode Island traffic stops conducted by Northeastern University's Institute on Race and Justice, non-White motorists were 2.5 times more likely to be searched than White motorists. However, when the traffic stop resulted in a search, Whites were more likely to be found with contraband.

The same issues and concerns need to be analyzed in the context of consumer racial profiling. While DWB involves law enforcement officers, the profiling of customers is done by store owners, managers, clerks, security guards, and/or other representatives of the seller. In some cases, CRP may involve police officers who are called to the scene in their capacity as law enforcement officers or who are employed as off-duty security guards serving in the capacity as private actors. Given that CRP typically occurs on the private premises of a commercial establishment, customers have fewer rights as "invitees" than they do as citizens traveling on public roadways.

Prevalence and Evidence of CRP

Racial profiling may be far more widespread than most people realize. According to a 2004 report by Amnesty International USA, there were 32 million victims of racial profiling in the United States. Furthermore, the report estimates that at least 87 million people—1 in 3—in the United States are at high risk of being victimized because they belong to a racial, ethnic, or religious group whose members are commonly targeted by police for unlawful stops and searches.

Since the early 1990s, the popular press has reported hundreds of accounts of CRP and marketplace discrimination against consumers of color. There have been a number of investigations by television newsmagazines such as *Dateline* and *20/20* using hidden cameras in attempts to document alleged marketplace discrimination at certain business establishments in an effort to substantiate the popular press claims. However, such investigations typically lack the scientific rigor to prove that marketplace discrimination exists. In fact, skeptics point to the anecdotal nature of the evidence in arguing that most of these incidents involve disgruntled consumers attempting to "play the race card."

While reliable data to confirm the regularity of CRP are not abundant, there are a number of studies that provide some insight into the frequency with which racial minorities experience this phenomenon.

A More Detailed Look at CRP

CRP can happen when individuals engage in marketplace activities involving goods and services. It is important to note that consumer activity extends beyond "shopping" and can encompass planning a purchase (e.g., browsing), making an actual purchase transaction, exchanging a purchase (e.g., returning an item that is defective), and disposing of a previous purchase (e.g., turning in items at a recycling center). CRP also extends beyond consumer activity in retail stores. For example, CRP can occur in other places of public accommodation, such as hotels, restaurants, gas stations, and other service providers, as well as retail establishments including grocery and food stores, toy stores, clothing stores, department stores, home improvement stores, and office equipment stores.

CRP is most often associated with African Americans, primarily because most highly publicized news accounts and court cases have involved African Americans. However, CRP can impact minorities from many different racial and ethnic backgrounds, including Hispanics, Asians, and Native Americans. In fact, since the terrorist attacks of September 11, 2001, there has been heightened interest and concern about CRP as it applies to anyone perceived as Middle Eastern. Arab Americans, in particular, are being scrutinized more carefully than other people, are questioned and detained more, are sometimes barred from boarding aircraft, and are even taken off planes by suspecting police and pilots.

To understand CRP, it is important to understand the law enforcement practice of "profiling." A *profile* is a coherent set of facts about an individual typically used to gain insight about whether a particular individual may be engaged in criminal activity. Originally, profiles were used *after* a crime was committed to assist police agencies in identifying the type of perpetrator they were seeking. Later, profiling became a tactic that law enforcement used *before* the crime. This altered use of profiling has now crept into the marketplace.

Overview of Research and Theory

Research on CRP and theory development is in the emerging stage, with very few published studies.

Empirical Research

At least one study dealing with marketplace discrimination can be traced back to the 1930s. In a cleverly designed study of that era, La Piere traveled widely in the United States with a Chinese couple, stopping at 66 sleeping places and 184 eating places. They were refused service only once. However, based on a follow-up mail questionnaire asking whether these same establishments would take "members of the Chinese race as guests in your establishment," 93% of the restaurants and 92% of the hotels said they would *not* serve Chinese people. The results of this study raised questions concerning discriminatory behaviors manifested in the marketplace and accompanying attitudes.

The La Piere study technically was not a CRP study, as it did not focus on criminal suspicion. A number of recent studies have examined CRP issues specifically. Several of these have analyzed legal cases in which retailers have been accused of engaging in CRP. In one of the studies, as many as 40% of cases involved allegations that customers were treated as criminals. Other studies have focused on the causes of CRP and on the psychological and emotional effects on CRP victims.

Theoretical Explanations

A number of researchers have offered theoretical explanations as to *why* ethnic/racial minorities, especially African Americans, are likely to be profiled. One explanation is that many merchants intentionally target ethnic/racial minority shoppers because they incorrectly believe them to be more likely to engage in shoplifting, to be less creditworthy, and so on. Retailers who see ethnic/racial minority customers as potential threats to company merchandise may attempt to discourage them from remaining in the store too long to prevent stealing. In this way, retailers can obfuscate their discriminatory motives with a perfectly legitimate and nonbiased rationale. This allows retailers to maintain control over ethnic/racial minorities who shop in their stores while continuing to see themselves as nonracist individuals. Such behavior coincides with theories of aversive racism, which suggest that racist feelings are more likely to be manifested when there is an easily justifiable explanation for the behavior.

Although much more difficult to identify and define, it also is likely that many instances of CRP are based on "subconscious racism." Unwittingly, some retailers make assumptions about their ethnic/racial minority customers based on stereotypes about African Americans that are fueled by ignorance and mistrust rather than by a conscious racist motive. *Labeling theory* states that society reacts to ethnic/racial minority people as criminals based on the labeling process that tags, defines, identifies, segregates, describes, and emphasizes them as such. Therefore, labeling theory suggests ethnic/racial minorities are more likely to be treated like potential shoplifters.

Legal Review

Aggrieved parties can file legal claims under various state and federal laws. In addition, plaintiffs rely on common-law claims that provide some measure of relief, although they prevent the racial aspect of the retailer's conduct from being exposed.

Common Law Claims

A typical tort law claim arises when retailers detain customers on suspicion of shoplifting. Retailers usually defend their conduct as permissible under merchant detention statutes that allow storeowners to protect their goods by detaining and searching. Next, racial discrimination of customers arguably violates contract law's duty of good faith and fair dealing. Some legal scholars advocate changes in contract law that would prohibit discrimination in the formation, performance, enforcement, and termination of a contract. While a plaintiff could bring a marketplace discrimination claim based on the "duty to serve," this property law doctrine has become ineffective in protecting individuals from racial discrimination in retail settings. In the past, owners of any commercial property held open to the public had a duty to serve all patrons. The common law rule has mutated so that it currently immunizes most businesses from the duty to serve all customers.

State Public Accommodations Laws

Forty-five states have enacted legislation prohibiting race discrimination in places of public accommodation. Only Alabama, Georgia, Mississippi, North Carolina, and Texas do not protect residents of color when they are treated unfairly in restaurants, hotels, gas stations, and other business establishments. Traditionally, state laws covered places used by travelers, such as transport facilities, restaurants, and lodgings as well as places of entertainment, amusement, or cultural contact. Today, most state statutes treat retail stores as "places of public accommodations"

although there is still some variation in terms of the type of establishments that are covered.

Forty-one states and the District of Columbia have established agencies to enforce their public accommodations laws. The role of the civil rights agencies varies, but in general they are responsible for studying discrimination and for educating the public about its rights and the business community about its duties. Most agencies have the authority to process complaints filed by individuals. State public accommodations statutes are underutilized for a variety of reasons, including the meager remedies available to plaintiffs who successfully prove discrimination.

Federal Laws

Victims of marketplace discrimination have advanced valid claims under the Civil Rights Acts of 1866 and 1964. The Civil Rights Act of 1866 was designed to ensure "that a dollar in the hands of a Negro will purchase the same thing as a dollar in the hands of a white man" (*Jones v. Alfred H. Mayer Co.,* 1968). Plaintiffs who successfully prove intentional discrimination under this act are entitled to both equitable (injunctive) and legal (monetary) relief, including compensatory and punitive damages. Equitable relief refers to the issuance of a court order prohibiting the defendant from engaging in discriminatory conduct. Section 1981 of the Civil Rights Act of 1866 provides that "All persons . . . shall have the same right . . . to make and enforce contracts . . . as is enjoyed by white citizens." The phrase "make and enforce contracts" includes "the enjoyment of all benefits, privileges, terms, and conditions of the contractual relationship." The U.S. Supreme Court has stated that the purpose of Section 1981 was "to remove the impediment of discrimination from a minority citizen's ability to participate fully and equally in the marketplace" (*Patterson v. McLean Credit Union,* 1989). To date, courts have narrowly interpreted the scope of Section 1981 by focusing on conduct that prevented the formation of the contract rather than conduct affecting the nature or quality of the contractual relationship. Many federal courts insist that Section 1981 plaintiffs must produce evidence that they were completely denied an opportunity to complete a retail transaction in order to state a valid claim.

Title II of the Civil Rights Act of 1964 is the federal public accommodations law, whose goal is "to ensure that all members of society have equal access to goods and services." It prohibits discrimination in "places of public accommodation," that is, privately owned institutions that are open to the public. Title II does not cover most retail stores. This means that the federal public accommodation law allows retail store personnel to discriminate against customers based on their race. There are some exceptions to this rule, since the act does cover retail stores that contain eating establishments as well as eating establishments that are "located on the premises of any retail establishment."

Under Title II, an individual is required to notify the appropriate state or local civil rights agency of the alleged discrimination prior to filing suit. Such notification must occur within a certain time frame established by the state's public accommodations statute. Plaintiffs who are not aware of it fail to meet the statutory deadline, and their claims are dismissed. The statute only permits a court to issue nonmonetary relief. The inability to recover monetary damages for violations of their rights undoubtedly discourages people of color from seeking redress under Title II.

Future Directions

Although significant strides have been made in eradicating discrimination in education, housing, employment, and other aspects of daily life since the passage of the civil rights legislation in the 1960s, discrimination still manifests itself in the marketplace in the form of CRP. Marketers, researchers, public policymakers, consumers, and law enforcement officials can take a number of steps to address concerns about CRP and any other vestiges of discrimination. First, all sales personnel should be trained to provide a more "welcoming" environment for all consumers, and particularly for consumers of color, including diversity training designed to sensitize employees to explicit or implicit prejudices that inhibit them from treating all customers with dignity and respect. Second, employee interactions with customers should be monitored to ensure that both positive outcomes and negative incidents are consistent across diverse subgroups. This can be accomplished by using mystery shopping audits or by employing "the demographic test" to detect and prevent discriminatory behavior among its employees, that is, using U.S. Census data to determine the racial/ethnic makeup of a store's trade areas and comparing data with store arrest and detention records. Given the increase in purchasing power among people of color, public policymakers could develop legislation that more effectively addresses CRP in today's economic climate.

Jerome D. Williams, Anne-Marie Hakstian, and Geraldine R. Henderson

See also Disproportionate Arrests; Profiling, Ethnic: Use by Police and Homeland Security; Profiling, Racial: Historical and Contemporary Perspectives

Further Readings

Crockett, D., Grier, S. A., & Williams, J. A. (2003). Coping with marketplace discrimination: An exploration of the experiences of Black men. *Academy of Marketing Science Review, 4,* 1–21.

Gabbidon, S. L. (2003). Racial profiling by store clerks and security personnel in retail establishments. *Journal of Contemporary Criminal Justice, 19,* 345–364.

Gabbidon, S. L., & Higgins, G. E. (2007). Consumer racial profiling and perceived victimization: A phone survey of Philadelphia area residents. *American Journal of Criminal Justice, 32*(1–2), 1–11.

Harris, A. G. (2003). Shopping while Black: Applying 42 U.S.C. § 1981 to cases of consumer racial profiling. *Boston College Third World Law Journal, 23,* 1–57.

Harris, A. G. (2006). A survey of federal and state public accommodations statutes: Evaluating their effectiveness in cases of retail discrimination. *Virginia Journal of Social Policy and the Law, 13,* 331–394.

Harris, A. G., Henderson, G. R., & Williams, J. D. (2005). Courting consumers: Assessing consumer racial profiling and other marketplace discrimination. *Journal of Public Policy & Marketing, 24,* 163–171.

Websites

Center for Consumer Equality: http://www.consumer equality.org

CONVICT CRIMINOLOGY

Convict criminology is an emerging school within the academic discipline of criminology that addresses scholarly social science research and public policy from the perspective of professors and graduate students who have previously been convicted of crimes, incarcerated, and who, as ex-convicts, continued their formal education, earned PhD degrees, and joined the ranks of academia in a variety of disciplines, including criminology, sociology, criminal justice, corrections, and public affairs.

In many respects, convict criminology grew out of a shared recognition and concern by a handful of ex-convict professors that the get-tough policies initiated through the War on Crime and War on Drugs had a disproportionate effect on racial minorities in the United States, especially on African American families, and had resulted in gross disparities within the criminal justice system. Convict criminologists are uniquely qualified to give a voice to the disenfranchised racial minorities who are imprisoned or are now ex-convicts suffering from the invisible punishments blocking the path to reentry following imprisonment, by merging scholarly methods and their own firsthand experiences as convicts to analytically discuss the issues.

Purpose and Objectives

The purpose of the school of convict criminology is to formally recognize the value that ex-convict social scientists add to the academy through their life events and perspectives that shape their view of the criminal justice system and, more specifically, corrections. There are two stated objectives of convict criminologists. First, convict criminologists seek to change the way in which research on prisons is conducted. Second, convict criminologists seek to influence the manner in which the American Society of Criminology (ASC) and Academy of Criminal Justice Sciences (ACJS) articulate criminal justice system policy reforms to make corrections more humane.

History and Development

The field of convict criminology was first developed and evolved through a panel assembled to speak at the 1997 conference of the American Society of Criminology. Since that time, interest in convict criminology has grown considerably, as has acceptance of ex-convict criminologists by many within the academy. There are currently several dozen professors and graduate students who regularly participate in convict criminology panels at academic conferences and whose scholarly research written in the convict criminology perspective is regularly published in peer-reviewed journals.

The "grandfather" of convict criminology is John Irwin, now a professor emeritus at San Francisco State University, who has long been recognized for his ethnographic scholarship involving prisoners. Irwin was the first criminologist to acknowledge publicly his status as an ex-convict (he served time in the 1950s for bank robbery in California). Although not recognized as a convict criminologist, primarily because he has not worked in academia or earned an advanced degree in criminology or a related field, Charles Colson has furthered the cause of convict criminology since the late 1970s. Colson, an attorney and White House staffer in the Nixon administration, was convicted in the Watergate scandal and served time as a prisoner in several federal prisons. For the past 3 decades, Colson has parlayed his personal experiences into the nonprofit organization Prison Fellowship Ministries and has been instrumental in lobbying for legislation to assist prisoners and ex-convicts.

Future Directions

In recent years it has become more common to find peer-reviewed journal articles in the literature authored by criminologists who affirmatively frame their social research in the perspective of convict criminology. Annual roundtables and discussion panels at conferences of professional organizations, namely ASC and ACJS, have continued to further recognition and perceived legitimacy of the school of convict criminology within academia. Numerous convict criminologists have obtained positions at universities throughout North America and the world in the past decade, in great part due to the greater awareness of the value of their individual and shared experiences in criminological research and public policy initiatives.

Philip Matthew Stinson

See also Black Criminology; Disproportionate Incarceration; Disproportionate Minority Contact and Confinement; Drug Sentencing; Drug Sentencing, Federal; Felon Disenfranchisement; Sentencing Disparities, African Americans; War on Drugs

Further Readings

Richards, S. C. (2008). USP Marion: The first federal supermax. *The Prison Journal, 88*(1), 6–22.

Richards, S. C., & Ross, J. I. (2003). A convict perspective on the classifications of prisoners. *Criminology & Public Policy, 2*(2), 243–252.

Ross, J. I., & Richards, S. C. (2003). *Convict criminology.* Belmont, CA: Wadsworth/Thomson.

Ross, J. I., & Richards, S. C. (2003). The new school of convict criminology. *Social Justice, 28*(1), 177–190.

Terry, C. M. (2003). Managing prisoners as problem populations and the evolving nature of imprisonment: A convict perspective. *Critical Criminology, 12,* 43–66.

CONVICT LEASE SYSTEM

The Thirteenth Amendment of the U.S. Constitution, while effectively ending slavery, eventually authorized the use of freed slaves for involuntary servitude with the following clause: "Neither slavery nor involuntary servitude, *except as a punishment for crime whereof the party shall have been duly convicted,* shall exist within the United States or any place subject to their jurisdiction" (italics added). Under the convict lease system implemented in the U.S. South after the Civil War, the state took advantage of this clause by leasing prison inmates to private companies that used them as forced laborers. This system of enforced labor ran from 1865 to 1920. This entry examines the convict lease system in the United States that emerged after the abolition of legal slavery. A brief history of the convict lease system is discussed, as is the social context surrounding its development.

Controlling Slaves in the Post–Civil War South

Scholars have suggested that after the passage of the Thirteenth Amendment, there was a concerted effort to control the labor of the new underclass of freed African Americans. Many laws—such as the Jim Crow statutes as well as numerous vagrancy laws targeted specifically at Blacks—were put into place to make sure former slaves were controlled. As a result of these acts, the close of the 19th century saw the population in southern prisons becoming primarily African American. These inmates provided a source of agricultural workers who could be used to alleviate the labor shortage while also lessening the pressure on the states to house prisoners.

Many former slaves found themselves with few options at the end of the Civil War and the subsequent aftermath; their former lives as slaves offered little in the way of survival skills beyond the confines of a plantation. As a result, many freed slaves were enticed by the agrarian labor system as a source of at least some form of sustenance, and many of them returned to work at the same plantations they had recently left. Under the convict lease system, other former slaves, often convicted for petty crimes, were leased out to private vendors to promote and undertake forced labor to drive White-owned businesses. Thus, many former slaves found themselves working in the same areas where they were once held captive. While some had chosen to return to the plantations for the sake of economic survival, others were compelled to work there as forced laborers under the convict lease system.

Differences From Slavery

Although similar to each other, the forced servitude conditions differed from slavery in several important respects. Those now forced to work under enforced servitude were mostly African American prisoners put behind bars due to their own actions, whereas slavery had simply branded many of them inferior and therefore fit to toil away. Moreover, it was possible for those forced to labor under the convict lease system to live free lives upon being released from confinement; escape from slavery was punished with physical torture or death in most cases. More than anything else, the convict lease system exemplified the dependence of the South on enforced labor in one form or another, usually involving the subjugation of minorities.

Freed slaves also gained new rights, such as the right to vote in county-level elections. The latter were particularly important for the recently freed, in that law enforcement frequently inflated and exaggerated charges against African Americans in the South. As many freed slaves were without residence or work, they often violated vagrant or trespass statutes; the new legal rights allowed Blacks to at least begin the process of contesting such charges. However, slavery-era racism still permeated southern culture and values; many Whites simply refused to accept the doctrine of emancipation that ultimately gave slaves their freedom. Much of the business interest in African Americans as reified commodities was related to maintaining an agrarian White-dominated system of cheap labor.

The Expansion of Forced Labor

Another primary motivation of the convict lease system was to make largely free labor available to White-owned business interests. Before the Revolutionary War, the use of forced labor for private profit was primarily the province of the Dutch and the British, who transported debtors and other "deviants" to the colonies for servitude. As the importation of forced labor declined, the American colonies increasingly relied on slave labor. After the close of the Civil War and the emancipation of slaves, the states passed laws that differentially affected the former slaves. Upon their imprisonment, many African Americans were leased out into forced servitude. The Thirteenth Amendment, in allowing for the extensions of racialized labor practices, promoted the interests of both industrial entrepreneurs and the agrarian planter class. The convict lease system, in legalizing this brand of forced labor upon African Americans, allowed "legitimate" types of work, such as coal mining and railroading, to be subsumed under the umbrella of enforced servitude. Finally, the unskilled and virtually free labor of African Americans was utilized not only by entrepreneurs in the South but by industrialists in the northern states as well.

Legacy

The convict lease system mirrors the racial divides and controversies within the current U.S. prison system. Many notable scholars have, in recent years, discussed the similarities between the rise in incarceration of African Americans in the post-slavery era and in the 1980s and 1990s. Both rises in imprisonment rates were the result of mass incarceration for largely petty crimes that had only been recently criminalized. In addition, several studies have found at least some link to economic and social disorganization of poor urban areas (which Blacks occupy at a rate 5 times that of Whites), similar to the hardscrabble conditions in the post–Civil War South.

Further, the seismic social and economic changes of the post–Civil War era mirror the increased global market economics of today, in which the search for cheap labor through outsourcing leads to an anomic sense of normlessness as wages and security are constantly shifting over time. The War on Drugs brought a greater emphasis on aggressive law enforcement tactics and led to a significant portion of the young Black male population being removed from many inner cities through mass incarceration. Finally, some scholars have noted the similarities between the use of punishment in both cases to reassert the normative order in times of massive social and economic change.

Brent Funderburk

See also Chain Gangs; Race Relations; Racial Conflict; Racialization of Crime; Racism; Slave Patrols

Further Readings

Du Bois, W. E. B. (1901). The spawn of slavery: The convict lease system in the South. *Missionary Review of the World, 14,* 737–745.

Garland, D. (2001). *The culture of control: Crime and social order in contemporary society.* Chicago: University of Chicago Press.

Hallett, M. (2002). Race, crime, and for-profit imprisonment: Social disorganization as market opportunity. *Punishment & Society, 4,* 369–393.

Myers, M. A. (1998). *Race, labor, and punishment in the New South.* Columbus: Ohio State University Press.

Oshinsky, D. M. (1996). *"Worse than slavery": Parchman Farm and the ordeal of Jim Crow justice.* New York: The Free Press.

Shelden, R. (2001). *Controlling the dangerous classes: A critical introduction to the history of criminal justice.* Boston: Allyn & Bacon.

COOL POSE

The Black male has been faced with many challenges since his arrival in America. Currently the Black community is in crisis due to poverty, poor education, high unemployment, and increasing morbidity rates. For example, in comparison to their White counterparts, Black males are 6 times more likely to die through violence. Among Black males ages 15 to 24 years old, homicide is the number one cause of death. The legacies of slavery, oppression, and discrimination have forced the Black male to adapt and reinvent himself, and the result has been the *cool pose*. The cool pose is the creation of an alternate persona that shields Black males against the constant barrage of racial discrimination in American society. On the one hand, it raises self-esteem, and, on the other, it further marginalizes him and may even reinforce negative stereotypes because it is outside the norm and is viewed as unacceptable.

The concept of the cool pose originated with the Harvard University Pathways to Identity Project during the 1960s and 1970s. Using the project data, one of the participants, Janet Mancini Billson, wrote an article in 1981 about how Black males in the inner city cope with everyday struggles. A decade later, her coauthor Richard Majors wrote a book chapter on the cool pose as it relates to Black males in sports. Their collaboration, titled *Cool Pose: The Dilemmas of Black Manhood in America,* provides an overall framework for the cool pose, its development, what it means, and its consequences.

Through a history of oppression of Blacks by Whites, Black males have been left powerless due to their lack of success in the familial, social, and financial realms. There is a huge gap between the desired status of the American dream and the means to achieve that station in life. The cool pose is a rejection of the definitions imposed upon the Black man by White dominant culture. It is the creation of a new identity. Further, it is the Black males' play on masculinity. This identity was formed out of a sense of survival and is the Black male presentation of self to greater society.

The cool pose is Black masculinity personified and involves role playing based on urban conventions of dress, speech, and behavior. Actors control interactions with an air that observers may view as arrogance but is grounded in honor and dignity. It embraces elements of the prison subculture, wearing pants low on the waist, poorly groomed hairstyles, and misogynistic comments. This stance is more prevalent among disadvantaged males and is a cultural, physical, and social detachment from everyday negative life. The cool pose, however, is an external projection and belies the internal pain and struggle of the actor.

The cool pose has its roots in West African culture, which is very expressive and emphasizes spirituality and strength. While the use of masks is prevalent among West African tribes, Black males create a symbolic mask through facial expressions and the overall image they portray. Outward symbols of expression are extremely important. Therefore, having the most stylish and expensive clothes, jewelry, cars, and hairstyles is very important. Verbalizations and body language also follow a script that epitomizes coolness, such as the way Black males greet one another with a hand clap, hand shake, and fast embrace. Cool pose is a response to the stress they face in society to mask their true inner feelings.

Effects of the Cool Pose

The cool pose has positive effects on the Black male psyche in that it brings a sense of pride, value, self-confidence, and personal control over their own lives. Adoption of the cool pose is a honed craft for the Black male. Conversely, the cool pose has negative effects. While slavery has changed Black male–female mating interactions, the cool pose stance has led to further changes in male–female relationships. One of the key components of the cool pose is an outward display of masculinity. One way to do this is to get involved with many women and have multiple children, but this negatively affects male–female relationships and has also led to an increase in the incidence of sexually transmitted diseases such as AIDS, which is plaguing the Black community at an alarming rate. Further, there is posturing between males on the street who will fight to the death to protect their image, as respect is a form of currency in inner-city communities. With so much lacking in other areas of their lives, respect is all they have, and as such they go to great lengths to protect it. One must be prepared to take a life or give up one's own life to save face and remain "cool."

Despite the positive effect the cool pose may have on Black male self-esteem, it has increased Black males' involvement in damaging behaviors. Thus, the race-crime connection is perpetuated through destructive behavior, maintaining high rates of violence among young Black males and the social ills of the Black community as a whole. Perhaps it is time to redefine this posture by holding onto that which is positive and rejecting the negative qualities that are currently sustaining the cultural, economic, and social blight. Re-mold the mask, change the posture, and save the community.

Laurie J. Samuel

See also Code of the Streets; Hypermasculinity; Self-Esteem and Delinquency

Further Readings

Anderson, E. (1999). *Code of the street.* New York: Norton.

Cool pose culture. (2007). *The Urban Dictionary.* Retrieved from http://www.urbandictionary.com/define.php?term=cool-pose+culture

Gibbs, J. (1988). *Young, Black, and male in America: An endangered species.* Dover, MA: Auburn House.

Kubrin, C., & Wadsworth, T. (2003). Identifying the structural correlates of African American killings. *Homicide Studies, 7,* 3–35.

Majors, R., & Billson, J. (1992). *Cool pose: The dilemmas of Black manhood in America.* New York: Simon & Schuster.

Samuel, L. (2005). *Self-cleaning ovens: The impact of police intervention and the code of the street on retaliation homicide in disadvantaged communities in Washington, D.C.* Unpublished doctoral dissertation, Howard University, Washington, DC.

Wallace, D. (2007). It's a m-a-n thang: Black male gender role socialization and the performance of masculinity in love relationships. *The Journal of Pan African Studies, 1,* 11–22.

CRACK BABIES

Crack babies is a term used to describe babies born to women who expose their fetuses to crack or powdered cocaine while pregnant. The name arose from a surge in cocaine and crack use in the United States; it was used in media outlets and in scientific research. The image most associated with a crack baby is a baby born to a minority woman, more specifically, an African American woman, living in poverty in the inner city.

Cocaine comes from the coca plant, whose leaves are chemically treated to produce a white powder. This white powder became a popular drug in the United States beginning in the 1960s and hit its peak of popularity in the 1980s. Cocaine can enter the human body through the vein or through the nose. To increase the potency of cocaine, users "freebase." This is a process to remove the hydrochloride. When the freebased cocaine is kept in its solid form, it is called *crack*, because of the cracking noises it makes when heated and smoked. People who use crack may experience some negative effects, including heart attack, stroke, convulsions, increased blood pressure, and depression. When a pregnant woman smokes crack, the drug affects not only the woman but also the fetus.

During the 1980s, greater attention was being paid by law enforcement, legislatures, and media sources to the increased use of crack. Although the War on Drugs had been in effect for many years, use of crack was still prevalent at this time. Hospitals in large metropolitan areas began reporting incidents of babies being born addicted to crack. Once newborns were found exposed to drugs or alcohol, law enforcement agencies and/or child protection agencies were contacted, and many newborns were removed from their mothers and placed with relatives or in foster care. As more incidents were reported, attention was focused on these children, who were predicted to become a societal burden. It was thought crack babies would be severely mentally and physically delayed and scarred from the mother's crack use. The imagery conjured by the media focused on poor, inner-city, African American women as the main perpetrators of this situation. The media outlets helped to perpetuate a fear of what crack babies would do to existing resources, including medical costs, educational costs, and overall societal stability. A genuine fear developed about the potential hazards that crack babies were going to cause socially.

Many governmental prevention programs were initiated to allow pregnant women abusing crack or cocaine a chance to stay "clean" until their children were born. The bulk of these drug prevention programs were voluntary, but the instilled fear of the reverberations of crack babies led many states to criminalize the use of crack and cocaine while pregnant. Many states enacted legislation that would allow prosecutors to charge women who gave birth to a baby testing positive for cocaine with child abuse or child endangerment. Several states also tried incarcerating crack-addicted pregnant women in a tactic to keep them from using the drug until their babies were born. A few states charged these women with criminal offenses because they delivered cocaine to a minor through the umbilical cord. The criminalization of women delivering crack babies was problematic because the majority of states and the federal government do not consider a fetus to be human until birth. Many of the criminal prosecution attempts were against disadvantaged African American women who had few available resources to assist in their defense.

Throughout the 1980s and into the 1990s, many scientific studies were conducted on the effects of crack on babies and the prevalence of crack babies. These studies had conflicting and inconsistent findings. There is unpredictable medical research on the effects of crack on fetuses. This research finds that crack babies may be more apt to be premature, have a low birth weight, have addiction withdrawals, and be more susceptible to sudden infant death syndrome, heart defects, and many other serious mental and physical effects. Although research finds that crack has a negative effect on in utero exposure, many studies concluded that the effects of crack cannot be specifically determined. Many substance-abusing women who use crack may also use alcohol, smoke cigarettes, and use other drugs. These same women usually live in poverty, which affects diet, health care, and many other aspects of life. Many published articles also found that crack babies were not limited to African American women but were born of women of all races, including Caucasians. Race was found to be one factor in understanding the prevalence of prenatal crack exposure. Many studies used large hospitals, in major cities, as the location to collect information on crack babies. These studies found major inconsistencies in who is and who is not drug tested at the hospitals. If the pregnant woman or the newborn showed signs of addiction, she or he was tested, but many tests were performed by hospital staff based on subjective factors like race. Because of costs, hospitals were not testing every woman delivering a baby at the hospital. Stereotypical images of the poor African American woman made this group more prone to drug testing than were women of other racial groups. This inconsistency creates skepticism about the number of crack babies, since there was no state or national guideline to support testing criteria.

The term *crack babies* reflects societal fears of a potential epidemic that did not occur. Although cocaine and crack are very harmful to unborn fetuses, their effects vary based on a number of factors that include drug use but are not limited to solely crack exposure. The term itself is controversial. Health care professionals have noted that there is no medical diagnosis to which it corresponds and have criticized the media for using a term that unfairly stigmatizes these infants. Minority women, but more specifically poor African American women, were depicted as villainous mothers who did not care about their unborn children, when research shows substance abuse crosses all racial and social class lines. The blame placed on African American women led to the removal of their crack-exposed newborns to foster care and the imprisonment of these women. Illegal drug use is a moral and legal battle but also a medical and social war because of the existence of crack babies.

Jennifer L. Gossett

See also Crack Epidemic; Crack Mothers; Family and Delinquency

Further Readings

Bopp, J., & Gardner, D. H. (1991). AIDS babies, crack babies: Challenges to the law. *Issues in Law and Medicine, 7*(1), 3–52.

Fulton, L. (2001). Protective custody of the unborn: Involuntary commitment of pregnant, substance abusing mothers for the protection of their unborn children. *Children's Legal Rights Journal, 21*(3), 8–16.

Glassner, B. (2000). *The culture of fear.* New York: Basic Books.

Kosta, W. (1996). *Crack babies are coming: What impact will 1980s crack babies have on police services by the year 2005?* (Publication No. 21-0434). Rockville, MD: National Institute of Justice/NCJRS.

Litt, J., & McNeil, M. (1997). Biological markers and social differentiation: Crack babies and the construction of dangerous mother. *Health Care for Women International, 18*(1), 31–42.

Lyons, P., & Rittner, B. (1998). The social construction of the crack babies phenomenon as a social problem. *American Journal of Orthopsychiatry, 68*(2), 313–321.

Twohey, M. (1999). The crack-baby myth. *National Journal, 31*(46), 3340–3345.

U.S. Sentencing Commission. (2002). *Report to Congress: Cocaine and Federal Sentencing Policy* (pp. 1–155). Washington, DC: Author.

Welch, M. (1997). Regulating the reproduction and morality of women: The social control of body and soul. *Women and Criminal Justice, 9*(1), 17–38.

CRACK EPIDEMIC

Crack epidemic refers to the significant increase in the use of crack cocaine in the United States during the early 1980s. Crack cocaine was popularized because of its affordability; its immediate euphoric effect, which helped individuals escape their social and economic dilemmas; and its high profitability, which provided opportunities for some to move up the "economic ladder." The relevance of the crack epidemic to the topic of race and crime lies in the increase of addictions, deaths, and drug-related crimes that took place mostly within the African American community of the inner city. This entry discusses crack cocaine, its arrival in America, its effects on crime in the African American community, and the efforts made to curtail its use.

Crack Cocaine

Cocaine is a fine white crystallized powder substance that is referred to by numerous names, including "coke," "snow," "freeze," and "blow." Before the dangerous effects of powdered cocaine were known, it was often used as a painkiller in the fields of medicine and dentistry. Once powdered cocaine was legally restricted and banned from soft drinks and medication, its price increased tremendously, ranging from $50 to $100 per gram.

As the demand for cocaine increased, so did the availability of supplies, which caused a substantial decrease in pricing. As a result, drug dealers discovered a way to convert powdered cocaine into a smokable form that could be sold in smaller portions but distributed to more people. This addictive version of cocaine became known as "crack." The name *crack* is attributed to the crackling noise that is made when the substance is smoked. Crack was produced by dissolving cocaine hydrochloride into water with sodium bicarbonate (baking soda), which precipitates solid masses of cocaine crystals. Unlike powder cocaine, crack was easier to develop, more cost efficient to produce, and cheaper to buy, which made it more economically accessible. Crack sold for anywhere between $5 and $20 per vial (a small capsule that contains pebble-sized pieces of crack that were approximately one tenth of a gram of powdered cocaine). Crack cocaine was noted for its instantaneous and intense high, which kept users craving for more, thus causing an upsurge in crack cocaine addictions. In 1985 alone, the number of cocaine users increased by 1.6 million people. Crack cocaine causes weight loss, high blood pressure, hallucinations, seizures, and paranoia. Emergency room visits due to cocaine incidents such as overdoses, unexpected reactions, suicide attempts, chronic effects, and detoxification increased fourfold between 1984 and 1987.

Arrival in America

Cocaine hydrochloride or powdered cocaine was a major cash crop for South American countries, especially Columbia. Up until the 1960s, very few people knew about cocaine, and the demand was very limited. As the desire for the drug increased, Colombian trafficking organizations, such as the Medellin cartel, instituted a distribution system of cocaine imported from South America into the U.S. market through the Caribbean and the South Florida coast. The successful trafficking of cocaine was aided by South American and Cuban refugees who smuggled the illicit drug by sea and air. Trafficking organizations oversaw all operations, including the conversion, packaging, transportation, and the first-level distribution of cocaine in the United States.

Crack cocaine first appeared in Miami, where Caribbean immigrants taught adolescents the technique of converting powdered cocaine into crack cocaine. These teens eventually brought the business of producing and distributing crack cocaine into other major cities of the United States, including New York City, Detroit, and Los Angeles. That trafficking continues today.

Crack Cocaine in the African American Community

The initiation of crack cocaine into socially eroded communities took place during President Ronald Reagan's term in office, when there was a structural shift that caused huge manufacturing industries to move outside the cities. Their relocation created workforce competitions that further widened the gap between social and economic segments in the inner cities of America.

Few skills and resources were needed to sell crack. Many small-time drug dealers worked independently of and outside the control of organizations, like the Medellin cartel. The rewards clearly outweighed the risk, and drug dealers immediately realized that their success depended on their survival. A small-time drug dealer who sold crack daily earned a median net income of $2,000 per month. The increase in the demand for crack cocaine caused intense competition between drug dealers as they fought to profit from the same customers. Consequently, violence became linked to crack cocaine as these small-time drug dealers defended their economic boundaries.

Murder and nonnegligent manslaughter rates had increased by approximately 19% after the emergence of crack cocaine in inner cities. There was also a 27% increase in robbery and a 50% increase in aggravated assault, which indicated the significant effect that crack cocaine had on crime. Ultimately, the prison population doubled due to the arrest of drug dealers and their customers. One in every four African American males was either incarcerated or on probation or parole by the year 1992, giving the United States the highest incarceration rate in the world. The incarceration ratio of African American males later progressed to 1 in every 4. In federal prison, between 1981 and 1986, prison admission for drug offenses had risen by 128%.

The War on Drugs

The *War on Drugs* refers to the governmental strides made internationally to impose drug laws that were declared by U.S. President Ronald Reagan in 1982. The War on Drugs efforts aimed to end the crack cocaine epidemic that was responsible for destroying so many lives. These efforts included the passing of federal anti-drug laws, increased federal anti-drug funding, the initiation and expansion of prison and police programs, and the establishment of private organizations, such as Partnership for a Drug-Free America, to campaign on its behalf. The idea of the War on Drugs was grounded in deterrence theory, whereby the implementation of legislation and harsher penalties would deter or discourage the use of drugs. The 100-to-1 ratio between powdered cocaine and crack cocaine was used as a guideline for minimal mandatory punishment. For instance, a minimum penalty of 5 years was administered for 5 grams of crack cocaine or 500 grams of powdered cocaine.

The War on Drugs played a major role in modifying incarceration rates and mandating severe sentencing. Yet, there was an immense growth in court caseloads and the prison population. The War on Drugs focused on small-time drug dealers, who were generally poor, young Black males from the inner city.

Indeed, the crack cocaine epidemic was an American prodigy. Although the consequences of crack cocaine today are not as substantial as they were during the early 1980s, there still is a crusade against the effects of crack cocaine as it continues to plague communities around the world.

Deonna S. Turner

See also Crack Babies; Crack Mothers; National African American Drug Policy Coalition; Scarface Myth; War on Drugs

Further Readings

Belenko, S. (1993). *Crack and the evolution of anti-drug policy*. Westport, CT: Greenwood.

Chatlos, C., & Chilnick, L. (1987). *Crack: What you should know about the cocaine epidemic*. New York: Putman.

Reinarman, C., & Levine, H. (Eds.). (1997). *Crack in America: Demon drugs and social justice.* Berkeley: University of California Press.

CRACK MOTHERS

Crack mothers illustrates how the overexposure of a racial or ethnic stereotype can wrongfully influence the treatment of a specific group of people. This entry examines the social construction of crack mothers, media portrayals, prenatal effects of cocaine, and legal issues. Crack mothers are pregnant women who use cocaine. The term emerged during the mid-1980s as a part of the War on Drugs crusade launched by President Ronald Reagan. The media was mainly responsible for bringing to light the images of crack mothers as mostly Black and Hispanic, economically underprivileged urban women. Television news teams showed these women smoking crack and openly describing their drug use. This led to the stereotype of crack mothers as poor women of color who were indifferent to the health of their babies.

Cocaine became popular in the mid-1980s as a highly addictive stimulant. Cocaine users report feelings of euphoria, high energy, and erratic behavior. Crack and powder cocaine are different forms of cocaine, but they are equally addictive. The term *crack* refers to the crackling sound cocaine makes when it is heated. Crack remains a popular drug because it is easy to produce, very inexpensive, and the feeling of euphoria is reached in less than 10 seconds when smoked. Powdered cocaine is more expensive, and the high from snorting it is reached at a slower pace.

The social construction of crack mothers illustrates the intersection among race, class, and gender. The profile of maternal crack use was a Black woman in her mid-20s who came from the inner city and was on Medicaid. This bias played an important role in the unfair drug testing of mothers and continues to play a part in the criminalization of poor women of color in the War on Drugs. Moreover, the media also distinguished between mothers who used cocaine and those who used crack. Criminologist Drew Humphries, in her book *Crack Mothers,* analyzed network news images and found that cocaine mothers, mostly White middle-class women, were televised as remorseful mothers caring for their children and conforming to a life of recovery. Conversely, crack mothers were portrayed as irresponsible and reprehensible mothers.

The detrimental effects of prenatal cocaine exposure are difficult to isolate because of multiple confounding factors that may influence a child's development in the womb. For instance, mothers who use cocaine may also use other drugs and differ in prenatal care, prenatal nutrition, and socioeconomic conditions. Babies born to crack cocaine–addicted mothers were often referred to as "crack babies." This was another popular term that surfaced in the midst of the crack cocaine era of the 1980s and early 1990s. Empirical studies found that babies exposed to cocaine have higher risks of mortality, low birth weight, and patterns of neurobiological damaging effects that can affect their scholastic and physical development. However, these studies also revealed that the effects on a child's motor skills and intelligence may not be as long lasting and severe as previously suggested. Nonetheless, these children need increased assistance in everyday learning and developing sound communication and interpersonal skills.

Unlike other drug offenders, many crack mothers entered the criminal justice system via hospital testing. Hospital suspicion of drug use by pregnant women would often lead to drug testing. If a woman tested positive, hospitals would alert criminal justice officials. These women were often charged with child abuse or drug distribution. This resulted in a controversial discourse on gender, race, drugs, and the criminal justice system. A Florida study found that hospitals drug-tested pregnant Black women at higher rates than White women. The overselection of Black pregnant women was a result of a prevailing stereotype fueled by the media and reinforced by federal policies. Moreover, there was an upsurge of legal arguments about the authority of hospitals' drug-testing policies and the legitimacy of indicting these women in criminal court. The U.S. Supreme Court case *Ferguson et al. v. the City of Charleston et al.* argued that drug testing of pregnant women without their consent for the sole reason of obtaining evidence for law enforcement purposes was an unreasonable search in violation of the Fourth Amendment. In 2001, the Supreme Court ruled in favor of the women and decided that this procedure was unconstitutional.

The media portrayal of crack mothers induced fear and alarmed the general public. Concomitant with this were the publicized War on Drugs debates, which introduced stringent and punitive policies that adversely affected minorities and had a direct impact on destitute crack-addicted mothers. The movement against crack mothers was just one chapter in the wide-ranging War on Drugs. The augmented attention to crack mothers disproportionately criminalized women of color and perpetuated the negative gendered stereotype of this racial group. However, by the mid-1990s the media had changed their outlook on crack mothers and began portraying them as women who were remorseful and in need of drug treatment. More drug treatment programs for drug-addicted mothers began to emerge, and the crack mother stigma began to fade away. In the end, the crack mother phenomenon is another example of the marginalization of people on the basis of race/ethnicity and of the partialities in the criminal justice system in the United States.

Vivian Pacheco

See also Crack Babies; Crack Epidemic; Drug Use; Media Portrayals of African Americans; War on Drugs

Further Readings

Ferguson v. City of Charleston, 532 U.S. 67, 149 L. Ed. 2d 205, 121 S. Ct. 1281, 2001 U.S. LEXIS 2460 (2001).

Humphries, D. (1999). *Crack mothers: Pregnancy, drugs and the media.* Columbus: Ohio State University Press.

National Institute of Drug Abuse. (2004). *Cocaine abuse and addiction: Research Report Series.* Rockville, MD: National Institutes of Health.

CRIME STATISTICS AND REPORTING

A prominent feature of the race/crime nexus in the United States is the racial disparity found in arrest statistics. Although self-report surveys suggest fewer racial differences in offending than do police-generated statistics, the media frequently focuses on crimes known to the police. To facilitate a better understanding of the relationship between race and crime, this entry focuses on two sources of national crime statistics: the Uniform Crime Reporting (UCR) Program, administered by the Federal Bureau of Investigation since 1930, and the National Crime Victimization Survey (NCVS), conducted by the U.S. Census Bureau since 1973 for the Bureau of Justice Statistics.

The UCR collects data on murder and nonnegligent manslaughter, forcible rape, robbery, aggravated assault, burglary, larceny-theft, motor vehicle theft, and arson (traditionally known as Part I crimes), in addition to 21 other criminal offenses. Beginning in the late 1980s, the National Incident-Based Reporting System (NIBRS) was inaugurated to provide in-depth information on six types of data segments: administrative, offense, victim, property, offender, and arrestee. Nonetheless, these data provide little usable information, as only 36% of the reporting agencies are currently certified for NIBRS participation. An annual report, *Crime in the United States,* documents information on crimes known to the police, crime trends, law enforcement personnel, and characteristics of homicides. Also published annually by this program are *Law Enforcement Officers Killed and Assaulted* and *Hate Crime Statistics.*

In 1993, the NCVS was modified to collect more detailed information on rape, sexual assault, personal robbery, aggravated and simple assault, household burglary, theft, and motor vehicle theft. A nationally representative sample of persons ages 12 and over from approximately 43,000 households is interviewed twice annually. Unlike the UCR, the NCVS includes crimes not reported to law enforcement. Results of the survey are reported annually in *Criminal Victimization in the United States.*

The *Uniform Crime Reports*

The Federal Bureau of Investigation's publication *Crime in the United States* employs four racial categories: White, Black, American Indian or Alaskan Native, and Asian or Pacific Islander. Not included in the data is ethnicity. Beginning in 1960, a Crime Index was calculated using the first seven crimes listed in the Part I crimes cited previously. The Crime Index was later modified to include the crime of arson. Criticism of the Crime

Index led to the suspension of the Crime Index category in 2004. The eight Part I offenses are still used in the calculation of violent crime and property crime rates in the United States.

Table 1 enumerates the arrests for Part I offenses by race for the year 2006. Racial differences in arrests are readily apparent. Examining arrest percentages separately for each racial group highlights one of the controversies surrounding these statistics. Three of the highest arrest percentages for Whites involve offenses from the property crime index. Arson (76%), burglary (69%), and larceny-theft (68.6%) represent the top three offenses for which Whites are arrested. A different picture emerges when Blacks are examined. Three of the top four crime categories are violent crimes: robbery (56.3%), murder and nonnegligent manslaughter (50.9%), and aggravated assault (34.5%). Only motor vehicle theft (34.9%) involves a nonviolent crime. Moreover, the violent crime and property crime indexes reflect these racial differences: the higher index for Whites is the property crime index (68.2% for property crimes versus 58.5% for violent crimes), whereas the higher index for Blacks is the violent crime index (39.3% for violent crimes versus 29.4% for property crimes). Because the percentages for the racial categories of American Indian or Alaskan Native and Asian or Pacific Islander provide little variation

(from 0.7% to 1.4%), these racial groups tend to be largely ignored in the criminal justice literature. Consequently, researchers focus on racial differences between White and Black arrestees.

Placing Racial Differences in Offending in Perspective

Interest in racial differences in offending has generated research aimed at explaining the ostensibly greater propensity of African Americans to engage in violent behavior. Theories such as Wolfgang and Ferracuti's (1967) subculture of violence theory have suggested differences in cultural values between minorities and nonminorities. Yet such explanations fail to capture the many similarities that exist between African American and White offenders while exaggerating their differences. A more critical examination of this issue is therefore warranted.

The eight offenses of the violent crime and property crime indexes comprised only 15.1% of the total arrests in the United States for 2006. To generalize from such a small number of arrests may not be prudent. An alternative to this is to examine all 29 offenses contained in the UCR to determine the most common offenses for which Whites and African Americans are arrested. Excluding the miscellaneous category "all other

Table 1   Part I Offense Arrests in the United States in 2006 by Race

Offense charged	Percentage Distribution				
	Total	White	Black	American Indian or Alaskan Native	Asian or Pacific Islander
Murder and nonnegligent manslaughter	9,801	46.9	50.9	1.1	1.1
Forcible rape	17,042	65.3	32.5	1.1	1.1
Robbery	93,393	42.2	56.3	0.7	0.9
Aggravated assault	326,721	63.2	34.5	1.2	1.1
Violent crime	446,957	58.5	39.3	1.1	1.1
Burglary	221,732	69.0	29.2	1.0	0.9
Larceny-theft	798,983	68.6	28.9	1.2	1.3
Motor vehicle theft	100,612	62.7	34.9	1.0	1.4
Arson	11,972	76.0	21.6	1.0	1.4
Property crime	1,133,299	68.2	29.4	1.1	1.2

Source: U.S. Department of Justice, Federal Bureau of Investigation (2006), Table 43.

offenses (except traffic)," Table 2 lists the most common crime categories involving arrest separately for Whites and African Americans. By ranking each crime category according to the number of arrests separately for Whites and African Americans, one can see a *pattern* of offending for each group. When viewing the 10 most common crimes that led to arrest, one is struck by the similarities rather than the differences. Eight of the 10 most common offenses leading to arrest are the same for each group: aggravated assault, burglary, larceny-theft, other assaults, drug abuse violations, driving under the influence, drunkenness, and disorderly conduct. Although the relative rank may vary somewhat (e.g., drug abuse violations are the most common crime for which Blacks were arrested in 2006, whereas drug abuse violations represented the second most common crime for Whites), the racial groups are more homogeneous than would be anticipated if only Part I crimes were analyzed. It thus appears that the typical crimes for which Whites and Blacks are arrested are more similar than dissimilar, thereby raising questions about the earlier assumption that African Americans and Whites differ substantially in their propensities toward violent and property crimes.

That being said, the UCR clearly reveals racial disparities in arrests. Despite comprising less than 13% of the general U.S. population, Blacks represented 28% of those arrested in 2006. When broken down by age, younger Blacks are somewhat more likely than their older counterparts to be arrested. In 2006, Blacks under the age of 18 constituted 30.3% of all youths arrested. For persons 18 and over, Blacks comprised 27.6% of the adults arrested. For Whites, who account for nearly 80% of the general population in the United States, the percentages were 67.1% and 70.1%, respectively, suggesting that White adults were somewhat more likely than White youths to be arrested.

When focusing on the property crime and violent crime indexes, an interaction between race and age is found. Whereas only 37% of adults arrested for a Part I violent crime were Black, 51% of youths (under 18 years of age) arrested for a Part I violent crime were Black. Conversely, White adults (60.8%) were more likely than White youths (47%) to be arrested for a Part I violent crime. Age does not appear to play a major role in Part I property crime arrests, however. Whereas

Table 2	Most Common Offenses Resulting in Arrest by Race in the United States for 2006

Whites		
Rank	Offense charged	Number of arrests
1	Driving under the influence	914,226
2	Drug abuse violations	875,101
3	Other assaults	619,825
4	Larceny-theft[a]	548,057
5	Liquor laws	398,068
6	Drunkenness	344,155
7	Disorderly conduct	325,991
8	Aggravated assault[b]	206,417
9	Vandalism	165,518
10	Burglary[a]	152,965

Blacks		
Rank	Offense charged	Number of arrests
1	Drug abuse violations	483,886
2	Other assaults	306,078
3	Larceny-theft[a]	230,980
4	Disorderly conduct	179,733
5	Aggravated assault[b]	12,645
6	Driving under the influence	95,260
7	Burglary[a]	64,655
8	Weapons: carrying, possessing, etc.	59,863
9	Fraud	59,087
10	Drunkenness	54,113

Source: Calculated from data from U.S. Department of Justice, Federal Bureau of Investigation (2006), Table 43.

Note: Excluding "all other offenses (except traffic)."

a. Included in the property crime index calculated by the Federal Bureau of Investigation.

b. Included in the violent crime index calculated by the Federal Bureau of Investigation.

30.9% of all youths arrested in 2006 for a Part I property crime were Black, 28.9% of all adults arrested that year for a Part I property crime were Black. Similarly, White youths accounted for 66.3% of those arrested for a Part I property crime compared to 68.9% of their adult counterparts.

Nevertheless, inferring criminal behavior from arrest statistics should be treated with caution, as the UCR data contain numerous shortcomings.

Because the UCR includes only crimes known to the police, failure on the part of police to detect crime and underreporting by the public may distort the racial distribution of offending. Self-reports of offending by juveniles suggest that the police are perhaps aware of only 10% to 20% of all youthful misbehavior. Moreover, since not all offenses known to the police become part of the official record, police discretion may influence the racial distribution of arrests. Criminologists have observed that police discretion may be influenced by the presence or absence of a complainant, preferences of the complainant (e.g., to release the suspect or take the suspect into custody), the demeanor of the suspect, and departmental policies, among others. Critics of the data also note that the War on Drugs, being focused on inner-city neighborhoods in general and crack cocaine in particular, disproportionately affects people of color. Powdered cocaine, more expensive to purchase and therefore more likely to be used in affluent suburbs, is more difficult for the police to detect than crack cocaine, whose drug transactions are more likely to occur on the street.

Differential treatment by law enforcement has been documented by numerous researchers. For example, an analysis of aggravated assault charges in Duvall County (Jacksonville), Florida, disclosed that police routinely overcharged African Americans with violent crime. During the 3 months covered in the investigation, more than three fourths of the initial charges of aggravated assault (a Part I offense used in calculating the violent crime index) were downgraded either to simple assault or to a misdemeanor. Most recently, the differential handling of African American and White youths in Jena, Louisiana, illustrates the need to approach official crime data with some skepticism.

The National Crime Victimization Survey

The National Crime Victimization Survey (NCVS) provides some additional information on crime. Although crime victims may fail to report their victimizations to the NCVS, and the perceived race of the offender is subject to human error (including racial stereotypes), the NCVS can be used to estimate the extent to which crime is intraracial (between persons of the same race) or interracial (between persons of different races). An examination of the survey for 2005 reveals that Whites are only slightly more likely than their Black counterparts to identify the race of the offender as a person of the other race for crimes of violence (rape or sexual assault, robbery, and assault). In violent crimes against Whites, the perceived race of the offender was Black in 13.5% of the single-offender victimizations. By contrast, 10.4% of the Black victimizations involved White offenders. Overall, the statistics demonstrate the intraracial nature of much violent crime. Although 27.7% of the White victimizations and 20.5% of the Black victimizations resulted in the race of the offender not being identified, 49% of the White victimizations were perceived to be perpetrated by Whites, whereas 63.5% of the Black victimizations were perceived to be perpetrated by Blacks.

Summary

Although both data sources have shortcomings, some racial differences are apparent. African Americans tend to be more likely to be arrested for crimes against the person, whereas Whites tend to be more likely to be arrested for property crimes when limiting the analysis to Part I offenses. When all 29 offenses contained in the UCR are included, however, the most common offenses for which Whites and African Americans are arrested are quite similar. Nonetheless, given the subjective nature of arrest data, generalizations should be drawn with caution. Victimization data further reveal that whereas White victims of violence are slightly more likely to identify their perpetrator as Black than Black victims of violence are to identify their perpetrator as White, violent crime in general tends to be intraracial in nature.

Marvin D. Free, Jr.

See also Death Penalty; Disproportionate Arrests; Disproportionate Minority Contact and Confinement; Hate Crimes; Interracial Crime; Jena 6; Juvenile Crime; Profiling, Ethnic: Use by Police and Homeland Security; Profiling, Racial: Historical and Contemporary Perspectives

Further Readings

Miller, J. (1996). *Search and destroy: African American males in the criminal justice system*. New York: Cambridge University Press.

U.S. Department of Justice. (2006). *Criminal victimization in the United States, 2005*. Washington, DC: Bureau of Justice Statistics.

U.S. Department of Justice, Federal Bureau of Investigation. (2007). *Crime in the United States, 2006*. Retrieved from http://www.fbi.gov/ucr/cius2006

Wolfgang, M., & Ferracuti, F. (1967). *The subculture of violence*. London: Tavistock.

CRIMINALBLACKMAN

The term *criminalblackman* refers to the myth of the Black man as a criminal. Katheryn Russell-Brown first used this expression when referring to the stereotyping of minorities as criminals. The term exemplifies the culmination of fear that many Whites have of Black men. Stereotyping of the Black race began with slavery. A portion of the justification for slavery included the idea that Blacks were inferior and animal-like. Shortly after the emancipation of slaves, stereotyping depicted members of the Black race as dangerous people, prone to criminality. This type of stereotyping was used to keep Blacks in their place and provide a form of justification for violence against the Black race. The image of the Black man as a rapist fueled both fear and violence. During the 1970s and 1980s, the Black male became labeled as a criminal predator, otherwise referred to as the "criminalblackman."

Fear of the Black man has been created by those in a position to benefit from such fear. For decades, politicians have emphasized their "tough on crime" approaches in running for office. Perhaps the most popular example of dislodging an opponent is George H. W. Bush's use of Willie Horton as a criminal poster child to discredit his opponent, Michael Dukakis, during the 1988 presidential campaign. A rape committed by Horton, a Black man, while out of prison on work furlough focused fear of crime on the Black race and further stereotyped Black men as predators. It especially enhanced the stereotype of the Black male as a rapist who seeks out White women to victimize.

It is well established that the media perpetuates myths and misconceptions about crime and criminals. Newspapers and news broadcasters have overemphasized the Black male as criminal. Statistically, Whites commit the majority of crimes, yet the public perceives the Black male as the greater threat for crime. There is more negative than positive representation of the Black male in newspapers, in magazines, and on television newscasts. Ted Chiricos and Sarah Eschholz found that Black males are 2.4 times as likely to be represented as criminal on local news broadcasts than are White males. The media shapes images for the public to adopt into thought, thus contributing to society's stereotyping of the Black male as criminal.

The myth of the criminalblackman is perpetuated by governmental policies and a system that targets the Black male as a criminal. The entranceway for the criminal justice system begins with the police. Police efforts are dictated by the "War on Drugs," "War on Crime," and the "War on Gangs." All of these "wars" depict the young inner-city Black male as the enemy and further stereotype the Black male as a criminal. The police carry these stereotypes into work, sometimes unconsciously. In part because of legislation such as the War on Drugs, police primarily target minority youth in urban areas. Discretion given to the police under the "war" directives allows them to focus investigative efforts toward minorities and away from the more affluent. These "wars" have also provided enough grounds in some states for pulling over cars driven by Black males. This "driving while Black" is more accurately called "racial profiling."

The media's depiction of the Black crack user is a prime example of how society adopts a stereotype. Cocaine was already widely used in America, primarily by Whites, when the more affordable form, known as "crack," became popular among Blacks. As the media paid special attention to the emergence of the new drug in the 1980s, it brought society's focus to the "crack epidemic" that was supposedly sweeping through the country. The media depicted Black crack users as violent, psychotic drug users, out of their minds, and willing to commit violent crimes in order to support their habit. Due to media attention of this nature, society began to associate crack with crazed and dangerous Blacks. The media just contributed to the stereotypes associated with the War on Drugs.

There have been cases in which White offenders have used fear of the Black male to their advantage by creating a racial hoax in which they accuse a Black male of committing the crime in order to deflect suspicion. Stereotyping and fear of the Black male can result in the authorities believing that there was a Black perpetrator when in fact the individual providing the description actually committed the crime. A 1994 example of a racial hoax involved Susan Smith, a South Carolina woman, who reported that a Black man stole her car and her children who were still in the car. For several days, she spoke in front of television cameras pleading for their safety. She later confessed to murdering her children.

Stereotyping and treatment that leads to the myth of the criminalblackman may be outwardly insignificant in any one area of society; it is rather an accumulated result of history, politics, media, and social policies. Within the legal system, racism begins with police surveillance focused primarily on poor minority youth and culminates with sentencing that is harsher and disproportionately applied to this stereotyped class. Media coverage and society's fear further contributes to the myth of the criminalblackman.

Patricia L. Brougham

See also Consumer Racial Profiling; Media Portrayals of African Americans; *Powell v. Alabama*; Profiling, Racial: Historical and Contemporary Perspectives; Racial Hoax; War on Drugs

Further Readings

Barlow, M. (1998). Race and the problem of crime in "Time" and "Newsweek" cover stories, 1946 to 1995. *Social Justice*, 25(2), 149–184.

Kappeler, V., & Potter, G. (2005). *The mythology of crime and criminal justice* (4th ed.). Long Grove, IL: Waveland.

Merlo, A., & Benekos, P. (2000). *What's wrong with the criminal justice system: Ideology, politics, and the media*. Cincinnati, OH: Anderson.

Petersilia, J. (2004). Racial disparities in the criminal justice system: A summary. In B. Hancock & P. Sharp (Eds.), *Public policy, crime, and criminal justice* (pp. 80–95). Upper Saddle River, NJ: Prentice Hall.

Russell-Brown, K. (1998). *The color of crime: Racial hoaxes, White fear, Black protectionism, police harassment, and other macroaggressions*. New York: New York University Press.

Tonry, M. (1995). *Malign neglect: Race, crime, and punishment in America*. New York: Oxford University Press.

Walker, S. (2006). *Sense and non-sense about crime and drugs* (6th ed.). Belmont, CA: Thomson Wadsworth.

Welch, K. (2007). Black criminal stereotypes and racial profiling. *Journal of Contemporary Criminal Justice*, 23(3), 276–288.

Zatz, M. (2000). The convergence of race, ethnicity, gender, and class on court decisionmaking: Looking toward the 21st century. In *Criminal justice 2000: Vol. 3. Policies, processes, and decisions of the criminal justice system* (pp. 503–552). Washington, DC: U.S. Department of Justice, Office of Justice Programs.

CRITICAL RACE THEORY

Despite the relatively recent appearance of critical race theory (CRT) in academia, it has become an indispensable perspective on race and racism in America. CRT launched what many race scholars now take as a commonsense view: the view that race, instead of being biologically grounded and natural, is socially constructed. However, unlike some views that argue that aspects of race should be eliminated from everyday speech, thought, and scholarship, CRT maintains that race, as a socially constructed concept, functions as a means to maintain the interests of Whites who construct(ed) it and is an indispensable lens from which to view the problem of racism. According to CRT, racial inequality emerges from the social, economic, and legal differences Whites create between "races" to maintain elite White interest in labor markets and politics, and as such create the circumstances that give rise to poverty and criminality in many minority communities. In this regard, CRT holds that the laws and policies in the United States will always be geared toward people of color's detriment and as such have focused their scholarship on the ways in which people of color are punished by White legal institutions. CRT is interested in both in how the actions of White institutions create and maintain the conditions of "racial criminality," and, more important, how White structures and governing entities punish and persecute these constructions of "racial criminality" on the gendered bodies of racialized people.

Though the intellectual origins of the movement go back much further, the movement officially organized itself in July 1989, marking its separation from critical legal studies (CLS). Instead of drawing theories of social organization and individual behavior from continental European thinkers like Hegel and Marx or psychoanalytic figures like Freud as its theoretical predecessors (CLS and feminist jurisprudence), CRT was inspired by the American civil rights tradition through figures like Martin Luther King, Jr., and W. E. B. Du Bois, and from nationalist thinkers such as Malcolm X, the Black Panthers, and Frantz Fanon. Being steeped in radical Black thought and nationalist thinking, critical race theory advanced theoretical understandings of the law, politics, and American socio- logy that focused on the efforts Whites have historically used to maintain colonialism and White supremacy against people of color.

Given the ways in which race is defined and contoured by the interests of Whites in American society, CRT exposes a sociocultural component of the American race problem and the rampant incarceration of people of color. CRT holds a guarded pessimism about the racial conditions in the United States; even though Whites seek to maintain power and keep America a White republic, people of color, especially Blacks, are demonized as criminals and victimized by the courts, the police, and the everyday stereotypes of White America. Critical race theorists maintain that racism in America is normal, not aberrant, and as such, the laws, policies, and justice system are all built to maintain the power and historical stature of Whites. Though crime and criminal justice comprise a relatively small portion of CRT scholarship, critical race theorists have introduced novel claims that range from arguments maintaining the criminal justice system is fundamentally racist to positions that contend that White male experiences form the basis of the actions committed by a reasonable person under duress. This entry briefly discusses the origins of CRT and outlines some of its major theoretical contributions to analysis of race and crime.

Origins of the Movement: Bell's Interest Convergence and Racial Realism

The foundational writings of critical race theory began in the late 1960s from the legal scholarship of Derrick Bell and Alan Freeman. These writings focused specifically on the reduction of gains of the civil rights era thought to be won in 1964 and the rollback of the integrationist agendas set forth in *Brown v. Board of Education* (1954). In Derrick Bell's earlier works (throughout the 1970s), Bell argued the gains of Blacks were inextricably wed to the temporary alignment of the self-interests of elite Whites and the interests of Blacks or the interest convergence between White interests and Black aspirations. This body of work led to a critical examination of integration, school desegregation, and the newly instilled privileges of the civil rights era and maintained that integration was a political consequence of U.S. attempts to maintain soft power legitimacy against communism during the cold war.

This argument, however, was mild in contrast to the thesis Bell introduced in the early 1990s. In 1992, Bell authored "Racial Realism," an article in which he argued that equality was both impossible and illusory in the United States; he argued that Blacks must accept that racism and Black subordination is a permanent and integral part of American society. In two subsequent articles titled "The Racism Is Permanent Thesis" and "Racism Is Here to Stay: Now What?" published the same year, and his 1993 book titled *Faces at the Bottom of the Well: The Permanence of Racism,* Bell reinforced his argument over the nature of anti-Black racism and urged Blacks to resist the idea that automatic progress in race relations accompanied the civil rights era.

Though this view does not explicitly attend to a specific analysis of crime and criminality, it lays the foundations for the perspectives many critical race theorists hold to be the philosophical underpinning of their perspectives that link the sociocultural to institutional and structural racism. In the years to follow, many of the theories articulated by Derrick Bell were used in the perspectives of emerging critical race theorists in looking to the legal aspects of the criminal justice system.

Critical Race Theories of Crime

Building on the normalness of racism, critical race theorists have taken various approaches in the analysis of criminality that seek to investigate how minority populations in the United States become majority populations in the criminal justice system. According to Richard Delgado's 1994 article "Black Crime, White Fears—On the Social Construction of Threat," Black crime is constructed to be a problem by Whites. While it is undeniable that some Blacks, Latina/os, and other minorities commit crimes, it is not the case that this crime is race specific. CRT wants to point out that there is a sociocultural construction that creates the ideas of Black crime, Hispanic crime, and so on, and the mythology of race-specific crime (i.e., Black crime) is a means by which Whites justify the historical vulnerability people of color suffer at the hands of dangerous Whites. By constructing crime as race specific, American society and its White beneficiaries make crimes involving Blacks or other minorities seem natural and endemic to that group, making punishment a far more likely course of action than rehabilitation. Under these conditions, judges, lawyers, and law enforcement agencies would be more likely to treat various racial groups differently based on the prevalent racial stereotype playing out in the national imagination and justify their actions on that constructed threat.

Given this sociocultural construction of racial criminality, some authors have asserted a particularly nationalist or separatist analysis of race and crime. These authors claim that the dereliction of the U.S. government in protecting Black communities, and the lives of people of color both from White violence and violence within their communities, justifies pushing "The Second Amendment: Towards an Afro-Americanist Reconsideration." While very few authors have pursued Robert Cottrol and Raymond Diamond's course of action, which argued for a radical interpretation of the Second Amendment in the U.S. Constitution that justifies Blacks to take up arms to protect their communities, subsequent writings in CRT have continued to confirm the unchanging reality of racism in the criminal justice system.

In Paul Butler's infamous 1995 article "Racially Based Jury Nullification: Black Power in the Criminal Justice System," he argues that it is better for some nonviolent Black offenders to stay in the Black community rather than be sent to prison. Accepting that the criminal justice system is fundamentally racist and will seek unjust means of punishment rather than rehabilitation, Butler argues that jury nullification, or the practice by which a jury acquits an offender they believe is guilty for political or racial considerations, is the best way to challenge the White supremacy of the criminal justice system. By making rehabilitation rather than punishment the focus of Black deviance, Butler argues that Blacks can begin to protect their own communities without dependence on or interference from White intervention.

Other scholars like Cynthia Lee and David Harris have discussed the actions that Whites take against people of color they perceive as threats. In Lee's work, she discusses the overt privilege White male reactions, some of which included murder, have in determining reasonable actions in criminal cases involving people of color, while Harris focuses on the irrationality and myth making that sustains racial profiling.

Gender Analyses of Crime in CRT

As an analytical perspective, CRT is primarily housed in the legal academy, and as such the analysis of gender and race in questions of criminality is largely dictated by the effects the law and other legal entities have on particular people of color, both male and female. Despite the predominant effects that the criminal justice system has on African American and Hispanic males, most CRT scholarship on gender focuses on the critical race feminist perspective.

Kenneth B. Nunn's article titled "Race, Crime and the Pool Surplus of Criminality: Or Why the War on Drugs Was a War on Blacks" is a classic work that articulates a gendered reality of racial criminality. Nunn argued that the War on Drugs is in reality a political program designed specifically to incarcerate African American males. Borrowing from the work of Michael Tonry, Nunn argues that the U.S. government knowingly instituted a War on Drugs despite the overall decrease of drug use in the United States and the drastic decline of drug use in White middle-class communities. According to Nunn, the choice of the U.S. government to focus on supply reduction (those who sold the product) over demand reduction (those who produced and wanted the product) was the consequence of a specific anti-Black cultural and racist political regime. As such, racial profiling became a surefire way to increase the presence of Black and Hispanic males, since the political climate presupposes they deal drugs. As CRT, Nunn's work exemplifies the structural analysis of crime. Nunn focuses on the structure and intent of the criminal system and then the effects that system has on people of color by enforcing racial bias.

Other CRT analyses speak directly to the experiences of women of color and have included feminist perspectives in their analysis of race and crime. In Kimberle Crenshaw's groundbreaking essay on intersectionality titled "Mapping the Margins: Intersectionality, Identity Politics and Violence Against Women of Color," Crenshaw argues that racial politics overlook the role of sex in antiracist strategies. In domestic violence and rape cases, Crenshaw argues that Black women's identities are measured up against the experience of White women. In such cases, Crenshaw argues that remedies to reduce the occurrence of domestic violence and rape in minority communities are ineffective because they do not address the intersection of race and sex in battery. Crenshaw's work argues for a unique Black female perspective that should be used when investigating Black women.

Following the success of intersectional analysis in CRT, Dorothy Roberts wrote *Killing the Black Body: Race Reproduction and the Meaning of Liberty.* Expounding on her argument in "Punishing Drug Addicts Who Have Babies," Roberts argued that Black female sentencing in the criminal justice system frequently involves some type of birth control and in some cases forced sterilization. According to Roberts, Black women are often encouraged to relinquish their reproductive liberties in exchange for reduced jail times and lesser offenses. Continuing the argument from her earlier work, Roberts also contends that Black pregnant mothers found to be on drugs were blamed for the cycle of poverty in Black communities, and as such, long-term birth control contraceptives such as Norplant were seen as a remedy to Black economic woes.

Current Trends

Recent scholarship in CRT has failed to attend to the structural and sociocultural explanations of crime, poverty, and Black victimization. Recent scholars like Reginald Robinson have argued for

psychoanalytic and existential positions that hold that Blacks are the root cause of their own suffering. Robinson maintains that Blacks' marriage to racial identity is the root cause of poverty.

CRT has adamantly maintained the involvement of White institutions and White political and cultural interest in defining the relationship between race and crime. Rather than abandoning the rich racial realist tradition that defined more than 2 decades of CRT scholarship, future work in CRT could expand on the constructive ways in which people of color can adequately challenge the permanence of racism in America.

Tommy Curry

See also Conflict Theory; Domestic Violence; Jury Nullification; Racism

Further Readings

Bell, D. (1980). *Brown v. Board of Education* and the interest convergence dilemma. *Harvard Law Review, 93*, 518–533.

Bell, D. (1992). Racial realism. *Connecticut Law Review, 24*, 363–379.

Bell, D. (1992). Racism is here to stay: Now what? *Howard Law Journal, 35*, 79–93.

Bell, D. (1993). *Faces at the bottom of the well: The permanence of racism.* New York: Basic Books.

Butler, P. (1995). Racially based jury nullification: Black power in the criminal justice system. *Yale Law Journal, 105*, 677–725.

Butler, P. (2004). Much respect: Toward a hip-hop theory of punishment. *Stanford Law Review, 56*, 983.

Cottrol, R., & Diamond, R. (1991). The Second Amendment: Toward an Afro-Americanist reconsideration. *Georgetown Law Journal, 80*, 309–361.

Delgado, R., & Stefancic, J. (2001). *Critical race theory: An introduction.* New York: New York University Press.

Nunn, K. (2002). Race, crime and the pool surplus of criminality: Or why the War on Drugs was a war on Blacks. *Journal of Gender, Race, and Justice, 6*, 381–445.

Robinson, R. (1991). Punishing drug addicts who have babies: Women of color, equality, and the right of privacy. *Harvard Law Review, 104*, 1419–1482.

Robinson, R. (2000). Expert knowledge: Introductory comments on race consciousness. *Boston College Third World Law Journal, 20*, 145–182.

CRITICAL WHITE STUDIES

The centrality of race in social, economic, and political discourse has been devoid of much discussion of White identity or the experience of being a White person. Whites have primarily been the subject of studies examining their prejudices toward a given group as opposed to a more phenomenological account of the experience of being White. However, these works mainly discuss how power is maintained among Whites and the importance of race relations in the current social milieu. In order to understand the White experience as a distinct identity, many scholars, particularly in sociology and cultural studies, have called for an examination of how Whiteness shapes social life. The field is still incipient, but a few clear concepts and themes have emerged in recent years.

It is important to note that theorizing and deconstructing Whiteness has not been completely neglected in critical race theory. Several sociologists note the work of seminal scholars W. E. B. Du Bois, bell hooks, and Molefi Kete Asante, among others, as central to understanding Whiteness as a unique identity and position of social privilege. In other words, these thinkers tried to expose Whiteness as an identity that must be discussed in relation to other racial groups; Whiteness should not be approached as the absence of color but another political category worthy of thorough analysis. In addition, many groups, such as Jewish and Hungarian immigrants, were not considered "White" as a central part of their identity upon arriving in America. For example, Black people were often referred to as Irishmen in American racial slang, while Jews were often discriminated against as non-White or even referred to with racial slurs often directed at African Americans. Thus, the mercurial nature of what and who is considered "White" suggests the conflict and ambiguity surrounding American racial identities. Many European Americans were not initially considered.

Theorizing Whiteness

Particularly in the 1980s, as groups such as Native Americans and African Americans began to clearly assert a multicultural racial identity in the public domain, some discussion of the White identity began to emerge in academe. Much of this discourse did not unfold into a cohesive body of theory, and only recently have more lucid themes emerged.

The key premise upon which critical White studies is based suggests that Whiteness is simply a social construction as opposed to a natural outcome but nonetheless with consequences for both Whites and non-Whites. Whiteness is, for these theorists, more of a social and cultural marker, a barrier between groups that creates distinct spaces between racial constructions and their resultant influence on identities. In addition, because racial identities are about the separation of groups into power structures and hierarchies, they are often inextricably linked to politics.

More precisely, Whiteness arises only in relation to that which is non-White; one depends on the other to extract cultural meaning. For White people, the meaning of this idea is linked to a certain "privilege" linked to skin color; thus, the skin serves as a marker about the status of a given individual or group of people. In the case of Whiteness, this racial marker represents, for critical White studies, a marker of dominance. That is to say, White people dominate many public institutions throughout many parts of the world; the White person is seen as a kind of baseline for human righteousness.

Because Whiteness can be theorized as a generalized social privilege, there are ways of dressing and behaving that are seen as ideals of Whiteness. Particular values and ways of behaving are championed as "White" and part of a dominant racial identity. For example, homosexual or infirm White men may sacrifice the inherent privilege of Whiteness. Further, some sociologists have drawn a parallel from growing scholarship on masculinity in that there are hegemonic standards of conduct for dominant groups in society (e.g., heterosexuality). Many times in the media, these ideals of masculinity and Whiteness are visible in body types, fashion, and general behavior, with many notable celebrities personifying these ideals.

Inequality Within Whiteness

Critical White studies seek to deconstruct this baseline in the hopes of understanding what standards underpin this White ideal and how they might be altered. In addition, recent works have examined how the category and identity of Whiteness is stratified and the source of inequity from within its own racial ranks. Many of the inequalities that exist between Whites and other races, such as wealth or social status, are present among Whites. Although a general social privilege of being White may exist, the race itself contains many tensions and inequalities.

Moreover, specific areas or states or nations may promote one form of dominant White ideals over another. There exist certain phenotypes and ways of comportment for Whites that may gain ascendancy over another. Different segments of the same White population may become opposed as one form of White standards attempts to come to the forefront of discourse at the expense of another. Thus some scholars have discussed dominant forms of Whiteness in certain media outlets and political discourses; thus being able bodied, White, male, and married would be an example of an ascendant or ideal type. This example illustrates a constellation of certain traits and social designations that bestow privilege and a dominant status.

Conclusion

Critical White studies seek to understand the origins and importance of Whiteness and its significance in social life. Both inter- and intraracial conflict fall within the domain of this field as the ascendant forms of social, economic, and even physical discourse are many times dominated by a paradigm of Whiteness. In order to create a more just society, Whiteness and White privilege must be removed from this privileged position, and a new authority encompassing a multicultural framework must emerge. Finally, Whiteness stands in relation to inequality and must be recognized as a privileged and distinct identity.

Brent Funderburk

See also Critical Race Theory; Immigrants and Crime; White Crime; White Privilege

Further Readings

Du Bois, W. E. B. (2006). *The souls of Black folk*. West Valley City, UT: Walking Lion Press. (Original work published 1903)

hooks, b. (1989). *Talking Black*. Boston: South End Press.

Stefancic, J., & Delgado, R. (Eds.). (2001). *Critical race theory*. New York: New York University Press.

CULTURAL LITERACY

E. D. Hirsch, Jr., published the national bestseller *Cultural Literacy* in 1987, thereby sparking a lively debate about the value and desirability of a national educational canon. This debate was based, in part, on an incomplete understanding of Hirsch's proposition; nevertheless, many concluded that the foundation of his argument was rooted in a privileging of the educational worldview of the White, Protestant, and male. A few years later, Terence Thornberry and then Larry Siegel and Marvin Zalman published separate articles on cultural literacy within the study of criminology and criminal justice, respectively. Their arguments were similarly met with criticism for the perceived overreliance on the works of White male scholars in their respective fields. This entry defines cultural literacy in the general sense, discusses the nature of the criticism against it, then turns to the specific cultural literacies of criminology and criminal justice, along with the criticism against them.

Cultural Literacy and General Education

Cultural literacy as conceptualized by Hirsch relates to one's ability to participate in one's culture at a highly competent level. As such, many view this definition of cultural literacy as having roots in anthropological notions of culture. That is, *culture* is defined as the shared meanings, values, behaviors, expectations, and beliefs, among other things, that people living in the same society participate in. As such, to be literate in one's culture assumes a shared experience and understanding of that culture and an ability to draw on and extend from that shared understanding when communicating with others of the same culture. The shared communication and understanding are based on the notion of the schema. A *schema* is a person's sense of what is happening, and what should happen, based on past experience and knowledge. New schemas may be created from existing ones by expanding or linking them to create new meaning. In this sense, schemas are rooted in the individual and form the basis of one's understanding of the world. However, schemas also exist on a cultural level, and a shared understanding of cultural schemas is the basis of the concept of cultural literacy. For example, jokes about public figures, sports teams, or other cultural icons make sense only to people who are familiar with those icons—people who share those cultural schema. When people living in the same society do not share cultural understanding, communication between them is limited and thereby limiting to those whose cultural knowledge is narrow and/or different from others. Cultural communication is most effective when all participants share the same knowledge and understand cultural schemas in the same or similar ways.

The cultural literacy movement sparked by Hirsch's book was an attempt to address a perceived lack of general shared cultural knowledge in U.S. society. However, the shared cultural knowledge he assumed many Americans lacked was modeled on a Western, classical, and traditional educational foundation seen as belonging mainly to upper-middle-class, White males, which many define as the mainstream of American culture. One of the outcomes of the movement was the creation of a series of lists of what every American should know (sometimes referred to in subsequent debates as Hirsch's "canon"). Critics of the cultural literacy movement contend that the United States is a plural or at least multicultural society and that there is no single culture, but rather multiple cultures all with their shared understandings and schemas. Advocates for the multicultural understanding of U.S. society claim that cultural literacy unfairly privileges the Western canon at the expense of other coexisting cultural heritages.

Cultural Literacy and the Study of Crime

Applying the term *cultural literacy* to criminology and criminal justice necessarily narrows the scope from general cultural knowledge to specific foundational frameworks in these disciplines. In 1990–1991, two articles were published as a result of a general discussion of what would constitute a cultural literacy of criminology and criminal justice. The first, written by Thornberry (1990), alters the use of the term *cultural literacy* to mean a core body of knowledge that advanced students and scholars in the field of criminology should be expected to know. That core of knowledge is further divided into core ideas and core literature, thereby incorporating both the idea of cultural literacy and its accompanying "canon." The ideas (or subareas) addressed by Thornberry included the "origins of criminological thought, the measurement of crime and delinquency, and theories of crime and delinquency" (p. 38), each of which has a corresponding body of literature thought to comprise the core knowledge within that area. The following year, Siegel and Zalman published a similar article on the cultural literacy of criminal justice. Expanding on the work of Thornberry, their definition of *cultural literacy* attempts to further define core concepts within the study of criminal justice, including policy, enforcement, adjudication, punishment, and corrections, all of which are accompanied by corresponding bodies of literature considered seminal to the understanding of each concept.

Critics of these conceptualizations of criminal justice and criminology cultural literacies (CJCL) contend that they, like their general cultural literacy counterpart, are in essence based in a Eurocentric and patriarchal understanding of crime, delinquency, and the criminal justice system. As with criticisms of cultural literacy, critics of CJCL argue that such a narrowly constructed view of the meaning of *literacy* within criminal justice and criminology effectively limits further inquiry within these disciplines by omitting other, different literacies, or different experiences or understandings of crime and the criminal justice system.

All agree that there is and should be a foundational body of literature that all who work in the fields of criminology and criminal justice should be expected to know; however, whether a knowledge of that body of literature constitutes something that can be called "cultural literacy" is debated.

Elizabeth M. Fathman

See also Code of the Streets; Culture Conflict Theory; Inequality Theory; IQ; Social Capital

Further Readings

Banks, J. (1993). The canon debate, knowledge construction, and multicultural education. *Educational Researcher, 22*(5), 4–14.

Barak, G. (1991). Cultural literacy and a multicultural inquiry into the study of crime and justice. *Journal of Criminal Justice Education, 2*(2), 173–192.

Bizzell, P. (1990). Beyond anti-foundationalism to rhetorical authority: Problems defining "cultural literacy." *College English, 52*(6), 661–675.

Hirsch, E. D. (1987). *Cultural literacy: What every American needs to know.* Boston: Houghton Mifflin.

Siegel, L., & Zalman, M. (1991). "Cultural literacy" in criminal justice: A preliminary assessment. *Journal of Criminal Justice Education, 2*(1), 15–44.

Thornberry, T. (1990). Cultural literacy in criminal justice. *Journal of Criminal Justice Education, 1*(1), 33–49.

CULTURALLY SPECIFIC DELINQUENCY PROGRAMS

In the United States, minority group members are disproportionately represented as victims and offenders in the criminal justice system. Culturally specific delinquency programs have as their objectives to prevent and/or stop delinquent behavior.

Culturally specific delinquency programs consist of both prevention and treatment modules whereby the racial and/or ethnic identities of youths are incorporated as a necessary component of the response to delinquent behavior. To that end, specific elements of a culture (e.g., language, family norms, religion, gender, work ethic) are used such that adolescents from various backgrounds may more readily identify with program objectives and goals within the context of their own social experiences. President John F. Kennedy in 1964 termed the United States a "nation of immigrants." Once thought a melting pot whereby racial, ethnic, and various subordinate groups would "give up" their cultural heritage and conform to an Anglo-Protestant core culture, the United States has evolved more into a culturally pluralist society whereby various groups retain elements of their cultural heritage. Thus, culturally competent organizations recognize that one size does not fit all when it comes to establishing effective delinquency prevention and/or treatment programs and include diverse culturally relevant elements in their approaches to delinquency.

Early immigrants inherited the city's inner core and found themselves experiencing higher levels of disease, death, and crime than residents who lived outside of the city's inner sphere. To that end, programs intent on relieving these social ills focused upon emerging cultural and social class elements among inhabitants of the areas. Similar types of programming are needed today.

Tobler in 1992 reported that culturally specific delinquency programs designed to address delinquency among African American adolescents are often Afrocentric in focus and multilevel, involving various entities of the community, including families, schools, churches, and the juvenile justice system. Moreover, Boyd-Franklin in 1990 and Turner in 1995 noted that such programs focus upon transitions to manhood and womanhood while incorporating cultural elements that highlight spirituality and religion, flexibility and adaptability of familial roles, extended family networks, educational attainment, effective economic and social coping strategies, and a strong work ethic.

Caetano in 1989 noted that Hispanics or Latinos in the United States originate from at least 50 different countries, with major cultural, language, geographical, and social differences among them. Additionally, Dumka, Lopez, and Carter in 2002 proposed that delinquency programs focusing upon Hispanic and/or Latino youth consider the aforementioned factors as well as socioeconomic, acculturation, and gender differences while denoting the emphasis placed upon family, familial support, and the use of family as their primary reference group.

Lee in 1990 noted that Asian populations in the United States encompass more than 60 distinct groups, many with very disparate cultures. Thus, Ho in 1992 recommended that prevention programs targeting Asians consider acculturation, bicultural, and class differences in conjunction with family traditions, structure, and help-seeking behavior.

Edwards and Edwards in 1990 noted that delinquency intervention programs for Native adolescents should incorporate family, clan, and/or tribal members in both planning and delivery of the program. Additionally, Oetting, Beauvais, and Edwards in 1988 suggested such programs include cultural pride and competency, problem solving, recreational, academic, leadership development, and alcohol- and drug-free lifestyle components.

While we see an increase among culturally specific delinquency programs, the effectiveness of such programs is still questionable. Wilson, Lipsey, and Soydan in 2003 note that more researchers from diverse backgrounds and more research on culturally specific intervention programs are needed to determine the effectiveness of such programming.

Charles Corley

See also Center for the Study and Prevention of Violence; Delinquency Prevention; Evidence-Based Delinquency Prevention for Minority Youth; Faith-Based Initiatives and Delinquency

Further Readings

Boyd-Franklin, N. (1990). Five key factors in the treatment of Black families. In G. W. Saba, B. M. Karrer, & K. V. Hardy (Eds.), *Minorities and family therapy* (pp. 53–69). New York: Haworth.

Caetano, R. (1989). Concepts of alcoholism among Whites, Blacks, and Hispanics in the United States. *Journal of Studies on Alcohol, 50*, 580–582.

Dumka, L. E., Lopez, V. A., & Carter, S. J. (2002). Parenting interventions adapted for Latino families: Progress and prospects. In J. Contreras, K. A. Kerns, & A. M. Neal-Barnett (Eds.), *Latino children and families in the United States: Current research and future directions* (pp. 203–233). Westport, CT: Praeger.

Edwards, D., & Edwards, M. E. (1990). American Indian adolescents: Combating problems of substance use and abuse through a community model. In A. R. Stiffman & L. E. Davis (Eds.), *Ethnic issues in adolescent mental health* (pp. 285–302). Newbury Park, CA: Sage.

Ho, M. K. (1992). Differential application of treatment modalities with Asian American youth. In L. A. Vargas & J. D. Koss-Chioino (Eds.), *Working with culture: Psychotherapeutic interventions with ethnic minority children and adolescents* (pp. 182–203). San Francisco: Jossey-Bass.

Lee, E. (1990). Assessment and treatment of Chinese-American immigrant families. In G. W. Saba, B. M. Karrer, & K. V. Hardy (Eds.), *Minorities and family therapy* (pp. 53–69). New York: Haworth.

McKinney, K. (2003). *OJJDP's Tribal Youth Initiatives* (Bulletin). Washington, DC: U.S. Department of Justice, Office of Justice Programs, Office of Juvenile Justice and Delinquency Prevention.

Oetting, E. R., Beauvais, F., & Edwards, R. W. (1988). Alcohol and Indian youth: Social and psychological correlates of prevention. *Journal of Drug Issues, 81*, 87–101.

Park, R. E. (1950). *Race and culture*. Glencoe, IL: The Free Press.

Tobler, N. S. (1992). Drug prevention programs can work: Research findings. *Journal of Addictive Disease, 11*(3), 1–28.

Turner, W. L. (1995). Healthy Black families: Protectors against substance abuse. *Employee Assistance Journal, 8*, 30–31.

Wilson, S. J., Lipsey, M. W., & Soydan, H. (2003). Are mainstream programs for juvenile delinquency less effective with minority youth than majority youth? A meta-analysis of outcomes research. *Research on Social Work Practice, 13*(1), 3–26.

CULTURE CONFLICT THEORY

Criminologists have studied the relationship between race and crime and what role conflicting cultures might play in the etiology of crime. As defined by criminologist Thorsten Sellin, culture conflict is a condition that occurs when the rules and norms of an individual's culture conflict with the role demands of conventional society. Sellin believes that in any culture, the behavior of the individuals in that culture comes to be accepted, and behavior that does not conform to these social norms is seen as a violation of them. From a sociological perspective, Sellin's approach to the causation of crime was centered on what he called the "conduct norm" governing normal and abnormal behavior. Conduct norms vary from society to society, so an action may be a violation in one society but not in another. The potential for culture conflict exists when the dominant culture sets the standards for acceptable behavior; thus, anyone whose actions do not conform to these standards will be considered deviant and/or criminal.

Each one of us is born into a unique culture whose ideas, customs, and beliefs we accept. It is through this process that conduct norms are formulated. These norms, which are present wherever social groups are found, help form the foundation of one's character and personality. The power of the dominant culture tends to establish certain criteria for the behavior of society that is accepted as "the law." In order to preserve social norms, societies establish laws with specific penalties for those who violate the norms. This power that the dominant group possesses tends to create the idea that nondominant cultures are more likely to be deviant and take part in criminal activities as a way of life.

Subcultural conduct can and sometimes does conflict with the norms of the dominant culture.

Culture Conflict in America: Mass Immigration to the United States

Mass immigration from Europe to the United States during the late 19th and early 20th centuries helps explain the role that culture conflict can play in relation to race and crime. For example, from 1880 to 1920, 24 million immigrants arrived in the United States from southern and eastern European nations including Italy, Croatia, Greece, Poland, Czechoslovakia, Hungary, and Russia. These "new immigrants," like the previous ones, were leaving their country for reasons such as low wages, unemployment, disease, and religious persecution, just to name a few. As they fled from poverty and persecution, they experienced difficulties in assimilating into American culture. The immigrants maintained their own culture by forming communities consisting of stores in their area of expertise, restaurants, churches, schools, and even their own newspapers, all in their native languages. For the most part, they could not speak English, which complicated their situation, and since they came from a nondemocratic government, they were very distrustful of the U.S. government.

The problems immigrants faced in trying to assimilate into unknown surroundings and the discrimination inflicted by native-born Americans were just the start of the difficulties they encountered. Evidence shows that because of their origin and economic and political status, the immigrants were subject to differential treatment concerning law enforcement due to the difference in *culture norms*. The likelihood of conflict due to the breach of rules often exists when it involves a very diverse and heterogeneous society; and the breaking of such rules could open the door to possible criminal activity.

Impact of Culture Conflict on Crime

Although Sellin makes a strong point referring to conduct norms as the causation of crime, Marxist theory would explain the correlation between culture conflict and race and crime better than any other theory. Here, a power struggle exists between two different groups of people, the *haves* and the *have nots*. With reference to race and crime,

discrimination is significant in the enforcement of laws and the distribution of punishment by the White power structure. The difficulties of assimilation faced by southern Blacks who moved to the northern United States during the period of the Great Migration between 1910 and the mid-20th century is another example of a significant event that produced cultural conflicts and likely contributed to the overrepresentation of Blacks in criminal justice systems in northern cities.

The Great Migration of Blacks overlapped one of the largest periods of European immigration to the United States; however, the difference was that Blacks' movement was directly from the rural South to the urban North. In all, approximately 6 million Black people migrated north to secure their freedom and avoid the lynching and mob violence against them as a result of the rise of Jim Crow laws. With the end of World War I and the decrease in European immigration to the United States, jobs were plentiful in the North. While some of the conflicts subsided throughout the last quarter of the 20th century, urban areas continued to struggle with culture conflicts that sparked conflicts, riots, and crime.

Wherever there is a heterogeneous society with varying conduct norms and the lack of accessibility to improve living conditions, there is also likely to be cultures that *have* and cultures that *have not*, creating conflict. Such a conflict, as seen by the history of the United States and predicted by culture conflict theory, has the potential to contribute to crime and disorder.

Ella Henderson

See also Conflict Theory; Du Bois, W. E. B.; Hate Crimes; Social Disorganization Theory

Further Readings

Barak, G., Flavin, J., & Leighton, P. (2006). *Class, race, gender, and crime: Social realities of justice in America* (2nd ed.). Lanham, MD: Rowman & Littlefield.

Du Bois, W. E. B. (1899). The Negro and crime. *The Independent, 51,* 1355–1357.

Gabbidon, S. L. (2007). *Criminological perspectives on race and crime.* New York: Routledge.

Sellin, T. (1938). *Culture conflict and crime.* New York: Social Science Research Council.

Wyle, S. (2003). *Revisiting America: Readings in race, culture, and conflict.* Englewood Cliffs, NJ: Prentice Hall.

DAVIS, ANGELA (1944–)

Prison abolitionist, political prisoner, Black Panther, Communist, radical activist, Black feminist, critical resistor, public intellectual, intellectual activist, and university professor are just some of the labels by which Angela Davis has been known throughout her lifetime. Davis was the face of Black Pride in the 1970s, was a candidate for vice president on the Communist Party ticket in 1980 and 1984, and is a major feminist scholar. Today's generation knows her as a critic of the criminal justice system, particularly the prison-industrial complex, and as a prison abolitionist. Davis is currently a full professor at the University of California, Santa Cruz, where she holds a joint appointment in the History of Consciousness and Women's Studies departments.

From the beginning, Davis has combined theory and practice through scholarship and participation in the grassroots movements of 1960s Black Liberation to the more recent prison abolition movement. Through 4 decades Davis has critiqued the "broken" criminal justice system through global, racial, gender, and class lenses. She urges us to think about the connections between the racialized figures of the "terrorist," the "criminal," and the "immigrant." Noting that crime is socially constructed, Davis reminds us that the "criminal" in the United States is stereotypically portrayed as a young Black man and that not only White people but Black people alike believe this stereotype. Crime in the United States is racialized, according to Davis. Yet her critique goes beyond race in that it includes global, gender, and class analyses, and her racial analysis includes not only Blacks and Whites but also Native Americans, Latinos, and other people of color.

Education

Angela Davis was born and raised in the "cradle of the confederacy," Birmingham, Alabama, during the end of segregation in the 1940s and 1950s. Although she attended segregated schools through junior high, she came from a privileged Black middle-class family. Davis then received an American Friends Service Committee scholarship to attend Elizabeth Irwin High School, a private school in Greenwich Village, New York. At Irwin High, she was exposed to Marxist-Leninist socialist ideology through conversations with teachers who had been blacklisted for their Communist membership. After having graduated from Irwin High School, Davis received a scholarship to Brandeis University, where she was one of only a few Black students. Extensive international travels while at Brandeis gave Davis a worldview of oppression, which she maintains to this day. During the summer of 1962, she attended the Eighth World Youth Festival in Helsinki, Finland, and met Cuban students with whom she was enthralled. For her third year at Brandeis (1963–1964), Davis studied at the Sorbonne in Paris. There, she engaged in political dialogue with Algerian students who were protesting French colonialism. Davis returned to Brandeis for her senior year and arranged an independent study in philosophy with the famous Herbert Marcuse, a radical philosopher of the Frankfurt school of critical theory who was teaching at Brandeis. Davis decided to pursue her graduate studies in philosophy. Upon graduation from Brandeis, she returned to Europe to do graduate work in philosophy at the Johann Wolfgang von Goethe University in Frankfurt, Federal Republic of Germany. In 1967, she returned to the United States to attend graduate school at the University of California, San Diego, where she received her master's degree in philosophy in 1969, again working with Marcuse, who had come there from Brandeis. During her international travels and while pursuing her degrees, she was always politically active and often arranged her classes so that she could have full days to work in the Black Liberation movement.

Political Activism and Criminal Justice

While pursuing her master's degree at the University of California, San Diego, Davis participated in antiwar demonstrations and was an active member of the Black Panther Political Party (BPPP), the Los Angeles Student Non-Violent Coordinating Committee, and the Communist Party USA. Unlike Bobby Seale's Black Panther Defense Party, the BPPP was composed of young Black intelligentsia. Davis came to national attention when she was fired from her first teaching job as an acting assistant professor in the philosophy department at the University of California at Los Angeles for being a member of the Communist Party. Although the school president supported her, the Board of Regents ordered that she be removed. Ronald Reagan, who was then governor of California, vowed she would never again work in the University of California system. From the beginning, Davis's activism revolved around issues of racial discrimination and the criminal justice system. In *Abolition Democracy* she reflects that she has been involved with prisoners' rights ever since she became a member of the BPPP. Davis worked to free the Soledad Brothers (George Jackson, John Clutchette, and Fleeta Drumgo) from prison, arguing that they had been imprisoned on fraudulent murder

charges. To this day, Davis includes George Jackson in her speeches and points out the discriminatory sentencing of Black men along with the disproportionate incarceration of minorities in the United States, which existed in the late 1960s and continues to the present. Perhaps the defining moment of her activism happened when she wasn't even there. Jonathan Jackson, George's young brother, used Davis's gun in an attempt to free three San Quentin prisoners when they appeared in the Marin County Courthouse, on August 7, 1970. In the ensuing gun fight, Jonathan Jackson and two of the three prisoners died, along with the presiding judge. The authorities found the gun registered in Davis's name and charged her with murder and kidnapping. Driven underground by an intensive police search, Davis was placed on the Federal Bureau of Investigation's (FBI's) 10 most wanted fugitives list. The FBI found her in New York. She was incarcerated at the New York Women's House of Detention and later extradited to California, where she was held in jail, in solitary confinement, to await trial. Davis was acquitted and released almost 18 months after arrest, following an international "Free Angela Davis" campaign. Davis has continued to be involved with organizations that criticize racism in the criminal justice system, work to release prisoners, and ultimately question the very institution of prison. She is a member of the advisory board of the Prison Activist Resource Center. She was instrumental in organizing Critical Resistance: Beyond the Prison Industrial Complex in 1998, a grassroots conference held annually, which works to develop strategies that will ultimately abolish the prison-industrial complex. She works with Justice Now, an organization that provides legal assistance to women in prison. Davis is also affiliated with Sisters Inside, a similar Australian organization based in Queensland.

Ideas

Prison issues have literally and figuratively defined Angela Davis's life. In her work with George Jackson and the Soledad Brothers, she realized that the prison system serves as a "weapon of racist and political repression" (Davis, 1999). While jailed in the early 1970s, Davis wrote about the relationship between the institutions of prisons and slavery, focusing on how the prison system maintained racism. Today, she emphasizes the ways in which prison reproduces forms of racism. She recognizes concerns related to young Black men in Black communities, almost one third of whom are under the jurisdiction of the criminal justice system—either in prison, on parole, or on probation. However, as a Black feminist, she warns us that focusing on young Black men alone can result in a failure to address the criminalization of young Black women and the increasing incarceration rate for women.

Davis is also recognized for popularizing the concept of the prison-industrial complex. The prison-industrial complex is a interconnected group of public and private entities that have an economic stake in maintaining prisons throughout the world, not just in the United States. In a speech given at Colorado College in 1997 titled *The Prison Industrial Complex*, she described how corporations that move overseas disrupt both the communities they leave and the new ones they inhabit.

Her most recent discussion of prison abolition, in *Are Prisons Obsolete?* questions why American society takes prisons for granted. She points out that the frequent and discriminatory imposition of prison sentences is an ordinary fact of life for the poor, Black, and Latina/o young people in the United States. Davis examines the consequences of living with prison as punishment, arguing that continuing to build prisons creates a vicious cycle: Funds that are used to build prisons are not available to the communities from which the prisoners come, and thus those communities experience greater economic stress.

Finally, Davis asks us to think about a society without prisons. Why are they necessary at all? It is difficult to envision a society without prisons, because this would be a more complicated endeavor than simply replacing the prison with a single alternative. Davis challenges us to create a "new terrain of justice," where one in every three young men of color is not destined to become imprisoned.

Contrary to former Governor Ronald Reagan's proclamation, Davis has been working as a university professor in the state of California for over the past 20 years.

Marianne Fisher-Giorlando

See also Black Panther Party; Prison Abolition; Racialization of Crime

Further Readings

Davis, A. Y. (1982). *Women, race and class*. New York: Random House.

Davis, A. Y. (1988). *Angela Davis. An autobiography*. New York: International Publishers. (Original work published 1974)

Davis, A. Y. (1988). *Women, culture, and politics*. New York: Random House.

Davis, A. Y. (1998). *Blues legacies and Black feminism: Gertrude "Ma" Rainey, Bessie Smith and Billie Holiday*. New York: Random House.

Davis, A. Y. (1999). *The prison industrial complex* [CD]. San Francisco: AK Press Audio. (Lecture recorded at Colorado Springs, CO, on May 5, 1997)

Davis, A. Y. (2003). *Are prisons obsolete?* New York: Seven Stories Press.

James, J. (Ed.). (1998). *The Angela Davis reader*. Malden, MA: Blackwell.

D.C. Sniper

On October 2, 2002, at approximately 5:20 p.m., the window of a Michaels craft store in Aspen Hill, Maryland, was shattered by a single bullet. This bullet continued through the store, barely missing the cashier on duty and embedding into a rear wall of the store. Less than 1 hour after this incident, a 55-year-old man was shot and killed while walking across a parking lot in Wheaton, Maryland. Although these shootings were initially perceived to be separate and random, law enforcement authorities later recognized these two acts of violence as the first among 13 linked shootings that took place over the next 23 days in what was ultimately known as the D.C. Sniper case. This shooting spree was one of the largest multijurisdictional criminal cases in the history of the United States, spanning Montgomery County, Maryland, the District of Columbia, and as far south as Ashland, Virginia. More than 30 different law enforcement agencies on the local, state, and federal levels worked together to track, identify, and capture the parties responsible for the attacks across the D.C. region. In 2003, two African

American males, John Muhammad and Lee Boyd Malvo, were convicted of murder and weapons charges in connection with the shootings. This entry reviews the sequence of shootings, the criminal investigation, and the outcome in the case.

By the end of the day on October 3, five more victims had been shot and killed in the D.C. metro area, and law enforcement agencies across the region had created a task force to combat the parties responsible for the seven shootings that had occurred. Witnesses of one shooting on the second day reported seeing a white box truck close to the crime scene. Witnesses at another shooting on the same day reported seeing a dark Chevrolet Caprice in the vicinity at the time of the crime. On the third day, the Department of Alcohol, Tobacco, Firearms and Explosives (ATF) reported that ballistics tests indicated that bullets from several of the first seven shootings were fired from the same weapon—most likely some type of hunting rifle. On the morning of the sixth day, a 13-year-old was shot and injured in front of his middle school in Bowie, Prince Georges County, Maryland. The shooters left a tarot card with a note to law enforcement written on it. No demands were contained in this note; however, witnesses reported seeing a white van parked outside the school around the time of this shooting. By the 10th day of the investigation, there had been 11 shootings.

Other than the conflicting reports of a white van, a white box truck, and a dark Chevrolet Caprice near the scenes of earlier incidents, police had no leads on the identity of the parties responsible for this string of shootings. Law enforcement profilers assisting in the investigation predicted that the snipers were most likely Caucasian males with a rural background. On October 9 and October 11 two males were killed while pumping gas in Virginia. In another incident in Virginia, a female loading her vehicle outside of a Home Depot was killed on October 14.

Eighteen days after the first incident, the 13th shooting occurred at a Ponderosa Steak House in Ashland, Virginia. Law enforcement officials found a second note from the snipers at this crime scene. In this note, the snipers demanded money and instructed the police to call them at a certain time and place. The phone number provided in the note was not a working phone number; however, technicians at the U.S. Secret Service crime lab

were able to link the handwriting on the second note to the handwriting on the tarot card left at the scene of an earlier shooting. Police received additional information in the form of phone calls to local police stations and the FBI tip line. These tips yielded an important lead—one advised the police to look into a robbery-homicide at a liquor store in Montgomery, Alabama, that had taken place in September 2002. A fingerprint lifted off a magazine from a gun used in the Montgomery incident was linked to Lee Boyd Malvo, who had been fingerprinted previously by the Immigration and Naturalization Service. Further investigation found that Malvo was last seen traveling with a man named John Muhammad. Investigators uncovered evidence that Muhammad was a former army infantryman with marksmanship training. Additionally, Muhammad and Malvo had been target practicing at a residence they stayed at in Tacoma, Washington, further linking them to the sniper case. An ATF arrest warrant was issued for Muhammad on a federal firearms violation, and the police identified the make, model, and tag number of the Chevrolet Caprice he was driving. Photos of Muhammad were obtained from the Department of Motor Vehicles. Law enforcement was surprised to find that the snipers were African American men and not Caucasian men from a rural background, as had been originally predicted by the profilers. The police released the car description to the media on the 22nd day of the investigation. Later that evening a citizen at a rest stop off Interstate 70 near Frederick, Maryland, spotted a vehicle matching the descriptions reported on the radio. He called 911 and reported the vehicle. Within 3 hours the members of SWAT teams from the task force agencies surrounded the car in which the subjects were sleeping and took them into custody.

In the fall of 2003, approximately 1 year after their arrest, John Muhammad and Lee Boyd Malvo faced trial in Virginia and were convicted of murder and weapons charges. Muhammad received a death sentence for his role in the sniper killings. Malvo received a sentence of life in prison without parole because he was 17 years old at the time the crimes were committed, thus making him ineligible for a death sentence.

One unique aspect of the D.C. Sniper case is the choice of victims. Typically, serial killers target one type of person so that the victims share a common characteristic. However, in the case of the D.C. Sniper, victims were men and women as young as 13 years old and as old as 72 years old. The race of the victims ranged from Caucasian to Hispanic to African American. The random nature of the sniper shootings instilled high levels of fear into the citizens of the Washington, D.C., metropolitan area.

Rachel Philofsky

See also Juvenile Waivers to Adult Court; Violent Crime

Further Readings

Davies, H. J., Murphy, G. R., Plotkin, M., & Wexler, C. (2004). *Managing a multijurisdictional case: Identifying lessons learned from the Sniper investigation* (Report prepared by the Police Executive Research Forum). Washington, DC: U.S. Department of Justice.

Mauriello, T. P. (2007). *Criminal investigation handbook: Strategy, law and science: Appendix 2. The 2002 Washington, D.C. area sniper shootings—a case analysis of the multi-jurisdictional investigation.* Albany, NY: Matthew Bender.

DEATH PENALTY

Anthony Porter spent 15 years on death row in Illinois for a crime he did not commit. Porter came within 2 days of execution; his IQ was 51. It was not until a group of journalism students investigated his case that Porter was exonerated, after another man confessed to the double murder that put Porter on death row. Porter's exoneration spurred Illinois Governor George Ryan to declare the nation's first statewide moratorium on executions. Since 1977, Illinois had freed more prisoners than it had executed. Just before Ryan left office, he commuted the state's 167 death sentences to life sentences because he felt the death penalty could not be administered fairly.

The Illinois example is illustrative of the many problems that plague the death penalty in the United States. Race permeates all aspects of the U.S. capital punishment system. It plays a role in how cases are prosecuted from beginning to end, ranging from the choice of which cases to charge as capital cases to the empanelling of a jury who decides the ultimate fate of life or death. The entry provides a brief history of the death penalty, highlighting problems of race as it intersects with innocence, execution of juveniles and the mentally retarded, gender, public opinion, and the international community.

Historical Background

The Supreme Court has struggled to interpret capital punishment in light of the Eighth Amendment, which prohibits cruel and unusual punishment. The landmark case, *Furman v. Georgia*, was one among four 1972 cases in which the Court ruled that juries had particularly untrammeled discretion to let an accused live or die, violating the Eighth and Fourteenth Amendments. The unprecedented decision removed death sentences of approximately 600 prisoners awaiting execution and was based almost exclusively on what the Court found to be discretionary power that fostered arbitrariness and inconsistent sentencing.

Only 4 years after *Furman*, the Court, in *Gregg v. Georgia* (1976), held that states that removed arbitrariness of capital outcomes could resume the death penalty with guided discretion. From the reinstatement of the death penalty in 1976 to October 15, 2008, 1,125 death row inmates have been executed by means of firing squad, hanging, electrocution, lethal injection, and lethal gas.

Capital Punishment in the States

In addition to the federal government and the military, 36 of the 50 states have the death penalty. As of January 1, 2008, 3,309 inmates await execution, with inmates in California, Florida, Texas, and Pennsylvania making up more than one half of the death row population. From 1976 to October 15, 2008, Texas led in the number of executions with 415 inmates put to death, followed (distantly) by Virginia (102) and Oklahoma (88). The southern region of the United States makes up a disproportionate number of total executions.

The role of race in capital punishment is prominent. Although the majority of death row inmates are White, the race of the victim matters most. Despite Blacks making up only 12% of the nation's population, death row is composed of 42% Blacks and 45% Whites. Since 1976, 57% of prisoners executed were White and 34% were Black. Although Blacks and Whites are murder victims in almost equal number, nearly 80% of those executed since reinstatement were executed for murdering a White victim. From reinstatement of the death penalty in 1976 to October 15, 2008, 228 Black inmates were executed for killing White victims, whereas just 15 White inmates were executed for killing Black victims.

The Supreme Court took up the race issue in two important cases: *Batson v. Kentucky* (1986) and *McCleskey v. Kemp* (1987). *Batson* examined the role of race in removing prospective jurors from the jury pool, and *McCleskey* considered the effects of racism in the administration of the death penalty system.

McCleskey established that even if racism affects the administration of the death penalty (in particular, if race of victim and race of defendant serve as significant predictors of sentencing decisions in capital cases), there is no violation of the equal protection clause of the Fourteenth Amendment so long as there is no evidence of intentional racial discrimination against the defendant. The Court held that the defendant in *McCleskey* failed to establish that the risk of racial bias in sentencing was intolerable under the Constitution. Further, the Court declared that exceptionally clear proof is required before the Court will infer that discretion has been abused. McCleskey presented the Baldus study to the Court to support his claim of racial discrimination. The Baldus study focused on patterns of racial disparities in death penalty sentencing in Georgia, specifically focusing on the victim's race. The study offered statistical evidence showing that defendants alleged to have killed White victims were 4.3 times more likely to be sentenced to death than defendants charged with killing Black victims. The Court found that the requisite intentional racial discrimination had not occurred in McCleskey's case, and it further rejected McCleskey's argument that when race is a factor in capital punishment cases, the death penalty is cruel and unusual punishment. The Court reasoned that

the Baldus study failed to prove that the death penalty was applied arbitrarily.

The Supreme Court also considered racism in jury selection. *Batson v. Kentucky* held that prospective jurors can be removed only for race-neutral reasons. If a prosecutor chooses to strike a disproportionate number of people of the same race, he or she is required to rebut the inference of racial discrimination by showing neutral reasons for the removal. Despite the ruling in *Batson*, discrimination in jury selection can still be a problem. The rule in *Batson* is often circumvented when prosecutors offer race-neutral reasons as a pretext for challenging Black jurors. Observers comment that *Batson*'s toothless holding makes it ineffective in eliminating discrimination for all but the most obvious forms of discrimination, partly because it assumes that courts are able to detect purely race-based challenges. Others argue that few claims are actually raised based on *Batson* because of the infrequency in which the claim is victorious. Nevertheless, discrimination in choosing a jury, discrimination from within the jury room, and wide discretion granted to the trial court are still major hurdles for almost any minority capital defendant.

Innocence

In the imposition of the death penalty, racial discrimination is often coupled with other errors. The Supreme Court addressed the innocence issue in *Herrera v. Collins* (1993), holding that, in the absence of other constitutional violations, newly discovered evidence alone is insufficient to require a new trial. That is, a legally guilty defendant is one who has been afforded every available legal protection (at least in principle) and found guilty by a jury of his or her peers. Such a case does not violate the U.S. Constitution. Actual innocence must be based on irrefutable evidence not available during trial. The Court did allow for the possibility that the Constitution prohibits executing a person who can irrefutably show actual innocence, although it recognized that such a showing would be rare. Since 1973, 130 people have been exonerated in 26 states. Recent developments in DNA (deoxyribonucleic acid) evidence increasingly challenges the claim that wrongful convictions on death row remain rare.

Juveniles and Mentally Retarded Persons

Historically, the United States has allowed the execution of juveniles and the mentally retarded. In *Thompson v. United States* (1988), the Supreme Court held that the Constitution prohibited the execution of juvenile offenders under the age of 15. One year later, the Court ruled in *Stanford v. Kentucky* (1989) that the Eighth Amendment did not prohibit the execution of 16- and 17-year-olds, seeming to confirm the age boundary for capital punishment at 16. However, in 2005, the Court reversed its position, ruling in *Roper v. Simmons* (2005) that to impose the death penalty on a person who had committed a capital crime while under the age of 18 constitutes cruel and unusual punishment. Prior to *Roper*, 71 prisoners (all men) were on death row for crimes they had committed as 16- and 17-year-olds, 41% of whom were Black. Mirroring adult counterparts, juvenile offenders' victims were 64% White and only 8% Black. Between 1976 and 2005, 22 juvenile offenders were executed in the United States.

Following much of the same reasoning, the Court banned executions of mentally retarded defendants. The Court held in *Atkins v. Virginia* (2002) that the Eighth Amendment's prohibition of cruel and unusual punishment dictated that mentally retarded offenders should not be subjected to capital punishment. Experts argue that an accused person who is mentally retarded is prone to suggestibility, and their willingness to please can often lead to false confessions. Between the reinstatement of the death penalty and the Supreme Court ban of the mentally retarded, 44 such prisoners were executed—27 (or 61.4%) of whom were Black.

Gender

In comparison to men on death row, the female death row population and rate of execution for women is minute. As of December 31, 2007, 51 women reside on death row, making up only 1.7% of the entire death row population and 0.1% of the female prison population. Eleven women have been executed since the 1976 reinstatement. There have been 568 documented executions of women in the United States since 1608, constituting only 2.8% of total executions. Of the 11 women executed since 1976, 2 were African American and 9 were White. Only 3 of the 11 women executed in recent times did not know their victims. The remainder of the women's victims were either husbands, significant others, ex-boyfriends, or children. In fact, 38% of the victims of all of the women currently on death row were under the age of 10, and another 7% were between the ages of 11 and 17.

Public Opinion

Officials and lawmakers remain deeply divided on the appropriateness of the death penalty, and public opinion reflects ambivalence about its application. Gallup polls indicate that in the 1930s, support for the death penalty was at 61% but fell to an all-time low of 42% in 1966. Thereafter, support steadily rose, which culminated in an all-time high in 1994 when 80% of the population reported favoring capital punishment. A May 2006 Gallup poll revealed that 65% of the public favor the death penalty, but that support drops to 48% when life imprisonment without parole is given as an alternative. Additionally, the role of public opinion often permeates elections, particularly judicial elections. For example, three justices on the Supreme Court of California were defeated in a retention election because they publicly opposed the death penalty. In June 2008, the U.S. Supreme Court noted a turning tide in public opinion, which seems to reject the death penalty for all but the most heinous murders. In *Kennedy v. Louisiana*, the Court ruled that evolving standards of decency prohibit capital punishment for nonhomicide offenses, even that of child rape.

International Community

The United States is the leader in executions among the industrialized Western world; in 2006, 91% of the world's executions were carried out in only six countries: China (1,010), Iran (177), Pakistan (82), Iraq (65), Sudan (65), and the United States (53). Though executions consistently take place in these countries, there has been a worldwide decline. In 2006, the Philippines became the 99th nation to abolish the death penalty; a total of 128 countries have abandoned capital punishment either in law or in practice. Increasing efforts to universalize anti–capital punishment policies have important implications for the United States. As the United States becomes a global community, international law is being applied more widely, and human rights violations on the part of large, powerful nations are increasingly recognized. For example, the Council of Europe and the European Union made abolition of capital punishment a requirement of all of its member states and a prerequisite for those nations wishing to join.

L. Susan Williams

See also Baldus Study; Capital Jury Project; *Furman v. Georgia*; *Gregg v. Georgia*; Innocence Project; *Kennedy v. Louisiana*; Martinsville Seven

Further Readings

Bright, S. B. (1995). Discrimination, death and denial: The tolerance of racial discrimination in infliction of the death penalty. *Santa Clara Law Review, 35,* 433–484.

Ogletree, C. J., Jr. (2002). Black man's burden: Race and the death penalty in America. *Oregon Law Review, 81,* 15–38.

Radelet, M. L., & Borg, M. J. (2001). More trends toward moratoria on executions. *Connecticut Law Review, 33,* 845–860.

Websites

Death Penalty Information Center: http://www .deathpenaltyinfo.org

DECRIMINALIZATION OF DRUGS

Decriminalization of drugs involves the removal or reduction of criminal penalties associated with the use of specific substances. Full decriminalization occurs when the government does not consider drug use a criminal matter. Partial decriminalization involves some degree of governmental regulation regarding the type and amount of substance. Under this type of policy, the government may regulate the types of substances for which use or possession are permissible and control the situations in which drug use is acceptable (e.g., medical marijuana or drug maintenance programs). Decriminalization of drugs is not the same as legalizing a substance; decriminalization normally means that an infraction (such as possession of a small amount of marijuana) is a civil, rather than a criminal, law violation and would result in a civil penalty (such as a fine).

The issue of decriminalization is of relevance to the intersection of race and crime because drug laws and subsequent sentencing have significant impacts on communities of color. Whereas most scholarly research reveals consistent rates of drug use across racial and ethnic groups, drug use in communities of color is more visible to law enforcement; this visibility results in disproportionate arrest and prosecution. For example, an examination of state incarceration facilities reveals that 56% of drug prisoners are African American and 23% are Hispanic, numbers far higher than their representation in the general population. This entry examines arguments for and against drug decriminalization. While some scholars advocate the decriminalization of all illegal substances, the decriminalization debate most frequently revolves around the use of marijuana.

Arguments for Drug Decriminalization

Proponents of drug decriminalization believe strongly that the criminalization of drugs is the result of a historical moral opposition to drug use and the subsequent overapplication of criminal law. From this perspective, the extension of criminal law to an issue that does not have a strong public consensus overburdens the criminal justice system through the arrest, prosecution, and imprisonment of nonviolent offenders at a cost to society of billions of dollars each year. Today many Americans view the use of at least some currently illegal substances as a victimless crime. Approximately 100 million Americans indicate they have tried marijuana, and 72% believe that incarceration for marijuana use is an unreasonable and excessive punishment. Current laws vary dramatically from state to state for simple possession offenses. Some states treat possession of small amounts of marijuana as a civil matter (essentially a decriminalization position), whereas other states, like Alabama, impose a sentence of 15 years to life for a third conviction for marijuana possession. If drug use were decriminalized, it would be treated as a civil matter, and citizens would not be incarcerated for possession of a regulated amount of a decriminalized substance. This would allow law enforcement to refocus its efforts on high-level drug dealers and traffickers.

Related to this is the argument against the effectiveness of imprisonment in "solving" prevalent drug issues. Many public health experts believe that substance abuse would best be resolved through the use of a variety of medical and social services, as opposed to incarceration. This is the essence of the harm reduction model, in which the goal is to reduce the harm that results from both drug use and current drug policies. With decriminalization, there would be proportional penalties for the recreational act of substance use that even drug authorities assert can never be entirely eliminated.

Scholars focusing on the medicalization of marijuana point to its effectiveness in alleviating the side effects of chemotherapy, stalling AIDS-related wasting, reducing the pain associated with multiple sclerosis, and preventing epileptic seizures. It has been argued that legal drugs (such as alcohol, tobacco, and prescription drugs) are more dangerous in terms of social, psychological, and health costs than are illegal substances.

Advocates of decriminalization note that many legal drugs have been approved by the U.S. Food and Drug Administration but shown to be potentially harmful (e.g., Vioxx); nevertheless, there is little political opposition to such drugs. They also call attention to the pharmaceutical industry, which is the number one industry donor to U.S. political campaigns and has the ability to influence public policy in ways that growers cannot. In contrast, manufacturers of illegal drugs do not exert such influence. The result is a more favorable view of legal substances, regardless of whether this view is warranted in terms of adverse health consequences.

Advocates of drug decriminalization suggest that such a policy would further result in a decrease of secondary criminality. The relationship between drug use and crime is portrayed as straightforward in the media: Drug use causes involvement in crime. However, some researchers have found that this relationship is much more complex, and they suggest that a policy of decriminalization would lower the cost of drugs, so that some individuals would not resort to committing crimes such as theft and burglary (secondary criminality) to support their habit.

Arguments Against Drug Decriminalization

Moral entrepreneurs and others who campaign against the use of illegal substances argue that a decriminalization policy would send the wrong message to America's youth. The government spends millions of dollars per year creating public service announcements that aim to dissuade people from using illegal substances, stressing the adverse social and health consequences of drug use. To decriminalize marijuana would undermine this message of abstinence. Decriminalization would indicate at least implied societal acceptance of use and a subsequent decrease in the legitimacy of the informal controls such as family and community that act to deter drug use and abuse. A decline in the number of marijuana users is often attributed to public service announcements, the continuation of "get tough" drug policies, and the effectiveness of informal social controls.

The experiment of decriminalization of small amounts of marijuana for personal use in Alaska between 1975 and 1990 provided a further argument against decriminalization. During the period of decriminalization, the rate of high school students admitting to marijuana use in Alaska was significantly higher than the national average. Such findings no doubt contributed to the recriminalization of marijuana in 1990. It is believed that decriminalization would increase the number of users, thereby increasing drug availability, which would lead to increased abuse. As well, the decriminalization of "softer" drugs is believed to be a "gateway" to the use of "harder" drugs. Those who argue against decriminalization suggest that drugs are harmful and can impair cognitive abilities; contribute to behavioral problems, health complications, and poor mental health; as well as impair the long-term social and economic potential of users. As such, those against decriminalization focus on the adverse social costs of drug use and abuse. Those against decriminalization believe that currently illegal substances must remain illegal to minimize addiction and violence levels.

The Debate Continues

Shortly after the passage of the Comprehensive Drug Abuse Prevention and Control Act of 1970, several states adopted positions of decriminalization with respect to marijuana. This position stalled in the 1980s, however, and states that had previously decriminalized small amounts of marijuana, such as Alaska and Oregon, have recriminalized this behavior. Currently, approximately 12 states have marijuana decriminalization policies for minor possession and 8 states permit the regulated use of medical marijuana. On a federal level, however, such practices remain illegal.

The debate between those who favor and those who oppose decriminalization will likely continue as strong political forces are involved. While most Americans would assert that the United States is plagued by a "drug problem," the alternatives proposed to address this issue vary dramatically. There is no exemplar nation that serves as a model in this regard, and there are no simple ways either to determine whether decriminalization would work with specific types of drugs or to identify the circumstances in which it would be effective. After decades of research in the criminal justice and public health fields, many scholars advocate models based on medicalization, harm reduction, and decriminalization. The goal of such policies is to minimize long terms of imprisonment for nonviolent drug offenders and to implement a model that would reduce the adverse consequences of drug use. Advocates of decriminalization of illegal substances also argue that this approach would help reduce the significant and negative impact of disproportionate arrest and prosecution policies against communities of color.

Lisa Anne Zilney

See also Drug Courts; Drug Sentencing; Drug Use; Drug Use by Juveniles

Further Readings

Goldberg, R. (2006). *Taking sides: Clashing views in drugs and society* (7th ed.). Dubuque, IA: McGraw-Hill.

Gray, J. P. (2001). *Why our drug laws have failed and what we can do about it*. Philadelphia: Temple University Press.

Husak, D., & de Marneffe, P. (2005). *The legalization of drugs: For and against*. Cambridge, UK: Cambridge University Press.

Inciardi, J. A. (2002). *The War on Drugs III*. Boston: Allyn & Bacon.

King, R. S., & Mauer, M. (2002, September). *Distorted priorities: Drug offenders in state prisons*. Retrieved from The Sentencing Project: http://www.sentencing project.org/Admin/Documents/publications/dp_ distortedpriorities.pdf

DEHUMANIZATION OF BLACKS

To dehumanize means to deprive a person of human qualities, attributes, and rights. It is the psychological process of demonizing a person, making that person seem less than human and hence not worthy of humane treatment. In addition, dehumanization morally excludes individuals from the basic norms of society. In dehumanizing, one sees the other as subhuman in order to legitimize increased violence or justify the violation of basic human rights. Dehumanization has existed since races and ethnic groups culturally clashed on the soils in America. Understanding the historical implications of dehumanization through the analysis of race and gender provides a foundation for understanding complex issues surrounding the many identities in society as a whole. This entry examines the concept of dehumanization as it relates to the victimization of Blacks in American society (both physically and psychologically) and describes both historical and contemporary instances of dehumanization.

Typically, those who choose to dehumanize perceive others as a threat to their well-being, values, or position of power in society. Race, skin color, gender, and social status are attributes used by individuals to dehumanize others. These attributes come under attack through stereotyping, objectifying, "othering," or all of these acts. Objectification distinguishes a person as different, inferior, or both, and is central to the process of oppositional difference. Stereotypes are oversimplified perceptions, opinions, or racial epithets about a specific ethnic or cultural group of people. People who are dehumanized are often defined as "other," and stereotypes play a role in the objectification.

In American society, many ethnic and gender groups have been victims of dehumanization. Among those groups are Black people, who have been victims of these acts since their arrival to America in the early 1600s and who still face dehumanizing incidents today. Although there are other ethnic groups who have suffered acts of dehumanization (Native Americans, Hawaiians, Jews, Japanese, and others), Black people are the focus of this entry.

Past Acts of Dehumanization (1619–1960s)

The primary existence of slavery in America began in Jamestown, Virginia, in 1619. In 1638 an African male who had been taken from his homeland in Africa, forced into slavery in America, and treated as property could be bought for about $27. In 1640 whipping and branding Africans became common practice in the American colonies, and in 1641 Massachusetts legalized slavery. At the time of emancipation, over 90% of Black people were illiterate in America. This was largely the result of slaves being whipped and killed if they tried to read and write. Even those who were free—although the degree of freedom depended on whether they lived in the North or South—found it difficult to secure an education. In addition there are 2,805 documented victims of lynch mobs between 1882 and 1930 in 10 southern states. Hanging Blacks from trees and treating them as objects instead of humans are dehumanizing acts that have tarnished America's history. Although most of these acts were targeted toward Black men, Black women experienced dehumanization as well.

Black women slaves were classified as laborers, child bearers, nannies, doctors, field hands, breeders, wives, mothers, and mistresses, and their children were often taken away from them at birth and sold to other plantation owners. Women slaves were raped by their masters, husbands, and other male slaves. Often, they were accused of being promiscuous and, as a result, were labeled as whores although they were victims.

During this time, skin complexions began to fade for African Americans, as the White master's blood flowed through the veins of the Black females—thus originated the term *mulatto*. *Mulatto* is defined as a person who has both Black and White ancestry, which often gives her (or him) a lighter complexion and straighter hair texture. Lighter skin color did not lessen the dehumanization of Black people. Black singers and performers in the entertainment industry who were mulatto or of lighter complexions were allowed to perform in White-owned venues, but they still confronted dehumanization because of their race. An example is Dorothy Dandridge, who was considered one of the most beautiful women in Hollywood during the 1940s and 1950s and had a light complexion and what was perceived to be good hair texture. She performed in nightclubs and was the first Black woman to perform at the Waldorf Astoria in New York. She achieved international respect and fame, performing in Paris at prestigious clubs such as Café de Paris and La Vie en Rose. Nevertheless, she faced continuous dehumanization because of her race. Despite an Oscar nomination and wide recognition, she continued to experience the effects of stereotyping and objectification. Dandridge died of a drug overdose in 1965.

Even Black people with White skin were dehumanized; for example, as early as the 18th century, showmen exhibited Blacks with albinism and vitiligo in circus sideshows, taverns, and dime museums, subjecting them to public labels such as "freak" and "White Negro."

During this period, racial stereotypes dominated the public perception of Blacks in the United States. Newspapers in 1886 referred to all Black people, regardless of skin color, as "niggers," "coons," and "colored," and by 1890 the word *nigger* was the primary term used to refer to Blacks in America. It remains one of the most controversial words in America today.

Transition, 1960s–1990s

As the century turned, Black people began to fight not only for their right to an equal education, but other rights as well. During the 1960s, the civil rights movement laid the foundation for Blacks who wanted to eliminate the "separate but equal" laws that had been imposed upon them after slavery, including (but not limited to) illegal voting practices, segregation in schools, and Jim Crow. Jim Crow laws in the South forbade Black people from sitting and eating in White restaurants and required them to drink from labeled water fountains and to sit only in designated areas on public transportation. During this time, Black people were publically beaten, lynched, and ridiculed when they defied these laws. As time progressed, acts of dehumanization continued.

Examples of Dehumanization in the United States, 1998–2007

In the 21st century, the ignorance, objectification, racial epithets, othering, and stereotyping of earlier eras continue to exist in American culture. The following are among the examples of contemporary dehumanization of African Americans.

- On June 7, 1998, three White men with suspected ties to the Ku Klux Klan chained James Byrd, Jr., a young Black man residing in Jasper, Texas, to the back of a pickup truck and dragged him by his neck to his death. His head, neck, and right arm were found about a mile from his mangled torso.
- Presently, a disproportionate number of Black males are in U.S. prisons and jails. According to the Bureau of Justice Statistics, Black men comprised 37% of all inmates held in custody in the nation's prisons and jails on June 30, 2006. About 4.8% of all Black males in the general population were in prison or jail, compared to 1.9% of Hispanic males and 0.7% of White males.
- In 2006, references to lynching surfaced when six teenage Black men, now known as the Jena 6, discovered three nooses hanging from the "White tree" at their high school in Jena, Louisiana.

- On April 4, 2007, talk-show host Don Imus referred to the mostly Black Rutgers women's basketball team as "nappy-headed hos" (the word *ho* derived from *whore*). His comments were widely denounced by civil rights and women's groups.

Kimetta R. Hairston

See also Alienation; Discrimination–Disparity Continuum; Jena 6; Race Relations; Race Riots; Slavery and Violence

Further Readings

Feagin, J. R. (2000). *Racist America. Roots, current realities, and future reparations*. New York: Routledge.

hooks, b. (1992). *Black looks: Race and representation*. Boston: South End Press.

Kennedy, R. L. (2002). *Nigger, the strange career of a troublesome word*. New York: Pantheon Books.

Maiese, M. (2003, July). Dehumanization. In G. Burgess & H. Burgess (Eds.), *Beyond intractability*. Boulder: University of Colorado, Conflict Information Consortium. Retrieved September 22, 2008, from http://www.beyondintractability.org/essay/dehumanization

Morton, P. (1991). *Disfigured images: The historical assault on Afro-American women*. New York: Praeger.

DELINQUENCY AND VICTIMIZATION

In recent years, increasing attention has been given to the connection between victimization and delinquency in the United States. Scholars in the fields of criminology and psychology have begun to recognize the cycle of violence that exists among America's youth and the impact of victimization. This entry examines the connection between delinquency and victimization, the subsequent emotional and psychological impact, and the structural and cultural explanations for the recent trends. Attention is also paid to the impact of race on patterns of violence and victimization among youth.

Prevalence of Delinquency and Victimization

Official reports of delinquency indicate that juveniles accounted for 380,000 Part I arrests and

1.2 million Part II arrests of the overall 14 million arrests made in 2005. Although these rates are alarming, it is also important to note that reports indicate that delinquency rates have been declining over the past few years. With regard to victimization and the estimated 23 million criminal incidents that occur yearly, national survey data indicate that youth are more likely than adults to be victims of crime in the United States; this further subjects youth to the critical and long-term consequences of victimization, such as emotional, physical, and mental trauma. Moreover, the results from recent victimization surveys have noted that victimization is not random but is a function of personal and ecological factors.

Although delinquency rates are declining overall, there has been a recent increase in violent crime arrests among juveniles. In 2005 scholars noted that murder rates among juveniles increased by 20% and robbery charges increased by 11.5%. Thus criminologists have focused research on exploring and identifying factors that have shaped these recent changes and trends in delinquency rates.

Recent Studies Examining Juvenile Delinquency

A recent study declared that delinquency among adolescents and young adults can be predicted mainly from early peer relations, more specifically from not getting along with others. Furthermore, the need to belong is a great hunger and thirst for the female adolescent, yet she may not be socially accepted because of belonging to a discriminated racial group, because of inner problems, or because of difficult family relationships. Friendship groups for females are normally closed, or the requirements are so great she can't handle them, leading her to eventually give up on making friends. In a case study on male and female offense repeaters, it was found that more female than male offenders quarreled with their peers and were "lone wolves." From this study it was concluded that female adolescents possess delinquent behavior as a result of being "isolates and misfits," as well as possessing the tendency of getting lost in the crowd.

In another study, higher levels of peer rejection were found to be associated with delinquent behavior and psychological problems. It was suggested that lacking close friendships during childhood leads to high levels of problem behaviors later in life. Social rejection was viewed as a cause of antisocial outcomes. Acceptance into peer groups provides children with the chance to grow physically, mentally, and socially with people of similar age. However, if children are rejected and deprived of physical, mental, and social growth, this may lead to feelings of anger and resentment, which may further lead to aggression and delinquency during their adolescence.

Explanations for Delinquency and Victimization

Scholars have attempted to explain the phenomena of crime and victimization since the early 1940s. These explanations often focused on the relationship between the victim and offender and included typologies of responsibility based on relationship and situations. Modern theorists have simply revised the earlier ideologies while continuing to focus on culture, behaviors, associations, spatial relationships, lifestyles, and situations. In response to community and school violence, traits such as toughness and recklessness appear to exist in conjunction with extreme levels of fear. This is particularly problematic for younger children residing in "war zone" environments; many of these children are African American. Similarly, negative identity and low self-esteem are often products of racism and economic inequality, which in turn generate antagonism and aggressive behavior. Hostility and low self-esteem also lead to toughness and recklessness. Additionally, impairments in both school performance and intellectual development are viewed as the result of hostility and withdrawal experienced by youth who have been continually exposed to violent situations. Many studies have also indicated significant changes in children's behavior, many of whom become more aggressive and hyperactive after a violent experience. In addition, difficulties in concentration often occur because of the intrusion of thoughts relating to violence. Escalating levels of violence are also considered to be the result of an association with drugs, gangs, and sophisticated weaponry in urban settings. The lack of legitimate economic and educational opportunities, coupled with the emergence of a powerful drug economy, further exacerbates the linkage between exposure to chronic community violence and stress reactions. Research studies have clearly established a connection between increased exposure to violence and youth adaptation to stressful situations.

Sociologists and psychologists have explored many potential explanations for the abuse–crime connection among adolescents that note the relationships between victimization and an adolescent's likelihood to commit a crime. The extent of authority within a household can lead to negative outcomes in a child's behavior. Failure to set clear expectations for behavior, lax supervision, excessively severe and inconsistent discipline, and other poor parenting practices are factors that predict violence in children. Parents who are not involved in their child's life, who have poor communication skills, and who do not provide support are putting their children at risk for developing behavioral problems.

Interventions and Research Suggestions

Juvenile violence is related to many factors. Interventions are helpful and successful when utilized to address more than one factor that causes problem behaviors. Programs that are used to reduce risk factors across several domains are the most effective. Intervention programs that are implemented in the school and home environments simultaneously are extremely effective. It is essential to conduct early intervention in high-risk environments as well, to help decrease the chances of violent behavior within the community. Later interventions, such as counseling and behavior training, can help decrease the chances of recidivism among juvenile delinquents.

Zina McGee and Ebone' Joseph

See also Child Abuse; Drug Use by Juveniles; Juvenile Crime; Self-Esteem and Delinquency; Victimization, Youth; Violence Against Girls; Violent Juvenile Offenders

Further Readings

Bernard, T. (1999). Juvenile crime and the transformation of juvenile justice: Is there a juvenile crime wave? *Justice Quarterly, 16,* 336–356.

McGee, Z. (2003). Community violence and adolescent development: Assessing risk and protective factors among African American youth. *Journal of Contemporary Criminal Justice, 19,* 293–314.

McGee, Z. (2003). Weapons, violence, and youth: A study of weapon-related victimization among urban high school students. In J. Joseph & D. Taylor (Eds.), *With justice for all: Minorities, women, crime, and criminal justice* (pp. 191–208). Upper Saddle River, NJ: Prentice Hall.

U.S. Department of Justice, Federal Bureau of Investigation. (2006). *Crime in the United States, 2005.* Washington, DC: Author.

DELINQUENCY PREVENTION

Delinquency prevention refers to intervening in the lives of youth to deter involvement in unlawful acts. It includes programs or policies that involve daycare providers, nurses, teachers, social workers, recreation, youth mentors, parents, faith-based groups, and criminal and juvenile justice agencies. Delinquency prevention is important to understanding race and crime because many youth who are at risk for delinquency are members of minority groups that are overrepresented in juvenile justice. This entry presents a brief history of delinquency prevention and identifies different approaches to prevention, including those representing public health and developmental perspectives.

History of Delinquency Prevention

The history of the prevention of juvenile delinquency in the United States parallels the history of juvenile justice in the United States. Preventing delinquency has been of interest since the first houses of refuge that opened in the early 1800s. More recent developments, including passage of the federal Juvenile Justice and Delinquency Prevention Act of 1974, continued to emphasize prevention.

One of the earliest juvenile delinquency prevention programs was the Chicago Area Project, which began in 1933. It was designed to produce social change in communities that suffered from high delinquency rates. Qualified local leaders coordinated social service centers that promoted community solidarity. More than 20 programs were developed. Some evaluations indicated positive results; others showed that this project did not reduce juvenile delinquency.

Another well-known delinquency prevention program was the Cambridge-Somerville Youth Study. The program's focus was to prevent the early onset of delinquency. The study was divided into a control group and an experimental group. The experimental group received regular, friendly attention and were given medical and educational services. An evaluation of the program 30 years after it ended found that those in the experimental group committed more crime than those in the control group.

In the 1950s a popular trend of delinquency prevention was to make connections with youth who were unlikely to use community centers. Individuals referred to as "detached street workers" were sent to inner-city neighborhoods to create close relationships with juvenile gangs and delinquent groups. The Boston Mid-City Project was the best-known program that used detached street workers. Trained social workers were dispatched to reach out to gang members in their own areas. The workers attempted to connect gang members to job and educational opportunities. An evaluation of the program found that the program resulted in no significant reduction in delinquency.

During the 1960s more federally funded programs emerged that were based on social structure theory. The best-known program of this era was created in New York City. The program, Mobilization for Youth, received more than $50 million in funds from the U.S. government. The program attempted to provide legitimate opportunities for at-risk youth by providing employment and social service programs; the program also promoted voter registration. The program ended as a result of lack of funding. During this era, Head Start was created (and still exists today) for preschoolers who came from lower-class families to help them improve their social, emotional, physical, and mental development. Evaluations of the program found that participants of Head Start averaged more than 10 points higher on their IQ scores than their peers who did not participate in the program. During the 1980s delinquency prevention was viewed as a positive outcome of Head Start program participants.

Prevention Approaches

Successful prevention programs target multiple risk factors, are theory driven, and have measurable goals and objectives at the outset of the program. Community-based programs that include the public health approach and the developmental perspective are important today.

The public health approach utilizes the three prevention categories: primary, secondary, and tertiary. Primary prevention focuses on improving the general well-being of individuals by providing easy access to health care services. Secondary prevention refers to intervening with at-risk children by creating neighborhood programs. The third category is tertiary prevention and focuses on intervening with offenders through, for example, substance abuse treatment, to reduce recidivism.

The developmental perspective is a more popular approach to dealing with delinquency. This model is supported by human development theories and longitudinal studies. It is designed to prevent the criminal potential in juveniles and targets at-risk factors and protective factors against delinquency. The approach addresses both families and children and is implemented in stages over the life course, including childhood, early school years, adolescence, and young adulthood. Other delinquency programs include early intervention strategies, such as home-visitation programs, parenting skill programs, and daycare and preschool programs. Primary-grade programs include school-based programs that assist teachers to use innovative teaching tools to help students learn and understand social norms. Prevention programs in teenage years include mentoring programs such as the Big Brothers/Big Sisters program and after-school programs. Other types of programs for teenagers and young adults include job training programs.

The final type of prevention programs for teens and elementary school students are community-based programs. These programs target socially disorganized areas and provide at-risk youth with alternatives to delinquency. These programs have activities, tutors, mentoring, and community policing.

Liza Chowdhury

See also At-Risk Youth; Mentoring Programs

Further Readings

Curtis, L. A. (1995). *The state of families: Family, employment and reconstruction: Policy based on what works.* Milwaukee, WI: Families International.

Farrington, D. P. (1995). Early developmental prevention of juvenile delinquency. *Criminal Behavior and Mental Health, 4,* 209–227.

Gottfredson, D. C., Gottfredson, G. D., & Weisman, S. A. (2001). The timing of delinquent behavior and its implications for after-school programs. *Criminology and Public Policy, 1,* 61–86.

Grossman, J., & Gary, E. (1997, April). *Mentoring—A proven delinquency prevention strategy.* Washington, DC: OJJDP Juvenile Justice Bulletin.

Lundman, R. J. (2001). *Prevention and control of juvenile delinquency* (3rd ed.). New York: Oxford University Press.

Welsh, B. C. (2005). Public health and the prevention of juvenile criminal violence. *Youth Violence and Juvenile Justice, 3,* 1–18.

DEPORTATION

Increasingly, deportation, a routine state practice comprising various social and political exclusions, banishment, or expulsion of noncitizens or forcible removal of nationals from a country, has become the panacea for migrant management. The policy of deportation is not new, nor is its use confined to a specific epoch, determinate groups, or particular countries. Nations have used deportation as a form of punishment and as a scapegoat mechanism to "cleanse society" of persons deemed "dangerous" or "undesirable" but disproportionately to expel ethnic or racial groups deemed unfavorable. Used extensively worldwide, deportation has been justified by, among other factors, political beliefs, health status, race or ethnic membership, religion, and sexual orientation. Deportation policies highlight historical links between racialization and immigration as evidenced by targeting individuals often based on their physical characteristics whether they are legal immigrants or not.

Statistics

The *Yearbook of Immigration Statistics* shows that between 1892 and 2005, a period of 113 years, 3.5 million people were deported from the United States—1.5 million of those people were deported between 1997 and 2005. In 1995 prior to implementation of new legislation, 50,924 persons were deported. In 1997, after implementation of new and more restrictive legislation, deportations increased to 148,618 and reached 208,521 in 2005. Immigrants in the United States come from all over the world; however, the population of the deported is composed predominantly of immigrants from Mexico, the Caribbean, and Central and South America.

U.S. immigration statistics show variations in the rates of deportation that are influenced by social, economic, political, and cultural factors. Nonetheless, current mass deportations, rationalized as a panacea for crime control and deterrence to illegal immigration, disproportionately affect people of color. This raises the question of what stimulates current exclusionary policies and selective expulsion from the United States.

Legislative Framework

The United States is currently undergoing a period of mass deportation that began with implementation in 1996 of the Anti-Terrorism and Effective Death Penalty Act and the Illegal Immigration Reform and Immigrant Responsibility Act. The latter, applicable to noncitizens, expanded the grounds for deportation, increased the likelihood of removal, eliminated an immigration judge's ability to waive deportation, and limited judicial review in deportation cases. It also made reentry after deportation an offense punishable by a term of 2 to 20 years. These changes also restrict access to appeal. Anyone deemed an aggravated felon is barred from applying for a waiver of deportation. These apply to both legal permanent residents who have committed an offense (criminal law violations) and individuals who have overstayed their visas or entered illegally (administrative violations).

Prior to 1965, immigrants came predominantly from Europe. Although legislative changes occurring in 1965, 1980, 1986, 1988, 1990, and 1996 have had varying effects on immigrants, the Immigration and Nationality Act Amendments of 1965 weakened earlier restrictions on non-White immigrants by opening immigration to persons from Asia, Africa, and Latin America. The Immigration and Nationality Act Amendments, together with broader social changes in the United States—such as a healthier economy, labor shortages, geopolitics, civil rights advocacy, greater tolerance of ethnic minorities, and the political environment—produced a demographic transformation. These changes increased the population of non-White immigrants. This shift in immigration source countries affected changing ethnicities of persons entering the United States and led to greater discussion of the relationship between race, ethnicity, and immigrant status in criminology. This shift further entrenched the racialization of immigration.

Racialization of Immigration

Exclusion on the basis of race commenced in 1790 when naturalization laws required that applicants be "free White persons." The Alien and Sedition Acts of 1798 gave the president power to oust any noncitizen deemed dangerous. Laws such as the Immigration and Naturalization Act of 1924 are evidence of the racialization that has long been an integral part of America's immigration laws, policies, and practices. In 1882 the Chinese Exclusion Act placed restrictions on Chinese entering the United States. Later extended to all Asians and other categories of persons, it was not repealed until the 1940s. Over the years, legislation created a system of racial restrictions that became entrenched during the 1950s.

The 1965 change in ethnic composition has been derogatorily labeled the "Browning of America." A resurgence in xenophobic sentiments and complaints that immigrants disproportionately contribute to America's crime and violence have accompanied this label. Research and the preponderance of scientific evidence empirically disproved the perception that immigrants are responsible for increasing the crime rate in the United States.

Indeed, decades of research have proven that immigrants do not disproportionately engage in criminal activity; on the contrary, in many instances, immigrants commit fewer crimes than native-born individuals. Since 1994, violent and property crimes have fallen. Simultaneously, the illegal immigrant population has increased from 5 million to 12 million. However, increased spending on border control has given the false impression that current immigration policy is effective in reducing both the flow of migrants and the incidence of crime in the United States.

Globalization has increased the flow of people across borders with European and North American nations receiving more and more migrants. It is the prerogative of each nation to allow or deny access to another country's people and to exclude or deport noncitizens. The issue is not whether the United States should keep "deportable" felons but, instead, whether deportations from the United States are consistent with U.S. values and with human rights laws. Equally important is the effectiveness of these policies. It remains unclear what the current policy hopes to achieve, as it is debatable whether deportation of illegal migrants is effective in reducing crime in the United States. The illegal migrant population is increasing while immigration enforcements, such as the erection of walls, are making matters worse. Despite the penalty for reentry, deportation has become a revolving door through which many simply reenter the United States after deportation. Enforcement has only displaced the point of entry into the United States and exacerbated social problems such as the death of persons who attempt to cross the border under dangerous conditions.

The United States has, throughout history, permitted the removal of noncitizens. However, due in part to the influence of social, economic, political, and cultural structures, the definition of *removable* is malleable and nebulous with danger being historically specific. Now *danger* seems synonymous with people of color.

Marlyn J. Jones

See also Immigrants and Crime; Immigration Legislation; Immigration Policy; Racialization of Crime

Further Readings

Bloch, A., & Schuster, L. (2005). At the extremes of exclusion: Deportation, detention and dispersal. *Ethnic and Racial Studies, 28*(3), 491–512.

Brimlow, P. (1995). *Alien nation. Common sense about America's immigration disaster.* New York: Random House.

Chan, W. (2005). Crime, deportation and the regulation of immigrants in Canada. *Crime, Law and Social Change, 44*(2), 153–180.

Dougherty, M., Wilson, D., & Wu, A. (2006, November). *Immigration enforcement actions: Annual report 2005.* Department of Homeland Security. Retrieved from http://www.dhs.gov/xlibrary/assets/statistics/yearbook/2005/Enforcement_AR_05.pdf

Greenblatt, A. (1995, April 15). History of immigration policy. *Congressional Quarterly Weekly, 53,* 1067.

Hong, N. (1990, Summer). The origin of American legislation to exclude and deport aliens for their political beliefs, and its initial review by the courts. *Journal of Ethnic Studies, 18,* 1–36.

Horowitz, C. (2001, April). *An examination of U.S. immigration policy and serious crime.* Retrieved from http://www.cis.org/articles/2001/crime/toc.html

Johnson, K. R. (1996). Fear of an "alien nation": Race, immigration, and immigrants. *Stanford Law and Policy Review, 7,* 111–118.

Martinez, R., Jr., & Valenzuela, A., Jr. (2006). *Immigration and crime: Race, ethnicity and violence.* New York: New York University Press.

Schrecker, E. (1996–1997, Winter). Immigration and internal security: Political deportations during the McCarthy era. *Science & Society, 60,* 393–426.

U.S. Department of Homeland Security. (2006, December 8). *Yearbook of immigration statistics: 2005.* Retrieved from http://www.dhs.gov/ximgtn/statistics/publications/YrBk05En.shtm

U.S. Department of Justice. (n.d.). *Drugs and border security* [Fact sheet: FY2008 budget]. Retrieved August 13, 2007, from http://www.usdoj.gov/jmd/2008factsheets/pdf/0803_border_security.pdf

U.S. Government Accountability Office. (2006, August). *Illegal immigration: Border crossings have doubled since 1995* (Report No. GAO-06-770). Retrieved from http://www.gao.gov/new.items/d06770.pdf

U.S. Government Accountability Office. (2006, September). Estimating the undocumented population (Report No. GAO-06-775). Retrieved from http://www.gao.gov/new.items/d06775.pdf

U.S. Immigration and Naturalization Service. (1999). *Statistical yearbook of the Immigration and Naturalization Service, 1997.* Retrieved from http://www.dhs.gov/xlibrary/assets/statistics/yearbook/1997YB.pdf

DETROIT RIOT OF 1967

The 1967 Detroit riot marked a point in U.S. history at which racial tensions between African Americans and Whites reached deadly proportions. Prior to the 1967 riot, allegations of police brutality, racial tension, and racial discrimination prompted a string of racial riots, including the riots in Rochester and Philadelphia in 1954 and in the Watts residential district of Los Angeles in 1965. The underlying causes of the succession of riots included social, political, and economic factors that led to disparate treatment of African Americans. The Detroit riot began on Sunday, July 23, 1967, in a predominantly African American neighborhood located at 12th Street and Clairmount Avenue. Like the riot on Detroit's Belle Isle in 1943, the 1967 riot was the result of political unrest, racial unrest, and turmoil. The 1967 Detroit riot lasted for 5 days and resulted in the death of 43 people. Thirty-three of the individuals were African American, and the remaining 10 were White. According to the writings of historian Sidney Fine, numerous individuals were injured, over 7,000 people were arrested, and over 1,000 buildings were burned in the uprising.

The immediate events leading to the riot involved a police vice squad raid of an illegal after-hours drinking club (also known as a "blind pig"). The location was the site of a welcome home party for two returning Vietnam War veterans. The vice squad, known as the "Big Four," arrested all patrons in attendance. Within 1 hour, all of the 82 African American patrons were arrested in the raid. Local residents who witnessed the raid protested. Several Detroit residents vandalized property, looted businesses, and started fires. Police responded by blocking a square mile of the city street, but outraged local residents drove through the blockade. The protesting and rioting spread to other areas of the city as local police lost control of the situation. Over the next several days, more than 9,000 members of the National Guards were called, along with 800 Michigan State Police. President Lyndon B. Johnson sought federal support and mobilized military troop involvement in the raid.

To understand the immediate events leading up to the 1967 Detroit riot, it is important to understand the social context. Deindustrialization, geographical and emotional isolation from mainstream society, lack of access to legitimate opportunities, and unemployment were all barriers that African Americans endured during this time in history. Deindustrialization resulted in the loss of industrial jobs that had been filled by young, minority, and unskilled workers. Such jobs were replaced with skilled positions requiring formal education. Car manufacturers in the city of Detroit automated assembly lines and outsourced some of their production. "White flight" and a shift in the tax base to the suburbs also contributed to deindustrialization. The loss of industrial jobs resulted in the decline of the Black middle class as industrial jobs were replaced with low-paying service jobs. Poverty and welfare had been pervasive in Detroit's inner-city neighborhoods as African Americans were left behind when manufacturing jobs moved to the suburbs. Detroit's 12th Street neighborhood residents lived in persistent and extreme poverty. They were isolated from mainstream society and lacked the mobility to end the cycle of poverty. African Americans lived under intense racial segregation, concentrated within certain areas and grouped together within certain pockets of the city. Urban renewal or freeway construction had eradicated areas in which African Americans once thrived and forced them into densely populated areas of the city. Housing shortages, housing discrimination, barriers to homeownership, and exclusion from certain areas forced many African Americans to remain in impoverished housing. Although African Americans in the city of Detroit fared better than African Americans in a number of other areas of the United States, they wanted equal housing opportunities.

Police brutality and racial profiling were ordinary occurrences in Detroit's inner-city neighborhoods. Neighborhood residents were subjected to unwarranted searches, harassment, and excessive use of force by Detroit police. Several controversial shootings and beatings of African Americans occurred during this time and resulted in citizen mistrust of the police department and a belief that police did not care about African Americans. It appears that police brutality and overall racial inequality led to frustration and ultimately a revolt against what African American citizens deemed the establishment, or representative thereof. The 1967 Detroit riot is considered to be a catalyst for the Black Power movement.

Traqina Quarles Emeka

See also Harlem Race Riot of 1935; Los Angeles Race Riot of 1965; Los Angeles Race Riots of 1992; Police Use of Force; Race Riots

Further Readings

Fine, S. (1989). *Violence in the model city: The Cavanaugh administration, race relations, and the Detroit riot of 1967.* Ann Arbor: University of Michigan Press.

Hershey, J. (1998). *The Algiers Motel incident.* Baltimore: Johns Hopkins University Press. (Original work published 1968)

Kenyon, A. M. (2004). *Dreaming suburbia: Detroit and the production of postwar space and culture.* Detroit, MI: Wayne State University Press.

Sugrue, T. J. (1995). Crabgrass—roots politics: Race, rights, and reaction against liberalism in the urban north, 1940–1964. *Journal of American History, 82*(2), 551–578.

Sugrue, T. J. (1996). *The origins of the urban crisis: Race and inequality in postwar Detroit.* Princeton, NJ: Princeton University Press.

Thompson, H. A. (2001). *Whose Detroit? Politics, labor, and race in a modern American city.* Ithaca, NY: Cornell University Press.

Discrimination–Disparity Continuum

The discrimination–disparity continuum designates a typology of discrimination attributable to the criminal justice system. This continuum provides a means to determine the degree of discrimination in the processes, procedures, and outcomes of the criminal justice system through examination of the employees, institutions, and policies of the system. This entry identifies and defines key terms related to the discrimination–disparity continuum and describes the continuum in full. It also discusses various scholarly viewpoints regarding placement of the criminal justice system on the continuum, at the levels of systematic discrimination, institutionalized discrimination, contextual discrimination, and individual acts of discrimination.

Key Terms and Definitions

Discrimination and disparity are topics actively addressed in criminology that are often misunderstood or misrepresented because of differences in terminology usage and operationalization. Before the discrimination–disparity debate can be understood, key terms must first be identified and defined. Race and ethnicity are two causal characteristics of discrimination and disparities in criminal justice. *Race* is an individual's biological and physical characteristics but is usually socially constructed. Race is often simplified as a color, separated by Black and White. It is important to understand that not only do other skin colors exist but other features, such as facial characteristics, height, and weight, aid in the determination of race. *Ethnicity* is an individual's nationality or culture identification and is usually defined by the individual. It is constructed through language, country of origin, religion, and other important traditions. *Prejudice* is a belief or biased opinion that others are unworthy or less than human because of an identifiable characteristic such as race or ethnicity.

The difference between discrimination and disparity can be simplified by the following statement: All discrimination is a disparity, but not all disparities are discrimination. *Disparity* is a differential outcome due to natural forces rather than unequal treatment. In criminal justice, disparities are based on legal factors or aspects related to law, including seriousness of the offense and prior criminal record. For example, if police perform traffic stops with more African Americans in neighborhoods that are predominantly African

American than in other neighborhoods, the difference is a disparity because African Americans are more readily available and arguably committing more traffic violations. If police perform more traffic stops on African Americans in neighborhoods that are predominantly European American and where European Americans are committing more traffic violations, the difference would constitute discrimination. Thus, *discrimination* is an inequality due to purposive actions whereby individuals receive differential treatment as a result of belonging to a descriptive category such as race, sex, or age. Discrimination is the acting out of prejudicial attitudes. In the previously given example, police officers' active pursuit of African Americans when European Americans are committing more traffic offenses illustrates discrimination in which officers base stops on extralegal factors (i.e., African American race) and not legal circumstances (i.e., type of traffic violation).

It is important to note that results in and of themselves cannot resolve the disparity–discrimination debate. The causal processes of outcomes must be scrutinized to determine if discrimination exists. Accordingly, in the example presented earlier, if police officers were stopping more African Americans because their offenses were perceived to be more serious (e.g., driving while intoxicated versus speeding), then the stops may not be a result of discrimination. On the other hand, if officers were conducting more traffic stops on African Americans because of a belief that African Americans carry illegal drugs and a traffic stop will lead to an arrest for a more serious offense, then stops would constitute discrimination. A more concrete example of discrimination would be if police officers conduct traffic stops on African Americans because of an informal departmental policy to stop all minorities. In summation, discrimination is an act or behavior based on prejudicial beliefs about extralegal factors, whereas disparities occur "just because" of legal factors. Discrimination reflects differential treatment of minorities, whereas disparities occur due to differential criminal involvement of minorities. Distinguishing between specific instances of discrimination and disparity requires background information on the situation and reasons why decisions were made.

The Discrimination–Disparity Continuum

Samuel Walker, Cassia Spohn, and Miriam DeLone created the discrimination–disparity continuum to simplify and understand the debate over whether the criminal justice system is discriminatory and, if so, to what degree. As highlighted earlier with the police traffic stop example, discrimination and disparities are complex phenomena with varying degrees and levels. The continuum is depicted in Figure 1.

The highest level of discrimination, *systematic discrimination*, refers to intentional and complete discrimination throughout the criminal justice system—in all the procedures, processes, policies, and institutions, as well as by individuals. It depicts all criminal justice system institutions (i.e., law enforcement, courts, and corrections) as collectively engaging in purposive discriminatory practices. One example from history is the Jim Crow laws, which were solely against and limited actions of people of color.

Institutionalized discrimination frames the criminal justice system as a set of interrelated organizations (i.e., law enforcement, court, corrections) that perform actions using conventional procedures that yield disparate outcomes. Unlike systematic discrimination, where intent to be discriminatory exists, institutionalized discrimination operates more subtly. Often termed *de novo* discrimination, the regulatory policies were originally created with prejudicial intent that is now absent. The prejudice is now ingrained in the organization's framework, and disparities result from mere practice of conventional norms and rules. One example of institutionalized discrimination is drug laws. Drug laws, including those against the use of marijuana, heroin, and opiates, were originally enacted to control people of color and limit their freedoms and cultural expressions. For instance, in the late 1800s and early 1900s, laws were passed banning heroin and other opiates and providing severe penalties for violations. This legislation was intended to discourage emigration from China to the United States. Other laws governing drug use and sale are in effect today and often create disparities in arrest and incarceration rates; however, in the absence of an intent to discriminate, it is questionable whether such laws and outcomes can be considered to be discriminatory.

Contextual discrimination roots discrimination in certain situations or environments (e.g., one police district but not the whole force) to an extent greater than individual action. The environment supports discriminatory acts and may be incorporated into the socialization process and informal rules that define particular situations, but discrimination does not characterize an entire institution at every place and time. Biased behavior is highly dependent on the context, and not every policy or procedure is clouded by discrimination or prejudice. One example of contextual discrimination would be traffic stops targeting all African Americans who drive expensive cars when all other drivers are treated equally.

Individual acts of discrimination are disparities that result from a particular person's actions (e.g., one police officer is discriminatory, but others do not perform duties in a discriminatory manner). Most scholars agree that because humans are social beings and work as agents of the criminal justice system, this is the minimum level of discrimination present in the system: Some individuals are biased, which encompasses beliefs, values, and actions in their personal and professional lives.

Finally, *pure justice* represents a criminal justice system that is free from all disparities and has no possibility of being discriminatory. Few, if any, argue that this characterizes criminal justice; hence, it is not discussed in the next section.

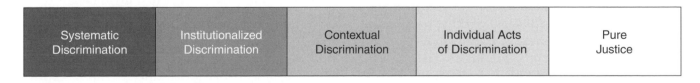

Figure 1   Discrimination–Disparity Continuum

Source: Walker, Spohn, and DeLone (2007).

Discrimination–Disparity Debate

This section highlights four levels of the discrimination–disparity continuum by providing scholars' viewpoints on systematic, institutionalized, contextual, and individual discrimination. It showcases the general debate of whether the United States is characterized by discrimination or disparity.

Systematic Discrimination

Coramae Mann is a proponent of the discrimination thesis, which holds that the criminal justice system is based on systematic discrimination. According to this thesis, not only is the United States a nation built on discrimination against African Americans, Hispanics, Native Americans, and other minorities, but the criminal justice system purposively perpetuates this belief structure in all of its procedures and policies. From the processes of law creation to incarceration and with everything in between, criminal justice institutions ensure that outcomes are discriminate against minority populations. This hinders assimilation of minority cultures into the United States because others become fearful and untrusting of those who have been typecast as criminals, murderers, rapists, and the like. Under the systematic discrimination viewpoint, justice becomes a fight against the myth of the minority criminal.

Institutionalized Discrimination

William Julius Wilson argues that the criminal justice system is based on institutionalized discrimination. The agenda of the criminal justice system is to be honest and fair, but because of structural characteristics of society, it is improbable for the system to be truly egalitarian. The structure of society in its education, employment, and housing markets has forged an unequal society, leaving certain members behind. These members are often termed the *poverty-stricken, underclass, proletariat,* or *truly disadvantaged.* In the United States these are frequently minorities. The criminal justice system sets laws that are enacted against those who cannot conform to the norms and rules of the majority society. Discrimination becomes institutionalized because procedures of criminal justice organizations are enforced in disparate manners against impoverished minorities, who are unable to live by conventional standards and are punished because society is incapable or unwilling to provide aid.

Contextual Discrimination

Walker, Spohn, and DeLone propose that the criminal justice system has been accurately portrayed on the continuum as systemic and institutionalized in the past, but the current status is more reflective of contextual discrimination. The criminal justice system has disparate outcomes at most processing levels (i.e., arrest, charging, and sentencing) but statistical significance normally disappears when the system is examined at a state or national level. If jurisdictions or localities are examined individually, statistics vary between no disparities to high levels of disparity. The reasoning for this is that not all police departments, prosecutorial attorney offices, courtrooms, and correction departments act in manners that result in disparity. Instead, disparities and discrimination are interwoven into particular situations and environments so that particular processes produce disparities.

Individual Acts of Discrimination

William Wilbanks has been portrayed as a leader of the nondiscriminatory thesis, which states that the criminal justice system is not discriminatory but individual actors employed by the system act in discriminatory manners that contribute to disparate outcomes. Confusion of the level of discriminatory practices in the criminal justice system is due to an inability to agree on key terms such as *race, ethnicity, racism,* and *discrimination.* Multiple theories and the need of a continuum exist because of this inability to define terms with precision and care. The system does not perpetuate racist behaviors; rather, it is an individual effort by those who act on personal biases while employed as agents of criminal justice institutions.

Conclusion

The discrimination–disparity continuum is a tool to be used when describing outcomes of the criminal justice system. The continuum suggests that outcomes cannot be simplified into categories of discrimination or no discrimination, because varying levels exist throughout the United States as a result of jurisdictional differences. The discrimination–disparity debate is highly dependant on definitions of key terms as well as an understanding and conception of process statistics including arrest and incarceration rates. This entry highlights pieces of the debate but more research should be accomplished to draw a personal conclusion regarding where the criminal justice system lies on the continuum.

Jennifer L. Huck

See also Crime Statistics and Reporting; Disproportionate Minority Contact and Confinement; Myth of a Racist Criminal Justice System; Racism

Further Readings

Bell, D. (1992). *Faces at the bottom of the well: The permanence of racism*. New York: Basic Books.

Gans, H. J. (1995). *The war against the poor: The underclass and antipoverty policy*. New York: Basic Books.

Mann, C. R. (1993). *Unequal justice: A question of color*. Bloomington: Indiana University Press.

Walker, S., Spohn, C., & DeLone, M. (2007). *The color of justice: Race, ethnicity, and crime in America* (4th ed.). Belmont, CA: Thomson/Wadsworth.

Wilbanks, W. (1987). *The myth of a racist criminal justice system*. Pacific Grove, CA: Brooks/Cole.

Wilson, W. J. (1987). *The truly disadvantaged: The inner city, the underclass, and public policy*. Chicago: University of Chicago Press.

DISPROPORTIONATE ARRESTS

African Americans and members of other racial minorities are arrested at rates disproportionate to their numbers in the U.S. population. Criminologists have debated whether this pattern can be explained by such factors as disparities in rates of offending or whether it reflects racial discrimination in law enforcement. Law enforcement officials have considerable discretion to decide in which geographical areas they will focus their activities and how to deal with individuals that

they apprehend in the course of these activities, including whether to arrest and charge them. For much of U.S. history, legal structures upheld slavery, segregation, and discrimination against racial minorities. Because the role of the police was to enforce these laws, some scholars argue that this established a pattern of police behavior and attitudes toward minority communities that still persists. Whatever the truth of this analysis, a growing body of evidence points to significant and unjustifiable racial disparities in arrest rates in the United States.

Arrest Rates

African Americans constitute about 12% of the U.S. population, but in 2003 made up about 27% of all arrests, 33% of arrests for crimes on the Federal Bureau of Investigation *Uniform Crime Reports'* index of serious crimes, and 37% of arrests for violent crimes. Similar patterns have persisted for as long as the relevant statistics have been gathered. Hispanics also experience disproportionate arrest rates. Debate has centered on whether these figures indicate racial bias by police officers or in the methods they employ, or whether they can be explained in other ways.

Some criminologists have argued that disparities in arrest rates can be accounted for on the assumption that Blacks are more likely to commit serious crimes than the general population and more likely to be disrespectful and hostile to the police in potential arrest situations. Many others have countered that such factors cannot explain all of the differences. One extensive study of more than 20 large police departments concluded that suspects were more likely to be arrested if they were Black and the victim was White. A California study found that African Americans and Hispanics were much more likely to be arrested on the basis of weak evidence, because charges were later dropped more often in their cases. The rate of unfounded arrests for Blacks was 4 times that of Whites. For Hispanics the rate was more than double the White rate. In major cities the disparity was greater. In Los Angeles the rate of unfounded arrests for African Americans was 7 times greater than the White rate, and in Oakland, 12 times greater. A more recent study of racial profiling in traffic stops found that, after controlling for other relevant factors, young minority men were still more likely to receive citations, be searched and arrested, and have force used against them. A 2005 official study by the Department of Justice reported similar findings (although the head of the Bureau of Justice Statistics was demoted after he attempted to publicize this). Studies of juvenile detentions have also found that after controlling for other relevant factors (such as seriousness of the offense and social background), African American and Hispanic youths are more likely to be arrested.

An extensive 1988 overview of numerous studies of race and the criminal justice system by the *Harvard Law Review* concluded that the race of the suspect was a significant factor in arrest decisions. National statistics add support to these studies. In 2003 the National Criminal Victimization Survey reported that in about 23% of violent crimes, victims said their assailants were Black, compared to a 37% Black arrest rate for such crimes.

Drug Arrests

Evidence of racial bias is perhaps strongest in the case of arrests for drug offenses. Between 1980 and 2000, the number of arrests nationwide for drug offenses rose from 581,000 to 1,579,566, despite an apparent decline in drug use during the same period. The best available data indicate that the rate of drug use among African Americans is the same as among Whites and slightly higher than the rate for Hispanics. Yet at the beginning of this period, Blacks accounted for 21% of arrests for drug possession and at the end of it, 32%. In 2000, African Americans made up 16% of recent cocaine users but 45% of arrests for cocaine possession. Blacks are also disproportionately arrested for selling drugs. In 1980 they represented 35% of such arrests; by 2000 the number had jumped to 47%. There is no evidence that Blacks are more likely to sell drugs than Whites, and a study of drug transactions in six major cities found that drug users typically buy drugs from a member of their own racial or ethnic group.

These high arrest rates appear to be the result of decisions by police departments to target Black inner-city neighborhoods for drug sweeps.

Compared to suburban neighborhoods, inner-city drug deals are more likely to take place on the street. But racial disparities exist even with respect to outdoor arrests. African Americans use crack cocaine at a much higher rate than do Whites (ranging from 4.5 to 11 times the White rate, depending on the year in which the survey was carried out). But while a study in Seattle found that crack was involved in about one third of outdoor sales of serious drugs, and that crack sales were much less likely to involve violence than outdoor sales of other drugs, fully 75% of outdoor arrests were for crack. This study concluded that there was a definite racial bias in the way that law enforcement was conceptualizing the drug problem, reflected in the very different arrest rates.

Philip Gasper

See also Disproportionate Arrests; Racialization of Crime; Sentencing Disparities, African Americans; Sentencing Disparities, Latina/o/s; Sentencing Disparities, Native Americans; Violent Crime; War on Drugs

Further Readings

Free, M. D., Jr. (2001). Racial bias and the American criminal justice system: Race and presentencing revisited. *Critical Criminology, 10,* 195–223.

Gabbidon, S. L., & Greene, H. T. (2005). *Race and crime.* Thousand Oaks, CA: Sage.

Mauer, M. (2006). *Race to incarcerate* (2nd ed.). New York: The New Press.

Walker, S., Spohn, C., & DeLone, M. (2007). *The color of justice: Race, ethnicity, and crime in America* (4th ed.). Belmont, CA: Thomson/Wadsworth.

DISPROPORTIONATE INCARCERATION

African Americans, Hispanics, and members of other minority racial and ethnic groups are incarcerated in federal and state prisons and in local jails at much higher rates than their numbers in the U.S. population. Although some criminologists have argued that this pattern can be explained by such factors as disparities in arrest rates, there is growing consensus that a significant portion of it reflects unwarranted racial bias (both direct and indirect) in the workings of the criminal justice system and systemic racism in the wider society. This entry reviews rates of incarceration for minorities compared with those for Whites and for the general population in the United States, as well as the historical context of these differences. It then examines explanations of these disproportionate incarcerations that go beyond an appeal to higher arrest rates for minorities.

Statistics

African Americans constituted about 12.4% of the U.S. population in 2006, but they constituted over 37% of those in federal and state prisons and almost 39% of those in local jails—about 3 times their percentage in the population as a whole. Hispanics made up 14.8% of the general population but over 20% of those in prison and nearly 16% of those in jail. By contrast, non-Hispanic Whites were 66% of the total population but only about 35% of the prison population and 44% of the jail population. (In 2006 there were over 1.5 million prisoners and about 760,000 jail inmates in the United States.) One in every 41 Blacks and 1 in 96 Hispanics were incarcerated, compared to 1 in 133 of the total population and 1 in 245 Whites; this means that Blacks are incarcerated at approximately 6 times the rate of Whites. One in 9 African American men between the ages of 20 and 34 were behind bars, almost 15 times the incarceration rate for the population as a whole (which is itself the highest in the world—almost 7 times the rate in Europe) and 8 times the rate for all men.

History

Statistical disparities do not by themselves demonstrate discrimination (because it may be possible to explain them in terms of legitimate factors), but given the long history of racial inequities and institutionalized discrimination in the United States, many scholars believe that the burden of proof lies with those who would deny that a significant portion of the differences in incarceration rates today is the result of racism. In the antebellum South,

"slave codes" denied Blacks most legal rights and prohibited them from gathering unless a White person was present. Punishments for many crimes were determined by race in both the North and the South. In Pennsylvania, for example, the penalty for an African American man convicted of raping a White woman was death, whereas a White man convicted of the same crime faced no more than 7 years in prison. A White man convicted of raping a Black woman in Georgia could escape with a fine.

After the Civil War, the former Confederate states introduced "Black Codes," designed to maintain White supremacy and ensure a supply of cheap labor. For example, unemployed Blacks of no fixed abode could be arrested for vagrancy and, if unable to pay a fine, required to perform labor. These codes were struck down by the passage of the Fourteenth and Fifteenth Amendments to the Constitution during the period of Reconstruction, but these codes came to an end in 1877, southern states enacted Jim Crow segregation laws under the fiction of "separate but equal," and Blacks and other minority racial groups continued to be treated unequally by the police and courts, despite the Constitution's promise of equal treatment. During the late 19th century, incarceration expanded dramatically in the South, with many Blacks arrested for "crimes" such as vagrancy and loitering and the creation of an extensive convict-lease system, which rented mainly Black prisoners to private landowners and businesses—a system that many regarded as worse than slavery, as employers were not concerned if their prison-laborers died. When the convict-lease system finally ended in the early 20th century, it was replaced in many states by the use of prisoners in chain gangs to build roads and labor on other public works projects. Meanwhile, pervasive racism ensured that members of minority groups continued to receive unequal treatment in the criminal justice system.

Much has changed since the first half of the 20th century, but the rise of the civil rights movement and the end of legalized segregation in the 1950s and 1960s provoked a backlash in which leading political figures played on racial fears to advance a conservative "law and order" agenda, resulting in a dramatic increase in incarceration rates that has disproportionately affected people of color. In 1972, the incarceration rate in the United States was 160 per 100,000, with 190,000 behind bars. Over the next 35 years, the incarceration rate increased almost fivefold and the number of prisoners more than tenfold. By 2003, twice as many African American and Hispanic men were incarcerated than were enrolled in higher education.

Explaining the Disparities

Criminologists have investigated the extent to which the racial differences in incarceration rates might reflect factors such as arrest rates, prior criminal records of those arrested (which would affect both the likelihood of imprisonment and the length of sentence), and the seriousness of the crimes with which defendants are charged. According to several studies, most—although not all—of the racial disparities can be explained in these terms.

However, explanations of this sort may mask some forms of discrimination. For example, there is evidence that there is racial bias in arrest rates themselves, reflecting the discretion of law enforcement officials to decide which locations to police and whether to arrest and charge individuals who are apprehended. The same considerations mean that minority defendants may be more likely to have accumulated prior criminal records. Moreover, arrest and incarceration rates may also reflect racial bias if the law itself unfairly criminalizes, or mandates harsher punishments for, activities that are more likely to be engaged in by members of minority groups. Higher arrest rates are also partly the result of greater poverty, higher unemployment, worse educational opportunities, and other symptoms of institutional racism in minority communities. African American and Hispanic minors are also significantly more likely to be suspended and expelled from schools, increasing their likelihood of becoming involved in the criminal justice system.

Even setting aside these considerations, Blumstein's research leaves 24% of the disparity in incarceration rates unexplained, which in 2006 amounted to over 200,000 African Americans in prison or jail. In fact numerous studies have documented the existence of significant racial disparities at every stage of the criminal justice

process after arrest. For example, Black and Hispanic defendants are more likely to be detained before trial than are White defendants, substantially increasing the likelihood of receiving a prison sentence. Some studies have found evidence that unfavorable racial stereotypes sometimes play a role in court decisions about who will receive bail and how high it will be set. Other studies have concluded that the defendant's economic status is often the deciding factor, disproportionately affecting African Americans and Hispanics, who are more likely to be poor than Whites.

There is also evidence that racial bias sometimes plays a role in prosecutors' decisions about whether to charge suspects, what charges to file, whether to offer plea bargains, and what deals to offer in such cases. For example, a study of King County, Washington, which controlled for factors such as past criminal record and seriousness of the crime, found that African Americans were 1.15 times more likely, and Native Americans 1.7 times more likely, to be charged with a felony than were Whites. Researchers have also shown that charging decisions are often affected by the race of the defendant and the race of the victim, particularly in cases of murder and sexual assault, with Black-on-White crimes being dealt with more harshly than White-on-White, Black-on-Black, or White-on-Black crimes. This may reflect both the prejudice that Black defendants are more dangerous and the prejudice that Black victims are less worthy. Additionally there is evidence that minority defendants are offered plea bargains less often than are Whites and are offered worse deals.

Finally, there is evidence of racial bias in court proceedings, including the use of peremptory challenges by prosecutors (and sometimes defense attorneys) to remove people of color from the jury pool on the assumption that they will be less likely to convict minority defendants (and more likely to convict White defendants), manipulation of the racial prejudices of jurors, and the imposition of harsher sentences on minority defendants. Numerous studies have confirmed that, even when other factors are controlled for, African Americans and Hispanics are more likely to receive prison and jail sentences than are Whites and are sentenced to longer terms. However, the studies also reveal that the importance of race can vary considerably from one jurisdiction to another and may depend on the nature of the crime and on other defendant characteristics (such as age and employment status).

The War on Drugs

Much of the large increase in incarceration rates since the early 1980s has been due to an escalation of the War on Drugs, which has disproportionately impacted African American and Hispanic communities. Drug arrests climbed from 581,000 in 1980 to 1.89 million in 2006, with more than 80% of the total for simple possession. But although drug use rates in various racial and ethnic groups are roughly comparable, the drug arrest rate for African Americans in 43 of the biggest cities in the United States during this period has grown by 225% yet only 70% for Whites. In 11 of the cities, the African American arrest rate increased by over 500%. A study of sentencing outcomes in 34 states found that Black men are nearly 12 times more likely than White men to be imprisoned on drug charges, and Black women are 4.8 times more likely than White women to be imprisoned. In 2003, over 53% of those imprisoned for drug offenses were African American and a further 20% were Hispanic.

Sharp differences in drug arrest rates in different U.S. cities show that much of the racial disparity is the result of decisions by local law enforcement officials to concentrate enforcement in minority inner-city neighborhoods rather than, for instance, in majority White suburbs. Laws that disproportionately impact minority groups skew the numbers further. Federal legislation enacted in the 1980s mandates a 5-year sentence for possession of 5 grams of crack cocaine, most commonly used by African Americans, and the same sentence for selling 500 grams of powder cocaine, the variant of the drug used by more affluent Whites. Several states maintain similar sentencing disparities. "School zone" drug laws, passed by many states, provide another example. These laws increase the penalties for drug offenses committed within a specified distance of schools, playgrounds, youth centers, and similar facilities. African Americans and Hispanics live disproportionately in more densely populated urban locations, where large areas of cities fall within the enhanced penalty zones. By comparison, far fewer locations in majority White suburbs and rural areas fall within these zones. As a consequence, most of those penalized by such laws are Black and Hispanic.

Philip Gasper

See also Disproportionate Arrests; Sentencing Disparities, African Americans; Sentencing Disparities, Latina/o/s; Sentencing Disparities, Native Americans; War on Drugs

Further Readings

Fellner, J. (2008). *Targeting Blacks: Drug law enforcement and race in the United States.* Retrieved from Human Rights Watch: http://www.hrw.org/reports/2008/us0508

Gabbidon, S. L., & Greene, H. T. (2005). *Race and crime.* Thousand Oaks, CA: Sage.

King, R. S. (2008). *Disparity by geography: The War on Drugs in America's cities.* Retrieved from The Sentencing Project: http://www.sentencingproject.org/PublicationDetails.aspx?PublicationID=614

Mauer, M. (2006). *Race to incarcerate* (2nd ed.). New York: The New Press.

Walker, S., Spohn, C., & DeLone, M. (2007). *The color of justice: Race, ethnicity, and crime in America* (4th ed.). Belmont, CA: Thomson/Wadsworth.

DISPROPORTIONATE MINORITY CONTACT AND CONFINEMENT

Disproportionate minority contact is the unequal involvement and participation of minorities with agents of the criminal justice system such as police officers, judges, and probation officers. Disproportionate minority confinement is the unbalanced incapacitation of minorities in secure detention facilities, jails, and prisons. Contact and confinement statistics are considered disproportionate when a higher percentage of a population is present in criminal justice than the proportion in the general population. Overrepresentation of minorities is examined through discretionary decision points of the system (e.g., arrest, sentencing) with the understanding that no single decision creates disproportional statistics; rather it is a cumulative effect of all decisions.

This entry provides an explanation of disproportional involvement and treatment along with statistics on adult and juvenile populations. Evaluation of police and court practices will offer a substantive and procedural background on disproportionate minority contact and confinement. An illustration on the use of drug laws is offered to demonstrate the cumulative effect of decision points. To conclude, approaches that can lessen disparities are discussed.

Disproportional Involvement and Treatment

Criminal justice statistics do not mirror those of the general population; minorities are more likely to have contact with, and be confined in, the criminal justice system. According to the 2006 *Uniform Crime Report,* Black adults accounted for 28% of arrests but were only 12% of the general population (Hispanic statistics were not included in this report). Additionally, according to the Bureau of Justice Statistics, Black men comprised 41% of prison and jail populations; 4.8% of Black men in the United States were behind bars. Further, almost 2% of Hispanic men were incarcerated, but only 0.7% of White men were incarcerated. Similarly for adult women, Blacks were 4 times more likely to be incarcerated than Whites and 2 times more likely than Hispanics.

Juvenile statistics are just as disparate: According to the 2006 *Uniform Crime Report,* Black juveniles were 15% of the general population but 30% of total arrests or 51% of violent arrests and 32% of property arrests. In 2003 per the Office of Juvenile Justice and Delinquency Prevention, Black youth were almost 4 times more likely than White youth to be incarcerated and 2 times more likely than Hispanics. Overall, minorities were held in custody at a per capita rate of 502, whereas the per capita rate for Whites was only 190. These juvenile and adult statistics suggest that disproportional minority contact and confinement exist in the United States.

Disproportionate minority contact and confinement have been explained by two opposing viewpoints of differential involvement and differential treatment. *Differential involvement* argues that whether for biological, sociological, or psychological reasons, minorities are more prone to criminal tendencies and commit more criminal acts. In other words, it is contended that minorities are more prevalent in criminal justice because by committing more deviant acts, minorities have a higher chance of being caught and subsequently arrested, sentenced, and incarcerated. Differential involvement is an offender-oriented explanation.

Differential treatment proposes that the criminal justice system operates in a discriminatory manner by selectively enforcing policies and procedures to harass minority populations. Minorities are overrepresented in criminal justice because decision makers respond to individuals in a prejudicial manner due to extralegal factors such as race and ethnicity. Differential treatment is a systemic explanation.

Law Enforcement and Disproportionate Contact

Law enforcement act as gatekeepers of the criminal justice system enabling their actions to strongly impact who is placed into the system. Law enforcement procedures and policies allow for disproportionate minority contact through decision points of stopping, detaining, arresting, and booking individuals. Police not only have more initial contact with minorities, but minorities are also more likely to proceed through all police decision points. One reason for these disparities is minorities are more likely to have other risk factors that contribute to law enforcement perceiving situations involving minorities as more serious. A higher level of concern and fear permits officers to use more discretion, which increases minority arrests and bookings.

Law enforcement involvement has changed throughout history in response to community structures and resident demands. Policies such as community policing, problem-oriented policing, zero tolerance policing, and hot-spot policing have positioned police directly into communities. Law enforcement has become more concentrated in minority areas due to residential patterns of poorer areas containing more minority groups and criminogenic concerns. Thus, police have more contact with minority citizens because officers are closer to residents and focus on removing civil disobediences and crimes. These foci contribute to police placing more minorities into the system because of differential involvement or differential treatment.

Court Systems and Disproportionate Confinement

Arrest statistics do not fully explain confinement statistics disparities. Disparities often worsen as minorities penetrate deeper into the system, especially when risk factors (Figure 1) are present. Prosecutorial decisions and judicial sentencing decisions are two court processes that aid in the explanation of disproportional minority contact and confinement. Prosecutorial decisions include charging (whether to charge and for what offense) and plea negotiations. Overall, adult and juvenile minorities are indicted with more-serious offenses, but nonminorities receive better plea negotiations resulting in adjudications of less-serious offenses. This has been explained by bias in the system, ineffective assistance of public defenders, and a belief that minorities lack social capital. These and other factors make minorities appear as unprivileged candidates for less-serious charges and the corresponding nonincarceration sentencing options.

A second court system decision point is judicial sentencing decisions. In both adult and juvenile courts, judges are more apt to sentence minorities to incarceration and to longer, harsher sentences. This occurs for legal and extralegal reasons. Legal reasons include seriousness of the offense, prior criminal record, requirements of mandatory minimums, and use of sentencing guidelines. Extralegal reasons include offender demographics, risk factors, and lower social capital that make minorities unable to secure nonincarceration or shorter sentences. Consequently, minorities are disproportionately confined in detention centers, jails, and prisons due to the cumulative effect of discretionary decisions.

A third decision point specific to juveniles is the decision to waive or transfer juveniles into adult court. This decision can be made by prosecutors, judges, or legislation, and determined by various factors including age of offender, seriousness of offense, weapon involvement in the offense, and prior criminal history. The previous discussions provide reasoning to why more minorities are waived into adult court, including presence of risk factors and violent arrest rates.

Case in Point: The War on Drugs

The War on Drugs in the United States has a history of over 100 years. Starting in the late 1800s and early 1900s, heroin and other opiates were banned to hinder Chinese immigration. To control Mexican immigration, marijuana became illegal in the 1930s, and then in the 1980s, crack cocaine received stiffer penalties than powder cocaine as a result of a "crack epidemic" in minority communities. This brief history exemplifies that drug laws were produced to target minorities and have continued to impact minority contact and confinement. According to the Bureau of Justice Statistics in 2006, Blacks were 35% of all drug abuse arrests, and in 2004, Blacks and Hispanics represented 29% and 21%, respectively, of state prison inmates incarcerated for drug offenses.

Two hypothetical scenarios highlight how process decision points create a cumulative effect to enhance disproportionate minority contact and confinement.

Criminal Justice System	Socioeconomic Conditions
Racial/ethnic bias in use of discretion	Low-income jobs
Insufficient diversion options	Few job opportunities
System "labeling"	Urban density/high crime rates
Poor community integration	Few community support services
Inability to afford justice	Inadequate health/welfare services
Educational System	**Family Unit**
Inadequate early childhood education	Single-parent households
Inadequate dropout prevention	Limited parental supervision
Inadequate overall education quality	Unmarried/single adult status
Lack of cultural education/role models	Economic stress/deprivation

Figure 1   Risk Factors That Contribute to Disproportionate Minority Representation in the Criminal Justice System

Source: Adapted in part from Devine, Coolbaugh, and Jenkins (1998).

Scenario 1: Tyrone Johnson is a young Black male who lives in an underclass neighborhood in Urban City, United States. He does not have a high school diploma and is unemployed, as legitimate opportunities are hard to locate. He moves around between family and friends. Tyrone uses marijuana recreationally and occasionally sells in order to help provide for his family. Due to the neighborhood, police concentration is high and Tyrone is known by police because of past convictions, including possession of marijuana.

Tyrone was involved with a drug bust and although he was not selling, the police arrested and booked him. He was charged with possession of marijuana with intent to deliver. He was unable to afford private representation and his public defender, although a good attorney, did not have time to treat clients individually. The public defendant and prosecutor failed to negotiate a plea acceptable to Tyrone. During this whole process, he had been in custody because he did not have the resources to post bail. Tyrone went to trial in a system that often does not tolerate drug trials because they are perceived as a waste of resources. Tyrone was found guilty. The sentencing judge—constrained by mandatory minimum sentences and other sentencing guidelines and by Tyrone's criminal history and lack of education, employment, and stable living environment—sentenced him to an 18-month prison term with no chance of parole or other community release alternatives.

Scenario 2: Carl Martin is a young White male who lives in a middle-class contemporary neighborhood in Suburban City, United States. He is currently enrolled in college and holds a part-time job at a coffee shop in his neighborhood. He lives with his parents and siblings to save money for his education. Carl uses marijuana recreationally, especially at college parties, but he has no criminal background. Police in his area use a community-oriented social work approach to justice as opposed to crime fighting.

The police busted a party he was attending and found marijuana in his pockets while questioning him. The police decided not to arrest or book Carl and instead wrote a citation for underage drinking. Carl's parents hired an attorney for the minor infraction, as they were concerned what it would do to his record and employability. The defense attorney was able to negotiate with the city attorney to hold the case open for 1 year with the stipulation that if Carl received no more infractions, the case would be dismissed.

Approaches to Address Minority Overrepresentation

Approaches to address disproportionate minority contact and confinement can be divided into direct services, training and education, and system change; each is discussed separately in this section.

Direct Services

Direct services are typically strategies that aid at-risk youth in order to prevent criminal justice involvement by building prosocial tendencies and developing skills to maintain healthy family and peer relationships. These programs can also include diversion to at-risk youth or those in the system for minor offenses (e.g., truancy), alternatives to secure confinement or incarceration, and advocacy to help individuals navigate through systemic processes. Examples of each are as follows:

- *Prevention/Intervention:* Head Start programs, academic achievement programs, vocation/job skills training, family therapy
- *Diversion:* restitution, community service, alcohol and other drug abuse programs, mental health services, pretrial release programs
- *Alternatives to Secure Detention/Incarceration:* foster homes, boot camp, electronic monitoring, house arrest, probation
- *Advocacy:* Office of Juvenile Justice and Delinquency Prevention, various state and local programs such as those that aid in language interpretation, family advocate programs, and lawyer assistance programs

Training and Education

Training approaches center on agency personnel to reduce and control the use of discretion at all decision points. This is usually accomplished through cultural responsibility training where employees learn norm, belief, and value distinctions of different ethnicities to improve cultural sensitivity.

Education includes the learning process of employees including new hires and before and during procedural changes. It is imperative that employees are not only properly trained but that training methods are evaluated and retraining is provided as necessary. Education also incorporates the vast resources made available through research initiatives such as those of the Office of Juvenile Justice and Delinquency Prevention and the National Criminal Justice Research Service.

System Change

System change comprises those policies, procedures, and processes that should be altered to aid minorities in the criminal justice system to reduce levels of minority overrepresentation. Changes are not a matter of leniency but adoption of appropriate means to avoid disadvantaging minorities involved with the criminal justice system. Examples of how the system has attempted to lower disparities in recent history include the following:

- *Law enforcement:* community policing, problem-oriented policing, removal of quotas in citations and arrest rates, formal policies against discriminatory practices of officers
- *Juvenile court system:* Juvenile Justice and Delinquency Prevention Acts of 1974 and 1992, which require states to address disproportionate contact and confinement
- *Adult court system:* determinate sentencing, sentencing guidelines, retraction of mandatory minimums, retraction of crack cocaine and powder cocaine laws
- *Corrections:* community corrections, restorative justice programs, "broken windows" probation

These approaches and others still require research to determine not only the causes of disproportionate minority contact and confinement but also what works to reduce them. For system change to occur it is necessary to address both differential treatment and differential involvement by incorporation of community and social-justice welfare agencies in the process, just as other institutions must be corrected to repair the criminal justice system.

Jennifer L. Huck

See also Crime Statistics and Reporting; Discrimination–Disparity Continuum; Disproportionate Arrests; Disproportionate Incarceration; Mandatory Minimums

Further Readings

Austin, R. L., & Allen, M. D. (2000). Racial disparity in arrest rates as an explanation of racial disparity in commitment to Pennsylvania's prisons. *Journal of Research in Crime and Delinquency, 37*(2), 200–220.

Blumstein, A. (1982). On the racial disproportionality of the U.S. states' prison populations. *Journal of Criminal Law and Criminology, 73*(3), 1259–1281.

Devine, P., Coolbaugh, K., & Jenkins, S. (1998, December). Disproportionate minority confinement: Lessons learned from five states. *OJJDP Juvenile Justice Bulletin* (Report No. NCJ 173420). Retrieved from National Criminal Justice Reference Service: http://www.ncjrs.gov/94612.pdf

Provine, D. M. (1998). Too many Black men: The sentencing judge's dilemma. *Law & Social Inquiry, 23*(4), 823–856.

Short, J., & Sharp, C. (2005). *Disproportionate minority contact in the juvenile justice system.* Washington, DC: Child Welfare League of America.

Ulmer, J. T., Kurlychek, M. C., & Kramer, J. H. (2007). Prosecutorial discretion and the imposition of mandatory minimum sentences. *Journal of Research in Crime and Delinquency, 44*(4), 427–458.

DNA PROFILING

The advent of DNA profiling has significantly enhanced the criminal investigative process. The use of DNA to convict the guilty and acquit the innocent has been promulgated by the media, and the value of DNA profiling is further highlighted when used to address miscarriages of justice. However, not so well publicized is the potential for DNA profiling to exacerbate existing racial bias in the American criminal justice system and subject ethnic minorities to disproportionate surveillance by law enforcement agencies. This entry provides a brief overview of the operation of DNA databases and draws attention to some of the disparate effects that DNA profiling may have on ethnic minorities.

The Development of DNA Databases

The United Kingdom pioneered the use of DNA as an investigative tool when it introduced its National DNA Database in 1995. Shortly thereafter in 1998, under the authority of the DNA Identification Act of 1994, the United States also introduced a DNA database, the Combined DNA Index System, which combines the National DNA Index System with local and state databases. The aim of such databases is to identify suspects by conducting electronic searches in an attempt to match DNA profiles of samples taken from crime scenes with DNA profiles of individuals stored on the database. As of May 2007, DNA had been used in 50,343 criminal investigations in the United States, and with at least 4,582,516 convicted offender profiles currently on record, reliance on the database will only increase.

Racial Issues

Those concerned about the impact of DNA profiling on minorities note that its increasing use takes place in the context of fractured relationships between law enforcement and ethnic minority groups. Troy Duster has hypothesized that given the historical police corruption, prejudice, and sometimes blatant racism that African Americans have suffered at the hands of the criminal justice system, minority groups may be more inclined to view DNA profiling and databases with anxiety and distrust. In 2005 the American Civil Liberties Union wrote a letter to the Senate Judiciary Committee, warning that the willingness of minority communities to cooperate with criminal investigations would be hindered by the passing of the Violence Against Women Act of 2005. The passage of the Violence Against Women Act, which included the DNA Fingerprint Act of 2005, widened the categories of individuals from whom DNA samples can be taken. Anyone arrested by the federal government or any foreign citizen detained by federal agencies will now have their profile uploaded onto the database. This includes individuals detained for immigration violations, many of whom are Hispanic. This will significantly increase the number of ethnic minority profiles, which will be added to the database on a yearly basis. Critics argue that DNA legislation continues to expand without consideration of its potential discriminatory effects.

At present, at least six states have the ability to take and maintain DNA samples in the database from individuals who are merely arrested for certain offenses. Given that non-Whites have a higher probability of being arrested than Whites, more widespread use of DNA sampling could criminalize a large percentage of minorities who have not yet been and may never be charged with, or convicted of, the offense for which they were arrested.

Another point of contention is the ability to conduct "familial searches." These searches create the potential for surveillance of family members similar to that of an individual who has his or her profile on the database. In other words, because close relatives share similar DNA, individuals who are related to someone on the database but may never have come into contact with the police nevertheless may become the subject of "genetic monitoring" each time a search is done on the database. Thus, as David Lazer and Michelle Meyer have pointed out, given the proportion of African Americans who are arrested, charged, or convicted each year, it is reasonable to surmise that many, if not most, African Americans would at some point in the near future be included on the database, whether directly or indirectly. Additional factors that may add to racial inequity arising from DNA profiling include DNA dragnets, the corrupt planting of DNA evidence and research into the correlation of genetic racial markers and criminality.

At 32%, the U.K. database already holds a disproportionate number of profiles from its Black male population. Given the rate of widening legislation, it is plausible that African Americans and Hispanics will become overrepresented on the Combined DNA Index System. One solution to eradicating any potential bias is by including the DNA profile of every citizen on the database. However, it has been argued that this would not resolve racial bias and would indisputably raise serious civil liberty issues for everyone, not just ethnic minorities.

Research Directions

In the United Kingdom, the Human Genetics Commission, in partnership with other organizations, will be conducting a "citizen's inquiry" on the use of genetic information, including DNA, in the prevention, investigation, and resolution of crime. The inquiry will focus particularly on obtaining the views of the general public on social and ethical concerns arising from the existing and potential use of DNA in the criminal justice system. There is a desperate need for such an inquiry in the United States, particularly with the growing number of categories of individuals whose profiles are retained. Any formal public discussion in the United States should examine the nexus between race and the taking of DNA samples, the use of DNA databases, and the very difficult, if not virtually impossible, task of having profiles removed from the database. Additionally, research should be conducted on how race and the use of DNA evidence in court correlate with acquittals, convictions, retrials, and exonerations.

The unfavorable aspects of DNA databases, which may disproportionately affect minorities, must be publicly and adequately discussed and solutions sought to limit injustice. Without such debate, any further expansion of police powers in relation to the forensic use of DNA will only undermine confidence in what is otherwise a very powerful and useful tool in the criminal justice armory.

Julia E. Selman-Ayetey

See also Criminalblackman; Disproportionate Arrests; Disproportionate Incarceration; Profiling, Ethnic: Use by Police and Homeland Security; Wrongful Convictions

Further Readings

Byravan, S. (2006). DNA typing: A technology of fear. *Development*, 49(4), 28–32.

Duster, T. (2006). Explaining differential trust of DNA forensic technology: Grounded assessment or inexplicable paranoia? *Journal of Law, Medicine and Ethics*, 34(2), 293–300.

Gosline, A. (2005, April 8). Will DNA profiling fuel prejudice? *New Scientist*, 186(2494), 12.

Lazer, D., & Meyer, M. N. (2004). DNA and the criminal justice system: Consensus and debate. In D. Lazer (Ed.), *DNA and the criminal justice system: The technology of justice* (pp. 877–949). Cambridge: MIT Press.

Rushlow, J. (2007, May). *Rapid DNA database expansion and disparate minority impact*. Retrieved from Council for Responsible Genetics: http://www.gene-watch.org/DNADatabases/RushlowPaper.html

Simoncelli, T. (2006). Dangerous excursions: The case against expanding forensic DNA databases to innocent persons. *Journal of Law, Medicine & Ethics*, 34(2), 390–397.

DOMESTIC VIOLENCE

Countless numbers of people have been affected by domestic violence at the hands of spouses, intimate partners, and boyfriends or girlfriends. This violence causes physical and emotional harm, costs billions of dollars in medical care and lost wages, and sets the stage for future domestic violence. People of all races are affected by domestic violence, making it a salient public issue. This entry defines domestic violence, discusses factors contributing to domestic violence, examines the characteristics of victims and perpetrators of domestic violence, and considers racial differences in the experience of domestic violence.

Domestic violence can be defined as behaviors exhibited by one person, called a batterer or an abuser, which are used to control or manipulate a spouse, partner, boyfriend, or girlfriend. These behaviors can be physical (hitting, kicking, choking, etc.) or they can be mental, psychological, and emotional (name-calling, put-downs, threats, stalking, etc.). Although both men and women can be batterers and victims, most frequently females are the victims of domestic violence and males are the batterers.

In most relationships in which domestic violence occurs, the batterer is not generally violent early in the relationship. It tends to take time for physical violence to occur, and when it does, victims are often shocked and frightened. Emotional and psychological abuse frequently occurs before physical violence and may manifest themselves in the form of jealousy and controlling behavior. This begins the "cycle of violence," which describes what happens when domestic violence occurs within a relationship.

The cycle of violence begins with a period of time during which tension builds between the people involved. There may be psychological or emotional abuse during this period. The next part of the cycle is the act of violence. Sometimes the violence will continue to be psychological or emotional during this part of the cycle, while escalating in severity. The final part of the cycle is commonly referred to as the honeymoon phase. This phase is characterized by apologies from the batterer for his or her behavior and promises to change. During this phase, life is a "honeymoon," and victims of domestic violence frequently feel as if the batterer has truly changed. Victims often blame themselves for the behavior of the batterers and feel if they (the victims) change, then the batterer will change as well. However, the cycle begins again, and the behaviors of the violent person may escalate over time, increasing in frequency, severity, or both. All of these behaviors are designed to control the victim.

Victims of domestic violence do not leave their battering partner for a variety of reasons. Batterers frequently threaten to harm the victim, to harm their children, or to take their children away. Victims may stay with batterers due to the inability to support themselves and their children. Victims of domestic violence also fear being rejected by family members and by society. In American society there is a stigma that surrounds not only domestic violence but also failed relationships. Victims who are married may not want the stigma of being divorced, and some victims feel that children should be raised in a two-parent household no matter what the circumstance.

There are many risk factors for domestic violence. Witnessing domestic violence in the home increases the risk that children will be victims or batterers as adults. Belief in gender roles and stereotypes, such as the belief that women are subordinate to men and are considered property, is a characteristic of many male batterers. Poverty, unemployment, and other life stresses are considered risk factors for being victims and perpetrators of domestic violence. Drug and alcohol use and abuse are also associated with a higher risk for domestic violence.

People who are victims of domestic violence can seek assistance from many sources. They can call the police, contact a crisis hotline, or seek emergency shelter at specialized organizations. Many people in violent relationships do not seek help out of fear of retaliation, fear of what will happen when they leave, financial difficulties, and because of worrying about what people will think. Leaving a violent relationship is difficult to do, however, and most people experiencing domestic violence will stay in the relationship. There is also assistance to batterers, who may undergo counseling or attend a batterer's intervention program.

There is some indication that there may be racial differences regarding domestic violence; however, the evidence remains mixed. For example, some information suggests that African Americans experience domestic violence at higher rates than Whites, while other information suggests that African Americans and Whites experience domestic violence at similar rates. There is evidence that rural minorities experience domestic violence very differently from their White counterparts, having limited access to services that fit their needs. The severity of violence may also vary by race, with African American women experiencing more severe violence than women of other races. Finally, there is evidence suggesting that socioeconomic status may impact the prevalence of domestic violence, with poorer minority women at the highest risk for victimization; this suggests that structural and social factors contribute to domestic violence.

Given the mixed evidence related to race and domestic violence, this topic represents an area in need of additional research. Additional research could provide insights into the experiences of Asian Americans and Native Americans.

Wendy Perkins

See also Domestic Violence, African Americans; Domestic Violence, Latina/o/s; Domestic Violence, Native Americans; Victimization, African American; Victimization, Asian American; Victimization, Latina/o; Victimization, Native American; Victimization, White; Violence Against Women

Further Readings

Dutton, D. G. (1999). *The domestic assault of women: Psychological and criminal justice perspectives* (4th ed.). Vancouver: University of British Columbia Press.

Elias, R. (1986). *The politics of victimization: Victims, victimology, human rights.* New York: Oxford University Press.

Frias, S. M., & Angel, R. J. (2005). The risk of partner violence among low-income Hispanic subgroups. *Journal of Marriage and Family, 67,* 552–564.

Hampton, R., Oliver, W., & Magarian, L. (2003). Domestic violence in the African-American community. *Violence Against Women, 9,* 553–557.

Schechter, S. (1982). *Women and male violence: The visions and struggles of the battered women's movement.* Boston: South End Press.

Tjaden, P., & Thoennes, N. (2000). *Full report of the prevalence, incidence, and consequences of violence against women.* Washington, DC: U.S. Department of Justice.

DOMESTIC VIOLENCE, AFRICAN AMERICANS

Numerous explorations have revealed the complexity and dynamics of intimate partner violence within African American communities. This entry includes a more critical examination that borrows from well-established theoretical paradigms, including structural and cultural explanations, and integrates a rapidly emerging critical race perspective. The concept of domestic violence is broader than that of intimate partner violence and captures a greater range of victimization experiences; however, for purposes of this entry, the terms *domestic violence* and *intimate partner violence* are used interchangeably to refer to acts of violence that occur between current and former spouses, boyfriends, or girlfriends. It also includes violence between persons who have a current or former marital, dating, or cohabitating relationship. The entry first compares offending, victimization, arrest, and homicide rates for intimate partner violence among African American and White populations. It then examines ways in which critical race theory, Black feminist theory, and critical race feminist theory offer alternatives to structural and cultural explanations of intimate partner violence. Using these perspectives, the entry explores ways in which the convergence of racism with other social forces, including cultural deviance and structural inequality, may exacerbate the plight of Black victims and offenders within justice systems.

Offending and Victimization Rates

More than 30 years ago, the first National Family Violence Survey found Black husbands had higher rates of overall and severe violence toward their wives than did White husbands. Blacks' rate of severe violence was 113 per 1,000, whereas in White families the rate was 30 per 1,000. The second National Family Violence Survey, conducted 5 years later, revealed similar disparities in the prevalence of intimate partner violence. More recently, African American women were 1.23 times as likely to experience minor violence and more than 2 times as likely to experience severe violence as White women.

Beyond experiencing similar levels of violent victimization in all other age categories as compared to White women, Black women also experienced slightly more intimate partner violence. As for racial/ethnic comparisons, between 1993 and 1998 African Americans were victimized by intimate partners at significantly higher rates than persons of any other race/ethnicity. According to a 2002 study, the number one killer of African American women ages 15 to 34 is homicide at the hands of a current or former intimate partner. African American women experienced intimate partner violence at a rate 35% higher than that of White women and about 22 times the rate of other women. Likewise, African American men experienced intimate partner violence at a rate about 62% higher than White men and about 22 times the rate of men of other races.

Although intimate partner violence among African Americans is complex, a major premise of this entry is that it is a partial reflection of racism within American society. The convergence of racism with other social forces, including cultural deviance and structural inequality, tends to exacerbate the plight of both Black victims and Black offenders within justice systems.

Intimate Partner Violence and Arrest Rates

As of this writing, arrest rates for Blacks were disproportionately higher (approximately 2 to 3 times) than the national average. They represented 23% of all spouses arrested for partner abuse and 35% of all boyfriend/girlfriend arrestees. This translates into about 300,000 arrests each year for allegations of intimate partner violence. While African American men represented 6% of the total population, they represented 44% of all male inmates in state and federal prisons and jails. This overrepresentation is a partial reflection of state laws that mandate arrest for domestic abuse; currently, 22 states mandate arrest. Another eight states encourage arrest in response to domestic violence—even when the abuse is characterized as either minor or mutual. The continued criminalization of domestic violence has led to mass incarceration of men while decimating marginalized communities. Arguably, these laws have a disparate impact on African Americans.

Homicide and Intimate Partner Violence

The Federal Bureau of Investigation's annual *Supplemental Homicide Reports* reveal a disproportionate number of African American homicide victims. From 1976 to 2002, African Americans did not constitute more than 15% of the population, yet they comprised more than 46% of all homicide victims. Important correlates of Black homicide rates include high percentages of Black households headed by females and high levels of divorce. Studies find that various forms of social structural oppression, including institutional racism, stereotypical images, and sexism, impact the quality of life for battered Black women, erecting barriers that prevent them from leaving abusive relationships. At times, Black female victims of intimate partner violence are distrustful of the concern and ability of helping professions deliver adequate and culturally competent services. Arguably, if others were subjected to the same degree of racism, social pressures, and structural disadvantages faced by minority populations, they, too, would exhibit high rates of homicide.

Explanations of Domestic Violence and Intimate Partner Violence

Scholars across disciplines offer competing explanations of intimate partner violence. Traditional explanations fall into two categories: *structural explanations* and *cultural explanations*. Structural explanations suggest social pressures disproportionately increase levels of frustration

and aggression. In contrast, cultural explanations suggest that the historical experiences of some, especially African Americans, promote attitudes that value and condone violence. Some African Americans believe that taking matters into their own hands (i.e., using violence) is an appropriate way to handle conflict. These explanations, however, are not exhaustive and there is ample room for other perspectives, including the burgeoning influence of *critical race theory*. The next section provides empirical evidence for these perspectives.

Structural Explanations

Sociological theories emphasize the role of structural factors in explaining criminal activity. Within the context of race and intimate partner violence, scholars suggest that Blacks are disproportionately exposed to criminogenic structural conditions. For instance, they are more likely than Whites to be poor and unemployed, to grow up in single-parent homes, and to live in segregated, poor, crime-ridden neighborhoods. Racial disparities in median household income, wealth accumulation, poverty, and unemployment rates further characterize their economic conditions.

Theoretically, the economic underdevelopment of African American men has always been a source of anger and frustration. Beginning with the American slavery era, African American men have experienced intense anger, hatred, and frustrations that they often displaced toward wives and lovers. This condition, referred to as frustrated masculinity syndrome, describes how some African American men respond to perceived racism and other institutional barriers that block opportunities for equal access to the designated legitimate means of achieving manhood. When blocked from conventional avenues of achievement, their economic dependence on working wives, girlfriends, and others is predictable. Conceivably, their dependence affects their self-esteem and sense of manhood in a way that can be characterized as a form of subordinated masculinity.

Critical Race Explanations

Historically, the victimization of African American women, Latinas, Native American women, and other women of color was seen not as a form of gender violence but as deeply rooted in issues of structural racism and poverty. Consider, for instance, the "universal risk" theory of domestic violence. Some regard it as a rhetorical paradigm resting on a false sense of unity that suggests violence can happen to anyone regardless of race/ethnicity and social status. This idea that *any woman* can be battered attempts to avoid individualizing the problem of domestic violence and to resist the stigmatization of race and class commonly associated with mainstream responses to social problems. When we view all women as equally vulnerable, race and class distinctions are ignored and economically marginalized women—especially women of color—are removed from the dominant view.

Critical race theory emphasizes the role of racism and classism in the construction of reality among people of color. Officially emerging as a theoretical genre in 1989, at least four aspects help to explain intimate partner violence within African American communities. The first aspect, *social construction*, holds that race and races are not real, per se, but products of social thought and relations. The second aspect, *essentialism and intersectionality*, conveys the notion that all oppressed people share something in common, but the forms of oppression vary considerably. A third aspect concerns *the rule of law*, as both critical race theory and feminist jurisprudence describe the rule of law as merely a mask for White male power relations. At times, it is virtually indistinguishable from politics. *First person narrative* is the fourth aspect. It enables persons of color to tell the story of their condition, while helping them realize the nature of oppression and subjugation. Each aspect is discussed further throughout the following sections.

Black Feminist Perspectives

Feminist scholarship places patriarchy at the center of any explanation for woman battering. In short, male dominance and control in the family and society as a whole perpetuates violence against women in the family. Dealing with historical oppression, negotiating intersectionalities, eradicating malignant images of Black women, and incorporating an activist perspective reflect the essential nature of Black feminism. Based on socially constructed perceptions of Black women,

Black feminist criminology scrutinizes how stereotypical images of these women affect the ways in which others respond to them. Some might question whether we can examine African American women's encounters with domestic abuse using theory based on victimization experiences of White women. The anticipated negative response to this question fosters a recognition of interconnected identities—shaped by larger social forces—as paramount. An intersectional approach explores how inequalities put some societal members at risk of being regarded as deviant and how law and state institutions both challenge and reproduce these inequalities. Intersectionality recognizes that systems of power such as race, class, and gender do not act alone to shape our experiences but rather are multiplicative, inextricably linked, and simultaneously experienced. Ignoring distinctions in identity and experiences may perpetuate indifference toward Black women and their plight. Historically, Black women have found that their interests as Blacks have taken precedence over their interests as women. Of particular relevance to intimate partner violence, albeit on a more critical note, some Black feminist theorists suggest that White women feminists forgot that for the Black woman, issues of gender are always connected to race. Moreover, Black women cannot choose between their commitment to feminism and the struggle with their men for racial justice. This primacy of concern for racism over sexism may partially account for the fact that there was relatively little special interest in minority spouse abuse and domestic violence—even among minority researchers—prior to 1980.

Critical Race Feminist Perspective

Developed in the 1990s, critical race feminist theory follows the tradition of Black feminist theory, critical legal studies, and critical race theory. Critical race feminists, however, are more interested in how domestic and international legal and social policies (e.g., welfare, education, and immigration, among others) assist or oppress racial/ethnic women and their families. Racism, in its many manifestations, is often subtle, covert, and not easily discernible.

A noticeable similarity between critical race feminist theory and Black feminist theory is that both consider women of color as individuals with multiple intersecting identities where one identity does not eclipse another. Critical race theory is particularly useful to researchers examining how various institutions with which Black women (and men) must interact daily reinforce social inequalities. Both perspectives purport that researchers of race/ethnicity have unique competencies to speak about the negotiation of intersectionality.

Battered Women's Syndrome

American cultural institutions have consistently distorted and exaggerated the images of African American men and women. Some researchers suggest that stereotypical perceptions of Black women as aggressive, resilient, and immune to the effects of violence have prevented them from receiving equal and sympathetic treatment in the criminal justice system, particularly by police officers. In some cases, these same stereotypes of Black women have prevented them from successfully using certain legal defenses, including battered women's syndrome (BWS).

BWS is a pattern of psychological and behavioral symptoms found in women living in battering relationships. According to the American Psychological Association, it is not a mental illness but a form of posttraumatic stress disorder. Acknowledged in some courts since the 1970s, at least 31 states allow expert testimony to establish its admissibility in a given case. Among those Black women who kill their abusers, most do not invoke BWS as a defense, reflecting in part the dynamics of racism, classism, and sexism. For purposes of this entry, discussions of BWS advance on the premise that White women, by virtue of membership in the dominant race, are more valuable than Black women are. Therefore, it is unreasonable to expect these two groups of women to receive equal treatment within social and criminal justice systems. Most Black women do not have equal access to the types of support services received by Whites. These include equal access to shelters, responsive 911 operators, sympathetic police officers, and objective emergency room workers. Black women are perceived as familiar, adaptable, and somewhat comfortable within their subcultures, and there is a silent reluctance to validate them as bona fide

victims of severe violence and equally worthy of rescue. Similar forces operate when these same women—unable to escape repeated cycles of violence—kill in (alleged) self-defense. The failure to validate Black women as victims calls into question whether they can prevail with a BWS defense.

Perception as Reality

Within the context of intimate partner violence, stereotypical representations of African American women as aggressive, domineering, castrating, independent, sexually promiscuous, and money hungry run rampant throughout the literature. These images tend to reduce socialized inhibitions against hitting a woman or treating a woman like a man. Even more, negative representations of African American women may lead some Black men to rationalize that violence is required to control women perceived as physically dangerous and capable of taking away their manhood. These perceptions, at times, could affect the criminal justice response to intimate violence. One study found police were more likely to comply with arrest policies when the victims were affluent, White, and lived in the suburbs. Policies were likely enforced, however, when the victims were African American, poor women living in urban areas.

Since the advent of mandatory and pro-arrest policies, women of color in the antiviolence movement have warned against investing too heavily in arrest, detention, and prosecution as responses to violence against women. In fact, there is evidence to suggest that poor women have not universally benefited from criminal justice interventions, as separation and arrest do not necessarily create safety for survivors of violence.

For myriad reasons, the criminal justice system has always been brutally oppressive toward communities of color. Unless one understands this and the historical impact of institutional racism, it may be difficult to understand why Black women are more reluctant than their White counterparts to report physical abuse to police or social service agencies. Moreover, Black women victims express reservations with trusting authorities in the criminal processing. This reality of this legacy creates both tension and dilemmas for poor women of color.

A critical race perspective underscores the magnitude of this dilemma when we consider, for example, the application of the principle *equality before the law* when sentencing domestic battery offenders. Whether conservative or liberal, many believe in color-blindness and neutral principles of constitutional law. Critical race theorists hold that color-blindness allows us to redress only extremely egregious racial harms, ones that everyone would notice and condemn. In the case of determinate sentencing, *equal treatment*—designed to reduce race- and class-based disparities—further exacerbates the problem. Its application to female offenders yields equality—but with a vengeance (i.e., a higher rate of incarceration and for longer periods of time than in the past).

Consequently, a number of scholars suggest that the racial factor has confounded the administration of justice, where, in some instances, neither defendants nor victims benefit from these arrangements. In a sense, abuse works in conjunction with the societal institution of the law via the courts, operating to help reduce the quality of life for both African American women and, in another context, African American men.

Research Directions

Despite the appeal of a critical race perspective, there are many important questions left unanswered. If race is a social construct, why focus on its primacy to the exclusion of other intersectional components of oppression? Moreover, as African Americans are culturally diverse, who decides whether mandatory arrest policies are in their best interest? How do certain institutions legally and economically interact with Black men and women in abusive relationships? Should a theoretical perspective consider the intersectionality of Black men as victims of intimate partner violence? Answers to these questions are not easy. A growing contingent of scholars and practitioners have serious reservations regarding the wisdom and propriety of mandatory and pro-arrest policies within African American communities. Some have even questioned whether we should implement (presumptive) prosecution practices in White communities and (nonpresumptive) prosecution practices within communities of color. Others argue that the efficacy of domestic violence policies should be measured by a material resource test and that assessment should be informed by the circumstances of those women who are in the greatest need. Given existing research that demonstrates that intimate partner violence victims of color prefer to handle their problems without official intervention, future examinations should center on whether victims of color would be more satisfied with a nonmandatory arrest policy.

Overall, this entry suggests that various perspectives are useful toward answering many of these questions. Perhaps, however, a critical race perspective is better suited than other perspectives, given its potential to trace the evolution of specific legislation or institutional policies related to intimate partner violence. Unlike structural and cultural explanations, its capacity to deconstruct cases of racial and sex discrimination, by focusing on its execution and enforcement, carries tremendous research potential.

Lee E. Ross

See also Black Feminist Criminology; Critical Race Theory; Domestic Violence; Domestic Violence, Latina/o/s; Domestic Violence, Native Americans

Further Readings

Ammons, L. L. (1995). Mules, madonnas, babies, bathwater, racial imagery, and stereotypes: The African-American woman and the battered woman syndrome. *Wisconsin Law Review, 5,* 1003–1080.

Belknap, J., & Potter, H. (2005). The trials of measuring the "success" of domestic violence policies. *Criminology and Public Policy, 4,* 559–567.

Burgess-Proctor, A. (2006). Intersections of race, class, gender, and crime. *Feminist Criminology, 1,* 27–47.

Coker, D. (2005). Shifting power for battered women: Law, material resources, and poor women of color. In N. Sokolof & C. Pratt (Eds.), *Domestic violence at the margins: Readings on race, class, gender, and culture* (pp. 369–388). New Brunswick, NJ: Rutgers University Press.

Crenshaw, K. (1991). Demarginalizing the intersection of race and sex: A Black feminist critique of antidiscrimination doctrine, feminist theory, and antiracist politics. In D. Weisberg (Ed.), *Feminist legal theory* (pp. 383–411). Philadelphia: Temple University Press.

Delgado, R., & Stefancic, J. (2001). *Critical race theory: An introduction.* New York: New York University Press.

Hampton, R., Oliver, W., & Magarian, L. (2003). Domestic violence in the African-American community. *Violence Against Women, 9*(5), 533–557.

Oliver, W. (2003). The structural cultural perspective: A theory of Black male violence. In D. F. Hawkins (Ed.), *Violent crimes: The nexus of race, ethnicity, and violence.* New York: Cambridge University Press.

Potter, H. (2006). An argument for Black feminist criminology. *Feminist Criminology, 1,* 106–124.

Richie, B. (2005). A Black feminist reflection on the antiviolence movement. In N. Sokoloff & C. Pratt (Eds.), *Domestic violence at the margins: Readings on race, class, gender, and culture* (pp. 50–55). New Brunswick, NJ: Rutgers University Press.

Ross, L. E. (2007). Consequences of mandatory arrest policies: Questions, comments, and concerns. *Law Enforcement Executive Forum, 7*(5), 73–85.

Ross, L. E. (2009). *The war against domestic violence.* Westport, CT: Greenwood Press.

Sherman, L. W., Schmidt, J. D., & Rogan, D. P. (1992). *Policing domestic violence: Experiments and dilemmas.* New York: The Free Press.

Sokolof, N. J., & Dupont, I. (2005). Domestic violence at the intersections of race, class, and gender. *Violence Against Women, 11*(1), 38–64.

DOMESTIC VIOLENCE, LATINA/O/S

Domestic violence is an issue that affects many people not only in the United States but worldwide. Numerous victims and their children experience this situation in isolation and fear. The cycle of domestic violence includes emotional, physical, and sexual abuse in the context of an intimate relationship. Although this cycle may be similar in different populations, the way in which power and control is exerted may be different based on ethnic group membership and what it represents to be part of that specific culture. This entry focuses on how domestic violence is experienced in the Latina/o population and how concurrent oppressions contribute to perpetuating this problem.

Relationships where domestic violence is present may be similar in diverse populations. There is a relationship of abuse when one person has power and control over the other. It is in this realm that the victim and the perpetrator are identified. In the United States, policy and program development has progressed in terms of services for both victims and perpetrators. As a result there has been improvement in service provision, law enforcement, and prevention. However, these efforts have not been enough to eliminate domestic violence.

Prevalence

A major consideration that must be taken into account when looking at domestic violence in Latinos has to do with the number of victims and the actual reporting of intimate partner abuse. Official reports have shown that one out of every four U.S. women has been assaulted by an intimate partner. It is clear that domestic violence is an issue that affects victims regardless of their ethnicity or cultural background. However, minority ethnic groups who are in positions of social disadvantage face great challenges in dealing with social problems such as domestic violence. In respect to Latinos, prevalence of reported domestic abuse is similar to reports by non-Latinos, especially African Americans. However, it is imperative to keep in mind that with Latinos there may be a misrepresentation of the data when two factors are considered: (1) underreporting of abuse and (2) violence among undocumented immigrants.

Contributing Factors and Barriers

There are issues that are particular to the Latina/o population that challenge the elimination of the problem. These factors create barriers to the use of services and resources, such as the criminal system, law enforcement, batterer education programs, and shelters, which are more accessible to some populations rather than others. They include barriers such as poor education; socioeconomic disadvantage; limited knowledge of legal provisions; and lack of bilingual personnel at the service provision level, law enforcement, and in the justice system. Another major barrier has to do with lack of cultural understanding at all levels. Cultural norms such as *machismo, marianismo,* and a patriarchal societal structure may also reinforce the idea of gender inequality and dominance in intimate relationships. Even though it would be inappropriate to state that domestic violence is socially acceptable in the Latina/o culture, it is important to emphasize that in a sociopolitical structure that has been tainted by colonization and patriarchy, the likelihood of resisting gender equality may be higher.

Other issues particular to the Latina/o population are the migration process and undocumented immigration. Even though a large portion of Latina/o immigrants live in the United States legally with visas, legal residency papers, and U.S. citizenship, many others are in the country without legal documentation. This represents a major challenge, especially for domestic violence victims. Research on undocumented battered women has found that requesting medical, legal, psychological, or other types of services is perceived as almost impossible because these women fear being referred to the Immigration and Naturalization Services (INS). In fact, threatening to turn the victim into the INS is a major victimization strategy used by perpetrators to perpetuate violence in the relationship. Victims often feel helpless because they believe that there is no escape from their situation. Even though many victims have been able to access services despite their immigration status, the fear of being deported is widespread.

Acculturation

Latinos who migrate to the United States go through particular processes of acculturation that could have repercussions for future generations. It has been found that Latinos who are more acculturated have higher rates of domestic violence. On the other hand, it has also been found that regardless of the acculturation process, many battered Latinos face numerous challenges in accessing services.

Oppression

Issues related to concurrent oppressions experienced by Latinos have to do with the aftermath of socioeconomic disadvantages, which include unemployment, underemployment, undereducation, poverty, and inability to cover expenses. Latinos who are socioeconomically disadvantaged also suffer the consequences when nonprofit organizations lack funds to provide legal aid, shelter, counseling, and advocacy.

Another factor is added when political disadvantage encourages stereotypes of this population. This may be linked to direct and indirect discrimination and institutional practices that interfere with help-seeking for those who experience domestic violence. Another element involves the internal struggle of what it represents to be a Latina/o, especially for battered women. In addition, fear of agencies and organizations, alienation from the justice system, and a perpetuation of the domestic violence cycle all contribute to making the situation worse.

The relationship between race and issues such as the perpetuation of domestic violence and the administration of justice is undeniable. Improvements to institutional policies, cultural competent practices, and social equality must be considered to move closer to effective intervention with Latina/o victims and batterers as well.

Elithet Silva-Martínez

See also Domestic Violence; Domestic Violence, African Americans; Domestic Violence, Native Americans

Further Readings

Adames, S. B., & Campbell, R. (2005, October). Immigrant Latinas' conceptualizations of intimate partner violence. *Violence Against Women, 11*(10), 1341–1364.

Dutton, M., Orloff, L., & Aguilar-Hass, G. (2000, Summer). Characteristics of help-seeking behaviors, resources, and services needs of battered immigrant Latinas: Legal and policy implications. *Georgetown Journal on Poverty Law and Policy, 7*(2), 245–305.

Klevens, J. (2007). An overview of intimate partner violence among Latinos. *Violence Against Women, 13*(2), 111–122.

Salcido, O., & Adelman, M. (2004). "He has me tied with the blessed and damned papers": Undocumented-immigrant battered women in Phoenix, Arizona. *Human Organization, 63*(2), 162–172.

Tjaden, P., & Thoennes, N. (2000, July). *Extent, nature, and consequences of intimate partner violence: Findings from the National Violence Against Women Survey* (Report No. NCJ 181867). Retrieved from Office of Justice Programs: http://www.ojp.usdoj.gov/nij/pubs-sum/181867.htm

Domestic Violence, Native Americans

Domestic violence, defined as harmful verbal, physical, or sexual abuse committed by one intimate against another, is a widespread and unfortunate problem encountered across virtually every society. Historically, domestic violence was viewed as a private matter. However, in the 1970s the public, as well as policymakers and other professionals, began to define this matter as a serious social and legal health problem that needed to be addressed. Still, it was not until the 1980s and 1990s that criminal justice and community agencies began to respond to the matter through practices, programs, and legislation. Furthermore, it was not until this past decade that researchers began to explore different variables, such as race/ethnicity, in studying domestic violence. This entry examines domestic violence victimization of Native Americans/American Indians (NAAIs) as well as NAAI culture, risk factors, and consequences related to victimization. The NAAI population discussed in this entry includes those individuals who are Native American or American Indian and live in the United States, whether on reservations, nonreservation rural land, or nonreservation urban land.

Victimization Rates

Although both NAAI males and females are victims of domestic violence, females are victimized at much higher rates and suffer greater injury. NAAI women experience extremely high rates of domestic violence victimization. According to various self-reports, NAAI women consistently record the highest rates of violence against them by an intimate compared to other racial/ethnic groups in the United States. These women report a rate of violent victimization over twice that reported by African Americans and Whites. Moreover, NAAI women have reported higher levels of physical violence by a partner than any other group. Similarly, official records reveal that NAAI women have the highest rates of falling victim to intimate partner homicide than any other group. All these differences have been found significant.

Culture

Native cultures are similar to mainstream cultures in that they both prohibit violence among family members. Yet, native cultures are distinctive in the way they are subjected to and the way they handle the matter. Traditionally, violence against women in NAAI communities has been rare. Prior to colonization, many tribes practiced gender equality and held strong social and ethical norms against such violence, resulting in low rates of victimization. After colonization, this violence has become increasingly frequent and is now recognized as one of the largest ills facing NAAI communities.

As a result of this historical trauma, the policing of domestic violence among NAAIs has become quite convoluted. An incident of domestic violence was typically handled by members in the same community. Often times, males in the victim's family would mediate until the offender had changed his ways. In extreme cases, elected tribal officials handled the matter. Law enforcement typically did not get involved. This reflects the use of informal sanctions in dealing with the crime. However, the family's ability to intervene has decreased due to colonization and the involvement by the U.S. government. Additionally, the lack of teaching and education of native culture caused by forcing children to attend boarding schools has contributed to the failure of the family to acknowledge and address the problem. It has also disrupted family structure. Consequently, domestic violence, among other related forms of family violence, has increased among NAAI communities.

Risk Factors

Although there have been few studies on domestic violence of NAAI women when compared to other groups, research has indicated that there are risk factors that make these women vulnerable to domestic violence. Among these include institutional prejudice, in the form of racism and sexism, and oppressive practices that resulted from colonization, such as the removal of Indian people from ancestral lands and their subsequent treatment, which can foster negative feelings and behavior. In addition, the introduction of alcohol and other substances into the NAAI community has largely been associated with the rise in domestic violence, as their use has long been noted to relate to violent behavior.

Other correlates of domestic violence among NAAIs include the following:

- Gender
- Age
- Income
- Unemployment
- Previous victimization
- Lack of education
- Pregnancy at an early age
- Low self-esteem

Young females living with an intimate partner who is the main or sole provider tend to be at high risk of experiencing domestic violence. These women may rely on their partner for financial or economic support. Previous victimization also has been linked to future victimization. Additionally, research has found that women with low self-esteem and women with poor education experience high rates of violence.

Consequences

Domestic violence has been associated with many negative consequences. These include, but are not limited to, poor health, illness, anxiety, depression, posttraumatic stress disorder, mental health problems, and even suicide/death. In addition, domestic violence has been found to be interrelated with the acquisition of HIV/AIDS. In a larger context, domestic violence has been linked to child abuse, elder abuse, and sibling violence. Thus, it perpetuates a cycle of violence.

Resources for NAAI Women

NAAI women represent a disproportionate number of those experiencing domestic violence and its related consequences. NAAI women consistently report experiencing higher rates of domestic violence than other racial/ethnic groups and thus warrant further attention and investigation. There has been limited access to shelters, counseling, and other services for these women, especially those living on reservation and nonreservation rural land. NAAI women are in need of referrals to services in their areas as well as appropriately tailored interventions that take culture and risk factors into account.

Alison Marganski

See also Domestic Violence; Domestic Violence, African Americans; Domestic Violence, Latina/o/s; Violence Against Women

Further Readings

Oetzel, J., & Duran, B. (2004). Intimate partner violence in American Indian and/or Alaska Native communities: A social ecological framework of determinants and interventions. *American Indian & Alaska Native Mental Health Research: Journal of the National Center, 11*(3), 49–68.

Vernon, I. S. (2002). Violence, HIV/AIDS, and Native American women in the twenty-first century. *American Indian Culture and Research Journal, 26*(2), 115–133.

Yuan, N. P., Koss, M. P., Polacca, M., & Goldman, D. (2006). Risk factors for physical assault and rape among six Native American tribes. *Journal of Interpersonal Violence, 21*(12), 1566–1590.

DRAFT RIOTS

See Race Riots

DRED SCOTT CASE

In the annals of the history of the U.S. Supreme Court, there is one case that is consistently ranked as the worst decision ever made by the Court. This is the *Dred Scott* case, officially known as *Dred Scott v. Sandford* (1857). The decision was widely discussed in the 1858 debates for the U.S. Senate seat from Illinois between Senator Stephen A. Douglas, Democratic incumbent, and Abraham Lincoln, Republican congressman. The debates were complicated by the 1857 Supreme Court ruling that had every tavern in the country buzzing with the words "Dred Scott." The Court ruled that Congress could not prohibit slavery in the territories (those areas west of the Mississippi River not yet states) and struck down the Missouri Compromise of 1820, even though the law had already been repealed by the Kansas-Nebraska Act of 1854, which Douglas had sponsored. As a result, the Court fueled the growing divisions between North and South over slavery, providing a significant factor for the outbreak of the War Between the States, or, as it is known in the South, the War of Northern Aggression, from 1861 to 1865. The decision also tarnished the prestige of the Court and the reputation of Chief Justice Roger B. Taney.

Background

Dred Scott was a Missouri slave who had accompanied his master, Dr. John Emerson, an army surgeon, to Illinois in 1834 and to Wisconsin Territory, present-day Minnesota, in 1836. Because both areas were free of slavery according to the Missouri Compromise, Dred Scott claimed to have been automatically freed by his presence there. Scott and Emerson returned to Missouri in 1838. In 1850, after Dr. Emerson's death, a court in St. Louis, Missouri, agreed with Scott's view, citing Missouri precedents dating from 1824, that Dred Scott had become free while living in non-slave jurisdictions and remained free, despite his return to Missouri. However, Scott's plea was lost on appeal in the Missouri Supreme Court. Reflecting the proslavery ideology of the South, the Missouri Supreme Court disavowed the old precedents in *Scott v. Emerson* (1852) and ruled that Dred Scott was not a citizen and could not sue for his freedom from Emerson's widow. After remarrying, the widow subsequently passed ownership of Dred Scott and his wife and two daughters through friends to her brother, John F. A. Sanford (incorrectly spelled in the case as Sandford), a native-born Southerner residing in New York.

By arranging the sale of the slave Dred Scott and his family to a New Yorker, Mr. Sanford, Dred Scott's friends hoped to argue the case in the federal courts on the grounds that it had become a case of a citizen of Missouri suing a citizen of New York. In 1854, Scott sued in the U.S. District Court in Missouri, arguing that as a "citizen" of Missouri, he was entitled to sue a citizen of another state in federal court, because Article III of the Constitution gave the federal courts jurisdiction over cases "between citizens of different states." The hope of Dred Scott and his supporters was to carry the case to the Supreme Court, where the entire question of slavery in the territories might be decided. Therefore, the essence of the case centered on the power of Congress to exclude slavery from the territories belonging to the nation. The Republican contention that Congress had always possessed this power, and exercised it in the Northwest Ordinance of 1787 and in the Missouri Compromise of 1820, was at issue. Southerners were confident that the Court would uphold Douglas's 1854 Kansas-Nebraska Act repeal of the Missouri Compromise restriction on slavery and deny the power of Congress to exclude slavery from the territories. (Both slave owners and abolitionists sent "settlers" into Kansas to intimidate the voters in such cases as the 1855 sacking of Lawrence by a posse of proslavery "Border Ruffians" and the immediate retaliation by abolitionist John Brown, whose group of seven men, including four sons and his son-in-law, shot to death one slave owner and hacked four others to death in the so-called Pottawatomie Massacre. Therefore, "Bleeding Kansas" became the catchphrase in the 1850s over the issue of popular sovereignty, whereby the residents of the given territory themselves would vote on slavery or "free soil.") Seven of the nine justices were Democrats, in the days when the Democratic Party had strong contingencies of proslavery advocates, five of whom were from the South. Moreover, there were indications that a majority of the Court was eager to remove the entire subject of slavery from Congress.

The Decision

In the subsequent 1857 Supreme Court decision, Chief Justice Taney, who had been appointed by President Andrew Jackson in 1836 and served until his death in 1864, ended all hope at that time for any kind of possible advancement by the Black race in the United States, slave, free, or presumed free, as was the case with Dred Scott. Speaking for the seven Democratic justices, Taney declared that the lower federal court lacked jurisdiction, because, under the laws of Missouri, Scott was not a citizen. Taney, writing in vivid language that many Northerners, both Black and White, found offensive, declared that Blacks could never be citizens of the United States. The following is a verbatim citation from Taney's *Dred Scott* decision:

The question is simply this: Can a negro, whose ancestors were imported into this country, and sold as slaves, become a member of the political community formed and brought into existence by the Constitution of the United States, and as such become entitled to all the rights, and privileges, and immunities, guaranteed by that instrument to the citizen? One of which rights is the privilege of suing in a court of the United States in the cases specified in the Constitution.

The words "people of the United States" and "citizens" are synonymous terms, and mean the same thing. They both describe the political body who, according to our republican institutions, form the sovereignty, and who hold the power and conduct the Government through their representatives. . . . The question before us is, whether the class of persons described in the plea in abatement compose a portion of this people, and are constituent members of the sovereignty? We think they are not, and that they are not included, and were not intended to be included, under the word "citizen" in the Constitution, and can therefore claim none of the rights and privileges which that instrument provides for and secure to citizens of the United States. On the contrary, they were at the time [1787] considered as a subordinate and inferior class of beings, who had been subjugated by the dominant race, and, whether emancipated or not, yet remained subject to their authority, and had no rights or privileges but such as those who held the power and the Government might choose to grant them. . . .

The question then arises, whether the provisions of the Constitution, in relation to the personal rights and privileges to which the citizen of a State should be entitled, embraced the Negro African race, at that time in this country, or who might afterwards be imported, who had then or should afterwards be made free in any State; and to put it in the power of a single State to make him a citizen of the United States, and

endue him with the full rights of citizenship in every other State without their consent? Does the Constitution of the United States act upon him whenever he shall be made free under the laws of a State, and raised there to the rank of citizen, and immediately clothe him with all the privileges of a citizen in every other State, and in its own courts?

The court thinks the affirmative of these propositions cannot be maintained. And if it cannot, the plaintiff in error could not be a citizen of the State of Missouri within the meaning of the Constitution of the United States, and, consequently, was not entitled to sue in its courts.

Furthermore, citing the Fifth Amendment, Taney said that no slaveholder could be deprived of his property without "due process" and that Scott, therefore, remained a slave.

Taney's message, like that conveyed by Douglas as chief sponsor of the Kansas-Nebraska Act, affirmed that the Missouri Compromise was null and void. He wrote:

The act of Congress, upon which the plaintiff relies [to claim his freedom], declares that slavery and involuntary servitude, except as a punishment for crime, shall be forever prohibited in all that part of the territory ceded by France, under the name of Louisiana, which lies north of thirty-six degrees thirty minutes north latitude, and not included within the limits of Missouri. And the difficulty which meets us at the threshold of this part of the inquiry is, whether Congress was authorized to pass this law under any of the powers granted to it by the Constitution; for if the authority is not given by that instrument, it is the duty of this court to declare it void and inoperative, and incapable of conferring freedom upon any one of the States.

Reaction to the Decision

The *Dred Scott* decision set off a firestorm of indignation and protest, especially in the North. Abolitionist Horace Greeley, editor of the *New York Tribune*, called the *Dred Scott* decision "the closing in of an Arctic night in our history, abominable, false, detestable hypocrisy." Abraham Lincoln's Republican Party called it a "wicked and false judgment," and Lincoln himself feared that the ruling could be construed to refer to Illinois as well as to Wisconsin as potential slave states.

Lincoln also saw that *Dred Scott* was in conflict with Douglas's own favored idea of popular sovereignty, the ability granted to residents of territories under the Kansas-Nebraska Act to vote on the right to admit slavery or to be "free soil." At a debate in Freeport, Illinois, Lincoln asked Douglas to explain how the people of a territory could exclude slavery if slaves like Scott were simultaneously permitted there. Douglas's response, both subtle and pragmatic in its cleverness, was the following: "Slavery cannot exist a day or an hour anywhere unless it is supported by local police regulations." This statement was true, but it did not help Dred Scott. The so-called Freeport Doctrine alienated Douglas from committed slave owners, but it won him reelection to the U.S. Senate from Illinois. Lincoln, now no longer a congressman, in turn, would have to wait until the election of 1860 to return to Washington as president. In another irony of the *Dred Scott* case, Scott's owner freed him shortly after the decision, but Dred Scott died 1 year later in St. Louis.

Dred Scott's case is a landmark in constitutional history as an example of the Supreme Court's attempt to impose a judicial solution on a political problem. Some Americans, in particular those who resided in the South or Northern Democrats who were apathetic to the horrors of slavery, lauded the decision as an important attempt to end the heated debate over the expansion of slavery into the territories. However, overall, in the North, people denounced the Court's decision and Chief Justice Taney. The Northern response quickly made the Republican Party the most powerful political institution in that part of the country. It set the stage for the election of Abraham Lincoln as the 16th president of the United States in 1860, the subsequent secession of the Southern states, led by South Carolina, and almost 5 years of bloody and devastating civil war.

Actions to Overturn *Dred Scott*

During the war, Congress and President Lincoln took steps to eradicate slavery and its evils. Many of their actions in 1862 and 1863 eviscerated the two main principles announced by Chief Justice Taney in *Dred Scott*: Congress could not prohibit slavery in the territories, and Blacks could not be citizens. Several years later, *Dred Scott* was formally overturned by the three Civil War amendments to the U.S. Constitution, ratified from 1865 to 1870.

In 1862, Congress passed a number of statutes directed against slavery. It offered financial compensation to states that agreed to abolish slavery gradually, abolished slavery in the District of Columbia, and prohibited slavery in the territories, thus rejecting a central principle of *Dred Scott*. Congress also passed legislation that freed slaves from all those who had committed treason against the United States or incited or engaged in any rebellion or insurrection against the United States. On January 1, 1863, Lincoln issued his Emancipation Proclamation, which freed the slaves in the states in rebellion.

In 1862, Attorney General Bates released a long opinion stating that neither color nor race could deny American Blacks the right of citizenship, denying a second central tenet of *Dred Scott*. He pointed out that "freemen of all colors" had voted in some of the states. The Constitution, noted Bates as he rejected *Dred Scott*, was "silent about *race* as it is about *color*." Bates concluded: "The free man of color, if born in the United States, is a citizen of the United States" (10 Op. Att'y Gen. 382 [1862]).

Following the War Between the States, Congress passed the Thirteenth Amendment, adopted in 1865, which abolished slavery in the United States as an institution. The Fourteenth Amendment, ratified in 1868, provided for the equal protection of Blacks and Whites before the law and specified in Section 1 that "all persons born or naturalized in the United States, and subject to the jurisdiction thereof, are citizens of the United States and of the State wherein they reside." Finally, the Fifteenth Amendment, which took effect in 1870, gave Blacks the right to vote. Under the express language of these amendments, Congress was empowered to enforce them "with appropriate legislation."

The *Dred Scott* ruling ruined the reputation of one of the longest-serving chief justices in American history, Roger B. Taney. It is a landmark case, widely condemned in the North at the time. Scott's diligence and perseverance in claiming his freedom as a citizen of the United States and the State of Missouri played an important role in ending slavery. As a result of the Fourteenth Amendment, in particular, descendants of former slaves in the South and the North are today U.S. citizens and subject to court decisions and laws—above all, *Brown v. Board of Education of Topeka, Kansas* (1954), a unanimous ruling that called for the desegregation of the public schools and overruled the "separate but equal" doctrine enunciated in *Plessy v. Ferguson* (163 U.S. 537 [1896]), as well as the Civil Rights Act of 1964 and the Voting Rights Act of 1965—protecting their due process rights, equality, and privileges and immunities throughout the land.

Stephen E. Medvec

See also Slave Patrols; White Supremacists

Further Readings

Basler, R., et al. (Eds.). (1953–1955). *The collected works of Abraham Lincoln* (9 vols.). New Brunswick, NJ: Rutgers University Press.

Brown v. Board of Education of Topeka, Kansas, 347 U.S. 483 (1954).

Dred Scott v. Sandford, 60 U.S. (19 How.) 393 (1857).

Fisher, L. (2005). *Constitutional law* (6th ed.). Durham, NC: Carolina Academic Press.

Hall, K. L., Finkelman, P., & Ely, J. W., Jr. (2005). *American legal history: Cases and materials*. Oxford, UK: Oxford University Press.

Klarman, M. J. (2004). *From Jim Crow to civil rights: The Supreme Court and the struggle for racial equality*. Oxford, UK: Oxford University Press.

Miner, C. (2003). *Kansas, The history of the sunflower state, 1854–2000*. Lawrence: University of Kansas Press.

Paludan, P. (1994). *The presidency of Abraham Lincoln*. Lawrence: University of Kansas Press.

Plessy v. Ferguson, 163 U.S. 537 (1896).

Scott v. Emerson, 15 Mo. 576 (1852).

Wiecek, W. M. (1978). Slavery and abolition before the United States Supreme Court, 1820–1860. *Journal of American History*, 65, 34.

DRUG CARTELS

Since the 1980s, much of the trafficking of drugs to the United States was, and is, attributed to the drug cartels of Colombia. Through the use of violence and established smuggling routes into the United States, Colombian cartels controlled much of the distribution of cocaine to America. The cartels' presence led to the evolvement of local gangs to sell and control the drugs, which in turn threatened communities and encouraged further drug use. This entry focuses on the nature of drug cartels and how the drug trade became institutionalized in poor communities predominated by racial and ethnic minorities (see Filippone, 1994; Tonry, 1994). Although the proportion of minorities directly involved with drug cartels is unknown, their involvement in drug dealing (indicated by arrests and convictions) indicates a substantial influence.

The Rise and Impact of Drug Cartels

Since the 1980s, Colombia has been responsible for 80% of the cocaine that annually enters the United States (Filippone, 1994). The geographic location of Colombia made it a perfect base of operation from which to monopolize the international drug trade. Coca, the plant from which cocaine is derived, is harvested mainly from Bolivia and Peru, which are in close geographic proximity to Colombia. Additionally, Colombia has ready sea and air access to the United States, which became established ways to smuggle drugs. During the 1980s, the Medellin cartel, based in the Colombian city of Medellin, was the best-known cartel, controlling at least 60% of the Columbian international drug trade. This cartel was controlled by Pablo Escobar, who further established the Medellin cartel as a violent, highly structured organization supplying cocaine to the U.S. drug market.

Other countries, such as Mexico and Jamaica, also produced drug cartels. Much like Colombia, Mexico and Jamaica serve as major transit points for marijuana and cocaine shipments entering the United States. Several primary Mexican cartels linked to increased drug trafficking include the

Gulf cartel, the Juarez cartel, and the Tijuana cartel. Although not typically called cartels, Jamaican drug-smuggling organizations compete with Colombian and Mexican cartels.

The Drug Enforcement Agency and Customs and Immigration Enforcement have reported a link between Jamaican drug organizations and criminal drug activity within the United States. As reported by several researchers (Jones, 2002; Maingot, 1989; McDonald, 1988; Stone, 1991), Jamaica is responsible for a substantial percentage of the marijuana imported into the United States. Jamaican drug organizations, known as posses, are believed to have been operating as early as the 1970s, distributing guns and marijuana into the United States. These posses began to deal in crack cocaine upon its onset in the mid-1980s. The influence of Jamaican posses is concentrated in the northeast United States around New York, New Jersey, and Philadelphia, and in Miami.

Initially, Jamaican posses used substantial violence when their drug-selling territory was challenged. Jamaican posses have more recently forged relationships with West Coast gangs and traditional organized crime, and they have strengthened ties with Colombian cartels to further aid in the distribution of drug flow into American markets. Once the drugs have entered the United States, cartels establish a distribution network to pass the drugs on to users. To do this, the cartels organize drug dealers. Although it is difficult to determine exact numbers of minorities utilized by cartels, specifically African Americans and Hispanics, it is logical to argue that cartels have exploited such minorities to distribute drugs (Hebert, 1997; Tonry, 1994).

One explanation posited by researchers regarding the high level of minority involvement in the drug trade is socioeconomic status (Tonry, 1994). With many young, minority juveniles experiencing economic hardships, it has been suggested that they see the drug trade as a way to ease their economic burden. The allure of making large sums of money makes minority juveniles particularly amenable to drug trafficking.

As cocaine shipments increased in the 1980s and more minorities were in place to distribute the drugs, turf war violence ensued among minority groups. Specifically, Florida experienced an influx of Cuban refugees during the early 1980s. This resulted in a war between Colombians and Cubans in Florida. Similar patterns of violence were also seen throughout different minority communities as subgroups attempted to gain control of drug markets.

Although cocaine remained popular, crack cocaine soon became the new drug epidemic, becoming more prominent and widespread beginning in 1985. Crack cocaine costs less and gives the user a faster high than powder cocaine. As a result of the price difference between the two drugs, powder cocaine became the drug of choice for more economically advantaged users, while crack became the drug of choice for economically disadvantaged minorities. Further increasing the negative influence on minorities, it was easier for policing efforts to address crack cocaine offenses than powder cocaine. Powder cocaine users are not typical targets for arrest in that they do not engage in their criminal activity in public. It is likely to occur in suburban or upper-class areas, and the dealers are likely to be involved with the same contacts. Unlike powder cocaine users, crack users and dealers often perform their illegal activity in areas that are more public. These types of crimes are typically committed in alleys and streets in poor minority areas that are easier for police to observe. Further, the dealers in disorganized areas have no choice but to sell to strangers, who could easily be undercover police. Juvenile and young minority adults were easy targets for the drug cartels because the minorities were economically depressed, and drug use and distribution provided them with the means to overcome their economic disadvantage. Because minorities are more likely to be involved with crack and crack is likely to be policed more efficiently than powder cocaine, minority arrest rates started to increase. Although there have been efforts of governmental agencies to stop the illegal drug trade on various fronts, Colombian and other cartels continue the drug flow into the United States. The increase in cocaine distribution and legislative changes that ensued have had long-lasting consequences on minorities in terms of sentencing disparities and overrepresentation within the prison system.

Jeffery T. Walker and Joseph B. McSherry

See also Anti–Drug Abuse Acts; Disproportionate Arrests; Disproportionate Incarceration; War on Drugs

Further Readings

Filippone, R. (1994). The Medellin cartel: Why we can't win the drug war. *Studies in Conflict and Terrorism,* 17, 323–344.

Gay, B., & Marquart, J. (1993). Jamaican posses: A new form of organized crime. *Journal of Crime and Justice,* 16(2), 139–170.

Hebert, C. G. (1997). Sentencing outcomes of Black, Hispanic, and White males convicted under federal sentencing guidelines. *Criminal Justice Review,* 22(2), 133–156.

Jones, M. J. (2002). Policy paradox: Implications of U.S. drug control policy for Jamaica. *Annals of the American Academy of Political and Social Science,* 582, 117–133.

Leigey, M., & Bachman, R. (2007). The influence of crack cocaine on the likelihood of incarceration for a violent offense: An examination of a prison sample. *Criminal Justice Policy Review,* 18(4), 335–352.

Maingot, A. (1989, July). The drug menace to the Caribbean. *The World and I,* 7, 128–135.

McDonald, S. B. (1988). *Dancing on a volcano: The Latin American drug trade.* New York: Praeger.

National Drug Intelligence Center. (2005, February). *National drug threat assessment, 2005 summary report.* Retrieved from http://www.justice.gov/ndic/pubs11/13846/marijuana.htm

Ousey, G., & Lee, M. (2004). Investigating the connections between race, illicit drug markets, and lethal violence, 1984–1997. *Journal of Research in Crime and Delinquency,* 41(4), 352–383.

Stone, C. (1991). Hard drug use in a Black island society. *Caribbean Affairs,* 4(2), 142–161.

Tonry, M. (1994). Racial politics, racial disparities, and the war on crime. *Crime and Delinquency,* 40(4), 475–494.

U.S. Drug Enforcement Administration. (n.d.). *Marijuana.* Retrieved July 18, 2008, from http://www.usdoj.gov/dea/concern/marijuana.html

Drug Courts

In a drug court, a trial court judge is assigned a docket of cases involving offenders whose crimes are related to their dependency on alcohol or illegal drugs. There are two major types of drug courts: drug case management courts and drug treatment courts. *Case management courts* are those courts that consolidate all of the drug cases in one court system in order to more efficiently and consistently dispose of (i.e., adjudicate) those cases. This entry focuses on drug treatment courts and their operation. In addition, the entry examines issues concerning race and ethnicity, as they relate to drug courts.

As the term implies, *drug treatment courts* emphasize intensive supervision and treatment of offenders with drug or alcohol problems. Drug treatment courts in different jurisdictions address defendants with varying legal situations. Pre-plea programs are aimed at relatively minor offenders who wish to avoid pleading to a charge, going through trial, and being convicted. The prosecutor will drop the charges against defendants who successfully complete the drug court program. The defendant may have to admit his or her guilt even though no formal plea is entered. In post-plea programs, the defendants plead guilty to the crime of which they are accused and seek to avoid adjudication of guilt, incarceration, or both, by agreeing to participate in treatment programs under the court's supervision. In community transition programs, offenders have already served a part of their sentence in prison and seek early release and a return to the community.

Characteristics of Drug Treatment Courts

The first drug treatment court was established in Miami, Florida, in 1989 as a response to the increasing caseloads resulting from prosecutions for crack cocaine. The Miami court was created by Judge Herbert M. Klein, and his method of active judicial involvement with each client is a hallmark of the drug courts. It is this judicial involvement that is the distinguishing characteristic of drug treatment courts as well as other problem-solving or therapeutic courts. Clients in the early phase of the programs are required to attend weekly court sessions, where the judge will review their progress and distribute rewards and punishments as warranted.

As befits the emphasis on treatment, the relationship between the court professionals and the defendants is nonadversarial, and the judge, prosecutor, defense counsel, treatment providers, and other practitioners assigned to work with the drug court are to function as a team to review cases and arrive at decisions regarding the disposition of defendants. Defendants are tested frequently for drugs and must participate in drug treatment programs and other programming relevant to their individual needs. Defendants who comply with the court's requirements are rewarded with advancement through the phases of the treatment in the courts, which usually implies greater freedom and fewer mandatory treatment or court sessions. Defendants who fail to comply, such as by relapsing or by missing treatment group sessions, may be punished by brief stays in jail or loss of advanced status. Defendants who commit new crimes, repeatedly relapse, or commit other serious infractions of program rules may be instantly terminated. Many courts hold graduation ceremonies for those who successfully complete the program, which may take at least 1 year and as much as 2 years.

Drug treatment courts are hailed by their advocates as an effective alternative to either incarceration without treatment or treatment without intensive supervision. Advocates refer to a drug court "movement" and note the rapid increase in the number of jurisdictions with drug courts as a positive development. Despite their popularity, drug treatment courts present serious concerns about their subversive effects on the adversary system of justice, the validity of claims of effectiveness, and their impact on racial and ethnic minority groups.

Issues of Jurisprudence and Ethics

Coerced Treatment

Drug treatment courts exist to facilitate the coerced treatment of alcoholics and drug addicts. This purpose is legitimated by the fact that defendants in drug courts have violated the law and are therefore doomed to some form of coercion—incarceration, treatment, home confinement, and so forth—as a result. Given their criminal liability, advocates of the drug court argue that it is better to coerce defendants into acquiescence in a course of treatment that works than it is to punish them

by incarceration or other methods that have not proven effective.

Underlying this argument are two assumptions: (1) that the criminalization of drug possession and, for all practical purposes, of drug addiction and alcoholism is inevitable if not desirable, and (2) that the purpose of coercing defendants is to prevent future crimes rather than to punish past crimes. Both assumptions are controversial. The first assumption makes drug courts complicit in the perpetuation of a War on Drugs that is condemned by its opponents as a wasteful, racist, repressive failure. The second assumption opens the door to a brave new world in which the principle is in jeopardy that the state must be restricted to punishment based on the past criminal conduct of the offender.

The practitioners who work in drug courts see things much differently. For them, concerns about drug courts as the velvet glove on the iron fist of repression seem abstract. They are dealing with the immediate loss of freedom and autonomy that are the essence of addiction and alcoholism. They see the offenders in drug court not as defendants at the mercy of the state, but as sick persons at the mercy of a fatal disease. The drug court can serve as a bridge for clients from resistance to acceptance of their problem and willingness to collaborate in its treatment. Practitioners also see drug courts as a way of reducing reliance on incarceration.

This implies that the legitimacy of coerced treatment depends, in part, on the validity and reliability of the methods used to classify defendants as substance abusers. Given ethical limits on the use of coercion and the need to make the most effective use of limited resources, it makes little sense to impose treatment on defendants who do not need it and cannot benefit from it. This is especially important where drug court treatment involves a longer, more costly, and more intrusive intervention in the life of the defendant than would have occurred if the defendant were sentenced in an ordinary court.

Adversarial Justice

In a system of adversarial justice, the truth regarding the guilt of the defendant is arrived at in a contest in which the state is represented by a prosecutor and the defendant by defense counsel. The judge serves as neutral referee who makes sure that the advocates for both parties follow elaborate rules of evidence and procedure. Drug treatment courts subvert the adversarial ideal in a number of ways. Instead of serving as neutral referee, the judge becomes the primary actor, involved in a therapeutic relationship with the defendant (the "client") and directing the course of treatment. The prosecutor and defender become members of the drug court team and, as team players, are expected to lay down their arms and join together with the judge to ascertain the best interests of the defendant, whatever his or her stated preferences might be.

Critics have noted that this model also departs from the ideal for a therapeutic relationship, one that is based on the voluntary decision of the client to collaborate with a therapist to achieve mutually agreed on goals. Drug courts are authoritarian by nature: The client's continued involvement with the drug court requires the client to comply with the requirements imposed by the court, or face termination from the program.

There are a number of specific ethical challenges posed by the tension between adversarial and therapeutic justice, but much of it boils down to the role of the drug court judge. Because the role of the judge is so enlarged in this setting, drug court judges must have a high level of competence, integrity, compassion, and knowledge. Neither therapeutic nor adversarial courts have satisfactorily addressed the issue of what to do with a bad judge.

The risk of departure from the adversarial ideal is linked to the issue of valid classification of defendants as substance abusers. Such departures may be justified if the goal is to save persons from a fatal, progressive disease of addiction, but the "doctors" should be sure of their diagnosis. One role that defense counsel can play is to promote the use of evidence-based practices in assessment of potential drug court participants, a stance that is also in the interests of the other members of the team.

Issues of Effectiveness

As one of the most studied innovations in criminal justice, drug courts have a strong basis for claiming to be effective. An authoritative study by the General Accounting Office found that the evidence supports the conclusion that drug courts produce a reduction in recidivism, but the evidence of an effect on the likelihood of relapse is mixed. The General Accounting Office found that the effects of the specific components of drug courts, such as the role of the judge or the effectiveness of drug treatment strategies, have not been adequately investigated. A complicating factor in assessing the effectiveness of drug courts is the wide variation in rates of program completion, for it is program completers whose recidivism rates are usually compared to a control or comparison group.

Evidence that some drug courts are effective should not be taken as evidence that all drug courts are effective. Other research has shown wide variation in the quality of drug courts, as measured by their adherence to the practices of successful programs.

Race and Ethnicity

Any consideration of issues concerning race and ethnicity must take place in the context of not only the overrepresentation of persons of color in prison and jail populations but also the effects of severe sentences for possession and sale of drugs on overrepresentation. It is in light of these concerns that drug courts are sometimes regarded as a partial solution to the problem of extremely high incarceration rates for African Americans and Americans of Hispanic origin. The issues become whether minority group members succeed in drug court programs and, if not, whether barriers to success may be identified and removed.

In comparisons of criminal justice processing and outcomes for different racial and ethnic groups, the following variables are present: admission to drug court, length of involvement, graduation rates, recidivism rates, and relapse rates. Very little research has been conducted that explicitly addresses issues of differences by race and ethnicity on these variables. The handful of studies that are available focus on graduation rates, and many show that African American defendants are significantly less likely to graduate from drug court programs than are White defendants.

No available research provides evidence of overt discrimination against Black defendants.

Instead, racial differences are attributed to differences in other variables—such as employment, education, drug of choice, and age—that are related to race and also predictive of graduation or termination from drug courts.

A second line of research emphasizes the cultural differences between African American and White drug court participants. In particular, African American clients may attribute their problems to racism and poverty, rather than to their substance abuse. African Americans may also have negative attitudes toward mental health treatment and toward didactic styles of treatment delivery. African American males may be better served by single-gender groups. A study by Beckerman and Fontana (2001) suggests that treatment that provides for such cultural differences is associated with persistence and retention in the drug court program.

Jerome McKean

See also Drug Treatment; Drug Use; Intermediate
    Sanctions; Juvenile Drug Courts

Further Readings

Beckerman, A., & Fontana, L. (2001). Issues of race and gender in court-ordered substance abuse treatment. *Journal of Offender Rehabilitation, 33*, 45–61.

General Accounting Office. (2005). *Adult drug courts: Evidence indicates recidivism reductions and mixed results for other outcomes*. Washington, DC: U.S. Government Printing Office.

Nolan, J. R. (Ed.). (2002). *Drug courts in theory and in practice*. New York: de Gruyter.

Websites

National Association of Drug Court Professionals: http://www.nadcp.org

DRUG DEALERS

During the 1980s, under the leadership of President Ronald Reagan, the U.S. government commenced its War on Drugs. Due to the highly skilled media onslaught engineered by the Reagan administration, many White Americans saw Hispanics, Black Americans, and other people of color as the primary culprits behind the exponential growth in crime. Federal, state, and local law enforcement agencies grew increasingly punitive regarding the use and sales of illegal drugs, eventually causing America's prisons to overflow with individuals sentenced to several years' incarceration for relatively minor offenses.

Sociologists speculated that the differences in the way Blacks and Whites dealt drugs were likely reasons for minority overattention; that is, legal authorities found it easier to apprehend minorities because of the dysfunctional nature of inner-city life. Smalltime White drug dealers tended to sell their wares in privacy, whereas smalltime Black drug dealers sold theirs on the street; this situation made it easier for the police to arrest Black dealers than to arrest White dealers. Ironically, someone committing a violent crime, such as aggravated assault or assault with a deadly weapon, could receive a much lighter sentence and/or probation more quickly than someone caught selling crack cocaine, because prison sentences for those convicted of selling drugs are mandatory.

For instance, until very recently, someone caught selling 5 grams of crack, 500 grams of powder cocaine, or 100 kilograms of marijuana, or merely possessing 100 grams of precursors needed for crystal methamphetamine could receive a sentence of 5 years in a correctional facility. If the police catch someone selling 50 grams of crack, 5 kilos of powder cocaine, or 1,000 kilograms of marijuana, or possessing 1,000 grams of precursors, the sentence would be 10 years.

Even though government pundits stated that organizations like the Medellin cartel in Colombia were still the true focuses of legal investigations, individuals of color living within the inner cities of major metropolitan American citizens were the ones most affected. Americans grew accustomed to the idea that minorities (meaning Blacks and Hispanics) were immeasurably harming the country by selling drugs, as was shown on American network news on a nightly basis. Viewers were not told, however, that law enforcement officers disproportionately concentrated their focus on racial minorities, making it seem that drug dealing was localized and endemic in minority populations.

Overpolicing was justified by the belief that most drug deals occurred in primarily Black areas, and thus police should focus their activities there. Police thought that if they centered their attention upon legal behaviors (e.g., groups of Black youth congregating together), then they could unearth criminal behavior. For instance, police cars began spending inordinate amounts of time in Black neighborhoods, looking for any behavior that could possibly mask the selling of drugs.

Prosecutors frequently offer major drug kingpins a deal for a lesser charge (thus, drawing a lesser sentence) because they often have crucial information for the police regarding drug cartels, drug deals, and so on. Because minor dealers—for instance, someone who sells marijuana inexpensively to his fraternity brothers in college on an intermittent basis—have nothing of interest to tell the authorities, they may receive stiffer sentences than those who become extremely wealthy selling drugs to anyone wishing to purchase them. Thus, the manner in which our system is structured usually means that the key drug dealers, those grossing millions of dollars per year in profits, often draw lesser prison sentences.

Many researchers point to economic factors as an explanation for why individuals choose to sell illegal substances, even when they realize that being caught could mean jail time. Individuals (especially adolescents) living in abject poverty often have little or no access to jobs, adequate housing, or education, and they may have poor or broken social networks. Such individuals may habitually turn to crime as they may feel it is impossible to ever achieve the "American dream." Moreover, the various problems often seem to reinforce each other; someone who has little opportunity to go to college may be unable to find a decent, well-paying job and as a result may live in substandard housing. Quite often, many feel that the only way out of this vicious cycle is crime, and thus many turn to illegally selling drugs.

On a global scale, the drug trade generates enormous sums of money. During 2000, the U.S. Drug Enforcement Administration estimated that the monetary value concerning worldwide trafficking in illicit drugs equaled approximately $400 billion (U.S. dollars). If the amount of money circulated with legal drugs is added, then the global trade value for drugs would surpass the total amount expended for food. The 2005 United Nations World Drug Report reported that the overall value of the worldwide illegal drug market for 2003 (in U.S. dollars) was approximately $13 billion at the manufacturing level, $94 billion at the level where the cartels sell the drugs to their respective buyers, and over $322 billion at the retail level.

Cary Stacy Smith and Li-Ching Hung

See also Discrimination–Disparity Continuum; Drug Sentencing; War on Drugs

Further Readings

Adler, P., & Adler, P. (1983). Shifts and oscillations in deviant careers: The case of upper level drug dealers and smugglers. *Social Problems, 31*(2), 195–207.

Gray, M. (2000). *Drug crazy: How we got into this mess and how we can get out*. London: Routledge.

Jacobs, B. (1999). *Dealing crack: The social world of streetcorner selling*. Boston: Northeastern University Press.

United Nations Office on Drugs and Crime. (2005). *World drug report*. Retrieved from http://www.unodc.org/pdf/WDR_2005/volume_1_web.pdf

DRUG SENTENCING

Since the advent of the War on Drugs in the 1980s, sentencing for drug offenses has been the predominant force driving expansion of criminal punishment in the United States. The increased use of criminal sanctions has disproportionately affected people of color. This entry addresses the impact of state-level (in contrast to federal) sentencing for drug offenses by race/ethnicity.

Theoretical and Policy Background

The goals of sentencing for drug offenses are commonly based in ideas of deterrence and incapacitation. In theory, the threat of criminal punishment deters people from possessing illegal drugs as well as dealing them. For those who are not deterred, criminal punishment serves to restrain (incapacitate) them in a physical way, for example, by keeping them in prison so they lack access to drug markets in the free world. Likewise, when people see the pain meted out to drug users and dealers through criminal sentencing, fear of receiving similar pain should deter the public from engaging in drug offenses.

These goals are particularly difficult to achieve in the case of drugs, however, because of market factors. As long as consumer demand for illegal drugs remains high, suppliers become available to fill vacancies left when existing suppliers (dealers) are incapacitated via imprisonment. Sentences that are based on type and quantity of drug do very little to disrupt demand or the lure of quick wealth among potential dealers, particularly in impoverished communities.

Another potential goal of sentencing is rehabilitation, but until recently that goal has been given relatively little attention with regard to drug crimes. Rehabilitation includes approaches such as treatment programs for substance abusers. The "war" metaphor that has been so potent in drug policy tends to embrace rehabilitative approaches quite sparingly.

There are more policy alternatives for structuring sentencing for drug offenses than for violent or property offenses. Policy prescriptions directed at sentencing can have major economic ramifications, as well as impact on particular communities. For example, among state prisoners, in 1980 there were approximately 19,000 inmates (6% of total inmates) incarcerated for drug offenses (Mauer, 1999). By 2003, largely as a consequence of the War on Drugs, this figure rose to approximately 251,000 (20% of all inmates; Mauer & King, 2007). Recently, about 25% of Black inmates and Hispanic inmates are incarcerated for a drug offense, compared to 13% of White inmates (*Sourcebook of Criminal Justice Statistics Online*, 2002).

Finally, in contrast to the utilitarian emphases in sentencing, retributive values also come into play. Retribution focuses on a kind of quid pro quo: The offender must be punished because of the evil he or she has inflicted on society. Because interpretations of drug use as evil have varied historically, retribution is somewhat more difficult to apply when sentencing drug offenders than when sentencing violent or property offenders. One central tenet of retribution is proportionality of punishment: The punishment must "fit" the degree of evil of the crime, and similar offenders must be punished similarly. Proportionality has been one of the most debated issues in drug sentencing.

State-Level Sentencing

Sentencing processes vary from state to state, and for state-level drug offenses there is considerable variation in the quantity of criminal punishment imposed from one state to another.

Drug sentencing is most commonly the result of a guilty plea rather than a trial. About 95% of convicted felons in state courts plead guilty, in lieu of a trial, and approximately one third of felony convictions in state courts are for drug offenses.

Many states use sentencing guidelines, which seek uniformity in sentencing by directing judges to impose sentences within a prescribed range that is based on criminal history and seriousness of the current offense. Some states mandate by statute that the judge sentence within the guideline range; others make the range an advisory for the judge. Additionally, all states have laws prescribing that judges must impose mandatory minimum sentences for certain crimes, and these most commonly apply to drug crimes.

Sentencing under "mandatory minimum" statutes requires that the judge disregard details about the offense and the defendant, and it usually precludes early release in the form of parole. Mandatory minimums for drug offenses tend to be based on the type and amount of the drug rather than on any particular defendant's level of involvement in illegal drug activity. Thus, so-called delivery "mules" who carry drugs for dealers—and who are disproportionately female—tend to be punished at least as severely as higher-level dealers. Over a third of women incarcerated in state prisons are drug offenders. The impact is particularly significant for women of color, who constitute at least two thirds of all female inmates in state prisons.

New York's "Rockefeller drug laws" (those passed when Nelson Rockefeller was governor) are an example of mandatory sentencing. In contrast to their avowed purpose of shutting down high-level drug dealers, most persons sentenced under these laws have been convicted of possession or low-level sales. Almost 40% of the state's prisoners are drug felons, most of whom have no prior convictions for any type of violent felony. Over 90% of the state's drug felons are African American or Latino (Human Rights Watch, 2002).

Drug Offenders Sentenced to Prison

Nationally, at least 20% of inmates in state prisons are incarcerated specifically for a drug offense. Over three fourths of these inmates are personsof color (e.g., approximately 56% are African American and 23% Hispanic; King & Mauer, 2002). This contrasts with rates of drug use in the general population, where it is estimated that 13% of monthly drug users are African American and 11% Hispanic. Though nearly three quarters of monthly drug users are White, only about 20% of drug offenders in state prisons are White (The Sentencing Project, 2001).

Drug offenders in state prison commonly have criminal histories; over three quarters have a prior sentence of incarceration or probation, and half are on probation, parole, or escape status at the time of their arrest. More broadly, well over half of all state prison inmates report having used drugs in the month prior to their arrest. Likewise, over half of all state prisoners experienced symptoms consistent with the psychological criteria for drug abuse or dependence in the 12 months prior to admission to prison. White inmates (59%) are somewhat more likely to meet these criteria than Hispanic (51%) or Black (50%) inmates. Nearly 40% of recent drug users in state prison report participating in drug-abuse programs, though the great bulk of the programs are self-help group/peer counseling or educational programs. Only about 10% report participating in actual drug treatment (e.g., professional counseling, residential unit, maintenance drug) in prison (Bureau of Justice Statistics, 1999).

Those sentenced to state prison for drug offenses tend not to have a history of violence or high-level drug activity. Over 40% are convicted of possession; 27% of these are for simple possession, and 16% are for possession with intent to deliver (King & Mauer, 2002). At the time of their crimes, violent offenders in state prisons are more apt to have been under the influence of alcohol than of other psychoactive substances.

Nonprison Sentences

Probation is another common sentence for persons convicted of drug crimes. Of the more than 4 million persons on state probation, the most common underlying crime (over 25% of probationers) is a drug offense. Nearly half of all state probationers are persons of color (Bureau of Justice Statistics, 2006). All states also use so-called intermediate sanctions that are intended to be harsher than regular probation but not as harsh as prison. These include residential programs and intensively supervised probation, and they commonly involve provision for relatively frequent drug testing.

It is generally recognized that drug treatment is more cost-effective in reducing crime and drug abuse than prison is. One promising alternative related to drug sentencing is drug treatment court, which combines a more holistic approach to drug treatment with the threat of criminal sanctions for noncompliance. Treatment staff work closely with the court, drug testing is frequent, and the threat of incarceration remains for those who fail to comply with court and treatment directives. For persons charged with drug possession, drug treatment courts have shown appreciable reductions in rearrest rates, as well as reduced drug use among participants, when compared with other sentencing options.

Racial/Ethnic Disparity

The fact that persons of color are punished more frequently for drug crimes is evident. In general, for drug offenses, both Hispanic and Black defendants have a higher likelihood of receiving a sentence of incarceration than White defendants, though there are not appreciable differences in lengths of prison sentences among racial/ethnic groups.

For example, it has been found that state mandatory sentences for drug crimes have tended significantly to result in increased sentences for Blacks and Mexican Americans for possession of narcotics, though for very small quantities of narcotics, Blacks were less likely to be incarcerated than Whites. Likewise, with sentencing guidelines, Whites (and females) are more apt to receive downward departures (from sentencing guidelines) than racial/ethnic minorities, with Hispanics least likely to receive such relatively favorable sentences.

Additionally, research in the sentencing of Black drug offenders found that Black women's custodial parenting responsibilities, or their caring for an adult family member, significantly reduced their likelihood of incarceration, but such mitigation was not afforded similarly situated Black men.

Criminologists have suggested a variety of explanations for racial/ethnic disparity in drug sentencing. One of the most common involves the interpretation of offense and offender by sentencing decision-makers. Here, stereotypes and social status can play a significant role. For example, because Hispanics generally have fewer resources and may be more culturally dissimilar from those sentencing them, they may be seen as more threatening and hence receive more severe punishment. Likewise, Blacks who are dealers and/or who have a prior criminal record may be stereotyped as more dangerous by sentencing decision makers.

Disparate sentencing by race/ethnicity also reflects earlier criminal processes that can be especially affected by factors like poverty and unemployment. For example, the unemployed and those who have previously come to the attention of the police are likely to be subject to higher bail and so are more likely to spend time in jail while awaiting further criminal processing. Likewise, poverty has a direct effect on the ability to retain a private lawyer for one's defense.

Socioeconomic disadvantage, which in the United States is correlated with race and ethnicity, also contributes indirectly to sentencing by influencing which social groups tend to enter the criminal process. Persons faced with relatively high levels of economic deprivation may see drug use or drug dealing as an appealing escape, and their disillusionment and alienation with regard to conventional society may enhance the lure of illegal gain that the drug world represents.

Finally, it is important to recognize that sentencing for drug offenses can implicate a variety of indirect but not insignificant side effects. For example, a drug conviction may collaterally involve loss of college financial aid, loss of public welfare benefits, a state of temporary disenfranchisement from voting, and inability to obtain professional licensure. Thus, even aside from time spent in institutional or community corrections, drug sentencing can involve major opportunity costs in terms of work, school, and parenting. If social groups are disproportionately subject to drug sentencing, the deleterious impact on entire communities can be substantial.

Frank Butler

See also Drug Courts; Drug Sentencing, Federal; Mandatory Minimums; Sentencing; Sentencing Disparities, African Americans; Sentencing Disparities, Latina/o/s; Sentencing Disparities, Native Americans; War on Drugs

Further Readings

Bureau of Justice Statistics. (1999). *Substance abuse and treatment, state and federal prisoners, 1997* (Report No. NCJ 172871). Washington, DC: U.S. Department of Justice.

Bureau of Justice Statistics. (2006). *Probation and parole in the United States, 2005* (Report No. NCJ 215091). Washington, DC: U.S. Department of Justice.

Demuth, S., & Steffensmeier, D. (2004). Ethnicity effects on sentence outcomes in large urban courts: Comparisons among White, Black, and Hispanic defendants. *Social Science Quarterly, 85,* 994–1011.

Flavin, J. (2001). Of punishment and parenthood: Family-based social control and the sentencing of Black drug offenders. *Gender & Society, 15,* 611–633.

Gainey, R. R., Steen, S., & Engen, R. L. (2005). Exercising options: An assessment of the use of alternative sanctions for drug offenders. *Justice Quarterly, 22,* 488–520.

Human Rights Watch. (2002). *Collateral casualties: Children of incarcerated drug offenders in New York.* New York: Author.

King, R. S., & Mauer, M. (2002). *Distorted priorities: Drug offenders in state prisons.* Washington, DC: The Sentencing Project.

Mauer, M. (1999). *The crisis of the young African American male and the criminal justice system* (Prepared for the U.S. Commission on Civil Rights). Washington, DC: The Sentencing Project.

Mauer, M. (2006). *Race to incarcerate* (Rev. ed.). New York: The New Press.

Mauer, M., & King, R. S. (2007). *A 25-year quagmire: The War on Drugs and its impact on American society.* Washington, DC: The Sentencing Project.

The Sentencing Project. (2001). *Drug policy and the criminal justice system*. Washington, DC: Author.

Sourcebook of criminal justice statistics (31st ed.). (n.d.). Retrieved September 21, 2007, from http://www .albany.edu/sourcebook

Steen, S., Engen, R. L., & Gainey, R. (2005). Images of danger and culpability: Racial stereotyping, case processing, and criminal sentencing. *Criminology, 43*, 435–520.

Tonry, M. (1995). *Malign neglect: Race, crime, and punishment in America*. New York: Oxford University Press.

DRUG SENTENCING, FEDERAL

Sentencing practices for federal offenders have been altered significantly over the past several decades. Those charged with drug-related offenses at the federal level have experienced the harshest treatment within the criminal justice system. Though the Sentencing Reform Act of 1984 was designed to support more equitable sentencing practices, sentencing disparities continue, sending minorities to prison with much longer sentences than those of their White counterparts. While drug use remains widespread in the United States, criminal justice professionals and policymakers have an opportunity to develop strategies to tackle this problem. This entry reviews federal laws relating to drug use and presents evidence of disparities in the sentencing of minorities convicted of drug offenses. Such evidence highlights the importance of developing strategies and interventions that address the problem of drug use without inequitably penalizing vulnerable populations.

Federal drug sentencing refers to penalties given to individuals convicted of drug-related offenses at the federal level. Drug offenses are treated harshly at the federal level. Ever since the Sentencing Reform Act of 1984 was implemented, the number of individuals incarcerated for drug-related offenses at the federal level has increased substantially. This has had a negative impact particularly on minorities.

The number of incarcerated individuals has increased by 500% since the 1970s. Between 1980 and 1996 alone, state and federal incarceration rates increased by over 200%. Between 1984 and 1999, the number of offenders convicted for a federal drug-related offense almost tripled from 11,854 to 29,306. Many attribute substantial increases in the number of incarcerated individuals to the War on Drugs and its implementation. Approximately 60% of those incarcerated in federal prisons are drug offenders.

The War on Drugs

The War on Drugs has stubbornly persisted in guiding sentencing mandates since the 1980s, calling for stiffer penalties for drug offenders, including those found guilty of possession, and trafficking. Since the initiation of the War on Drugs, tens of thousands of individuals have been incarcerated on drug-related charges, most of whom are African American males.

Even though African Americans reportedly are less likely than Whites to use drugs, they are more likely to be arrested on drug-related charges. African Americans are more than twenty times more likely to be incarcerated for a drug-related offense. More specifically, Blacks, males, and less-educated offenders from socially disadvantaged backgrounds are more likely to receive substantially longer sentences.

In 2004, measures of drug abuse and dependence were included for the first time on the annual survey conducted by the Bureau of Justice Statistics, the research arm of the National Institute of Justice. The findings indicated that over three fourths of the recent arrestees were under the influence of illicit drugs during the commission of their crime(s). Minorities often get longer sentences than White offenders for committing similar offenses. Much of this disparity is as a result of the implementation of increasingly punitive federal drug laws aimed at controlling the use of illegal substances.

Federal Drug Laws

Over the past several decades, penalties for drug use and trafficking have increased substantially. Largely due to legislative changes during the 1980s and 1990s, the vast majority of federal drug offenders were subjected to statutory minimum prison terms. A pivotal piece of legislation, the Sentencing Reform Act of 1984, was designed to alleviate the disparities that were evident in traditional sentencing practices. This act mandated mandatory sentencing minimums for federal offenses and also shifted sentencing discretion from judges to prosecuting attorneys, resulting in a nationwide shift. This act was applied toward any federal offense committed on or after November 1, 1987.

Though the Sentencing Reform Act of 1984 was designed to eliminate racial disparities in standard sentencing practices, researchers have reported that this act actually increased disparities between Blacks and Whites. The Sentencing Reform Act also limited the number of incentives that federal offenders received for good behavior while incarcerated; this required the development of guidelines to restructure sentencing procedures. Accordingly, federal offenders are required to complete at least 87% of their sentence before being released.

The implementation of the Sentencing Reform Act of 1984 has been particularly harsh to federal drug offenders. From 1986 to 1999, both the number of individuals incarcerated for drug-related offenses and the length of their sentences increased substantially; drug offenders involved in crimes related to crack cocaine received the longest sentences. Supporters of this act initially expected it to be instrumental in eliminating sentencing disparities. Supporters of this act also insisted that it would create a more just and equitable environment, mostly due to shifting the discretion that judges normally possessed to prosecuting attorneys. However, sentencing disparities have stubbornly persisted.

Sentencing Disparities

Since the implementation of more punitive sentencing practices and penalties for drug-related offenses, the number of minorities incarcerated has increased substantially. Disparities in sentencing for federal offenses have continued beyond legislative action designed to eliminate them. African American and Hispanic defendants charged with drug-related offenses experience discrimination at various phases in the criminal justice system, including during sentencing.

Researchers examining sentencing disparities have used a variety of theoretical models and explanations to probe this issue. Disparities are especially evident in cases involving drug offenders, and nowhere is the disparity seen more prominently than sentencing patterns for individuals caught with crack cocaine versus those possessing powder cocaine. Individuals convicted of possessing crack cocaine are at a distinct disadvantage, as the penalties for individuals convicted of possession of crack cocaine versus powder cocaine are much stiffer.

Crack Cocaine Sentencing Disparities

Crack cocaine is especially popular in urban areas and has resulted in law enforcement agencies resorting to aggressive strategies and techniques to capture crack cocaine users and sellers. Crack cocaine is especially popular in inner-city areas where many minorities, particularly African Americans, reside. Since African Americans tend to be charged with using or distributing crack cocaine, they are particularly vulnerable and it is quite evident in the statistics on the prison population. The prison population has continued to increase; federal prisons are currently operating 34% over capacity. African Americans are incarcerated disproportionate to their representation in the general U.S. population. They currently comprise almost half of the prison population.

Tawandra L. Rowell

See also Sentencing; Sentencing Project, The; War on Drugs

Further Readings

Albonetti, C. A. (1997). Sentencing under the federal sentencing guidelines: Effects of defendant characteristics, guilty pleas, and departures on sentence outcomes for drug offenses, 1991–1992. *Law & Society Review, 31,* 789–822.

Bertram, E., Blachman, M., Sharpe, K., & Andreas, P. (1996). *Drug war politics: The price of denial.* Berkeley: University of California Press.

Blumstein, A., & Beck, A. (1999). Factors contributing to the growth in U.S. prison populations. In M. Tonry & J. Petersilia (Eds.), *Prisons* (pp. 17–61). Chicago: University of Chicago Press.

Brent, S. L., & Damphousse, K. R. (1996). Punishing political offenders: The effect of political motive on federal sentencing decisions. *Criminology, 34,* 289–321.

Free, M. D. (1997). The impact of federal sentencing reforms on African Americans. *Journal of Black Studies, 28,* 268–286.

Iguchi, M. Y., London, J. A., Forge, N. G., Hickman, L., Fain, T., & Riehman, K. (2002). Elements of well-being affected by criminalizing the drug user. *Public Health Report, 117*(Suppl. 1), S146–S150.

Mauer, M. (2006). *Race to incarcerate.* New York: The New Press.

Mumola, C. J., & Karberg, J. C. (2006). *Drug use and dependence, state and federal prisoners, 2004.* Washington, DC: U.S. Department of Justice.

Mustard, D. B. (2001). Racial, ethnic, and gender disparities in sentencing: Evidence from the U.S. federal courts. *Journal of Law and Economics, 44,* 285–314.

Scalia, J. (2001). *Federal drug offenders, 1999 with trends 1984–99* (Report No. NCJ 187285). Washington, DC: U.S. Department of Justice.

Spohn, C., & Holleran, D. (2000). The imprisonment penalty paid by young, unemployed Black and Hispanic male offenders. *Criminology, 38,* 281–526.

Ulmer, J. T., & Kramer, J. H. (1996). Court communities under sentencing guidelines: Dilemmas of formal rationality and sentencing disparity. *Criminology, 34,* 383–408.

Wooldredge, J., Griffin, T., & Rauschenberg, F. (2005). (Un)anticipated effects of sentencing reform on the disparate treatment of defendants. *Law & Society Review, 39,* 835–874.

DRUG TRAFFICKING

Drug trafficking involves the commercial trading, smuggling, or distributing of illegal drugs and/or the paraphernalia used to produce or consume these illegal substances. Drug trafficking and corresponding drug use are, and have been, two persistent concerns to law enforcement agencies. Drug trafficking, drug users, and drug offenders involve many different racial groups and vary from street-level dealings to large-scale drug trafficking organizations. This entry describes the history of drug trafficking and contemporary drug transporting and distribution threats to the United States.

America's first drug epidemic can be traced to the 1850s when the Chinese, bringing with them opium, began migrating to the United States to work in the gold mines and on the railroads. Opium began spreading steadily east across the nation, and soon Americans of all ages were addicted to opium as well as other opiates, such as morphine, and newfound drugs, like cocaine and heroin, often used for pain management. Cities and states began passing antidrug laws in an effort to combat the epidemic. Simultaneously, the federal government initiated a movement to limit opium and coca plant production.

By the end of World War II, drugs were seen as only a minor social problem. At this time, the United States could find no legitimate linkage between drugs and racial/ethnic minorities. The decade of the 1960s brought with it drugs like marijuana, amphetamines, psychedelics, and a generation who had long forgotten the first drug epidemic. This generation of recreational drug users believed drugs were part of the "hip" social culture of the time. During the 1960s, the drug culture exploded and opened the United States and the world to major drug trafficking. These new concerns involving illegal drugs and their trafficking caused the U.S. government to create the Drug Enforcement Administration in 1973, in an attempt to quell the growing problem.

Drug use was not suppressed as hoped, and use has continued since its peak in 1979. This peak came about due to the resurgence of powder cocaine use during the 1970s and 1980s and the Colombian drug mafia's introduction of crack cocaine in the 1980s. The combination of crack and powder cocaine cast America into its most devastating drug crisis yet. The 1990s saw the War on Drugs, in which there was a push by society to target crack and powder cocaine use and trafficking. New laws, strategies, and tactics were put in place in a strong attempt to crush the drug dilemma of the 1970s and 1980s.

Today, the United States' largest drug threats arise from drug trafficking organizations (DTOs), which are primarily Mexican and Colombian associations and have a clear hierarchy of command. These operations manufacture, smuggle, and distribute multiple illegal substances. This then creates a huge challenge to law enforcement across the country. In the 2008 National Drug Threat

Assessment, Mexican DTOs were considered the most insidious organized drug groups threatening the United States today. This is primarily because these DTOs tend to control every aspect of the drug trafficking industry. For example, in Florida, the Mexican DTOs have replaced street-level distribution by African American gangs and have taken over the entire drug market.

Asian DTOs are seen as an emerging concern to law enforcement. They are based in Canada and are primarily Vietnamese in origin. They traffic highly potent marijuana and methylenedioxymethamphetamine (MDMA, also called ecstasy). Both marijuana and ecstasy are produced in Canada and smuggled into the United States through vehicles crossing the Canada–U.S. border. Recently, Asian DTOs have moved their production sites inside the United States to avoid losing drug shipments at border crossings.

Other than by the Mexican DTOs, most of the transporting and distributing of illegal drugs is done by Colombian, Dominican, Cuban, and Jamaican groups. Colombian DTOs are known for their transportation and distribution of South American heroin and cocaine in the Northeast and Florida. Due to several large confiscations and arrests made against Colombian DTOs, they are now channeling much of their transporting and distributing to the Mexican DTOs in order to foil law enforcement interdiction. The Dominican DTOs operate in the same regions as the Colombians and tend to work alongside the Colombians in distribution of South American heroin and cocaine. Cuban DTOs work primarily in Florida and the southeastern states, distributing highly potent marijuana. Finally, Jamaican DTOs focus on the distribution of marijuana to the New York–New Jersey area and to Florida and the Caribbean Islands.

Colombian DTOs retain the control not only of the U.S. cocaine supply but also that of the world. Cocaine is trafficked mainly by the Colombian organizations with help from Mexican DTOs. Alternatively, crack cocaine is distributed by African American gangs and smaller criminal organizations such as Dominicans, Puerto Ricans, or Jamaicans. Heroin comes mainly from South America (Colombia), Southeast Asia (Burma), Mexico, and Southwest Asia/Middle East (mainly Afghanistan) and is trafficked by a specific group in each one of those regions/countries. Methamphetamine is also chiefly trafficked by Mexican DTOs. Marijuana is trafficked by the Asian DTOs through the U.S.–Canada border and by the Mexican DTOs through the U.S.–Mexican border. Lastly, ecstasy originally had a low demand but has recently experienced a staggering increase in demand and users. Ecstasy is a hallucinogenic drug that is manufactured in Europe and is trafficked by both international and U.S. trafficking groups for consumption primarily by middle-class adolescents.

Although illegal drugs are being trafficked by certain racial and ethnic groups, they are consumed by all demographics. The most recent data on drug use by race/ethnicity are from 2006, when there was a total U.S. population of 299,398,485 people of which almost 74% were White, 12.4% were Black, almost 15% were Hispanic/Latina/o, 0.8% were American Indian/Alaska Native, almost 4.5% were Asian, 0.1% were Native Hawaiian/other Pacific Islander, a little over 6% were some other race, and 2% reported being two or more races. Of the 299 million people, it was recorded that 20.4 million people, 12 and older, admitted to being current illegal drug users. The group using the most illegal drugs overall in 2006 (relative to their population size) was American Indians/Alaska Natives, followed by Blacks/African Americans, and people listing that they were two or more races; coming in fourth were Whites, followed by Hawaiians/other Pacific Islanders, Hispanics/Latinos, and finally Asians.

The War on Drugs can no longer be viewed as a demographically specific fight because drugs affect all races from all levels of society. Drug use and trafficking have a lengthy history in the United States, and unfortunately an end to that history is not in the foreseeable future. Although today's drug problem is not viewed as prolific an issue as it was in the 1970s and 1980s, there is still a strong societal demand to see drug trafficking and drug use quelled.

Marigny Hluza

See also Drug Cartels; Drug Dealers; War on Drugs

Further Readings

Drug Enforcement Administration Museum and Visitors Center. (n.d.). *Illegal drugs in America: A modern history*. Retrieved February 28, 2008, from http://www.deamuseum.org/museum_ida.html

Drug Policy Alliance Network. (2008). *Drug policy around the world: Drug trafficking & interdiction*. Retrieved from http://www.drugpolicy.org/global/drugtraffick

National Institute on Drug Abuse. (2003, September). *Drug use among racial/ethnic minorities: Revised* (NIH Publication No. 03-3888). Retrieved from http://www.drugabuse.gov/pdf/minorities03.pdf

Office of National Drug Control Policy. (n.d.). *Minorities and drugs* [Fact sheet]. Retrieved March 7, 2008, from http://www.whitehousedrugpolicy.gov/drugfact/minorities/index.html

Substance Abuse of Mental Health Services Administration, Office of Applied Studies. (2007). *Results from the 2006 National Survey on Drug Use and Health: National findings* (NSDUH Series H-32, DHHS Publication No. SMA 07-4293). Retrieved from http://www.oas.samhsa.gov/nsduh/2k6nsduh/2k6Results.cfm#2.7

U.S. Drug Enforcement Administration. (n.d.). *Drug trafficking in the United States* [Fact sheet]. Retrieved February 18, 2008, from http://www.usdoj.gov/dea/pubs/state_factsheets.html

U.S. Drug Enforcement Administration. (2002). *Get it straight! Words you'll run across*. Retrieved from http://www.usdoj.gov/dea/pubs/straight/words.htm

U.S. Drug Enforcement Administration, National Drug Intelligence Center. (2007, October). *National drug threat assessment 2008: Drug trafficking organizations*. Retrieved from http://www.dea.gov/concern/18862/dtos.htm#Top

DRUG TREATMENT

The primary goal of drug treatment is commonly called "recovery," which is usually defined as the abstinence from mind-altering chemicals; however, recovery also involves changes in drug users' physical, psychological, social, familial, and spiritual areas of functioning. For this metamorphosis to take place, an efficacious treatment plan needs to be designed, but before it is made, a thorough assessment needs to be carefully conducted by well-trained mental health professionals. Such an assessment is aimed at making an accurate diagnosis, as well as obtaining the client's history of drug use. The criteria should include how drug use affects the clients' behavioral characteristics (job or school performance, relationship with others, legal problems, medical problems, etc.).

Treatment Settings

Drug treatment can take place in a variety of locales. These treatment settings differ with respect to the treatment services provided, treatment requirement, treatment length, and the frequency of meetings. This section provides basic information about some of the most common treatment settings.

Free-Standing Rehabilitation and Residential Programs

Free-standing, non-hospital-based rehabilitation and residential programs include three treatment phases: detoxification, rehabilitation, and aftercare. The detoxification phase is a process of relieving the symptoms of intoxication and takes place either in a hospital or in nonhospital settings. Although some patients may be detoxified prior to being admitted, many programs have their own detoxification facilities. Once detoxification is completed, the patient is formally enrolled into treatment.

During the rehabilitation phase, the client receives an intervention, where facets include peer interaction as well as a supportive atmosphere. During this time period, patients receive different types of therapeutic intervention (individual, group, or family), and active participation is required by the facility. The treatment length for inpatients lasts approximately 21 to 28 days, but if the patient is not making progress, a more restricted environment may be implemented.

Aftercare is the third phase, which is designed as a transition period for clients before they reenter daily life. The environment is not as restrictive as the other two phases, but patients are still required to attend 12-step meetings.

Intensive Outpatient Programs

This type of program provides daily treatment-related activities to once-weekly meetings. Clients are expected to attend three evenings of 3-hour group therapy with 1 hour of family therapy. In addition, they are expected to attend Alcoholics Anonymous or Narcotics Anonymous meetings.

Partial Hospitalization

In partial hospitalization programs, also called day treatment, clients are allowed to live at home but are still required to attend at least one treatment activity during the day. The environment is less restrictive than some treatment settings and is between hospital impatient and intensive outpatient.

Temporary Recovery or Halfway Homes

This setting is a community-based home near a rehabilitation facility. These homes provide minimally structured transitional living in a recovering environment. Patients are required to stay abstinent, find employment, and attend 12-step recovery meetings.

Dual-Diagnosis Hospital Inpatient Program

The dual-diagnosis hospital inpatient program has the following characteristics: Services are provided in psychiatric hospitals and are designed to help clients with more-serious drug use or dependency. These services include onsite, 24-hour medical and psychiatric care with limited family and friend visitation, intensive assessment services, and daily intensive group contact with other clients. This environment is very restrictive.

Medical Detoxification and Stabilization

This type of treatment setting is designed for individuals with a severe type of addiction. Usually, most employees in this setting have training in pharmacological detoxification and thus can work with patients' concomitant medical conditions. Patients are treated to lessen the physical and psychological symptoms caused by heavy drug use.

The treatment length usually lasts 2 weeks, and the first step is detoxification.

Treatment Plans

Once a treatment setting is selected, a detailed treatment plan needs to be completed by the mental health service providers. The treatment plan is designed to help mental health service providers clarify their objectives while working with clients who have a history of drug use. A basic treatment plan should have the following elements:

1. Type of plan: must be specific and behaviorally oriented

2. Problem statement: a statement of the client's problem(s)

3. Evidence to prove the statement of problems

4. Treatment goals: long-term and short-term goals

5. Objective: needs to be realistic and measurable

6. Methods: interventions designed to address specific behaviors

7. Frequency of services provided: types of therapy and when the intervention would be implemented during the treatment

8. Signature from clients, indicating their consent to, and understanding of, the entire treatment plan

Although there are differences, some treatments offer very similar services, and any treatment might be the best choice for a particular client under certain circumstances. Thus, it is essential for the client to consider the following factors when selecting the type of treatment: ability to pay, method of payment, previous treatment experiences, and current emotional and behavioral state.

Treatment Therapy

Individual Therapy

During individual therapy sessions, counselors provide interventions designed and chosen to help their clients reach treatment goals. Individual therapists are more likely to choose the following treatment approaches: cognitive-behavioral therapy, solution-focused brief therapy, reality therapy, Gestalt therapy, and aversion therapy.

Group Therapy

This is the most frequently used drug treatment. It costs less than individual therapy and has reliable treatment outcomes. A typical group consists of six to eight members and is either closed or open to new members. Family therapy is a highly recommended option and involves other family members.

Treatment Concerns

Regardless of how effective the type of treatment setting is, some researchers have argued that the most common drug treatment outcome is relapse. As a result, relapse prevention has become a critical issue and has caught the attention of many mental health care professionals. Relapse is determined by an individual's personality and the environment he or she is in. Thus, it is important for professionals to prepare relapse intervention strategies as part of the treatment plan.

Cary Stacy Smith and Li-Ching Hung

See also Drug Courts; Drug Use; Drug Use by Juveniles

Further Readings

Fletcher, B. W., Horton, A., & Inciardi, J. A. (1994). *Drug abuse treatment: The implementation of innovative approaches.* Westport, CT: Greenwood Press.

Laban, R. L. (1997). *Chemical dependency treatment planning handbook.* Springfield, IL: Charles C Thomas.

Stevens, P., & Smith, R. L. (2005). *Substance abuse counseling: Theory and practice* (3rd ed.). Upper Saddle River, NJ: Pearson/Merrill Prentice Hall.

DRUG USE

Drug use refers to individual behaviors that involve the consumption of alcohol and use of other illicit drugs including nonprescription drugs. Some individuals use drugs for recreational purposes, others have a more serious problem of drug abuse, while the extreme form of drug use is addiction. Drug use can have serious consequences not only for individuals but for families, schools, communities, social institutions, the criminal and juvenile justice systems, and the private sector. This entry examines the extent of drug use, drug of choice, drugs and race, and drug use and crime.

During the first decade of the 21st century, drug use continues to be a social problem. According to the National Survey on Drug Use and Health (NSDUH), during 2007, approximately 19.9 million Americans age 12 and older, used illegal drugs. The rate of illicit drug use has remained fairly stable since 2002, ranging from 8.3% to 8.1% in 2005, and 8% in 2007. Binge drinking, driving under the influence, marijuana use, prescription drug use, and cocaine use continue to present challenges for all Americans, especially youth and young adults. For example, almost 10 million persons age 12 or older reported they drove under the influence of illicit drugs in 2007, 2.1 million used cocaine, and 6.9 million reported using prescription-type drugs for nonmedical purposes during the past month when surveyed. According to the NSDUH, 3.9 million people age 12 or older received treatment for alcohol or illicit drug use in 2007.

Each drug user is unique. Recreational drug users are not easily characterized. They are less likely to use alcohol and/or drugs on a regular basis and, therefore, may not view themselves as either drug abusers or drug dependent. They are less likely to view their drug use as interfering with their interpersonal relationships, employment, or other endeavors. Most drug abusers and those experiencing addictions are dependent on drugs and are thought to share some common characteristics, including personality disorders, an unhealthy physical appearance, as well as engaging in risky behaviors and social activities. Some lack adequate hygiene, have an imbalance in sleeping habits, experience loss of appetite, have weight problems (too thin or too heavy), and experience an overabundance of hyperactivity or lethargy. From a personality and social activity perspective, the following behaviors tend to occur: (a) verbally and physically abusive to others, (b) frequent change in mood, (c) constant lying and stealing, (d) depression, (e) loss of interest in social activities, and (f) poor concentration or memory.

Drug Choice Information

Drug choices have varied over time. During the past several decades, marijuana has been the most commonly used illegal drug. According to the most recent data, 14.4 million Americans reported using marijuana in the past month.

Cocaine is second only to marijuana as the drug of choice for many. For example, an estimated 23 million (10.6%) Americans age 12 or older have used cocaine. In 2007, an estimated 1 million (0.4%) Americans had tried hallucinogens, including ecstasy.

According to the National Institute on Drug Abuse (NIDA), prescription medications such as pain relievers (hydrocodone, oxycodone, and morphine), depressants (tranquilizers and sedatives), and stimulants (amphetamines, methamphetamines, and Ritalin) are beneficial when used responsibly. When these drugs are not taken as directed or given to others to use, serious problems, including addiction, can occur. Even though the number of persons abusing prescribed medications is unknown, the rates of the nonmedical use of prescription pain relievers have not changed very much between 2002 and 2007. In the 2007 NSDUH survey, 2.1% (5.2 million) of respondents reported using prescription pain relievers nonmedically during the past month. Over-the-counter medications, such as cough and cold medicines containing dextromethorphan, are also abused.

Drugs and Race

According to the NSDUH, illicit drug use varied by race and ethnicity in 2007 and the specific drug in question. Despite media portrayal of African Americans and drugs, they were not the group most likely to report illegal drug use. The largest ethnic group was that of American Indians or Alaska Natives (12.9%), followed by those reporting to belong to two or more races (11.8%), Blacks or African Americans (9.5%), and Whites (6.6%). The smallest categories were Hispanic and Latinos (6.6%) and Asians (4.2%). Although these numbers might be surprising, the NSDUH reports no significant changes in the rates of use between 2006 and 2007. Use of alcohol was highest among Whites (56.1%) and binge alcohol use was more likely to be reported by American Indians or Alaska Natives (28.2%).

Drug Use and Crime

During the late 20th century, drug-related crimes became a serious problem in the United States, as did crimes such as theft and assault. For example, between 1980 and 1995, more than 50% of all federal prisoners were convicted of drug offenses. Evidence from these prisoners indicated they were more likely to commit crimes after using alcohol, cocaine, heroin, or methamphetamine. In addition, heavy drug users were more likely to commit crimes than were irregular drug users. According to data obtained from the 2004 Bureau of Justice Statistics report on drug use and dependence among state and federal prisoners, 50% of federal prisoners and 56% of state prisoners committed their offenses under the influence of drugs. Forty percent of state and 49% of federal inmates were either drug abusers or drug dependent, and 26% of federal inmates reported using drugs at the time of their offense. Moreover, the majority stated that the most common drug of choice was either marijuana or cocaine (both powder and crack). The report also stated that one in four violent offenders used drugs when they committed their offenses. Among minority groups, African Americans were more likely than Whites and others to be victims of drug-related homicides between 1976 and 2005. The highest levels of drug use in the month the offense was committed were reported by burglary, robbery, and larceny offenders. Adults on probation (28.4%) and parole (24.1%) reported much higher illicit drug use than adults not on probation (7.4%) or parole (7.7%) in 2007.

Drug use continues to be an important societal issue. Even though misperceptions about race and drug use continue, drug use among Whites now receives more media attention. Future research should examine evidence-based education and prevention efforts that deter drug use and abuse.

Cary Stacy Smith and Li-Ching Hung

See also Drug Courts; Drug Sentencing; Drug Treatment; Drug Use by Juveniles

Further Readings

Karberg, J. C., & James, D. J. (2005, July). *Substance dependence, abuse, and treatment of jail inmates, 2002* (Report No. NCJ 209588). Retrieved from U.S. Department of Justice website: http://www.ojp.usdoj .gov/bjs/pub/pdf/sdatji02.pdf

Mumola, C. J., & Karberg, J. C. (2006, October). Drug use and dependence, state and federal prisoners, 2004. *Bureau of Justice Statistics Special Report* (NCJ 213530). Retrieved March 7, 2009, from U.S. Department of Justice website: http://www.ojp.usdoj .gov/bjs/pub/pdf/dudsfp04.pdf

Provine, D. M. (2007). *Unequal under law: Race in the War on Drugs.* Chicago: University of Chicago Press.

Substance Abuse and Mental Health Services Administration. (2008). *Results from the 2007 National Survey on Drug Use and Health: National findings* (Office of Applied Studies, NSDUH Series H-34, DHHS Publication No. SMA 08-4343). Rockville, MD: Author. Retrieved March 7, 2009, from http://www.oas.samhsa.gov/nsduh/2k7nsduh/ 2k7Results.pdf

Substance Abuse and Mental Health Services Administration, Office of Applied Studies. (2009). *Trends in nonmedical use of prescription pain relievers: 2002 to 2007.* Retrieved March 7, 2009, from http://www.oas.samhsa.gov/2k9/painRelievers/ nonmedicalTrends.cfm

U.S. Department of Justice, Bureau of Justice Statistics. (2007). *Homicide trends in the U.S.: Trends by race.* Retrieved March 7, 2009, from http://www.ojp.gov/ bjs/homicide/race.htm

Websites

National Institute on Drug Abuse: http://www .drugabuse.org

Office of National Drug Control Policy: http://www .whitehousedrugpolicy.gov

Streetdrugs.org: http://www.streetdrugs.org

Substance Abuse and Mental Health Services Administration: http://www.SAMHSA.gov

DRUG USE BY JUVENILES

Psychoactive drug use is a mainstay of American culture, with use dating to the nation's founding. Most adult drug users report adolescence as the time in which drug initiation occurred for them. Due to the potential negative consequences that juvenile drug use poses, considerable effort has been made toward understanding the consequences, prevalence, and causes of this public health problem. This entry provides a brief overview of each of these dimensions. Where applicable, components are discussed within the context of race.

Consequences

Psychoactive drug use poses considerable negative consequences for individual users, families, and society in general. On the economic front, costs are astronomical. In 2002, costs stemming from adult and juvenile drug treatment, drug law enforcement, lost productivity, and insurance totaled $180.8 billion. Underage drinking alone costs taxpayers $62 billion a year.

On the health front, considerable life is lost to drug abuse and dependence, particularly that concerning alcohol and tobacco. While hard drug use is indicated in the deaths of 8,000 Americans each year, alcohol and tobacco use is implicated in the deaths of 130,000 and 440,000 individuals, respectively. Of the 50,000 12- to 17-year-olds who sought emergency department treatment for medical problems stemming from drug use in 2005, Drug Abuse Warning Network data indicate that 9,000 sought medical aid for cocaine use.

Adolescent drug use negatively impacts cognitive, emotional, and social development; has the potential to stunt memory and learning skills; and is indicated in a plethora of health-risk behaviors and conditions. Adolescent drug use constitutes a salient risk factor for psychiatric disorders, suicide, accidents, pregnancy, truancy, school dropout, delinquency, and drug abuse and dependence during both adolescence and adulthood. According to the National Survey of Drug Use and Health, less than 200,000 of the 2.1 million adolescents estimated to need drug treatment in 2005 actually received it.

Epidemiology

The incidence and prevalence of drug use among juveniles are captured and monitored by two major surveys: the Monitoring the Future study, which collects data from 8th-, 10th-, and 12th-grade students, and the National Survey on Drug Use and Health, which collects data from juveniles ages 12 to 18. Alcohol, tobacco, and marijuana use (collectively referred to as soft drugs) are the three most commonly used drugs among youth. In 2004, for example, almost 20% of youth were estimated to have used alcohol within the past month.

Rates of drug use differ along demographic lines. Incidence and prevalence rates increase as youth navigate through adolescence. Hard drugs typically are initiated at older ages than are soft drugs, and alcohol and tobacco initiation typically occurs prior to marijuana initiation. Adolescent females are initiated to alcohol and tobacco use at slightly earlier ages than are their male counterparts, but male youth engage in more frequent drug use. American Indian and Caucasian youth consistently report the highest levels of drug use of all racial groups; rates of use are lowest among Asian adolescents. Rates of drug use among Hispanic and African American youth generally fall in the middle.

Etiology

Over 40 theories of adolescent drug use have been developed. Most theories are environmental in nature, positing that risk factors emanating from peer, family, school, and community domains of influence increase youth's risk for drug use. The most empirically supported theories include Hirschi's social control theory, Akers's social learning theory, and Hawkins and colleagues' social development model.

Research consistently has documented the following risk factors for youth drug initiation and use: poor school performance; prodrug norms and attitudes; delinquency; positive drug expectancies; poor relationships with parents; parental conflict; and association with peers, parents, and other adults who use drugs or espouse prodrug norms and attitudes. Protective factors that decrease risk for drug use include attachment to prosocial others; commitment to conventional pursuits; and a belief in and respect for laws and authority.

Prevention and Control

Two major lines of action are taken to prevent juvenile drug use: the employment of youth drug prevention programs and the enforcement of drug laws. Youth drug prevention programs typically are school-based and utilize primary prevention strategies designed to prevent juvenile drug initiation. Drug prevention programs shown to have the most promise for preventing or delaying drug use include those founded on the social influence model.

The enforcement of drug laws does not appear to elicit a sizable deterrent effect among juveniles. According to Federal Bureau of Investigation (FBI) data, for example, roughly 334,000 juvenile arrests were made in 2003 for liquor law and illegal drug

violations. During this same year, data from the National Survey on Drug Use and Health indicate that without taking into account the illegal use of drugs, 10.9 million 12- to 20-year-olds violated liquor laws.

Racial disparity exists in the arrest and formal case processing of juveniles for drug law violations, with the largest disparity observed between Caucasian and African American youth. Although the average juvenile arrested for violating liquor or illegal drug laws is a Caucasian 16- to 17-year-old male, African American youth have historically been formally processed at significantly higher rates. Some of this racial disparity appears systemic in nature. Caucasian youth are less likely to have their drug cases petitioned, be detained and incarcerated, and have their drug cases waived to adult court than youth of other races. In 2002, for example, FBI data indicate that 65% of African American juvenile drug cases were petitioned, compared to 55% of Caucasian juvenile drug cases. During this year, the proportion of African American youth detained for drug offenses was more than 2 times that of Caucasian youth (33% vs. 16%), and nearly 2 times that of youth of other races (17%).

Rebecca J. Boyd

See also At-Risk Youth; Drug Use; Juvenile Crime

Further Readings

Johnston, L. D., O'Malley, P. M., Bachman, J. G., & Schulenberg, J. E. (2006). *Monitoring the Future national survey results on drug use, 1975–2005: Vol. 1. Secondary school students*. Bethesda, MD: National Institute on Drug Abuse.

Snyder, H. N., & Sickmund, M. (2006). *Juvenile offenders and victims: 2006 national report*. Washington, DC: U.S. Department of Justice, Office of Juvenile Justice and Delinquency Prevention.

DU BOIS, W. E. B. (1868–1963)

William Edward Burghardt Du Bois was one of the most prolific and profound social scientists of the 20th century. Du Bois' writings on race have influenced scholars from across the social sciences, including political science, psychology, and economics. In recent years, prominent sociologists have recognized Du Bois' contributions as a founding father of American sociology. Over the past decade, scholars of race, crime, and justice have also acknowledged his significant contribution to American criminology.

Du Bois was raised by his mother in Great Barrington, Massachusetts. Like many of the few Black Americans who lived in the small and mostly immigrant mill town, Du Bois' mother worked as a domestic. Despite his mother's modest social position, Du Bois was regularly exposed to the ways of life of the town's well-to-do White citizens, some of whom took a special interest in the academic and social development of the young, intellectually advanced Du Bois. This somewhat bifurcated childhood experience marked by exposure to the elite, despite his skin color, and social proximity and distance from the immigrant mill worker, along with later racial encounters in university settings, informed Du Bois' early writing on the "double consciousness" that characterizes the social experience of Black Americans.

After graduating from high school in Great Barrington, and with the help of the elite White citizens of his hometown, Du Bois received a college scholarship to Fisk University, now a historically Black university in Nashville, Tennessee. Three years later, Du Bois received his B.A. from Fisk. He applied to Harvard University, which he had longed to attend as a boy, and was accepted to Harvard as a junior. He received a B.A. in philosophy from Harvard before continuing on to earn a Ph.D. During his period of graduate study, Du Bois spent 2 years in Germany, where he studied with a founding father of sociology, Max Weber (author of *The Protestant Ethic and the Spirit of Capitalism*, as well as many other works). After completing his dissertation, which was a well-respected and still-cited study of the suppression of the African slave trade, Du Bois directly encountered race prejudice from White colleges that refused to hire him for faculty positions. Du Bois was eventually offered an academic position at Wilberforce University, an all-Black school near Dayton, Ohio. Shortly thereafter, he was invited to conduct a social study of

the Black community in Philadelphia, commissioned by the University of Pennsylvania.

Du Bois in Philadelphia

Du Bois offers his earliest substantial statement on the problem of crime in the African American community in "The Negro Criminal," which appeared as a chapter in *The Philadelphia Negro* (1899). From the beginning, Du Bois was aware that this commissioned study was inspired by the perceived problem of crime that originated—in the minds of the "better class of White citizens" in Philadelphia—in the city's African American population: "It was the fear of crime that commissioned this study.... Philadelphia had a theory that this rich municipality was gone to the dogs because of Negro crime" (Du Bois quoted in Anderson, 1996, p. xvi). Du Bois' analysis, which blended urban ethnography with social history, census data, and descriptive statistics, highlighted the complexity of the problem of crime in Philadelphia and challenged the popular pseudoscientific arguments of Italian physician and "founding father" of the positivist school of criminology, Cesare Lombroso, a creator of the "new science" of criminal anthropology.

Lombroso's theory that criminals were *born* and not made was widely circulated in the popular and scientific press during the late 19th and early 20th centuries in both Europe and the United States. In contrast, Du Bois recognized crime as a problem that was inherent in society: "Crime is a phenomenon of organized social life, and is the open rebellion of an individual against his social environment" (Du Bois, 1899/1996, p. 235). It was Du Bois' definition of what was problematic—not the Negro, per se, but the social context in which the Negro population of Philadelphia sought to make a life—that shaped his understanding of the problem of crime in Philadelphia. For Du Bois, crime was a social problem and not an immutable characteristic of an individual or a community. Such an assertion brought attention to the recursive relationship between an individual and his or her environment; to truly understand the problem of crime, Du Bois suggested, one had to shift one's attention from the individual context to the social context. In light of the popularity of the racist pseudoscience of the time, this approach to understanding the problem of race and crime, which would become more popular with the rise of the Chicago school of sociology, was not only sociologically sophisticated but also remarkably progressive.

In contemporary terms, Du Bois' "The Negro Criminal" highlights the dialectical relationship between the individual and his or her structural circumstances that, in turn, reveals the culture of a particular place. Throughout his chapter, Du Bois shifts our attention from the "criminal" to those charged with performing acts of punishment; in these descriptions Du Bois repeatedly, though subtly, highlights the distorted lens of race prejudice through which his benefactors viewed the problem of Negro crime. Du Bois situated discussions of increases and decreases in crime within particular social-historical circumstances. While positivist criminologists of the time argued that the prisons were full of prisoners because of an increase in "born criminals," Du Bois offered an early argument for the use of incarceration as a mechanism of state control over problematic populations. For example, Du Bois connects what he described as the "worst period of Negro crime ever experienced in the city" (Du Bois 1899/1996, p. 238) to the disenfranchisement of the Negro in 1837, which was initiated, in part, by the actions of the White citizens of the city who were shaken by the Nat Turner slave revolt. Du Bois also introduces a discussion of how discrimination influences the complexion of the prison population.It is only after a serious consideration of the historical circumstances that Du Bois comes to consider the current problem of Negro crime in Philadelphia.

In his careful presentation of the social history of crime in Philadelphia, Du Bois repeatedly undermines assumptions underlying claims of a "Negro crime wave" and undermines the logic of biologically deterministic theories of race and crime. Du Bois' criminological perspective is bold not only in its inclusion of White citizens in fostering and overdramatizing the problem of Negro crime but also in its eventual accusation of the "moral weakness" of some segments of the Black community in Philadelphia. This strand of his early writing precedes the development of "subculture" analyses within American criminology.

Du Bois in Atlanta

After completing his field research on *The Philadelphia Negro*, Du Bois published a social study of Black Americans in northern cities. He also completed several studies for the Bureau of Labor Statistics. Each of these works highlighted how the problems encountered by African Americans were shaped by race and class. The failure of White Americans to allow for the full incorporation of African Americans into mainstream American life was repeatedly revealed as a barrier to the full economic and social development of African Americans. While Du Bois remained a stern critic of the moral deficiencies of certain "classes" of the Black population in the North and the South, these deficiencies did not fully explain the problem of crime in the Black community. Rather, Du Bois argued that crime was symptomatic of the Black American's inability to effectively adapt to the restricted freedom that followed the end of slavery; both White Americans and Black Americans shared the burden of responding to crime in responsible and ethical ways.

In 1898, Du Bois accepted a professorship at Atlanta University. Du Bois' contributions to the Atlanta school of sociological study, which predated the Chicago school, are revealed in the Atlanta University Studies, a series of research publications on race and American life, with a special emphasis on the participation of the Black American in family, civic, and economic life. Du Bois's writing and research on race and crime during this time echoed his findings in *The Philadelphia Negro*. Du Bois highlighted the moral failings and differing worldviews of White and Black Americans and how race prejudice restricted the full participation of Black Americans and validated feelings of alienation among some segments of the Black population, which ultimately encouraged a criminally involved class within the Black population.

In 1904, Du Bois published one of the earliest crime polls in American history. This statewide crime poll preceded the contemporary National Crime Survey and other general opinion polls conducted today. Du Bois surveyed police chiefs, officials, and Black and White citizens, including hundreds of youth (ages 9–21) on perceptions of crime in the African American community. Du Bois' survey instrument included questions on the disproportionate representation of Black Americans in courts and on the chain gang.

Responses to Du Bois' survey revealed that a large number of citizens identified moral or cultural deficiencies such as "laziness" or "lack of home training" as reasons for Black Americans' representation in the criminal justice system of the day. It is likely that these perceptions reflected widely held stereotypes. Du Bois also solicited qualitative responses, which revealed racial differences in perceptions of fairness in the courts: Many Whites reported that Black people were treated fairly in the eyes of the court, whereas Black people generally reported that the courts did not treat them fairly at all. Du Bois' analysis also revealed that the demographic composition of a geographical area might influence public perceptions of crime. He found that in counties where the Black population approached equilibrium with the White population, more crime was charged to the Black population. This was true even when the facts disputed such perceptions. In this regard, Du Bois' poll was one of the first to highlight how public opinion can contradict official statistics, a phenomenon that remains a feature of contemporary public opinion polls on crime. Du Bois' writings on race and crime in the early 20th century also offered potential remedies that are consistent with policy recommendations from today's most prominent criminal justice experts and race scholars, with better employment at the top of the list shortly followed by educational and social development.

Du Bois' early writings on race and crime also linked the conditions of confinement to the economic conditions of the region. Du Bois' study of the convict lease system in the South, which preceded the rise and expansion of the penal institution, revealed an early Marxist analysis that is reflected in some contemporary writings on the prison-industrial complex. Du Bois argued that legislators of the Black Codes, which designated specific crimes for recently freed Blacks such as unemployment at the first of the year, and southern courts colluded to produce a secure and steady source of cheap labor after the collapse of slavery in the South. The large-scale leasing of Black convicts to pick cotton, cut plants for rubber production, and construct roads and railroads confined men and women to harsh sentences for menial crimes in inhumane conditions that were considered by some to be worse than slavery. Men and women who were leased out as convicts often died as a result of the conditions of their confinement. Du Bois' early writing on the convict lease system concluded that the system was "another form of slavery" (Gabbidon, 2001, p. 587).

Du Boisian Criminology

W. E. B. Du Bois died on August 27, 1963. His passing was announced to a crowd of 250,000 people who gathered in the nation's capital on August 28 for the historic March on Washington. Du Bois chose to meet his final days in Ghana rather than in an America that he once believed would do better by the Black American if the truth, based on facts and systematic study, were revealed. Du Bois left a substantial intellectual legacy for scholars from a variety of disciplines in the social sciences and the humanities. In 1910, Max Weber identified Du Bois as "the most important sociological scholar anywhere in the Southern States in America, with whom no scholar can compare" (Gabbidon, 2000, p. 167). Today, the most prominent sociologists recognize Du Bois as a founding father of American sociology. Du Bois' contribution to American criminological thought is also being resurrected. In doing so, scholars reveal Du Bois' prescience and pragmatism in his study of the problem of crime and the African American experience.

Du Bois' criminological perspective was informed largely by his understanding that in the minds of many people, the "Negro problem" was equivalent to the problem of crime. Consistent with his early belief that upper-class White citizens were thinking wrong about race, Du Bois set out to dispel the myths of Negro criminality, often bolstered by the biological determinism that characterized the popular pseudoscience of the time. Over a century since the publication of *The Philadelphia Negro*, Du Bois' scholarship encourages us to turn away from the contemporary guises of biological determinism that are the legacies of Lombroso and other, less enlightened "founding fathers" of criminology. Embracing Du Bois as a founding father of American criminological thought will allow future criminologists to inherit a scholarship committed to the study of crime as a social problem and not a biological or genetic deficiency. As a sophisticated and committed social scientist, Du Bois set off on a course of rational and systematic study that the best social scientists of our time continue to follow.

Nikki Jones

See also Atlanta University School of Sociological Research; Biological Theories; Historically Black Colleges and Universities; Race Relations

Further Readings

Anderson, E. (1996). *Introduction.* In W. E. B. Du Bois, *The Philadelphia Negro: A social study* (Reprint ed., pp. ix–xxxvi). Philadelphia: University of Pennsylvania Press. (Original work published 1899)

Du Bois, W. E. B. (1996). *The Philadelphia Negro: A social study* (Reprint ed.). Philadelphia: University of Pennsylvania Press. (Original work published 1899)

Gabbidon, S. L. (2000). An early American crime poll by W. E. B. Du Bois. *Western Journal of Black Studies, 24*(3), 167–174.

Gabbidon, S. L. (2001). W. E. B. Du Bois: Pioneering American criminologist. *Journal of Black Studies, 31*(5), 581–599.

Gabbidon, S. L. (2007). *W. E. B. Du Bois on crime and justice: Laying the foundations of sociological criminology.* Burlington, VT: Ashgate.

Gabbidon, S. L., Greene, H. T., & Young, V. (2002). *African American classics in criminology & criminal justice.* Thousand Oaks, CA: Sage.

Lewis, D. L. (1993). *W. E. B. Du Bois: Biography of a race.* New York: Holt.

Lewis, D. L. (2000). *W. E. B. Du Bois: The fight for equality and the American century 1919–1963.* New York: Holt.

Wright, E., III. (2002). Why Black people tend to shout! An earnest attempt to explain the sociological negation of the Atlanta Sociological Laboratory despite its possible unpleasantness. *Sociological Spectrum, 22*(3), 335–361.

Zuberi, T. (2004). W. E. B. Du Bois's sociology: *The Philadelphia Negro* and social science. *Annals of the American Academy of Political and Social Science, 595,* 146–156.

DUKE UNIVERSITY ASSAULT CASE

In March 2006, a female exotic dancer accused members of the Duke University lacrosse team of rape and sodomy. Three players, all men, were quickly indicted on charges of rape, sexual offenses, and kidnapping. The case quickly gained national media attention, with particular interest paid to the race of the victim and the accused offenders: the alleged victim is Black and the accused men are White. In addition to the media, minority groups also took a vested interest in the case. This entry provides a brief review of the events that took place on the night the sexual assault allegedly occurred, the subsequent investigation and findings, and the final decision by North Carolina Attorney General to drop all charges against the men accused.

The woman accusing the Duke players of assault was a poor, Black, local single mother working at an escort service while attending the predominantly Black North Carolina Central University in Durham, North Carolina. The accused players were White Duke University students from middle- to upper-class families who attended private all-boys high schools in their home states. The NAACP took an instant interest in the case and many other groups came forward criticizing the off-field behavior of athletes at colleges and universities across the nation and called for an investigation into their conduct.

On the night of March 13, 2006, members of the Duke University lacrosse team held a party at an off-campus house in Durham, North Carolina. Two exotic dancers were booked by the party hosts for what they claimed was "a small bachelor party." When the dancers arrived, however, they found over 40 people in attendance; the vast majority were members of the Duke lacrosse team. Despite the large number of party attendees, they consented to perform. When the performance began, one dancer appeared to be unsteady on her feet and fell to the floor during the performance.

This is the same woman who would later allege that she was raped while at the party. During the performance, the women engaged in sexual banter with the party attendees but the performance ended abruptly when one of the attendees held up a broomstick and suggested that it be used as a sexual object for the dancers.

The dancers then retreated to the back of the house where they were followed by some of the party attendees who attempted to convince them to resume their performance. The women refused and shut themselves in the bathroom for a period of time. After emerging from the bathroom, the woman who alleged that she was sexually assaulted was photographed having difficulty walking steadily, talking incoherently to no one in particular, and lying in a prostrate position on the back porch. After observing these behaviors, a party attendee assisted the woman in walking from the back porch to the other dancer's car where he placed her in the front passenger seat. Before driving away, the other dancer yelled a sexually and racially motivated comment at a group of party attendees standing across the street. She then called 911 and reported that a group of White men were yelling racist comments at individuals passing by the party.

The woman then drove to a grocery store where she went inside and asked a security guard to notify the Durham Police Department that the other woman refused to get out of her car. When the police department arrived, the officer witnessed the accusing woman lying unconscious in the front seat of the car. After rousing her, the officer took her to a center that provided victim's services. It was here that the woman stated that she was raped; this was the first time that she had indicated to anyone that she had been the victim of sexual assault. After she was transported to the Duke University Medical Center, the woman recanted her statement that she had been sexually assaulted. A short time later, she changed her story again and restated that she had been raped. Three party attendees, Colin Finnerty, Reade Seligmann, and David Evans, who were all lacrosse players, were charged with the rape, as well as kidnapping. The players consistently proclaimed their innocence and had concrete evidence that placed them elsewhere when the woman alleged that the rape occurred.

The ensuing investigation was plagued with problems from the outset. The accusing woman constantly changed her story, contradicted herself, and was inconsistent in picking out her attackers from a line-up. The rape kit also detected traces of sperm from several men, none of whom was Finnerty, Seligmann, or Evans or even any of their teammates in attendance at the party that night. Other evidence, including ATM receipts, cell phone records, and restaurant receipts, indicated that Finnerty, Seligmann, and Evans were no longer at the party when the woman alleged that the rape occurred. Despite these inconsistencies, the District Attorney, Michael Nifong, did not drop the charges. Nifong also further complicated the already troubled case by making disparaging remarks to the media about the three defendants and deliberately participating in the withholding of exculpatory evidence from a DNA laboratory report. Nifong's strongest critics accused him of pursuing a fruitless case for political gain.

Nifong eventually dropped the rape charge against the three defendants in December 2006 as a result of the failure to match any DNA evidence obtained from the rape kit to any of the defendants. Although the rape charge was dropped, the defendants still faced charges of kidnapping and sexual offenses and were facing extensive prison sentences if they were convicted. Shortly after the rape charges were dropped, the North Carolina State Bar filed ethics violations charges against Nifong as a result of his conduct during the course of the case. As a result, Nifong asked to be removed from the case and the North Carolina Attorney General took over. Upon Nifong's removal from the case, the Attorney General's office conducted a new review of the evidence and completed an additional investigation into the charges and the allegations made by the woman.

The subsequent report compiled by the State Attorney General concluded that there was no credible evidence to support the allegation that the crimes occurred. Subsequent investigation also revealed additional weaknesses in the state's case. As a result, the State Attorney General's office dropped all charges against Finnerty, Seligmann, and Evans.

Carly M. Hilinski

See also Interracial Crime; Victimization, African
American; Violence Against Women

Further Readings

Baydoun, N., & Good, S. M. (2007). *A rush to injustice:
How power, prejudice, racism, and political
correctness overshadowed truth and justice in the
Duke lacrosse rape case.* Nashville, TN: Thomas
Nelson.

Taylor, S., & Johnson, K. C. (2007). *Until proven
innocent: Political correctness and the shameful
injustices of the Duke lacrosse rape case.* New York:
Thomas Dunne Books.

Yeager, D., & Pressler, M. (2007). *It's not about the
truth: The untold story of the Duke lacrosse rape case
and the lives it shattered.* New York: Threshold
Editions.

DYER BILL

The Dyer bill, proposed in 1918 by Congressman
Leonidas Dyer of Missouri, was the first major
attempt by Congress to eliminate the practice of
lynching. The purpose of the bill was to hold
state and local governments accountable for their
support of intimidation against Blacks, including
lynching, which largely went unpunished by l
aw enforcement officials during the post–
Reconstruction era in the South. This entry examines the history and context surrounding the
pioneering bill.

Historical Context of Dyer Bill

In 1922, the U.S. House of Representatives passed
the Dyer bill. Due to a filibuster by mostly White
southerners, the bill was defeated in the U.S.
Senate. Some critics of the Dyer bill argued that
the legislation would interfere with states' rights.
Although the Dyer bill failed to pass Congress, it
was a major political achievement that laid the
foundation for future antilynching legislation.
For example, the Costigan-Wagner antilynching
bill proposed in 1935 garnered support from
many members of Congress, but the support was
insufficient to defeat the opposition of southern

senators. However, the Costigan-Wagner bill was
another historical moment that brought attention
to the practice of lynching and failure of law
enforcement officials to punish those who initiated it.

Lynching, although not limited to the South,
was highly concentrated in southern states.
Statistics indicate that between 1882 and 1968,
lynching occurred most often in Mississippi,
Georgia, and Texas. Lynching was primarily a
response used by southern Whites to express their
dissatisfaction with the outcome of the Civil War,
which many Whites believed had led to too much
freedom for African Americans. However, lynching was a common occurrence across the United
States. In Nebraska, for example, William Brown
was beaten unconscious, dragged by an automobile, and burned for allegedly robbing a White
man. States where lynching was reported not
to have occurred during that time period
include Alaska, Rhode Island, New Hampshire,
Massachusetts, and Connecticut. False criminal
charges, such as alleged rapes or whistling at a
White woman, were common tactics used by police
to promote lynching. Some African Americans
were lynched simply because of the color of their
skin. Although to a much lesser extent, Whites
were also lynched. Generally, the lynching of
Whites occurred in western states, where they were
suspected of murder or stealing cattle. Consequently,
the extent and circumstances by which African
Americans and Whites were the victims of lynching
were very different.

On a daily basis, African Americans were the
direct targets of violence and intimidation at the
hands of Whites. Lynching was embedded throughout American culture, and it is documented that
more than 4,700 African Americans were lynched.
Although estimates vary, figures from Tuskegee
Institute and the records of National Association
for the Advancement of Colored People (NAACP)
director Walter White indicate that nearly 5,000
lynchings occurred in the United States between
1882 and 1927, and about two thirds of the victims were young Black men. Lynching took many
forms, ranging from hanging to dismembering the
victim's body. Public announcements were often
issued about the time and location of a scheduled
lynching. Public squares and parks were prime

locations for lynching. It was common practice for families to watch and cheer, as if they were spectators attending their favorite sporting event. Memorabilia, including pictures, postcards, fingers, toes, and other body parts belonging to lynching victims, were often preserved to commemorate a lynching, while also serving as a method of intimidation against African Americans.

To hold on to their economic and political power, White supremacy groups were formed to circumvent the freedoms that African Americans gained after the Civil War. Supremacy groups, such as the Ku Klux Klan, used lynching and various other forms of intimidation to strip away the rights and dignity of African Americans. Lynching was a threat to all African Americans, even pregnant women and persons who were disabled or mentally ill. Due to inadequate historical records, we may never have a true account of all who fell to their demise under the practice of lynching.

The NAACP, founded in 1909, became a major force behind the antilynching campaign and deemed it the organization's most pressing priority in 1916. The organization centered its platform on vigorously awakening America's consciousness to the prevalence of lynching and supporting the Dyer bill.

Women also figured prominently in the efforts to change the social climate of African Americans. For example, militant Black women such as Ida B. Wells-Barnett, a journalist, put pen to paper to highlight the indignities that African Americans endured. In the 1890s, Wells-Barnett's *Red Record* (a statistical report on lynching) and her book *On Lynching* were a few of the many publications used to raise awareness about the treatment of African Americans. By 1922, African American women assumed positions of leadership in the NAACP and entered the antilynching crusade. Led by Mary Talbert, these courageous women called themselves the Anti-Lynching Crusaders, whose slogan was "A Million Women United to Stop Lynching." The Crusaders set forth an agenda that included three major areas: fundraising, awareness, and promoting legislation to eradicate lynching. They traveled for miles giving speeches to drum up support for Dyer's antilynching bill. To support their fundraising efforts, the Crusaders attempted to recruit 1 million women to donate $1 each to the NAACP in support of their antilynching campaign. Talbert understood that in order for the Crusaders to meet their fundraising goal, they had to garner the support of all women, not just African American women. Therefore, Talbert's strategy was to seek the financial support of White women and recruit them to advocate for ending lynching. However, their invitations to encourage White women to join in their crusade to end lynching were not welcomed. Although the Crusaders' efforts did not lead to legislative reform or significant financial gains to support the movement, their awareness campaign gained international attention when Ida B. Wells visited Great Britain in 1893 and 1894. These international visits were highlighted in a series of articles that Wells published in a Chicago newspaper, which ignited international pressure to end lynching.

As the United States entered World War II, racist attitudes continued to flourish. African American soldiers had hoped that their patriotic service in the war effort would help elevate their social status and help them achieve their dream of greater equality. While serving in the military, African American soldiers were kept in the lowest ranks, received inferior equipment, and continued to face persistent violence and racism. Once the war was over, soldiers returned home to intensifying hostility and violence, including lynching. Whites continued to design ways to maintain racial divides, thus further solidifying their economic and political control.

Responses in the 21st Century

Today, race relations in the United States have improved. The healing process for all Americans, particularly African Americans, is a long and complicated journey. It is apparent that no action can right the wrong endured by African Americans under the practice of lynching. As a result, debates continue surrounding the role, if any, the government should play in acknowledging past atrocities. In 2005, an antilynching resolution was introduced into the U.S. Senate apologizing to victims of lynching for the Senate's historical and consistent failure to outlaw lynching. Republican

Senator George Allen of Virginia, who instituted Confederate History Month during his tenure as governor, was one of the cosponsors of the resolution. Although the antilynching resolution of 2005 passed in the Senate, it did not receive unanimous support.

Jacqueline Smith-Mason

See also Ku Klux Klan; Lynching; National Association for the Advancement of Colored People (NAACP); Rosewood, Florida, Race Riot of 1923; Till, Emmett

Further Readings

Ginzburg, R. (1988). *100 years of lynching*. Baltimore: Black Classic Press.

Hixson, W. B., Jr. (1969). Moorefield Storey and the defense of the Dyer anti-lynching bill. *New England Quarterly, 42,* 65–81.

Hogan, D. J. (Ed.). (2003). *Civil rights chronicle: The African-American struggle for freedom.* Lincolnwood, IL: Legacy Publishing.

Zangrando, R. (1980). *The NAACP crusade against lynching, 1909–1950.* Philadelphia: Temple University Press.

ELAINE MASSACRE OF 1919 (PHILLIPS COUNTY, ARKANSAS)

The year 1919 was marked by race riots in cities across the United States, including Chicago, Washington, D.C., and Omaha. The deadliest incident occurred in rural Phillips County, Arkansas, that autumn. This entry analyzes the underlying causes of the violence; provides a chronology of the riot itself; describes the biased character of the official response, which resulted in the conviction of innocent African Americans; recounts how civil rights groups sought redress; and identifies legacies of the conflict.

Causes

Like many of the riots elsewhere, the violence in Phillips County erupted against a backdrop of labor strife, growing African American militancy, and elite fears of leftist radicalism. But the vast scale of the bloodshed was an outgrowth of the repressive nature of plantation agriculture in the Jim Crow South.

Landownership in the Arkansas Delta was highly concentrated among a small number of White plantation owners. Their workforce consisted largely of Black sharecroppers who were entitled to a portion of the cotton harvest as compensation for their labors. The sharecropping system was rife with abuse. Croppers often received less than market price for their cotton because they were forced to rely on the planters as middlemen. In addition, planters frequently delayed payment or reneged on their obligations altogether. Blacks who dared question such practices risked bodily harm, for which planters and their agents were rarely punished.

In the spring of 1919, Black sharecroppers in Phillips County formed branches of the Progressive Farmers and Household Union of America (PFHUA), hoping to improve their lot through mutual aid and collective action. Several developments influenced their decision to organize. Inflated cotton prices at the end of World War I enabled some sharecroppers to purchase plots of land and raised others' aspirations for greater economic independence. Many PFHUA members had recently been released from military service, and their experiences outside the Deep South fighting to "make the world safe for democracy" may have emboldened them to challenge injustice at home. The *Chicago Defender*, which circulated widely in Phillips County, reinforced such sentiments with stories of Black upward mobility, sharp criticism of conditions in the South, and sympathetic coverage of labor union struggles.

Fear of leftist agitation was widespread among business owners in the aftermath of the Russian Revolution, and the strike wave that swept the United States after the war contributed to their unease. Local newspapers warned that the Industrial Workers of the World had its sights set on Arkansas. Although it is unclear whether the "Wobblies" had any support in Phillips County, planters took the threat seriously.

The Riot

On the evening of September 30, members of the fledgling PFHUA met in a remote church in Hoop Spur to discuss hiring a sympathetic White attorney to help them sue their employers. Spies fired shots into the church, and union members fired back, killing a White man. Over the next several hours, hysteria swept the White population of Phillips County as rumors of a Black insurrection spread.

Early the next morning, local authorities deputized hundreds of White men to put down the "uprising." Planters organized private posses, and the American Legion mobilized armed units from nearby counties, including several in Mississippi and Tennessee. Over the course of the day, Whites rampaged through homes and combed the countryside in search of suspected PFHUA members, terrorizing the African American population of Phillips County. Eyewitnesses recalled that in Elaine, the putative epicenter of the alleged insurrection, Black corpses were dragged through the streets, their toes and ears removed as souvenirs. White snipers indiscriminately shot at Blacks from moving cars and trains. Fearing for their lives, many Blacks hid in thickets, while others, including PFHUA organizer Robert Hill, fled the state. Some fought back, though they were heavily outgunned.

On October 2, Governor Charles Brough personally escorted a detachment of 583 federal troops to Phillips County. Colonel Isaac Jenks ordered White vigilantes to disarm and announced that Blacks who refused to surrender their weapons would be shot. The posses were soon dispersed, and Brough departed on October 4, confident that the situation was under control. However, anecdotal evidence suggests that groups of soldiers continued to brutalize Blacks during the ensuing military occupation of the county. A prominent landlord later recalled watching soldiers shoot one sharecropper in the back and burn another alive.

By the time the violence had finally subsided, five Whites and many more African Americans lay dead. Although the exact number of Black fatalities is unknown, it is clear that the official count of 20 was a gross underestimation. Contemporary scholarship suggests that over 75 African Americans were killed, possibly 200 or more.

Prosecution of African Americans

Though none of the White rioters was apprehended, several hundred Blacks were detained. An all-White "Committee of Seven," composed of local officials and businessmen, oversaw interrogations in the Helena jail, where many prisoners were tortured with chemicals and electricity until they signed false confessions. A total of 122 Blacks were indicted, 73 on charges of murder.

When trials began in early November, mobs of angry Whites ringed the Phillips County courthouse. The defendants were represented by court-appointed attorneys, who did little to prevent the railroading of their clients. Counsel failed to request a continuance or change of venue; did not contest the selection of all-White juries; and generally refrained from calling defense witnesses. Jurors returned guilty verdicts after just minutes of deliberation. In the end, 12 men were sentenced to death, and 67 others received prison terms ranging from 1 to 21 years.

Campaign for Justice

Owing to the courageous on-the-scene reporting of antilynching crusader Ida B. Wells and Walter White from the National Association for the Advancement of Colored People (NAACP), African American newspapers and the independent press debunked the myth of a sharecropper insurrection and exposed the trials as miscarriages of justice. Arkansas activists and the national NAACP launched a defense campaign on behalf of the condemned men, who came to be known as the "Elaine 12": Alf Banks, Jr., Ed Coleman, Joe Fox, Albert Giles, Paul Hall, Ed Hicks, Frank Hicks, Joe Knox, John Martin, Frank Moore, Ed Ware, and Will Wordlow. Protest meetings were held, and donations were solicited to defray legal costs. Scipio Jones, who rose from a childhood in slavery to become Arkansas' most respected Black attorney, anchored the new defense team. White lawyer U. S. Bratton, whose willingness to collaborate with the PFHUA almost got him and his son lynched during the riots, also played a key role in the defense effort.

A major breakthrough occurred in 1921, when two White prosecution witnesses, H. F. Smiddy and T. K. Jones, admitted that they had personally tortured suspects to obtain confessions. In 1923, the U.S. Supreme Court set aside the convictions of six defendants on the grounds that a mob atmosphere pervaded their original trials. The Supreme Court's ruling in *Moore v. Dempsey* established an important precedent, strengthening federal habeas corpus rights. Though it would take another 2 years of legal maneuvering to secure the release of the Elaine 12, by early 1925 all of the Phillips County riot defendants were free.

Legacies

The victory was a major boon to the NAACP and raised the stature of Walter White, who went on to become NAACP executive secretary. For his part, Scipio Jones spent the next 2 decades fighting attempts by White Republicans to purge Blacks from leadership roles in the Arkansas GOP. Planter E. M. Allen, who headed the Committee of Seven, and John Miller, the prosecutor in the original trials, were subsequently elected to the U.S. Congress.

Though the PFHUA was crushed, Black sharecroppers in Phillips County continued to seek collective solutions to their plight. During the 1920s, some joined Marcus Garvey's back-to-Africa movement. In 1934, two veterans of the PFHUA helped found the interracial Southern Tenant Farmers Union, which succeeded in pressuring the federal government to intervene on behalf of poor farmers.

Matthew F. Nichter

See also Moore v. Dempsey; Race Riots

Further Readings

Cortner, R. (1988). *A mob intent on death: The NAACP and the Arkansas riot cases.* Middletown, CT: Wesleyan University Press.

Stockley, G. (2001). *Blood in their eyes: The Elaine race massacres of 1919.* Fayetteville: University of Arkansas Press.

Taylor, K. (1999). "We have just begun": Black organizing and White response in the Arkansas Delta, 1919. *Arkansas Historical Quarterly, 58,* 264–284.

Whayne, J. (2001). Low villains and wickedness in high places: Race and class in the Elaine riots. *Arkansas Review: A Journal of Delta Studies, 32,* 102–118.

Woodruff, N. (2003). *American Congo: The African American freedom struggle in the Delta.* Cambridge, MA: Harvard University Press.

ELDER ABUSE

Elder abuse is a serious public problem. According to the National Center for Victims of Crime, 20% of people over 50 years of age in the United States have experienced crime since reaching age 50. Elder abuse occurs not only among those living either alone or with families but also in nursing home and assisted living settings. Abuse of the elderly is grounded in the same realities as abuse of any other age group—power and control. For older people, power and control become serious issues when those preying upon the elderly see them as easy targets. Frequently, public safety issues impacting the elderly go unnoticed by the general population until there is a significant incident drawing public attention.

There is a lack of significant scholarship on the subject of elder abuse, although fortunately more attention is being placed on this issue—perhaps because seniors are one of the fastest-growing demographic groups within the United States. Even though research scholarship on elder abuse has not been a priority historically, for professionals working with elder abuse, the term *abuse* is often used as part of the larger construct of "abuse, neglect, or exploitation" (ANE). Often, race plays an important role as a variable that is either discounted or factored in on the basis of societal stereotypes. This entry reviews the types of elder abuse, identifies ways in which racial differences impact such abuse, and describes resources for addressing it.

Types of Elder Abuse

There are several types of elder ANE. One type is neglect by a caregiver; this is the refusal or failure to provide essential needs (e.g., food or assistance with finances). A second type of ANE is self-neglect, which is an adult's inability due to physical or mental impairment or capacity to take care of him- or herself. Because of stereotypes about the aging, those who are uninformed about elder ANE may assume that most elder problems are instances of self-neglect. A third ANE type is financial exploitation, which refers to improper, illegal, or unauthorized use of assets or property for benefit of the perpetrator. A fourth type of ANE, physical abuse, is the most visible form of abuse. It involves restrictive or intrusive behavior intended to effect power or control over another. Those outside of the professional ranks of elder care often may fail to consider the improper use of medication in order to control behavior and/or confine the elderly. A common stereotype is that seniors need to be medicated to keep them from "being a nuisance." A fifth ANE type is sexual abuse, which is any unwanted or illegal sexual act on another. Both society and seniors themselves may accept the stereotype that seniors are not viable targets of sexual abuse. Sexual assault of seniors may be intended to instill fear and a sense of powerlessness and to carry out a further goal of enabling the perpetrator to gain access to the victim's house, car, or financial resources.

Elder Abuse and Race

Research and other information on elder abuse and race are limited for several reasons. First, there is not enough interest in this topic among criminologists. Second, elder abuse is difficult to uncover because of the underreporting of what many view as a private matter. Third, victims may be reluctant to report abuse to police and social service agencies. The effect, if any, of race and institutional racism on ANE of the elderly is impacted by both historical inequities associated with education and the lack of access to information about care for the elderly. Anthropologists and geneticists have made clear that "race" is a social (rather than biological) construct; thus, notions that ANE of elderly is connected with racial propensities to either inflict or receive ANE are questionable. Any discussion of race and elder ANE must recognize that cultural norms play a role in how communities and individuals perceive this issue. Historically, lack of awareness of financial matters is tied to cumulative disadvantage and lower rates of disposable income. Often this means that financial aspects of ANE are not openly discussed. It is important to avoid generalizing about race and elder abuse. Practitioners involved with ANE must consider racial realities for majority and minority elderly, taking into account historical legacies, cultural norms, and differences along racial lines of existing resources.

Resources for Addressing ANE

Many practitioners consider the resources available to address ANE of the elderly to be less than adequate or even virtually nonexistent. From a policy perspective, one problem with regard to elder ANE is that in many U.S. jurisdictions, even at the federal level, resources are allocated largely within a public health framework. In contrast, significant efforts to address child ANE exist primarily within a law enforcement framework. The lack of official focus on elder abuse as a law enforcement issue leads to significant disparities with respect to funding, personnel, and, in many cases, authority to address ANE. This is not to imply that child ANE has sufficient resources, merely that elder ANE receives significantly less.

Advocacy groups play an important role in addressing elder ANE, specifically groups involved with aging, disabilities, and health. For instance, disability-related conferences often have some material dedicated to elder ANE. Several universities, especially some law schools, have made significant efforts to address elder law and educate the public and practitioners about the salience of elder ANE. More effort is needed to educate seniors and to foster a culture of interest with respect to elder ANE. Some efforts toward this end have been made at the undergraduate level. For example, the Senior Justice Center at the University of Arkansas in Little Rock uses undergraduate student interns to directly address elder ANE via education and conducts research to address perceptions on elder crime generally. Recent preliminary findings from 1 year of survey data collection indicate that in counties with largely different racial demographics, perceptions about elder ANE and resources to address elder ANE are different.

U.S. Census data indicate that demographic trends for the next 15 years will significantly increase the proportion of seniors, thus elder ANE will likely increase rather than decrease and the issue of resources to address elder needs, including ANE, will likely be impacted by resources allocated to this growing population. Campbell (1996) predicts that by the year 2025, the percentage of elderly Americans will double. According to this same source, specifically in ranked order, the Asian American population is growing the fastest, followed by the Hispanic/Latino population, American Indian population, African American/Black population, and European American/White population. The allocation of resources to address elder ANE will need to take account of these trends.

The complexity of technology in the 21st century makes some forms of abuse easier to carry out. For example, online banking may contribute to some forms of check fraud by a caregiver. Many adult protective services agencies nationally rely on tips from concerned neighbors and friends to identify elder ANE on the part of family members. Adding racial realities to this equation further compounds the importance of making elder ANE more of a societal priority. Finally, the list of mandated reporters who are legally required to report suspected elder ANE (e.g., bank tellers and nurses) is literally increasing each year in many jurisdictions. This valuable tool in the law helps provide needed attention by professionals who are directly involved with seniors or those who need to interact with the reporters in order to carry out elder ANE (e.g., unusual bank transactions). Everyone in society should participate in addressing elder ANE, and appropriate consideration of race is important in properly addressing this societal problem.

David R. Montague and Patricia Wilkerson

See also Domestic Violence; Domestic Violence, African Americans; Domestic Violence Latina/o/s; Domestic Violence, Native Americans; Institutional Racism

Further Readings

Arkansas Senior Citizen Crime Survey: Preliminary findings report. (2007, Fall). Little Rock: University of Arkansas, Senior Justice Center.

Arkansas 2020: The changing demographics and challenges facing Arkansas' state government in 2020. (2006). Little Rock: University of Arkansas, Senior Justice Center.

Brown, E. (2000). *Elder mistreatment in the African American community.* Unpublished manuscript, University of Michigan. Retrieved July 14, 2008, from http://www.rcgd.isr.umich.edu/prba/perspectives/springsummer2000/ebrown.pdf

Campbell, P. R. (1996). *Population projections for states by age, sex, race, and Hispanic origin: 1995 to 2025* (Report No. PPL-47). Washington, DC: U.S. Bureau of the Census, Population Division.

Dimah, A., & Dimah, K. P. (2002). Gender differences among abused older African Americans and African American abusers in an elder abuse provider agency. *Journal of Black Studies, 32*(5), 557–573.

Kertzer, D. (1984). *Age and anthropological theory.* Ithaca, NY: Cornell University Press.

McNamee, C. C., & Murphy, M. B. (2006, November). Elder abuse in the United States. *NIJ Journal 255.* Retrieved from http://www.ojp.usdoj.gov/nij/journals/255/elder_abuse.html

National Center on Elder Abuse. (1998, September). *National Elder Abuse Incidence Study, Final Report.* Retrieved from http://www.aoa.gov/eldfam/Elder_Rights/Elder_Abuse/AbuseReport_Full.pdf

National Clearinghouse on Abuse in Later Life, Wisconsin Coalition Against Domestic Violence. (2006). *Abuse in later life wheel.* Retrieved from http://dhs.wisconsin.gov/caregiver/pdfscenarios/barb_abuse.pdf

Rogerson, P. A. (1998, January). The geography of elderly minority populations in the United States. *International Journal of Geographical Information Science, 12*(7), 687–698.

Websites

National Center for Victims of Crime: http://www.ncvc.org

ENVIRONMENTAL CRIME

Environmental crime has been described as consisting of acts that cause harm to the natural environment, typically involving the handling of hazardous wastes and the contamination of the air and water. Environmental crime is important to the topic of race and crime because its occurrence affects low-income groups and people of color at a far greater rate than more-affluent White groups. However, defining environmental crime has been rather difficult because of the fluctuating nature of how environmental crimes are characterized and the fact that environmental laws are relatively recent creations that are constantly being reevaluated and modified. The most immediate events that come to mind when most think of environmental crime are incidents such as the Love Canal toxic waste disaster, the Three Mile Island nuclear power plant radiation leak, and the Exxon *Valdez* oil spill. However, the emerging concern of environmental justice has to do with the disproportionate burden that poor and minority groups bear when it comes to environmental hazards. This entry discusses the perception of environmental crime; its disproportionate effect on poor and minority groups; and the attempts, through laws and other efforts, to prevent it.

Most crimes are perceived by society as violent crimes that involve direct and immediate physical acts such as rape, robbery, and murder. As such, this perception has not afforded much room for environmental crimes, whose elements evolve at a much slower and more inconspicuous pace. For example, the health effects of a polluted environment may take years to surface and a link to the environment may not be readily apparent, whereas the harm from violent crimes is immediate. Also, environmental crimes are often perceived as lesser crimes because many take place during the course of otherwise beneficial activities. For example, a coal plant may emit tons of pollution while producing energy that keeps thousands of households running. Furthermore, environmental crimes differ in that they are typically committed by the most socially and economically powerful, which goes against the common notion of crimes being committed by the poor and underprivileged. Environmental crimes are often tolerated up until a certain point; therefore, striking a balance between what is beneficial to society and what is harmful is a difficult undertaking. Lastly, environmental crimes are often thought of in the same context as corporate and white-collar crimes. There is often no one particular person at whom to point the finger, as environmental crimes stem from organizations or entities rather than individuals. Pollution of the environment by corporations has been suggested as the most common form of environmental crime. Crimes such as illegal dumping into rivers and lakes in violation of the Clean Water Act, or nighttime air emissions that violate

the Clean Air Act, are common violations committed by corporations either for profit or out of ignorance of the resulting harm.

It has also been recognized that many environmental crimes take place in poor or minority communities. Early environmental groups, such as the National Wildlife Federation and Friends of the Earth, were mostly concerned with preserving the wilderness; however, local grassroots organizations eventually emerged to deal with environmental hazards in poor and minority neighborhoods. Public attitudes toward environmental crimes began to shift away from viewing environmental crimes as the cost of doing business and toward viewing them as crimes against humanity. From a legal standpoint, environmental crimes are defined in terms of certain statutory definitions, but many others analyze environmental concerns from a more social approach. Social justice advocates believe that environmental hazards should be distributed in such a way so that no one group should bear the burden of environmental health threats. A 1987 study by the Commission for Racial Justice found that of the five largest hazardous waste facilities located in the United States, three were sited in low-income, African American communities. It further found that three out of every five African Americans and Latinos lived near uncontrolled toxic waste sites.

Many environmental justice issues emerged around so-called locally unwanted land uses (LULUs) that frequently affected poorer communities without the resources or voice found in wealthy communities needed to stave off LULUs. As a result, hazardous polluting facilities are disproportionately located near low-income minority neighborhoods. Many activists have gone so far as to characterize this phenomenon as "environmental racism" because of the interwoven role that race and class play in LULUs. Factors such as the distribution of wealth, housing and real estate practices, and land use planning have been blamed for environmental inequities that place minorities at a greater health risk than the rest of society. However, attempts to rectify environmental slights against poor minorities have not been made easy in the courts. A 1979 environmental lawsuit filed in Houston, Texas, attempted to show a pattern of racially discriminatory siting decisions. This suit, *Bean v. Southwestern Waste Management*

Corporation, alleged that the siting of a hazardous waste facility in a largely African American community was a violation of civil rights on equal protection grounds. The suit was eventually unsuccessful but, more importantly, it highlighted the difficulty of proving racial discrimination using a constitutional argument. Given this difficulty, many activists turned to alternative approaches using statutory law.

The Environmental Protection Agency (EPA) regularly works with state regulatory agencies to enforce environmental laws. State agencies must adopt federal environmental protection standards, although the state may impose much stricter standards. This has, however, led to huge variations among states' enforcement practices. Many environmental interest groups complain that weak and limited enforcement of environmental laws contributes to continued pollution and impunity for the offenders. Despite this, there has been a tremendous growth in environmental legislation over the past 40 years. Legislation designed to protect public health and safety, such as the Safe Drinking Water Act and the Community Right to Know Act, requires EPA to limit contaminants in public water systems and to disclose releases of specific chemicals by chemical and refinery companies. Additionally, the National Environmental Policy Act offers mechanisms to challenge official decisions. Title VI of the 1964 Civil Rights Act has also been used to deny federal monies to states that take part in environmental decisions that have discriminatory effects. During the Clinton administration, EPA announced that Title VI applied to environmental policies, which has led to investigations concerning the controversial placement of hazardous waste facilities in poor or minority neighborhoods. The term *environmental equity* has been adopted by EPA in an attempt to distribute environmental risks over various populations.

Today, a majority of environmental statutes have penalties attached for violating them. Most environmental statutes contain two criminal categories: strict liability and "knowing" violations. Strict liability crimes require only that a violation occur without regard to the intention of the wrongdoer, whereas "knowing" violations require that the wrongdoer have intention of committing the wrong. Individuals and corporations convicted of environmental crimes face various penalties: monetary criminal fines; payments to government agencies or affected parties; nonmonetary penalties, such as corporate probation, suspension, or debarment from government contract; and jail sentences for individuals.

Environmental crime continues to be a serious public health problem that threatens the well-being of millions of Americans every day. The current focus of policymakers and industries is to seek ways to protect the environment by guiding economic growth in an environmentally sound manner. Although environmental laws are continuously evolving, there are laws at both state and federal levels designed to curb violations and strike a balance between industry needs, health risks, and environmental equity.

Tracy S. Penn

See also Environmental Racism

Further Readings

Burns, R. G., & Lynch, M. J. (2004). *Environmental crime: A sourcebook.* New York: LFB Scholarly.

Camacho, D. (Ed.). (1998). *Environmental injustices, political struggles: Race, class and the environment.* Durham, NC: Duke University Press.

Clifford, M. (1998). *Environmental crime: Enforcement, policy, and social responsibility.* Gaithersburg, MD: Aspen.

ENVIRONMENTAL RACISM

The term *environmental racism* has been defined in several ways. The definitional variations of this term are subtle and involve difference between related concepts (e.g., environmental justice, equity, and discrimination). More important than these terminological variations are the main ideas expressed by this term, its history and use. This entry not only defines the term but also reveals how environmental racism and the disproportionate exposure of racial and ethnic minorities to hazardous materials and conditions have serious implications for the health and well-being of such communities.

Defining Environmental Racism

Environmental racism can be defined as a form of differential treatment affecting minorities (who are often also low-income groups) in ways that produce environmental disadvantages. These disadvantages include (a) differentials in exposure to a variety of environmental hazards, such as air, water, and soil pollution, hazardous waste facilities, and toxic waste sites; (b) the unequal placement or siting of hazardous waste or toxic waste facilities in minority communities; (c) unequal detrimental health impacts associated with exposure or proximity to pollution-producing or hazardous waste sites and facilities; (d) inequity in government responses toward the dangers, hazards, and conditions posed by pollution and hazardous waste sites in minority communities; (e) the distribution of, or access to, environmental advantages such as parks and recreational areas as well as aspects of the urban environment, including public transportation; and (f) inequities in the design and implementation of environmental laws, regulations, and responses. The goal of environmental racism research is to expose the relationship between race (and often ethnicity and social class) and environmental inequities that focus on the intersection of "race, space and place" (Bullard, 2007) in an effort to generate awareness of these discrepancies and public policies designed to alleviate these conditions.

Environmental Racism and the Environmental Justice Movement

The term *environmental racism* emerged from the environmental justice movement, which is linked to three key events that occurred during the 1980s. The first study of environmental justice, performed by Robert Bullard during the late 1970s, examined the relationship between the distribution of solid waste facilities in Houston and the spatial proximity of those sites to Black communities. Bullard, a leading scholar and activist in this area and often referred to as "the father" of the environmental justice movement, was also instrumental in writing Executive Order 12898 on environmental justice ("Federal Actions to Address Environmental Justice in Minority Population and Low-Income Populations"), issued in 1994 under the Clinton administration.

Another important development in the history of this term was the emergence of the first environmental justice protest in Warren County, North Carolina, in 1982. Local residents from a primarily African American, low-income community challenged the placement of a state PCB (polychlorinated biphenyl) landfill within its boundaries. This event, which included the arrest of 500 protestors, led to the first governmental study of environmental justice by the Government Accounting Office, which exposed a pattern of inequitable hazardous waste facility siting. This study was followed by a national report on these issues by the United Church of Christ, which established the basic elements for the definition of environmental racism.

There are two broad approaches taken to the study of environmental racism: the institutional model and the pure discrimination model. The primary difference between these two approaches for defining environmental racism rests on the recognition of intent. In the institutional model, the key indicator of environmental racism is evidence of disparity or disproportionate outcomes rather than intent. In this view, evidence of racial disparity in the distribution of, or proximity to, hazardous waste sites or pollution-emitting facilities, or in the implementation or enforcement of environmental policies, serves as evidence of environmental racism. This approach is associated with the work of Bullard.

In the pure discrimination model, the intent of the actors who create a hazard or inequity is key to determining the existence or nonexistence of environmental racism and therefore requires that the actor's intent be examined before environmental racism can be established. This definition is derived from legal principles related to legal challenges to remedy alleged instances of environmental racism under the U.S. Constitution's Equal Protection Clause or Title VI of the Civil Rights Act.

Environmental Racism Research

The research addressing environmental racism is difficult to summarize succinctly. The results of environmental equity, discrimination, and justice research (e.g., proximity to hazardous waste facilities, the siting of hazardous waste facilities, patterns of exposure to toxic or hazardous waste) often depend on five factors: (1) the types of facilities examined; (2) the types of toxic hazards examined; (3) region of the country examined; (4) the inclusion or exclusion of social class indicators, which are highly correlated with race; and (5) the level of analysis (census tracts, zip codes, block groups, radial buffer zones, or distance measures; see Liu, 2001). Despite the potential impact of these factors, the majority of studies indicate the existence of significant racial effects. Yet, it should be kept in mind when examining this research that the correlation between race and social class is sometimes difficult to disentangle and can lead to both the under- or overestimation of race effects depending on the methodological approaches employed in individual studies (Liu, 2001).

The few studies that employ elementary schools as the basis for analysis, for example, find significant evidence of racial disparities related to proximity to hazardous waste sites, the siting of hazardous waste facilities, and exposure to and deleterious impacts from air pollution. Studies of exposure to cancer-producing toxins have also demonstrated strong racial associations that support a finding of environmental racism. Prior research also indicates racial disparities in proximity to hazardous waste treatment, storage, and disposal facilities; Superfund sites, and in relationship to penalties imposed by the Environmental Protection Agency. In a recent study, Mohai and Saha (2006) indicate that the use of advanced methods for modeling distance relationships can help clarify conflicting findings. Indeed, these researchers discovered that using various buffer zone measures rather than census track, zip code, or traditional hazard-coincidence approaches increased the strength of race associations.

Conclusion

In sum, environmental racism is an important concern. This issue has been largely absent from criminological discussions of crime and justice. Yet, environmental racism has numerous criminological implications. For example, environmental racism is a means of measuring the extent of racial biases in the processing of regulatory infractions

and can be related to issues pertinent to the study of racial biases in justice mechanisms. In addition, the uneven distribution of environmental harms is not simply a matter of justice: Exposure to environmental toxins may also impact behavior and may be an important element in explaining the distribution of crime or even racial differences in crime across communities. The issue of environmental racism has only recently been addressed by criminologists, and further attention to this issue appears warranted based on research findings from other disciplines.

Michael J. Lynch

Further Readings

Been, V. (1994). Locally undesirable land uses in minority neighborhoods: Disproportionate siting or market dynamics? *Yale Law Journal, 103*(6), 1383–1422.

Bullard, R. D. (1983). Solid waste sites and the Houston Black community. *Sociological Inquiry, 53*, 273–288.

Bullard, R. D. (Ed.). (2007). *Growing smarter: Achieving livable communities, environmental justice and regional equity.* Atlanta, GA: Environmental Justice Resource Center.

Government Accounting Office. (1983, June 1). *Siting of hazardous waste landfills and their correlation with racial and economic status of surrounding communities* (GAO/RCED-83-168). Washington, DC: Author. Retrieved from http://www.gao.gov/docdblite/info.php?rptno=RCED-83-168

Liu, F. (2001). *Environmental justice analysis: Theories, methods and practice.* Boca Raton, FL: Lewis.

Lynch, M. J., Burns, R. G., & Stretesky, P. B. (2008). *Environmental crime, law and justice.* New York: LFB Scholarly.

Mohai, P., & Saha, R. (2006). Reassessing racial and socioeconomic disparities in environmental justice research. *Demography, 43*(2), 383–399.

United Church of Christ Commission for Racial Justice. (1987). *Toxic wastes and race in the United States: A national report on the racial and socioeconomic characteristics of communities surrounding hazardous waste sites.* New York: Author.

ESCOBEDO V. ILLINOIS

Escobedo v. Illinois (1964) was decided by the U.S. Supreme Court during the era of Chief Justice

Earl Warren. It is part of what has come to be known as the "due process revolution," one of a series of cases that granted many protections of the Bill of Rights to state defendants, to whom these rights had historically been denied. The case was decided during the civil rights movement of the 1960s, when concerns about state abridgment of the rights of minorities, the poor, and other disadvantaged populations reached a peak. *Escobedo* for the first time recognized a suspect's Sixth Amendment right to counsel during police interrogation. Although *Escobedo* has little value as a precedent today, it is considered by many to be the precursor to the Supreme Court's landmark decision 2 years later in *Miranda v. Arizona,* which placed significant Fifth Amendment limitations on police efforts to obtain confessions from suspects.

Facts of the Case

Danny Escobedo, a 22-year-old Mexican American laborer, was arrested on the night of January 19, 1960, for the murder of his brother-in-law, but was released several hours later when his attorney filed a writ of habeas corpus (a legal instrument alleging that Escobedo's detention was unlawful because there was insufficient evidence to hold him). Upon his release, Escobedo was advised by his attorney that he should not answer any questions if the police arrested him again.

Eleven days later, Escobedo was rearrested after another suspect in the case, Benedict DiGerlando, told police that Escobedo fired the shots that killed his brother-in-law. En route to the police station, and without advising him that he had a right to remain silent, the police told Escobedo that DiGerlando had identified him as the shooter, and urged him to admit to the crime. Escobedo requested that he be permitted to talk with his attorney. The police denied this request. During questioning at the stationhouse, Escobedo repeated this request several times. His attorney, who had been informed of Escobedo's arrest by another family member, arrived at the police station and asked to see his client. The police denied this request. The attorney sought permission to see his client from at least three other higher-ranking officials but was informed that he would

not be permitted to talk to his client until the police interrogations were complete. When Escobedo noticed his attorney in an adjoining room, the police told him that the attorney did not want to see him. An officer who knew the Escobedo family and who spoke Spanish came into the room and asked Escobedo if he would like to confront DiGerlando. Escobedo said that he would. He claimed that the police told him that he could go home if he identified DiGerlando as the culprit and that he would only be called as a witness in the case. When the two were brought face-to-face, Escobedo said, "I didn't shoot Manuel. You did it." He was unaware that his statement implicated him in the crime and made him an accomplice under Illinois law, the same as if he had fired the fatal shots. He was subsequently convicted of murder and appealed the verdict.

Background

When *Escobedo* was decided, the admissibility of stationhouse confessions was governed by a "voluntariness test," under which trial courts examined the "totality of the circumstances" to determine whether the suspect made the confession of his or her own free will. In the early part of the 20th century, courts were concerned about police use of torture and other unsavory methods to obtain admissions from suspects. In *Brown v. Mississippi,* for example, the Supreme Court invalidated the confessions of African American suspects whom sheriffs acknowledged they had hanged from a tree, let down, hanged again, whipped, and threatened with continued whipping until they confessed. The concern in such cases was about the reliability of the confession. Anyone tortured or threatened or questioned incommunicado for long hours (or even days) might confess to a crime he or she did not commit. Most of the suspects in cases involving confessions obtained through torture and threats were poor, uneducated, racial and ethnic minorities, often from the South.

In the 1950s, the Supreme Court began to address the use of more subtle forms of coercion. Gradually, the voluntariness test came to focus less on the unreliability of confessions and more on police interrogation techniques. Police interrogation tactics had become more psychological than physical. The psychological nature of the interrogation tactics made it difficult for courts to determine whether a confession reflected the unfettered will of the suspect. The factors courts were required to consider were numerous (including suspect characteristics, interrogators' behavior, and context of the interrogation) and often difficult to assess (e.g., suspect's intelligence, education, psychological condition, emotional state, and sleep deprivation), and they were not given any instruction regarding how heavily to weigh one factor versus another. The result was a lack of consistency in the application of the voluntariness test.

Just 1 month prior to *Escobedo,* the Supreme Court had decided *Massiah v. United States,* which limited the admissibility of pretrial confessions. Winston Massiah had been indicted in a narcotics conspiracy, had retained counsel, and had made incriminating statements to an accomplice who was cooperating with police. Massiah was not in police custody at the time, and he talked freely to his accomplice. There were no threats and no pressure. Nevertheless, the Supreme Court held that the statements were inadmissible. The Court ruled that once a suspect has been accused of crime (in this case, Massiah had been indicted), the right to counsel attaches, and once the right to counsel has attached, the police may not attempt to elicit information from a defendant in any way when counsel is not present. The Court reasoned that the right to counsel at trial would mean little if police could obtain uncounseled confessions from defendants prior to trial and subsequently admit them into evidence. The Court explained that in the U.S. system of justice, the government bears the responsibility of amassing evidence sufficient to establish guilt, without assistance from the defendant.

The *Escobedo* Decision

The *Escobedo* Court overturned the conviction, ruling that Escobedo's incriminating statements had been taken in violation of his right to counsel guaranteed by the Sixth and Fourteenth Amendments. In reaching this decision, the Court focused on the fact that the police were no longer in an investigatory mode when they

questioned Escobedo. Suspicion had focused squarely on Mr. Escobedo: Police believed that they had solved the crime, that they had their shooter. Writing for the majority, Justice Arthur Goldberg likened Escobedo's situation to Massiah's. Because the government was in an accusatory mode in both cases, Goldberg reasoned that it was immaterial that Massiah had been indicted when he made incriminating statements whereas Escobedo had merely been arrested. It thus appeared to some commentators that the *Escobedo* case stood for the proposition that police were prohibited from questioning any individual who had become the focus of suspicion unless counsel was present. Further, because defense attorneys rarely, if ever, encourage their clients to speak to police, the case might spell the end of stationhouse interrogations and confessions. Whereas opponents of police interrogation techniques might have applauded such a result, law enforcement officials would surely decry the loss of what they viewed as a vital crime control strategy.

In fact, the *Escobedo* decision was not nearly so straightforward. While the Court's opinion included expansive statements likening this case to *Massiah* ("The interrogation here was conducted before petitioner was formally indicted. But in the context of this case, that fact should make no difference."), it also included limiting ones, such as the following:

> where, as here, the investigation is no longer a general inquiry into an unsolved crime but has begun to focus on a particular suspect, the suspect has been taken into police custody, the police carry out a process of interrogation that lends itself to eliciting incriminating statements, the suspect has requested and been denied an opportunity to consult with his lawyer, and the police have not effectively warned him of his absolute constitutional right to remain silent, the accused has been denied The Assistance of Counsel in violation of the Sixth Amendment to the Constitution as made obligatory upon the States by the Fourteenth Amendment . . . [N]o statement elicited by the police during the interrogation may be used against him at a criminal trial. (*Escobedo v. Illinois,* 387 U.S. 478, at 491)

In the 2 years following *Escobedo,* courts were split over how to interpret it. Did it mean that, prior to interrogation, police had to furnish counsel to all arrestees upon whom suspicion had focused? The limiting language in the opinion suggested that the answer was "no." Alternatively, the ruling could be read more narrowly to apply only to arrestees upon whom suspicion had focused and who had not been apprised of the right to remain silent. Narrower still, the ruling might apply only to arrestees who had not been apprised of the right to remain silent and who requested to consult with an attorney. Even narrower still, it might be limited to arrestees upon whom suspicion had focused who had not been apprised of their right to remain silent, who requested to consult with an attorney, and whose counsel was denied access to them.

The ambiguity of the *Escobedo* ruling was clarified in 1966, with *Miranda v. Arizona.* The Court in *Miranda* shifted the analysis from the Sixth Amendment right to counsel to protection of the Fifth Amendment privilege against self-incrimination. That shift was more in keeping with the purpose of the *Escobedo* decision—to protect a suspect's right to remain silent by providing for the assistance of an attorney to help secure that right. In *Miranda,* the Court struck a middle ground, not prohibiting all stationhouse interrogations but requiring police to explicitly inform suspects of their rights and requiring an affirmative waiver of those rights prior to any interrogation.

After the Supreme Court decided *Miranda, Escobedo* lost most of its value as a legal precedent. Nevertheless, it remains an important stepping stone in a line of cases that responded to concerns that police interrogation techniques were being used to exploit the vulnerabilities of disadvantaged suspects.

Donna M. Bishop

See also Brown v. Mississippi; Miranda v. Arizona

Further Readings

Brown v. Mississippi, 297 U.S. 278 (1936).
Escobedo v. Illinois, 387 U.S. 478 (1964).
Kamisar, Y. (1965). Equal justice in the gatehouses and mansions of American criminal procedure. In A. E. D. Howard (Ed.), *Criminal justice in our time.* Charlottesville: University Press of Virginia.
Kamisar, Y., LaFave, W. R., Israel, J. H., & King, N. (2005). *Modern criminal procedure: Cases, comments, and questions* (11th ed.). New York: West.
Massiah v. United States, 377 U.S. 201 (1964).
Miranda v. Arizona, 384 U.S. 436 (1966).

ETHNICITY

Based on the Office of Management and Budget (OMB) standards, ethnicity is generally defined as the heritage, nationality group, lineage, or country of birth of an individual or an individual's parents prior to their arrival in the United States. Specifically, OMB standards specify two minimum categories of ethnicity: Hispanic or Latino and not Hispanic or Latino. According to the OMB, race is a socially or culturally defined concept and does not conform to purely biological, anthropological, or genetic criteria. Furthermore, race is considered a separate concept from Hispanic origin (ethnicity), and persons who identify as Hispanic or Latino can be of any race. In addition to Hispanics or Latinos, some broad and commonly recognized ethnic groups in the United States include African Americans, Asian Americans, American Indians, and European Americans. Each of these groups has a unique personal history related to experiences in the United States.

This entry provides a brief background of ethnic groups in the United States; examines some of the research regarding ethnic involvement in offending, incarceration, and victimization; and reviews general theoretical explanations for this involvement. Research directions are also discussed.

Background

In the earlier part of 20th-century America, European immigrants had become well settled in communities throughout the United States, and the general expectation was that certain ethnic groups would exhibit higher crime rates as compared to native-born Americans. Despite research findings to the contrary, concerns related to subsequent immigrant populations persisted. After 1965 a new wave of immigration began, this time including a large influx of Asians, Afro-Caribbeans, and Latinos. In concert with a largely uninterrupted flow of legal and illegal (undocumented) immigrants from Mexico that intensified after 1980, a second major wave of Latina/o immigration occurred during the 1980s; this wave included the Marielito refugees from Cuba and further large-scale emigration from other war-torn areas in Central America. (The term *Marielito* refers to Cuban refugees who fled to the United States from the Cuban port of Mariel in 1980 to escape political unrest and gain asylum.) By the early 1990s, Latina/o immigration had reached its peak; however, current population estimates indicate that Hispanics/Latinos are the largest and fastest-growing minority group in the United States. Although more recent attempts have been made to close the borders, the U.S. Latina/o population has continued to grow.

According to the census, as of 2000, there were 35.3 million Hispanics or Latinos, 34.7 million African Americans or Blacks (which can include Hispanics reporting their race as Black), 11.9 million Asians, 2.5 million American Indians, and almost 200 million European Americans living in the United States. This increased ethnic diversity has led to a plethora of political and social issues, one of the most controversial being the real or perceived relationship between immigration and crime. Given that Latinos are the largest ethnic group in the United States, ethnicity-centered crime analyses typically reference Latinos, at the exclusion of other ethnic groups.

Offending, Incarceration, and Victimization

Race and ethnicity are often cited as the most important predictor variables of crime and delinquency in the United States. Contemporary criminological research, however, has generally focused on race rather than ethnicity—with Blacks and Whites as the two major groups under examination. Although the social implications and controversies pertaining to race and ethnicity are largely shared, ethnicity should be differentiated from race in criminological research.

Research findings based on official data should be interpreted with caution. For example, classic criminological studies largely relied on official records to determine the extent to which ethnic groups are involved in crime or delinquency; however, such records were often inaccurate and

prejudicial against immigrants and other ethnic minorities. A specific obstacle often faced by researchers is the failure of official crime data statistics to account for distinctions between immigration generations, ethnic subgroups (ethnic origin or country of origin), and race.

The available research indicates that, relative to their representation in the U.S. population, ethnic minorities (particularly Blacks and Latinos) are overrepresented in prison and jail statistics. According to official reports, the incarceration rate for Latino males incarcerated in U.S. prisons and jails in 2006 was an estimated 1.9% (per 100,000 residents for each state and the federal system), compared to 0.7% of non-Latino White men. Based on current incarceration statistics, the lifetime chance of a Latino going to prison was estimated at 10%, compared to 3.4% for a non-Latino White.

Ethnic minorities are also more likely to be victims of violent and property crimes. For instance, between 1992 and 2001, rates of violent victimization among Native Americans were more than twice that of non–Native American Blacks and Whites, and 4½ times that of Asians. During 2005, Latinos were victims of overall violence at rates higher than non-Latinos. Specifically, while Latinos age 12 or older made up 13% of the total population that year, they experienced 15% of all violent crime. Compared to non-Latinos, 2005 statistics indicate that the rates for property crimes were also higher among Latinos (210 vs. 148 per 1,000 households).

Theoretical Explanations for the Ethnicity–Crime Link

Some of the major criminological theories have predicted high levels of criminal involvement among ethnic minorities, particularly immigrants. Based on these theories, some of the factors attributed to the immigrant crime problem have included settlement patterns and poverty, blocked economic opportunities, culture conflicts, language barriers, relative youth and a preponderance of males, and problems associated with assimilation.

Researchers have often attempted to study the link between ethnicity or immigration and violence in the context of criminogenic structural conditions. Earlier work of sociologists connected with the University of Chicago investigated the development of delinquency areas in the city of Chicago to find support for a theory of social disorganization. Specifically, theoretical expectations were based on an interplay of rapid industrialization, urbanization, immigration processes (heterogeneity), and the subsequent breakdown of community controls. Findings indicated that high delinquency rates persisted in the same urban areas despite ethnic composition. For example, at the turn of the century, the predominant ethnic groups in high delinquency areas were of northern European background (e.g., Irish and German), whereas eastern and southern Europeans (e.g., Italian and Polish) predominated by 1920. On the basis of these findings, it has been suggested that ethnicity may contribute more in the way of social disorganization and delinquency in its negative impact on neighborhood organization, particularly in terms of the amount of population turnover, ethnic heterogeneity, social cohesion, and integration.

Although the evidence weighs heavily against a finding that certain ethnic groups are prone to criminality, it has been argued that children of immigrants are more represented in crime statistics (as offenders and victims) when compared to their parents. Moreover, research pertaining to crime among the second-generation children of immigrants indicates that there is something about the process of acculturation that may be conducive to crime and delinquency—particularly, the development of street gangs. Crime among immigrants and ethnic minorities has been attributed to problems associated with forced assimilation into mainstream American culture and the subsequent breakdown of traditional cultural norms that usually serve to mediate any conflict experienced.

Research Directions

Given inconsistencies in findings and the lack of contemporary research, more studies are needed. A limitation, however, is that data which are more suitable to this type of exploration are not readily available. One of the complaints offered by researchers who have previously studied ethnic or immigrant populations in the United States is the failure of official crime data to include a general ethnicity distinction.

A major source for data pertaining to race and ethnicity is the decennial census. In 1997, the OMB modified the standards for the classification of federal data on ethnicity to include a minimum of two categories: "Hispanic or Latino" and "not Hispanic or Latino." This revision was incorporated into the 2000 decennial census as a question pertaining to identification of Hispanic ethnicity. Despite the changes made in the questionnaire to distinguish ethnicity from race, there were issues raised with respect to data quality for the Hispanic question. Concerns included the reasonableness of changes in population growth, response rates, response inconsistencies, and inaccuracies resulting from poor question wording and format.

The Census Bureau is addressing Hispanic data quality issues for the 2010 census. For instance, preliminary test results indicated that the inclusion of the word *origin* in question wording and the provision of detailed examples for an "Other Spanish, Hispanic, or Latino" category will improve reporting of more specific Hispanic ethnicity information. Given the complexities associated with the development of a composite measure of Hispanic ethnicity, however, there are additional philosophical issues to be considered. Whereas the Census Bureau has relied upon the principle of self-identification as the best approach for counting the Hispanic population, the primary issue has become one of balancing the need to understand the diversity of Hispanic groups versus a general trend among respondents who wish to self-identify in more general terms.

Despite any data limitations, numerous studies and reports have surfaced indicating discriminatory practices in arrest, sentencing, and incarceration—albeit in violation of both suggested and mandated policies. Whether disparities are related to discrimination or bias among criminal justice system actors or disproportionate offending by certain ethnic groups is subject to debate. Because of the complexity and controversy associated with the issues, interest in studying ethnic and racial disparities within the criminal justice system seems to rise and fall throughout different periods and developments. Given more recent policies designed to combat discretion among criminal justice actors (i.e., sentencing guidelines), and the call for studies that break through the Black–White dichotomy, there is a renewed interest in research.

Michele P. Bratina

See also Immigrants and Crime; Latina/o/s; Sentencing

Further Readings

Martinez, R., Nielsen, A. L., & Lee, M. T. (2003). Reconsidering the Marielito legacy: Race/ethnicity, nativity, and homicide motives. *Social Science Quarterly, 84,* 397–411.

Peterson, R. D., & Krivo, L. J. (2005). Macrostructural analyses of race, ethnicity, and violent crime: Recent lessons and new directions for research. *Annual Review of Sociology, 31,* 331–356.

Sellin, T. (1938). *Culture conflict and crime.* New York: Social Science Research Council.

Shaw, C. R., & McKay, H. D. (1942). *Juvenile delinquency in urban areas.* Chicago: University of Chicago Press.

ETHNORACIAL PRISON GHETTO

See Ghetto, Ethnoracial Prison

EUROPEAN AMERICANS

European Americans are defined as persons of European descent living in the United States. The term *European American* is often used synonymously with *White, Anglo,* or *Caucasian;* however, there are differences among these groups. Both *White* and *Caucasian* denote larger groups and include persons of non-European descent (currently those tracing their ancestry to some eastern areas of the former Soviet Union and historically those from the Middle Eastern countries and Asian Indians). *Anglo* is a more specific term, referring to those of English descent. Additionally, there are many "racial" minorities, such as Blacks from France and the United Kingdom, Asians from the Netherlands, and Middle Easterners from Germany. Upon immigration to the United States, these "racial" minorities become subsumed under the umbrella of European Americans.

Most European Americans trace their ancestry to three waves of immigration: (1) colonial stock (English, Scottish, Irish, Welsh, German, and Dutch) arriving in the United States prior to and within a few decades of the Revolutionary War; (2) first-wave immigrants (Irish, German Catholics, British, Dutch, and Scandinavians) arriving between 1820 and 1890; and (3) second-wave immigrants (southern and eastern Europeans, including Italians, Greeks, Poles, Slavs, Portuguese, and Jews) arriving between 1880 and the 1920s.

There have been some changes in the ethnic characteristics of the European American population. Data from the U.S. Census between 1980 and 2000 indicate that the percentage of Americans claiming European American descent (by specific ethnicity) has declined for virtually all groups, with the exception of Basques, Belgians, Greeks, Italians, Norwegians, Portuguese, Romanians, Serbians, Slovenians, Spaniards, and Ukrainians. The greatest increases were among Romanians, Slovenians, Ukrainians, and Basques. This trend is worth addressing, as historically Europeans who immigrated to the United States as a result of destabilized homelands (whether due to war, famine, or religious persecution) tended to exhibit, by the second generation, higher-than-average crime and delinquency rates.

Historical Overview of European American Crime

Although as a group, European Americans today are among the most privileged groups in the United States, with the lowest poverty rate and with levels of education, household income, and personal income second only to Asian Americans, historically this has not always been the case. Although British colonies, including those in North America, were used as a repository for criminals and other undesirable members of society, others immigrated in search of religious tolerance or economic opportunity. These early immigrants were, for the most part, Protestant, and no one European ethnic group appears to have been singled out for differential or discriminatory treatment. However, subsequent immigrants, including Irish, Jewish, and Italian immigrants, did experience stereotyping and discrimination.

Irish Americans

The potato famine of the mid-1800s and the subsequent Irish Diaspora resulted in the immigration of approximately 4 million Irish Catholics, most of whom settled in the Northeast. Irish immigrants, who were poor and Catholic, were the first European Americans to be considered a separate and inferior "race." As such, they were the targets of widespread discrimination (direct and indirect) as well as the victims of prejudice and negative stereotyping. Employment advertisements would include the phrase "No Irish Need Apply," and political cartoons of the day portrayed Irish Americans as apes.

Many Irish traditions, such as alcohol use and a tendency to settle disagreements with violence, ensured frequent and unpleasant contact with law enforcement and other criminal justice agencies. Police wagons used to transport offenders to the police station earned their nickname "paddy wagons" because the bulk of their occupants were Irish (Paddies).

While racism certainly played a part in the high rates of arrest and conviction for Irish Americans, discrimination contributed to higher rates of offending. Shut out of legitimate employment and consigned to substandard housing, Irish Americans turned to crime as a means of survival. The birth of the ethnic street gang in the United States can be traced to 1820s New York City and the Forty Thieves gang in Five Points. Originally formed as a social support club, members turned to organized criminal activity, ultimately establishing Tammany Hall as a political wing and controlling the Irish section of New York City.

By the early 1900s Irish street gangs had developed into what is now known as organized crime. Irish organized crime predominated in New York and in Chicago, peaking in the years leading up to Prohibition. Although Irish dominance of organized crime waned with the rise of Jewish and Italian organized crime during and after Prohibition, some Irish crime syndicates remained active through the latter part of the 20th century, including the Winter Hill Gang and the Charleston Mob in Boston, the Westies in New York City, and the K & A Mob in Philadelphia. Some Irish mobs (the North Side Gang) competed with Al Capone in Chicago during the Prohibition years, but Irish influence in Chicago's organized crime was negligible by the end of Prohibition.

Shortly after the American Civil War, Irish Americans began to assimilate. With the rise of the Tammany Hall political machine and Boss Tweed in the 1870s, Irish Americans began to gain social, political, and economic power. The Irish political machine opened new and legitimate opportunities to Irish Americans, and many members of this ethnic group moved into employment in factories, politics, and even the criminal justice system. This upward social and economic mobility prompted many Irish to move out of neighborhoods like Five Points, making way for the next wave of immigrants.

Jewish Americans

Jewish Americans, predominantly from Russia and eastern Europe, began immigrating to the United States en masse in the 1880s, escaping the pogroms and religious persecution of their homelands. Settling primarily in the Five Points area, Jewish Americans experienced negative stereotyping, prejudice, and discrimination. Ulysses S. Grant, during the Civil War, issued an order expelling Jews from some areas in some Southern states. Although this order was soon rescinded by President Lincoln, it illustrates the anti-Semitic attitudes of the time. In the early years of the 20th–century, Jews were excluded from social clubs, subject to enrollment quotas at colleges and universities, forbidden to purchase certain properties, and discriminated against in employment. Between 1880 and 1920 approximately 2 million eastern European and Russian Jews immigrated to the United States.

Although Jewish Americans may not have faced poverty as severe as that of Irish immigrants, they quickly filled the void left in major urban areas with the assimilation of Irish Americans. Criminal enterprises left vacant when Irish Americans assimilated and relocated were filled by other immigrants, mostly Jews and Italians. Young Jewish Americans were involved in traditional street gang activity, including stealing from vendor carts, pickpocketing, and other minor crimes. Adult and young adult Jewish Americans gravitated to traditional organized crime activities, including prostitution, extortion, and robbery.

Jewish American mobsters also branched into new enterprises. They were the first group to get involved in labor racketeering, providing muscle for both the union and management, beating, intimidating, and terrorizing "scabs." Through labor racketeering Jewish and Italian gangsters met and formed the nucleus of the mega crime syndicates of the Prohibition and post-Prohibition eras.

The Jewish mobs of the early 1900s were the first crime syndicates to make the transition from bands of organized street criminals to criminal enterprise, employing lawyers and accountants, and operating in a manner similar to legitimate business. Arnold Rothstein (nicknamed "The Brain") is generally credited with initiating this change. Rothstein was the mastermind behind the infamous 1919 World Series scandal, with the Chicago White Sox players accepting a payoff from Rothstein to throw the World Series. This incident heralded the entry of criminal enterprises into sports betting.

Jewish American organized crime reached its zenith during Prohibition through the end of World War II. Active in most major U.S. cities, including New York City, Philadelphia, Newark, Cleveland, Detroit, Minneapolis, and Los Angeles, Jewish mobsters, including Meyer Lansky and Bugsy Siegel, controlled illegal activities nationwide. Near the end of Prohibition (1931) Lansky and Siegel joined forces with the up-and-coming Lucky Luciano. The relationship among the three dated back to their teens, when Siegel ran afoul of Luciano when one of Luciano's prostitutes failed to charge Siegel for sex. Lansky, then an apprentice, intervened in the ensuing fight. The relationship among the three ultimately resulted in the creation of the murder for hire business, known as Murder, Inc.

Jewish American crime syndicates are also responsible for the creation, and more importantly marketing, of Las Vegas. All major casinos of the 1940s and 1950s were built with Jewish mobster money and supervised by Jewish American mobsters, most notably Bugsy Siegel.

The entry of Jewish Americans into organized crime was the result of social and geographical dislocation, poverty, and discrimination. By the end of World War II anti-Semitism had decreased, Jewish Americans (by now the third and fourth generations) had pursued and achieved legitimate opportunities, and Jewish Americans had moved out of the slums of large cities and into the suburbs. Intermarriage with Gentiles hastened assimilation, and by the 1960s Jewish Americans had gone from accounting for one sixth of all felony arrests in New York City to being stereotyped as one of the most law-abiding ethnic groups in the country. Currently, Russian and Israeli mobsters claiming Jewish descent have been active in the Northeast, engaging in real estate fraud, oil tax evasion scams, arms dealing, and narcotic (particularly Ecstasy) trafficking; however, many allegedly Jewish Russian gangsters claimed Jewish status to facilitate immigration to the United States. It is also interesting to note that the newest wave of Jewish mobsters, like Lansky before them, have formed alliances with Italian organized crime.

Italian Americans

Italians immigrated to the United States primarily between 1880 and 1920 and, like the Irish and Jews before them, were subjects of stereotyping, prejudice, and discrimination. In the late 1880s Italians were one of the ethnic groups most likely to be lynched, with 11 being killed by a lynch mob in New Orleans in 1891. Stereotyped as violent, criminal, and involved with the Mafia, Italian Americans were, like earlier ethnic minorities, discriminated against in employment and housing. Additionally, most Italian immigrants during this time period were rural, poorly educated, and poor farmers and peasants from southern Italy and Sicily. About one third of these immigrants intended to remain in the United States only for a brief period of time, and about one fourth ultimately returned to Italy; the remainder, however, either opted to remain in the United States or were prevented from returning because of World War I.

Settling in the slums of major cities such as New York and Philadelphia, some of the 4 million Italian immigrants to the United States, finding themselves shut out of legitimate employment and other opportunities, turned to crime. While Italian American youth were involved in street gangs, engaging in many of the same activities as their Irish and Jewish predecessors, Italian American adults came with a ready-made organized crime structure, "La Mano Nera" or The Black Hand, the precursor to the American Mafia. Early on, The Black Hand limited itself to extortion; however, as the Italian American population grew, Italian gangsters branched out into loan-sharking, murder, kidnapping, robbery, and commercialized vice (gambling, drugs, alcohol, and prostitution).

Prior to prostitution, Italian American organized crime was neither as well organized nor as extensive as Jewish American organized crime, operating less as organized crime and more as a street gang. One of the earliest Italian Americans to operate a truly organized crime syndicate was Paolo Antonio Vaccarelli, a former prize fighter who changed his name to Paul Kelly and offered his services to the Irish American mob and Tammany Hall. Kelly founded the Five Points gang, recruiting and mentoring many of Prohibition's most successful Jewish American and Italian American mobsters. By the time of Prohibition, Italian American mobsters, under the leadership of Al Capone, Lucky Luciano, and Salvatore Maranzano, consolidated their operations, becoming the dominant organized crime syndicate of the day.

The Italian American Mafia continued to thrive throughout World War II; the United States even brokered a deal with Lucky Luciano to use his influence with Sicilian Mafiosos to facilitate the Italian campaign. After the war Italian American organized crime moved in to control the unions (previously the territory of Jewish American organized crime). Other recent business ventures include pornography, numbers, sports betting, tax fraud, and stock manipulation schemes.

As with the Irish and Jewish immigrants to the United States, Italian Americans ultimately assimilated into American society. With assimilation came increased legitimate opportunities and a subsequent decline in both delinquent and criminal behavior. However, stereotyping of Italian Americans as gangster continues and is in fact exacerbated by the media, including books (*The Godfather*), television (*The Sopranos*) and movies (*Casino, Goodfellas, A Bronx Tale*). A study by the Response Analysis Corporation found that nearly three fourths of Americans believe that Italian Americans have a connection to the Mafia; the actual number of Mafia members, at any given time, is about 2,000.

Theoretical Perspectives on Crime by European Americans

Much of the early criminological research on race and crime focused on the delinquent and criminal behavior of European Americans, particularly on Irish, Jewish, and Italian immigrants. While the subjects in these studies were European American, some of the theories on which the earlier studies of European American crime were based are still used today to explain apparent higher-than-average rates of offending among non-European immigrants.

One of the more popular theories used to explain European organized crime during the mid-20th century was the alien conspiracy theory. Simply put, this "theory" suggests that organized crime in the United States had its start in the mid-1800s in Sicily and is centralized through a national commission that allocates territory and governs disputes. This model, popular with law enforcement and politicians at the time of the Kefauver hearings, implies that Italians and Italian Americans bear responsibility for bringing organized crime to the United States; however, there is limited evidence to support the idea that Italian American organized crime is truly centralized, and historically organized crime had existed in the United States (most notably the Irish American mobs) decades before the influx of Italian immigrants in the late 1800s.

Some sociological theories that can be applied to organized crime and European American criminality include anomie, social learning theory, and social disorganization theory.

Anomie theory attributes criminal behavior to an individual's method of coping with economic strain. Individuals find themselves shut out of traditional avenues of economic success and may adapt in a number of ways: innovation, ritualization, retreatism, and rebellion. The innovator, while still adopting culturally valued goals (the American dream) eschews socially approved means of goal attainment and instead engages in illicit or criminal activity to achieve the same goals to which mainstream society aspires.

Social learning theory states that criminal behavior, like all other behavior, is learned from our primary groups. In the case of criminal behavior, children (and adults, as learning is a life-long process) learn three things: (1) deviant, delinquent, or criminal norms and values; (2) how to engage in deviant, delinquent, or criminal behavior; and (3) the "vocabulary of motives" used to rationalize or justify one's behavior. Children living in neighborhoods with a strong criminal tradition are more likely to be exposed to, and more likely to adopt, criminal norms and values. Additionally, they will have the opportunity to learn the mechanics of criminal behavior. It is therefore assumed that these individuals not only will be willing to accept or approve of criminal behavior but also will have the necessary skills to engage in crime. If presented with a criminal opportunity, he or she will be more likely to engage in crime than someone who is less exposed to crime and deviance.

At a more macro level, social disorganization theory focuses on the conditions inherent in center city neighborhoods, such as the Five Points area of New York City. Historically, European immigrants have flocked to the inner city areas of major cities. Five Points and other urban slums offered not only inexpensive housing but a ready-made immigrant community offering friends, support, and familiarity. Inevitably, these neighborhoods were rundown, poor, and overcrowded. Faced with a rapid influx of immigrants, many speaking unfamiliar languages, the institutions in these communities (churches, schools, police, economic organizations) became overwhelmed and found themselves unable to function. Faced with impotent social agencies, unemployment, and disorganization, immigrants living in these communities turned to crime. However, rather than placing the onus for criminal behavior on the immigrant (as in anomie and social learning theory), social disorganization theory states it is the neighborhood, not the individual, that is deviant (deviant areas). With the breakdown of legitimate social institutions in areas like Five Points in New York City, deviance, delinquency, and criminality became the norm. Residents not engaged in crime came to be considered abnormal.

Of the three theories, social disorganization may offer the best explanation for European American crime; as each group assimilated and moved away from the inner city, crime and delinquency rates for the group dropped. However, as one group moved out, another group of immigrants moved in. Irish crime rates, particularly in New York City, were high in the early to late 1800s. As the Irish moved away from Five Points, Jewish immigrants moved in and subsequently experienced high crime and arrest rates. As Jewish Americans assimilated and moved out of the city, Italian immigrants moved into what is now known as Little Italy, with some of the first

and second generations becoming involved in street and organized crime. Again, as Italian Americans assimilated and moved to the suburbs, their crime and delinquency rates dropped; however, new immigrants, including new European immigrants have moved into these delinquent areas.

Current Trends in European American Crime: The Russian Mafia

The majority of European immigrants to the United States today are from eastern European and former Soviet bloc countries. Romanians living in the United States have been implicated in cybercrime (most notably phishing), and Armenians in grocery coupon fraud. However, the current successors to the Irish, Jewish, and Italian American crime syndicates are Russian mobsters, operating primarily out of the Brighton Beach area in Brooklyn but also out of Denver, Seattle, Cleveland, Minneapolis, Chicago, Dallas, Boston, Los Angeles, and Phoenix. While Russians immigrated to the United States in large numbers in the mid-1800s, the most recent wave began with the fall of the Soviet Union in 1991, followed by extreme poverty (between 40% and 50%) and political instability. About 250,000 Russians immigrated to the United States between 1991 and 1995, with approximately another 30,000 entering the country or remaining in the United States illegally.

The Soviet Union, by the time of its collapse, had a thriving black market and extensive crime networks. Like the Italian immigrants, some Russian émigrés may have brought criminal traditions with them to the United States. Many immigrants to the Brighton Beach area came from Odessa, a seaport on the Black Sea with a history of pirate activity and criminal subculture. Although there is limited evidence pointing to the existence of a nationwide Russian crime syndicate similar to the Italian Mafia in the mid-1900s, Russian gangsters have been involved in and arrested for extortion, counterfeiting, forgery, confidence schemes, drug trafficking, gasoline bootlegging, insurance and medical fraud, real estate scams, weapons trading (including nuclear), and money laundering. In 1999 U.S.-based Citibank was investigated as a participant in a Russian Mafia money laundering scheme.

Kenney and Finkenauer (1995) have likened the Russian Mafia to the Italian Mafia from a century ago. Clearly, there are similarities. Both groups came from politically unstable countries with histories of organized crime. Both the Italians and the Russians have been more open to criminal violence and more serious violence than many of their predecessors. Both have shown themselves open to emerging criminal opportunities (the Italians and bootlegging liquor, the Russians and cybercrime). Cultural and religious minorities, Italians and Russians settled in urban ethnic enclaves. Russian immigrants, however, were more likely to have come from urban areas and to have more education and more experience with law enforcement. (One Russian mobster, when asked if he feared the police in the United States, responded that he had already dealt with the KGB, what else could they do to him in America?) Still very much a mystery to law enforcement and scholars, the future of Russian American crime remains to be seen.

Regardless of the past, present, or future of European American criminal activity, the past 2 centuries have, through the experiences of the Irish, Jews, Italians, and Russians, illustrated the importance of not just race but also ethnicity (language, religion, and culture) in the rise of criminal behavior within an ethnic group. Political, social, and economic upheaval, coupled with poverty, overcrowding, prejudice, and discrimination, create a climate where crime and deviance are not only tolerated, they are rewarded.

Pamela Preston

See also Chicago School of Sociology; Critical Race Theory; Immigrants and Crime; Immigration Legislation; Immigration Policy; Victimization, White; White Crime

Further Readings

Abadinsky, H. (2006). *Organized crime*. Belmont, CA: Wadsworth.

Gabbidon, S. L., & Greene, H. T. (2005). *Race and crime*. Thousand Oaks, CA: Sage.

Hess, H. (1996). *Mafia & Mafiosi: Origin, power and myth*. New York: New York University Press.

Kenney, D. J., & Finckenauer, J. O. (1995). *Organized crime in America*. Belmont, CA: Wadsworth.

Kleinknecht, W. (1996). *The new ethnic mobs: The changing face of organized crime in America*. New York: The Free Press.

Lyman, M., & Potter, G. W. (1998). Organized crime and the drug trade. In *Drugs and society: Causes, concepts and control*. Cincinnati, OH: Anderson.

Lyman, M., & Potter, G. W. (2006). *Organized crime*. Upper Saddle River, NJ: Prentice Hall.

Mahan, S. (Ed.). (1998). *Beyond the Mafia: Organized crime in the Americas*. Thousand Oaks, CA: Sage.

EVIDENCE-BASED DELINQUENCY PREVENTION FOR MINORITY YOUTH

A number of general approaches and specific programs have been found to be effective in reducing delinquent behaviors among youth. The first studies conducted to these ends, however, largely relied on samples of White males, as did the study of crime in general. Criminologists are making progress in this respect, however, implementing violence- and delinquency-prevention programs in urban, ethnically diverse areas. More recently, scholars are investigating gender-specific programs, or those designed to meet the specific needs of youth of a particular gender, assuming that males and females have differing experiences of crime and its consequences. Some evidence also suggests that youth of different racial and ethnic backgrounds differ in their experiences of crime, though "race-specific programming" has yet to emerge as a unique field of criminological study. Programs have been developed specifically for youth of particular racial and ethnic backgrounds, to meet their specific needs in a culturally sensitive manner. Not all of these and other programs targeting youth of all races have been evaluated to determine their effect. It is important to examine the various evidence-based approaches currently used to deal with juvenile delinquency for evidence that they are effective when used with minority youth.

The Push for Evidence-Based Delinquency Prevention

In 1996, the U.S. Congress mandated the Attorney General to evaluate the effectiveness of crime-prevention strategies with independent analyses and scientifically rigorous methods. Evidence-based prevention approaches are those with "proven" effects, supported by a body of scientific research. The National Institute of Justice commissioned this congressionally mandated independent review, which was ultimately carried out by Lawrence Sherman and his colleagues at the University of Maryland. This broad review examined a wide range of crime-prevention strategies, from those based in the community, schools, and family to those utilized by police and correctional systems. These scholars found a variety of approaches to be effective, such as increasing police patrol of high-crime areas, incarcerating repeat offenders, arresting abusive partners in their homes, and providing therapeutic treatment for incarcerated substance abusers. More specific, effective treatment methods included family therapy, parenting training, home visitation for preschoolers, and school-based social competency training.

A number of other approaches were determined to be ineffective, including police follow-ups with abusive couples, neighborhood watch and community mobilization programs, outdoor wilderness programs and electronic monitoring for juvenile offenders, and school-based leisure and peer counseling programs. Sherman and colleagues also argued that the more widely used D.A.R.E., boot camp, and Scared Straight programs did not work.

At the same time, other university-affiliated and government-funded agencies developed their own initiatives to research "what works." The Office of Juvenile Justice and Delinquency Prevention funded the Blueprints for Violence Prevention initiative; the Department of Education funded the Safe, Disciplined, and Drug-Free Schools Panel; the Center for Substance Abuse Prevention funded the Strengthening America's Families project; and the Surgeon General also released a report. Though comprehensive in nature, these reports were still preliminary because they did not investigate how well the program worked with individuals and groups of different social backgrounds (gender, age, race/ethnicity, etc.). Nonetheless, a new era focusing on the development, implementation, and continued evaluation of evidence-based programs was born.

Determining What Works

An evidence-based delinquency-prevention program is one that has produced evidence that it can reduce delinquency or impact factors that put individuals at risk for delinquency. There are multiple levels of prevention, however, that must be considered. Primary prevention methods target the general population, preventing them from ever becoming involved in delinquent behaviors. Secondary prevention targets those determined to be at risk for future delinquency. Tertiary prevention focuses on those who have already committed crimes, treating them in order to prevent them from reoffending.

Risk and Protective Factors for Delinquency

Many different factors put an individual at risk of engaging in delinquent behavior. These risks present themselves in nearly every domain of social life. In the community, neighborhood disorganization; high rates of violence; poverty; and the high presence of firearms, gang activity, and drugs place individuals at risk. In schools and peer groups, individuals who are uncommitted to school, who experience academic failure, and who associate with delinquent peers are at higher risk. Antisocial attitudes and behaviors at the individual level, as well as conflict, lack of supervision, and poor management and parenting practices at the family level also increase risk.

Similarly, there are factors that appear to "protect" an individual from developing delinquent behaviors. Some protective factors, such as commitment to school, appropriate parental supervision, good parenting practices, and association with nondelinquent peers, appear to be the opposite of risk factors. Others, including positive future orientation, intolerant attitudes toward deviance, attachment to parents, and self-esteem, are argued to act independently because they have been found to exert their own impact on outcomes related to delinquency. Risk and protection may be more clearly understood as working with and also against one another, changing over time and across contexts. For example, a child may experience a persistent lack of supervision while simultaneously feeling strongly attached to parents for other reasons. Changes in one or both of these factors over time may change an individual's overall risk level.

Regardless of this debate, prevention programs must consider these factors and, when appropriate, incorporate into their curriculum specific methods to treat them. Failure to understand the factors that lead to delinquency, or that protect one from becoming involved in it, will complicate attempts to prevent and treat it at any level.

Criteria for Determining What Works

An evidence-based program has demonstrated it works through experimental evaluation and statistical analysis. Experimental evaluations are those that compare a group of youth who receive a program (the "treatment group") to a group of youth who receive no treatment ("control group") or an alternative treatment ("comparison group"). These two groups are compared both before and after the program is implemented, and statistical tests examine differences between groups over time. Ideally, participants will be randomly assigned to groups but, when random assignment is not used, it is important that the two groups are "matched" or statistically similar before the program is delivered. This is the best way to ensure that the program itself, rather than outside factors, is responsible for the changes seen over time. Evidence-based approaches have multiple evaluations of this nature, all of which support the notion that they are effective in reducing delinquency.

Disseminating Information on What Works

Today, some of the research agencies mentioned earlier in this entry continue to review and evaluate youth programs to identify "what works." Several, including the Blueprints for Violence Prevention program and the Substance Abuse and Mental Health Services Administration, offer public access to their program databases. Each of these and other "information houses" created different criteria and rating systems; some are more rigorously defined than others. There are consistencies across these various listings, though, regardless of the specific methods used to determine how well the programs work. In fact, the Blueprints program created a cross-listing of all programs rated by twelve different agencies.

Delinquency Prevention for Minority Youth: What Works

Thirty of 299 listed programs were rated as "effective" or "promising" by five or more of the twelve agencies. Seven evaluated program effectiveness in studies with largely Caucasian youth. The remainder delivered program services to youth of multiple ethnic groups, four with samples consisting almost entirely of African American and/or Hispanic youth. One of these four programs, Brief Strategic Family Therapy, impacted delinquency outcomes, reducing behavioral and emotional problems and marijuana use across several different samples of Latina/o youth.

Evaluations of these, and hundreds of other programs, are readily available, as they are published as articles, book chapters, or technical reports. Though the information houses referred to earlier often provide summaries of these program evaluations through their websites, many summaries do not report effects by race. Nine of the twelve programs mentioned, however, conducted race-specific analyses of program effects, and seven of these impacted delinquency outcomes. Participation in Big Brothers, Big Sisters of America delayed the onset of drug use among non-Caucasian youth and alcohol use among non-Caucasian females. Minority participants in Project Northland experienced some of the strongest effects on reduced alcohol, tobacco, and marijuana use. The Adolescent Transitions Program, CASASTART (the Striving Together to Achieve Rewarding Tomorrows program from Columbia University's Center on Addiction and Substance Abuse), Life Skills Training, the Midwestern Prevention Project, and Multisystemic Therapy all worked equally well in reducing substance use for youth of all ethnicities. Multisystemic therapy also reduced the frequency and seriousness of recidivism among participating youth, regardless of ethnicity, and CASASTART reduced violent crime and, for Hispanic youth relative to African American youth, the use and sale of drugs.

Multiple programs have been created specifically for use with minorities. Sometimes referred to as rites of passage or culturally specific programs, they build upon culturally specific values and norms, but many have yet to prove their effects. In fact, some rites-of-passage programs are outdoor-based and, as discussed previously, scholars have questioned or rejected the impact of wilderness programs for use with delinquent youth.

The Aban Aya Youth Project and the Strong African American Families Program, however, show promise. Both are specifically designed for African Americans, are informed by Afrocentric theories, and incorporate African American cultural values into their curriculum. Aban Aya has been shown to reduce violence, school delinquency, sexual behavior, and substance use, but only among boys. The Strong African American Families program has demonstrated positive impacts on youth alcohol use.

Project FLAVOR is a school-based, primary-level, smoking-prevention program designed for implementation in multicultural settings. Evaluations reveal reduced tobacco smoking after one program year among Hispanic boys and similar reductions for all Hispanic youth when implemented in schools with at least 40% Hispanic in population. The program proved ineffective for Asian Americans, however.

The Bicultural Competence Skills Program is a drug-prevention program adapted for use with Native Americans from the Life Skills Training Program. Evaluations show long-term reductions in the use of smokeless tobacco, alcohol, and marijuana, about 3 years after participation.

Though these programs do not appear on rating lists of agencies that conducted comprehensive program reviews in recent years, it is not necessarily due to flaws in methodological designs. All but the Strong African American Families program, now a Blueprints "Promising" program, randomized at the school level. Overall, the studies retained a good number of original participants over time, and groups were largely equivalent before the study period began. The program effects are not replicated and have not been tested for long-term sustainability, however. Some were developed and evaluated after agency reviews had been conducted.

In conclusion, the push for evidence-based programs has produced a wealth of knowledge as to "what works" in preventing delinquency. Some proven approaches appear to work equally well for youth of different ethnicities, some produce specific effects for Hispanic and/or African American youth, and some are designed just for youth of specific ethnic backgrounds. Relatively few programs, specifically those that target minority youth, have been evaluated with strong research designs, but scholars are working to build evidence that is scientifically sound, examining long-term and race-specific effects and conducting replications of past work. Overall, the "what works" field will benefit from continued research and development of programs that are specifically beneficial for children and families of minority racial and ethnic groups.

Allison J. Foley

See also Center for the Study and Prevention of Violence; Culturally Specific Delinquency Programs; Delinquency Prevention; Ethnicity; Juvenile Crime; Mentoring Programs

Further Readings

Brody, G. H., Murry, V. M., Kogan, S. M., Gerrard, M., Gibbons, F. X., Molgaard, V., et al. (2006). The Strong African American Families Program: A cluster-randomized prevention trial of long-term effects and a mediational model. *Journal of Consulting and Clinical Psychology, 74,* 356–366.

Sherman, L. W., Gottfredson, S., MacKenzie, D., Eck, J., Reuter, P., & Bushway, S. (1997). *Preventing crime: What works, what doesn't, what's promising.* Washington, DC: U.S. Department of Justice, Office of Justice Programs, National Institute of Justice.

U.S. Surgeon General. (2001). *Youth violence: A report of the Surgeon General.* Retrieved from http://www.surgeongeneral.gov/library/youthviolence

Websites

Center for the Study and Prevention of Violence, program matrix: http://www.colorado.edu/cspv/blueprints/matrix.html

Office of Juvenile Justice and Delinquency Prevention (OJJDP) model programs guide: http://www.dsgonline.com/mpg2.5/mpg_index.htm

FAITH-BASED INITIATIVES AND DELINQUENCY

Working in collaboration with federal, state, and local criminal justice agencies, faith-based community organizations have played a significant role in gaining and maintaining public trust, decreasing crime, and fostering neighborhood development. Faith-based initiatives that focus on delinquents are important in the study of race and crime because of the differential treatment and disproportionate contact and confinement of minority youth in juvenile justice. Faith-based initiatives can assist in primary, secondary, and tertiary delinquency prevention. This entry describes the rationale for faith-based initiatives, examples of such initiatives, and the role of community with respect to these programs.

The most important link between faith-based organizations and crime has to do with the location of those organizations in communities where crime prevails. In such high-crime, low-income communities, churches continue to have a significant presence. Independent of other factors, church-going individuals from high-poverty neighborhoods may have a greater chance to escape crime and other social ills by the guidance offered in faith-based programs that provide services such as mentoring, mental health counseling, job readiness training, employment opportunities, self-esteem building, parent support groups, and parent readiness classes for teen parents. Often a faith-based organization can help change people's lives

and motivate them to rise to new levels of caring for their neighbors. Faith-based organizations located in communities with high levels of delinquency provide an opportunity to engage youth in positive activities.

A basic tenet of faith-based initiatives is that a delinquent individual's association with a religious institution (church, mosque, synagogue, or other house of worship) can contribute to his or her success. Adolescents who participate in extracurricular activities have an advantage not only because those activities divert them from delinquency but also because such programs enable youth to develop positive relationships with the community. Faith-based initiatives give participants the opportunity to acquire skills and attributes that help them succeed. The activities that are associated with faith-based initiatives expose the delinquent individuals to social contacts that can serve as positive role models outside of the original family associations. The development of such contacts gives the delinquent a framework of positive activities that may reduce potential risky behaviors. The personal attention that participants receive also contributes to the reduction of delinquency.

Current discussions on church–state relations represent a new chapter in the living history of faith-based initiatives that seek to reduce crime. As a result of federal legislation, funding for faith-based initiatives has been greatly expanded over the past decade. "Charitable choice" provisions in the 1996 Welfare Reform Act identified several types of social service programming for which religious organizations could receive federal funding. The scope of such programs was further expanded during the George W. Bush administration and now includes agencies in the U.S. Department of Justice such as the Office of Juvenile Justice and Delinquency Prevention. Although some critics are concerned that the legislation violates First Amendment church–state provisions, a number of states and cities have also adopted their own faith-based initiatives.

Faith-Based Initiatives: Mentoring

Clergy using faith-based initiatives have served as mentors or have become key players in mentoring programs aimed at addressing delinquency in their communities. The goals of such mentoring programs range from identifying positive role models to recruiting and training clergy to serve as volunteers.

The use of mentors is a key component of personalized services for individuals who are at risk or maintain a self-destructive lifestyle. Faith-based organizations have used individuals as mentors to counter any socially destructive lifestyles within the community. Mentors, who are raised in the same community or neighborhood, understand how the community can be a positive force in the lives of those who are delinquents. Faith-based initiatives have always used mentors as the bridge between the community and delinquent individuals.

Examples of Faith-Based Initiatives

In Baltimore, an after-school tutoring program is run by a Christian community group called The Door. Although The Door has no direct church affiliation, it is intended to bring together those whose faith motivates them to help others. The Door helps bring children whose reading and math skills are below grade level up to standards. Federal funding has enabled The Door to upgrade their center, enlist certified teachers, buy up-to-date computer equipment, and administer standardized tests to measure progress of students reading below grade level.

Another example of a faith-based preventive program is the Youth and Congregations in Partnership program. Established in 1997, this program in Brooklyn, New York, matches teenage offenders with mentors from local religious organizations, with the aim of reducing juvenile and adult recidivism.

The programs mentioned in the previous two paragraphs provide safe haven for youth from high-risk communities and offer positive activities to help stem delinquency.

Faith-Based Initiatives and the Community: The Holistic Approach

The challenge for faith-based initiatives is to create public services that build on the traditions of church–community relations while preserving the unique religious character within the congregations. Faith-based initiatives have deep roots in serving the community needs. This belief in a communal bond with church and community is used in faith-based initiatives to deliver a variety of services to address delinquency while still maintaining religious undertones.

The ability of faith-based initiatives to use secular relationships is a unique aspect of a holistic approach to intervention with delinquent youth. A holistic approach is concerned with youth development as well as factors related to the family, school, and neighborhood. The reality of treating behavioral problems associated with delinquency emphasizes the importance of developing holistic treatment for such delinquencies as gang violence, substance abuse, and teen truancy. The services that are provided through these programs must be diverse to deal with the multicultural diversity within the delinquent population. The unique holistic approach of partnerships between faith-based initiatives partnerships and funding resources addresses the economic limitations encountered with past community initiatives. Faith-based organizations have tremendous advantages over the direct benefits by the federal or state government. The fact that they are closer to the problem allows them to better tailor solutions to those they serve. Such programs enable clergy and other faith-based leaders to address the special needs of disadvantaged youth.

Faith-based initiatives seek to elicit the support of the community in their efforts to strengthen the implementation and sustainability of delinquency programs. The strong ties between the community and the church help faith-based initiatives capitalize on spirituality as a resilience factor. The focus of the faith-based initiatives as they relate to delinquency is the reintegration of the delinquent youth back into the community. Usually this integration is accomplished through help from community leaders, local businesses, family members, and educators. Long-term collaborative efforts are important to the long-term effectiveness of faith-based initiatives.

Many faith-based organizations function as the central force that binds the community together. Churches, mosques, and other spiritual centers frequently become even more important in the lives of those who seek solutions to delinquency in the community. In a faith environment, the doctrine of compassion and service to the community has long been a principle of spiritual leadership.

In many troubled communities, clergy are often viewed as leaders who are called upon in the community to represent the community voice. For example, Martin Luther King, Jr., and other clergy were the driving force behind the voice of the civil rights movement. Faith-based initiatives are a means by which clergy in communities faced with problems related to delinquency can have a rallying effect on the lives within their own communities.

Faced with a national crisis of delinquency, with gang violence, truancy, and substance abuse, faith-based organizations can and do work in communities of crisis. Many communities use churches as their starting point to help resolve community issues. In the future, identifying and funding delinquency programs that work might lead to faith organizations and the initiatives playing a greater role in preventing and controlling delinquency.

Gilton Christopher Grange

See also Delinquency Prevention; Mentoring Programs; Youth Gangs, Prevention of

Further Readings

Black, A. E., Koopman, D. L., & Ryden, D. K. (2004). *Of little faith: The politics of George W. Bush's faith-based initiatives.* Washington, DC: Georgetown University Press.

Websites

Center for Faith-Based and Community Initiatives, Department of Health and Human Services: http://www.hhs.gov/fbci

The Door: http://www.thedoorinc.org
Faith-Based and Community Initiatives, Office of Juvenile Justice and Delinquency Programs, U.S. Department of Justice: http://ojjdp.ncjrs.gov/fbci/
Youth and Congregations in Partnership: http://www.brooklynda.org/YCP/YCP.htm

FAITH-BASED INITIATIVES AND PRISONS

Faith-based initiatives operate in federal and state prisons across the United States. This entry describes faith-based prison initiatives and discusses key issues surrounding these programs. A summary of Kairos Prison Ministry, Horizon Communities, and Prison Fellowship is provided, as these programs operate nationwide in the U.S. prison system. Most programs are Christian centered, and religions such as Islam, Judaism, Buddhism, and other non-Christian faiths are often neglected in faith-based prison programs. This issue of neglect is addressed along with suggestions for future research.

Prison Statistics

According to the Bureau of Justice Statistics there are over 2.2 million prisoners held in federal or state prisons or local jails. In 2006 the Bureau of Justice Statistics estimated the overall incarceration rate per 100,000 U.S. residents for each state and federal prison system. These statistics indicated that 4.8% of Black men were in prison or jail compared to 1.9% of Hispanic men and 0.7% of White men. Blacks are the most disproportionately represented minority group in the U.S. prison population, as they currently make up 12.3% of the U.S. population compared to Whites, who comprise 69% of the U.S. population, according to the U.S. Census Bureau. Considering their disproportionate representation, Black inmates have much to gain from faith-based prison initiatives. Unfortunately, their religious needs have often gone unmet.

Participating Agencies

The U.S. Department of Justice's National Institute of Correction Information Center conducted a survey in 2005 in which they contacted all departments of correction in 50 states and the Federal Bureau of Prisons for information on residential, faith-based programs for inmates. To be considered, programs had to be separately housed, residential inmate programs that utilize a faith-based approach. Of the 51 agencies surveyed, 21 (41%) operate or are developing at least one residential, faith-based program. Two agencies are currently developing programs, and faith-based programs are being added or expanded in at least 10 agencies of those surveyed. The Florida Department of Corrections represents one of the most unique faith-based prison initiatives in that it is currently operating three separate faith-and-character-based institutions: Lawtey Correctional Institute, Wakulla Correctional Institute, and Hillsborough Correctional Institute, which is designated specifically for female inmates.

Policy Issues

Religion has played an important role in the historical development of the U.S. penal system, and in recent years several factors have brought to light the issue of faith-based initiatives in prisons. In 1996 the U.S. Congress passed the Personal Responsibility and Work Opportunity Reconciliation Act. Contained in this legislation was the Charitable Choice requirement, which requires states to contract with faith-based social service organizations in the same manner as they contract with other nonprofit organizations. This was an important step because it allows faith-based organizations to compete for federal grant money in providing social services. It has also played a major role in allowing religious organizations to provide services to correctional institutions. At the same time it raises issues regarding the separation of church and state as decreed in the U.S. Constitution, which is currently being debated by many religious groups and constitutional rights organizations, such as the American Civil Liberties Union.

In 2001 Congress passed the Religious Land Use and Institutional Persons Act. This legislation greatly strengthens the constitutional right of inmates to practice their religion in prison. This law was challenged and later upheld by the U.S. Supreme Court in 2006. In addition, President George W. Bush created the White House Office of Faith-Based and Community Initiatives in 2001, which provided further support for faith-based organizations in providing social support services.

Faith-Based Prison Initiatives

Kairos Prison Ministry

Kairos Prison Ministry is the first faith-based prison initiative to operate in the U.S. correctional system. Kairos held its first weekend ministry program, Kairos Weekend, at Union Correctional Institution in Raiford, Florida, in 1976. Kairos Prison Ministry is a Christian organization that is led by volunteers who represent the Christian faith and present a Christian perspective to inmates. Kairos Prison Ministry is also ecumenical in that its many volunteers come from different Christian denominations, which allows volunteers to minister the core Christian principles to inmates. Although most Kairos volunteers are lay people, clergy also play an important role in this prison ministry. The main mission of Kairos Prison Ministry is to minister to incarcerated individuals, their families, and those who work with them.

Kairos Prison Ministry has three core programs that are provided to offenders and their families. One is the Kairos Weekend program for incarcerated men and women offenders. This 3-day program acts as a short course in Christianity and is presented by Kairos volunteers and clergy from the local faith community in conjunction with the prison chaplain. Kairos Weekend is an intensive program that provides 40 hours of programming, such as talks, meditations, and events. After the Kairos Weekend program is over, a follow-up program is provided for its participants; this program is called the Fourth Day. The Fourth Day is symbolic in meaning because it refers to the rest of the participants' lives. Program participants meet in small reunion groups where they can continue to deepen their fellowship and faith through prayer.

Kairos Prison Ministry also offers a program for spouses, parents, and other relatives of prisoners called Kairos Outside, which began in 1991. This program is designed as a 2-day retreat, which is led by Kairos volunteers, for family members who have a loved one in prison. Kairos Outside's goal is to provide spiritual healing to the families of incarcerated offenders. Kairos Outside allows program participants to share their personal experiences of having a loved one in prison and gain strength from a Christian community.

The third program that Kairos Prison Ministry offers is Kairos Torch. First implemented in 1997, Kairos Torch is aimed at youthful offenders between the ages of 18 and 25. Kairos Torch begins with a weekend retreat that is held inside the prison. This retreat centers on providing unconditional love and acceptance to these young participants. One of the main goals of Kairos Torch is to encourage young men and women to share their life journey through participation in a long-term mentoring process with Kairos volunteers.

Kairos Prison Ministry has been providing faith-based prison programming for over 30 years in the United States. Currently, Kairos Prison Ministry operates in 270 prisons in 33 states as well as internationally in England, Australia, South Africa, Costa Rica, and Canada. Since its inception in 1976, over 170,000 men and women offenders have participated in Kairos faith-based prison programs. The number of Kairos volunteers totals over 20,000 each year. Kairos Outside operates in 19 states and internationally in Canada, England, Australia, and South Africa, totaling over 35 programs worldwide. Kairos Torch is currently operational in 10 locations across the United States. In 2006 Kairos Prison Ministry held 618 weekend programs in 309 ministry locations, including 502 Kairos Weekends, 80 Kairos Outside Weekends, and 36 Kairos Torch Weekends.

Horizon Communities

Horizon Communities is a nonprofit organization that was founded to provide faith- and character-based residential programs in prisons. Horizon Communities is an outgrowth of Kairos Ministry and is now considered a separate, multi-faith-based prison initiative. The first Horizon Community was established in 1999 at Tomoka Correctional Institution in conjunction with the Florida Department of Corrections. Currently, there are Horizon Communities active in five locations and four states. Horizon's mission is to prepare prisoners to live responsibly with others. Horizon also focuses on the successful reentry of prisoners to life outside of prison by providing

time and opportunity for prisoners to practice new attitudes and behaviors.

The Horizon program consists of building respect for self and others and establishing a new link between the faith community and correctional institution for the rehabilitation of offenders. The Horizon program begins by holding a 2-day community event for participants. Volunteers play an important role as facilitators and mentors to the inmates throughout the program. Each Horizon program lasts for 12 months and has about 60 participants per class.

Horizon Communities has six core components that are provided during the completion of the program. These consist of individual weekly mentoring with volunteers; Journey, which is a 5-month small study group that focuses on manhood and fatherhood; Quest, a 7-month, volunteer-led, weekly small group that addresses the issues of anger, conflict resolution, relationships, and communication skills; Family Relations, which requires participants to write weekly letters to children and or family members; Transition Planning, a program that provides services to participants to increase their employability skills and successful reentry into the community; and Service to Others, which requires participants to perform some type of service to inmates who are disadvantaged in the correctional institution. Horizon Communities also encourages participation in faith-specific studies, which are available to all program participants. Participation in Kairos Outside is also encouraged for family members of incarcerated participants as a support system throughout the program.

Prison Fellowship

Prison Fellowship was founded in 1976 by Charles Colson, an ex-inmate who was imprisoned as a result of his involvement in President Richard Nixon's Watergate scandal. Colson, a born-again Christian, founded Prison Fellowship in collaboration with churches of all faiths and denominations. Prison Fellowship has become the world's largest outreach to prisoners, ex-prisoners, crime victims, and their families. Prison Fellowship has over 40,000 prison ministry volunteers and operates in over 100 countries worldwide. The goal of Prison Fellowship is for prisoners to become born again through Jesus Christ and to grow as faithful disciples of Christ. The prison chaplains work directly with prison ministry volunteers to provide programming to inmates such as Bible studies, seminars, and special events.

One of the main programs of Prison Fellowship is the InnerChange Freedom Initiative, which began in 1997 in Texas in collaboration with the Texas Department of Criminal Justice. The InnerChange Freedom Initiative is a Christ-centered, faith-based prison program that focuses on the successful reentry of inmates back into the community as faithful servants of Christ. The main goal of the InnerChange Freedom Initiative is to create and maintain a prison environment that encourages respect for God and others and fosters the spiritual and moral transformation of prisoners. Prisoners take part in this program 18 to 24 months prior to their release date.

The InnerChange Freedom Initiative is divided into three phases that are completed by program participants. Phase 1 is heavily centered on the prisoners' spiritual transformation, with special attention given to education, work, and support to build a new foundation for a productive life. Phase 2 of the program tests the inmates' value system in real-life settings and prepares them for life after prison. Inmates spend much of their time working in off-site prison work programs or participating in the reentry portion of the program. Phase 3 consists of inmates being transferred to halfway houses or work-release programs to continue their reentry process. An aftercare ministry is provided to inmates once they have been released, which provides assistance for the many obstacles that ex-inmates face as they begin their new, Christ-centered life in the community.

A preliminary evaluation of the InnerChange Freedom Initiative was conducted by Byron R. Johnson and the late David B. Larson in conjunction with the Texas Department of Criminal Justice and Prison Fellowship. While this is a preliminary evaluation and its findings should be treated with caution, it does provide information regarding the types of prisoners who are participating in faith-based prison programs. The study participants ($N = 177$) were 67% Black, 16% Hispanic, and 18% White. The majority of study participants (52%) were less than 35 years of age. Offense type indicated that 50% of participants were drug offenders, 36% were property offenders, and 12% were violent offenders. Program completion rates by race include 37% of Blacks, 61% of Hispanics, and 45% of Whites. It should also be noted that of the initial 177 study participants, a substantial number of inmates were paroled early ($n = 51$), quit ($n = 24$) or were removed ($n = 19$) from the program for disciplinary reasons.

Meeting the Needs of African American Inmates

A large number of African Americans in prison are Muslim and practice the Islamic faith. In 2000 there were approximately 350,000 Muslims in federal and state prisons, with an estimated 30,000 to 40,000 added each year. It took several court cases in the 1960s, 1970s, and 1980s before Islam was officially recognized as a legitimate religion in the prison system. Though Muslims now have the right to freely practice their religious faith in prison, faith-based prison programs generally do not address the needs of non-Christian religions such as Islam. Some programs are considered multifaith, but the majority of faith-based prison programs are Christian oriented and Christ centered. Even more important than providing faith-based prison programs to rehabilitate offenders is addressing the specific religious needs of inmates. This will not only benefit the inmates who participate in faith-based programs, but it should also increase the completion rates of these programs and provide for a more successful reentry back into the community.

Jamie L. Weldon

See also Faith-Based Initiatives and Delinquency

Further Readings

Ammar, N. H., Weaver, R. R., & Saxon, S. (2004). Muslims in prison: A case study from Ohio state prisons. *International Journal of Offender Therapy & Comparative Criminology, 48*(4), 414–428.

Burnside, J., Loucks, N., Adler, J. R., & Rose, G. (2005). *My brother's keeper.* Portland, OR: Willan.

Camp, S. D., Klein-Saffran, J., Kwon, O. K., Daggett, D. M., & Joseph, V. (2006). An exploration into a faith-based prison program. *Criminology & Public Policy, 5*(3), 529–550.

Clear, T. R., Hardyman, P. L., Stout, B., Lucken, K., & Dammer, H. R. (2000). The value of religion in prison. *Journal of Contemporary Criminal Justice, 16*(1), 53–74.

Jang, S. J., & Johnson, B. R. (2004). Explaining religious effects on distress among African Americans. *Journal for the Scientific Study of Religion, 43*(2), 239–260.

Johnson, B. R. (2004). Religious programs and recidivism among former inmates in prison fellowship programs: A long-term follow-up study. *Justice Quarterly, 21*(2), 329–354.

Kennedy, S. S. (2003). Redemption or rehabilitation? Charitable choice and criminal justice. *Criminal Justice Policy Review, 14*(2), 214–228.

Kerley, K. R., Matthews, T. L., & Schulz, J. T. (2005). Participation in Operation Starting Line, experience of negative emotions, and incidence of negative behaviors. *International Journal of Offender Therapy and Comparative Criminology, 49*(4), 410–426.

McDaniel, C., Davis, D. H., & Neff, S. A. (2005). Charitable choice and prison ministries: Constitutional and institutional challenges to rehabilitating the American penal system. *Criminal Justice Policy Review, 16*(2), 164–189.

FAMILY AND DELINQUENCY

Families are generally considered to be the primary agent of socialization. The impact of family on delinquency (defined here as a juvenile's violation of the penal code) has been theorized about and investigated for decades, across academic disciplines, and in diverse samples. As is the case with crime, minorities are often shown to be overrepresented in juvenile delinquency. Difference in family dynamics and structures is one of a number of potential explanations for this finding and, as such, has been heavily investigated. This entry summarizes theory, research, and findings regarding prevention and intervention.

Theories

There are numerous theories that focus on families as central to explaining crime. Control theories hold that delinquency results from inadequate controls instilled in a person by society. Families play a vital role in instilling values and norms

acceptable by the social order. Travis Hirschi's social control theory explains the importance of establishing secure connections to conventional social institutions to decrease delinquency. Self-control theory, developed by Michael Gottfredson and Hirschi, contends that primary caregivers must instill adequate amounts of self-control in children prior to a given developmental age because lack of self-control leads to delinquency. Another class of theories consists of learning theories, which argue that delinquency is learned in interactions with close others, like family members, similar to how other learning occurs. In addition to these direct connections, families are indirectly implicated in macro-level theories that examine the neighborhood and economic strain as causes of delinquency. For youth, these important factors are generally determined by familial circumstance.

Research

Criminal Family

Crime generally runs in families. Studies have shown that a large percentage of arrested family members come from a small percentage of families. In addition, parental criminality is one of the strongest and most consistent predictors of a child's delinquency. Juvenile delinquency is also predicted by the criminality of other family members, including siblings, aunts, uncles, and grandparents. The impact of familial criminality on youth is stronger within sex than across sex. In other words, father criminality has a larger impact on sons than daughters (and vice versa).

There are numerous potential explanations for why family has such a strong impact, and many of them have been supported by research. There is research to support (a) a genetic component to criminality, (b) intergenerational transfer of criminal ideology and learning, (c) antisocial parents producing children who are attracted to antisocial partners, (d) familial criminality resulting from conditions of the environment, and (e) justice system bias against criminal families.

Parenting

One possible explanation for the impact of parental criminality on children's delinquency is child rearing. Diana Baumrind theorized the importance of parenting styles (i.e., authoritative, authoritarian, neglecting/rejecting, or permissive) on children's behavior. Authoritative parenting is significantly related to a decrease in delinquency, and authoritarian parenting has been found to increase delinquency. However, there is good reason to believe the impact of parenting style is racially and culturally specific. Parenting styles that may be classified by Caucasian raters as authoritarian do not necessarily have the same impact on children of other racial and ethnic groups. In Chinese American families, authoritarian parenting has been shown to lead to better school outcomes, whereas it leads to poorer school outcomes for European American students. Similarly, authoritarian parenting is related to positive outcomes in African American children and is often interpreted by the child as parental warmth and concern.

Of factors related to child rearing, supervision/ monitoring is the strongest correlate of later delinquency and is the most replicated finding. The quality, not the quantity, of supervision has been found to be important. If a youth is adequately supervised, there is little to no impact of having a working mother.

Another important child rearing factor is the type of discipline used. Harsh or erratic/inconsistent discipline significantly impacts a child's delinquency. Research has made a distinction between light physical punishments (e.g., spanking) and physical abuse. The use of light physical punishments during developmentally appropriate times, and in conjunction with warm and supportive parenting, has not been shown to lead to later delinquency.

There are racial and cultural differences related to the effect of physical punishment on youth. Physical punishment is more strongly related to antisocial and delinquent behavior in Caucasian children than in African American children. Context also matters: Exerting more control on children, like confining them to their homes, escorting them from place to place, or sending them to live away from home, is effective in reducing delinquency in high-risk areas, but potentially harmful in low-risk areas. This may be a partial explanation for why African American children, who are more likely to live in disadvantaged neighborhoods, are more receptive to more restrictive disciplinary measures.

Another parenting factor that has been shown to be important is a parent's emotional relationship with the child. A warm relationship can buffer other negative life events like divorce. Also, active parent involvement can decrease delinquent behavior.

Exposure to Violence, Abuse, or Neglect

In contrast to studies on the impact of light physical punishments, most studies find a link between exposure to violence or being the victim of abuse (physical or sexual) and later offending. Childhood exposure to marital violence has been significantly associated with engaging in marital violence as an adult, but the quality of parenting is a more important factor.

An estimated 30% of abused parents abuse their children—a rate 15 times higher than non-abused parents. Abused mothers who did not abuse their children appear to have had nonabusive adults in their childhood or had stable romantic partners in adulthood. Women who were physically abused during childhood are also more likely to experience domestic violence as adults.

In addition, being a victim of sexual abuse as a child is linked to perpetration of sexual offenses later. One study found that 42% of sexual abusers had been sexually abused. Another study found that daughters of women who were sexually abused as children were 12 times more likely to be sexually abused (even if the mother did not participate in the abuse). Children that were sexually abused are at a greater likelihood for delinquency, suicidal ideation, and prostitution.

Family Structure

The structure of the family matters. Children of divorce have an increased rate of delinquency from children of two-parent homes. Family breakup has been linked to increased conflict, weakened attachment to parents, and more vulnerability to peer pressure and delinquency. The effect of divorce on children has been shown to be worse than the loss of a parent due to death. The impact of divorce is likely mediated by conflict in the home, less effective parenting, or increased stress caused by the challenge of single parenting. High-conflict but "intact" homes produce more delinquency than does divorce, but both scenarios produce more delinquency than low-conflict, intact homes. There are two important notes regarding these findings: First, results regarding the impact of divorce have been stronger in predicting minor forms of delinquency than more serious offenses. Second, there is a stronger link between official data and broken homes than self-report data, suggesting a bias by police and court officials. Studies have even shown that the absence of parents has a greater impact on juvenile justice officials' decisions than does the actual behavior of the child.

Single motherhood is predictive of delinquency in youth, but other factors likely mediate the relationship. There is support for the idea that single mothers suffer extreme stress due to economic disadvantage. About 60% of female-headed households live below the poverty line, and African American women are overrepresented. Extreme stress then leads to ineffective parenting, which leads to delinquency. In support of these findings, studies have shown that, as child support increases, problem behavior in children decreases. There is no evidence that the frequency of paternal contact is a good predictor of delinquency, but the type of parenting of the nonresidential father is related to the externalizing behaviors of daughters and sons.

As the divorce rate has increased, so has the rate of remarriage and the creation of "blended families." Hispanic and African American children are more likely than Caucasian children to be part of blended families. Remarriage has not been shown to alleviate the impact of divorce. In fact, the presence of stepfamilies has been found to increase delinquency and behavior problems in school, more so than for children whose parents never remarry. Numerous changes in parental figures further increase behavioral problems in youth. A positive relationship with the stepparent typically leads to better outcomes.

Other changes in the "typical" family structure include multigenerational families. One in five African American families live in multigenerational or extended-family households (i.e., families with or without parents that include grandparents or other family members in the home) as compared with one in ten Caucasian families. Studies show that youth have better outcomes, including conduct, in multigenerational families than in single-parent families.

Family Size

Larger families produce more delinquent children than do smaller families. Also, being a middle child is more predictive of delinquency than being either the eldest or youngest. One common explanation for this result is a straining of resources in larger families and an inability to provide appropriate monitoring and supervision. Scholars suggest that middle children are more likely to be present during the times of strain (i.e., older children leave the home first and younger children remain when there is not as much demand for parental resources).

Poverty

Poverty has been linked to crime. Approximately 18% of children under the age of 18 live in poverty. Children who grow up poor have a number of negative life outcomes, including delinquency. A closer look at the impact of socioeconomic status, however, suggests that economic strain plays an important role likely because increased stress decreases effective parenting, a situation that leads to delinquency in children.

Neighborhood

Research on neighborhoods has produced significant results. Collective socialization, or the participation of the community in raising the children, has a beneficial impact on the rate of delinquency among these youth. A longitudinal study of African American families showed that children who lived in a community high in collective socialization were less likely to associate with delinquent peers even when controlling for other important factors (e.g., parenting, poverty, school).

Prevention and Intervention

Given the important role families play in the socialization of children, numerous programs have been implemented to prevent familial contribution to delinquency or to intervene once a problem has been realized. Years of program evaluations have produced a number of effective family-based prevention programs. Parent training on appropriate and effective child-rearing techniques has been found to reduce delinquency by 20%. Home visitation with new parents, a program that educates parents about their infants, has reduced delinquency by 12%. Meta-analytic studies have also shown that intervening in the family once delinquency has been identified as a problem can have a significant impact on rates of recidivism. About three quarters of studies show significant improvement when families volunteer for intervention.

Kristy N. Matsuda

See also At-Risk Youth; Child Abuse; Juvenile Crime

Further Readings

Farrington, D. (2002). Families and crime. In J. Q. Wilson & J. Petersilia (Eds.), *Crime: Public policies for crime control* (pp. 129–148). Oakland, CA: Institute for Contemporary Studies.

Farrington, D. P., & Welsh, B. C. (2007). *Saving children from a life of crime: Early risk factors and effective interventions*. New York: Oxford University Press.

Latimer, J. W. (2001). A meta-analytic examination of youth delinquency, family treatment, and recidivism. *Canadian Journal of Criminology, 43*, 237–253.

Loeber, R., & Stouthamer-Loeber, M. (1986). Family factors as correlates and predictors of juvenile conduct problems and delinquency. *Crime and Justice, 7*, 29–149.

Simons, R. L., Simons, L. G., & Wallace, L. E. (2004). *Families, delinquency, and crime: Linking society's most basic institution to antisocial behavior*. Los Angeles: Roxbury.

FEAR OF CRIME

Definitional ambiguity regarding fear of crime is pervasive; however, most researchers relate it to being afraid of becoming a victim of crime when frequenting public areas. Fear of crime gained national recognition in the 1960s as a viable topic of social research when it was identified as a pervasive social problem whose impact was detrimental to the structure of civilized society. Long acknowledged as a public malady, it is believed to result in communities characterized by loss of solidarity and communal spirit. Communities overcome by fear of crime are places where individuals isolate themselves from one another and no longer live as the social animals they are. Left unchecked, fear of crime can result in people becoming suspicious of one another such that they willingly give up freedom and support for democracy. Understanding fear of crime is important to the study of race and crime because many crime victims and residents of communities plagued with violent crimes and drugs experience higher levels of fear; thus fear of crime has greater impact on their lives.

The public's perception of crime and their fear of crime differ significantly from the reality of crime. This disjuncture between fear of crime and the reality of crime is understandable when one recognizes that the fear of crime has become politicized in much the same way as has crime. Fear of crime has been used to convince the public that crime is rampant and that a society free of crime and its fear must submit to social control policies designed to alleviate the problem. Although fear of crime can be resolved with social control measures, excessive social control can result in an unjustifiable surrender of freedom. Living in a democracy that strives for maximum individual liberty and freedom dictates that society surrender only the amount of freedom or liberty that is necessary for society to function in a stable and orderly fashion. The difficult task is to prescribe only the amount of social control needed to resolve the specific problem without unnecessary loss of freedom and liberty. Development of public policies that enhance rather than reduce quality of life is an issue that is basic to the scientific understanding of the fear of crime.

An examination of the relationship between Americans' fear of crime and politics indicates that the 1960s witnessed the beginning of the politicizing of the fear of crime with a government report titled *The Challenge of Crime in a Free Society*, which reportedly became the basis for the Omnibus Crime Control and Safe Streets Act of 1967. Since that time, political strategists have exploited the public's suggestibility about crime and its capacity to incite human emotion. Evidence of its politicization is perhaps best exemplified through its past use in national presidential campaigns. For example, political strategists for Richard Nixon co-opted public fears stemming from the civil rights movement and protests against the war in Vietnam in the

1968 War on Crime campaign. Several years later, Reagan's strategists used the public's fear of crime in the War on Drugs campaign. In George H. W. Bush's 1988 presidential campaign, political strategists co-opted the public's ignorance of the criminal justice system and the emotional nature of one criminal incident to create a fear of crime that the public associated with the Willie Horton case. In George W. Bush's 2004 campaign for the presidency, the public's fear of criminal victimization by terrorists was used not only as a political platform but also to justify a war, that is, the War on Terror.

Even though researchers have been studying fear of crime since the 1960s, definitional ambiguity regarding fear of crime continues to be pervasive. Some of the more common measurement criticisms include lack of standardization of measures of fear of crime, intermingling of fear of crime with other fears, fear of anticipated victimization rather than fear of crime, and a confounding of fear of crime with risk or vulnerability to crime. Researchers suggest that the dimensions of fear can be biological, sociological, and psychological. Biologically, fear involves a series of complex changes in bodily functions that alert individuals to potential dangers. Sociological explanations tend to focus on fear as a social phenomenon, an event that takes place in a social setting that is performed by social animals whose lives and experiences are dominated by culture. On the other hand, psychological explanation of fear suggests that it is best described as the emotional reaction of anxiety to a sense of danger or a threatening situation. Because fear of crime is a multidimensional phenomenon that is not bounded by victimization, social interaction, or physical environment, its understanding requires an interdisciplinary approach that considers the physical environment, the state of the organism, and social interaction.

Even though there is little consensus about the best approach to measuring fear of crime, one of the most common, single-item indicators of fear of crime is whether there is any area within a mile of an individual's neighborhood where he or she would be afraid to walk alone at night. Most researchers recognize the validity problems associated with the preceding measure; that is, it lacks specificity with regard to fear of what, and its frame of reference (neighborhood) is open to interpretation. Most researchers recommend the use of multiple-item indicators such as indexes; however, consensus is still lacking on the most reliable or valid measure of fear of crime.

What people fear most is being a victim of a violent crime; however, they are more likely to be a victim of a property crime. The public's misperception of crime is believed to result from the media and government's portrayal of arrest statistics and prison populations as well as fictionalized presentations of crime that do not reflect an accurate picture of crime.

Fear of crime research indicates that the elderly, females, African Americans, the less educated, and property owners report the highest levels of fear of crime. Conversely, young adults, those at greatest risks for criminal victimization, report the lowest levels of fear of crime. Over the years researchers have explained why those with less chance of crime victimization report greater levels of fear. For example, the elderly are more fearful because they are probably less physically able to defend themselves, and women are more fearful because they may confound fear of crime with fear of being raped and also see themselves as less capable of defending themselves.

Even though much research on fear of crime has been conducted, continued research of fear of crime is necessary as fear can affect anyone, both victim and nonvictim. Additionally, it is often exaggerated such that it bears little relation to the reality of crime, thus having the capacity to negatively affect the quality of life experienced by all.

Elizabeth H. McConnell

See also Omnibus Crime Control and Safe Streets Act; President's Commission on Law Enforcement and Administration of Justice; Television News; Victimization, African American; Victimization, Asian American; Victimization, Latina/o; Victimization, Native American; Victimization, White; War on Terror

Further Readings

Chiricos, T., Padgett, K., & Gertz, M. (2000). Fear, TV news and the reality of crime. *Criminology, 38,* 755–785.

Ferraro, R. (1995). *Fear of crime: Interpreting victimization risk.* Albany: SUNY Press.

Lee, M., & Ulmer, J. (2000). Fear of crime among Korean Americans in Chicago communities. *Criminology, 38,* 1173–1206.

Smith, S. (1987). Fear of crime: Beyond a geography of deviance. *Progress in Human Geography, 11*(1), 1–23.

FELON DISENFRANCHISEMENT

Perhaps one of the most pertinent topics in the subject of race and crime is that of felon disfranchisement. Because felon disenfranchisement laws singlehandedly ban a large percentage of minority voters from participating in elections as a result of experiences with the criminal justice system, this topic is pertinent as it impacts not only these minorities but elections within the United States as well. This entry examines the current status of felon disenfranchisement laws in the United States, the historical background against which they emerged, and their impact on the African American population, partly as a result of the War on Drugs.

Current Felon Disenfranchisement Laws

Felon disfranchisement is a recent concern in the area of race and the criminal justice system. These state-level laws prevent people with felony convictions from voting in a particular state. The time period for which voting is banned may be the period of incarceration, the time on parole, or, in some states, the duration of an offender's life. This is a critical concern in ethnic studies because the individuals being affected by these laws are primarily minorities. The laws are of particular concern for African Americans, because national data demonstrate a disproportionate number of African Americans in prison: An estimated 13% of African American men are unable to vote as a result of a felony conviction. However, these policies also impact Hispanic voters and other minorities. Many of these offenders and former offenders have been incarcerated under drug laws in the United States.

According to the Drug Policy Alliance, the United States is the only democracy where citizens are banned from voting even after their sentence has been served. Currently, an estimated 5.3 million people in the United States cannot vote as a result of a felony conviction; this statistic includes individuals who are banned from voting because they are currently incarcerated for a felony conviction, individuals banned because they are currently on parole for a felony conviction, and individuals who are banned because they currently reside in a state whose felon disenfranchisement laws ban felons for the duration of their lives.

The Sentencing Project provides the most recent statistical information concerning felon disenfranchisement laws in the United States. Some of the most interesting findings relevant to the study of race and crime from the Sentencing Project include that 48 states and the District of Columbia prohibit inmates from voting while incarcerated for a felony offense; only Maine and Vermont allow inmates to vote. Thirty-five states prohibit felons from voting while they are on parole, and 30 of these states exclude felony probationers. Two states, Kentucky and Virginia, currently deny the right to vote to all ex-offenders who have completed their sentences; a third state, Florida, has now modified its policies to extend voting rights to some offenders who have completed their sentences; however, given the difficulty offenders face in order to have their rights restored in Florida, many individuals still consider this to be a third state of permanent disenfranchisement. Nine states disenfranchise certain categories of ex-offenders and/or permit application for restoration of rights for specified offenses after a waiting period (e.g., 5 years in Delaware and Wyoming and 2 years in Nebraska). Each state in the United States has developed its own processes of restoring voting rights, but, according to the Sentencing Project, most policies offering restoration of voting rights are extremely cumbersome and discourage many individuals from taking advantage of them. Table 1 shows disenfranchisement policies by state.

Many states in the United States have had felon disenfranchisement laws embedded into their individual state constitutions. As stated, these laws typically outline that felons are prohibited from voting during the time period for which they are incarcerated for a felony conviction, during the time period they are on parole for a felony conviction, and/or for their entire life span. In recent

Table 1 Disenfranchisement Categories Under State Law

State	Prison	Probation	Parole	All	Postsentence Partial
Alabama	X	X	X		X
Alaska	X	X	X		
Arizona	X	X	X		X (2nd felony)
Arkansas*	X	X	X		
California	X		X		
Colorado	X		X		
Connecticut	X		X		
Delaware	X	X	X		X (certain offenses 5 years)
District of Columbia	X				
Florida	X	X	X		X (certain offenses)
Georgia	X	X	X		
Hawaii	X				
Idaho	X	X	X		
Illinois	X				
Indiana	X				
Iowa	X	X	X		
Kansas	X	X	X		
Kentucky	X	X	X	X	
Louisiana	X	X	X		
Maine					
Maryland	X	X	X		
Massachusetts	X				
Michigan	X				
Minnesota	X	X	X		
Mississippi	X	X	X		X (certain offenses)
Missouri	X	X	X		
Montana	X				
Nebraska	X	X	X		X (2 years)
Nevada	X	X	X		X (except first-time nonviolent)
New Hampshire	X				

(Continued)

Table I (Continued)

State	Prison	Probation	Parole	All	Postsentence Partial
New Jersey	X	X	X		
New Mexico	X	X	X		
New York	X		X		
North Carolina	X	X	X		
North Dakota	X				
Ohio	X				
Oklahoma	X	X	X		
Oregon	X				
Pennsylvania	X				
Rhode Island	X				
South Carolina	X	X	X		
South Dakota	X		X		
Tennessee	X	X	X		X (certain offenses)
Texas	X	X	X		
Utah	X				
Vermont					
Virginia	X	X	X	X	
Washington*	X	X	X		
West Virginia	X	X	X		
Wisconsin	X	X	X		
Wyoming	X	X	X		X (certain offenses 5 years)
U.S. Total	**49**	**30**	**35**	**2**	**9**

Source: The Sentencing Project (2008).

* Failure to satisfy obligations associated with convictions may result in postsentence loss of voting rights.

years, many states in the United States have become virtual battlegrounds on felon disenfranchisement. This battleground has played out in print news reports, media coverage, attacks on the credibility of politicians in the states, as well as other prominent sources, all of which are examined in this entry. In the past few years, there have been policy changes in approximately 17 states.

The issue of voting rights in Kentucky, one of the two states that ban all ex-felons from voting, has been a prominent battleground in recent years and has led to attacks on the credibility of two of Kentucky's prominent governors, Paul Patton and Ernie Fletcher. Section 145 of the Kentucky Constitution states that people are disenfranchised if they have been convicted of treason, of a felony, or of bribery in an election, and also if they are imprisoned at the time of the election or if they are "insane." In 2008, the Kentucky House of Representatives passed a constitutional amendment that would extend voting rights to some ex-offenders and require the Department of Corrections to inform and help eligible offenders in completing the restoration process. However, the Senate must also pass it, and then it must be approved by citizens in a statewide election. In several other states, however, more extensive legal changes have been made. For example, the lifetime ban imposed on felons in the state of Delaware was changed in 2000 to allow for rights to be restored to these offenders following a 5-year waiting period following the completion of their sentence. The change implemented in the state of Delaware enabled an estimated 6,355 individuals convicted of a felony offense to regain their voting rights. In the state of Texas, a mandatory 2-year waiting period prior to voting rights being restored was removed, which resulted in approximately 316,981 offenders who were restored their voting rights. Connecticut restored voting rights to probationers, thus reinstating the voting rights of approximately 33,040 offenders.

Historical Background

Felon disenfranchisement laws can be linked to several different contexts throughout the history of the United States. Recent literature has attempted to analyze the origins and development of the state felon disenfranchisement laws by building on theories of group threat to test whether racial threat influenced the passage of such laws. Many of these felon disenfranchisement laws were passed in the 1860s and 1870s when there was great opposition to the extension of voting rights to African Americans. Although they initially appear to be race-neutral, they are not, because of disproportionate imprisonment rates for minorities, especially young African American men.

Perhaps the most interesting point during the time period of disenfranchisement laws in the United States is the Reconstruction period, in part due to the adoption of the Fourteenth Amendment to the U.S. Constitution, which extended citizenship to former slaves, and the Fifteenth Amendment,

which prohibited the use of race as a basis for denying the right to vote. The enfranchisement of African Americans and other minorities threatened to shift the balance of power in the United States. Some scholars suggest that disenfranchisement laws represented a backlash to the threat of a shift of power among racial groups in the United States. Recent literature makes a connection between disenfranchisement, lynching, and racial violence in the United States; some scholars argue that such violence was the forerunner to legislation establishing disenfranchisement in the United States.

Drawing on research on ethnic competition and criminal justice, some scholars consider several ways that felon disenfranchisement could be linked to racial factors such as the perceived threat of African Americans. Behrens, Uggen, and Manza, prominent researchers in this field, raise two critical questions that are essentially the foundation of their analysis. The first deals with the race neutrality, at least on the face, of felon disenfranchisement laws. The second pertains to the shift in racial politics. These scholars link current disenfranchisement laws in the United States to Jim Crow laws and the Black Codes, which represented efforts to minimize the political power of those minorities enfranchised by the Fourteenth and Fifteenth Amendments. In 1850, approximately one third of the states had ex-felon disenfranchisement laws in place, and this number continued to grow to three fourths of the states by the year 1920; however, several of these rights were restored during the 1960s and 1970s when many of these laws were amended.

Impact of Felon Disenfranchisement Laws

The Sentencing Project focuses its attention on the impact of felon disenfranchisement laws in the United States. As noted, it is estimated that more than 5 million people have lost their voting rights as a result of having a felony conviction on their record. It is important to keep in mind, however, that this statistic as well as the others accounted for individuals who have lost their voting rights for the time period during which they were incarcerated, the time period on probation, or for the remainder of their lives. Statistics provided by the Sentencing Project estimate that 5.3 million

Americans, or 1 in 40, have currently or permanently lost their voting rights; 1.4 million (13%) African American men are disenfranchised; and nearly 700,000 women are currently disenfranchised. Also, approximately 2.1 million disenfranchised individuals are ex-offenders who have served out their sentences.

Public Opinion on Felon Disenfranchisement

Critical to the issue of the ban of felony voters in the United States is the question whether this is actually what Americans want. Recent literature has examined public attitudes toward felon disenfranchisement. For example, in a 2004 telephone research survey in *Public Opinion Quarterly,* Manza and associates found a 72% endorsement rate for restoring voting rights to felons convicted of drug-related crimes. Further, this survey suggests that approximately 80% of those surveyed favored enfranchisement, with 52% favoring enfranchisement for former sex offenders as well. Additionally, 66% of those surveyed believed ex-felons who have served their entire sentences should have full voting rights. With these findings, one major question posits: If Americans are willing to extend civil liberties to felons, why are the state policies still denying these rights? This statistic provides evidence, at some level, that Americans are not afraid of the "Black criminal vote." Concerning the predicted future impact of disenfranchisement practices in the United States, the Sentencing Project predicts that 3 out of 10 of the next generation of African American men will be disenfranchised at some point in their lifetime. Furthermore, as many as 40% of African American men will lose their voting rights for the duration of their lifetime in states that disenfranchise ex-felons.

The War on Drugs and Politics

Felon disenfranchisement laws have a direct link to the War on Drugs because of the large number of minorities, especially African Americans, who are incarcerated as a result of felony drug convictions. The high incarceration rates for African American men are in large part a result of the War on Drugs in the United States. With a felony drug conviction

on their record, these African American men lose perhaps the most important right this nation offers—the right to vote. The modern effects of this punitive war have created many backlashes: The major concern here is the disenfranchisement of African Americans. The United States is the only democracy in the world to disenfranchise its citizens even after their sentences are complete. One of the most prominent researchers studying this link is Boyd, who discusses the impact of felon disenfranchisement in the 2000 presidential election as a result of the War on Drugs. At the time of the 2000 elections in the state of Florida, any drug offense was considered a felony, causing the offender to lose voting privileges for life. While the outcome of the election came down to only a few hundred votes in Florida, more than 200,000 African American men in Florida could not vote in that election as a result of a felony conviction. This number represented approximately 31% of all African American men in the state of Florida.

Sherry Lynn Skaggs

See also African Americans; Black Codes; Crime Statistics and Reporting; Disproportionate Incarceration; Drug Sentencing; Lynching; National African American Drug Policy Coalition; Sentencing Project, The; War on Drugs

Further Readings

Behrens, A., Uggen, C., & Manza, J. (2003). Ballot manipulation and the menace of negro domination: Racial threat and felon disenfranchisement in the United States, 1850–2002. *American Journal of Sociology, 109*(3), 559–605.

Benedict, W. R., & Huff-Corzine, L. (1997). Return to the scene of the punishment: Recidivism of adult male property offenders on felony probation, 1986–1989. *Journal of Research in Crime and Delinquency, 34*(2), 237–252.

Boyd, G. (2001). The drug war is the new Jim Crow. *NACLA Report on the Americas, 35.* Retrieved from http://www.aclu.org/drugpolicy/racialjustice/10830pub20010731.html

Drug Policy Alliance Network. (2005). *Drugs, police, and the law: Voting rights.* Retrieved from http://www.drugpolicy.org/law/felon

Giboney, S. (2004, June 28). *Challenge to felon voting ban fails, but fight goes on.* Retrieved from http://www.commondreams.org/headlines04/0628-10.htm

Graffam, J., Shinkfield, A., Lavelle, B., & McPherson, W. (2004). Variables affecting successful reintegration as perceived by offenders and professionals. *Journal of Offender Rehabilitation, 40,* 1–2.

Jablecki, L. T. (2005). Changing the lives of prisoners: A new agenda. *The Humanist, 65,* 6.

Kentucky Constitution, Section 145, Ratified November 8, 1955. Retrieved September 2, 2008, from http://www.lrc.ky.gov/Legresou/Constitu/145.htm

Manza, J., Brooks, C., & Uggen, C. (2004). Public attitudes toward felon disenfranchisement in the United States. *Public Opinion Quarterly, 68,* 2.

Nolan, J. L., Jr. (2001). *Reinventing justice: The American drug court movement.* Princeton, NJ: Princeton University Press.

Richards, S., Austin, J., & Jones, R. (2004). Kentucky's perpetual prisoner machine: It's about money. *Review of Policy Research, 21,* 1.

The Sentencing Project. (2005). *Felony disenfranchisement laws in the United States.* Washington, DC: Author.

The Sentencing Project. (2008, March). *Felony disenfranchisement laws in the United States.* Retrieved from http://www.sentencingproject.org/PublicationDetails.aspx?PublicationID=335

Uggen, C., Manza, J., Thompson, M., & Wakefield, S. (2002). *Impact of recent legal changes in felon voting rights in five states* (Briefing paper prepared for the National Symposium on Felony Disenfranchisement, September 3–October 1, 2002, Washington, DC). Retrieved from http://www.sentencingproject.org/Admin/Documents/publications/fd_bs_impactinfivestates.pdf

White, W. L. (1998). *Slaying the dragon: The history of addiction treatment and recovery in America.* Bloomington, IL: Chestnut Health Systems/Lighthouse Institute.

FEMALE GANGS

Much of the literature available on gangs has largely ignored the presence and significance of female gangs. Historically, researchers viewed female gangs as poor imitations of male gangs. The study of female gangs has become increasingly important because of the rise in the number of female gangs in recent years. It is appropriate that female gangs be included in this body of work because of the prevalent role that race plays in the makeup of both male and female gangs and because of the proliferation of the female gang in modern society.

History of Female Gangs

The recent history of female gangs can be traced back to the 1960s when female members acted as helpmates to male gang members. Although the females considered themselves to be authentic gang members, they were most often limited to duties such as sewing gang insignia on male members' jackets, running errands, and relaying messages, or they were restricted to the role of the girlfriend of a gang member. During the early years, this was sufficient for most female gang members, but as time progressed many of them began to desire a more prominent role within their gang.

As female gangs struggled to emerge from the shadows of their better-known counterparts, they fought to shed the image held by many outsiders that relegated them to the role of sexual partners for male gang members. Although some literature supports this assertion, some female gang members in surveys have strongly denied the claim that their primary value to the gang family was sexual in nature. Female gang members struggled not only to remove the stigma of being considered a sex object but also to prove their worth and value to the gang.

Female Gang Statistics

The 1980s brought an increase in the number of gangs across the United States, and the number of female gangs increased substantially during this period. This trend corresponded with the nationwide increase in juvenile delinquency, as the number of gangs proliferated and the level of gang violence rose to unimaginable heights. Although it was widely accepted among social scientists that female gang membership increased throughout the years, it has been difficult to accurately portray the number of females who hold membership in a gang because of the way that gangs and gang membership are defined and studied.

The methods used to research gang affiliation have contributed to the difficulty in accurately determining the number of female gang members across the United States. One of the most widely used methods of gang research is the survey method. Associated problems with this method include the exaggeration of gang membership and gang activities by those female members surveyed and conversely, the distrust that some gang members may have of the researcher. Criminologists have also suggested that it was possible for the number of female gang members to be underreported because some law enforcement agencies are hesitant to label females as gang members.

It has also been difficult to accurately portray the number of female gangs because of the way in which gangs are defined. While some female groups related to researchers that they were gangs, it has been difficult to distinguish whether they belonged to true gangs or loosely formed groups. Pop media has made the gang life attractive through portrayals of gang culture by means of insignia, clothing, gestures, and tattoos. Movies, music, and music videos present gang life in a way that captures the attention and fills a void for some juveniles. As a result, they copy what the pop media portrays as a gang and combine that with their limited ideas of what constitutes a gang. Not only are youth influenced by pop media's portrayal of gang members, so is the general public. Pop media contribute to perceptions that most gangs are overwhelmingly made up of minority youth. However, some groups are mistakenly identified as authentic gangs when they are merely loosely formed groups. It has also been difficult to accurately quantify the number of female gang members because of the propensity of researchers to focus only on researching the activities of male gangs. Miller suggested that up to 10% of all gang members were females. Recently, researchers have suggested that female gang membership has increased, albeit at a slower rate than male gangs.

Reasons for Gang Membership

Within the context of female gangs, several themes are commonplace in research on female gang formations, female gang members, and gang preservation. With respect to gang formation, in general, and female gangs, in particular, most findings suggest that gangs are formed for a variety of reasons, including physical protection, economic prosperity,

companionship, and drugs. Traditional gang members, consistent with today's female gangs, are the by-products of socially disorganized communities characterized by inferior living conditions, broken family structures, limited employment opportunities, and inadequate school systems. Gangs and their associated vices more easily emerge within these areas of dense poverty and hopelessness. In these socially disorganized communities, female gangs are greater in number and tend to use violence more readily. The emergence of a "drugs for profit" phenomenon also fosters gang formation. The ethnic composition of such neighborhoods is disproportionately minority.

Gangs also form and survive because of the characteristics of its members. The typical female gang members, like male gang members, tend to be by-products not only of inadequate community structures but also of severely dysfunctional homes. Typically, female gang members have been subjected to verbal, physical, or sexual abuse in both their community and home lives at very young ages. Within the context of the family as well as the community, these individuals typically saw problems resolved through violence. Thus, when they encounter problems in their lives, they employ violence as a solution. Further, for many female gang members, the gang is the nearest semblance to a family that most have experienced. In the eyes of the female gang member, the gang, like a family, provides protection, security, and an identity.

Preservation of the gang unit is common because gangs exist in neighborhoods that condone criminal and delinquent activities. From this perspective, gangs may more easily thrive because many people within the context of such communities feel helpless against the gangs.

Ethnicity and Gender Issues

Gender inequality is a significant theme in discussions of female gangs. Female gang members typically view themselves as equal to the male gang members with whom they have aligned themselves. Female gang members may also feel that through gang membership, they gain the respect of male gang members in their families and even the respect of persons outside the gang. Typically male gang members have treated females as lower-class citizens within the gang community. Despite the female gang members pledging unbridled loyalty to the gang, it is not uncommon for them to be sacrificed in some way, reportedly for the good of the gang. In some male gangs, the female members are expected to be available to satisfy the sexual needs and desires of the male members. In some cases, the test of loyalty to the gang involves the female member responding favorably to the request from gang leadership to welcome the newest gang member or to reward a member for acting satisfactorily on behalf of the gang. In most mixed gangs, female members have little power and are considered a disposable commodity.

Instances of gender inequality occur not only at the hands of male gang members but also female gang members. It is not uncommon for female members to refer to other females using derogatory names and to deny the ability of females to carry out positions of leadership or hold some measure of status or rank within the gang. Additionally researchers have found that female gang members do not value other female gang members who are initiated by "sexing in"—that is, engaging in sex with male members of the gang for the purpose of initiation. Although the activities of female gangs would suggest that they have little regard for social mores and values, they do have high expectations of their peers, especially regarding their conduct.

The racial makeup of female gangs has become more varied over time. The largest racial group represented has been African Americans, followed closely by Hispanics/Latinas. There are indications that White and Asian gangs are growing in number. Although rare, mixed ethnicity may occur in loosely formed gangs. There is a scarcity of research studies available on female gangs; those that exist have for the most part dealt with African American, Hispanic/Latina, and White gangs. Although different in racial makeup, these gangs have several commonalities, including the reasons for gang membership, similar academic challenges, and a history of physical, sexual, or domestic violence in their family backgrounds. In comparison to male gangs, available research has found that female gangs of all ethnicities tend to place a higher value on both the economic benefits and the emotional connectedness offered through gang membership.

Violence and Criminality

Past research has shown that in their quest to prove their toughness and value as gang members, females may mimic the behavior and actions of male members. Just like their male counterparts, female gang members show no reluctance to fight. It is not uncommon for female gang members to be just as violent in the commission of their delinquent or criminal activity in an effort to earn the acclaim that oftentimes is bestowed upon male gang members. In spite of their gender, females are intent upon presenting their gang as a true and genuine gang and not just an affiliate of a male gang. Some of the activities of modern female gang members include street fights, mugging, shoplifting, petty theft, assaults with weapons, and the distribution of illegal substances.

Although criminal acts by female gang members have traditionally been less violent than those of male gang members, current trends show increases in violence and criminality among female gang members with offenses like aggravated assault, drug offenses, prostitution, and weapon-related offenses. Drug offenses are common to female gangs, as selling drugs is often the primary source of financial support for female gangs.

Future Research and Policy

Female gangs have transitioned from an auxiliary component of male gangs to modern independent gangs increasingly prone to violent activities. Faced with the "get-tough movement," most female gang members subjected to harsher criminal justice sanctions are seeing their children become wards of the state. Thus society is faced with the problem of confronting more violent female gang members and simultaneously caring for their offspring. With the problem of female gangs expanding, solutions to suppress and reduce their influence in American society must come more readily, and the problem of female gangs must be addressed holistically.

By removing the root causes that contribute to gang membership through better jobs, better schools, and better businesses, society will be better positioned to curtail gang growth. The lack of current and available research on female gangs suggests that there is much for researchers to do to begin effectively combating the ever-increasing numbers of young girls joining female gangs and their violent subculture. Although there are similarities between male and female gangs, the differences between them are significant enough to warrant increased attention to female gangs.

Tonya Y. Willingham and Willie M. Brooks

See also Female Juvenile Delinquents; Violent Females; Youth Gangs

Further Readings

Decker, D. C. (1998). *Confronting gangs.* Los Angeles: Roxbury.

Miller, J. (2001). *One of the guys: Girls, gangs, and gender.* New York: Oxford University Press.

Molidor, C. E. (1996). Female gang members: A profile of aggression and victimization. *Social Work, 41*(3), 251–257.

Moore, J., & Hagedorn, J. M. (2001, March). Female gangs: A focus on research. *Juvenile Justice Bulletin.* Retrieved from http://www.ncjrs.gov/html/ojjdp/jjbul2001_3_3/contents.html

Sikes, G. (1994, February). Girls in the 'hood. *Scholastic Update, 126,* 20–22.

FEMALE JUVENILE DELINQUENTS

Girls are the fastest growing population in the juvenile justice system. In 2003, they accounted for 29% of all juvenile arrests, yet they are rarely the focus of research. In a correctional system designed for boys and men, girls have proceeded through the juvenile justice system as the "forgotten few." Historically, literature and research ignored girls, even though they were being referred to the juvenile justice system as long ago as 1900. It has been suggested that gender and race, separately and in conjunction, influence juvenile justice processing. This entry addresses the issues of female juvenile delinquents by reviewing the role of gender and race in the original juvenile court, exploring the offenses that are generally responsible for girls entering the system, and discussing the unique characteristics of female delinquents.

Gender is one of the single best predictors of crime. The juvenile justice system deals predominantly with boys, and until recently, female delinquency has not been considered a serious problem. Girls are generating more attention from law enforcement and the media, and the past decade specifically has witnessed a significant increase in the number of girls entering the system.

History

The first juvenile court was established in 1899 in Cook County, Illinois. Although fewer girls than boys appeared before the court, the number of girls increased in the early 20th century. During this time, the sexuality of girls was considered to be an appropriate issue for law enforcement, and nearly 80% of girls brought to juvenile court were charged with immorality. Similarly, the other common charge for girls was incorrigibility, which was frequently used to charge the girls in lieu of immorality as an attempt to protect their reputations. Activities such as riding in a closed automobile, loitering in a department store, inhabiting a furnished room with a young man, or even shimmying on a roadhouse dance floor were considered inappropriate for girls and could lead to charges of incorrigibility. The incarceration of girls was a measure intended to keep them safe and "pure." Unlike boys, girls were not eligible for probation, and consequently they were incarcerated at a higher rate than boys. Training schools were used to prepare the girls for their future roles as wives and mothers.

Court records indicate that the delinquent girls who first appeared in Chicago's Cook County courtroom were poor and working-class girls from immigrant and African American migrant families. African American girls were particularly affected by the overcrowded courts and delayed case processing. The only institution to which African American girls could be admitted was the State Training School for Girls at Geneva, which accepted only a few girls at a time. The State Training School at Geneva was a state-run institution where delinquent and dependent girls were confined, educated, and reformed. When the school was full, delinquent girls were held in the Juvenile Detention Home until spaces became available at the school.

This process could take as long as 6 months. As a result of segregation in these institutions for juveniles, African American girls were incarcerated longer than were their White counterparts.

This trend of longer incarceration periods for African American girls seems to have changed very little through time. Race continues to influence juvenile justice processing. For example, research contends that African American youth are 3 times more likely than White youth to end up in residential placement. It is well documented that, as with incarcerated adults in the criminal justice system, minority youth are overrepresented in the juvenile justice system.

Types of Offenses

As the juvenile justice system evolved over time, girls continued to be referred to the court for lesser offenses, particularly status offenses. Status offenses are offenses that would not be considered criminal if the youth had reached the age of majority, such as curfew violations, running away from home, truancy (not attending school), and drinking alcohol. In 2000, 58% of all status offenders were girls, and it is estimated that 72% of all status offenders are referred to the juvenile justice system by their parents, usually for things such as ungovernability. Like their adult female counterparts, girls are often arrested for nonviolent crimes. Today's juvenile system continues to exhibit the juvenile court's earliest focus on the morality of girls' behavior and the need to punish girls for being unruly; as a result of these concerns, girls continue to be disproportionately affected by the juvenile legal system's handling of status offenses.

Causes of Female Juvenile Delinquency

Female delinquents have unique needs, and unique causes underlie their delinquency. Most delinquent girls have histories of abuse and exploitation. In fact, approximately 73% of girls who enter juvenile institutions report being victims of abuse. Cathy Spatz Widom, an expert on the causes and consequences of child abuse and neglect, found that child abuse increases the risk of delinquency, violent behavior, and antisocial tendencies. According to Widom (1992), child abuse and neglect increase the likelihood of arrest by 53% and the likelihood of committing violent crime by 38%. Abuse is a stronger predictor for offending behavior in females than in males.

Not surprisingly, abuse is the primary reason girls run away from home. Girls often attempt to escape the abuse they receive at home and are subsequently arrested for running away, which is a status offense. This is often a girl's first involvement with the juvenile justice system. In 2003, girls accounted for 59% of the arrests for running away from home.

Delinquent girls who come from dysfunctional homes and experience abuse, neglect, and exploitation often grow up with a feeling of worthlessness and hopelessness that often results in low or damaged self-esteem. Self-report data indicate that more than half of the girls in juvenile facilities have previously attempted suicide.

Substance abuse is another important risk factor associated with female delinquency. Girls report that drugs and alcohol help them escape emotional pain caused by abuse. According to the National Survey on Drug Use and Health, in 2003, substance abuse was the most common delinquent behavior among girls ages 12 to 17.

Although the majority of arrests of girls are for nonviolent crimes and status offenses, the rate of arrests for violent crimes such as assault has increased in the past decade. There is evidence that girls' arrests for violent behavior have indeed increased. Between 1980 and 2003, female aggravated assault arrests increased from 15% to 24%, and simple assault arrests increased from 21% to 32%. However, it cannot be concluded that this increase establishes that girls are more violent today than they were half a century ago. This change might be related to policy changes rather than an increase in female juvenile violence. The perception that girls are more violent may also result in part from the media's focus on "bad girls" and media reports that girls are becoming increasingly violent.

Several factors may explain the increased arrest rate for these offenses. First, this increase may be attributed to law enforcement's change in handling domestic violence incidents. Mandatory arrest laws might account for the increase in girls arrested for assault, while having no effect on other violent crimes. Second, the arrest rates might be related to girls' involvement in gang offenses and the police attention toward the gang problem. Third, the increase might be attributed to zero tolerance policies in schools. Girls who were once sent to detention or suspended from class because they engaged in fighting at schools may now be arrested for assault. The increase in arrests at school might have contributed to an increase in the arrest rates for assault for females. Despite this increase, girls still lag behind boys by a significant margin for all offenses except running away.

Additionally, just as African American girls are overrepresented in the original juvenile court, research indicates that there is evidence of disproportionate minority contact in nearly every state in America. Disproportionate minority contact occurs when the percentage of minority youth who pass through the juvenile justice system exceeds the percentage of minority youth in the general population. It is estimated that two thirds of the girls in the juvenile justice system are either African American or Latina.

In general, girls have been ignored by the juvenile justice system and by researchers because the number and magnitude of the crimes they commit are significantly smaller than for boys. Nevertheless, female delinquents require attention. They have unique needs and histories and require effective programs and interventions that acknowledge their issues. It is hoped that with appropriate awareness and involvement from authorities and academics alike, girls in the system will be helped before they grow up to become women in the criminal justice system

Alison S. Burke

See also: Child Savers; Delinquency Prevention; Disproportionate Minority Contact and Confinement; Juvenile Crime; Status Offenses

Further Readings

Chesney-Lind, M., & Shelden, R. G. (1998). *Girls, delinquency, and juvenile justice*. Belmont, CA: Wadsworth.

Knupfer, A. M. (2001). *Reform and resistance: Gender, delinquency, and America's first juvenile court*. New York: Routledge.

Schaffner, L. (2006). *Girls in trouble with the law*. New Brunswick, NJ: Rutgers University Press.

Tannenhaus, D. S. (2004). *Juvenile justice in the making*. New York: Oxford University Press.

Widom, C. S. (1992). *The cycle of violence*. Washington, DC: Department of Justice, National Institute of Justice.

FERGUSON, COLIN (1958–)

Colin Ferguson was convicted of 6 murders and 19 attempted murders stemming from a December 7, 1993, incident on the Long Island Rail Road. Before trial, Ferguson's lawyers announced that his defense would be temporary insanity directly caused by their client living in America's "racist" society. However, this defense was never formally entered, as Ferguson chose to represent himself during trial and maintained that he was not the gunman. He is currently serving six consecutive life sentences at the Attica Correctional Facility, a maximum-security prison approximately 30 miles east of Buffalo, New York. This entry examines Ferguson's background as well as the details of the incident and his trial.

Ferguson was born on January 14, 1958, in Kingston, Jamaica, and immigrated to the United States in 1982. He lived in Flatbush, Brooklyn, taking business classes at local universities and community colleges in Nassau County while having periodic employment. On December 7, 1993, he boarded the 5:33 p.m. Hicksville-bound Long Island Rail Road train during the heavy commute from Manhattan to the suburbs of Nassau County. As the train approached the Merillon Avenue station in Garden City, New York, approximately 38 minutes into the ride from Manhattan, Ferguson rose from his seat and commenced firing his Ruger P89 9mm semiautomatic pistol. He walked along the aisle while discharging his weapon for approximately 2½ minutes at both seated passengers and those later scrambling for the exit once the train came to a halt at the station platform. After firing 30 rounds, he stopped to reload his pistol. During this period, Ferguson was physically confronted and restrained by three passengers. Police, railroad officers, and emergency personnel reached the scene to discover 23 people were wounded by gunfire in the attack and 2 injured by the stampeding for the doors of the train during the shooting. Six of the injured would die, all from gunshot wounds. Along with the weapon and nearly 100 rounds of ammunition, police officers found handwritten notes on Ferguson detailing his hatred for a wide scope of racial groups, including Whites, Hispanics, Asians, and certain segments of his own race, Blacks; in particular, Ferguson noted his displeasure with those he regarded as "Uncle Tom Negroes" or Blacks who kowtowed to Whites.

The charges brought against Ferguson included the 6 counts of murder and 19 counts of attempted murder, as well as numerous counts of civil rights violations based on the seemingly premeditated racial motive for the shootings. Attorneys William Kunstler and Ronald Kuby, who initially handled Ferguson's case, planned an insanity defense based on "Black rage." They argued that their client was made temporarily insane by the racial prejudice he faced in the United States for over 10 years since his immigration. They likened such a condition to posttraumatic stress disorder, which would have rendered Ferguson unable to appreciate the nature of his actions and would have resulted in a temporary disconnection from reality. They planned to argue that previous uses of posttraumatic stress disorder as a viable defense, particularly in cases of battered women, served as a justifiable precedent even though "Black rage" had itself never been used at trial. However, Kunstler and Kuby did not have a chance to introduce the defense. Ferguson insisted that he was not insane, and that he in fact was not the shooter though the prosecution had planned to introduce 40 witnesses identifying Ferguson as the offender; he then dismissed the attorneys and sought to defend himself at trial. Throughout the pretrial process, Ferguson refused to meet with psychiatrists, suggesting that they were part of the larger conspiracy against him. During pretrial motions, Ferguson was found mentally capable of standing trial in New York State by understanding the charges and being able to provide toward his defense, and thus was afforded the right to act as his own counsel if he so chose. Though he retained a legal advisor, Alton Rose, all courtroom decisions and actions were taken by Ferguson for the duration of the proceeding from jury selection to sentencing.

The trial began on January 27, 1995, in Mineola, New York. The essence of his defense focused on a racist conspiracy to blame him, as a Black male, for a crime that he did not commit. Ferguson claimed to be sleeping on the train when his weapon was stolen from his bag by a White male who subsequently began shooting; this woke Ferguson and he sought to avoid the gunman along with the other passengers. According to his argument, Ferguson was identified as the shooter because he was the sole Black passenger in the train car and the witnesses' larger cultural impetus, fueled by racism, aimed to destroy Black people and make them scapegoats for White crime. Ferguson suggested multiple theories to explain the details of the shooting in court, often in the context of open rants against the criminal justice system, society, and international organizations. One such theory noted CIA (Central Intelligence Agency) mind control technology and implanted microchips, though Ferguson's witness for this allegation did not appear at trial. In fact, the defense did not call a single witness in court for examination.

After approximately 3 weeks, the trial concluded on February 17, 1995. The jury deliberated for 10 hours and returned guilty verdicts on all murder and attempted murder charges but found Ferguson not guilty on the civil rights violations due to the fact that he aimed his weapon and injured all races of people and no one race was singled out. At sentencing on March 23, 1995, Ferguson was given the maximum prison term of 200 years to life (the death penalty was not available at the time of the crime and thus could not be pursued). Judge Donald Belfi noted that in his 2 decades on the bench, he had "never presided over a trial with a more selfish and self-centered defendant." When given the opportunity to speak on his own behalf, Ferguson likened himself to John the Baptist as the victims and victims' families walked out of the courtroom. On appeal, Ferguson had to argue that his case should be remanded due to "incompetent counsel" and subsequently relinquished control to appointed attorneys. He is currently serving his sentence at the Attica Correctional Facility.

The Ferguson case also led to a significant political change. Carolyn McCarthy, whose husband was murdered and son was seriously wounded in Ferguson's attack, became a vocal gun-control advocate during the course of the trial. This visibility resulted in a political career; in 1996 she was elected to the House of Representatives for New York's Fourth Congressional District as a Democrat.

Sean Goodison

See also Hate Crimes; McVeigh, Timothy; Skinheads; White Supremacists

FIRST PEOPLES

See Native American Courts; Native American Massacres; Native Americans; Native Americans: Culture, Identity, and the Criminal Justice System; Native Americans and Substance Abuse

FOCAL CONCERNS THEORY

Walter B. Miller presented a pure cultural theory of gang delinquency in 1958 that has been generalized to the lower class. His theory, proposed in a short article titled "Lower Class Culture as a Generating Milieu of Gang Delinquency," submitted that the lower class subscribed to a distinct criminogenic culture. Miller's explanation of delinquency is situated in depressed inner cities, wherein the majority of households are headed by females, implying that traditional values are not instilled because of inadequate discipline and role-modeling. Without middle-class values, the lower class operates according to *focal concerns*. Specified as trouble, toughness, smartness, excitement, fate, and autonomy, these concerns devalue conventional values and lead to gang formation. Smartness refers to the ability to "con" someone in real-life situations and brings respect for successful hustlers and con artists. A belief in fate—in predetermined outcomes—undermines the work ethic and sabotages self-improvement. Deviance is normal and to be expected in lower-class cultures because the focal concerns make conformity to criminal behavior as natural as acceptance of conventional mores for the middle class. Miller observed that juveniles accepting a preponderance of these "cultural practices which comprise essential elements of the total life pattern of lower class culture automatically violate legal norms."

Evaluation of the theory has centered around two significant criticisms. First, some of the focal concerns contended to be exclusive to the lower class are also observable in the middle class. A second and more controversial issue concerns the use of race rather than class in assessing the relationship between delinquency, matriarchal households, and an exaggerated sense of masculinity associated with physical aggression.

Whereas Miller's focal concerns and related subcultural theories largely dominated criminological thought during the 1950s, the 1960s ushered in a number of interrelated social movements (including the civil rights crusade, anti–Vietnam War protests, and the counterculture). In varying degrees they expressed the same themes: distrust and defiance of authority that was perceived to be used by elite factions to create and maintain a social hierarchy, exploitation of crime and delinquency, and opposition to the oppressiveness of the criminal justice system. As bandwagon shifts to the political left transpired, labeling theory soon replaced subcultural explanations as the leading perspective on crime.

Although historical developments set into motion a chain of events that moved criminological theorizing away from the subculture, the theory was further marred by paradigmatic shifts in social science research methodology. The rise of positivism was especially critical of the criminogenic saliency of the subculture and delivered focal concerns theory a would-be deathblow. There was suddenly a disjuncture between the subculture approach and the new preferred theoretical–methodological symmetry: variable assignment, measurement, and analysis congruent with causality as established by levels of statistical correlation. Critics of subculture theory focused on the growing belief that acceptable science must subscribe to particular precepts that subculture explanations did not meet. The theory could not, via a variable analysis format, be adequately tested.

Perhaps more consequential to the demise of the focal concerns perspective was the notion of the theory's inherent "classism" in a society where social class and racial minority status were (and still are) strongly correlated. Despite the focal concerns perspective being logically applicable to the discussion of minority representation in the justice system, there have been few attempts by criminologists to do so, perhaps because of the general liberal and politically correct ideology characteristic of American higher education. Interesting and somewhat ironic, the original lower-class subjects whose behavior and collective values served as the empirical basis for Miller's original framework were lower-class northeastern Caucasian youth.

The focal concerns perspective has been seldom used since the 1960s to explain crime and delinquency per se. Instead, scholars invoke a "focal concerns" framework (often little more than related conceptual elements germane to a central topic) to analyze justice system realities. Examples include parole decision making as a function of focal concerns specific to release outcomes and the "focal concerns" of judges in sanctioning according to combinations of race and ethnicity variables. Such uses further remove focal concerns theory away from its thesis on the cultural transmission of values to a less controversial and less coherent general conceptual framework for better understanding discretion in criminal justice contexts.

There has been, however, a revitalization of the focal concerns perspective that is truer to the seminal version in Elijah Anderson's now famous *Code of the Street: Decency, Violence, and the Moral Life of the Inner City*, which appeared in 1999. Although not self-proclaimed as such, the identification of "street codes" (essentially focal concerns), while original and groundbreaking ethnography, is a direct theoretical elaboration of the majority of values discussed by Miller in 1958. These codes, in a sense then, are neofocal concerns that are reflective of Black lower-class street culture, generally, and its symbiotic and contributive relation to crime.

Anderson's work is consequential in at least three respects: (1) It has revitalized the focal concerns perspective through demonstrating contemporary relevancy; (2) it righted, if unintentionally, longstanding erroneous assumptions regarding race and focal concerns; and, relatedly, (3) it has finally situated the focal concerns perspective in the context of race and crime. Several studies have sought to operationalize Anderson's codes for theory testing via variable analysis, and it is likely that additional applications in other minority and ethnic contexts (e.g., Hispanic cultural values, Appalachian code of honor subcultural adherents) will be forthcoming.

Focal concerns theory is typically referenced in the larger context of subcultural or cultural transmission theories of criminal behavior, although recent utilizations have been extended to also address the operational functioning of various criminal justice system components. Of the leading subcultural explanations of crime and delinquency, focal concerns theory is perhaps the most controversial—primarily because of its fundamental contention that crime is a function of group values that reify through cultural transmission (i.e., social learning) across stratified society.

Cultural transmission theories of crime and delinquency rest on the rudimentary postulate that people internalize values and beliefs. Learning is shaped by, and also perpetuates, values that collectively constitute a belief system reflecting social attitudes, preferences, and sense of group identification. Belief systems come to characterize social environments, but some environments are distinguished by atypical, criminogenic value and normative systems in which crime is condoned if not encouraged. Cultural variation is thus a fundamental assumption as is the power of conformity. Subscription to the unconventional is rewarded through increased social status and self-esteem denied subgroup members elsewhere in society where conventional values define the social.

As similarly situated people face rejection because of socioeconomic status, race, ethnicity, religion, or place of geographic origin, it is common practice and seems only natural that people from like backgrounds faced with similar problems choose to identify and bond together. This reality becomes more pronounced when the subgroup is outside of its native environment, largely because culturally specific practices and patterns of speech and behavior stand out as different. Noticeable differences in dialect, manners, and political or religious attitudes motivate the disadvantaged and disenfranchised into group settings wherein they are more familiar and comfortable.

The study of subcultures from a criminological orientation is necessarily integrated with the study of legal process. Although the production of law has been shown to be aligned with the interests of the populace, the criminal law is generally regarded (ironically, by the populace) as a product of a normative consensus, a parallel reinforced by both the myths and realities of democratic ideals. While the law thus denotes "conventional" or "dominant" culture, an important and paradoxical feature of the legal process is the disjuncture between the moral normative value system held by lawmakers and the positional norms of various societal groups.

Positional norms, defined by values correlated with combinations of class status, sex, age, race and ethnicity, religious affiliation, and similar variables, are often underrepresented in the formal definition of authority. That which is considered normal, appropriate, popular, and wrong varies considerably across different social groups throughout society. Repudiation of other groups' societal standards and norms, as specified in law and the rules governing societal institutions, fosters greater group cohesion and amplifies differences between the value systems of subcultures and the larger society. Thus, another defining characteristic of a subculture is cultural conflict. Accordingly, it is important to make the conceptual distinction between subculture and population segment. The subcultural values of a gang, for example, may intensify although membership is reduced through criminal justice system actions. In short, normative conflict is inherent in social structure, and subcultures are very much a manifestation of this conflict.

J. Mitchell Miller

See also Code of the Streets; Culture Conflict Theory; Structural–Cultural Perspective; Youth Gangs

Further Readings

Anderson, E. (1999). *Code of the street: Decency, violence, and the moral life of the inner city*. New York: Norton.

Cohen, A. (1955). *Delinquent boys*. Glencoe, IL: The Free Press.

Gabbidon, S. L. (2007). *Criminological perspectives on race and crime*. New York: Routledge.

Miller, J. M., Schreck, C. J., & Tewksbury, R. (2007). *Criminological theory: A brief introduction* (2nd ed.). Boston: Allyn & Bacon.

Miller, W. B. (1958). Lower class culture as a generating milieu of gang delinquency. *Journal of Social Issues, 14*, 5–19.

Vold, G. B., & Bernard, T. J. (1986). *Theoretical criminology* (4th ed.). New York: Oxford University Press.

Wolfgang, M. E., & Ferracuti, F. (1967). *The subculture of violence: Towards an integrated theory in criminology*. London: Tavistock.

Focal Concerns Theory, Labeling

According to focal concerns theory, three focal concerns have an effect on sentencing decisions: blameworthiness of the offender, protection of the community, and organizational restraints and consequences. Minorities are more likely to be labeled negatively when appearing in court based upon these three focal concerns. Debate has occurred on how prevalent this labeling is as well as how it might impact the sentencing and punishment of minority defendants. The entry examines the three focal concerns and how this labeling process results in disparities in minority sentencing and punishment.

Focal Concerns

The focal concerns perspective is a theoretical framework which states that judges sentence individuals based upon perceptions and stereotypes surrounding three foci. The first focus is how blameworthy the offender is. This focus reflects the nature and seriousness of the offense, the offender's involvement with the offense, and the offender's previous record. The more serious the offense, culpable the offender, and the more criminal offenses they have committed, the more blameworthy the offender appears.

The second focus judges consider when deciding a sentence is protection of the community. This focus is based on the judges' perception of recidivism and the dangerousness of the offender. The more dangerous an offender appears and the higher his or her likelihood for recidivism is, the more likely the sentence length or severity will increase.

Third, a judge will consider the organizational restraints and practical consequences of a judgment. Judges will determine the offender's ability to do time, cost of incarceration, impact on other social institutions such as family and the economy, and the effect on the courtroom relationships and workgroups. This last focal concern allows for the judge to consider organizational concerns, such as the reputation of the court, the stability of the courtroom workgroup, and overcrowding of local correctional facilities, as well as individual concerns, such as the offender's health, special needs, and family ties.

Labeling and Sentencing Disparities

Focal concerns theory posits that judges have very little information with which to make sentence determinations. Judges have a minimum amount of time with offenders and attorneys, yet they must be certain about their sentencing decisions. Overcrowded courtrooms and loaded dockets force judges to make swift decisions and avoid uncertainty based on a combination of the three focal concerns. As a result, judges will label or stereotype offenders based upon characteristics that are directly observable, descriptively neutral, and inherent in the status derived from gender, race, age, and social class. Focal concern theorists have called this "perceptual shorthand."

Studies show that the perceptual shorthand of judges has resulted in disparities within the criminal justice system. Criminal records of young Black males are defined as more serious, and the possibility for recidivism is deemed greater in comparison to other social categories. Women and older offenders are labeled as less dangerous and less of a risk to the general public than are other categories of offenders. Judges also are more likely to consider the possibility that women and older offenders might have been victimized themselves by individuals belonging to other social categories. They are also seen as a higher cost to the criminal justice system. Possibilities for pregnancy and age-related problems suggest that women and older offenders may present high social costs to correctional facilities. Lastly, women and older offenders are labeled as having more social ties. Women are viewed as the support system for children, and older offenders are perceived as more likely to be employed.

It has been suggested that consequences of this labeling process have resulted in inequalities in the criminal justice system. African American and Hispanics are more harshly punished than are Whites. Males receive more punitive sentences than do females. Younger offenders are more likely to be incarcerated and to receive longer sentences than are older offenders. Unemployed offenders and offenders located in lower social strata are more harshly punished than are offenders who are employed or offenders who belong to the middle or upper class.

The direct effect, as well as the complex interaction between gender, race, age, and social class, is most detrimental to young, Black and Hispanic minorities. Focal theorists claim that characteristics and attributions derived from the judges' perceptual shorthand reflect negative societal stereotypes. Judges assign meaning to behaviors consistent with their perception of societal stereotypes which are assigned to the offenders' association with a particular social category. When considering the three foci, a judge might resort to stereotypes and label young minorities as more blameworthy, more dangerous to the community, and more likely to recidivate. As a result, studies reveal that there is a high cost of being young, male, and of minority status in the criminal justice system.

Alana Van Gundy-Yoder

See also Disproportionate Incarceration; Focal Concerns Theory; Labeling Theory; Sentencing Disparities, African Americans; Sentencing Disparities, Latina/o/s

Further Readings

Gabbidon, S. L. (2007). *Criminological perspectives on race and crime*. New York: Routledge.

Kleck, G. (1981). Racial discrimination in criminal sentencing: A critical evaluation of the evidence with additional evidence on the death penalty. *American Sociological Review, 46,* 783–805.

Miller, W. (1958). Lower class culture as a generating milieu for gang delinquency. *Journal of Social Issues, 14,* 5–19.

Steffensmeier, D., & Demuth, S. (2000). Ethnicity and sentencing outcomes in U.S. federal courts: Who is punished more harshly? *American Sociological Review, 65,* 705–729.

Steffensmeier, D., Ulmer, J., & Kramer, J. (1998). The interaction of race, gender, and age in criminal sentencing: The punishment and cost of being young, Black, and male. *Criminology, 36,* 763–797.

FRAZIER, E. FRANKLIN (1894–1962)

E. (Edward) Franklin Frazier was a prolific Black sociologist whose pioneering research contributed to the foundation of Black sociological thought and challenged conventional wisdom by raising existential questions regarding the complexity of race relations in American society.

Frequently characterized as an "improper Negro," a nonconformist, a protestor, and a gadfly, Frazier represents a generation of Black sociologists who embodied the intellectual, political, and social zeitgeist that characterized the 1920s. At a historical juncture when issues centered on race, crime, and justice were at the forefront of the American discourse, Frazier ascended as a young scholar concerned with examining some of the most prevalent issues associated with the Black experience—the progression of racism endured by Blacks that included slavery, involuntary migration, emancipation, segregation, and urbanization. Whereas Frazier is most notably recognized as both a student and scholar of sociological thought, his contributions to criminological thought are less acknowledged but equally significant. Frazier's avid scholarship exemplifies his countless contributions to both sociological and criminological thought and illustrates his legacy as a scholar. Although his research on the Black family, critique of the Black middle class, and final address to the Negro intellectual are often considered the pinnacle of scholarly contributions, it is his examination of Blacks in the United States that has significantly enriched sociological and criminological thought. Frazier's extensive review of family disorganization, crime, delinquency, and other similarly related issues plaguing Black communities provides an informed understanding of the complexity of race in American society.

Edward Franklin Frazier dedicated a significant part of his life to opposing three things: racial injustice within the context of American society; the reluctance on the part of Blacks to satisfy and/or excel national standards; and the pretentiousness, superficiality, and embracing of false ideals among the Black middle class. Frazier, unlike more mainstream scholars of his time, challenged conventional wisdom by attempting to dispel the disingenuous assertions and stigmatizing labels that perpetuated myths and untruths about Blacks. Amid the mendacious assertions, Frazier was primarily concerned with dispelling the myth of Negro inferiority which dominated extant examinations of the Black experience. It is Frazier's

departure from mainstream explanations that have significantly contributed to a more informed understanding of the importance of sociologically based explorations of the Black historical experience.

Vestiges of Slavery: Race, Social Disorganization, and Crime

Race

The late 1920s witnessed the birth of an intellectual movement comprising Black scholars, intellectuals, and activists. Frazier exemplifies the intellectual ferment of this era. The racial climate, characterized by racial animus, segregation, and political and social turmoil, which permeated American society, illustrates the insidious racism that predominated and served as the impetus for Frazier to challenge examinations of Blacks. Frazier's research emerged in response to mainstream characterizations of Blacks as inferior, pathological, deficient, and criminally prone. According to Frazier, extant examinations of Blacks illustrated both an acceptance and overreliance on deficit models to explain issues plaguing the Black community, rather than a historical examination of the legacy of slavery, involuntary migration, emancipation, segregation, and urbanization experienced by Blacks in the United States. More specifically, Frazier argued that the cumulative effects of racism resulted in Blacks being afforded no more than second-class citizenship. As such, in an effort to identify the complexity of race relations in the United States, Frazier enunciated that the tumultuous relationship between Blacks and American society was best situated within a historical and ecological context.

Social Disorganization

A descendant of the Chicago School of Sociology, Frazier was significantly influenced by the theoretical and methodological approaches to sociology that emerged at the University of Chicago during the late 1920s. Rooted in a commitment to objective inquiry, ecological approaches to understanding social change, and social disorganization advanced as a theoretical approach to predict and explain the etiology of crime in urban locales plagued by physical decay and social disorder,

Frazier's research parallels both the theoretical and methodological approaches advanced during this era. However, critical of social scientific methods of inquiry, Frazier opined that attitudinal and quantitative methods, deemed optimal methods of objective inquiry, failed to yield meaningful data and precluded appreciable results. More specifically, Frazier asserted that conventional methods of inquiry were void of analyses of historicity, human ecology, and social relations. As such, Frazier employed both quantitative and qualitative methods of inquiry to examine the impact of social change on the Black family and community.

Although critical of conventional methods of inquiry, Frazier's research illustrates the utility of the ecological approach and social disorganization theory to explore family dissolution, crime, and delinquency. According to Frazier, the abysmal social conditions that plagued the Black community were a manifestation of urbanization and the resultant physical decay and social disorder. Employing a historical analysis, Frazier asserted that urbanization, akin to slavery, was a consequence of the systematic, intentional, and insidious racism experienced by Blacks. Moreover, social and economic forces undermined the strength and cohesiveness of the Black family and community and contributed to the absence of communal controls and the prevalence of crime and delinquency.

Crime

Amid his numerous contributions to the sociological body of knowledge, dispelling the myth of Negro inferiority by raising existential questions regarding disingenuous assertions premised on race serves as Frazier's greatest intellectual achievement. The assumption that crime and delinquency, akin to Negro inferiority, were attributable to deficiency and pathology of the Negro predominated in social science research and was underscored by deficit models which perpetuated myths and untruths. Frazier challenged this frame of thought by examining social disorganization, family dissolution, crime, and delinquency through a purely sociological lens, situating the Black Diaspora within an ecological and historical framework.

Frazier, challenging conventional wisdom, began with the presupposition that crime and delinquency among Blacks were attributable neither to deficiency nor to pathology but rather to social structural factors, economic conditions, family dissolution, and lack of community controls. Moreover, Frazier maintained that crime, delinquency, and similarly related social ills plaguing the Black community exemplified the vestiges of slavery, which remained ubiquitous in the U.S. emancipation, according to Frazier, serving as the catalyst for the states' increased interest in Blacks as criminal in an effort to maintain racial and class divisions. Urbanization, a manifestation of emancipation, further perpetuated crime and delinquency as a consequence of the disorganizing effects on the family and the community. The efficacy of both traditional methods of inquiry and personal narratives to explore crime and delinquency among Blacks illustrates Frazier's ardent desire to capture the uniqueness of the Black experience.

The Failure of the Negro Intellectual

E. Franklin Frazier illustrated his greatest intellectual fury in his 1962 publication *The Failure of the Negro Intellectual*. Frazier's indefatigable effort to advance the race is best exemplified by his unapologetic critique of the Black middle class in general and the Negro intellectual in particular. In his address, Frazier provides an assessment of the relationship of Blacks to American society and the catalytic force of racism. More specifically, Frazier examined the processes of integration and assimilation, as well as the associated costs.

Vehemently pessimistic about the fulfillment of ultimate assimilation, Frazier enunciated that it was necessary for Blacks to be integrated into American society both socially and economically as an initial stage toward a remedy of the "Negro problem." However, assimilation, a more fundamental challenge according to Frazier, remained a question unanswered.

Advancing his earlier critique of the emerging Black middle class, Frazier asserted that it was the preoccupation with integration and ultimate assimilation which illustrated the greatest failure of Black intellectuals. Moreover, the allure resulted in the loss of meaning as it related to the unique culture of Blacks and the progress of the race. Charging the intellectual periphery of the Black middle class, Black leaders, and the intellectual community with a spirit of anti-intellectualism tainted by the desire to achieve the "American dream," Frazier likened the Negro intellectual to an unconscious victim both unaware of and unconcerned with the fundamental impact of slavery. Moreover, Frazier argued that contempt and discrimination, despite integration, continued to be an enduring reality among the Black middle class who had sacrificed their identification, self-image, and sense of personal dignity. Frazier's contemptuous critique signifies an indelible warning to the Black intellectual as well as the Black community generally.

Academic Scholarship: A Vehicle for Social Change

Dedicated to producing scholarship as a means of advancing the race, Frazier remains one of the most extraordinary intellectual minds America has produced. Publishing, at times, controversial yet thought-provoking scholarship on issues related to the Black family, church, and community, Frazier's indefatigable ardor for examining the impact of social change on Blacks within the context of the United States remains one of his most significant contributions to the epistemology of sociology in general and the sociology of knowledge in particular. His audaciousness in raising existential questions regarding race relations in American society and his critique of the appropriateness of using social scientific methods to investigate the social realities of Blacks earned Frazier countless accolades for his contributions to the field of social science, advancing historically Black colleges and universities, and enriching the race.

Frazier's Legacy

Symbolic of the duality of both scholar and activist, Frazier's pioneering research has contributed to the emergence of Black sociology and to American sociology generally. In 1948, Frazier was the first Black male to serve as president of the American Sociological Society (later renamed the American Sociological Association). After an extended tenure at his alma mater, Howard University, Frazier retired as the chair of the Department of Sociology in 1959. On May 17, 1962, he died in Washington,

D.C., at the age of 68. In honor of Frazier's dedication to using education as a vehicle for social change, the *Journal of Negro Education* devoted its fall 1962 issue to his life's work. To honor his commitment and innumerable contributions to the institution, Frazier was named Professor Emeritus of the Department of Sociology and the African Studies Program, and on May 24, 2000, the Howard University School of Social Work established the E. Franklin Frazier Center in his honor. In the spirit of Frazier's legacy, the center is committed to conducting research that examines issues affecting families, communities, and geographic locales within the context of a diverse and racially heterogeneous environment.

Misha S. Lars

See also African Americans; Chicago School of Sociology; Harlem Race Riot of 1935; Historically Black Colleges and Universities; National Association for the Advancement of Colored People (NAACP); Racism

Further Readings

American Sociological Association. (2005). *E. Franklin Frazier*. Retrieved from http://www.asanet.org/page.ww?section=Presidents&name=E.+Franklin+Frazier

Balfour, L. (2005). Edward Franklin Frazier. In *Africana: The encyclopedia of the African and African American experience* (Vol. 2, p. 708). New York: Oxford University Press.

Bracey J., Meier, A., & Rudwick, E. (1988). The Black sociologists: The first half century. In J. A. Ladner (Ed.), *The death of White sociology: Essays on race and culture* (pp. 3–22). Baltimore: Black Classic Press.

Davis, A. P. (1962). E. Franklin Frazier (1894–1962): A profile. *Journal of Negro Education, 31*(4), 429–435.

Frazier, E. F. (1927, June). The pathology of race prejudice. *Forum, 70,* 856–862.

Frazier, E. F. (1932). *The Negro family in Chicago*. Chicago: University of Chicago Press.

Frazier, E. F. (1939). *The Negro family in the United States*. Chicago: University of Chicago Press.

Frazier, E. F. (1949, February). Race contacts and the social structure. *American Sociological Review, 14*(1), 1–11.

Frazier, E. F. (1957). *The Negro in the United States*. New York: Macmillan.

Frazier, E. F. (1962). *Black bourgeoisie: The rise of the new middle class in the United States*. London: Collier-Macmillan.

Frazier, E. F. (1998). The failure of the Negro intellectual. In J. A. Ladner (Ed.), *The death of White sociology: Essays on race and culture* (pp. 52–66). Baltimore: Black Classic Press.

Greene, H. T., & Gabbidon, S. L. (2000). *African American criminological thought.* Albany: State University of New York Press.

Howard University. (2001). *E. Franklin Frazier.* Retrieved from http://www.howard.edu/library/Social_ Work_Library/Franklin_Frazier.htm

Howard University. (2002). *E. Franklin Frazier Center for Social Work Research.* Retrieved from http://www .howard.edu/schoolsocialwork/SW/FrazierCenter.htm

FURMAN V. GEORGIA

In the 1972 case of *Furman v. Georgia,* the U.S. Supreme Court addressed the question of whether capital punishment constituted cruel and unusual punishment in violation of the Eighth and Fourteenth Amendments. The Court held that although the death penalty is not in itself cruel and unusual, the Eighth and Fourteenth Amendments imposed some limitations on state administration of the death penalty. The disproportionate application of the death penalty to the poor and to minorities was a central focus of the case.

Background

Since the ratification of the U.S. Constitution and the adoption of the Bill of Rights, support for the death penalty has waxed and waned. After World War II, abolitionist sentiment grew, and a number of state legislatures eliminated capital punishment. In the early 1960s, opponents of the death penalty turned to the courts, hoping that the success of constitutional litigation to rectify discrimination in other social and political institutions (e.g., cases involving school desegregation and reapportionment) would continue. In *Robinson v. California* (1962), the Supreme Court held that the Eighth Amendment's prohibition against cruel and usual punishment applied to the states, and in *Witherspoon v. Illinois* (1968), the Court held that a death sentence could not be carried out where the jury recommending it had been chosen by excluding "for cause" any prospective jurors who

had "religious or conscientious scruples" against inflicting the death penalty. But in *McGautha v. California* (1971), the Court found no constitutional infirmity where the jury imposed the death penalty without any governing standards, even in unitary proceedings in which the jury determined both guilt and punishment. One month later, the Court granted certiorari in *Furman v. Georgia* (1971) and in three other cases (*Aikens v. California,* 1971; *Jackson v. Georgia,* 1971; and *Branch v. Texas,* 1971) to determine whether imposing and carrying out the death penalty in these cases (involving convictions for rape or murder) constituted cruel and unusual punishment in violation of the Eighth and Fourteenth Amendments. (After certiorari was granted, but before the Court's decision in *Furman v. Georgia,* 1972, the Supreme Court of California declared that capital punishment in California was unconstitutional under the California Constitution and that the decision was fully retroactive. In light of this intervening decision, the U.S. Supreme Court dismissed certiorari in *Aikens v. California,* 1972.)

Opinion

In a one-paragraph per curiam opinion that offered neither an explanation of its decision nor guidance for state death penalty legislation, a sharply divided Supreme Court held that imposing and carrying out the death penalty "in these cases" (*Furman v. Georgia, Jackson v. Georgia,* and *Branch v. Texas*) constituted cruel and unusual punishment in violation of the Eighth and Fourteenth Amendments. Each of the justices in the five-four majority wrote a separate opinion (totaling more than 230 pages in the *United States Reports*), and no single analysis prevailed. The positioning of the justices left open the possibility that capital punishment could be upheld if properly structured in its application.

Justices Brennan and Marshall found the infliction of the death penalty constitutionally impermissible in all circumstances under the Eighth and Fourteenth Amendments. Justice Brennan's opinion explored the Framers' intent with respect to cruel and unusual punishment and set forth four principles for assessing the constitutional validity of challenged punishments: (1) "a punishment must not be so severe at to be degrading to the dignity of human beings," (2) "the States must not arbitrarily inflict a severe punishment," (3) "a severe punishment must not be unacceptable to contemporary society," and (4) "a severe punishment must not be excessive." Justice Marshall's concurrence focused on the origin and judicial history of capital punishment; argued that the average American citizen, if presented with all the facts regarding capital punishment, would "find it shocking to his conscience and sense of justice" and stated that "the measure of a country's greatness is in its ability to retain compassion in time of crisis."

Justices Douglas, Stewart, and White determined it unnecessary to decide the ultimate question of the constitutionality of capital punishment, concurring on narrower grounds. Justice Douglas described discretionary death penalty statutes as "pregnant with discrimination" and noted that the death penalty was disproportionately imposed on minorities and the poor. Justice Stewart found that the death penalty is "wantonly and so freakishly imposed," while Justice White focused on the fact that "there is no meaningful basis for distinguishing the few cases in which it is imposed from the many cases in which it is not."

Chief Justice Burger and Justices Blackmun, Powell, and Rehnquist dissented. Justice Powell found the death penalty constitutionally permissible, cautioned against injecting "personal predilections" into analysis of the language of the Eighth Amendment, reasoned that all of the arguments and factual contentions accepted in the concurring opinions had been rejected in *McGautha* and that that decision should be regarded as a controlling pronouncement of law, and thus concluded that the Court had "overstepped" its bounds. Justice Powell's dissent lamented "the shattering effect [of the concurring opinions] on the root principles of stare decisis, federalism, judicial restraint and—most importantly—separation of powers." Similarly, Justice Rehnquist focused on the role of judicial review and emphasized deference to State legislative judgment.

Aftermath

Because *Furman* did not hold that the death penalty is inherently cruel and unusual, it essentially created a moratorium on the death penalty. Thirty-five states responded to *Furman* by revising their capital sentencing procedures to satisfy the Court's objections and concerns. In 1976, the Court considered a representative group of these statutes, upholding three states' post-*Furman* death sentencing provisions and striking down two others.

In *Gregg v. Georgia* (1976), *Proffitt v. Florida* (1976), and *Jurek v. Texas* (1976), the Court upheld statutes that guided the exercise of discretion by a judge or jury in the imposition of the death penalty, finding constitutional those capital sentencing procedures that focused on the particularized circumstances of the individual offense and individual offender and that required a consideration of aggravating and mitigating factors.

In *Woodson v. North Carolina* (1976) and *Roberts v. Louisiana* (1976), the Court held that certain mandatory death sentences that did not provide for a consideration of the character, personal background, and criminal record of the individual offender or the circumstances under which the particular offense occurred violated the Eighth Amendment's prohibition of cruel and unusual punishment.

On January 17, 1977, Gary Gilmore of Utah became the first person executed after the reinstatement of the death penalty. Since Gilmore, there have been 1,125 other executions (as of October 15, 2008).

Avi Brisman

See also Death Penalty; Marshall Hypotheses; Sentencing Disparities, African Americans; Sentencing Disparities, Latina/o/s; Sentencing Disparities, Native Americans

Further Readings

Aikens v. California, 403 U.S. 952, 91 S.Ct. 2280, 29 L.Ed.2d 863 (1971).

Aikens v. California, 406 U.S. 813, 92 S.Ct. 1931, 32 L.Ed.2d 511 (1972).

Branch v. Texas, 403 U.S. 952, 91 S.Ct. 2287, 29 L. Ed.2d 864 (1971).

Carter, L. E., & Kreitzberg, E. (2004). *Understanding capital punishment law*. Newark, NJ: Matthew Bender.

Furman v. Georgia, 403 U.S. 952, 91 S.Ct. 2282, 29 L.Ed.2d 863 (1971).

Furman v. Georgia, 408 U.S. 238, 92 S.Ct. 2726, 33 L.Ed.2d 346 (1972).

Gregg v. Georgia, 428 U.S. 153, 96 S.Ct. 2909, 49 L. Ed.2d 859 (1976).

Jackson v. Georgia, 403 U.S. 952, 91 S.Ct. 2287, 29 L.Ed.2d 863 (1971).

Jurek v. Texas, 428 U.S. 262, 96 S.Ct. 2950, 49 L.Ed.2d 929 (1976).

McGautha v. California, 402 U.S. 183, 91 S.Ct. 1454, 28 L.Ed.2d 711 (1971).

Proffitt v. Florida, 428 U.S. 242, 96 S.Ct. 2960, 49 L. Ed.2d 913 (1976).

Rivkind, N., & Shatz, S. F. (2001). *Cases and materials on the death penalty.* St. Paul, MN: Thomson/West.

Roberts v. Louisiana, 428 U.S. 325, 96 S.Ct. 3001, 49 L.Ed.2d 974 (1976).

Robinson v. California, 370 U.S. 660, 82 S.Ct. 1417, 8 L.Ed.2d 758 (1962).

Streib, V. L. (2003). *Death penalty in a nutshell.* St. Paul, MN: Thomson/West.

Witherspoon v. Illinois, 391 U.S. 510, 88 S.Ct. 1770, 20 L.Ed.2d 776 (1968).

Woodson v. North Carolina, 428 U.S. 280, 96 S.Ct. 2978, 49 L.Ed.2d 944 (1976).

GAMBLING

Race and crime have played and continue to play a prominent role in the realm of gambling, most notably in the United States, where many religious groups maintain that gambling is sinful because it intrudes into God's domain. Religious considerations, combined with notorious episodes of criminal skullduggery, led to the outlawing of gambling in all American jurisdictions near the end of the 19th century. But states, hard-pressed for funds to provide adequate services to residents, subsequently returned to lotteries and other forms of wagering as a painless political move, much more acceptable to citizens than tax increases.

At first, gambling in the United States tended to be controlled by organized crime, but in recent years corporate interests have taken over big-time gambling enterprises, aware that such businesses could be operated legally and yield huge profits. All that is necessary is to arrange the odds—such as the percentage paid out by slot machines—to assure that the house takes away a satisfactory percentage of the money wagered.

Gambling has a strong appeal to the wishful, the oppressed, the naive, the credulous and, often, the bored. A particular attraction to deprived racial and ethnic minorities is the prospect, however unlikely, of an escape route from financial burdens. People fool themselves into believing that they can beat the odds, either through skill or, more likely, by good luck.

There are three major situations in which race, crime, and gambling have intersected. The first involves the striking appeal of gambling to Chinese, both at home and abroad. In Chinese culture, luck and chance are often viewed as mystical qualities. In addition, for Chinese Americans who may feel uncomfortable conversing in English, linguistic interaction is not necessary in the nonverbal world of slots and other gambling activities. The Chinese involvement in gambling has been marked by the construction of multimillion-dollar casinos in Macau, mostly by Las Vegas interests. Macau, a former Portuguese colony, was returned to China in 1999 and lies but a short jetfoil ride from Hong Kong. Since 2008, Macau has shown the highest gambling profits in the world, outpacing Nevada.

The second interaction among gambling, crime, and race has been the proliferation of gambling casinos operating on Native American reservations in the United States, from which Native American tribal members are reaping what were once unthinkable incomes. Several well-publicized criminal activities have surfaced in connection with efforts to establish and protect Native American casinos.

The third situation is the illegal neighborhood betting activity in American slum areas, largely engaged in by members of minority groups, notably Hispanics and African Americans. These arrangements persist despite the emergence of state-sponsored lotteries.

Chinese Gambling

There is no question that in general, persons of Chinese ethnic identity are more attracted to gambling than persons with other ethnic backgrounds. In 1897, the Reverend James S. Dennis wrote in *Christian Missions and Social Progress* that "China seems to lead the van of the gambling world." "The indulgence of the Chinese," Dennis went on to say, "is immemorial and inveterate; in fact, it is justly regarded as the most prominent vice in China." According to a 1998 survey by William Thompson, half of the money gambled in England's 120 casinos came from Chinese players. In the United States, a poll of 1,800 residents in San Francisco's Chinatown found that 75% regarded gambling as the most serious social problem in their midst. That view was buttressed by data indicating that 21% of Chinatown's people defined themselves as "pathological gamblers" and 16% considered themselves "problem gamblers."

There is no agreement on the reasons for the strikingly great attraction of gambling to Chinese. Most explanations point out that gambling behavior is learned by Chinese youngsters as a prominent part of their culture, manifest in games such as mah-jongg and pai-gow, which are played with tiles, and sic bo, a combination of roulette and craps. Importantly, there is no Chinese religious doctrine that defines gambling as sinful; it commonly is regarded as a form of recreation. In the United States, the condition of Chinese immigrants, aliens in a new and often confusing culture, was believed to be responsible for the illegal gambling dens that appeared in Chinese ghettos when the Chinese first came to the West Coast of the United States to work on the railroads. When these immigrants were liberated briefly from their back-breaking labor, visits to gambling halls, brothels, and opium dens provided a few hours of relief. Today, Las Vegas and Native American gambling sites are especially cordial and respectful to Chinese and often other Asian clients, knowing that they typically are their best customers.

Other Asian countries besides China, including Vietnam, the Philippines, Korea, and Cambodia, generally manifest a level of gambling that correlates with the infusion of Chinese culture into their population. On the China mainland, gambling is outlawed, but in Hong Kong the Jockey Club enjoys a monopoly on racetrack betting and is energetically working to keep Internet gambling from intruding. In March 2007, the police in Hong Kong discovered that organized crime groups had planted darts with tranquilizing drugs in the turf by the starting gates at a racetrack. The intent apparently was to mildly sedate horses favored to win and to place wagers on those spared from the drugging. The situation in Hong Kong emphasizes that crime and corruption, sometimes dormant but always lying in wait, tend to be associated with gambling.

Shanghai and other major Chinese cities are said to have a vibrant underground gambling economy. An English-language newspaper in China, the *Shanghai Sun*, recently observed half-facetiously that all Chinese are born with a gambling gene.

Other Asian American groups show particular gambling patterns. In southern California, an illegal gambling venture involves video poker games in cafés frequented by Vietnamese Americans. The tabletop equipment appears to be the same as that in a legitimate video parlor, but it can be altered into a gambling mode by use of a remote control gadget, making it difficult for the police to spot the illegal action. When a non-Vietnamese enters the café, any machine being used for gambling quickly is moved back into its innocent-appearing video mode.

Native American Gambling

Casinos run on tribal territory by Native Americans came onto the scene in the 1990s. In 2009, there were approximately 400 such casinos run by approximately half of the nation's 556 federally recognized tribes. The National Indian Gaming Commission, in its most recent report, indicates that in 2007 these sites accounted for $26 billion in revenues.

The initial step along the path toward the appearance of Native American casinos came in the federal appellate court decision in *Seminole Court Tribe v. Butterworth* (1981). The Seminoles were operating high-stake bingo games that the state of Florida sought to prohibit. The court came down in favor of the tribe. Six years later, in *California v. Cabazon Band of Mission Indians* (1987), the U.S. Supreme Court ruled that neither state nor local laws could be used to ban gambling on the Cabazon and Morongo tribal reservations in Riverside County because Indian tribes retain "attributes of sovereignty over their members and their territory" and that "this sovereignty is subordinate only to the federal government." In 1988, the Congress enacted the Indian Gaming Regulatory Act that legalized gambling on all Native American reservations.

Today, the Foxwoods Resort Casino in Connecticut, run by the Mashantucket Pequot tribe, is said to be the most lucrative gambling operation in the western hemisphere. Each day Foxwoods and its competitor Mohegan Sun dispatch 100 buses to the predominantly Asian neighborhoods in Boston and New York, with twice that many pressed into service on the Chinese New Year, Thanksgiving, and Christmas. It is estimated that one third of the customers at Foxwoods are Asian, and mostly Chinese. Not unusual is the case of Zheng Yuhu reported on Yahoo News on July 20, 2006. She came to New York about a decade ago. She works 6 days a week, 11 hours a day, preparing takeout food in a Chinese restaurant. On the seventh day, she takes the bus to Foxwoods, where she gathers with her friends. "Life in America is hard," she says. "There's nowhere else to go. We don't have cars."

Critics say that Foxwoods and some other reservation casinos were created by fraudulent tactics that identified as Native Americans numerous persons who did not truly belong on tribal rolls. Particularly notorious have been the well-publicized Native American lobbying efforts that often crossed the line into criminal behavior. Six tribes hired Jack Abramoff to press their interests, and Abramoff collaborated with a former aide to Tom DeLay, then the House of Representatives majority leader, to bilk the tribes out of $80 million in the years between 2001 and 2004. More than two thirds of the money went into the pockets of the lobbyists. In an ugly double-cross, Abramoff got the Texas legislature to shut down the Tigua tribe's Standing Rock casino and then gulled the tribal counsel into paying him $4 million on his promise that he would manage to get permission for it to resume operation. Abramoff pled guilty to three criminal charges and received a relatively light sentence of 5 years and 10 months in return for his agreement to cooperate with the prosecution in related cases. Also pleading guilty for making false statements under oath during the Abramoff investigation was Congressman Robert Ney of

Ohio, who, among others things, had been treated to a golfing excursion to Scotland financed by Abramoff's Native American clients. Ney was sentenced to 30 months' imprisonment.

Leaders of the Native American tribes were themselves not without guilt. The Choctaw, for instance, had agreed to launder the payments it made to evangelist Ralph Reed, who was part of the lobbying team, because Reed did not want to run the risk of having it become public knowledge that he had accepted money from gambling interests. The Choctaw's particular lobbying concern was an effort to keep the Alabama legislature from allowing slot machines to be installed at dog racing sites, which they saw as competition they wanted to head off.

Betting on Numbers

Betting on numbers, an illegal activity, is also known as "policy," "bolita," and "the figures," and is largely found in depressed urban ghettos where large numbers of minorities dwell. The odds of 600 to 1 for picking a winning three-digit number are better than those offered by the state-run lotteries. In addition, no taxes need to be paid on numbers winnings. In New York City, the police in 2006 uncovered a wide network of sites that sold chances on numbers, including hair salons and bodegas. Some numbers merchants took bets in their cars. Tens of thousands of New Yorkers are estimated to play the numbers each week. The winning figures are calculated from the last number of the total amount bet on winning horses in specified races at designated tracks.

In urban slum areas, where the numbers business flourishes, women send their children to a grocery store with some extra change to place on a number. Publications, so-called dream books, claim to provide clues to likely winning numbers. Competition from newcomers is eliminated either by mergers or by the police who are paid off for ignoring the activity.

Criminal Dynamics of Gambling

Crime, especially acts involving racial and ethnic minorities who have limited funds with which to wager, enters into the gambling scene when bettors are impelled to break the law in order to obtain funds to sustain their habit. Police records are replete with tales of robberies, murders to collect insurance, beatings by loan sharks, and similar depredations that are believed to have resulted from unmanageable gambling losses. Family tensions that erupt into domestic violence are also said to result from the stress associated with the squandering by gambling of the breadwinners' salaries. The opportunity to break the law has been particularly fueled by the careless issuance of credit cards by Visa, MasterCard, and other financial organizations that rely on exceptionally high interest rates to recoup any amounts that might be lost—and cannot be repaid—by persons who owe gambling debts.

There are no satisfactory statistical reports on the relationship between gambling and crime, either in general or in regard to minority groups. The Federal Bureau of Investigation *Uniform Crime Reports* database indicates that about the same proportion of Blacks and Whites are arrested for gambling offenses, but these are at best only a hint at the extent of illegal wagering.

Gilbert Geis

See also Immigrants and Crime; Native Americans; Organized Crime

Further Readings

Aasved, M. (2003). *The sociology of gambling.* Springfield, IL: Charles C Thomas.

Benedict, J. (2000). *Without reservation: The making of America's most powerful Indian tribe and the world's largest casino.* New York: HarperCollins.

Clotfelter, C. T., & Cook, P. J. (1989). *Selling hope: State lotteries in America.* Cambridge, MA: Harvard University Press.

Darian-Smith, E. (2004). *New capitalists: Law, politics, and identity surrounding casino gambling on Native American land.* Belmont, CA: Wadsworth.

Nguyen, T. H. (2004). The business of illegal gambling: An examination of the gambling business of Vietnamese cafes. *Deviant Behavior, 25,* 451–464.

Thompson, W. N. (1998). Casinos de juegos del mundo: A survey of world gambling. *ANNALS of the American Academy of Political and Social Science, 556*(1), 11–21.

GANG INJUNCTIONS

Gang injunctions, also known as civil gang injunctions, are court orders sought by public prosecutors to quell a specific gang or named gang members and associates' routine activities in a geographically defined space. The injunctions that have been granted primarily affect impoverished, minority neighborhoods and may actually serve to further stigmatize and oppress innocent minority youth who also live in these communities. This entry briefly explains the history of gang injunctions and the gang injunction process and touches upon the potential for abuse in acquiring gang injunctions.

History

The primary goal of a gang injunction is to eliminate a public nuisance caused by a gang or gang members within a specified target area. Although a couple of gang injunctions have been granted in Texas and Illinois, the overwhelming majority of injunctions have been obtained in southern California.

The use of gang injunctions can be traced back to Santa Ana, California, where, in 1980, a court issued a temporary restraining order that forbade gang members from gathering and drinking at a known gang hangout that was the source of widespread criminal activities in the surrounding area. Over the next couple of years, a few other building abatement injunctions addressing gang activity (i.e., graffiti, drinking, loitering, etc.) were obtained by both the Los Angeles County District and Los Angeles City Attorneys.

The success of these early abatements led to the first court order representing a gang injunction. Although it was quite controversial (even the judge questioned the use of civil sanctions against gang members), 23 named members and all other known members of the Playboy Gangster Crips were prohibited from certain activities, such as trespassing, vandalism, littering, and harassing and intimidating citizens, under civil law. The first injunction to prohibit defendants from appearing in public view with any other defendant within the target area was obtained in 1992 by the Burbank City Attorney's Office against members of the

Barrio Elmwood Rifa gang. It was this injunction that led to a constant course of filings over the next decade.

Strategy Against Gang Environments (SAGE)

A year after the 1992 injunction in Burbank, the Los Angeles County District Attorney's Office established the Strategy Against Gang Environments (SAGE) program. Although SAGE uses community outreach as well as other interventions, its focus is primarily on the use of injunctions. In fact, SAGE attorneys have even been involved in training or assisting prosecutors in other jurisdictions on the injunction process. Additionally, the Los Angeles County District Attorney's Office has published a guide to the SAGE program that includes more than multiple steps in the injunction process.

The Injunction Process

Because the process used to obtain gang injunctions may vary from jurisdiction to jurisdiction, the following discussion refers to the procedures in the SAGE manual. The injunction process usually consists of two phases: acquisition and implementation.

Acquisition Phase

The acquisition phase, also called the issuance phase, involves gathering evidence to build a case against the defendants and attempting to convince a judge to grant the injunction. The main goal of this phase is to demonstrate to the court that the targeted gang is responsible for creating and maintaining a public nuisance in a particular neighborhood. Declarations can be made by the police, community residents, or both, and are submitted to the court to support the claim that the gang is responsible for the public nuisance, as well as to show that the gang is an unincorporated association. Declarations are sworn statements that describe the activities of the targeted gang and the relationship between them, the individual defendants, and the public nuisance. Although they may be more difficult to obtain because of citizens' fears of reprisal, resident declarations are usually more persuasive because of their ability to better detail the implied threat to community well-being.

Once the declarations are collected, the prosecutor applies for a temporary restraining order (TRO) and/or a preliminary injunction that requests immediate relief from the nuisance, including such activities as vandalism, harassing residents, selling drugs, and clustering near certain locations. Whether or not a TRO is issued, an order to show cause (OSC) hearing date is set. The defendants are required to be notified of the hearing but are not required to attend. If the defendants choose to attend, they may have legal representation, but because of the civil nature of the proceeding, they have no right to public defenders. At the OSC hearing, the judge may revise the restricted activities or delete certain individuals' names from the application. If the TRO/preliminary injunction is issued, each defendant must be served, as must the gang, if it is named as a defendant. The TRO/preliminary injunction remains in effect if any defendant chooses to take the suit to trial; however, if no defendant files an answer to the suit (which is most often the case), a permanent injunction is issued by default.

Implementation Phase

The implementation phase, also called the enforcement phase, involves following up with defendants and enforcing the provisions of the injunction. Once defendants have been notified of the injunction against them, they can be arrested for violating any of the conditions of the injunction. It is then up to the prosecutor to decide to bring contempt charges in either criminal or civil court. Besides allowing for all of the constitutional rights given to a criminal defendant, including right to appeal, trial by jury, and court-appointed defense, a criminal contempt charge may carry a $1,000 fine, no more than 180 days in jail, and probation. Civil sanctions include no more than 5 days in jail and a $1,000 fine. Although a civil contempt conviction may seem easier to obtain, criminal contempt allows the prosecutor to seek certain probation conditions, including searches without probable cause and longer incarceration sentences for repeat offenders.

Potential for Abuse

Because civil law prohibits defendants from confronting or cross-examining witnesses, there is increased risk of injunctions being issued based upon perjured statements. Such was the case involving the Los Angeles Police Department's Rampart Division's Community Resources Against Street Hoodlums (CRASH) unit. CRASH officers had provided declarations providing evidence that led to the issuance of two injunctions against the 18th Street gang. It was later discovered that members of the CRASH unit had fabricated other allegations of improprieties against the 18th Street gang, and the enforcement of the two injunctions was suspended.

In addition to the potential for abuse just described, some legal scholars have argued that broadly worded injunctions may threaten innocent minority youths that live in those communities that the courts are attempting to protect. Because gang members have been popularly seen as members of lower-class racial and ethnic minorities, antigang civil injunctions may perpetuate racial stigmas through the labeling of minority youths as gang associates simply because they share racial backgrounds or public spaces with gang members or because they may actively associate with gang members but not participate in a gang's nuisance-causing activities. These individuals may then be arrested during the enforcement stage and have a difficult time proving their innocence due to a lack of financial and legal resources.

Christopher Bruell

See also Rampart Investigation; Youth Gangs; Youth Gangs, Prevention of

Further Readings

Allan, E. L. (2004). *Civil gang abatements: The effectiveness and implications of policing by injunction.* New York: LFB Scholarly.

Maxson, C. L., Hennigan, K., & Sloane, D. C. (2003). For the sake of the neighborhood? Civil gang injunctions as a gang intervention tool in Southern California. In S. H. Decker (Ed.), *Policing gangs and youth violence* (pp. 239–263). Belmont, CA: Wadsworth/Thomson Learning.

Stewart, G. (1998). Black Codes and broken windows: The legacy of racial hegemony in anti-gang civil injunctions. *Yale Law Journal, 107*(7), 2249–2279.

GENDER ENTRAPMENT THEORY

Gender entrapment theory is a specific micro-level theory that attempts to explain the involvement of battered African American women in crime. Gender entrapment directly refers to the process that African American women who commit illegal activities undergo in response to the threat of violence they receive from their intimate male partners. According to this theory, throughout the gender entrapment process, the African American woman experiences an identity shift (from one of privilege that stems from her household of origin to one of an absence of privilege in her intimate relationship). This identity shift is accelerated because of the violence she is threatened with and/or experiences at the hands of her male partner, ultimately resulting in her participation in illegal activities (such as prostitution, arson or property damage, drug use, or, in the most extreme cases, the killing of one's own intimate partner or children).

Development of Gender Entrapment Theory

Early attempts at studying domestic violence among African Americans focused on certain factors that contributed to domestic violence, primarily high rates of poverty, financial instability, and high levels of unemployment. Studies showed that African Americans were 400% more violent in the home when compared to White Americans and twice as likely to engage in intimate partner abuse. As studies progressed, more focus was placed on the consequences of domestic violence, including why so many battered African American women were committing crime. Studies indicated that African American women were engaging in crime because of several factors, including racism, sexism, classism, and identity development.

Beth E. Richie first introduced the concept of gender entrapment when researching the effects of domestic violence among incarcerated African American women. Richie observed a process where African American women are vulnerable to male violence in their intimate relationships. From the perspective of gender entrapment theory, this vulnerability underlies the women's experience of violence, which in turn leads the women to take part in illegal activities.

Development of Gender Identity

Prior research that has examined gender entrapment places great emphasis on African American women's gender identity in relation to their household of origin. Most women exposed to gender entrapment had a privileged status within their families as adolescents. Having a privileged status meant that as children these women were praised and given special privileges (e.g., extra spending money for leisure activities, clothing, and other possessions) for certain qualities (including being competent and resourceful, taking care of the household chores, and helping take care of younger siblings) and were used as positive role models for the other children in the household. This privileged status becomes an important contributing element to gender entrapment, as these African American women feel a particular burden and pressure to maintain their privileged status within the family. Furthermore, the gender entrapment process begins when the African American woman's household of origin identity is contradicted by the identity that is created with her intimate partner.

When attempting to explain the link between gender entrapment and gender-identity development, many criminologists suggest that African American women at a young age learn to believe that they are in a better position than African American men. Consequently, African American women learn to feel sorry for their intimate male partner and to always maintain great loyalty to their partner. These feelings leave African American women vulnerable to gender entrapment as they feel pressured and needed to maintain the privileged status that they once had in their childhood.

Intimate Partner Violence

Many criminological studies have indicated that most women stay in abusive relationships until it is too late to get out. Research shows that battered African American women become vulnerable to a cycle of physical, emotional, and sexual abuse. The African American woman chooses not to leave the abusive relationship but to work hard to save the relationship, while at the same time attempting to maintain order in the household. Furthermore, the African American woman blames herself, denies abuse, alienates herself from the world, and abandons any plans she may have made for the future.

A central aspect of gender entrapment is the avoidance of the criminal justice system. For example, some studies suggest that battered African American women view the police as the opposition and will not reach out for help or protection. As the abuse continues, their hope and self-worth are diminished. Research suggests African American women's avoidance of the criminal justice system helps explain how these women become easily lured into illegal activities.

Participation in Illegal Activities

Battered African American women witness a series of downfalls that include their commitment to family life, their tolerance of abuse, and their lack of assistance from criminal justice agencies. Studies suggest that African American women's resistance to criminal justice agencies while they were battered and breaking the law helped cement their gender entrapment.

For instance, Richie compared battered African American women and battered White American women. Her study concluded that White American women felt less stigmatized and less misunderstood than did the African American women. The White American battered women were more willing to reach out for assistance from criminal justice agencies during the time of their battering and breaking the law. Richie's study clearly shows how African American women resisted turning to the criminal justice system and continued to engage in illegal activities because of their strong loyalty to their abusive intimate partner.

Despite the recent interest in why battered African American women are compelled to commit crime, more research is needed. A key factor in gender entrapment that needs more recognition is the onset of violence and its ongoing effects. More focus needs to be placed on interaction among race/ethnicity, gender, class, and victimization to further understand the nature and scope of gender entrapment.

Lisa R. Muftić and Rebecca D. Foster

See also Black Feminist Criminology; Domestic Violence; Domestic Violence, African Americans

Further Readings

Bent-Goodley, T. B. (2001). Eradicating domestic violence in the African American Community. *Journal of Trauma, Violence, & Abuse, 2,* 316–330.

Oliver, W. (2000). Preventing domestic violence in the African American Community. *Journal of Violence Against Women, 6,* 533–549.

Richie, B. E. (1996). *Compelled to crime: The gender entrapment of battered Black women.* New York: Routledge.

Wesely, J. K. (2006). Considering the context of women's violence. *Journal of Feminist Criminology, 1,* 303–328.

West, C. M. (2002). *Violence in the lives of Black women: Battered, black, and blue.* New York: Haworth Press.

GENERAL THEORY OF CRIME

In 1990, *A General Theory of Crime* by Michael Gottfredson and Travis Hirschi was published. The theory described in this book is often thought of as a social control theory with its theoretical foundation in both earlier social bonding theory and learning theory. At its core, the general theory of crime asserts that crime is committed because individuals have no self-control. In other words, if an individual, through processes of social bonding and learning, does not come to behave within the bounds of social norms, this means that he or she has no self-control. When testing the general theory of crime, researchers most frequently include race/ethnicity as either a key independent variable or, along with other demographic variables such as gender, as a control variable. In other words, researchers seek to answer the question, "Are there differences between Whites and minorities when it comes to the role that low self-control plays in the commission of crime and/or delinquency?"

Parenting as a Means to Instill Self-Control in Children

For Gottfredson and Hirschi, self-control is learned primarily through typical processes associated with parenting. Thus it is the institution of the family that carries the most responsibility for ensuring that children learn the meaning of delayed gratification. In this sense, children learn that they cannot always have everything they want, when they want it. Rather, they must learn that good behavior will eventually lead to a positive outcome. Conversely, bad behavior will only lead to negative consequences such as punishment. These theorists argue further that working toward establishing self-control in offspring must begin early. In fact, if self-control is not in place by the time a child is about 8 years old, it is doubtful that the child will be able to refrain from engaging in risk-taking behaviors.

Behaviors Analogous to Crime and Delinquency

One of the underlying assumptions of the general theory of crime is that most people will engage in unacceptable behaviors if they have not developed a healthy sense of self-control. For example, when very young children act out in an aggressive manner toward other children or toward an adult, they have not learned how to control themselves when they become disgruntled with an individual. Adolescents who use tobacco or who engage in underage drinking do so because they have no self-control. Adults who cheat on their income taxes have no self-control. All of these behaviors are signs pointing toward more serious problems in the future. Other behaviors that may be deemed deviant but not yet codified into law and thus recognized as a crime, for example, sexual permissiveness, are all signs of low self-control. Gottfredson and Hirschi suggested that individuals who engage in these types of activities that are *analogous to crime and/or delinquency* are one step away from crossing the line into more serious criminal behavior.

A Critique of the General Theory of Crime

One of the measures of a theory is the empirical support it is able to garner in the research arena. To date, the general theory of crime has demonstrated support for its basic underlying assumption. Studies have shown, for example, that there is a relationship between cutting classes, consuming alcohol, and low self-control among college students. Other studies have shown that low self-control is related to marital problems, educational attainment, and the achievement of, or inability to achieve, career goals.

A major critique of the general theory of crime comes from an argument that the opportunities for crime, rather than low self-control, are more likely to determine whether a crime will occur. In other words, some people may be situated such that opportunities to engage in high risk taking or criminal behavior simply do not exist. This is based on notions from differential opportunity theory and structural positivist theories such as social disorganization theory.

Perhaps the most common critique of general theory of crime is its steadfast argument that the degree of self-control an individual is able to exercise is determined in early childhood and is very difficult to change at any later time. Well-known tests of the theory, however, have refuted such an argument and have shown that self-control varies across the life course. For example, Gottfredson and Hirschi saw race as a factor when it comes to adolescent self-control, suggesting that there is a great deal of variation in how Whites and minorities monitor and supervise their children. Further, according to Gottfredson and Hirschi, there are differences by race when it comes to efforts made by parents to correct inappropriate behaviors. Such an argument suggests that minority youth are less likely to exhibit self-control than are their nonminority counterparts and, as such, are more likely to engage in risk-taking behaviors.

Although some studies suggest that there are significant differences between White and minority youth when it comes to a propensity to engage in risk taking or offending behaviors, there is also evidence that this may be true for younger adolescents but that in older adolescents, the reverse is true. This was a finding related to a major study that utilized data from the National Evaluation of the Gang Resistance Education and Training program. White youth reported, in later waves of the data, engaging in more risk-taking behaviors than did African American youth. Thus it would appear that most researchers who suggest that Gottfredson and Hirschi are incorrect in their basic assumption that self-control does not fluctuate over time are on solid ground. Further, most researchers would argue strongly against the notion that African Americans or other minorities do not place as much emphasis on supervising their children and correcting inappropriate behaviors as do Whites. Assessing variations in the parenting practices of different groups is a complex matter, no less so than exploring the extent to which self-control varies over time.

Gottfredson and Hirschi purport to have developed a theory that can explain all crime at all times and in all places. From the perspective of the general theory of crime, the explanation is quite simple: People engage in such behaviors because they have very low or no self-control. For most theorists, their argument is flawed in that crime is caused by multiple factors. This is akin to seeing the argument "Crime occurs because people freely choose to engage in such behavior" as undersimplified. In both cases, the arguments do not go far enough. Proponents of either the low self-control model or the free will model neglect to consider the multiple rival causal factors that might lead to criminal behavior. What is it, for example, about *society* that creates family climates that are conducive to bonding and learning in some neighborhoods but not in neighborhoods torn apart by disarray and violence?

Summary

The general theory of crime asserts that people commit crime because they have no self-control. If a sense of self-control is not instilled in children in the early years, it is highly unlikely that it will ever be realized. This theory argues that it is a "general" theory of crime in that it can explain all crime (violent crime, property crime, White collar crime, etc.), regardless of the time or place. Some empirical support for the theory has been found, but it still receives a great deal of criticism from proponents of other equally viable theories (structural theories, conflict theories, etc.). Most modern-day theorists argue that crime/delinquency is much too complicated a social phenomenon to be reduced to such a simple theoretical explanation.

Barbara Sims

See also At-Risk Youth; Family and Delinquency

Further Readings

Evans, D. T., Cullen, F. T., Burton, V. S., Jr., Dunaway, R. G., & Benson, M. L. (1997). The social consequences of self-control: Testing the general theory of crime. *Criminology, 35,* 475–495.

Gabbidon, S. L. (2007). *Criminological perspectives on race and crime.* New York: Routledge.

Gibbs, J. J., & Geiver, D. (1995). Self-control and its manifestations among university students: An empirical test of Gottfredson's and Hirschi's general theory of crime. *Justice Quarterly, 12,* 231–255.

Gottfredson, M., & Hirschi, T. (1990). *A general theory of crime.* Stanford, CA: Stanford University Press.

Winfree, T. L., Taylor, T. J., He, N., & Esbensen, F. A. (2006). Self-control and variability over time: Multivariate results using a 50-year multisite panel of youths. *Crime and Delinquency, 52*(2), 253–286.

Ghetto, Ethnoracial Prison

The concept of the ghetto as an ethnoracial prison is intended to call attention to the relationships between the processes of ghetto prisonization and prison ghettoization. *Ghetto prisonization* refers to the process by which the ghetto has come to resemble a penal institution in which residents are segregated from the larger society and denied the privileges possessed by those outside. The related term—*prison ghettoization*—relates to the transformation of the penitentiary from a correctional institution guided by rehabilitative ideals to a prison "warehouse" characterized by cyclical oppression through racial divisiveness, miseducation, and violence within the prison walls. More specifically, incapacitation as a means of punishment operates like a ghetto in that it separates certain groups (overwhelmingly Black men and now, increasingly, Black women) from the larger society and keeps them confined but controlled by the larger societal apparatus. Still loosely used in research related to social policy, the exact definition of the term *ethnoracial prison ghetto* remains ambiguous at best. Loïc Wacquant often uses the term to describe the way in which both the ghetto and the prison have formally and informally incapacitated the descendants of slaves in the United States. This relationship has been best illustrated through work that analyzes the containment of African Americans, which has historically occurred through the use of "peculiar institutions" such as slavery, Jim Crow practices, ghettos, and the prison-industrial complex.

The Prisonization of the Ghetto

The evolution of the Black ghetto can be traced to the Great Migration, in which southern Blacks attempted to escape from the racial injustice of the southern Jim Crow practices. Though other rationales have been cited, this attempted escape is evidenced, statistically, by the greater numbers of migrants coming from southern counties with the highest rates of lynching. With promises of prosperity and freedom, Blacks fled to the industrialized midwestern and northeastern parts of the United States where they were ultimately subjected to less blatant but equally dangerous forms of social containment. The exploitation of Black labor was prevalent in the industrialized North, the economic and social conditions were poor, and discriminatory practices were apparent in housing, education, and public accommodations.

Ostracized by Whites and shut out of the more prosperous areas of the city, Blacks had no alternative but to take refuge in their own communities, which became "Black cities within the White world." These urban communities, in which African Americans were isolated behind invisible walls, became known as "Black Belts." Black Belts protected White America from any social contact with the ghetto and its occupants.

Research on the ghetto as ethnoracial prison has suggested that the ghetto, similar to slavery and Jim Crow, failed to completely incapacitate those living in the "Black cities within the White world." Rather, during the 1960s in the midst of urban riots and the civil rights movement, African Americans, both inside and outside of the ghetto, fought for and were legislatively granted the voting and civil rights already legally afforded to them by the U.S. Constitution. This inclusion resulted in more opportunities and alternatives to life in the ghetto. The response to this potential inclusion of northern Blacks was a combination of White flight, White opposition to social welfare programs, and White support for the use of law and order methods to control urban unrest. From this perspective, the ghetto began to function as a preparatory school for the prison system.

The prisonization of the ghetto is best captured by examining specific features that are said to be peculiar to the ghetto. The ghetto was a place of confinement for its inhabitants, primarily lower-class, undereducated minorities who were trapped by the boundaries of their community. This space erected to "maintain" Blacks and "keep them at bay" often provided both beneficial and destructive features. It gave a sense of pride to those who resided there because they had access to services from other Blacks, but at the same time it reminded them that segregation was ever present. The lives of ghetto residents were endangered by high levels of crime, there was a lack of police protection, and the ghetto was overpopulated and overcrowded. The ghetto seemed to deny its residents the pursuit of happiness because the outside world operated on a completely different system of economics, whereas the ghetto communities were blocked from economic growth; nevertheless, ghetto residents continued to work and remained resilient. Often, churches provided comfort. In short, within the ghetto, economic disparity and oppressive-exploitative systems of interlocking oppression controlled the lives of ghetto residents.

The Ghettoization of the Prison

The modern prison has taken on the role of other social institutions in its confinement of African Americans. Although the prison has been labeled as a "surrogate ghetto," one could argue that the incapacitation of African Americans through the penal system existed prior to the formation of the urban ghetto. This is particularly relevant to the history of criminal punishment in the South, where freed slaves were subjected to a set of criminal laws designed specifically for them and

applicable only to them. These crimes, referred to as crimes of moral turpitude, created a system by which the South could restore their cadre of free, Black labor through criminal convictions leading to convict leasing, prison farms, and chain gangs.

Unlike the original intent of the contemporary penal system, which was designed for economic profit, the post–Civil War southern penal system simply warehouses inmates, particularly socially constructed criminals of the post–civil rights movement era. However, more recently, the trend of mass incarceration for labor has increasingly become desirable for those in the private industries and the prison-industrial complex. The prison-industrial complex ensures that punishment remains a profitable business through collaborations between lawmakers, for-profit organizations, and the U.S. criminal justice system. For example, legislative bodies pass "tough on crime" policies that contribute to increases in incarceration; these policies are supported by the interested parties, such as private prison corporations who build and profit from the construction of prisons and for-profit businesses who use cheap prison labor to cut costs. The interested parties are afforded favors by governmental organizations such as State Departments of Corrections offering prison space (i.e., cheap rent) for the private companies to house their operations All the while, the inmates are receiving minimal wages despite the profits from their labor; thus the inmates and their community are caught in an economic stranglehold. This economic control ultimately creates a symbiotic relationship between the ghetto and the prison, with people caught in a cycle whereby they leave one system only to arrive in the other.

Thus the current penal system serves to exploit the same people that its sister "peculiar institution," the ghetto, attempted to incapacitate—people of color. The prison becomes an extension of the ghetto; in fact, they become almost synonymous. Although the history is different, disproportionality is greater with Blacks, and the concept was developed in the context of Blacks, the concept of the ethnoracial prison ghetto applies also to Latinos.

The most common factor leading to the disproportionate number of minorities being herded into the criminal justice system is the War on Drugs. Launched in the 1980s, federal law mandates minimum prison terms for "serious" drug crimes. In 1980, there were 4,749 sentenced drug offenders within the federal system. In 2005, 55% (86,972) of inmates under federal jurisdiction were incarcerated for drug violations. In addition, the Federal Bureau of Prisons reports one of the largest growths in the prison population at mid-year of 2006.

The use of tougher punishments such as mandatory minimums and three-strikes laws has led to the disproportionate confinement of lower-class and undereducated populations, namely, African Americans and Latinos. With the steady increased use of harsher penalties and decreased use of good time and parole, the prisons are operating above maximum capacity, keeping the targeted population in and society "protected." In short, prison acts as a surrogate ghetto, no longer with invisible walls but with steel ones, removing the occupants from the public's view.

Isis N. Walton and Cherie Dawson Edwards

See also African Americans; Davis, Angela; Disproportionate Incarceration; Felon Disenfranchisement; Great Migration

Further Readings

Wacquant, L. (2000). The new "peculiar institution": On the prison as surrogate ghetto. *Theoretical Criminology, 4*(3), 377–389.

Wacquant, L. (2001). Deadly symbiosis: When ghetto and prison meet and mesh. *Punishment & Society, 3*(1), 95–134.

GOETZ, BERNARD (1947–)

In the mid-afternoon of December 22, 1984, Bernard Goetz shot four African American males, Barry Allen, Darrell Cabey, Troy Canty, and James Ramseur, while riding the number 2 train in New York City. The incident began when Goetz was approached by Troy Canty, who asked how Goetz was doing. Goetz interpreted the inquiry as a prelude to a mugging. Canty asked for and then demanded money from Goetz. Goetz produced a

.38 caliber handgun and shot the four youth. Goetz was indicted on criminal charges, including attempted murder, but was convicted only of illegal possession of a handgun. However, in a civil trial, damages of $43 million were awarded to Darrell Cabey, who was paralyzed and suffered brain damage as a result of the shooting. This case generated great controversy, especially concerning the justification of vigilantism, and it is important to the study of race and crime because the incident was interracial (Goetz is White) and public statements made by Goetz were viewed by many people as highly offensive.

In testimony, Goetz stated that he shot Cabey a second time, after saying, "You don't look too bad, here's another." The shot severed Cabey's spinal cord and resulted in his paralysis. A passenger pulled the emergency brake, bringing the train to a stop. Goetz stepped from the train and disappeared into the subway tunnel after briefly checking on two nearby passengers. In media coverage, Goetz became known as the subway vigilante. Reports indicated that the youth had three screwdrivers in their possession and each had an arrest history. Reports of the screwdrivers being sharpened were unfounded but widely reported. Goetz had been the victim of a mugging 3 years earlier after which he attempted to get a license to legally carry a handgun. His permit to legally carry a concealed handgun request was denied, so he resorted to carrying a handgun illegally.

Goetz surrendered to authorities in Concord, New Hampshire, on December 31, 1984. Two confessions by Goetz, one taped in New Hampshire and one later taped in New York, were videotaped and played a role in grand jury proceedings, the criminal trial, and the subsequent civil proceedings against Goetz. A grand jury was convened in late January 1985, and he was indicted on three counts of illegal weapons possession. The grand jury failed to return an indictment on the more serious charges facing Goetz, including attempted murder and assault. The favorable public opinion Goetz enjoyed following the shooting began to wane, and political pressures on the prosecution increased. As a result, the case against Goetz was brought to a second grand jury. On March 27, 1985, Goetz was indicted by a second grand jury on a total of 13 charges ranging from illegal weapons possession to attempted murder. Prior to the start of the trial in the spring of 1987, a significant portion of the indictment was dismissed by the trial judge due to the instructions to the grand jury associated with the reasonable person standard for self-defense; the charges were later reinstated by the Court of Appeals. Goetz had the benefit of the legal defense of Barry Slotnick during his criminal trial.

Slotnick was able to successfully argue a claim of self-defense on behalf of Goetz. New York law allows deadly force in self-defense to thwart an attempted robbery. A key provision of the defense claim is that imminent force or threat of force was being used to take property from another person. When self-defense is used to ward off an imminent physical threat, legal traditions require that the use of force be necessary and proportionate to the threat posed to the individual. The person using self-defense also cannot be the initial aggressor. In the case of Goetz, the four men did not show the screwdrivers to Goetz, although Goetz testified that one of the men had his hand in his pocket and there appeared to be an unidentified object. The defense centered on Goetz's belief of an impending physical harm if he did not comply with their demands for money. The defense argued that a subjective test should be used to evaluate Goetz's belief so that his attitudes toward minorities and his experience in getting mugged could have been introduced to explain his fear of being robbed and beaten. However, the New York Court of Appeals required that an objective standard be used as the basis for determining the reasonableness of his actions.

Although New Yorkers faced violent crimes and social disorder, statistically, the subway did not pose a significantly high threat to their personal safety. In the criminal case, Goetz faced a jury that included several people who had had experience with crime and fear of crime. The charges Goetz faced were both serious and confounding to his claim of self-defense. Goetz faced a charge of criminal possession in the second degree; the penalty ranges from a mandatory minimum of 1½ years to 15 years. An interesting issue was whether the illegal possession of a handgun would imply the actor's intent to use it for an unlawful purpose. Also, the attempted murder charge addresses the defendant's intent and would focus on his state of mind. Slotnick was able to

portray the four shooting victims as predators and referred to them as the gang of four. Slotnick was able to portray Ramseur as a thug as he refused to cooperate on the witness stand and was also charged with contempt. Goetz did not take the stand in the criminal case, but both sides made use of the taped confessions. Goetz was convicted for criminal possession and found not guilty on the other charges; he served less than a year in jail.

Ron Kuby represented Cabey for his civil case against Goetz. There were several significant differences between the criminal case and the civil case. The civil case took place in 1996, almost 12 years after the shooting took place. Crime and social disorder problems in New York were markedly different. Both were in decline. The burden of proof is lower in a civil trial compared to a criminal trial. The criminal trial took place in Manhattan with a predominantly White jury, whereas the civil trial took place in the Bronx with an African American and Hispanic jury. In the criminal case, Goetz was defended by Slotnick, an experienced and skilled attorney, and in the civil case, Goetz was defended by Darnay Hoffman, who was a relatively inexperienced attorney. In the criminal case, Goetz could avoid the witness stand, but the protection against self-incrimination does not extend to civil cases. Goetz's views toward minorities were also more public. Goetz was found not guilty of the more serious criminal charges stemming from the shooting, but he was found responsible for the harm inflicted on Cabey. The jury awarded $18 million in damages for the physical harm and $25 million in punitive damages in a civil trial which concluded in April 1996.

David A. Mackey

See also Victimization, White; Vigilantism; Violent Juvenile Offenders

Further Readings

Brooks, M. (1998). Stories and verdicts: Bernhard Goetz and New York in crisis. *College Literature*, 25(1), 77.

Fletcher, G. P. (1988). *A crime of self defense: Bernie Goetz and the law on trial*. New York: The Free Press.

GREAT MIGRATION

At the end of the Civil War, about 90% of African Americans lived in the former slave-holding states of the south. But as Reconstruction ended and the promises of emancipation dimmed, Blacks began to leave the agrarian south for cities in the north like Chicago, Detroit, New York, and Philadelphia. It is estimated than more than 6 million African Americans left the South between 1910 and 1970. This population movement, especially the period between 1915 and 1930, is known as the Great Migration. Within this time frame, several waves of migration occurred; however, the largest wave of migration took place during World War I, as thousands of factory workers left to fight the war. This entry examines the causes of the Great Migration and discusses the social, legal, and economic challenges faced by African Americans in northern cities.

Causes of the Great Migration

After the Civil War and despite the end of slavery, some southern Whites continued to engage in racial targeting and lynching, especially in the post-Reconstruction era during the close of the 19th century. African Americans sought an alternative to the harsh life in the segregated South, where Jim Crow laws left them disenfranchised and without recourse when they experienced blatant discrimination and violence. Many African Americans envisioned the North as a place where they could escape these conditions and experience a better life.

During the latter half of the 19th century, changes took place that drastically altered the agrarian ways of life and production. New technology, manufacturing, and mass production contributed to the reshaping of the modern city. Immigrants, predominantly from European countries, poured into the United States, searching for cheap, habitable land and factory jobs. The industrial era also spurred the development of jobs for migrants from the South. In contrast, the sharecropping system implemented in the southern United States after the Civil War left many African Americans destitute. An infestation of boll weevils in the early years of the 20th century damaged the cotton fields, and devastating floods worsened conditions further. Moving to the North offered many African Americans the opportunity to find work and earn wages that were considerably better than what they could find in the South.

Another factor in migration was the role of labor agents who represented large companies such as railroads and recruited African Americans in the South for jobs in the North. Especially during World War I, when many White men left factory jobs to fight in the war, labor agents persistently exploited southern Blacks. They made promises of work and better living conditions that enticed Blacks from the South to move out of a region that offered them very little in comparison with the promising northern city life. The war also brought about the need for more products and war materials that were sold to European countries, and as a result labor agents hired masses of Blacks to maintain productivity levels. Labor agents also played a fundamental role in overcoming labor union strikes in the North by hiring southern Blacks to cross picket lines.

Finally, the North offered both men and women an opportunity to acquire work so that a couple could both earn wages. This was very different from the typical work arrangement among families in the South, where the burden of labor was spread across the entire family but there was only one source of income. In the North, an entire family could move with the hope of earning two wages. African American men were more likely than African American women to migrate, however. The typical scenario consisted of Black men leaving behind families, often sending back remittances, and eventually reuniting with their family some time later.

Anecdotal evidence of the benefits of the North was enticing for many Blacks and often provided a motivation for moving. African American newspapers such as the *Chicago Defender* provided information about jobs in the North, and Black churches provided material resources for migrants. Many newcomers to the North moved in with other family members or friends when they migrated, and this social support eased the transition to a new environment. Organizations such as the National Urban League helped newcomers find both jobs and housing. These sources of kinship and community support helped make migration seem feasible to southern Blacks seeking change.

Racial Discrimination in Northern Cities

Although Blacks sought opportunities to create a better life, they were often hindered by discriminatory and racist attitudes among northern Whites, in addition to housing policies that resulted in the isolation of Black neighborhoods. Migration itself, social inequalities, and limited opportunities in the North contributed to Black involvement in crime and delinquency in urban areas.

Most of the Black migrants who were able to find housing settled in overcrowded tenements in the center of the city where a majority of jobs were located. Immigration from Europe intensified the demand for housing. Northern cities rapidly became crowded and socially disorganized; as more Blacks migrated northward, the range of social pathologies increased. Many migrants lived in slumlike conditions, with little to no access to public resources such as water and sanitation. Furthermore, the shortage in housing only exacerbated the problem as landlords saw the potential to exploit these populations by subdividing apartments and charging higher rent. In most major cities to which Blacks migrated, the number of applicants for housing outweighed the number of available units. Subdivision and overcrowding were all too often the remedies to the problem.

Finding employment in factories became a daunting process for many migrants. White laborers were outraged by Black laborers who were not unionized and who were paid lower wages than Whites. Labor agents employed thousands of Black migrants, a situation that only fueled anger among Whites, especially during strikes. Black migrants were prevented from obtaining trade or skilled jobs by native Whites and other European immigrants, and as a result, Blacks were offered only jobs that required manual labor and few skills. Furthermore, migrants were exposed to longer work hours and poorly ventilated work areas, and they often suffered from health conditions that resulted in many deaths. Wages for Blacks lagged far below those of the middle class, and the lack of transportation prevented many Blacks from moving out of city slums. Children of migrants were denied equal access to education, and they often attended underfunded schools with few resources.

Deindustrialization and Ghettoization

The Depression brought the shutdown of many factories and contributed to the economic problems confronting African American communities. Blacks were affected most seriously by the decline of the manufacturing and industrial sectors and the resulting loss of industrial jobs.

Due to an onslaught of social, economic, and technological innovations that made it possible for Whites to escape the inner cities and move outward, Blacks in the North faced new modes of discrimination. Assisted by federal policies, Whites were steered into homeownership in the surrounding suburbs at the expense of Blacks. The Federal Housing Authority (FHA) of the 1930s was developed in order to assist homebuyers with loans. The FHA created an appraisal system with the use of mortgage redlining as a tactic to facilitate the out-migration of Whites from the inner cities, while preventing Blacks from moving entirely. By the mid-1920s, redlining had become an important factor that contributed to the decline of property values of city residences. Most often, the victims of these policies were migrants who were most concentrated in the areas considered of little value. Realtors, banks, and local city government contributed to "White flight" and often urged Whites to move out of Black neighborhoods. Wealthier Blacks also contributed to the segregation of migrant Blacks from the South by moving out of Black neighborhoods. As a result of this social separation, migrant Blacks were isolated in pocket enclaves, often with other migrants from the same regions of the South.

To worsen the problem, highway systems often tore through city centers and displaced thousands of inner-city residents, predominantly Blacks and other minorities with little or no assistance for relocation. If federal housing did become available, it was offered in cities and not in the suburbs, thus preventing Blacks from integrating in suburban neighborhoods. Once again race played an intricate role in this process. Further discrimination and acts of violence by Whites led to major riots by Blacks. Returning White veterans were in need of work and engaged in acts of discriminatory violence. All across major cities, riots of varying magnitude broke out and in some cases ended in the loss of Black lives. Setbacks such as these severely hampered Black life in the North, stalling the movement toward equality.

By the late 20th century, these shifts in population had brought about many negative consequences, especially for those left behind. The weakened tax base made it impossible to sustain the inner cities and led to a growing economic disparity between urban and suburban areas. The movement toward the suburbs resulted in structural shifts of income and left behind a new culture of poverty marked by isolation from mainstream society, residential segregation, and few chances for socioeconomic mobility.

Politics, Power, Privilege, and the Law

The isolation of poor Blacks in ghetto neighborhoods resulted in a lack of political power as the White majority created laws that were most beneficial to Whites. Mob violence, riots, and pushback against the structural forces of the political economy instilled negative images of Blacks among Whites. Exploited by the media and politically powerful, Blacks were progressively painted as criminals and dangerous to the community's well-being and safety. Driven by fear-mongering, law enforcement and police power became new tools to overcome criminality in the Black neighborhoods. Although the vast majority of African Americans do not commit crimes, negative stereotypes associated with Blacks have left a lasting impression upon the fabric of the United States. Racial profiling became a common method of policing inner cities, and over time, racial profiling was used to arrest and convict thousands of Blacks for nonviolent crimes.

The millions of Blacks who migrated northward in the hope of economic stability often had no capital resources or assets to build upon, and they were subjected to harsh treatment, poor pay, and structural barriers. Exploitation and victimization became common methods for crime control. Black criminals at the time faced White judges, all-White juries, and punitive laws created by Whites in political power, resulting in mass incarceration.

The culmination of policies affecting Blacks in particular has created a wedge in the American people along race and class lines. Although the Civil War ended slavery and granted freedom, a new kind of social control was effected in the North, one that utilized race as a divisive tool.

Leila Sadeghi

See also Black Criminology; Detroit Race Riot of 1967; Media Portrayals of African Americans; Structural–Cultural Perspective; War on Drugs; White Privilege

Further Readings

Arnesen, E. (2003). *Black protest and the great migration: A brief history with documents.* Bedford, MA: St. Martin's.

Gabbidon, S. L., Greene, H. T., & Young, V. D. (Eds.). (2002). *African American classics in criminology & criminal justice.* Thousand Oaks, CA: Sage.

Grossman, J. R. (1989). *Land of hope: Chicago, Black southerners, and the Great Migration.* Chicago: University of Chicago Press.

Hirsch, A. R. (1983). *Making the second ghetto: Race and housing in Chicago 1940–1960.* Chicago: University of Chicago Press.

Kusmer, K. (Ed.). (1991). *Black communities and urban development in America, 1720–1991* (10 vols.). New York: Garland.

Lemann, N. (1991). *The promised land: The Great Black Migration and how it changed America.* New York: Vintage Books.

Trotter, J. W., Jr. (Ed.). (1991). *The Great Migration in historical perspective: New dimensions of race, class, and gender.* Bloomington: Indiana University Press.

Trotter, J. W., Lewis, E., & Hunter, T. W. (Eds.). (2004). *The African American urban experience: Perspectives from the colonial period to the present.* New York: Palgrave Macmillan.

GREGG V. GEORGIA

In 1976, the U.S. Supreme Court's ruling in *Gregg v. Georgia* reestablished the death penalty as constitutional in certain circumstances. The ruling came after a 4-year moratorium resulting from the Court's 1972 decision in *Furman v. Georgia*, which had found the death penalty to be unconstitutional as it was then applied. Death penalty opponents had cited significant racial disparity in death sentences in *Furman*, but race was not cited by the *Gregg* Court as a justification for overturning the death penalty. Racial disparity, in both the race of the defendant and the race of the victim, remains a major concern of death penalty opponents.

Crime, Investigation, and Trial

Troy Gregg and a companion, Floyd Allen, were picked up while hitchhiking on November 21, 1973, by Fred Simmons and Bob Moore. Outside of Atlanta, Georgia, the four travelers took a rest stop by the side of the road, where the bodies of Simmons and Moore were found the next morning. They had been killed by a .25 caliber pistol. Based on a report from a third hitchhiker who gave a description of the car the four had driven in, police picked up Gregg and Allen on November 24 in North Carolina. Gregg and Allen were in the car described by the third hitchhiker, and Gregg had a .25 caliber pistol, later shown to be the one used in the shooting of Simmons and Moore.

Gregg admitted in a signed confession to shooting and robbing both Simmons and Moore. He initially claimed he had shot in self-defense, whereas Allen stated that the shootings happened during the course of the robberies and were deliberate. When detectives brought Gregg back to the crime scene, he confirmed Allen's version of the story.

At trial, Gregg claimed self-defense, but his contrary statements to detectives and a letter he wrote to Allen were put into evidence against him. Gregg was convicted by the jury of two counts each of murder and of armed robbery. In the separate sentencing phase of the trial, he was sentenced to death for each of the murders, based on the presence of two of ten aggravating factors required by the new Georgia capital murder statute; only one was required. On appeal, the Georgia Supreme Court upheld the sentence, and Gregg then appealed to the U.S. Supreme Court.

U.S. Supreme Court Ruling

The issues before the Supreme Court were whether the death penalty was a constitutional form of punishment for the crime of murder and, if so, whether the Georgia capital sentencing statute provided sufficient procedural safeguards against arbitrary and capricious imposition of the death sentence. In *Gregg*, the Court upheld the majority finding in *Furman* that the punishment of death for the crime

of murder did not, in and of itself, violate the Eighth or the Fourteenth Amendment. Next, the Court considered whether the procedural safeguards established by the Georgia State Legislature in response to the *Furman* decision were sufficient to minimize the risk of arbitrary and capricious imposition of the death sentence. These safeguards included a bifurcated procedure: First, a trial was held to determine guilt or innocence. The guilty verdict was then followed by a separate hearing to determine whether a sentence of death was appropriate. In this penalty phase of the trial, the jury was to consider aggravating and mitigating factors. The jury in *Gregg* in fact had found two of the aggravating factors defined by the new Georgia capital sentencing statute to be present: The murders were committed firstly while the defendant was engaged in another capital offense (armed robbery), and secondly in order to obtain the victims' property. The Supreme Court held that this statutory scheme and these findings were adequate justification for the imposition of the death penalty.

Meaning and Significance

The Supreme Court's opinion in *Furman v. Georgia*, which had found the death penalty unconstitutional as then applied, had caused confusion among the states. After the *Furman* decision, 35 states passed new capital sentencing statutes that attempted to comply with *Furman*; some states made capital punishment mandatory for specified offenses, whereas others enacted schemes of mitigation and aggravation.

The guidance from *Gregg* and the cases that followed it set boundaries within which states may choose their own statutory capital sentencing schemes. The formulas for aggravating factors may vary, they may be subjective, and they may "double count" the same fact under two different aggravating factors. The critical joint legacy of *Gregg* and *Furman* is the requirement that states legislatively guide the discretion of juries and judges; the methods vary, but the requirement remains.

Other capital sentencing schemes, which require the jury to weigh the aggravating factors against the mitigating factors, were specifically found to pass constitutional muster in *Jones v. United States*, where the federal death penalty statute was found to be constitutional.

Some historians argue that *Gregg v. Georgia* is the most important death penalty case in American jurisprudence, whereas others claim that *Furman v. Georgia* is the most important. Both cases helped to shape the landscape of the death penalty in the United States today. *Furman* set what was out of bounds in terms of applying the death penalty, *Gregg* gave an example of what was in bounds, and other cases since then have either clarified the boundary or tracked its shifting.

Under the Eighth Amendment, which prohibits cruel and unusual punishment, defendants sentenced to death must have been convicted of a crime for which the death penalty is proportionate, considering both the harm that was caused and the moral blameworthiness in causing such harm. The Constitution therefore requires some level of uniformity in the sentencing process. Reserving power to the legislature to set standards regarding public policy may be considered wise because it prevents judges from arbitrarily imposing their own moral standards in sentencing.

Sam Swindell

See also *Coker v. Georgia*; Death Penalty; *Furman v. Georgia*; Marshall Hypotheses; *McCleskey v. Kemp*

Further Readings

del Carmen, R. (2007). *Criminal procedure* (7th ed.). Belmont, CA: Wadsworth.
Furman v. Georgia, 408 U.S. 238 (1972).
Gregg v. Georgia, 428 U.S. 153 (1976).
Jones v. United States, 527 U.S. 373 (1999).

GRINGO JUSTICE

In his 1987 book *Gringo Justice*, Chicano sociologist, lawyer, and activist Alfredo Mirandé provided an alternative to mainstream explanations of Chicano criminality and its social control. His book, one of the most widely recognized works in the field of criminology and criminal justice, offers a sociohistorical explanation of the seemingly disparate treatment of Mexican-origin Latinos within the U.S. criminal justice system. The concept of gringo justice developed by Mirandé offers a perspective that is rooted in a Chicano worldview and responsive to the particularities of Chicano culture and history. Even so, labeling, conflict, and social constructionist perspectives inform this framework, which first appeared alongside the early developmental years of the scholarly legal movement now commonly referred to as critical race theory.

At the heart of the concept of gringo justice is an assertion that a dual standard of justice in the United States benefits Whites at the expense of Mexican Americans. Gringo justice points to the historical development and maintenance of a stereotypical image of Chicanos as inherently criminal, rather than looking toward internal shortcomings (biological, psychological, and/or cultural) of Mexicans to explain their criminal behavior and its societal regulation. It is the mobilization of this stereotype at suitable times by public and/or private actors that produces the conscious or unconscious disparate treatment of Chicanos at the hands of various criminal justice agents and legal authorities. This entry reviews the relationship between the United States and Mexico from the early 19th century to the present, highlighting the ways in which U.S. policy and socioeconomic interests contributed to the development of a stereotype of Chicano criminality.

The Development of Gringo Justice

To fully comprehend the negative manifestations of gringo justice, it is necessary to recognize and understand the legacy of social, economic, and political conflict between the United States and Mexico, which developed during the early 19th-century settlement of the northern Mexico borderlands now identified as the American Southwest. Ironically, Mexican authorities formally invited American immigration into their northern borderlands as early as 1822 to help stabilize the region, which basically was populated by a number of nomadic and warring indigenous tribes, despite over 200 years of Spanish and Mexican colonizing efforts. A trickle of legal immigrants recruited through *empresarios*, or land agents, soon turned into a tide of mostly southern, undocumented American immigrants who brought with them preconceived notions of

Anglo superiority and dominance. Not surprising, these Anglo American immigrants in the northern borderlands came to view Mexicans as a subhuman and inferior mongrel race due to their centuries-old African, Indian, and European *mestizaje*, or racial/ethnic mixing.

This negative view of Mexicans coincided with national desires of American expansionism that congealed into the concept of Manifest Destiny. This belief became the rallying inspiration and justification for God's chosen people to settle the North American continent in order to spread freedom through democratic institutions among those who could be self-governed. Unfortunately, non-Whites, and to a lesser degree, non–Anglo Saxon Protestant Europeans were excluded from the category of those who could be self-governed. Mexicans, with their mixed racial and cultural background and adherence to feudal and Catholic traditions, were the antithesis to emergent American core values.

Equally important as a push factor for American emigration to northern Mexico was the issue of slavery. In 1820 the Missouri Compromise allowed Missouri to enter the union as a slave state, but barred the further spread of slavery in any U.S. state or territory located north of Missouri's southern border. This forced slave owners to push westward for additional territory to expand the booming cotton industry made extremely profitable by free slave labor. After Mexican independence from Spain, however, Mexico's constitution of 1824 outlawed the growth of slavery, and in 1829 a presidential proclamation abolished slavery completely. Southern slave owners who immigrated to Mexico's northern borderlands before this time period through empresario grants lobbied the Mexican government for exemptions, with later immigrating slave owners disdaining any and all Mexican laws abolishing slavery. This disregard for slave laws pitted American immigrant land grant holders against Mexican land grant holders who were without the advantages of slave labor to compete in the growing capitalist world market.

Non–slave owning American immigrants' disdain for any formal Mexican governance was manifest in the overall advantages provided to Mexican land grant owners. First of all, American immigrants applying for Mexican land grants had to formally decree their allegiance to the Mexican government by agreeing to become Spanish-speaking, Mexican Catholic citizens. Even then, American immigrant land grant applicants were at a disadvantage in securing large portions of the best arable land that were reserved for Mexican citizens, which included mestizos, de-tribalized Indians, and Afromestizos, as well as even more favored peninsulares and criollos. This limitation to smaller parcels of less arable land was particularly troublesome for American speculators and developers immigrating to the region. In fact, it was quite evident to all Americans that Mexican lands were a fountain of resources for a burgeoning U.S. society bent on spreading modern capitalist society around the globe.

U.S.–Mexican War and the Treaty of Guadalupe Hidalgo

Social, economic, and political conflict on the northern Mexican frontier came to a head through several successful and unsuccessful American filibustering endeavors that led up to the largely American immigrant declaration of Texas's independence from Mexico in 1836. Mexican officials' refusal to recognize this pronouncement burst open violent hostilities between Anglos and Mexicans over land and political power. Oddly enough, it was Mexican resistance to American aggression and illegal colonizing efforts that led to the evolution of the Mexican "bandido" stereotype. This negative icon portrayed Mexicans as bloodthirsty savages filled with wanton lust for American land and women and worked to justify sustained skirmishes in disputed lands. This provided the rationale for the formal U.S. protection of American emigrant "freedom fighters" through the annexation of Texas in 1845. For Mexico, this was a violation of international law and a declaration of war between the United States and Mexico that lasted from 1846 to 1848.

Critical analyses of early criminological research notes the tendency for many scholars to discount the enduring impact that the violent mid-19th-century takeover of the southwestern United States had on Mexican Americans and agents of social control. More often than not, this legacy of mistrust was manifested in biased law enforcement and unjust legal practices that deleteriously impacted Mexicans. The dubious exploits of the famed Texas Rangers that rose up during this era provides an example: Whereas many scholars have loudly praised the Texas Rangers' heroic-like motivation and tactics, others have likened them to a private state militia employing vigilantism in the protection of Anglo interests from renegade Indians, Mexican bandidos, and runaway slaves. Furthermore, the 1848 Treaty of Guadalupe Hidalgo, which ended "official" hostilities between the United States and Mexico, became a pretense for a legal and extralegal land grab that left Mexicans powerless and transformed them into a dependent labor force for southwestern commercial agriculture and industrialization.

In particular, U.S. governmental officials diluted provisions in Article VIII of the treaty that guaranteed the social, economic, and political rights of Mexicans remaining in ceded Mexican territories that included present-day Arizona, California, New Mexico, Nevada, Texas, Utah, and parts of Colorado, Kansas, Oklahoma, and Wyoming. Article VIII stipulated that Mexican citizens who decided to stay in the ceded region within 1 year from the date of treaty ratification would be treated as American citizens and entitled to all U.S. constitutional rights. On the other hand, Article IX proved most problematic for Mexicans in that it made the U.S. Congress the final arbiters of full American citizenship rights for Mexicans, rather than those rights being granted automatically as stipulated in Article VIII. Especially contentious turned out to be whether or not Mexicans, with their mixed racial/ethnic heritage, were entitled to full American citizenship, which at the time was reserved for free White males first and foremost.

The U.S. Congress's total deletion of Article X, which guaranteed the validity of land grants distributed by Mexican authorities before the war, further disenfranchised Mexicans. It became extremely difficult and expensive to prove land grant ownership through Spanish-language documents brought forth in English-speaking tribunals. In effect, many scholars agree that the total disregard for the Spanish language and legal customs was commonplace. Annual property taxes added to the exorbitant legal expense Mexican land owners incurred while trying to legitimate their land grants in long, drawn-out land claims. Hence, many Mexican land owners would sell their lands at less than market prices to avoid total destitution. When the takeover of Mexican lands could not be accomplished legally, Anglos often turned to forceful extralegal means in their endeavors.

Informal and formal vigilante groups like the Texas Rangers became pitted against Mexican social bandits throughout the southwest like Gregorio Cortez, las Gorras Blancas, and Juan Cortina. These social bandits were perceived as heroes by the Mexican populace because they openly resisted the legal and extralegal takeover of Mexican lands, suppression of Mexican civil rights, and the violation of Mexican families. Nevertheless, the eventual landless status of the majority of Mexicans in the region hastened their downward spiral into second-class citizenry with little influence on social, economic, and political institutions that could rectify their situation.

20th-Century Gringo Justice

U.S.–Mexican relations at the turn of the 20th century proved critical in reinforcing and reshaping the border bandido stereotype. Class conflict in Mexico produced the first big wave of Mexican immigration to the United States. Included among these immigrants were Mexican revolutionaries who sought political asylum in large southwestern Mexican urban enclaves. From here, these individuals spoke out against U.S.-supported governmental officials and economic policies in Mexico. They also spoke out against the mistreatment of Mexicans and Mexican Americans within the United States and became instrumental in the early development of Mexican labor organizing in the United States. This, coupled with border skirmishes against Pancho Villa's revolutionary army of the north, gave rise to a notion of unpatriotic disloyalty among the U.S. Mexican-origin immigrant and nonimmigrant population.

Even so, the desire for Mexican immigrant labor swelled as Asian and southern, eastern, and central European immigrant labor became scarce with the implementation of restrictive immigration policies directed toward these groups. The *barrioization*, or hypersegregation, of the U.S. Mexican population solidified during this early 20th-century era, and at the same time, rural and urban barrios began to appear in regions outside of the Southwest. As is characteristic of most socially, economically, and politically neglected neighborhoods, illicit activities turned problematic in Mexican barrios. Compounding problems were cultural differences in the definition of unacceptable conduct. Research suggests that the appearance of the cruel Mexican macho alcoholic developed out of a divergence in attitudes toward alcohol consumption between Mexicans and Anglos. In response, early 20th-century reformers and powerful business elites used misdemeanor criminal codes as a means for further securing a dependent labor force for social, economic, and political gain. The arbitrary application of vagrancy, substance use, prostitution, guns, personal assault, and contraband legal codes against Mexicans amounted to outcomes similar to those of Jim Crow laws for southern Blacks.

The Great Depression era exacerbated historically tenuous relations between Anglos and Mexicans and brought about the highly questionable repatriation of Mexicans and Mexican Americans that many felt would help stabilize wide-scale unemployment and poverty in the United States. Regardless, a mostly young, U.S.-born Mexican American community began to organize politically in order to fend off both individual and institutional discrimination at the hands of mainstream society. Indeed, the pachuco zoot-suiters came to be seen as a plague to American culture and society by the 1940s. Their eccentric style of dress and associated youth subculture symbolically challenged anti-Mexican sentiments, which came to a boil in Los Angeles during World War II. With the aid of the local media spiraling nativist frenzy, American servicemen openly attacked Mexican zoot-suiters in the summer of 1943 with little intervention by the police, which amounted to arresting Mexicans for resisting the vicious attacks.

Gringo Justice Today

Today, *Gringo Justice* should be viewed as a seminal work for Latina/o critical theory, an offshoot of critical race theory. With the help of critical race feminism, LatCrit legal theory has helped illuminate further how Latina/o criminal stereotypes are tied to issues of race/ethnicity/culture, class, and gender. At the turn of the 21st century, popular images of Mexican criminality include ruthlessly violent "gang-bangers," "illegal alien

drug smugglers," and "illegal alien welfare queens." Be that as it may, current research contradicts private and public notions of increases in criminal activity due to Latina/o immigration. Further research is needed that examines how the internalization of criminal stereotypes impacts Latina/o criminal activity. Emerging research suggests that antisocial behavior tends to increase with increased generational exposure to American culture and society.

Ed A. Muñoz

See also Critical Race Theory; Latina/o Criminology; Latina/o/s; Media Portrayals of Latina/o/s; Minority Group Threat; Profiling, Ethnic: Use by Police and Homeland Security; Profiling, Racial: Historical and Contemporary Perspectives; Racialization of Crime; Zoot Suit Riots

Further Readings

Bender, S. W. (2003). *Greasers and gringos: Latinos, law, and the American imagination.* New York: New York University Press.

Martinez, R., Jr., & Valenzuela, A., Jr. (Eds.). (2006). *Immigration and crime: Race, ethnicity, and violence.* New York: New York University Press.

Mirandé, A. (1987). *Gringo justice.* Notre Dame, IN: University of Notre Dame Press.

Muñoz, E. A., Lopez, D. A., & Stewart, E. (1998). Misdemeanor sentencing decisions: The cumulative disadvantage effect of "gringo justice." *Hispanic Journal of Behavioral Sciences, 20*(3), 298–319.

GUARDIANS, THE (POLICE ASSOCIATIONS)

African American police officers around the United States began to form fraternal groups as early as 1922, when such groups were organized in the New York City Police Department (NYCPD). Many of the groups took the name Guardians, although, regardless of their names, the groups shared patterns of initially meeting for fellowship or benevolent support, generally without the approval of their departments, and finally gaining charters from their cities or departments as one of the many ethnically or racially based groups active in large departments. This entry highlights the history of the Guardians and other police organizations concerned with the advancement of Black police officers.

The first Guardians Club in the NYCPD comprised 31 officers, most of them assigned to the 32nd Precinct in Harlem, the city's largest African American neighborhood. One of the group's founders was Samuel Battle, who had been the first African American to pass the police officer civil service exam in New York City in 1910 and who was the department's first Black supervisor. In addition to Battle, who upon his retirement in 1941 became New York State's first Black member of the Parole Board, more than half the members had achieved at least one first for African American officers. Although sharing a name with the current Guardians, the forerunner group was strictly a social club and was one of a number of similar clubs for Black officers.

The development of organizations of Black police officers differed in the southern United States because of the explicit policies of racial segregation. Although southern and western associations of Black officers rarely used the word *Guardians* in their names, they were more actively involved in political action than were northern groups and they set a course that the Guardians would eventually embrace. One of the earliest such groups was Houston's Texas Negro Peace Officers Association, formed in 1935 by six officers who held a Black-only ball to raise money for a retirement and burial fund. These were the identical functions that had led earlier to the formation of Police Benevolent Associations, the vast majority of which prohibited or severely limited the participation of Black police officers. Because few police departments at the time provided suitable disability or death benefits for any officers regardless of race, but particularly for Black officers, African American officers from other cities in Texas joined their Houston colleagues. In 1938 the group lobbied unsuccessfully for appointment of Blacks to the Dallas Police Department. Despite this setback, the Texas Negro Peace Officers Association inspired similar groups, including the Miami Colored Police Benevolent Association, which was formed in 1946, only 2 years after Black officers joined the department and learned they would not be accepted into the Police Benevolent Association. Later, in

1953, North Carolina officers formed the Negro Law Enforcement Association.

Despite having achieved some measure of legal equality, beginning in the 1940s and 1950s, a new generation of Black police officers, many of whom had fought in World War II and had been disappointed in racial progress in the United States, formed associations that took on advocacy roles for better assignment and promotional opportunities for Black officers. By the 1970s and 1980s, when they supported affirmative action policies to increase the numbers of Black officers and the creation of civilian review boards to review incidents of police brutality, these groups came into conflict with the unions representing police officers, which have almost universally opposed these measures.

Organizations for more than solely social purposes in northern police departments began in the NYCPD; as the nation's largest police department, it had a larger number of Blacks than did police departments in other cities. The New York Guardians Association developed in the early 1940s, when there were approximately 150 Black officers in the NYCPD out of a total of 1,900. Black police officers were usually assigned to precincts in Black neighborhoods, with only a few scattered elsewhere. The group differed from earlier social groups, because a major aim was to eliminate so-called Black posts and to assist Black officers in gaining full participation in department activities. A major area of dispute was that Black officers were limited to foot posts while White officers were assigned to patrol in marked cars. The Guardians received its charter in 1949, only after New York Congressman Adam Clayton Powell helped pressure the city into issuing it.

Similar events occurred in Philadelphia, where there had existed, prior to 1940, a social club made up of Blacks who worked for the police, fire, and electric departments. One of the group's members, James N. Reaves, recalled that the city administrators opposed the group for fear it might become an action group, which turned out to be correct. As in New York, one of the first areas of discrimination addressed by the Guardians Civic League of Philadelphia (chartered in 1956) was the prohibition against Black officers using patrol cars. Relying on local Black politicians, the group succeeded in getting six Black officers assigned to patrol cars. Although the breakthrough did not benefit others beyond the original six, it was the first political action by the group and set the tone for later advocacy.

Another similarity between the two groups, and others like them, was the problem they experienced in organizing. Because many Black officers felt their positions in their departments were tenuous despite civil service protections, many feared reprisals for joining groups the departments viewed as radical. Generally, early members in both cities literally stood in front of precincts to identify Black officers after the departments refused to provide employee information. Despite these modest beginnings, leaders of the New York and Philadelphia Guardians achieved high ranks; in New York, Robert L. Mangum, a founder and the first president of the Guardians, who had been a corrections officer before becoming a police officer in December 1942, retired in early 1954 as a fourth deputy commissioner. In Philadelphia, Reaves in 1954 became the city's first Black precinct captain and was later named chief of the city's housing police department, which he helped in 1971 move from guards to police officers and to form their own Guardians Association.

In Cleveland, African American officers also met with hostility when they organized the Shield Club in 1946 to defend a Black officer who, after being shot by private guards, refused to surrender his weapon to White senior officers while hospitalized in a White area of Cleveland for fear of reprisals. Like the Guardians associations, the Shield Club ultimately undertook community activism and by the 1960s opposed a number of positions taken by the Cleveland chapter of the Fraternal Order of Police, the police officers union.

Black police officers associations were active in the 1950s in gaining promotional opportunities in cities where officers were unable to take civil service examinations for higher ranks. By the 1960s, at a time of rising expectations in part influenced by the national civil rights movement, African American police officers increased their organizational efforts. Detroit police formed the Guardians of Michigan in 1963, followed in 1967 by the Afro-American Policemen's League of Chicago. In 1968, with civil unrest and anti–Vietnam War protests visible in many cities, Black police also increased their activism. Groups formed that year included San Francisco's Officers for Justice and St. Louis'

(Missouri) Ethical Police Society. In Los Angeles, where Black officers had been appointed in small numbers since 1886, in 1968 they formed the Oscar Joel Bryant Association, named to honor the first Black member of the department to have been killed in the line of duty on May 13, 1968. By 1969, Atlanta police officers had created the Afro-American Patrolmen's League, and in Hartford (Connecticut) Black officers resorted to calling in sick to protest their inability to gain assignments anywhere but in the city's high-crime, ghetto areas.

Activism in a number of cities, including Miami, Atlanta, Detroit, Houston, and Chicago, centered on eliminating Black precincts and "Black posts" in nominally integrated precincts and on introducing race-neutral assignments of patrol car partners. By the 1970s, many of these cities had higher proportions of Black officers than ever before, including 35% in Detroit, 42% in Washington, D.C., and about 20% in San Francisco, Chicago, Philadelphia, Memphis, and Baltimore. In a number of cities, including New York, the Guardians played an active role in litigation against their department in areas such as discriminatory hiring and promotion policies and were often joined by associations of Hispanic officers and sometimes by policewomen, whose opportunities for advancement were also severely limited. Each of the groups, to a different extent and following different tactics based on local political considerations, lobbied for policies in recruitment, promotion, internal investigations and communications, and training that would enhance opportunities for Black officers.

The campaigns to increase the percentages of African American officers were opposed by police unions, who fought affirmative action plans, preferential hiring for city residents or cadet-style programs aimed at recruiting young minority-group members into police departments. The Guardians associations also became involved in community-wide issues, often supporting demands from within the minority community for civilian review of the police, placing them in adversarial roles with Police Benevolent Associations and other unions representing police officers.

The number of Black police officers associations was large enough by the 1970s for a national meeting in St. Louis (Missouri), which resulted in the formation of the National Black Officer

Association, which continues to hold annual conferences attended by hundreds of officers from around the nation. In many cities, Guardians also began to affiliate locally. For instance, because of the large number of law enforcement agencies in the New York City metropolitan area, a Grand Council of Guardians was incorporated in 1974 as an umbrella organization. By 2007 the Grand Council included a dozen police, corrections, sheriffs, and probation and parole Guardians associations and maintained close links with other African American civil service groups and with groups of Black firefighters.

From purely social support groups, Guardians associations developed into major forces contributing to the advancement of Blacks in American law enforcement. Although more attention has been paid to the roles of the federal government and courts in advancing equal opportunities in criminal justice agencies, associations of Black police officers, often at the risk of alienating White colleagues and city administrators, have been major forces in improving the work environment for minority officers and for supporting policies to enhance relationships with minority communities.

Dorothy Moses Schulz

See also National Association of Blacks in Criminal Justice; National Organization of Black Law Enforcement Executives

Further Readings

Abel, R. L. (2006). *The Black Shields*. Bloomington, IN: AuthorHouse.

Bolten, K., & Feagin, J. (2004). *Black in blue: African American police officers and racism*. New York: Routledge.

Broome, H. F., Jr. (1977). *LAPD's Black history: 1886–1976*. Norwalk, CA: Stockton Trade Press.

Dulaney, W. M. (1996). *Black police in America*. Bloomington: Indiana University Press.

Leinen, S. (1985). *Black police, White society*. New York: New York University Press.

Nicholas, A. (1969). *Black in blue*. New York: Meredith.

Reaves, J. N. (1991). *Black cops*. Philadelphia: Quantum Leap.

Harlem Race Riot of 1935

The Harlem Race Riot of 1935 was the culmination of racial tension and economic frustration that built in Harlem during the Great Depression. Although the entire nation was experiencing economic difficulties, Harlem was hit especially hard. While dealing with mounting obstacles such as inadequate health care, poor education, and mounting poverty, Blacks also had to face discrimination that made it harder for them to receive any of the limited social services that were available at the time. If there was assistance in the form of health care, food, or jobs, it was offered to the White community first.

Riots in other economically distressed urban centers with significant Black populations, such as Detroit, were viewed as a warning sign that similar disruptions could occur in New York City. With Harlem being one of the worst hit communities in America during the Great Depression and with racial tensions mounting, it took only one spark of misunderstanding to set off the tinderbox that became the Harlem Race Riot of 1935. It would end after the death of 3 people and the injuring of 125 more. This entry describes the social context in which the riot occurred, the incident that triggered it, the events during the March 1935 riot, and the work of the Mayor's Commission formed to investigate the riot.

Jim Crow and Harlem

When racial tensions are compounded by other issues, from acts of violence to economic deprivation, the conditions for riot often arise. During the first part of the 20th century, racial discrimination against African Americans was codified in law. The Supreme Court's upholding of the "separate but equal" doctrine in its 1896 ruling in *Plessy v. Ferguson* and Jim Crow laws at the end of the 19th century had legitimized discrimination against African Americans in the United States, and in the 20th century, African Americans continued to be banned from restaurants, movie theaters, schools, parks, and hospitals and required to use separate entrances, drinking fountains, and schools.

Harlem and the Great Depression

The economic devastation of the Great Depression was fully evident by 1935. This was particularly true in major urban centers across the country like Detroit and New York City. People across the nation were struggling to find jobs, and unemployment levels were especially high in Harlem, the urban center of African American life in New York City. Many Blacks lived in abject poverty, and many suffered from higher rates of illness than Whites. The health care and educational facilities were inadequate, poorly equipped, and unable to serve the mounting needs of its residents. The scarcity of employment opportunities for Blacks, coupled with discrimination and police brutality, helped fuel the insurgence of 1935.

Economic conditions in Harlem served to exacerbate the already increased level of racial tension between Blacks and Whites. In an era when Blacks were denied equal opportunities or the means to acquire ownership, Whites owned the businesses in primarily Black Harlem, which was characteristic of American society. Therefore, the elevated unemployment levels were blamed on White store owners who refused to hire Blacks, despite the fact that their clientele was primarily African American. Adding to racial tensions at the time was the fact that Blacks were routinely being discriminated against in housing and other aspects of existence. African American and White organizations that supported them organized pickets and boycotts of White businesses to protest racial discrimination in hiring. However, in 1935 a handful of shopkeepers filed an injunction against picketers, temporarily undermining the boycott movement.

These events angered Blacks, but what intensified tensions was the fact that police were hired to enforce the injunction, something many did with an increased measure of brutality. Allegations of police brutality were rampant in Harlem and further reinforced the belief that the police were in Harlem to protect Whites and White property and not Black residents. The disenfranchisement of African Americans through legal segregation, overt discrimination, combined with police callousness and the perceptions of it, augmented racial tensions and helped fuel the misunderstanding that led to tension that in turn led to rioting. The increased level of tension erupted in March 1935, when a riot in Harlem resulted from simmering racial tension and an unfortunate set of misunderstandings and circumstances.

The 1935 Riot

There are varied accounts of the exact flashpoint that culminated in the Harlem Race Riot of March 1935. Some accounts of the riot maintain that Lino Rivera, a teenage Puerto Rican, was caught shoplifting in the S. H. Kress Department Store. One account, however, maintains that the shoplifter was actually a 10-year-old Black youth. Whether the boy was Black or Latino, a series of unfortunate misunderstandings followed the detention of the suspect. Rumors quickly spread that the boy was being held and beaten by the storeowner. The police were called in, and allegations of police brutality and the boy's beating

quickly spread. In actuality, the boy was detained (in some accounts after a brief scuffle with a clerk) and ultimately released and sent home by the store personnel and police officials. However, this information was not available to the public, and rumors of the boy's beating and death spread through Harlem. At one point, a hearse scheduled to pick up a body at a funeral parlor next to the store was mistakenly thought by Blacks to be there to pick up the shoplifter, whom they assumed had been beaten to death. In fact, there had been no place to park the hearse, so the driver pulled in front of the department store with its ample spaces.

As rumors of the boy's beating and death spread through Harlem, matters were made worse by the fact that the department store, where the incident allegedly occurred, was notorious for discriminating against Blacks in employment. This did little to quash the rumors that were uniting Harlem Blacks in a call for violent action. Thinking that a young African American had been beaten to death at a department store known for its discriminatory practices against Blacks and by a police force suspected of outright brutality against Blacks, African American leaders, street orators, and groups such as the Young Communist League inflamed the residents of Harlem with angry rhetoric and written propaganda against Whites and police brutality.

The S. H. Kress Department Store incident served as the match to the tinderbox of racial tension that spread throughout Harlem. Soon Harlem was ablaze as Black residents took to the streets rioting. Most of the violence and destruction of property were aimed at White businesses. Windows of storefronts were smashed, property was stolen or destroyed, and fires were set. An angry mob of Blacks began to circle around the Kress store. By late afternoon, the store was forced to close its doors, and police were called in. Nevertheless, the crowd continued to smash windows and loot the department store. At one point a police car pulled up. When the officers exited the car, one officer pulled his gun and fired to disperse the crowd. Another aimed his gun at one of the African American looters and fired. The man was hit and died a few days later in a Harlem hospital.

The shooting only inflamed rioters. African American advocacy groups such as the radical defense organization the Young Liberators disseminated pamphlets about the incident, still maintaining the young shoplifter had been killed and that police and store officials were continuing to lie to favor Whites. The Harlem Race Riot signaled a change in the nature of violence between Whites and Blacks in 1930s America. In the past, racial disturbances had been confined to skirmishes between or among individuals or groups. With the increasing racial tension and economic deprivation of the 1930s, urban explosions began to be directed toward whole communities.

The Harlem riots were directed at the White community which, despite its relatively low numbers in Harlem, owned most of Harlem's stores and other institutions and was the main source of employment. This perception made many Blacks feel as if the Whites had direct control over Harlem law enforcement. In addition to the rumor about the boy being beaten and killed, other rumors also served as fuel for the riot. As outraged crowds continued to amass in front of White-owned targets, rumors spread that the police had also broken the arm of a Black woman who had tried to render aid to the boy accused of shoplifting. Such rumors were highly plausible and readily believed because of perceptions among the African American community of police brutality. Years of economic hardship and discrimination, coupled with perceptions of such abuse, undermined rational thought and removed restraint of Harlem residents.

The riot continued to rage as Harlem burned for the entire night and following day. Many more buildings were destroyed as Blacks moved from target to target, taking out their frustration and anger on White-owned property. In the violence that ensued, 3 African Americans were killed, and more than 60 individuals were seriously injured and treated at local hospitals. More than 100 people were arrested on a variety of charges, from inciting violence to looting and property destruction. Estimates of the total amount of damage wrought during the Harlem Race Riot approached $2 million, an exorbitant sum of money in the Depression era.

The Aftermath

Malcolm X maintained, in Chapter 19 of *The Harlem Riot*, that "Harlem has never been the same since the 1935 riot." Other intellectuals of the riot era also believed that the Harlem Race Riot of 1935 had provided important lessons on race relations not only for officials but also for society as a whole. In *Survey Geographic*, Alain Locke argued that the Harlem riot of 1935 demonstrated that "the Negro is not merely the man who shouldn't be forgotten; he is the man who cannot safely be ignored."

Despite the significant violent behavior and financial devastation wrought by the 1935 Harlem Race Riot, some positive changes occurred in the community. Mayor Fiorello La Guardia was determined to take action in the aftermath of the riots. Believing racial tensions were at the root of the riot, he created a biracial Mayor's Commission 8 months later that was charged with investigating the riot and the conditions in Harlem that preceded it. The 14-member biracial commission included scholars and expert sociologists like E. Franklin Frazier and Alain Locke. The outcome of the commission's investigation was provided on March 31, 1936, in a report titled "The Negro in Harlem: A Report on Social and Economic Conditions Responsible for the Outbreak of March 19, 1935." The report offered many recommendations for improving race relations and increasing social and economic opportunities for Blacks. Among the recommendations were significant antidiscrimination efforts in housing, employment, and education opportunities. Fair hiring in municipal jobs and antidiscrimination efforts among law enforcement were also recommended in the report by Frazier and the Mayor's Commission.

Social and infrastructure improvements in Harlem in the aftermath of the riots were also undertaken. Harlem Hospital was enlarged and updated with a number of improvements. Mayor La Guardia also ordered the development of more public housing for Blacks. Racial sensitivity training for police officers was also implemented among New York law enforcement. Efforts to undermine racism and discrimination in city agencies were also initiated. Nevertheless, violence would erupt in riot once more in Harlem in 1943.

Conclusion

Blacks no longer live in an era where Jim Crow discrimination is codified in law, and they have made major advances in social justice since the 1965 Civil Rights Act. Nevertheless, some of the issues that laid the foundation for the Harlem Race Riot of 1935 still plague contemporary American society; these include embittered police–community relations, economic disenfranchisement, perceived discrimination, and elevated unemployment. These conditions led to other civil disturbances in the 1960s in cities across the United States and in 1992 following the acquittal of officers involved in the Rodney King beating in Los Angeles.

Antonio Ford

See also Frazier, E. Franklin; Los Angeles Race Riots of 1992; Race Relations; Race Riots; Racial Conflict

Further Readings

Greenberg, C. (1992, August). The politics of disorder: Reexamining Harlem's riots of 1935 and 1943. *Journal of Urban History, 18,* 395–441.

Locke, A. (1936, August). Harlem: Dark weather-vane. *Survey Graphic, 25*(8), 457. Retrieved from http://newdeal.feri.org/survey/36457.htm

HARRISON NARCOTICS TAX ACT OF 1914

The Harrison Narcotics Act of 1914, sponsored by New York Congressman Francis B. Harrison and written in large part by Dr. Hamilton Wright, is regarded by historians and criminologists as the basis for drug policy in the United States. This legislation, which went into effect on March 15, 1915, was intended to control listed narcotic substances (e.g., opiates, cocaine derivatives) through taxation and commercial regulation. On its face, the Harrison Act was designed to eliminate the nonmedical sale and use of opiates and cocaine, which were widespread, over-the-counter, and unregulated. At the same time, the Harrison Act facilitated the construction of a discursive intersection of mainstream American feelings on race with the nature and mythology of mind-altering substances, with "drug laws" becoming a euphemism for the social control of non-Whites.

The law required supervised distribution to physicians, pharmacists, wholesalers, and manufacturers who, licensed by federal government, remitted an excise tax and maintained adequate records of all transactions involving the listed substances. In effect, the Harrison Act was a revenue measure whose wording also allowed Department of Treasury authorities, who were directly invested with its implementation, to determine the legitimacy of physicians' discretion in dispensing narcotics and empowered the federal government to prohibit the maintenance of persons addicted to opiates by the medical practitioners. The Department of the Treasury's interpretation of the law created literally overnight a class of criminals who on the day before had been merely opiate addicts. Although very similar in wording to the United Kingdom's "Dangerous Drugs Laws" crafted at nearly the same time, the Harrison Act was applied in a manner that criminalized addiction, imperiled physicians, and allowed federal authorities unprecedented discretion in enforcing U.S. law applied to the manufacture, trafficking, and sale of narcotics that lawmakers in the United Kingdom never sought.

In a series of high-profile U.S. Supreme Court rulings, including *Jin Fuey Moy v. United States* (1915), *Webb v. United States* (1919), and *Behrman v. United States* (1922), Department of the Treasury officials succeeded in handcuffing physicians, precluded the establishment of drug rehabilitation clinics, attenuated the operation of existing clinics, and in doing so moved the nation away from ambulatory addiction treatment to total prohibition. Addiction researcher and activist Alfred Lindesmith (1965, 1968), who studied opiate addiction in the 1930s, predicted that the use of the Harrison Act in such a manner would create an unenforceable and largely symbolic law, fill the prisons with addicted persons who should otherwise be in hospitals, and channel the massive proceeds from the illicit drug trade into the pockets of organized crime and corrupt public officials. It did exactly those things.

Even more damaging to the nation, the Harrison Act created a basis for prohibition organizations such as the Woman's Christian Temperance Union to influence likeminded federal officials, such as the Federal Bureau of Narcotics (FBN) Chief Harry J. Anslinger, who together created a decades-long drug panic that lasted into the 1960s. For his efforts between 1930 and his forced retirement in 1962, Anslinger can be credited with using the Harrison prohibitions as a foundation for criminalizing marijuana in 1937, linking drug use to communism during the McCarthy era, and advising the U.S. Congress to ratchet up narcotics penalties twice, in 1951 and 1956, thus setting the stage for the War on Drugs in its present form. Whereas Anslinger's campaign resulted in a decrease of federal narcotics prosecutions by 66% between 1930 and 1960 (numbers that Anslinger cited in his budget requests), state prosecutions over the same period increased over 500%.

The opiate addiction problem had always been one associated and imbued with American sentiments on race, a fact that was apparent in the original legislation, the Narcotic Drugs Import and Export Act of 1909. It specifically mentioned "smoking opium," thereby identifying the problem as one linked to Asian immigration to the U.S. West Coast. It should come as no surprise that through the 1930s, 1940s, and 1950s, the average age of addicts arrested decreased significantly and the demographic of addiction became concentrated among the urban poor. Between 1930 and 1957, Caucasians went from 77% to approximately 12% of the recorded addicts, while African Americans, who made up 17% of the addicted in 1930, became 87% of the same group by 1957. It was clear that enforcement strategies and urbanization had shifted the burdens of addiction heavily onto the shoulders of non-White populations in the United States.

In 1975, John Helmer described the sea change in addiction as a result of segregation, high birthrates among African Americans in the 1930s relative to Whites, and the FBN's portrayal of drug use as a function of diminished African American character. Through a text of thinly veiled racism, Anslinger capitalized on the "Black myth" of drug use and addiction widely held by Whites to justify continued funding of FBN programs. Anslinger, in his own right, was immersed in a highly contentious federal environment of fervent anticommunism, competing for funding with charismatic Federal Bureau of Investigation Director J. Edgar Hoover.

The Harrison Act also provided an anchor for Anslinger and the FBN to press the states for adoption of a Uniform Narcotic Drug Act, which was formulated and passed in 35 states by 1937. Mentions of marijuana were prominent in the drafts sent to each state, and the public information surrounding passage was again tied to racial bigotry and Mexican immigration in the western half of the country. While very few Americans in the 1930s knew anything about marijuana, the public campaign undertaken by Anslinger dwelt heavily on accounts of Mexican Americans, who were presumably illegal immigrants, gone mad and committing atrocious crimes after smoking a single joint. Similar to the Harrison Act, the Uniform Narcotic Drug laws passed in all 35 state legislatures without expert scientific testimony or serious contributions by medical authorities as to the impact of the policy on the general public.

David Keys

See also Drug Sentencing; Drug Treatment; Drug Use

Further Readings

Lindesmith, A. R. (1965). *The addict and the law.* Bloomington: Indiana University Press.
Lindesmith, A. R. (1968). *Addiction and opiates.* Chicago: de Gruyter.
Helmer, J. (1975). *Drugs and minority oppression.* New York: Seabury Press.

HARVARD, BEVERLY (1950–)

Beverly Harvard joined the Atlanta Police Department (APD) in 1973, a year before A. Reginald Eaves became the first African American public safety commissioner, when the department was a tense place for minorities and women. After a rapid rise through the ranks that slowed after she became a deputy commissioner, Harvard, who never expected to be a police officer, in November 1994 was confirmed by the city council as the country's first African American woman chief of a major city police department.

Harvard, born Beverly Joyce Bailey in 1950 in Macon, Georgia, was the youngest of six, four boys and two girls; she described her sisters as her best friends. Sheltered by her middle-class family, she attended local schools and in 1972 earned a bachelor's degree in sociology from Morris Brown College, a historically Black institution. In 1980, while in policing, she earned a master's degree in urban government and administration from Georgia State University.

Harvard joined the APD to win a $100 bet with her husband Jim, who had agreed with friends that a woman police officer would have to be big, strong, and boisterous, the opposite of his small, studious, and quiet wife. Harvard, who had expected Jim to support her view that any woman could become a police officer, had limited knowledge about the police and was unsure of the hiring process, but she set out to prove him wrong. When she joined the department, her plans were to remain only to learn police argot, constitutional law, and self-defense, but she was surprised to be able to help people, even on her first foot patrol assignment from 6 p.m. to 2 a.m. in one of Atlanta's high-crime areas. After she became chief, she revealed that her husband had followed her and her partner around in his car because he had trouble accepting she was able to do the job.

After only a few years on patrol, Harvard began a rapid rise through the ranks; in 1978 she oversaw the police, fire, and corrections departments' implementation of an affirmative action plan. Named director of public affairs in 1980, she held the position during the resolution of Atlanta's child murder cases in 1981 and 1982, when Lee Patrick Brown was public safety director. Within barely a decade of having joined the APD and only 31 years old, she became the first African American female deputy chief with assignments in career development, criminal investigations, and administrative services. In 1983 she became the APD's first female graduate of the Federal Bureau of Investigation's National Academy, an executive training course that has served for many as a stepping-stone to becoming a chief. After a maternity leave in 1988 to have a daughter, Christa, she was considered for chief in 1990, when she was voted city government's woman of the year, but instead the position went to Eldrin Bell, who she replaced on an interim basis for 6 months before being named chief in 1994.

Serving Atlanta During Noteworthy Events

At that time, Atlanta had about 1,700 police officers and was ranked by the Federal Bureau of Investigation as sixth in violent crimes per capita. During Harvard's first two years as chief, Atlanta hosted the Olympic Games, the Paralympics, and the Freedom Fest (formerly Freaknik). Freaknik placed Harvard in the spotlight in 1995, when a rowdier than usual crowd resulted in about 200 arrests. Reflecting her self-described strait-laced background, she criticized women for allowing themselves to be fondled by groups of men, noting that it was difficult to criticize men when women behaved as some of the attendees had. She was again in the spotlight when Atlanta hosted the 1996 Centennial Olympic Games and she served as co-chair of the Olympic Security Support Group, which coordinated federal, state and local, and private agencies' efforts to secure Olympic venues.

Harvard, who made corruption control and community policing her signature issues, lowered the crime rate but faced internal criticism from those who felt she lacked patrol experience and had been primarily an administrator, an accusation leveled against all of the first-generation women chiefs, and external criticism from those who felt she was overshadowed by Mayor Bill Campbell. Although Harvard tended to downplay race and sex throughout her career, her critics often seized on issues that were stereotypically female, such as a weak management style, an aloof personality, and a lack of street-policing experience. Despite this criticism, she served for 8 years, longer than most large-city chiefs of police. In 2002 she declined to apply for reappointment and retired after 29 years in the department. In August 2002 she was named the federal assistant director of security at Atlanta's Hartsfield International Airport, working with director Willie Williams, previously Philadelphia's police commissioner and chief of the Los Angeles Police Department.

As the first African American woman to lead a major city police department, Harvard's position was history-making, but her career was typical of big-city chiefs. Although she initially rose through the ranks rapidly, when named chief she had been in APD for more than 20 years and had spent her entire career there. Harvard was active in state policing groups and in the National Organization of Black Law Enforcement Executives and served on the Commission on Accreditation for Law Enforcement Agencies. In 1985 Morris Brown College named her alumna of the year; she received the Atlanta Chapter of the Top Ladies of Distinction award, the AAUW/National Conference for College Women Student Leaders Women of Distinction award, and the National Institute of Justice Pickens Fellowship in 1993.

A member of groups working to reduce violence and aid battered women and children, Harvard has rarely been closely associated in the media with national women's or African American policing groups. Yet, because of her unique status as the first African American woman to lead a major police department, it was difficult for her to transcend being "the woman chief" or the "African American woman chief," a point made by an Atlanta councilman who said when she retired that had she been a man, she would have been lauded and carried around city hall on people's shoulders. Rather than receiving these plaudits, she retired quietly, making it easy for Shirley Franklin, Atlanta's first African American female mayor with whom Harvard had worked during the Olympics Games, to replace her with an African American male from outside the department.

Dorothy Moses Schulz

See also Brown, Lee P.; National Organization of Black Law Enforcement Executives

Further Readings

Eddings, J. (1994, December 26). Atlanta's new top cop makes her mark. *U.S. News & World Report,* pp. 82–83.

First Black woman to run a big city police force cracks down on corruption. (1995, October 2). *Jet,* pp. 8–13.

Schulz, D. M. (2004). *Breaking the brass ceiling: Women police chiefs & their paths to the top.* Westport, CT: Praeger.

Smothers, R. (1994, November 20). Atlanta's police chief won more than a bet. *The New York Times,* p. C1.

Suggs, E. (2002, July 16). Former Atlanta top cop lauded; crime reduced in controversial era. *Atlanta Journal-Constitution,* p. 4D.

Whetstone, M. L. (1994, March). Atlanta's top cop. *Ebony,* pp. 92–95.

HATE CRIMES

Hate crimes refers to crimes motivated by an offender's dislike of a victim's belonging to a "socially undesirable" group. Many scholars, politicians, and law enforcement officials have argued, however, that using the term *hate crimes* is inaccurate as such crimes are often motivated more by the offender's biases than by hatred. Therefore, hate crimes are also frequently referred to as *bias crimes, civil rights crimes,* or *ethnic intimidation.* Although the definition of hate crime offending can include crimes against a variety of groups, race and religion are consistently embraced in the definition. Other group categories sometimes included are sexual orientation, physical or mental disability, gender, political affiliation, age, and national origin. Consistent, however, is the assumption of the existence of a predicate offense, or an underlying crime. Predicate offenses to hate crimes can include a range of crimes, from property destruction to homicide.

Although hate crimes have only come to the American public's attention in recent years, hate and intolerance are not strangers to the United States. From the beginning days of America's nationhood, hate crimes have existed in numerous forms. Slavery is often considered by many scholars to be one of the largest instances of hate crimes in U.S. history. Additionally, instances of racially motivated lynchings and cross burnings have occurred, but they were not labeled as hate crimes because the definition as we now know it now did not exist then. However, since the late 1970s and early 1980s, a flurry of attention has been given by the media, police, and legislators to crimes motivated by the hatred or bias of individuals based on their identification with a "socially undesirable" group. Much of this attention stems from several celebrated cases of hate crimes that occurred during the 1990s. One particularly vicious example occurred on June 7, 1998, in Jasper, Texas when three White supremacists chained James Byrd, an African American man, to the back of their pick-up truck and fatally dragged him by his ankles. James Byrd's death by White supremacists further exposed the gravity of such hatred and intolerance and prompted many to ask questions as to why such brutal acts of hatred are committed against minorities in America.

Although there are numerous issues worthy of discussion regarding hate crimes, this entry aims to provide an introductory overview of the topic. Included are relevant discussions of hate crime victims, offenders, and the debate surrounding hate crimes legislation.

Hate Crime Victims

Hate crimes that are as extreme as murder are rare. However, the Federal Bureau of Investigation recorded nearly 8,000 various hate crime incidents in the United States in 2006. Because many of these crimes go unreported for various reasons, such as a law enforcement officer's misclassification of a hate crime or a victim's fear of self-reporting, the actual figure of hate crimes in America is most likely much higher. As a result, it is difficult to determine the exact number and race/ethnicity of hate crime victims. However, three groups that are frequently victimized are African Americans; Jews; and gay men, lesbians, bisexuals, and the transgendered.

Race

African Americans are the most common victims of hate crimes in the United States. This should not be surprising given African Americans have been subject to intolerance, violence, racism, and inequality for centuries. American slavery is perhaps the most massive hate crime in U.S. history, and many consider it to have set the stage for more recent hate crimes. For decades after slavery, African Americans endured lynchings and other forms of violence nationwide, though much of the violence occurred in the South. Historically, these crimes were not necessarily recorded or viewed as hate crimes. Prejudicial views of African Americans are still present today and are made painfully visible every time a hate crime against an African American occurs. Incidents occur more frequently than one would presume, though they are not always as brutal as the James Byrd murder. For example, in the South hundreds of Black churches have been bombed or burned in recent years. Numerous cross burnings have occurred on the front lawns of African Americans as well. Researchers suggest that though considered

free speech, these cross burnings, usually carried out by Whites, often precede more direct and violent attacks. These incidents are equally troubling given that they are motivated by the same hatred and intolerance that took James Byrd's life.

African Americans are not the only race targeted for hate crime victimization, however. Although attacks on Asians and Asian Americans are far less common, they are a reality. Such is the case of the murder of Vincent Chin, a Chinese American victimized by angry autoworkers in Detroit, Michigan, during the rise of Japanese auto sales in the 1980s.

Religion

Anti-Semitism is perhaps among the oldest and deepest forms of hatred and intolerance in existence. Historically, Jews were persecuted by the Egyptians, Greeks, and Romans and have been confined to ghettoes and prohibited from owning land. The best-known account of anti-Semitism occurred during Nazi Germany when 6 million Jews were killed throughout Europe. On the American front, anti-Semitism often involves the extremist beliefs of people who blame Jews for economic troubles, communism, and disloyalty to the United States. Additionally, many fringe Americans believe that a Jewish conspiracy runs the country and that Jews have led various social movements, such as the feminist and civil rights movements. When these extremist beliefs are used to fuel intolerant acts, anti-Semitic incidents, ranging from swastika graffiti on synagogues to harassment and even more violent assaults, are the result. For instance, in 1994 a Lebanese immigrant shot at a van carrying 15 Hasidic Jewish students in New York. One student died and three were injured.

Since the terrorist attacks on September 11, 2001, far more attention has been paid to hate crime victimization of Americans who are or are presumed to be Muslim, Arab, or of Middle Eastern descent than had previously been the case. For example, researchers reported that in the first half of 2001 there were no instances of anti-Islamic hate crimes in Colorado. However, after September 11 of the same year, 17 anti-Islamic hate crimes were reported in that state.

Sexual Orientation

A social group often targeted by hate criminals is the gay, lesbian, bisexual, and transgender (GLBT) community. The GLBT community is often a minority group that does not receive full legislative protection from hate crime victimization. Consequently, the group's inclusion in hate crime legislation is often the basis for much controversy and debate. Historically, what is now known as homophobia has been acceptable around the world in many societies for centuries. In many circles, antigay bias is still socially acceptable and freely expressed, though many would argue that the bias has steadily decreased in the past several decades. This belief is particularly troublesome because the social acceptability of homophobia is likely one of the foremost causes of antigay hate crimes in the United States.

In addition to being confronted with verbal harassment and intolerance, many in the GLBT community face brutal attacks such as that of Rebecca Wright and Claudia Brenner. In 1988, the lesbian couple was murdered in a state park in Pennsylvania. Perhaps the best-known antigay hate crime was committed in Wyoming in 1998. Matthew Shepard, a gay University of Wyoming student, was brutally beaten and killed. His murder continues to be used as an example of the need for more inclusive hate crime legislation.

As is the case with hate crimes based on race or religion, biases and prejudice are present in antigay hate crimes as well. As many law enforcement officials and scholars have noted, the difference is that hate crimes against the GLBT community tend to be especially brutal and are often considered "overkill." This sends a particularly strong message of hate and intolerance to victims and to the entire GLBT community.

Hate Crime Offenders

When a hate crime occurs, organized hate groups such as the Ku Klux Klan, skinheads, or neo-Nazis are often blamed. However, in general, organized hate groups do not commit the majority of hate crimes. As noted in numerous studies, although hate crime offenders generally commit their crimes in groups, they are not usually affiliated with an organized hate group. These groups of offenders tend to comprise young, White males with no prior criminal record and from backgrounds that are generally not impoverished. Moreover, in many cases the offender may even be a neighbor or live in close proximity to the victim.

Hate crime offenders' motives can vary. However, the underlying factor found in all hate crimes is bigotry. Scholars suggest there are various motivating factors involved with hate crime offending. For instance, in certain hate crimes the offender is in search of a sense of power and excitement; these crimes are considered thrill crimes and are the most common. Other hate crime offenders feel the need to protect their territory or resources; these offenders are called defensive offenders. Others commit hate crimes in a reactive manner, avenging a perceived wrong; these offenders are regarded as retaliatory criminals. Those who victimize based on a desire to "cleanse the world of evil" are known as mission offenders.

With the motivations of hate crime offenders in mind, it is difficult to identify with any level of certainty the underlying reasons why bigoted individuals choose to commit hate crimes. However, many argue that what hate criminals do, intentionally or inadvertently, is to send a strong and hateful message to the group to which the victim belongs.

Hate Crimes Debate

Few would debate the harm caused by hate crimes, as most in the mainstream would denounce all forms of bigotry and hatred. However, the issue of hate crimes becomes open for debate when considering appropriate legislative protections for groups that become victims of hate crimes. Currently, there are federal and state laws that differ significantly in their scope, but all aim to protect various minority social groups from hate crime offending. Arguments both for and against such enhancements are considered legitimate, therefore causing the debate.

The controversy over hate crimes is primarily concentrated on laws that enhance the sentences of predicate offenses that were committed against members of included protected groups. Many believe that hate crimes are more serious than other types of crimes that are not inspired by hate and bigotry and therefore warrant a more serious punishment. It is argued that these crimes are much worse than other, non–hate-based crimes because of the hateful message that is sent to the community and the fear caused by it. Those that oppose hate crime legislation suggest that it is inappropriate, and at times unconstitutional, to punish an offender's motives or thoughts. Punishing motives and thoughts, it is argued, would violate the First Amendment. Moreover, some fear that hate crime legislation can criminalize others for their speech or thoughts. Yet another issue up for debate is which groups should be protected under hate crime legislation. Currently this varies by state, but groups based on race, ethnicity, and religion are often protected in most states. Sexual orientation and gender are two categories that are frequently omitted by states, though the inclusion of sexual orientation has been the subject of most of the debate.

Whatever a person's persuasion on the issue, every time a news report of a hate crime appears in the media, it becomes painfully clear that this topic warrants attention. From the definition of hate crimes to hate crime legislation, there are a multitude of issues and directions yet to be considered. However, significant progress has been made since hate crimes came to the public's awareness, and the issue is likely to continue demanding attention for years to come.

Ryan B. Martz

See also Anti-Defamation League; Anti-Semitism; Hate Crime Statistics Act; Ku Klux Klan; Ku Klux Klan Act; Lynching; Racism; Skinheads; Southern Poverty Law Center; White Supremacists

Further Readings

Gerstenfeld, P. B. (2004). *Hate crimes: Causes, controls, and controversies.* Thousand Oaks, CA: Sage.

Green, D. P., & Rich, A. R. (1998). White Supremacist activity and cross burnings in North Carolina. *Journal of Quantitative Criminology, 14*(3), 263–282.

Levin, J. (2007). *Violence of hate: Confronting racism, anti-Semitism, and other forms of bigotry.* Boston: Pearson Education.

Levin, J., & McDevitt, J. (2002). *Hate crimes revisited: America's war on those who are different.* Boulder, CO: Westview Press.

McDevitt, J., Levin, J., & Bennett, S. (2002). Hate crime offenders: An expanded typology. *Journal of Social Issues, 58*(2), 303–317.

Perry, B. (2001). *In the name of hate: Understanding hate crimes.* New York: Routledge.

U.S. Department of Justice, Federal Bureau of Investigation. (2007, November). Hate crimes statistics, 2006. *Uniform Crime Report.* Retrieved January 17, 2008, from http://www.fbi.gov/ucr/hc2006/downloadablepdfs/incidentsoffenses.pdf

HATE CRIME STATISTICS ACT

The Hate Crime Statistics Act (HCSA) was the first piece of federal legislation that directly acknowledged hate crime. Enacted by Congress and signed into law by then President George H. W. Bush on April 23, 1990, the HCSA (Public Law 101-275) mandated the U.S. Attorney General to collect data and produce an annual summary of "crimes that manifest evidence of prejudice" as well as establish guidelines and procedures for the collection of such data. The act required the reporting of eight crimes as hate crimes when they demonstrated bias based on race, religion, ethnicity/nationality, or sexual orientation. The crimes were murder, forcible rape, aggravated and simple assault, intimidation, arson, and the destruction, damage, or vandalism of property. The Department of Justice was given the authority to expand this list and was assured appropriations for the first decade of the effort.

Implementation of the HCSA was delegated to the Federal Bureau of Investigation's Uniform Crime Reporting (UCR) program. In 1991, the program issued the *Training Guide for Hate Crime Data Collection* and requested that law enforcement agencies report hate crime, defined as crimes motivated at least in part by the prejudices documented in the HCSA. Since 1993, information about hate crimes against person, property, and society have been collected and published, with an emphasis on those crimes identified in the initial legislation as well as robbery, burglary, larceny-theft, and motor vehicle theft. In 1994, the Violent Crime Control and Law Enforcement Act amended the HSCA to include crimes manifesting prejudice based on physical or mental disability. Pending legislation recommends that the HCSA be expanded further to include gender and homelessness. The rest of this entry discusses the act's legislative history, goals and concerns, and results.

Legislative History

The passing of hate crime legislation has been accredited to social movements, strong state initiatives, and dedicated advocacy groups. Social movements of the 1950s, 1960s, and 1970s spurred an antihate movement of the 1980s by highlighting the plight of minorities, violence, and victims' rights and their interconnectedness. As early as the 1980s, hate crime reporting as well as substantive and sentencing statutes were being enacted by states across the country, supported by a growing body of data from organizations created to address the issues of hate such as the Anti-Defamation League. In the mid-1980s those organizations testified before Congress about the increasing presence of hate crime and its consequences. As a result of such information and pressure, legislation designed to record hate crimes based on race, religion, and ethnicity was overwhelmingly passed by the House of Representatives in 1986.

However, delay in Senate voting and the subsequent addition of gay and lesbian groups to the coalition supporting such legislation led to a new version of the bill in 1987 that included sexual orientation. The bill passed the House in 1988 over strong conservative objections and again in 1989 with less controversy, owing to a surge of strong law enforcement support for such legislation. However, Senate passage of the bill was delayed by an amendment put forth by conservatives outlining the threat posed by gays and lesbians. In response, an alternative amendment highlighting the importance of the traditional family and its security and noting that the HCSA was not to be "construed . . . to promote or encourage homosexuality" was offered, which allowed for overwhelming Senate passage of the bill in 1990.

Goals and Concerns

Although the HCSA created no new rights or causes of action and, as such, had no direct effect on criminal law, its passage was viewed as a critical first step toward addressing hate crime. In particular, it was believed that such legislation would raise awareness and send a strong message of national concern while at the same time providing communities, politicians, and law enforcement with the information necessary to develop an effective response to the problem. However, the ability of the HCSA to collect accurate data has been questioned. Concern stems from several issues, including the subjective quality of identifying a prejudicial motivation; obstacles to citizen reporting resulting from self-identification of the nature of the crime and/or poor police-community relations; variation in federal, state, and local definitions and laws; and influences on police reporting such as political and internal pressures to demonstrate low or decreasing crime rates. To date, analysis of the law's effectiveness is scant.

Results

More than 12,000 law enforcement agencies, representing 90% of the U.S. population, are reporting hate crime data to the Federal Bureau of Investigation. Although no hate crimes are reported in the majority of jurisdictions, the data collected reveal a fairly consistent number of hate crimes and patterns regarding the nature, offender, and victim of such crimes. Since the initial reporting of hate crime statistics in 1993, the annual number of such incidents has been between 7,000 and 9,000 except for a low in 1994 of not quite 6,000 and a high of nearly 10,000 in 2001, likely a result of the September 11 attacks. The data suggest that the majority of reported hate crimes are committed by White men and involve low-level crimes against persons, primarily intimidation. Crimes motivated by racial bias generally account for over half of all reported hate crimes, while bias based on religion or sexual orientation are the next most frequent. However, recent research has revealed that when population size is considered, gays and lesbians are the most prone to hate-based victimization.

Terrylynn Pearlman

See also Hate Crimes

Further Readings

Fernandez, J. M. (1991). Bringing hate crime into focus. *Harvard Civil Rights–Civil Liberties Law Review*, 26(2), 261–293.

Grattet, R., & Jenness, V. (2001). The birth and maturation of hate crime policy in the United States. *American Behavioral Scientist*, 45, 668–696.

Jacobs, J. B., & Eisler, B. (1993). The Hate Crime Statistics Act of 1990. *Criminal Law Bulletin*, 29, 99–123.

Rubenstein, W. B. (2004). The real story of U.S. hate crimes statistics: An empirical analysis. *Tulane Law Review*, 78, 1213–1246.

U.S. Department of Justice, Federal Bureau of Investigation. (2007). *Hate crime statistics 2006*. Retrieved from http://www.fbi.gov/ucr/hc2006/index.html

Websites

Library of Congress, H.R. 1048: http://thomas.loc.gov/cgi-bin/bdquery/z?d101:HR01048:@@@L&summ2=m

Hate Crime Statistics Act of 1990, Pub. L. 101-275, 28 U.S.C. 534: http://www.qrd.org/qrd/usa/federal/1990/federal.hate.crimes.stats.act-04.23.90

HIGGINBOTHAM, A. LEON, JR. (1928–1998)

A. (Aloysius) Leon Higginbotham, Jr., was a lawyer, legal scholar, teacher, author, and federal judge for 29 years. When he retired in 1993 he had served on the U.S. Third Circuit Court of Appeals in Philadelphia for 13 years and had been named Chief Judge in 1992, only one of a handful of African Americans to achieve such a position at that time. A key figure in the civil rights movement and a supporter of affirmative action, Higginbotham was a continual force for equality and individual rights, using the law as his tool for attacking racism in the United States in the 20th century. In the legal process Higginbotham saw both the problem and the solution: the roots of much of the racial tension of the times and the hope for change. He received the Presidential Medal of Freedom in 1995.

As an undergraduate at Purdue University, Higginbotham, because of his color, was denied a place in the heated dormitories by President Edward Charles Elliot, who told him that the law did not require such accommodations. This personal experience showed him the connection between the law and racism, and crystallized his desire to fight racism from within the legal system. He eventually transferred to and graduated from Antioch College and subsequently from Yale Law School.

Writings

For Higginbotham the law was a lens and a tool for approaching the issue of racism so deeply embedded in the fabric of American life. He believed that racism was woven into the American legal system and that the legacy of slavery law was a cause of modern social unrest. Real change would not occur without facing this historical truth head on. He proposed to write a four-volume work to be titled *Race and the American Legal Process*. The overall trajectory of the work would demonstrate how the legal process at first actively upheld racist practices, more passively sustained them, and then eventually became an instrument for some change and for progress toward a "shade of freedom," a phrase he used as the title of the second book in the series.

Higginbotham never completed the project, but in 1978 he published the first volume in the series, titled *In the Matter of Color: Race and the American Legal Process: The Colonial Period*. In it, he chose six colonies as representative (Virginia, Massachusetts, New York, South Carolina, Georgia, and Pennsylvania) and analyzed statutes and cases in them in order to explore the deep vein of racial inequality in the American legal system. In the epilogue to that book, he wrote, "The poisonous legacy of oppression based upon the matter of color can never be adequately purged from our society if we act as if slave laws never existed."

The second volume, *Shades of Freedom: Racial Politics and Presumptions of the American Legal Process*, which appeared nearly 30 years later in 1996, dealt with the first of what Higginbotham called "The Ten Precepts of American Slavery Jurisprudence: Inferiority." In the appendix to the book, he laid out the 10 precepts and defined the first in this manner: "Presume, preserve, protect, and defend the ideal of the superiority of Whites and the inferiority of Blacks." Leaving the colonial period behind, this volume mostly emphasized the 19th century. In a notable chapter, "Unequal Justice in the State Criminal Justice System," Higginbotham examined criminal cases for examples of racist speech and conduct on the part of the prosecution and sometimes of the judiciary. He discussed such practices as segregated seating for spectators in courtrooms, forms of address used with Black witnesses, and arguments based on racial stereotypes. Although in some of the cases the decisions, when challenged, were overturned on grounds of racism, in many others they were not. The acceptance of such behaviors, Higginbotham argued, goes beyond the immediate injustice and creates further harm by serving as an implicit standard of acceptability in the court system and in society at large.

Later, in a 1997 article on the recently concluded murder trial of O. J. Simpson, Higginbotham wrote about the use of the "race card" in that trial, concluding that defense attorney Johnnie Cochran was acting responsibly in bringing a witness's attitudes on race to the attention of the jury. He argued that race always was an issue in the case, not an issue arbitrarily introduced into the case by the defense. To suggest that race was not an issue results in just the kind of denial of truth that, in Higginbotham's view, obstructs progress toward equality. The "larger societal racial attitudes" are what need to be examined.

Public Service

While Higginbotham made significant scholarly contributions with his books and more than 40 articles, he was also always engaged in events in the world around him. Early in his career he was a partner in the Philadelphia law firm of Norris, Green, Harris & Higginbotham, a rare all-Black law firm, which took on both criminal and civil cases. The firm helped make changes in Pennsylvania bar admission practices, resulting in more African Americans entering. While in private practice, Higginbotham was also a special Deputy State Attorney General from 1956 to 1962 and was president of the Philadelphia Chapter of the National Association for the Advancement of Colored People from 1960 to 1962. In 1962 he was appointed a commissioner

on the Federal Trade Commission. Through his work on the Federal Trade Commission he came to know Attorney General Robert Kennedy, who recommended him for a judgeship in the Eastern District of Pennsylvania in 1963; thus at the age of 35, he began his long judicial career. Higginbotham also served on various committees of the Judicial Conference and was involved in its examination of the jury system and the issues surrounding getting a "representative jury." He was made a member of the White House Conference on Civil Rights in 1995.

Higginbotham served as the vice chairperson for the high-profile National Advisory Commission on the Causes and Prevention of Violence (known as the Eisenhower Commission), which was formed in 1968 by President Lyndon Johnson in the wake of the assassination of Senator Robert Kennedy. It issued its final report on December 10, 1969; Richard Nixon had meanwhile become president. Higginbotham represented the liberal end of a politically diverse spectrum. In contrast to the National Advisory Commission on Civil Disorders (known as the Kerner Commission), which preceded it and which focused on the causes of collective violence, the Eisenhower Commission focused on the causes of individual crimes. Both commissions, however, came to the same conclusion: that the plight of the urban poor and the injustices they suffered in the inner cities were the roots of the violence sweeping the country at that time. The Commission on the Causes and Prevention of Violence recommended a large influx of federal funds to provide better job and educational opportunities in the inner cities. The Vietnam War was being fought at the time, and there was general recognition that the funding would not be available any time soon. One notable recommendation from the commission was for the licensing of handguns. At the commission's end, Higginbotham made it clear that he was in favor of more social action and less social study: The nation had been awash in federal commissions for years.

Current Affairs

Higginbotham's influence extended outside the United States. In 1994 he traveled to South Africa at the request of Nelson Mandela to serve as a mediator during the first elections in which Blacks were permitted to vote.

Although he saw progress during his lifetime toward racial equality, Higginbotham was saddened to see reversals of that progress as the political climate changed in the 1980s and 1990s. In reaction to the appointment of Justice Clarence Thomas to the Supreme Court, Higginbotham addressed an open letter to Thomas. Always a strong supporter of affirmative action, Higginbotham exhorted Thomas to recognize the debt he owed to affirmative action programs and to the civil rights movement. The letter created a stir and he remained an outspoken critic of Thomas. In a *New York Times* article written shortly before he died, he expressed his dismay at the court ruling striking down affirmative action at the University of Texas Law School.

Catherine Stern

See also O. J. Simpson Case; Race Card, Playing the; Slavery and Violence; Thomas, Clarence

Further Readings

Higginbotham, A. L., Jr. (1978). *In the matter of color: Race and the American legal process: The colonial period.* New York: Oxford University Press.

Higginbotham, A. L., Jr. (1992). An open letter to Justice Clarence Thomas from a federal judicial colleague. *University of Pennsylvania Law Review, 140,* 1005–1028.

Higginbotham, A. L., Jr. (1996). *Shades of freedom: Racial politics and presumptions of the American legal process.* New York: Oxford University Press.

Higginbotham, A. L., Jr. (1998, January 18). Breaking Thurgood Marshall's promise. *New York Times Magazine,* pp. 28–29.

Higginbotham, A. L., Jr., François, A. B., & Yueh, L. Y. (1997). The O. J. Simpson trial: Who was improperly "playing the race card"? In T. Morrison & C. B. Lacour (Eds.), *Birth of a nation'hood: Gaze, script, and spectacle in the O. J. Simpson case* (pp. 31–56). New York: Pantheon Books.

Hip Hop, Rap, and Delinquency

Hip hop is an artistic cultural expression that embodies music, language, dance, visual art, and fashion. Although it has its roots in the evolution of rap music during the early 1980s, it emerged as a major pop-cultural theme during the 1990s. Life and the artistic expressions of urban America have largely shaped the aesthetics of this art form. This entry provides a definition of hip hop and then presents a synopsis of the debate surrounding the nature of the influence of this cultural expression on aberrant behavior, especially among urban African American youth. It reviews claims that that there is a connection between hip hop and delinquency/crime, as well as the counterargument against the existence of such a connection.

Hip hop has experienced an enormous amount of acceptance and has had a major impact on popular culture. The popularity of this cultural form is evident in the sales records of the various commodities (e.g., CDs, clothing, and magazines) that have emerged from this art form. The influence of hip hop culture on the dominant culture can also be seen in the infusion of the hip hop vernacular into mainstream conversations, as well as the use of the music to sell products.

Although the term *hip hop* can refer to a variety of cultural forms, it is most commonly associated with music, and with rap music in particular. In spite of high record sales and widespread acceptance in the entertainment arena, this genre of music has come under a great deal of criticism for its use of offensive language, negative depictions of women, and adulation of criminal enterprises. It has been linked to a host of social pathologies involving crime and delinquency. The following section summarizes the perspective of critics who contend that hip hop encourages such deviant behavior.

Dancing to That Illicit Beat: The Link Between Hip Hop and Delinquency/Crime

The debates surrounding hip hop's connection to delinquency and crime hinge on the suggestion that rap, specifically *gangsta* (altered spelling of the word *gangster*) rap, encourages pessimistic, cavalier, and antisocial behavior. Gangsta rap is a subgenre of hip hop music that became popular after the first release of N.W.A.'s Straight Outta Compton CD in 1988. This genre of music has been accused of promoting procriminal and misogynistic attitudes through images that often glorify and legitimize involvement in criminal activities.

The accusation concerning the glorification of delinquency and crime largely stems from the music lyrics that contain references to the artists' participation in criminal activity, namely, drug dealing, pimping, and gang activity—commonly referenced as hustling. A history of involvement in gang and/or criminal activity provides what is considered "street creditability," which is a vital ingredient to being perceived as a serious contender in this genre of music. A quick review of the personas of the most famed rap artist demonstrates that they often make reference to their past experience in delinquency and crime. For example, artists such as Jay-Z and 50 Cent have highlighted their past involvement in drug dealing, while artists such as Snoop Dogg have made references to their past gang affiliation. These artists and others often present their past experience in criminal activity in a way that suggests that involvement in these activities is a viable means to obtaining money and fame. Those who criticize hip hop and rap claim that the preponderance of this theme in such music symbolizes not only acceptance of criminal behavior but high regard for it.

Additionally, whether it is a case of life imitating art or art imitating life, some artists continue their connection with the gangster lifestyle during the height of their music success. The late, famed rapper Tupac Shakur, who died in 1996 as the result of gunshot wounds following a drive-by shooting, was well known for his celebration of the "thug life." The "thug life" culture celebrates what is considered a hard-core lifestyle that includes possessing a cavalier attitude, flaunting money and material items, and accepting violence as a method of resolving conflict. All of these characteristics led themselves to illustrations of the link between thug life and delinquency/crime.

In presenting images of violence as an acceptable means of resolving conflict, rap artists such as T.I. and Snoop Dogg have also been in the media in connection with illegal activities such as possession of illegal drugs and firearms. The continued connection with criminal activity keeps alive the hardcore persona of these artists and demonstrates their procriminal attitudes, which are often illustrated in their music.

Past and current affiliations with criminal activity by famed gangsta rap artists have the potential to serve as a normalizing force. Critics of hip hop contend that the repetitive presentations of pro-criminal images in the music and videos, coupled with real-life scenarios, reinforce the notion that engaging in aberrant behavior is a common and acceptable practice. Such critics argue that hip hop's glorification of illegal activity in both song and real life encourages young people to get involved in delinquency and crime. Others suggest that because these individuals are in the limelight, they inadvertently have a tremendous appeal to young people, and their celebration of involvement in illegal activities serves as a marker that such activities are legitimate. This is particularly relevant for young people who do not have positive role models within their close circles, such that outside social agents can become replacement agents of socialization.

Some critics have argued that the power in the music lies in the impact the music has had not only on individuals but on society at large. Critics of rap music, such as newspaper columnist Stanley Crouch, argue that the negative ramification of the glorification of "thuggish behavior" extends beyond the individuals who listen to the music to impact the larger African American community. Hence, gangsta rap is being seen as having a devastating impact on the youth of today and the larger society.

Pointing the Finger in the Wrong Direction: Misplaced Blame of Hip Hop

While politicians and social critics have maintained that there is a connection between gangsta rap, procrime attitudes, and delinquency/crime, others question the social shaping effect of gangster rap. Supporters of gangsta rap argue that the music merely reflects the life experiences of the artists. It is a cultural form that mirrors the state of today's society, particularly that of urban youth. Scholars such as Michael Eric Dyson, Tricia Ross, and Clarence Lusane have defended hip hop, characterizing it as music with a higher purpose. Many of these supporters argue that hip hop artists are actually poets putting their prose to the beat of music, which has the power of transporting its listeners into the world of the artists.

Many supporters of this genre of music argue that contemporary rappers describe their reality just as rappers of the past (e.g., Kurtis Blow, Furious Five, The Sugarhill Gang) rhymed about issues that were salient in their times. As times change, so too does the music, and gangsta rap is a grittier, harsher musical form that reflects the grittier, harsher conditions of the urban poor in America today. Consequently, when rap artists rhyme about murder, drugs, and prostitution, they are expressing aspects of reality in urban centers. Many artists insist that their music reflects the harsh reality of their lived experiences, and in order to express themselves lyrically and be true to their art, they have to paint a picture of the realities of their lived experiences.

Some argue that the depictions of the harsh conditions of life and specifically the criminal aspects of life in the inner city are being romanticized by these artists. However, scholars such as Dyson and Ross contend that this is a misplaced criticism; on their view, hip hop artists do not seek to romanticize the physical geography of the ghetto; instead, they seek to uphold the intellectual by-products of the circumstances present in life in urban America and to erase the stigma associated with the ghetto. It can be argued that the music serves as a cathartic expression for the artists, as they use rhymes to describe life in their social world. Hence, when artists lament the harsh realities of the urban slums, their music can be seen as akin to a liberating experience that releases the toxins associated with this environment.

Whereas some critics argue that rhyming about crime and violence serves to legitimize these acts, others argue that while gangsta rap (or hip hop) is misguided at times, such music is more a description of the gangster world than an endorsement of this lifestyle. From this perspective, the suggestion that gangsta rap causes delinquency and crime is considered to be misguided; the artists should be regarded as sources of insight, not as role models who are leading the youth into a life of crime and destruction. According to this view, the artistic expression of gangsta rap functions to inform and entertain, not to make any judgment about the morality of criminal behavior. To claim that rap serves as an initiation into the world of crime and criminality is to put the cart before the horse; in reality, delinquency and crime existed before the evolution of gangsta rap. Supporters of this genre of rap suggest that it is used as a scapegoat for society's ills.

In response to the defense of hip hop, some social activists contend that the use of misogyny and negative name calling in hip hop contributed to social acceptance of racist language, such as radio host Don Imus's reference to members of the Rutgers University women's basketball team as "nappy-headed hos." The fact that the Don Imus incident brought the issue of misogyny and violence-laden lyrics into the public debate is illustrative of the link that has been made between the social ills of society and rap music. Newspaper columnist Crouch argues that Imus took cues from the rap idiom in his reference to the Rutgers team. However, other scholars argue that the use of words and imagery used in the art form is never an excuse for others outside of the African American community to use such idioms. Michael Eric Dyson has argued that there is an obvious distinction between the use of such language by Don Imus and the use of this language by Snoop Dogg.

The debate over the influence of hip hop on delinquency and crime was heightened as result of the Imus incident and continues today. Some artists have agreed that there needs to be a moratorium on the use of negative words and images in the music, whereas others fervently disagree. Many artists argue that they have a right to use terms that some find offensive, and the moral debate surrounding rap has done little to influence the views of some of the artists.

Conclusion

Both sides of the debate concerning hip hop and crime make valid points. There continues to be a divide between those who see hip hop as being a negative force and those who disagree with this assessment. While the debate rages on, it is important to note that while much attention is focused on gangsta rap artists, other rap artists present a more positive tone in their music. Artists such as Common, Mos Def, Queen Latifah, Lauren Hill, and M-1 produce music that is commonly referred to as "conscious" music because it often serves to educate and set a more affirmative tone for its listeners. These artists are often left out of the debate, but their influence on hip hop should be noted as they have served as the positive forces of hip hop.

Terri M. Adams

See also African American Gangs; Drug Dealers; Media Portrayals of African Americans; Violence Against Girls; Violence Against Women; Youth Gangs

Further Readings

Adams, T., & Fuller, D. (2006). Misogynistic lyrics and rap music: The words have changed by the ideology remains. *Journal of Black Studies, 36*(6), 938–957.

Dyson, M. (2007). *Know what I mean.* New York: Basic Civitas Books.

Goodman, A. (Interviewer), & Dyson, M. E. (Interviewee). (2007, July 18). *Professor and preacher Michael Eric Dyson on hip hop & politics, Don Imus, the "N"-word, and Bill Cosby* [Interview transcript]. Retrieved from Democracy Now! website: http://www.democracynow.org/2007/7/18/professor_and_preacher_michael_eric_dyson

Quinn, E. (2004). *Nuthin but a "G" thang: The culture and commerce of gangsta rap.* New York: Columbia University Press.

Rose, T. (1994). *Black noise: Rap music and Black culture in contemporary America.* Middletown, CT: Wesleyan University Press.

HISTORICALLY BLACK COLLEGES AND UNIVERSITIES

Historically Black colleges and universities (HBCUs) were founded to educate formerly enslaved people of African descent. Cheyney State University in Cheyney, Pennsylvania, was established in 1837 as the first historically Black institution of higher education. There are now 105 HBCUs scattered throughout the United States, the majority of which are located in the South. Many of these were built after the Morrill Act of 1890, which provided for state-supported land-grant HBCUs. The importance of these institutions to Black people is paramount, past and present. This entry provides a short history of

HBCUs and describes the challenges they have faced, the successes they have achieved, and future goals. It identifies reasons why a knowledge of HBCUs is important in understanding race relations in the United States and how Blacks have been self-determined in their efforts to educate themselves despite opposition. It also explores the growing role of degree programs in criminal justice at HBCUs.

After the enslavement of African-descended peoples was abolished, it was HBCUs that embraced the ideals for Black empowerment through education. More than 90% of people of African descent in college were enrolled in HBCUs until midway through the 20th century. However, the favorable impact of HBCUs was not immediate; initial opposition to Black education had to be dealt with before African Americans could truly benefit from the creation and implementation of HBCUs. Some Whites opposed Black education in the belief that education would put Blacks in direct competition with them for jobs. Despite this, HBCUs continued to be built.

Challenges Confronted by HBCUs

Over time, educators at a number of universities, including Fisk University, Howard University, and Atlanta University, expressed disdain toward HBCUs' lack of concern with the social, political, and economic realities facing Blacks. The institutions were criticized for not gearing their education to suit the needs of Black communities and for failing to prepare students for life and its hardships. Such critics argued that political and economic empowerment needed to be a critical part of the curriculum if Blacks were to elevate themselves from the second-class citizenship status imposed on them by the dominant culture.

Some HBCUs, including Bluefield State and West Virginia State universities, have come to have predominantly White student bodies. However, Black students have not become the majority at any historically White colleges and universities (HWCUs). HBCUs have struggled to assert their legitimacy to state legislators in Louisiana, Florida, Texas, Georgia, Mississippi, and Alabama. Additionally, state monetary appropriations to HBCUs have traditionally been markedly less than that given to HWCUs, sometimes constituting 10% or less. Some HBCUs also have issues with the quality of facilities, availability of academic programs, and the number of graduate programs. Despite these challenges, these educational institutions have experienced many successes, and Black students from across the nation continue to seek them out.

Success at HBCUs

Over the past 100 years or more, HBCUs have produced stellar students from multiple disciplines who are competitive in their respective fields. Additionally, the value of these schools is shown by increases in enrollment and in the number of bachelor degrees awarded. In 2004 the National Center for Educational Statistics reported that HBCUs have awarded 28% of all bachelor degrees earned by African Americans. In 2000 *Black Enterprise* surveyed more than 500 Black professionals and found that the five top-ranked colleges and universities in terms of best social and academic environment for Black students were HBCUs. Of the top 10 institutions graduating Black students who go on to earn a Ph.D., the United Negro Fund has reported that nine of them are Black colleges.

Researchers Kim and Conrad compiled the results of multiple studies to highlight the success of Black students who attend HBCUs in an article published in 2006. These studies indicate the increased involvement with faculty through mentoring experienced at HBCUs results in greater African American achievement. Additional studies included also suggest that Black students attending HBCUs have greater and deeper involvement with their communities and do as well as or better in standardized writing skills, science reasoning, and overall grade attainment than do Black students who attend HWCUs. However, in a 2006 study, Kim and Conrad found no differences in rate of degree completion whether Black students attended an HBCU or an HWCU.

Criminal Justice Programs at HBCUs

Relative to involvement in empowering Black communities is recognition of the current state of Black communities. The disproportionate incarceration of African Americans in the United States requires attention from researchers, activists, and educators who are familiar with this phenomenon and are trained in racially sensitive perspectives to seek change on a number of levels. Since the late 1960s, the existence and growth of criminal justice programs at HBCUs have been a testament to the desire of those institutions to tackle these issues. Graduates of these programs have diversified the criminal justice system, and their long unheard voices will continue to paint a more complete picture of the lived experiences of Black people and their interaction with the criminal justice system. According to Penn and Gabbidon, there are currently 48 criminal justice programs offering a bachelor's degree, with over 5,800 students enrolled, and 5 programs offering a master's degree, with approximately 500 students enrolled.

Criminal justice programs at some HBCUs have become the largest degree programs at those institutions. It is likely that such increased enrollment reflects a growing concern with addressing the disparities in the criminal justice system as well as a perceived opportunity to confront these issues. Moreover, in addition to the ever-increasing number of graduate programs in criminology and criminal justice at HBCUs, it is notable that there are now Ph.D. programs in justice-related areas at Prairie View A&M University (in juvenile justice) and Texas Southern University (in administration of justice). As a result of such programs, it is likely that there will also be increasing diversity on the faculties of criminology and criminal justice programs across the nation.

Future Challenges

In the age of technology, distance learning has become an ever-increasing alternative to traditional learning on many college campuses. Some HBCUs are embracing this form of education and, as a result, may increase enrollment if students are not required to be on campus full-time. An increase in enrollment may also be seen as a result of the decreased cost of distance learning programs.

The charge of HBCUs continues to be relevant as race relations have yet to exhibit equitable treatment of people regardless of race. HBCUs continue to produce graduates that utilize their skills to empower Black communities, and that empowerment continues to modify the landscape of America. For instance, HBCU graduates now have political leadership in government and can advocate for legislation to support the growth and maintenance of these institutions. Additionally, these institutions continue to produce graduates who are competitive in their respective fields while being cognizant of who they are and their ability to utilize their knowledge for Black empowerment and subsequently the betterment of all humanity.

Efua Akoma

See also Mentoring Programs

Further Readings

Ashley, D., & Williams, J. (2004). *I'll find a way or make one: A tribute to historically Black colleges and universities.* New York: HarperCollins.

Debro, J. (1981). Criminology and criminal justice education in historically Black colleges and universities. In R. L. McNeely & C. E. Pope (Eds.), *Race, crime, and criminal justice* (pp. 161–174). Beverly Hills, CA: Sage.

Distance education is coming to the Black colleges. (2004, October). *Journal of Blacks in Higher Education, 45,* 112–114.

Evans, A. L., & Evans, V. (2002). Historically black colleges and universities (HBCUS). *Education, 123*(1), 3–16.

Gabbidon, S. L., & Penn, E. B. (1999). Criminal justice education at historically Black colleges and universities: Past, present, and future. *The Justice Professional, 11*(4), 439–449.

Kim, M. M., & Clifton, C. (2006). The impact of historically Black colleges and universities on the academic success of African American students. *Research in Higher Education, 47*(4), 399–427.

Lemelle, T. (2002). The HBCU: Yesterday, today and tomorrow. *Education, 123*(1), 190–196.

Penn, E. B., & Gabbidon, S. L. (2007). Criminal justice education at historically Black colleges and universities: Three decades of progress. *Journal of Criminal Justice Education, 18*(1), 137–162.

Roebuck, J., & Murty, K. (1993). *Historically Black colleges and universities: Their place in American higher education.* New York: Praeger.

HIV/AIDS

HIV/AIDS is a devastating disease that disproportionately affects minorities. This entry defines HIV/AIDS, explains the routes of transmission, examines the disparities of HIV infection and AIDS diagnosis among racial and ethnic groups, and offers explanations for these differences. It also describes some recent HIV/AIDS and crime issues.

Overview

The human immunodeficiency virus (HIV) is a retrovirus that attacks the human immune system. It is transferred from an infected to a noninfected individual by bodily fluids, which include blood, breast milk, pre-ejaculate, semen, and vaginal fluid. HIV is transmitted by sexual intercourse, blood transfusion, mother to baby (known as perinatal transmission, including breast feeding, child birth, and pregnancy), and contaminated needles and syringes. The advanced or final stage of the fatal disease is known as acquired immunodeficiency syndrome (AIDS). There is no known cure for HIV/AIDS, but antiretroviral drugs have been successful in increasing the life expectancy of those who are infected. However, these drugs are expensive and often out of reach for people in underdeveloped countries. Recognized in 1981, HIV is believed to have originated in sub-Saharan Africa. Today HIV/AIDS is considered a pandemic. According to the World Health Organization, approximately 39.6 million worldwide are living with HIV. Although it is a global problem, sub-Saharan Africa carries the largest burden of cases, and females are disproportionately infected. It is estimated that 25 million people around the globe have died of AIDS since the virus was identified.

U.S. Data

Although the number of HIV infections and AIDS diagnoses in the United States has not been as prevalent as in sub-Saharan Africa, it remains a serious public health problem. The first HIV cases began appearing in gay men in 1981, and HIV was initially labeled a gay or homosexual disease.

According to the U.S. Centers for Disease Control and Prevention (CDC), the infection rate peaked in the 1980s with approximately 150,000 new infections annually, then dramatically decreased to 40,000 infections annually, where it has remained. As a result of antiretroviral drugs entering the market in 1996, AIDS cases began to decrease. In the United States, approximately 500,000 people have died from AIDS since 1981. Today over 1 million Americans are currently living with HIV and one quarter are unaware they are infected, indicating the need for more public awareness and additional prevention efforts.

Race

In terms of race and ethnicity, HIV/AIDS has affected minorities more than Whites, thus creating a health disparity. African Americans and Hispanics are disproportionately represented with HIV/AIDS. According to the CDC, although Blacks comprise 14% of the U.S. population (based on the 2000 U.S. Census), they account for 49% of HIV/AIDS cases diagnosed. In comparison, Hispanics comprise 14% of the population and make up 18% of HIV/AIDS diagnoses in 2005. The CDC reported that in 2005, the rate of AIDS diagnoses for Black adults and adolescents was 10 times greater than that of Whites and nearly 3 times greater than for Hispanics; the rate of AIDS diagnoses for Black women was nearly 23 times that of White women; and the rate of AIDS diagnoses for Black men was 8 times greater than that of White men, indicating the disparity among races. With regard to life expectancy, on average Blacks diagnosed with AIDS do not live as long as do non-Blacks. Moreover, AIDS is a leading cause of death for Black females. According to the CDC, in 2002 HIV/AIDS was the leading cause of death for Black women ages 25 to 34. Thus far, 211,000 Blacks have died from AIDS. The statistics for the Black population indicate a health crisis.

Explanations

Although Blacks have been the hardest hit of any race or ethnicity in the United States, it is important to note that race and ethnicity are not in themselves risk factors for HIV/AIDS. Socioeconomic factors such as poverty, high unemployment, lack of education, and incarceration are known risk factors for HIV/AIDS and other illnesses. Individuals who are poor may not have the resources to get tested for HIV or may lack health insurance to seek treatment. Minorities are more likely to be poor than are Whites. In terms of health, Blacks also have higher rates of sexually transmitted diseases (STDs) according to the CDC. This is significant because certain types of STDs increase the chance of infection. Individuals with STDS are 2 to 5 times more likely to become infected with HIV. Similarly, those with HIV who have an STD are more likely to infect their partner with HIV via sexual contact, revealing the importance of treating STDS.

Culturally there is a stigma attached to being HIV positive, which can make individuals less likely to get tested, seek treatment, or inform partners of their HIV status; this lack of action contributes to the spread of the disease. Oftentimes individuals live in denial, unable to admit to themselves or others they have the disease. Moreover, there is a stigma attached to being homosexual. The fear, discrimination, and hate crimes associated with homosexuality make it difficult for individuals to come forward with the disease. This is significant given that the majority of Black males become infected through male-to-male sex. The fact that Black females predominantly become infected through heterosexual contact compounds the problem and brings up the issue of sexual orientation. Homosexuality, bisexuality, and heterosexuality may not be openly discussed between partners due to shame and fear. In addition, there is a Black male shortage. Demographically, Black women face an unfavorable sex ratio, which potentially limits their selection of partners. These barriers increase the likelihood of spreading HIV.

HIV/AIDS, Crime, and Criminal Justice

HIV/AIDS transmission is a critical issue in criminal justice. According to the National Center for Victims of Crime, many states have enacted HIV/AIDS legislation that requires either preconviction or postconviction testing (or both) of sexual offenders and disclosure of test results to the victims. Victims of other violent crimes might also be at risk for HIV infection as a result of physical and sexual trauma. The transmission of HIV/AIDs among intravenous drug users has been a concern to criminal justice and public health officials since the 1980s.

Government Intervention

The U.S. federal government has responded to HIV/AIDS. In 1990, Congress passed the Ryan White Care Act, which is the largest federal HIV program serving 500,000 individuals. According to the U.S. Department of Human Services, it provides funding for low-income individuals with HIV who are uninsured or underinsured, promotes access to care, and provides primary health care. To address the disproportionate number of African Americans with HIV/AIDS, President Clinton created the Minority Aids Initiative in 1998, which provides new funds for HIV/AIDS services in minority communities. The goal of the program is to improve health outcomes and decrease health disparities for minorities with HIV/AIDS. Specifically, it addresses prevention, provides outreach to minorities with HIV/AIDS, and assures access to care and treatment.

Next Steps

Although government programs and treatment are available to those with HIV/AIDS, there is no cure for the disease. It is critical that new HIV infections be prevented by educating people, specifically minorities, about the transmission of HIV and the importance of practicing safe sex and getting tested regularly. For those already infected with HIV, quality health care and affordable treatment need to be sustained. Research needs to focus on successful prevention strategies in minority communities and ongoing surveillance of the disease.

Lorenda A. Naylor

See also Drug Treatment; Drug Use; Hate Crimes; National Association for the Advancement of Colored People (NAACP); Victim Services

Further Readings

Centers for Disease Control and Prevention. (1998, July 31). HIV prevention through early detection and treatment of other sexually transmitted diseases—United States recommendations of the Advisory Committee for HIV and STD Prevention. *Morbidity and Mortality Weekly Report, 47*(RR/12), 1–24. Retrieved from http://www.cdc.gov/mmwr/preview/mmwrhtml/00054174.htm

Centers for Disease Control and Prevention. (2006, June 2). Twenty-five years of HIV/AIDS—United States, 1981–2006. *Morbidity and Mortality Weekly Report, 55*(21), 585–589.

Centers for Disease Control and Prevention. (2007, June). *HIV/AIDS among African Americans* [Fact sheet]. Retrieved July 8, 2007, from http://www.cdc.gov/hiv/topics/aa/resources/factsheets/aa.htm

Centers for Disease Control and Prevention. (2007, June). *HIV/AIDS surveillance report, 2005* (Vol. 17, Rev. ed.). Retrieved from http://www.cdc.gov/hiv/topics/surveillance/resources/reports/2005report/pdf/2005SurveillanceReport.pdf

Joint United Nations Programme on HIV/AIDS (UNAIDS). (2006). *2006 report on the global AIDS epidemic.* Geneva: UNAIDS. Retrieved from http://www.unaids.org/en/KnowledgeCentre/HIVData/GlobalReport/2006/default.asp

National Center for Victims of Crime. (1999). *HIV/AIDS legislation.* Retrieved from http://www.ncdsv.org/images/HIV-AIDSLegislation.pdf

Simoni, J. M., Sehgal, S., & Walters, K. L. (2004). Triangle of risk: Urban American Indian women's sexual trauma, injection drug use, and HIV sexual risk behaviors. *AIDS and Behavior, 8*(1), 33–45.

HOMICIDE SERIOUSNESS DYAD

Homicide seriousness dyad refers to the way in which courts have historically evaluated the seriousness of homicides committed by Blacks against Whites versus those committed by Whites against Blacks. This entry describes Guy Johnson's analysis of the impact of cultural and social factors, such as slavery and racial discrimination, on the seriousness with which homicides are perceived in the slave era and discrimination based on offender–victim characteristics. Next, the entry summarizes research by sociologist Darnell Hawkins on explanations for disproportionately high rates of homicide among African Americans.

Hawkins points to situational, structural, and institutional factors that should be considered in understanding the causes of Black homicide.

The Slave Era

Slavery dehumanized African Americans in such a way that they were seen as subordinate individuals per the degradation of slavery. Blacks were unable to establish a stable family, stable economic organization, or a stable community life. Sociologist Guy Johnson, in 1941, argued that slavery elicited a certain set of behaviors in the Negro, such as lack of self-respect, lack of self-confidence, a distaste for hard work, and a distrust for White man's laws. These behaviors caused strain and resulted in violent or criminal acts. During the slave era, it was not considered a crime when a White slave owner killed a Black slave. In addition, a White person was allowed to cause injury to a Black slave without any criminal repercussions. However, when a Black slave killed a White person, this was considered one of the worst crimes imaginable and carried a heavy punishment. Punishment was swift and severe for the Black slave who found himself in this position, as the probability of the destruction of social order was feared. Throughout the slave era in the South, several local and state ordinances and statutes defined criminal offenses that were strictly slave-specific. Some state statutes made the punishment for an offender dependent on a comparison of offender–victim characteristics.

Offender–Victim Characteristics

Johnson noted that the murder of a White person by a Negro and the murder of a Negro by a Negro were not the same kind of murder from the standpoint of the upper caste's scale of values, even though official crime statistics categorized them together. Johnson proposed four offender–victim categories. He called his four offender–victim categories the "hierarchy of homicide seriousness model." This model rank-ordered crimes by seriousness of crime, from most serious to least serious, as follows:

1. Negro versus White

2. White versus White

3. Negro versus Negro

4. White versus Negro

In studies of three states in the South, Johnson found that Blacks who killed Whites were more likely to be sentenced to death and executed than were Whites who killed Whites. Furthermore, Blacks who killed Blacks were given lighter sentences overall. Whites who killed Blacks were seldom prosecuted. Blacks learned rather quickly that harsher punishment was in store if they killed a White person versus a Black person. They also learned that when a White person killed a Black person it was seldom reported, and such a case was even less likely to be prosecuted in a court of law.

Drawing on Johnson's model, Hawkins proposed three theoretical propositions to explain the fact that rates of Black criminal homicide were higher than those for Whites or other non-Black Americans:

1. American criminal law: Black life is cheap, but White life is valuable.

2. Past and present racial and social class differences in the administration of justice affect Black criminal violence.

3. Economic deprivation creates a climate of powerlessness in which individual acts of violence are likely to take place.

The first proposition states that throughout American history, a Black life was treated as less valuable than a White life. Hawkins expanded Johnson's work and created a racial hierarchy of homicide offenses which listed most serious to least serious types of homicide (Hawkins, 1983, pp. 420–421):

Hawkins' Hierarchy of Homicide Seriousness

Rating	Offense
Most Serious	Black kills White, in authority
	Black kills White, stranger
	White kills White, in authority
	Black kills White, friend, acquaintance
	Black kills White, intimate, family
	White kills White, friend, acquaintance
	White kills White, intimate, family
	Black kills Black, stranger
	Black kills Black, friend, acquaintance
	Black kills Black, intimate, family
	White kills Black, stranger
	White kills Black, friend, acquaintance
Least Serious	White kills Black, intimate, family

Furthermore, Blacks learned that killing another Black carried little if any prison time; Hawkins postulated that this devaluation of life contributed to Black-on-Black homicide.

The second proposition speaks to the numerous factors preceding a homicide event, such as assault. Hawkins argued that when such prehomicide events occur in the Black community, they are overlooked, or law enforcement and other administration of justice agencies do not respond adequately; for example, there may be no response, or police response times may be unacceptably slow. This ineffective intervention, in turn, caused Blacks to fail to report prehomicide behavior.

The third proposition states that criminal violence is caused in part by economic deprivation and powerlessness, and thus, homicide rates will occur at a higher rate among the Black underclass than among the Black middle class. Hawkins felt the association between Black homicide rates and low socioeconomic status was characterized by lower-class Blacks seeing violent crime as a way to have some sort of control in a society that rendered them powerless socially, politically, and economically. Consequently, Blacks are disproportionately represented in the prison system for acts of criminal violence.

Over the past 25 years since the publication of Hawkins's suppositions, countless death-penalty studies have shown support for the "race-of-victim" effects. In short, in line with the homicide seriousness dyad, Black offenders have been more likely to receive a death sentence when the victim is White than when the victim is non-White.

Monica B. Pinalez

See also Black Criminology; Capital Jury Project; Center for the Study and Prevention of Violence; Dehumanization of Blacks; Inequality Theory; Interracial Crime; John Jay College Center on Race, Crime and Justice; Sentencing Disparities, African Americans; Sentencing Project, The

Further Readings

Farrell, R. A., & Swigert, V. L. (1978). Legal disposition of inter-group and intra-group homicides. *Sociological Quarterly, 19,* 565–576.

Green, E. (1964). Inter- and intra-racial crime relative to sentencing. *Journal of Criminal Law, Criminology and Police Science, 55,* 348–358.

Hawkins, D. F. (1983). Black and White homicide differentials: Alternatives to an inadequate theory. *Criminal Justice and Behavior, 10*(4), 407–440.

Johnson, G. B. (1941). The Negro and crime. *Annals of the American Academy of Political and Social Science, 217,* 93–104.

Kleck, G. (1981). Racial discrimination in criminal sentencing. *American Sociological Review, 46,* 783–805.

Ross, P. H., Bose, C. E., & Berk, R. E. (1974). The seriousness of crimes: Normative structure and individual difference. *American Sociological Review, 39,* 224–237.

Wolfgang, M. E. (1958). *Patterns in criminal homicide.* New York: Wiley.

HOUSES OF REFUGE

The housing of delinquent youth in America has been a major concern throughout history. With the influx of immigrant families entering the United States in the late 1700s and early 1800s, increased juvenile presence and delinquency quickly became a social concern. As the result of increased juvenile presence on the streets, houses of refuge were proposed as a solution to juvenile delinquency. Throughout history, houses of refuge have been consistently defined as care facilities developed by the child savers (reformers who developed programs for troubled and neglected youth). Although houses of refuge existed ostensibly to protect potentially criminal youth from being easily influenced by the negative aspects of society, some critics argue that the use of houses of refuge was discriminatory, affecting only poor White immigrants while excluding Blacks. Particular attention has been given to historical discrimination and segregation of Black and White youth in juvenile facilities, as well as the existence of separate facilities for Blacks. This entry examines the history of the development of houses of refuge in America and consequently reviews the role of social reformers and court decisions in their existence.

In the 17th and 18th centuries, recognition of child rights in England sparked a new era of recognition of childhood as a status to be protected in America. This newfound status was identified as a special stage during which children were considered innocent but also corruptible. During this time, there were no laws governing or protecting children's rights; rather, chancery courts addressed the issue of neglected and poor children.

In the early 1800s, many White immigrant youth came to the United States from England as indentured servants or apprentices. Once these youth were in America, reformers were concerned with the moral training of those who exhibited behaviors such as drinking, vagrancy, delinquency, and running away. The doctrine of parens patriae, the power of the state to act on behalf of the child, was adopted by the courts to address children in need of supervision. This adoption marked a new direction in America, in which parents became second to the state when considering the well-being of children. Reformers believed that juvenile crime was the direct result of exposure to poverty, immigration, and lack of parental guidance. In their attempt to address these conditions, child savers supported removing children from their homes and placing them in houses of refuge to offer them better opportunities.

On January 1, 1825, the first house of refuge opened in New York. The main purpose of the house of refuge was to provide youth with firm discipline and a strong work ethic to compensate for what the family was not doing. Throughout the 18th century, many states followed New York in an attempt to address the newfound social concern surrounding juvenile delinquency. In 1826, Boston opened its first house refuge, and by 1828 many youth were being transported across the country.

Unlike their White counterparts, Black youth continued to be treated as, and housed with, adults in jail for years after the first house of refuge was established. Black youth were often hard to place as apprentices, and they were excluded from the opportunities provided by houses of refuge because of their skin color. Although delinquency concerns were similar for both Black and White youth, arguments surfaced that White child savers were interested only in saving White youth. And while facilities in New York and Boston accepted Blacks, they were segregated from the White youth. In other states, however, Black youth were excluded altogether from the houses of refuge. In 1849, Philadelphia established a separate house of refuge for Black youth. Even so, continued concern surrounding unequal race-based treatment led to the establishment of the Black Child Savers organization in 1907.

The relationship between the houses of refuge and law are depicted in two annotated court decisions: *Ex Parte Crouse* (1838) and *People v. Turner* (1870). In the 1838 case of Mary Ann Crouse, a female believed to be incorrigible was presented to the court. Even though her father petitioned the court for her release, Mary Ann Crouse was sent to live in a house of refuge in Pennsylvania as the result of her family's economic status. This was the first case where a child who had not committed a crime was committed to a house of refuge. In a similar case, *People v. Turner* (1870), Daniel O'Connell was sent to live in a house of refuge because the court believed he was likely to offend in the future. On appeal, this case was overturned by the Illinois Supreme Court, which ruled that O'Connell was not being treated and was being imprisoned without due process.

Despite the original intent of reformers to care for youth, abusive treatment of youth became apparent. Houses of refuge were marked with filth, danger, and discrimination, and they were not equipped to supervise youthful populations. Over the years, the existence and persistence of disproportionate minority confinement have been linked to discriminatory practices of this time. For over 50 years, houses of refuge were the dominant facilities that housed juvenile delinquents in America, and during this time, more than 50,000 children were displaced.

Tiffiney Y. Barfield-Cottledge

See also Child Savers; Delinquency Prevention; Juvenile Crime; Reformatories

Further Readings

Bernard, T. J. (1992). *The cycle of juvenile justice.* New York: Oxford University Press.

Bernard, T. J. (2006). *Serious delinquency: An anthology.* Los Angeles: Roxbury.

Del Carmen, R. V., Parker, M., & Reddington, F. P. (1998). *Briefs of leading cases in juvenile justice.* Cincinnati, OH: Anderson.

Gabbidon, S. L., & Greene, H. T. (2005). *Race and crime.* Thousand Oaks, CA: Sage.

Parent, D. G., Lieter, V., Kennedy, S., Livens, L., Wentworth, D., & Wilcox, S. (1994). *Conditions of confinement: Juvenile detention and correctional facilities*. Washington, DC: Office of Juvenile Justice and Delinquency Prevention.

HOUSTON, CHARLES HAMILTON (1895–1950)

Charles Hamilton Houston, an African American attorney and teacher, was known as the architect of civil rights legislation. It was Houston's strategy for defeating racial segregation through the courts that led to the *Brown v. Board of Education* decision of 1954. He is responsible for training or influencing the nation's early civil rights attorneys, including Thurgood Marshall, Spottswood Robinson, William Hastie, James Nabrit, and Oliver W. Hill. This entry reviews Houston's life, his academic training, and his substantive contributions to the civil rights movement.

The Early Years

Charles Hamilton Houston was born September 3, 1895, in Washington, D.C., to William LePre Houston, an attorney, and Mary Ethel Hamilton Houston, a beautician. His birth came 1 year before the infamous U.S. Supreme Court case of *Plessy v. Ferguson* (1896), which sanctioned racial segregation. William Houston was a renowned attorney who moved to Washington, D.C., in search of economic and cultural opportunities for his family. Charles Houston was an exceptionally intelligent child. He graduated first in his class from the M Street High School in Washington, D.C., which was known nationally for its high academic standards and prestigious Black graduates. Alumni of M Street include Charles Drew, M.D., Congresswoman Eleanor Holmes Norton, and the first Black graduate of the Harvard Business School, Dr. Howard Naylor Fitzhugh. Charles Houston then attended Amherst College, where he graduated magna cum laude at age 19. The only Black person in the class of 1915, he was elected to Phi Beta Kappa and was class valedictorian.

Finding Destiny

In 1917, in the advent of the U.S. entry into World War I, Houston joined the military, enlisting in the U.S. Army's officer training program. The U.S. military was segregated and steeped in a tradition of hostility toward Blacks. Charles Houston rose to the rank of second lieutenant in the army's field artillery unit. The depth of racism he faced in America's military led Houston to make an oath that would change his life and the direction of civil rights litigation. He wrote, "I made up my mind that if I got through this war I would study law and use my time fighting for men who could not strike back." After the war, Houston returned to Washington, D.C., and applied to Harvard Law School. It was 1919. Race riots engulfed the nation leading that summer to be known as the "Red Summer," so named for the blood that ran through the streets.

Charles Houston was admitted to Harvard Law School and became known as a brilliant student. Houston was elected an editor of the *Harvard Law Review*, the first Black person to achieve this honor. He graduated from Harvard in 1922 and in 1923 received a Doctor of Juridical Science, the first Black person at Harvard to be awarded this degree. After graduating from Harvard Law School, Houston traveled to Africa before returning to Washington, D.C., to practice law with his father.

Attorney, Professor, Strategist

Charles Houston argued the U.S. Supreme Court case of *Nixon v. Condon* (1932), which successfully challenged a Democratic Party policy in Texas prohibiting Blacks from participating in primary elections. Soon Charles Houston determined that the fight against racial segregation required the training of Black attorneys at Black law schools. In 1929, in addition to the practice of law, Houston taught at Howard University, which at the time had a fledgling law school. Houston is chiefly responsible for raising the prestige and quality of education of Howard Law School. Through his efforts, by 1931, Howard Law School attained full accreditation by the Association of American Law Schools and the American Bar Association, the first Black law school to do so.

When the American Bar Association refused membership to Blacks, Houston helped found the National Bar Association, the first national organization for Black attorneys.

At Howard Law School, Houston created a rigorous curriculum featuring substantive law as well as trial advocacy and appellate practice. He viewed the Fourteenth Amendment to the U.S. Constitution as the Black *Magna Carta* and trained Howard University law students in the use of the equal protection and due process clauses to fight racial discrimination. He urged law school graduates to return home and challenge discriminatory practices. To Charles Houston, a "lawyer is either a social engineer or a parasite on society." Houston would become a professor and the dean of Howard University Law School.

In 1935, Houston left the dean's post at Howard Law School to become the first special counsel to the NAACP, leading the organization's legal committee until 1940. It was during his tenure at the NAACP that Houston began to implement a strategy to defeat the *Plessy v. Ferguson* (1896) legal doctrine of "separate but equal'" in education. Houston brilliantly surmised that the requirement to build and maintain a separate facility for Blacks would be financially prohibitive for state governments. He then assisted dozens of attorneys around the country in an orchestrated plan to challenge racial discrimination in public education. Charles Houston, with Thurgood Marshall, led the litigation of *Murray v. Pearson* (1936), integrating Maryland's law school, and *Missouri ex rel. Gaines v. Canada* (1938), in which a Black applicant was denied admission to the University of Missouri Law School based solely on his race. Houston successfully argued that Gaines must be admitted into the state's law school or be provided with a law school for Blacks. In 1938, the U.S. Supreme Court ruled in favor of Gaines.

In 1940, Houston returned to Washington, D.C., leaving his position at the NAACP to his assistant and former student, Thurgood Marshall. In private practice at his father's firm, Charles Hamilton Houston continued to challenge racial discrimination. Despite threats to his life and his livelihood, he represented Blacks from trial through appeal, applying his constitutional strategy to both civil and criminal cases. Houston was responsible for two renowned labor law cases: *Steele v. Louisville & Nashville R.R. Co.* (1944) and *Tunstall v. Brotherhood of Locomotive Firemen & Enginemen* (1944), which forced unions to represent the interests of Black employees fairly. Houston argued several state criminal cases challenging the exclusion of Blacks from juries. In *Legions v. Commonwealth of Virginia* (1943) and *Hale v. Kentucky* (1938), Houston argued that Black defendants were denied due process rights because of the exclusion of Blacks from juries. In *Shelley v. Kraemer* (1948) and *Hurd v. Hodge* (1948), Houston successfully argued that a court is prohibited from enforcing racially discriminatory provisions in the deeds and contracts known as restrictive covenants.

Houston died on April 22, 1950. His death would come 4 years before the U.S. Supreme Court's ruling in *Brown v. Board of Education of Topeka* (1954) denouncing the doctrine of "separate but equal" in public education. Although he did not live to see the fruit of his labor, Houston remains *the* architect of civil rights litigation. Civil rights law, featuring his legal precedents, has become a course of study in every law school in the country. Houston's legacy is the political, economic, social, and educational progress within the Black community. Charles Hamilton Houston is an American hero whose contributions as scholar, writer, lawyer, activist, and professor are evidenced by advocacy groups, of all walks of life, which continue to utilize his strategies in their quest for justice under law.

Gloria J. Browne-Marshall

See also NAACP Legal Defense Fund

Further Readings

Anderson, J. F. (2006, Spring). The criminal justice principles of Charles Hamilton Houston: Lessons in innovation. *University of Baltimore Law Review, 35*(3), 313–345.

Browne-Marshall, G. J. (2007). *Race, law, and American society: 1607 to present.* New York: Routledge.

Carter, R. (2004). The long road to equality. *The Nation, 278*(17), 28–30.

Carter, R. (2007, Summer). Brown's legacy: Fulfilling the promise of equal education. *Journal of Negro Education, 76*(3), 240–249.

McNeil, G. R. (1983). *Groundwork: Charles Hamilton Houston and the struggle for civil rights.* Philadelphia: University of Pennsylvania Press.

HUMAN TRAFFICKING

Nearly 700,000 people a year are transported globally across national boundaries by force or deception for the purpose of labor or sexual exploitation. Of these victims, an estimated 18,000 to 20,000 are trafficked into the United States, which is the second largest destination for victims of the sex trafficking trade. While human trafficking is recognized as a growing transnational phenomenon, a uniform definition has yet to be internationally adopted; in several countries human trafficking is not even a crime. The fact that individual countries often adopt their own definition of human trafficking leads to an international inability to measure its occurrence, which gives the perception of a lack of trafficking activity. This entry examines human trafficking, which can be considered a form of modern-day slavery based on cultural instability and economic deprivation.

Whereas several countries have adopted the definition of human trafficking introduced by the United Nations, the United States has adopted a different and detailed definition, which divides human trafficking into two categories: sex trafficking and labor trafficking. More specifically, the United States acknowledges human trafficking as an individual induced by force, fraud, or coercion to engage in the sex trade, or the harboring, transportation, or obtaining of a person for labor service. The United Nations has expanded this definition to include the removal of organs—a circumstance that remains unacknowledged in the U.S. definition. Although the definitions of the crime may vary, the elemental factors they describe remain the same: the purposeful transportation of an individual for the purpose of exploitation.

The Trafficking Scheme

Human traffickers create transnational routes that facilitate the transportation of migrants who are driven by unfavorable living conditions to seek the services of a smuggler. Human trafficking starts in origin countries, namely, Asia, the former Eastern Bloc, and Africa, where recruiters seek migrants through various mediums such as the Internet, employment agencies, the media, and local contacts. Middlemen who recruit from within the origin country commonly share the same cultural background as those migrating. Migrants view the services of a smuggler as an opportunity to move from impoverished conditions in their home countries to more stable, developed environments.

Because such circumstances make it difficult for victims to obtain legitimate travel documents, smugglers supply migrants with fraudulent passports or visas and advise them to avoid detection by border control agents. Transporters, in turn, sustain the migration process through various modes of transportation: land, air, and sea. Although victims often leave their destination country voluntarily, the majority are unaware they are being recruited for a trafficking scheme. They may be kidnapped, coerced, or bribed by false job opportunities, passports, or visas. Transporters involved in trafficking victims from the origin country are compensated only after bringing migrants to the responsible party in the destination country. Immigration documents, whether legitimate or fraudulent, are seized by the traffickers. After this, victims are often subjected to physical and sexual abuse, and many are forced into labor or the sex trade in order to pay off their migratory debts.

The cause of human trafficking stems from adverse circumstances in origin countries, including religious persecution, political dissension, lack of employment opportunities, and poverty. Wars and natural disasters also influence a migrant's decision to seek the services of a smuggler. Another causal factor is globalization, which has catapulted developing countries into the world's market, increasing the standard of living and contributing to the overall growth of the global economy. Unfortunately, globalization is a double-edged sword in that it has shaped the world's market for the transportation of illegal migrants, affording criminal organizations the ability to expand their networks and create transnational routes that facilitate the transporting of migrants, while technological advances have transformed large criminal enterprises into manageable, diversified groups.

U.S. Legal Response

Before the establishment of U.S. laws specifically targeting crimes of human trafficking, smugglers were prosecuted under softer and less germane statutes. For instance, the White Slave Traffic Act, also known as the Mann Act, was enacted to prevent the use of interstate commerce facilitating prostitution or other forms of immorality. The Thirteenth Amendment established antislavery laws while providing the individual's right to freedom from involuntary servitude. The U.S. Congress also criminalized peonage, or the act of enslaving an individual until a debt is paid off, yet the U.S. courts penalized only those captors who imposed physical force or threats on their victims. As efforts to combat human trafficking were limited by the inability to compete with the evolving forms of enslavement, the United States recognized the need to adopt legislation more capable of addressing this growing transnational crime.

Although the practice of trafficking humans is not new, concerted efforts specifically to curtail human trafficking did not emerge until the mid-1990s when public awareness of the issue also emerged. The first step to eradicating this problem was to persuade multiple stakeholders that human trafficking was a problem warranting government intervention. As antitrafficking rhetoric gained momentum, efforts to address human trafficking crossed ideological and political lines. In 1999, motivated by the issue of slavery in Sudan, U.S. Senators Sam Brownback (R–KS) and Paul Wellstone (D–MN) proposed the first antitrafficking legislation. Similar bills concerning human trafficking were proposed in both the House and the Senate. In recognizing the inadequacy of existing laws, the U.S. Congress passed, and President William Jefferson Clinton signed into law, the first comprehensive federal legislation specifically addressing human trafficking, the Trafficking Victims Protection Act of 2000 (TVPA). The primary goal of the TVPA is to provide protection and assistance to trafficking victims, to encourage international response, and to provide assistance to foreign countries in drafting antitrafficking programs and legislation. The TVPA seeks to successfully combat human trafficking by employing a three-pronged strategy—prosecution, protection, and prevention.

Prosecution and Treatment of Human Trafficking as Organized Crime

The TVPA provides more fitting criminal statutes that assist in distinguishing human trafficking from human smuggling. This difference is often misunderstood or ignored. While the two crimes share common elements, they are distinguished in the latter phases of the crime, as the determination is made once the migrants have reached the destination country. The smuggler's involvement ceases after helping the person cross the border illegally, whereas a trafficker's participation does not. Smuggled migrants are free to leave their smugglers once they arrive in the destination country, and they are not victimized.

Although the definitions of *human trafficking* and *human smuggling* differ, they share common elements, as both crimes are highly structured and organized. The criminal enterprises need to transport a large number of migrants over a substantial distance, have a well-organized plan to execute the various stages of the crime, and possess a substantial amount of money for such undertakings. Human traffickers and smugglers have developed a multibillion-dollar industry by exploiting those forced or willing to migrate. For this reason, migrant trafficking is increasingly recognized as a form of organized crime. Trafficking networks may encompass anything from a few loosely associated freelance criminals to large organized crime groups acting in concert.

Human trafficking is a lucrative form of organized crime, and its profits are surpassed only by drug trafficking. In fact, the trafficking of narcotics and the trafficking of humans are often intertwined, using the same actors and routes into a country. Migrant trafficking is one of the fastest-growing criminal enterprises, grossing an estimated $3 billion to $10 billion annually. Traffickers resort to other illicit activities to legitimize these proceeds, such as laundering the money obtained not only from trafficking but also from forced labor, sex industries, and the drug trade. To protect this investment, traffickers use terroristic threats as a means of control over their victims and demonstrate power through the threat of deportation, the seizing of travel documentation, or violence against the migrants or their family remaining in the origin country.

Although the TVPA of 2000 recognized human trafficking as a form of organized crime, it was not until the TVPA's reauthorization that human trafficking was officially acknowledged as a type of racketeering activity, which is a Racketeering Influenced and Corrupt Organization Act (RICO) predicate offense. The purpose of the RICO legislation was to assist in prosecuting organized crime figures. Successfully prosecuting human trafficking under RICO further enhances criminal penalties. Additionally, the TVPA's implementation has enhanced criminal and civil penalties, allowing the seizure of assets and criminal forfeiture. The TVPA diverges from prior legislation by providing clarity and focused definitions. It also has specified new crimes in an effort to regulate labor exploitation and the commercial sex trade, thus addressing prior failed attempts of existing legislation.

Protection of Trafficking Victims Through the TVPA

Victims can petition for a T visa, a newly created visa under the legislation, which allows victims to apply for permanent residency, receive federally funded benefits, and petition to have family members relocated to the United States. To qualify for this visa, the individual (a) must be a victim of a "severe form" of trafficking (sex or labor trafficking), (b) must comply with requests of law enforcement, (c) must be physically present in the United States as a result of trafficking, and (d) would suffer extreme hardship involving unusual and severe harm if deported. A downside to this process is that it is a subjective and lengthy endeavor, and many criticize that the protection of victims is secondary to furtherance of criminal prosecution. For instance, to increase the victim's assistance with investigations, the TVPA has placed conditions on their federally funded benefits that are contingent upon their cooperation. Another criticism of domestic protection efforts is that the TVPA puts forth a narrow definition of victimization. While a person may be a legitimate trafficking victim, the U.S. government may not view a victim's situation as severe enough to merit protection under the TVPA.

Prevention and Control of Human Trafficking

Trafficking is a transnational crime that requires international cooperation, and the United States has taken a lead in promoting intercontinental cooperation. The TVPA provides assistance to foreign governments in facilitating the drafting of antitrafficking laws, strengthening investigation, and prosecuting offenders. International countries of origin, transit, and destination of trafficking victims are encouraged to adopt minimal antitrafficking standards. As outlined in the TVPA, these minimal standards consist of prohibiting severe forms of trafficking, proscribing sanctions proportionate to the act, and making a concerted effort to combat organized trafficking.

Foreign governments are to make a sustained effort to cooperate with the international community, assist in the prosecution of traffickers, and protect victims of trafficking. If governments fail to meet the minimum standards or fail to make strides to do so, the United States will only provide humanitarian and trade-related aid. Financial assistance of any other form from the United States is prohibited. Furthermore, these countries will face opposition from the United States in obtaining support from financial institutions such as the World Bank and the International Monetary Fund. The U.S. Department of State annually reports antitrafficking efforts in the *Trafficking in Persons Report* on countries considered to have a significant trafficking problem.

Strengthening Antitrafficking Efforts

Without knowing how prevalent the crime is, the true scope of the problem is difficult to assess, and programs addressing the needs of victims are difficult to implement. Regardless of the number of unknown victims, there remains a need to better assist known trafficking victims who remain fearful of deportation, retaliation, and incarceration. Although the TVPA has created a strong platform for combating human trafficking, barriers in investigating and prosecuting trafficking cases remain, both domestically and internationally.

Alese C. Wooditch

See also Organized Crime; Slavery and Violence; Violence Against Women

Further Readings

Kangaspunta, K. (2003). Mapping the inhuman trade: Preliminary findings of the database on trafficking in human beings. *Forum on Crime and Society, 3,* 81–103.

Schloenhardt, A. (1999). Organized crime and the business of migrant trafficking: An economic analysis. *Crime, Law & Social Change, 32,* 203–233.

Stoltz, B. A. (2007). Interpreting the U.S. human trafficking debate through the lens of symbolic politics. *Law & Policy, 29,* 311–338.

U.S. Department of State. (2008, June). *Trafficking in persons report.* Retrieved from http://www.state.gov/g/tip/rls/tiprpt/2008

Victims of Trafficking and Violence Protection Act of 2000 (Pub. L. 106-386), 114 Stat., 1464–1548.

HURRICANE KATRINA

Hurricane Katrina made landfall along the U.S. Gulf Coast on August 29, 2005, and is deemed one of the top five deadliest storms in U.S. history and the deadliest since 1928. The ensuing impact of Hurricane Katrina revealed significant social concerns, including matters related to race, crime, and justice. Katrina was a Category 5 storm (though weakening to Category 3 before making landfall) whose physical devastation resulted more from the flooding of substandard infrastructures than from the hurricane itself. Parts of Louisiana, Mississippi, Alabama, and Florida suffered human, structural, and property destruction as a result of Katrina; however, New Orleans, Louisiana, endured the greatest losses. Even though the precise death toll is still not known, 1,836 individuals are reported to have perished as a result of Katrina, including 1,577 who hailed from Louisiana and 238 from Mississippi. An additional 705 people are still reported as "missing." In an analysis of data on deaths in New Orleans, Sharkey found that the number of Blacks who died as a result of Katrina was greater than would be expected given their population and age distribution in and around New Orleans. In addition, the great majority of the 705 people still reported as missing are African American.

This entry examines aspects of Hurricane Katrina that are related to crime and race, specifically in regard to the disparate impact of the hurricane on African Americans.

Criminal Behavior in the Aftermath of Katrina

Hurricane Katrina resulted in distraught victims committing desperate actions to survive the aftermath of the catastrophe. One such response by many residents to the consequences of Katrina was their involvement in activities considered to be criminal in nature and defined as crime by legal policy. News media accounts depicted many acts of looting and violence. Although similar acts took place in other cities, such as in Biloxi, Mississippi, the majority of the news media reports (some of which were later determined to be unfounded) focused on the deviant behaviors of New Orleans residents. The concerns of racial identity, race relations, and racial implications related to the storm were heavily influenced by the images fed to the general public of the impact on the New Orleans area and on the cities that welcomed large numbers of evacuees (such as Houston, Texas, and Baton Rouge, Louisiana).

It is clear that survivors in the areas most affected by Katrina engaged in looting. Looting can be defined as taking the property of others, without prior approval, during and after a natural disaster or human-caused catastrophe or uprising, such as what occurred after the 1992 riots in Los Angeles, California. What is undetermined about the looting that took place following Katrina is the extent to which it occurred and the majority of the types of items stolen. Research has found that in the aftermath of disasters in the United States, looting is an unusual occurrence. Because of the destruction and chaos following Katrina, much of what is known about any looting is from anecdotal accounts and ethnographic interviews. Although many Katrina survivors may have been engaged in acts that would generally be deemed illegal, it is useful to carefully consider the types of acts and motivations for committing them (e.g., survival).

Some survivors in affected areas physically broke into stores, whereas others entered stores that had already been broken into or otherwise opened (e.g., doors and windows unsealed or broken by the force of the floodwaters). As was evident from ethnographic interviews and news media reports concerning these acts, individuals and groups seemed to rest on one of two sides of the debate about the usefulness of the looting that took place in the aftermath of Katrina and may have further qualified their assessment of the acts by deeming what was allowed to be taken (food and water) and what was not allowed to be taken (guns and luxury items such as televisions and stereos). The act of police officers (particularly in New Orleans) also breaking into stores and otherwise aiding residents in acquiring supplies was seen as further justifying the looting behaviors of Katrina survivors.

Within days of the storm, shocking tales were spread about murderous rampages by young male (African American) "thugs," brutal rapes of small children, and gangs of men armed with guns prowling New Orleans and the temporary shelters. Many of these accounts were reported as fact by city officials, including New Orleans Mayor Ray Nagin and then Police Chief Eddie Compass. These tales were repeated and disseminated worldwide through television and print media. Again, not until weeks later were the majority of reports of rapes and murders found to be unsubstantiated. Speculation is made that such stories of savage brutality were so easily accepted because of the large population of poor African Americans in New Orleans, the high rates of street crime in the city (with New Orleans having previously been known as the "murder capital of the nation"), and the overrepresentation of African Americans in correctional facilities throughout Louisiana.

Beyond the criminal and violent behavior attributed to Katrina evacuees, some individuals established fraudulent schemes, particularly through the use of the Internet, to deceive unsuspecting donors into contributing to what the donors believed was a legitimate source to support victims of the storm. Donors and potential donors were lured with fraudulent e-mails requesting assistance and illegitimate websites claiming to provide financial assistance to Katrina survivors. These Katrina-related scams reportedly occurred at higher rates than similar deceptive acts associated with previous disasters.

Public Safety Responses

Local police officers in Katrina-affected areas were faced not only with being (or feeling) obligated to remain in the sites to be affected by the storm and challenged with damaged equipment and stations but with facing the storm as victims as well. For example, members of the New Orleans Police Department (NOPD), more than half of whom were African American at the time of Hurricane Katrina, were required to live within city limits, and, as a result, approximately 80% of the police force's homes were ravaged by the flooding. In the immediate aftermath of Katrina, Louisiana officials, specifically Governor Kathleen Blanco and New Orleans Mayor Ray Nagin, stressed the importance of search and rescue efforts for New Orleans victims; however, within 3 days after the storm hit, these officials ordered public safety officers to focus their efforts on pursuing law violators.

Serving dual roles as survivors and rescuers placed a unique burden on NOPD officers; some chose to abandon their jobs. Although a number of NOPD officers (approximately 250) deserted their jobs soon after the storm, the majority of the 1,668 NOPD officers remained on the job to assist with evacuation efforts and crime control. The officers who abandoned their posts were caring for their own families, handed over their badges to indicate their resignation from the force, or simply left the job without notice. At least two officers committed suicide. Because the NOPD had been plagued with an unfavorable reputation due to the action of several corrupt officers during the 1990s, some public opinion concluded that the actions of the NOPD officers who deserted their jobs and who engaged in alleged acts of looting and unnecessary use of force were to be expected of these NOPD officers.

It took more than a year after the storm for the NOPD to replace police-related equipment that had been ruined by the storm. In addition, evidence from more than 3,000 criminal cases that was housed in the New Orleans police headquarters and the courthouse was destroyed.

Shelter and Trailer Park Management

As looting activities of Katrina survivors were continuously replayed in news outlets, African

Americans were stereotyped as "criminal" and treated accordingly when they arrived at some of the shelters created to assist the survivors. Housing a large number of people in open areas of a facility not designed for sheltering disaster survivors unavoidably warranted some level of security. However, the level of safety measures and the inconsistency in who faced security screening led many Katrina evacuees to believe these operations were likely based on racially motivated biases. These biases most likely resulted from the numerous harmful rumors spread after Katrina and the preexisting stereotype of African Americans as a group believed to possess violent and otherwise criminal tendencies.

Three of the largest facilities used as shelters were the Superdome, the Astrodome, and the Baton Rouge River Center. The Superdome—referred to by Mayor Nagin as the "refuge of last resort"—is a sports facility in New Orleans that housed up to approximately 30,000 people from a day before the storm until September 3, 2005. The Ernest N. Morial Convention Center in New Orleans was used as an overflow shelter for those who could not get into the Superdome; it housed more than 20,000 people. The Astrodome, a sports stadium in Houston, Texas (350 miles west of New Orleans), housed as many as 27,000 between September 1 and 20, 2005. The Baton Rouge River Center, a multiuse event center, housed more than 5,000 evacuees from the beginning of the storm until mid-October 2005.

The shelter residents were largely African American. The rampant rumors of scores of dead bodies (up to 200) in the Superdome were later found to be greatly overstated. In the end, six deceased individuals were retrieved from the Superdome, none of whom died due to violent acts. Four died of natural causes, one of a drug overdose, and one of an apparent suicide. With regard to the reports of rape, NOPD officers arrested two people for attempted sexual assault. (However, reports of sexual assault or rape are typically underreported, so substantiating rumors of these crimes would not be as accurate as murder, where a body is likely to exist.) Even though the extent of violence that took place in the Superdome was much less than believed, the rumors continued for some time and affected the administration of other shelter facilities.

Entrance into the Baton Rouge and Houston shelter facilities was gained through one or a small number of secured doors. The entrances were controlled by National Guard soldiers, most of whom were men. Each entrant was to pass through a free-standing metal detector and had to have her or his bags physically searched by a National Guard soldier. If an individual continued to trigger the metal detector, she or he was scanned with a hand-held metal detector to deem the entrant was not carrying anything that would be harmful to those inside the shelter (i.e., contraband). It was standard procedure that each National Guard member, dressed in full military uniform, was armed with a rifle, which connected to a strap and was draped over his or her chest or back, and a handgun, which was stored in a hip holster. Trailer parks that had been set up by the Federal Emergency Management Agency (FEMA) had similar security measures in place. The reaction by many African American evacuees was that the National Guard was present to maintain control over African American evacuees, many of whom were from New Orleans. These security procedures elicited multiple references by evacuees that the shelters and trailer parks resembled an incarcerative setting (such as a jail or prison), as opposed to a place to assist lawful citizens who had been displaced from their homes due to a natural disaster.

Correctional Facilities and Disaster Management

An institution that rarely is considered in regard to disaster preparation is the correctional facility. Jails in the areas affected by Hurricane Katrina were not spared from the effects of the storm. In particular, two facilities that faced staggering tales of distress were the Orleans Parish Prison and the Plaquemines Parish Prison, both of which are, technically, county jails (i.e., a facility used to incarcerate offenders for short periods of time and to detain persons suspected of committing crimes until their cases are resolved).

The Orleans Parish Prison (OPP) consisted of 12 buildings located in the downtown New Orleans area known as Mid-City. Prior to Hurricane Katrina, OPP was the eighth largest jail in the United States. New Orleans, prior to Katrina, had the highest incarceration rate among large cities in the United States, consisting of more than 6,000 inmates. This included the housing of almost 2,000 inmates confined for state prison sentences and over 200 federal detainees, all of whom were housed due to the lack of space in Louisiana state prisons and federal facilities. OPP had been under federal court oversight since 1969 as a result of the case of *Hamilton v. Morial*, where more than 3,000 inmates filed suit against OPP for inadequate conditions of confinement.

Soon after Katrina made landfall, the Orleans Parish sheriff, Marlin Gusman, reported that all inmates had been safely evacuated from the OPP facilities by boat and transported to other jail and prison facilities throughout the state. Weeks after the storm, Sheriff Gusman maintained this statement even though he issued arrest warrants for several fugitive inmates and even though numerous reports were made by inmates and staff that many inmates were abandoned in locked and flooding cells. All evidence made available to date indicates that there was no adequate evacuation plan for OPP facilities in the event of a natural disaster. The Louisiana Department of Corrections (the prison system) offered evacuation assistance to OPP in the days leading up to the storm. However, New Orleans officials refused the assistance, believing they could withstand the impending storm. Further, nearly 2,000 inmates from nearby county jails (i.e., "parish prisons") had been transferred to OPP, assuming the OPP structures were strong enough to withstand any ensuing effects of Katrina.

Thousands of children, men, and women were abandoned in OPP facilities, most of whom were poor, African American pretrial detainees held for minor offenses. Only small amounts of food and drinkable water had been available for the stranded inmates to consume. The OPP facilities lost electrical power soon after Katrina made landfall, leaving the inmates in cells with little ventilation, no sanitation, and nights in complete darkness. The rising water in the cells was contaminated with sewage from nonworking toilets. Inmates remained in the Katrina-flooded facilities for 4 days. Although many OPP workers maintained their posts, inmates later reported that officers from several of the facilities abandoned the inmates during and after the storm. Many inmates took it upon themselves to break free of the flooded cells. Although Sheriff Gusman states that no deaths occurred at OPP during or after the storm, several reports have since been made—by both inmates and officers—depicting escaping inmates being killed by officers who had been ordered to shoot and kill escapees.

After going days without food, water, and other needs, the trapped inmates were rescued over a 3-day period by officers of the Louisiana State Penitentiary in Angola (known as Angola). The rescued inmates remained on a highway overpass anywhere from several hours to several days. While the rescue efforts were welcomed by the trapped inmates, their eventual transfer to state prisons did not necessarily eliminate their concerns. It was not until September 9, 2005, that prison officials received a list of all pre-Katrina OPP inmates with the release dates for those serving jail sentences. However, many inmates whose release dates had passed had not been released. As a result, a group of lawyers volunteered its services to the inmates and filed habeas corpus motions requesting that the courts release the represented inmates or show cause for their continued confinement. Even still, for reasons that have yet to be clarified, not all OPP inmates eligible for release were freed from Department of Corrections confinement.

During the immediate recovery efforts of Katrina, New Orleans public safety officials created a makeshift jail in a bus station to have a place to detain suspected offenders, including those involved in looting, particularly in towns neighboring New Orleans. With approximately 90% of New Orleans evacuated, this effort is reported as having been the first official city function to resume after Katrina made landfall, erected within a week with the assistance of prison inmates and administered by the warden of the Angola prison, Burl Cain. For several days, inmates reportedly were not afforded their civil rights, as they were not allowed to make phone calls or contact attorneys. For those who were herded through the makeshift jail's justice process, mainly for charges of looting, possession of stolen property, and violation of curfew, they were often only offered a choice of continued incarceration in one of the state prison facilities or to plead guilty and perform between 40 and 80 hours of "community service."

Sheriff Gusman began to refill OPP facilities soon after the flooding waned, even though officials had not yet determined if the city and its infrastructure were safe. By spring 2008, five facilities and a number of temporary jails, holding approximately 800 inmates, had been reopened in New Orleans.

Crime Rates in the Aftermath of Katrina

Many cities experienced a significant increase in their residential populations due to mass evacuations before, during, and after Hurricane Katrina. In particular, Baton Rouge, Houston, Dallas, and Atlanta received a large number of survivors. Rumors spread through formal and informal channels increased the fears of many original residents in several evacuation cities. The rumors included tales of murder, looting, and other crimes. Residents in the host cities began to fear for their lives and their property, resulting in a noteworthy increase in gun sales and increased police patrols.

Katrina survivors who were involved in illicit drug markets prior to the storm had little difficulty locating new sources to secure drugs in their relocation sites. In Houston, while evacuee drug users reported that the shelter conditions in the Astrodome were safe and provided for their basic needs, they could easily access illicit drugs in the immediate areas surrounding the temporary shelter. However, as reported by Baton Rouge law enforcement officials, there was initially a concern that drug-related violence might increase as Katrina-evacuated drug sellers attempted to reestablish their enterprises among territories already controlled by existing drug sellers. Although Katrina evacuees committed criminal acts in their relocation cities, it remains unclear as to the extent to which the crime rates have risen, if at all, in these cities and can be attributed to the evacuees.

Hillary Potter

Further Readings

Bates, K. A., & Swan, R. S. (Eds.). (2007). *Through the eye of Katrina: Social justice in the United States*. Durham, NC: Carolina Academic Press.

Brunsma, D. L., Overfelt, D., & Picou, S. J. (Eds.). (2007). *The sociology of Katrina: Perspectives on a modern catastrophe*. Lanham, MD: Rowman & Littlefield.

Dunlap, E., Johnson, B. D., & Morse, E. (2007). Illicit drug markets among New Orleans evacuees before and soon after Hurricane Katrina. *Journal of Drug Issues, 37*, 981–1006.

National Prison Project and American Civil Liberties Union. (2007). Abandoned and abused: Prisoners in the wake of Hurricane Katrina. *Race and Class, 49*, 81–92.

Potter, H. (Ed.). (2007). *Racing the storm: Racial implications and lessons learned from Hurricane Katrina*. Lanham, MD: Lexington Books.

Roman, C. G., Irazola, S., & Osborne, J. W. L. (2007, August 28). *After Katrina: Washed away? Justice in New Orleans* (Research report). Washington, DC: Urban Institute, Justice Policy Center. Retrieved September 18, 2008, from http://www.urban.org/UploadedPDF/411530_washed_away.pdf

Sharkey, P. (2007). Survival and death in New Orleans: An empirical look at the human impact of Katrina. *Journal of Black Studies, 37*, 482–501.

Sommers, S. R., Apfelbaum, E. P., Dukes, K. N., Toosi, N., & Wang, E. J. (2006). Race and media coverage of Hurricane Katrina: Analysis, implications, and future research questions. *Annals of Social Issues and Public Policy, 6*, 39–55.

Tierney, K., Bevc, C., & Kuligowski, E. (2006). Metaphors matter: Disaster myths, media frames, and their consequences in Hurricane Katrina. *Annals of the American Academy, 604*, 57–81.

HYPERMASCULINITY

The term *hypermasculinity* is believed to have been established by Ashis Nandy in her writings on colonialism and gender in the 1980s. The term is widely used in the social sciences and has evolved in meaning, but no standard definition exists. At its core, hypermasculinity is an adoption of extreme machismo in males. According to Matt Zaitchik and Donald Mosher, it is an exaggerated form of masculinity, virility, and physicality, as well as a tendency toward disrespecting women. Furthermore, any embrace and exhibition of emotions is feminized as inherently weak. Mosher suggested that three distinct characteristics identify the hypermasculine personality: (1) the view of violence as manly, (2) the perception of danger as exciting and sensational, and (3) callous behavior toward women and a regard toward emotional displays as feminine. This entry explores the various contexts in which hypermasculinity has been found.

Examples of Hypermasculinity in Film

Clint Eastwood's character in the films *The Outlaw Josey Wales* (1976) and *A Fist Full of Dollars* (1964) was a strong, silent man who exhibited no emotion as he dispatches his enemies. In addition, the films depicted an extremely feminine or hyperfeminine female lead character who supported the Eastwood characters. This is referred to as encouraging hypermasculinity through women who prefer strong, silent, emotionless men.

In the early 1970s, martial arts films starring the Asian American actor Bruce Lee became popular within the United States. Lee's characters often demonstrated a sense of emotion only during fight scenes. The animalistic sounds and his going berserk on anyone who exacted a blow that drew blood are examples of hypermasculinity.

D. W. Griffith's 1915 film *The Birth of a Nation* was one the first of its genre to depict both Black and White male characters in a hypermasculine context. The theme was based on Thomas Dixon's novel *The Clansman* in which the post–Civil War remnants of Southern leaders invoked the spirits of their ancestry, the "clansmen" of old Scotland. The film depicted Black males as sexually aggressive and criminal. Collectively these images were presented as the Black male rapist and Black politicians who committed larceny against the government. In contrast, the "Invisible Empire" of the Ku Klux Klan was created to combat the breakdown of law and order to which Black male criminality contributed, to restore the chastity of Southern womanhood, and to save the South from tyranny. The Klansman, dressed in White with his face covered so as to not display any emotions, is depicted as the hero.

Historically, overexaggerated male behavior was often considered countercultural and primarily applied to the prowess of African American males. Examples of such characteristics in Hollywood films are evident in the 1970s blaxploitation era of the Shaft and Superfly film series.

Hypermasculinity and Newer Forms of Communication

Today socialization occurs on a broader scale via the media with assistance of rapid technological advancements of cell phones, PDA (personal digital assistant) devices, Internet access, and cable satellite television. Such sources provide unfiltered exposure to images of hypermasculinity. Although some researchers hold that socialization is the primary contributor toward the development of hypermasculinity, these media images may also contribute to the emergence of hypermasculine traits. Thus, the fact that African Americans view television more than any other racial groups may be significant in understanding the origins of hypermasculinity among Blacks.

Hypermasculinity and Hip Hop

The commercial mainstream hip hop entertainment arena presents one of the most exaggerated forms of masculine behavior. It has become the current medium that portrays criminal prowess as a cultural embrace of criminality by African American youth and thus forms a "rite of passage" toward Black male authenticity. Black women are seen as licentious, sexual "props" on a video set, while Black men are depicted as virile, self-absorbed, superphysical, and anti-intellectual. Within this context, men seeking intellectual development are rejected and feminized.

Hypermasculinity and Marketing Strategies

Commercial marketers are among the biggest promoters of hypermasculinity. For example, the late rappers Tupac Shakur and Biggie Smalls served primary roles in fostering the "East Coast versus West Coast" hip hop rivalry during the 1990s. This rivalry was based on the perpetuation of hypermasculine thug images. Furthermore, rapper 50 Cent's commercialized marketing campaign included being promoted as a "gangsta." This strategy included marketing the fact that he had been shot nine times and survived.

Hypermasculinity and Loyalty

Although the concept of loyalty to colleagues exists across class, gender, and racial lines, it is more pervasive and promoted by males within the hip hop community. Violating loyalty can often result in retaliation or, in worst-case scenarios, being killed. For example, female rapper Lil' Kim was awarded a reality television program titled *Countdown to Lockdown*, which aired on the Black Entertainment Television network. The show followed her daily life as she prepared to enter a federal correctional facility. She was convicted of lying to a federal grand jury to protect associates involved in a 2001 shootout outside a Manhattan radio station, fined $50,000, and required to serve a year and a day in prison. Upon her release from prison, she held a press conference outside of the correctional facility. Lil' Kim's actions demonstrate hypermasculine characteristics—more specifically, her willingness to show no emotion, endure incarceration, and maintain the social construct reinforcing credibility (e.g., "street cred") through the current "stop the snitching" phenomenon.

Conclusion

Existing research shows that social conditions in depressed communities combined with exposure to television violence increase the likelihood that conflicts will result in violence. This is especially the case when television and video games are the stimuli. In the case of Black males, these conditions and stimuli, as highlighted throughout this entry, result in an overactive hypersexual and hypermasculine super ego.

Ronald O. Craig

See also Stop Snitching Campaign

Further Readings

Maybach, K. L., & Gold, S. R. (1994). Hyperfemininity and attraction to macho and non-macho men. *Journal of Sex Research, 31*(2), 91–98.

Rome, D. (2004). *Black demons: The media's depiction of the African American male criminal stereotypes.* Westport, CT: Praeger.

Scharrer E. (2005). Hypermasculinity, aggression, and television: An experiment. *Media Psychology, 7,* 353–376.

Spencer, M., Fegley. S., Harpalani, V., & Seaton, G. (2004). Understanding hypermasculinity in context: A theory-driven analysis of urban adolescent males: Coping responses. *Research in Human Development, 1,* 229–257.

Wilson, A. (1990). *Black on Black violence: The psychodynamics of Black self-annihilation in service of White domination.* New York: African World Infosystems.

Zaitchik, M., & Mosher, D. L. (1993). Criminal justice implications of the macho personality constellation. *Criminal Justice and Behavior, 20,* 227–239.

ILLINOIS V. WARDLOW

One of the freedoms guaranteed under the Fourth Amendment is the right "to be secure . . . against unreasonable searches and seizures," and Americans expect the government to enforce this right. *Illinois v. Wardlow* raised the question of whether police violated this Fourth Amendment right in stopping a man as he ran from police in an area known for high rates of narcotics trafficking and other crime. The U.S. Supreme Court held that the nature of the surroundings and the suspect's "unprovoked flight" created reasonable suspicion that justified the police in making an investigatory stop (*Illinois v. Wardlow*, 2000).

Facts of the Case

William "Sam" Wardlow was standing next to a building on West Van Buren in a part of Chicago known for high crime and narcotics trafficking. When entering the area, the police "anticipated encountering a large number of people . . . including drug customers and individuals serving as lookouts." As four police cars entered the area and passed Wardlow, an officer in the last car made eye contact with Wardlow and observed him holding a white, opaque bag. When the last car had passed, Wardlow turned and ran from this area. Wardlow's flight in the presence of police cars made the officers suspicious. They intercepted him and conducted an investigative stop. For their safety, one of the officers immediately performed a pat-down for weapons, based on his past experience that weapons were likely to be present during drug trafficking. (A pat-down involves the touching of a person's outer clothing, including any packages that the person is holding, to determine if that person is armed. The U.S. Supreme Court had held in the 1968 case of *Terry v. Ohio* that such an action is permitted to ensure an officer's safety during an investigative stop.) An officer took the bag that Wardlow was holding and, without opening the container, felt what appeared to be a handgun. A handgun was subsequently removed from the bag, and Wardlow was arrested.

At the trial, Wardlow's counsel moved to suppress the handgun as the fruit of an illegal search that violated the defendant's Fourth Amendment rights. The Illinois court denied the suppression motion, and Wardlow was convicted of the unlawful use of a weapon. The Illinois Court of Appeals reversed the trial court, and its decision was upheld by the Illinois Supreme Court. The case was then appealed to the U.S. Supreme Court, which granted a writ of certiorari.

The Issues

The U.S. Supreme Court's ruling in *Terry v. Ohio* (1968) established that police may conduct a brief investigatory stop of an individual when there is "reasonable, articulable suspicion of criminal activity." This must be more than a "hunch." In *United States v. Sokolow* (1999), the Court also noted that the Fourth Amendment requires a minimal level of objective justification—reasonable suspicion—for making an investigative stop. While a person's mere presence in a high-crime area alone is not sufficient for reasonable suspicion, the Court in *Brown v. Texas* (1979) held that police officers could look to the totality of the circumstances, including a high-crime area (*Adams v. Williams*, 1972) and nervous, evasive behavior (*United States v. Brignoni-Ponce*, 1975), in order to develop reasonable suspicion of criminal activity. In the case of *Michigan v. Chesternut* (1988), the court noted that police officers' "investigatory pursuit" of a fleeing suspect did not constitute a seizure. Determining reasonable suspicion is based on "commonsense judgments and inferences about human behavior" (*United States v. Cortez*, 1981).

The Decision

The Illinois Supreme Court had held that sudden flight in a high-crime area does not create a reasonable suspicion justifying an investigative stop of the sort authorized by *Terry*. It also had rejected the argument that flight combined with the fact that it occurred in a high-crime area supported a finding of reasonable suspicion because the "high-crime area" factor was not sufficient standing alone to justify a *Terry* stop. Finding no independently suspicious circumstances to support an investigatory detention, the Illinois court held that the stop and subsequent arrest violated the Fourth Amendment (*Illinois v. Wardlow*, 2000).

In rejecting the Illinois Supreme Court ruling, the U.S. Supreme Court found that the police had reasonable suspicion to stop Wardlow. It noted that the officers, based upon their experience, were "justified in suspecting that Wardlow was involved in criminal activity, and . . . investigating further" (*Illinois v. Wardlow*, 2000). The Court determined that Wardlow was doing more than freely walking through an area. His flight created a suspicion of criminal activity in the eyes of the experienced law enforcement officers. A pat-down for weapons was appropriate under the circumstances, and the discovery of the weapon was legal. The stop by the officers did not constitute a violation of Wardlow's Fourth Amendment rights.

Keith Gregory Logan

See also Drug Dealers; *Terry v. Ohio*; *United States v. Wheeler*

Further Readings

Adams v. Williams, 407 U.S. 143 (1972).

Brown v. Texas, 443 U.S. 47 (1979).

Darmer, M. K. B., Baird, R. M., & Rosenbaum, S. E. (Eds.). (2004). *Civil liberties vs. national security in a post-9/11 world.* Amherst, NY: Prometheus Books.

Illinois v. Wardlow, 528 U.S. 119 (2000).

Michigan v. Chesternut, 486 U.S. 567 (1988).

Terry v. Ohio, 392 U.S. 1 (1968).

United States v. Brignoni-Ponce, 422 U.S. 873 (1975).

United States v. Cortez, 449 U.S. 411 (1981).

United States v. Sokolow, 490 U.S. 1 (1999).

IMMIGRANTS AND CRIME

In the American imagination, immigrants and criminal activity are linked. The social reality of immigrant involvement with crime is actually mixed. First, one needs to consider whether crime unrelated to immigrant status (ranging from shoplifting to homicide) is the type of act being considered. Second, one has to decide whether entrance into the United States without required documents should be considered different from other civil and criminal offenses. Finally, there are visitors who legally enter the United States and then "overstay" their visas, thus becoming undocumented and illegal residents. When considering the criminality of immigrants, a differentiation needs to be made between traditional crime and crimes involving national sovereignty. The government classifies the first entry by an undocumented migrant as a civil violation. A second attempt is a felony offense. This entry provides an overview of the critical issues related to the immigration and crime debate.

Undocumented Entry and Deportation

Current estimates are that there are 10 million to 12 million undocumented immigrants in the U.S. population. Politicians, government administrators, and media accounts often refer to undocumented entrants as criminals; for both undocumented immigrants and legal immigrants with temporary or permanent resident status, the desire to avoid deportation is a strong motivation to avoid committing crime. Even legal immigrants lack the full rights of citizens and are subject to deportation if they commit a type of crime designated as an aggravated felony. Since the beginning of the War on Drugs, federal legislation successively and retroactively designated a series of offenses as grounds for "institutional removal." Institutional removal involves deportation upon completion of a sentence. Even a misdemeanor charge of shoplifting has been made grounds for removal. Commission of an aggravated felony carries a collateral civil penalty of deportation for noncitizens. The right to due process is suspended for noncitizens. The two terrorist attacks on the World Trade Center are connected to designation of new aggravated felonies by federal law, increased incarceration, and then deportation of both legal and undocumented noncitizen residents.

Federal Imprisonment

Statistics released by the U.S. Government Accountability Office (2005b) show that "criminal alien" imprisonment has moved steadily upward. In 1991, 14,475 immigrants were ordered removed as compared to 42,000 in 2001. In 2004, 49,000 were deported.

According to John Scalia and Marika Litras, from 1985 to 2000, two thirds of the growth in the federal prison population were noncitizens. Government Accountability Office figures indicate that by 2003, immigration offenses were the cause of 68% of federal criminal alien convictions (2005a). In 2003, 24% of criminal aliens were charged with drug-related crimes, and less than 5% were convicted of violent crimes (2005a). In other words, immigration offenses are the predominant cause of federal incarceration.

Traditional Crime

Rubén Rumbaut and colleagues (2006a, 2006b) used 2000 U.S. Census data to establish that immigrants have a lower crime rate than people born in the United States. In the United States, the prototypical arrestee has a low level of education, is aged 18 to 39, and is of minority background. The youthfulness of the immigrant population predicts a higher crime rate, particularly among Mexicans. In fact, 3.51% of the U.S.-born population was incarcerated as compared to less than 1% (0.86%) of the foreign-born population (Rumbaut et al., 2006a, 2006b). Non-Hispanic Whites have higher crime rates than first-generation Latin American, Asian, or other immigrants. This statistic includes Puerto Ricans, who are U.S. citizens. When Puerto Ricans are excluded from the analysis, only 0.68% of all immigrants have been convicted and incarcerated for a crime. It is important to consider that Salvadorcans/Guatemalans (0.52%) and Mexicans (0.70%) have the lowest level of education and the lowest rate of incarceration—atypical when compared to education level of other inmates. First-generation Mexicans and other Latin American immigrants are often stigmatized as a criminal element by the media.

Underreporting of Immigrant Victimization

One factor that affects immigrant group crime rates is unwillingness to deal with the police. The desire to avoid deportation gives immigrants a motive not only to avoid committing crime but also to avoid reporting criminal victimization. Immigrants can fear personal, family, or acquaintance deportation or retaliation by the criminal or their friends or family. Immigrants may also believe that individual problems should not be known outside of the family. Less well understood is the fact that bad experiences with corrupt police in immigrants' countries of origin can carry over to fear of U.S. police officers. The result is that immigrant crime victimization is underreported; but because immigrants are motivated to avoid criminal acts, this is likely to have only a tiny influence on the crime rate.

1.5- and Second-Generation Gang-Related Delinquency and Crime

Criminality is more likely to be expressed by the 1.5-generation (foreign-born children and adolescents) and the second generation born to immigrant parents. Second-generation children are sandwiched between the parent's traditional culture and exposure to Americanization. For youth in impoverished areas with underfunded public schools, the gang can represent a status-gaining alternative to academic achievement, a source of protection, and a source of exposure to criminal activities and recruitment. This implies that, as a host society, the United States does a poor job of culturally and economically assimilating poverty background immigrant youth. Carl Horowitz refers to the increased crime rate in the second generation as the "echo effect." High birth rates in low-income immigrant groups are connected to the echo effect.

The post-1965 new immigrant population is very diverse in national origins, and second-generation crime varies according to the social characteristics of these groups.

Rumbaut et al. (2006a, 2006b) found that only the second and later generations of the following ethnicities had a higher percentage of criminal conviction than the native-born percentage (3.51%): Laotians and Cambodians (7.26%), Mexicans (5.9%), Vietnamese (5.6%), Puerto Ricans (5.37%), Cubans (4.20%), and Dominicans (3.71%).

In the United States, lack of a high school degree is a strong predictor of criminality. Dropouts (6.91%) have higher incarceration rates than high school graduates (2.0%). Nevertheless, native-born high school dropouts are at much greater risk of imprisonment (9.76%) when compared to immigrants who did not receive a high school education (1.31%).

Regardless of ethnicity, being native-born is a stronger predictor of criminality than is immigrant status. Rumbaut and colleagues consider that Americanization involves being exposed to divergent norms and consumer culture. Second-generation youth experiencing educational difficulty and the consequent lack of social mobility may be motivated to commit acts of delinquency and then crime.

Theories of Intergenerational Crime Among Immigrant Groups

Social Disorganization Theory

Robert Sampson has used social disorganization theory to predict crime in high-poverty neighborhoods. This theory predicts higher crime rates in high-poverty neighborhoods with a younger population. Nevertheless, research indicates that immigrant neighborhoods have similar or lower rates of crime when compared to similar nonimmigrant areas. Ramiro Martinez and several colleagues believe that immigrants revitalize deteriorating neighborhoods and exercise informal social control that would produce or prevent crime. The first generation's ability to adapt to poverty and desire to succeed in this society are strong.

Segmented Assimilation Theory

Ramiro Martinez and his colleagues found that, in San Diego and Miami, Latina/o crime did increase in the second generation when the process called segmented assimilation was occurring. Segmented assimilation refers to an inability to become socially mobile due to a lack of economic opportunity while undergoing a process of cultural assimilation to American society. It refers to a process of assimilation in which national origin immigrant groups vary in degree of human capital. Assimilation is segmented because immigrant groups entering with more education, assets, and social ties will be better able to achieve social mobility than will immigrant groups struggling at the bottom.

For example, research shows that impoverished neighborhoods with more young Mexican male immigrants who lack education have a higher incidence of drug-related homicides. Yet Martinez and his colleagues indicated that economic conditions may be the strongest predictor of drug-related homicide. One reason is that drug-related homicide rates were lower in San Diego neighborhoods in which Mexican families were poor yet had jobs. This acted as a buffer against crime.

Another aspect of segmented assimilation theory is the prediction that some immigrant parents arriving with a low level of education will experience conflict with their children as the children adopt American values. The traditional cultures of these ethnic groups extend discipline to prevent the delinquency of Asian immigrant youth. The differences between traditional ethnic culture and American norms create friction and misunderstanding between Asian parents and their children.

For example, Laotian parents use harsh discipline, and their children can see that American discipline is more lenient. Misunderstandings between parents and children contribute to problems in dealing with youth–police interactions.

Similarly, Mexican immigrants practicing traditional views experience similar conflict with their children. However, marginalization and discrimination against this population, approximately half of whom are undocumented, lead to a situation in which parents are not likely to cooperate with police because they do not see them as helpful allies. Parents fear that Mexican youth in trouble will be stereotyped as delinquents and future criminals (Waters).

The process of segmented assimilation is connected to poor schooling outcomes and consequent lack of opportunity. Rumbaut et al. indicate that a series of social factors are associated with immigrant crime across the generations. Risk factors include having a single parent, having a low grade point average, experiencing a series of school suspensions, experiencing physical threat or being invited to use drugs on more than two occasions in high school, and not obtaining a high school degree. Initial acts of delinquency include school fights that cause injury, attempt or threat to fight, being defiant toward school authority or causing class disruption, perpetrating property damage, and possessing weapons. Basically, school failure is connected to attempts to achieve through crime which leads to the second failure: imprisonment.

Organized Crime

One consequence of restricted economic opportunity among certain immigrant nationalities has been the evolution of certain gangs into transnational crime organizations. According to Jim Fickenauer and Jay Albanese, globalization has fostered organized immigrant crime groups connected to drug and human trafficking. These groups include the Russian Mafia, the Mexican Mafia, the Central American Mara Salvatrucha (MS-13), the Chinese Fuk Ching, and international drug cartels such as the Mexican Arellano-Felix and Carrillo Fuentes organizations.

Organized criminal activities include forced prostitution, smuggling, and money laundering.

Crossing a border is one way of escaping prosecution that has been used by serious offenders and organized criminals connected to drug and human trafficking. Deportation of organized criminals to their homeland is often ineffective because trafficking organizations can help them quickly return.

Conclusion

In the media, news about conflict creates interest. News about exceptional crimes, such as those of serial murderer Rafael Resendez, stories about migrants attempting border crossings, fears about terrorist entry, and stories about the cost of incarcerating undocumented migrants scare the public. The fact that the United States has the highest imprisonment rate in the world, primarily the native-born, is not emphasized. News stories sympathetic to immigrants are few. As a result, it is not surprising that American citizens fear an immigrant crime wave and want immigration reform.

Conservatives suggest that limiting immigration based on family reunification and encouraging skilled professional entrants can prevent the 1.5- and second-generation delinquency and crime problem. Alienated youth gangs would be prevented from forming. Because of undocumented immigrants, both border security and visa-overstay tracking would need to be improved. The costs of policing and incarcerating delinquent populations that develop due to blocked social mobility would be an issue in considering immigration reform.

A liberal interpretation would advocate improving public education and economic opportunities in the inner-city neighborhoods so that the experience of 1.5- and second-generation youth would lead to their becoming better integrated into U.S. society. Although the employers who hire undocumented immigrants and promote mass immigration are seldom highlighted, these employment practices are a major cause of the post-1965 immigrant wave.

Judith Ann Warner

See also Delinquency Prevention; Family and Delinquency; Immigration Legislation; Immigration Policy

Further Readings

Horowitz, C. (2001). *An examination of U.S. immigration policy and serious crime*. Washington, DC: Center for Immigration Studies.

Martinez, R., Jr., Lee, M. T., & Nielsen, A. L. (2004). Segmented assimilation, local context and determinants of drug violence in Miami and San Diego: Does ethnicity and immigration matter? *International Migration Review, 38*(1), 131–157.

Menjivar, C., & Bejarano, C. (2004). Latino immigrants' perceptions of crime and police authorities. *Ethnic and Racial Studies, 27*(1), 120–148.

Rumbaut, R., Gonzales, R. G., Komaie, G., & Morgan, C. V. (2006a). *Debunking the myth of immigrant criminality: Imprisonment among first- and second-generation young men*. Retrieved from http://www.migrationinformation.org/USfocus/display.cfm?ID=403

Rumbaut, R., Gonzales, R. G., Komaie, G., Morgan, C. V., & Tafoya-Estrada, R. (2006b). Immigration and incarceration: Patterns and predictors of imprisonment among first- and second-generation young adults. In R. Martinez, Jr., & A. Valenzuela (Eds.), *Immigration and crime: Race, ethnicity and violence* (pp. 64–89). New York: New York University Press.

Sampson, R. J., Raudenbush, S. W., & Earls, F. (1997). Neighborhoods and violent crime: A multilevel study of collective efficacy. *Science, 277*, 918–924.

Scalia, J., & Litras, M. F. X. (2002). *Immigration offenders in the federal criminal justice system, 2000* (Report No. NCJ 191745). Retrieved from Bureau of Justice Statistics: http://www.ojp.usdoj.gov/bjs/abstract/iofcjs00.htm

U.S. Government Accountability Office. (2005a). *Information on certain illegal aliens arrested in the United States* (Report No. GAO-05-646R). Retrieved from http://www.gao.gov/new.items/d05646r.pdf

U.S. Government Accounting Office. (2005b). *Information on criminal aliens incarcerated in federal and state prisons and local jails* (Report No. GAO-05-337R). Retrieved from http://www.gao.gov/new.items/d05337r.pdf

Waters, T. (1999). *Crime and immigrant youth*. Thousand Oaks, CA: Sage.

IMMIGRATION LEGISLATION

Categories of racial difference have always been important in the regulation of immigration. Racial distinctions can no longer be found in the legislation itself, but they live on in its administration. This entry considers the evolution of immigration policy, including refugee policy, and its political and practical impact. The openness of the United States to both legal and illegal immigration has produced a backlash that has significant implications for the quality of life of citizens and noncitizens who are perceived to be immigrants.

Race as a Criterion of Membership

During the first century of its existence, the United States paid little heed to who entered the country. The issue was who would be entitled to citizenship through "naturalization." A 1790 law set a uniform residence requirement and also specified that only "free White persons" could be naturalized, a restriction that stayed in place, remarkably, until 1952 when the McCarren-Walter Act finally swept it away. Decades of jurisprudence interpreting the "Whiteness" requirement were suddenly moot.

Congress began to take piecemeal steps toward immigration regulation in 1819, with the adoption of federal reporting rules. No one was excluded until 1875, when prostitutes and convicts were barred. The excluded categories expanded in 1882 to include "lunatics," "idiots," and "those likely to become a public charge." Race also became a ground for exclusion in the aptly named Chinese Exclusion Acts of 1882 and 1888. Approximately 110,000 Chinese laborers entered the United States between 1850 and 1882 to do the arduous work of building the nation's railroads and developing its mines. However, once this work was completed, Chinese immigration was no longer seen as desirable.

Racism was a defining feature of the debate over Chinese labor. Whites in the western states made their views known with riots that destroyed Chinese homes and businesses and through discriminatory legislation. California and other western states lobbied vigorously for the Chinese Exclusion Acts. They found a receptive audience in Congress, whose members spoke of these residents as "locusts," "rats," "flies," and "leeches" in debating the bill. Race-based restrictions on Chinese, Indian, and other Asian immigration survived until 1943. The Japanese were also unwelcome. A 1907

"Gentleman's Agreement" severely limited their immigration.

During this period of increasing restrictions and racialized criteria for entry, the U.S. federal government was creating a bureaucratic apparatus to carry out its laws, including the power to deport persons already present. Congress enacted a series of national quota laws in the 1920s, limiting admissions for each nationality based on the proportion already in the United States. This system helped to maintain the nation's White, northern European character. In 1952 Congress limited immigration from the eastern hemisphere, leaving the western hemisphere unrestricted. The Senate Judiciary Committee claimed that it was not "giving credence to any theory of Nordic superiority" but was developing "a rational and logical" means to "best preserve the sociological and cultural balance of the United States."

The need for agricultural workers in the Southwest, however, necessitated exempting Mexicans from the federal quota system. These workers entered the United States in large numbers, legally and illegally, during the prosperous 1920s. Local laws segregated them from Anglo residents, and employers paid them a lower, "Mexican" wage. Their right to remain in their ancestral homeland was never secure. When hard times hit in the Depression, they were forcibly repatriated. It was a system of "imported colonialism" arising out of Mexico's subordinated relationship to the United States.

The government put a federal stamp of approval on this exploitative relationship in 1942, when it signed a bilateral agreement with Mexico establishing the bracero program, which provided for guest workers from Mexico. This program displayed the disadvantages characteristic of such guest worker agreements: harsh admission procedures, poor working conditions, and vulnerability caused by the constant possibility of deportation. The United States ended the program in 1964 when mechanization had reduced the need for Mexican labor.

At no time during this period was there an expectation that the Mexicans who labored in the United States would become citizens. Their status as cheap, exploitable labor was clear when the government undertook Operation Wetback in 1954, unceremoniously deporting over 1 million undocumented Mexican workers and some U.S. citizens. Congress could take such drastic action without fear of a lawsuit from these displaced people because the Supreme Court had ruled a few decades earlier that Congress has sovereign, undisputable, unreviewable power in matters of immigration. The plenary power doctrine, established in a series of cases challenging the exclusion of Chinese laborers, has been much criticized but still has significant sway in immigration cases.

Refugees

The government's approach to political refugees has followed a much different trajectory. The United States was, at first, slow to get involved in accepting refugees, refusing even to take significant numbers of European Jews fleeing the Nazi regime. But in 1948, 400,000 eastern Europeans were invited to the United States as refugees. In 1957 the United States offered special status to refugees fleeing communist countries. Seeking refuge because of war and escaping persecution in communist countries have remained grounds for admission. The United States accepted 700,000 anti-Castro Cubans, for example, between 1960 and 1980. The fall of Vietnam and Cambodia to communism brought more than 400,000 Indochinese refugees. Victims of persecution in "friendly" regimes, however, have great difficulty getting refugee status. The flow of refugees has been slowed in recent years by the passage of the USA PATRIOT Act.

Race Recedes as a Criterion for Admission

The United States finally abandoned its effort to control admission on the basis of national origin with the Immigration and Nationality Act of 1965, also know as the Hart-Celler Act. Although this legislation created a slightly higher ceiling on admissions of 290,000 people annually, it still differentiated between the eastern and western hemispheres. Eastern-hemisphere nations could send no more than 20,000 people per year. The new rules favored family reunification, permanent resident aliens with needed occupational skills, and refugees. With this change, the number of Asian, Mexican, and Latin American admissions began to increase dramatically. Refugee admissions also began to increase when the United States adopted the UN definition of *refugee* and put refugees in a separate category from other immigrants.

The trend toward more generous admissions that began in the 1960s continues, despite growing public resentment. The 1986 Immigration Reform and Control Act granted permanent residence to nearly 3 million undocumented residents who had lived in the United States since 1982. This law initiated a temporary agricultural worker program that allowed some farm workers to opt for citizenship. Discrimination against immigrants was forbidden, with a Justice Department agency set up to enforce this stricture. The quid pro quo was supposed to be new controls on undocumented immigration. Employers were required to check immigration status upon hiring. Part of the responsibility for enforcing immigration laws had, for the first time, been shifted to the private sector.

Immigration quotas have continued to be adjusted upward, based on both expert analysis that it is in the national interest and lobbying by a strong coalition of free-market conservatives, cosmopolitan liberals, and, more recently, interested ethnic groups. In 2006, more than 1.2 million immigrants were granted legal residence in the United States.

Congress dealt with public resentment against increasing numbers of immigrants by limiting their rights rather than their numbers. The Personal Responsibility Act and the Illegal Immigration Reform and Individual Responsibility Act, both adopted in 1996, limited access of noncitizens to welfare benefits, strengthened border enforcement, and expedited deportations. This was the first time the United States had limited the rights of legal resident aliens and subjected them to deportation for minor criminal offenses that may have occurred years before. The government was also moving toward an enforcement-based approach to immigration control. The border with Mexico was the focus of almost all of the attention, which included authorization of a 140-mile fence and funds for fingerprinting apprehended aliens.

Unauthorized Immigration

Unauthorized immigration is a long-standing pattern in the United States. According to the Office of Immigration Statistics, an estimated 11.8 million unauthorized residents were living in the United States in January 2007, an increase of nearly 40% from 2000. That number is likely to increase, despite recent efforts to reduce undocumented immigration through vigorous enforcement. An estimated 7 million of these residents were born in Mexico.

About 60% of these immigrants crossed a land border to the United States without authorization. The remainder entered legally with visas that subsequently expired. Unauthorized immigration is generally a poor peoples' phenomenon, reflecting the huge inequities in wealth between the global north and the poorer south. These immigrants are responding to America's enormous appetite for cheap labor. Strict limits on legal admissions from Latin America indirectly encourage undocumented immigration, which leads to increased rates of deportation.

Weak constraints on employers facilitate undocumented immigration. Industry groups successfully lobbied Congress to water down the employer sanctions provisions of the 1986 Immigration Relief and Control Act, which remains in effect. The industries that are organized around low-wage work remain committed to keeping borders as open as possible.

The new emphasis on enforcement at the border and in the workplace has increased the rate of expulsions somewhat, but the more significant impact may be increased levels of surveillance of all persons who look "foreign." Because Mexicans constitute over half of the undocumented population in the United States, and because of long-standing prejudice, the issue has been defined in the media, and even in the law, as a Mexican problem. "Hispanic appearance" has been authorized by the Supreme Court as a relevant ground for stops to ascertain immigration status. Hispanic appearance is not supposed to be the sole criterion, but complaints suggest that it often operates that way. This problem occurs not only at the border but also throughout the United States, as local police increasingly work with federal immigration-control officials to expel unauthorized aliens. The 44 million people of Hispanic ancestry who live lawfully in the United States, 15% of the population, are thus affected on a regular basis by current U.S. immigration legislation.

Beliefs about race and ethnicity are also implicated in the methods used to intercept would-be immigrants. Walls have been constructed in California and Texas that deflect people to dangerous desert crossings. Desperate Haitians are being intercepted on the high seas and forcibly returned to their dangerous homeland.

Unauthorized immigration and the federal government's inability to control it have spawned a grassroots anti-immigration movement across the United States. Cities, towns, and many states are enacting laws to deflect undocumented immigrants from their jurisdictions. They are following the early example of California, which adopted Proposition 187 by large margins in 1994. The idea was to deny a broad range of public services to people who could not prove their legal status. A court found the law unconstitutional, but it has nevertheless inspired other communities to follow California's example. Some communities, in addition to cutting off services, are directing their local police force to probe the immigration status of persons suspected of being undocumented immigrants. These developments create new opportunities for mistaken identification, racially based harassment, and strained relations among ethnic and racial groups.

Conclusion

Race will continue to be part of immigration law for the foreseeable future. The long-standing association of Mexicans with undocumented immigration and the criminalization of this status help perpetuate racial stereotypes and encourage racial profiling by police and immigration authorities. Muslims in the United States now face some of the same problems because of fear of terrorism. The cycle becomes self-perpetuating as public attitudes are shaped by racialized law-enforcement priorities and whole populations are placed under suspicion.

Doris Marie Provine

See also Chinese Exclusion Act; Deportation; Immigrants and Crime; Institutional Racism; Japanese Internment; Latina/o/s; Operation Wetback; Racism

Further Readings

Calavita, K. (2006). Collisions at the intersection of gender, race, and class: Enforcing the Chinese exclusion laws. *Law & Society Review, 40,* 249–282.

Hattam, V. (2007). *In the shadow of race: Jews, Latinos, and immigrant politics in the United States.* Chicago: University of Chicago Press.

Johnson, K. R. (2004). *The "huddled masses" myth: Immigration and civil rights.* Philadelphia: Temple University Press.

Kanstroom, D. (2007). *Deportation nation: Outsiders in American history.* Cambridge, MA: Harvard University Press.

Ngai, M. M. (2004). *Impossible subjects: Illegal aliens and the making of modern America.* Princeton, NJ: Princeton University Press.

Tichenor, D. J. (2002). *Dividing lines: The politics of immigration control in America.* Princeton, NJ: Princeton University Press.

IMMIGRATION POLICY

Illegal immigration has rapidly become one of the most debated issues in the United States today. Some of the most commonly cited reasons for illegal immigration include war, family reunification, and abject poverty as well as drug and human smuggling. While illegal immigrants to the United States come from many countries, the overwhelming majority come from Mexico, Southeast Asia, and Central America. Various proposals are currently being considered, but all revolve around one central question: To what extent should the United States support or oppose an open borders policy?

Arguments for an Open Borders Policy

Advocates of an open borders policy raise both ethical and economic issues in support of their position. Some open borders (aka free migration) proponents argue that the very concept of the nation-state is archaic and should come to an end. With the advent of high-tech means of travel, rigidly enforced borders unnecessarily impede free migration, thus rendering international travel cumbersome. Moreover, some advocates of open borders believe that Americans simply have no right to refuse access to the land known as the

United States to people from Mexico and Central America. In addition, supporters of open borders also point to the fact that many immigrants are actively participating in the U.S. military.

Another argument made by supporters of open borders is that using law enforcement to guard the southern border should be a low priority given the much greater problems of terrorism, world hunger, homelessness, the national debt, and global warming. They believe that it is unwise to dedicate massive amounts of resources to preventing the immigration of people who simply want to live and work here. In addition, replacing undocumented workers who do not pay income taxes with workers who do would result in immediate increases in revenues in the form of payroll taxes. At the same time, immigrants from poorer nations such as Mexico and elsewhere in Latin America would be able to send funds back to their native lands that would serve as a form of foreign aid. The end result of this would be an improvement in Mexican and Central American economies that would ultimately reduce the number of immigrants who come to the United States simply because they cannot provide for their families in their home countries.

According to supporters, an open borders policy will substantially reduce labor shortages resulting from a declining native-born U.S. birthrate by providing workers for assembly line work, construction, agricultural labor, and the service industry. Further potential benefits of open borders include increased union membership in the United States, as the number of low-wage workers increases, and healthy competition for lower-level jobs.

Others note that an open borders policy would reduce problems associated with illegally smuggling human beings across the border. In addition, open borders remove the need for American citizens to function as informants to assist in identifying undocumented workers and turning them over to federal authorities. Finally, open borders advocates also point to the contributions to American culture made by immigrants who have positive values, such as a strong work ethnic and a sense of community.

Arguments Against Open Borders

Groups opposing an open borders policy make several arguments. A central focus is the economic costs to U.S. taxpayers. For example, opponents of open borders cite data indicating that illegal immigrants are more likely than native-born Americans to carry some communicable diseases, including Chagas, tuberculosis, herpes, and syphilis. Thus, they may present a challenge to the health care system, especially for institutions where the economic resources are limited. A number of hospitals along the southern border of the United States have closed because federal U.S. law prohibits them from turning people away because of lack of insurance and they are unable to meet the demand for care. Critics of open borders also point to the relatively high number of illegal immigrants who have not completed high school and to the costs of public assistance for illegal immigrants on the welfare rolls.

Another concern raised by critics of an open borders policy is the cost of criminal offending by illegal immigrants. Southwestern states in particular struggle with massive expenditures needed for law enforcement and the operation of the criminal justice system. Substantial increases in spending for court personnel (e.g., prosecutors, defense attorneys, judges, clerks) have also strained state and local budgets.

The average cost to house an inmate for 1 year is approximately $24,000. Currently, the Government Accountability Office estimates that there are over 100,000 illegal aliens in federal and state prisons in the United States, at a cost of approximately $1.5 billion per year to the American taxpayer. The average number of arrests for illegal aliens currently in confinement is eight. Critics of open borders policy also note the social costs of violent and property crimes committed by illegal immigrants.

Finally, the anti–open borders lobby argues that illegal immigration has led to a balkanization of American society. They cite research data suggesting that residents of primary source countries of illegal immigrants into the United States harbor negative views of Americans. By extrapolation, they suggest that it will be very difficult to assimilate the tens of millions of poor aliens who come into the United States illegally and that this will exacerbate the problem of social disorganization. This, it is argued, typically weakens the bonds between neighbors and also results in lower participation in voluntary organizations. In sum, it is argued that illegal immigration is leading to a much weaker sense of community in American neighborhoods, which increases the possibility of street crime.

Enforcement Options to the Illegal Immigration Problem

If the United States ultimately chooses an open borders policy, illegal immigrant enforcement will largely become a moot point. The primary consideration will then be how to prevent entrance by those posing a clear national security threat to the United States. However, in the absence of an open borders policy, several approaches to reducing illegal immigration have been advocated.

The Security Fence

The Secure Fence Act of 2006 provides for a multilayered fence along the southern border complete with high-tech ground sensors, unmanned aircraft, and the use of Cyclops (manned towers using infrared to detect heat). Supporters of the fence note that in the areas where the fence has been completed, illegal alien crossings have been significantly reduced.

Elimination of Incentives for Illegal Immigration

One proposal to reduce incentives for illegal immigration is a national ban on welfare payments (e.g., free medical care, cash payments, food stamps) to illegal immigrants. Other opponents of open borders have proposed a change in the policy under which all children born in the United States are U.S. citizens. These advocates of border security argue that this change would not require a constitutional amendment but simply a reinterpretation by the federal courts so that only children born to individuals in the United States legally would be granted automatic citizenship.

Enhanced sanctions for U.S. employers who continually hire illegal aliens also are a consideration. This would require substantial funding increases for personnel assigned to this task. Most currently discussed plans include a $10,000 fine for the first offense of hiring an illegal alien, $30,000 for the second offense, and the loss of a business charter for the third offense. It is argued that this would lead to voluntary repatriation of illegal aliens to their countries of origin. The recently passed REAL ID program, which calls for a national ID card for all American citizens, may improve the government's ability to identify illegal aliens working in the United States by streamlining the process of examining citizenship status. This program is set to go into effect in December 2009.

Sanctuary City Policies

A sanctuary city is a city where local police are prohibited from asking suspects about their immigration status. This policy is based on the reasoning that illegal aliens will be more likely to report crime to the police if they are not afraid of being deported. Opponents of open borders, however, argue that sanctuary cities serve as magnets for illegal aliens because they are essentially granted immunity from prosecution. Some advocates of strict immigration laws propose that government withhold federal funds for various projects (e.g., roads, bridges, education, police) for any city or state deemed to be in violation of the ban on sanctuary cities. Some also suggest that local and state police officers be deputized to be allowed to enforce federal immigration laws, as is the case in Canada.

Billy Long

See also Immigrants and Crime; Immigration Legislation; Latina/o/s; Race Card, Playing the

Further Readings

Hayworth, J. (2006). *Illegal immigration, border security and the War on Terror*. Washington, DC: Regnery.

Tarver, M. (2002). *Multicultural issues in the criminal justice system*. Boston: Allyn & Bacon.

U.S. Government Accountability Office. (2005). *Information on certain illegal aliens arrested in the United States* (Report No. GAO-05-646R). Retrieved from http://www.gao.gov/new.items/d05646r.pdf

INDIAN CIVIL RIGHTS ACT

The Indian Civil Rights Act (ICRA), enacted by Congress in 1968, is federal legislation that transfers key provisions of the Bill of Rights to criminal justice processes that occur in Indian Country. This legislation is important in the study of race and crime because it ensures due process to defendants in tribal justice systems. This entry describes the ICRA, its impact in Indian Country, and strengths and weaknesses of the legislation.

For more than a century, the protections in the Bill of Rights were viewed as governing only federal prosecutions. Just as its provisions had to be extended to the states through the process of selective incorporation, the rights included in the Bill of Rights were not automatic for individuals on tribal lands. The logic was that tribal governments were not governed by the U.S. Constitution because they had entered into treaty relations with the United States prior to the adoption of the Constitution and Bill of Rights, so they did not participate in the ratification process, and the later Fourteenth Amendment's due process clause did not apply to tribal governments. In *Talton v. Mayes* (1896), a Native American defendant on trial in Cherokee territory challenged the number of grand jurors on his indictment and other issues of trial fairness as insufficient under the Constitution (specifically the Fifth Amendment), but the U.S. Supreme Court ruled that he was not entitled to relief, saying, "as the powers of local self-government enjoyed by the Cherokee Nation existed prior to the constitution, they are not operated upon by the fifth amendment, which, as we have said, had for its sole object to control the powers conferred by the constitution on the national government" (p. 384).

The passage of ICRA by Congress occurred in the same general time period as the "due process revolution" in the 1960s, when the U.S. Supreme Court handed down a series of rulings mandating that protections in the Bill of Rights apply to investigations and prosecutions at the state level rather than just in federal proceedings. During the 1960s, complaints about violations of civil rights in general were heard and considered by the Senate Subcommittee on Constitutional Rights, and that committee conducted a series of hearings specifically devoted to tribal justice. The result of those hearings was ICRA, which imposed most of the provisions of the Bill of Rights on tribal governments.

Bill of Rights Protections Mandated by ICRA

The Bill of Rights protections mandated by ICRA are among the most cherished rights in American legal history, and those of the First through Eighth Amendments are enumerated in the ICRA with some omissions.

The First Amendment rights to freedom of religion, free speech and press, peaceable assembly, and the ability to petition the government for redress of grievances appear nearly verbatim in ICRA, except for one conspicuous absence. Whereas the U.S. government was enjoined from making laws "respecting an establishment of religion," ICRA omitted this requirement because it was felt that some Native American tribes consider religion to be inseparable from their government and social life ways. So, while tribes cannot deprive citizens of a general freedom of religion, they may have official established religions, which guide their legal and social systems.

The Second Amendment right to bear arms is not guaranteed by ICRA because it was felt that tribes should have the ability to regulate firearms within their reservations. The Third Amendment ban on quartering of soldiers was not included because tribes do not have a professional military that could seek shelter in private homes. Of interest, neither of these amendments was incorporated, meaning they also do not apply to the states.

The Fourth Amendment protection against unreasonable searches, seizures, and warrants sought without probable cause is nearly verbatim from the Bill of Rights and guarantees all these bedrock rights to individuals residing in Indian Country.

The Fifth Amendment protections against double jeopardy and self-incrimination are extended through ICRA in addition to the ban on taking private property for public use without fair compensation, but the clause relating to grand juries in capital or otherwise infamous crimes is not included in ICRA. The grand juries clause has not been incorporated, so it does not apply to the states, either.

The Sixth Amendment provisions for speedy and public trials and those that guarantee defendants the right to confront witnesses against them, compel witnesses to testify in their cases, and to know the charges against them are also part of

ICRA. The Sixth Amendment right to counsel is included in ICRA but specifies that a defendant in Indian Country may have such assistance "at his own expense," meaning that defendants are guaranteed the ability to have an attorney represent their interests, but the government is not obligated to provide an attorney for them. Some scholars lament that failing to provide attorneys for those in tribal justice systems amounts to unacceptable injustice, but that right was not included in ICRA due to the feeling that poor tribes would not be able to endure such an expensive burden. Some tribes, such as the Navajo Nation, provide public defenders, but they are not mandated by ICRA to do so. The Sixth Amendment right to a trial in the district in which the offense occurred is not part of ICRA, in part due to complex legal jurisdiction that results in many defendants in Indian Country being tried off-reservation depending on the type of crimes they are accused of committing.

The Seventh Amendment right to jury trials is not part of ICRA, but this right has also not been extended to the states through incorporation.

The Eighth Amendment prohibitions against excessive bail or fines and cruel or unusual punishment are part of ICRA. Of interest, the ban on excessive bail has not yet been extended to the states through incorporation, so this is one of the rare constitutional protections mandated for tribal citizens but not for their counterparts in state justice systems. In addition, ICRA states that tribal governments cannot impose sentences more severe than 1 year in jail and a fine of $5,000. This additional guarantee has been criticized because it limits the ability of tribal governments to establish penalties for violations of their laws. It also means that tribal courts are essentially limited to adjudicating misdemeanors.

The Ninth and Tenth Amendments are not part of ICRA, nor are they extended to the states through incorporation.

In addition to the above Bill of Rights guarantees, ICRA includes verbatim text from the Fourteenth Amendment guaranteeing equal protection to all citizens and due process to accused individuals. ICRA also includes the mandate from Article 1 of the Constitution banning bills of attainder and ex post facto laws. Then, ICRA guarantees those accused of offenses for which they may be jailed the right of trial by jury of six or more persons; the right to jury trials for serious cases was extended to the states by the U.S. Supreme Court ruling in *Duncan v. Louisiana* in 1968 (the year ICRA was enacted). Finally, ICRA directs the creation of a model code to govern justice processes for tribes that rely on federally operated Courts of Indian Offenses (rather than those created by their own governments) and changes the guidelines for state assumption of jurisdiction over tribal justice systems to require tribal consent to state takeovers and making retrocession of jurisdiction back to tribes possible.

Taken as a whole, ICRA made many significant changes to the way justice was handled in Indian Country by guaranteeing individuals accused of crimes on tribal lands many of the same basic due process rights that their counterparts in state courts obtained through selective incorporation of the Bill of Rights. Though agreeing with those guarantees in theory, critics of ICRA feel it amounts to unnecessary oversight and meddling in tribal affairs. Some lament about imposing "White man's justice" on tribal governments and trying to make tribal justice systems mirror those of their White counterparts. Some tribes already had substantial due process guarantees in place in their common law provisions. Navajo Nation common law, for example, mandates that attorneys be knowledgeable about the type of law they are practicing, which is a protection that many off-reservation defendants may desire. ICRA also wreaked havoc with traditional legal practices, such as peacemaking and other culturally appropriate mediation schemes, by guaranteeing rights that can be seen as working against the goals of mediation (e.g., most tribes prohibit attorneys from acting in an official capacity during traditional mediation hearings).

A significant weakness in ICRA is that the only remedy guaranteed to tribal defendants is that of habeas corpus, meaning they may use alleged violations of ICRA to challenge their incarceration, but they cannot use ICRA to seek other remedies, including injunctions against tribal governments, changes to tribal laws or legal processes, or even financial compensation. In addition, defendants may not file habeas corpus proceedings until exhausting all potential avenues of remedy within their respective tribal legal systems. The U.S. Supreme Court has allowed non–habeas corpus proceedings in only a handful of situations since ICRA's passage more than 4 decades ago. Citizens who are not incarcerated, then, are essentially denied any guarantees under ICRA. So, while some critics charge that ICRA is meddling in tribal affairs, others charge that it does not provide any real protections for tribal citizens. More and more tribes are now including ICRA-like guarantees in their own constitutions and governing documents, however, so citizens in Indian Country may soon have the same protections as their off-reservation counterparts.

Jon'a F. Meyer

See also Indian Self-Determination Act; Native Americans; *United States v. Antelope*

Further Readings

Canby, W. C., Jr. (2004). *American Indian law in a nutshell* (4th ed.). St. Paul, MN: West Publishing.

Deloria, V., & Wilkins, D. E. (1999). *Tribes, treaties, and constitutional tribulations.* Austin: University of Texas Press.

Garrow, C. E., & Deer, S. (2004). *Tribal criminal law and procedure.* Walnut Creek, CA: AltaMira Press.

Indian Civil Rights Act of 1968 (25 U.S.C. §§ 1301-03).

Talton v. Mayes, 163 U.S. 376 (1896).

INDIAN SELF-DETERMINATION ACT

The Indian Self-Determination Act can be seen in historical context as a recent policy perspective by the U.S. government among several shifting policies on what to do about Indians. The U.S. government has approached the issue of Indians in several manners, including extermination, allotment and assimilation, the New Deal, termination of tribal status, and self-determination. Extermination involved the denial of Native American culture, subsistence, and land rights. The allotment and assimilation approach was a policy of placing Indians on reservations and gave individual Indians parcels of land in an effort to transition them into independent farmers. The New Deal began a reversal of previous allotment and assimilation policies and sought to

give Indians some role in managing their own affairs. With termination, the U.S. government sought to eliminate all federal responsibility over Indian affairs and to terminate tribal status. Finally, self-determination sought to foster autonomy and community for Native American tribes. This policy toward self-determination was exemplified by the 1975 Indian Self-Determination and Education Assistance Act (Public Law 93-638), which allowed tribes to administer their own service programs. The act was amended in the 1980s and 1990s to allow for greater self-governance.

Extermination

Native American lands were obtained by the U.S. government in a variety of ways, including betrayal of trust as expressed in formal treaties. As settlers expanded their land interests and Native Americans were in the way, the U.S. government engaged Indians in a number of treaties that were eventually revoked or ignored to gain control over Indian lands. Initially, many of the treaties allowed Indians to exclusively occupy vast areas of land that provided them with subsistent hunting and gathering, and seasonal or wandering encampments. In exchange for their land, the Indians were granted peace. When settlers wanted and encroached upon these additional lands, the U.S. government failed to enforce the treaties and used troops to force native inhabitants into relinquishing their lands. In addition, the troops and settlers destroyed Indian assets and food sources such as the buffalo.

Allotment and Assimilation

The U.S. government began a policy of placing Indians on reservations and gave individual Indians parcels of land in an effort to transition them into independent farmers and to keep them out of the way of settlers. The allotment and assimilation era began in 1871 and was marked by refusal by Congress to deal with Indian tribes as separate and sovereign nations. In 1887, Congress passed the General Allotment Act, which divided reservation land into family plots; the titles to these lots were held in trust by the U.S. government. It, indeed, may be that dividing reservation land into plots was the only way to protect it from White divestiture. Even so, the parcels of land and life within the reservations were very poor, and the best tracts of land ended up in White hands. In addition to dividing up and privatizing Indian land, other policies sought to wipe out native languages and stamp out tribal cultures.

Native people who refused to be placed upon reservations or who engaged in resistance were hunted down by U.S. troops and returned to the reservations by force. In some noteworthy cases, there were massacres of Indian women and children. Indian resistance was effectively quashed by 1890, and the "Indian Wars" ended.

The New Deal

While Indians on the reservations retained minimal rights of self-determination and organization, the federal government ruled over reservations through the Bureau of Indian Affairs and congressional legislation and oversight. In 1934, Congress enacted the Indian Reorganization Act as part of the Indian New Deal under President Franklin Roosevelt. The Indian Reorganization Act began a reversal of previous allotment and assimilation policies. New policies sought to give Indians an active role in managing their own affairs. The Secretary of the Interior was authorized to negotiate funding and contracts with any state for Indian social services, including education. Congress sought to allow Indians living on reservations local self-government and tribal corporations to manage reservation resources. Continued allotments of Indian lands were prohibited, and allotted lands were consolidated for community purposes.

Termination of Tribal Status

Despite the initiatives contained in the Indian Organization Act, the federal government reversed itself again in 1953, with a new era of federal Indian policy known as the termination era. Congress declared its intent to eliminate all federal responsibility over Indian affairs and to terminate tribal status. In doing so, tribal sovereignty was to be replaced with state law, and communal tribal lands were to be disposed of into private,

individual hands. As a result, 109 tribes were terminated, and thousands of Native Americans lost tribal affiliation. Federal responsibility and jurisdiction were turned over to state governments. Land held in trust by the federal government for Indians was removed from protected status and sold to non-Indians. The policy of termination had disastrous consequences. The loss of tribal status was associated with high unemployment, a decline in educational levels, and a loss of homes and welfare enrollments.

Self-Determination

The plight of Indians was reexamined in the 1960s as the result of several factors, including Indian activism. This led to yet another change in Indian policies called the era of Indian self-determination. Self-determination began to form during President John F. Kennedy's administration. Self-determination found support with President Johnson and the War on Poverty, and President Richard Nixon's perspectives on Indian policy included an adamant repudiation of termination. Nixon recommended that Congress support self-determination and foster autonomy and community for Native American tribes.

In 1975, Congress passed Public Law 93-638, the Indian Self-Determination and Education Assistance Act, in an effort to maximize Indian participation in the government and education of the Indian people. Even though neither the Bureau of Indian Affairs officials nor the tribes were particularly happy with the implementation of the program, it was widely hailed as an improvement in federal Indian policy and a meaningful step toward self-determination. Prior to this act, the federal government controlled the planning and administration of services such as hospitals, schools, and community centers, intended to benefit Native Americans, without their input or involvement. The legislation gave tribes the funding amount that the government would have spent to plan, conduct, and administer the programs. As a result, tribes could negotiate contracts with the Bureau of Indian Affairs to administer their own service programs, including hospitals, health clinics, dental services, mental health programs, and alcohol and substance abuse programs.

The Indian Self-Determination and Education Assistance Act was amended in the 1980s and 1990s to allow for greater self-governance. For example, instead of discrete individual grants, tribes received bloc grants from the Indian Health Service and the Bureau of Indian Affairs to support several programs and were given discretion as to how to allocate funds. Further tribal role was expanded to include programs with the Environmental Protection Agency and the Department of Housing and Urban Development. The intent has been to cultivate independence and leadership within the Native American tribal communities. Finally, while Congress and the Executive Branch provide indications of support for self-determination, and there have been some modest improvements to existing tribal programs, the last major legislative initiative aimed at self-determination was enacted in 1996. No significant new legislation has been enacted since then.

J. Michael Olivero

See also Bureau of Indian Affairs; Domestic Violence, Native Americans; National Native American Law Enforcement Association; Native American Courts; Native American Massacres; Native Americans; Native Americans and Substance Abuse; Tribal Police; *United States v. Antelope*

Further Readings

Canby, W. C., Jr. (2004). *American Indian law in a nutshell* (4th ed.). St. Paul, MN: West Publishing.

Castile, P. (1998). *To show heart: Native American self-determination and federal Indian policy, 1960–1975.* Tucson: University of Arizona Press.

Churchill, W. (2002). *Acts of rebellion: The Ward Churchill reader.* Milton Park, UK: Routledge.

Collins, R. (2006). A brief history of the U.S.-American Indian Nations relationship. *Human Rights, 33*(2), 3–4.

Cross, R. (2004). Reconsidering the original founding of Indian and Non-Indian America: Why a second American founding based on principles of deep diversity is needed. *Public Land & Resources Law Review, 25,* 61.

Dean, S., & Webster, J. (2000). Contract support funding and the federal policy of Indian tribal self determination. *Tulsa Law Journal, 39,* 349.

Fredericks, J. (1999). America's First Nations: History and future of American Indian sovereignty. *Journal of Law and Policy, 4,* 347.

Glazer, E. (2004). Appropriating availability: Reconciling purpose and text under the Indian Self-Determination and Education Assistance Act. *University of Chicago Law Review, 71,* 1637.

Janik, C., Malcolm, J., & Iott, S. (1999, October). *Indian Self-Determination Act: Shortfalls in Indian contract support costs need to be addressed.* Collingdale, PA: Diane Publishing.

Kersey, H. (2005). Buffalo Tiger, Bobo Dean, and the "Young Turks": A Miccosukee prelude to the 1975 Indian Self-Determination Act. *American Indian Culture and Research Journal, 29*(1), 1.

Reid, B., & Winton, B. (2004). *Keeping promises: What is sovereignty and other questions about Indian Country.* Tucson, AZ: Western National Parks Association.

Skibine, A. (1995). Reconciling federal and state power inside Indian Reservations with the right of tribal self-government and the process of self-determination. *Utah Law Review Society, 1995*(4), 1105.

Walch, M. (1983, July). Terminating the Indian termination policy. *Stanford Law Review, 35,* 1181.

Washburn, K. (2006, May). Tribal self-determination at the crossroads. *Connecticut Law Review, 38,* 777.

Wright, D., Hirlinger, M., & England, R. (1998). *The politics of second generation discrimination in American Indian education: Incidence, explanation, and mitigating strategies.* Westport, CT: Bergin & Garvey.

INEQUALITY THEORY

Social inequality is the giving of privileges and obligations to one group of people while denying them to another. Inequality theory is a system in which groups of people are divided into layers according to their relative power, prestige, and property. It is a way of ranking large groups of people into a hierarchy according to their relative privileges. Social inequality affects individuals' life chances, the way they see the world, and even the way they think.

Every country in the world has inequality; some societies have greater inequality than others, but inequality theory states that inequality is universal. In addition, every country uses gender as a basis for its inequality. On the basis of gender, people are either allowed or denied the good things offered by their society.

In no society is gender the sole basis for inequality, but the categories into which people are sorted and given different access to the good things in their society always favor males. The lower status of women is almost universal and timeless; few societies have been found where women habitually dominate men. For example, in every society in the world, men earn more money than women. In addition, according to UNESCO estimates, 64% of the world's illiterates are women, a figure unchanged since 1990.

Inequality theory does not limit inequality to gender. Gender inequality affects females and males throughout their lives, and it starts when they are young. Childhood differs structurally from adulthood; children are subject to additional levels of social control (by parents, teachers, and other adults). Adults are structurally positioned to take advantage of available resources; they create and use power to their advantage, and they control access to valued resources. Also, adults have accumulated advantages over time that children have not had the opportunity to achieve. Moreover, children's economic utility makes them a drain on resources, and both behavioral and attitudinal variables (female infanticide, son preference, affection, the social inclusion and evaluation of boys and girls) are specific to childhood gender inequality.

Inequality theory recognizes that skin tone is a paramount criterion of social acceptance in America and that race often supersedes the influence of class, background, religion, or language in terms of access to the good things offered by society. The darker a person's skin is, the greater his or her social distance is from the dominant group and the more difficult it is to make personal qualifications count. Racial disproportionalities in American rates of arrest, imprisonment, and capital punishment are indisputable, although debate about the sources of these disproportionalities persists. There is evidence that race is more important than social class for explaining variation in urban American arrest rates. In support of this view, researchers point to the intense surveillance of Black neighborhoods, the relative absence of surveillance in White neighborhoods, and differences in punishments for White and Black offenders that reinforce perceptions of a racist and unequal criminal justice system designed to oppress Black people.

Race is also a salient comparative point of reference for understanding perceptions of the criminal justice system in America. African Americans overwhelmingly perceive these differences in the criminal justice system as unjustifiable, and the massive numbers of African Americans (especially youth) who come into contact (or conflict) with the criminal justice system perceive it as unjust. This has led to a growing concern that perceived injustice itself causes criminal behavior, which adds urgency to developing a better understanding of racial and ethnic differences in the criminal justice system. Middle-class African American professionals distrust the criminal justice system. Low-income African Americans are more inclined to restrict their frame of reference to their immediate community when judging their experiences. The separateness of the African American urban experience may make police harassment so common that they are less outraged than would be expected.

African Americans perceive inequality and discrimination in education, employment, health care, and housing as a result of racism, due mainly to the long history of public humiliation of African Americans. Neighborhood, school, and workplace experiences provide further context for racial subordination. Affluent and better-educated Blacks view African Americans as worse off than White Americans. Economically successful African Americans can compare more easily their experiences with Whites and other racial groups, so they may be more inclined to perceive injustice among African Americans as a group. In addition, middle-class Blacks may be surprised when their economic status does not protect them from police harassment, whereas African Americans who are economically disadvantaged may be conditioned to expect that type of treatment. This places middle- and upper-class African Americans in a heightened state of sensitivity to differential treatment.

Inequality theory states that for a society to maintain its inequality, the powers that be must either control ideas and information or use force. Coercion often breeds hostility and rebellion, so those in control focus on controlling people's ideas by developing an ideology (a belief that justifies the way things are) to justify its position at the top. For example, around the world schools teach that their country's form of government (regardless of what form that is) is the best. Inequality theory also posits that to maintain their positions of power, elites try to control information by manipulating the media or withholding information. However, as can be seen in the disproportionate treatment by the criminal justice system, coercion is not ruled out as a means of maintaining unequal access to the good things offered by a society.

Although programs exist to help level the playing field (e.g., affirmative action, college scholarships) and provide more equal opportunity, such programs encounter structural inequality in which inequality is built into economic and social institutions. Examples of structural inequality are unemployment and differences in wages. Inequality theory states that the consequences of inequality include a quality of life that goes to the core of one's being. Inequality affects the way people think, behave, and severely limits their life chances.

PJ Verrecchia

See also Black Feminist Criminology; Conflict Theory; Disproportionate Arrests; Disproportionate Minority Contact and Confinement; Gender Entrapment Theory; Racism

Further Readings

Baunach, D. M. (2001). Gender inequality in childhood: Toward a life course perspective. *Gender Issues, 19*(3), 26–87.

Chambliss, W. J. (2000). *Power, politics, and crime.* Boulder, CO: Westview Press.

Curtis, R. F. (1986). Household and family in theory on inequality. *American Sociological Review, 51*(2), 168–183.

Hagan, J., Shedd, C., & Payne, M. R. (2005). Race, ethnicity, and youth perceptions of criminal justice. *American Sociological Review, 70,* 381–407.

Hagan, J., Simpson, J. H., & Gillis, A. R. (1979). The sexual stratification of social control: A gender based perspective on crime and delinquency. *British Journal of Sociology, 30*(1), 25–38.

Huber, J. (1990). Micro-macro links to gender stratification. *American Sociological Review, 55,* 1–10.

Lipset, S. M. (1979). *The third century: America as a post-industrial society.* Stanford, CA: Hoover Institution Press.

Reiman, J. (2001). *The rich get richer and the poor get prison: Ideology, class, and criminal justice.* Boston: Allyn & Bacon.

Rogers, S. J., & Amato, P. R. (2000). Have changes in gender relations affected marital quality? *Social Forces, 79,* 731–748.

Toffler, A. (1980). *The third wave.* New York: Morrow.

United Nations Educational, Scientific and Cultural Organization. (2006). *Education for All global monitoring report.* Paris: Author. Retrieved from http://unesdoc.unesco.org/images/0014/001416/141639e.pdf

INNOCENCE PROJECT

Established by Peter J. Neufeld and Barry C. Scheck (civil rights attorneys) in 1992, the Innocence Project started at Benjamin N. Cardoza School of Law located at Yeshiva University in New York City. The mission of the Innocence Project is to aid inmates who have the chance of being established innocent through the technology of deoxyribonucleic acid (DNA) testing.

The Innocence Project, which has the status of a nonprofit organization, was based at Yeshiva University until 2003, when the group moved to its own location. The affiliation between the university and the Innocent Project remains solid. Both Neufeld and Scheck are members of the faculty. The project has five full-time lawyers working on cases, and each year, students of Cardoza School of Law work with the Innocence Project. Their responsibilities include investigating cases and locating evidence that might hold DNA and assisting lawyers in drafting motions for the court. Along with the help of the law students, the Innocence Project employs 38 other people, including a policy and an intake department.

History of Exoneration

The act of exoneration is not a new element in the U.S. criminal justice system. According to Rob Warden of Northwestern Law, the first case of documented exoneration was in Vermont in 1820. Jesse and Stephen Boorne were sentenced to hang for the murder of their brother-in-law Russell Colvin in 1812. Although Colvin's body was not found, Silas Merrill, Jesse's cell mate, claimed that Jesse had confessed to the murder. After the police confronted Jesse about the statement, he confessed to the police while laying the principal culpability on Stephen. After the trial both Jesse and Stephen were sentenced to death by hanging. The legislature in Vermont commuted Jesse's sentence to serving life in prison but did not do the same for Stephen. Not long before Stephen was to die, Russell Colvin was found alive in the state of New Jersey. He returned to Vermont, and both Stephen and Jesse were exonerated of the murder.

According to Amanda Buck, the first group devoted to exonerating the innocent from prison was the Court of Last Resort. It was started in 1947 by Erle Stanley Gardner, a lawyer and a mystery novelist who was well known for his character of Perry Mason, a fictional lawyer. Gardner established a panel of experts to examine cases in which an innocent person may have been convicted. His first case was that of William Marvin Lindley. Lindley was convicted on the charge of murder in the state of California. Gardner and his panel proved Lindley was innocent. Gardner's work stopped in 1960, but he estimates that through the course of his work, the Court of Last Resort looked into 8,000 cases of innocent people who were incarcerated.

Centurion Ministries was the first organization that worked nationally. The Centurion Ministries was established by James McCloskey in Princeton, New Jersey, in 1983. McCloskey worked as a chaplain in Trenton State Prison. He chose to leave the position as junior chaplain and the ministry in order to focus his attention solely toward the goal of freeing innocent inmates. Centurion Ministries is still based in New Jersey and has five full-time employees and a network of forensic experts and lawyers throughout the United States and Canada. The organization also has a dedicated network of volunteers who work with the Innocence Project.

The work of the Innocence Project was groundbreaking. Inspired by the work of people who came before them, the Innocence Project staff were the first to work toward the goal of exonerating inmates based on DNA evidence. They took a concept that is quite old, an inmate's plea of innocence, and combined it with the breakthrough technology of DNA.

There is currently a network of organizations that are working toward the identical objective. According to the Innocence Project website, there are approximately 53 locations in 40 states across the nation, including Texas, Washington, Virginia, California, District of Columbia, Ohio, Kentucky, and Maine. There are also international locations in Canada, England, and Australia. These organizations work together to achieve two main objectives: for innocent people to be released from prison and for laws and statutes to change to safeguard more innocent people from ever seeing the inside of a cell.

Applying for Consideration by the Innocence Project

To be considered by the Innocence Project, an individual must submit a letter including a brief summary stating the facts of the case and the evidence that was used in the trial. The lawyers for the Innocence Project will then review the case. It is made clear that if the case does not have evidence pertaining to DNA, the inmate or individual has the option of contacting other institutions that help in proving innocence.

If the Innocence Project decides to accept a case, the inmate is required to fill out a very detailed questionnaire and provide the organization with all of the information that the inmate and his family can obtain. If there is DNA evidence, then the organization will send it for testing. According to Neufeld, approximately 50% of the cases reviewed by the Innocence Project result in inmates' innocence.

Results

The first exoneration based on DNA evidence occurred in 1989. On April 23, 2007, the Innocence Project celebrated their 200th exoneration when Jerry Miller was released after serving 24 years for kidnapping, rape, and robbery of a Chicago woman in 1982.

Inmates have been exonerated in over 32 states across the nation, including Washington, D.C. As of November 7, 2008, the Innocence Project has helped exonerate 223 wrongly convicted inmates across the country, including 17 inmates on death row. Of those 223 exonerated, 138 are African American, 59 are Caucasian, 19 are Latino, 1 is Asian American, and 6 are of unknown race. Over 70% of the exonerated are members of a minority race or ethnicity. Of the exonerated, about 50% have been financially compensated. The average time spent incarcerated before exoneration is 12 years, and the average age of those exonerated at the time of their conviction is 26.

According to Elisabeth Salemme of *Time* magazine, the Innocence Project receives approximately 200 requests for assistance each month. Every year, the Innocence Project has to reject approximately 33% of cases that are submitted due to lost or misplaced or destroyed evidence. At any given time, the Innocence Project is actively working on approximately 160 cases.

After Exoneration

The Innocence Project has established a program to help the people who are exonerated. The program employs a social worker who helps the exonerated adjust to life outside of prison; the program accepts donations to help the exonerated start a new life. The Innocence Project staff is also working on passing state legislation establishing fair compensation to those who have been exonerated. Only 22 states and the District of Columbia currently have some sort of compensation statute in place, and several of the compensation statutes in place are inadequate. The Innocence Project's goal is to see that all states in the nation have sufficient compensation statutes in place.

Federal Legislation

Due to the number of incarcerated inmates exonerated through the work of the Innocence Project and others like it, Congress has taken a new look at the laws dictating the conditions under which inmates can have old evidence retested and addressing the right of exonerated inmates to compensation for their time behind bars.

The Advancing Justice Through DNA Technology Act was signed into law in 2003. It authorizes for $1 billion over a period of 5 years to help both federal and state governments understand and appreciate the capability of DNA testing when it comes to solving crimes while protecting the innocent. There are four separate titles to the bill. Titles I and II are the DNA Sexual Assault Justice Act and the Rape Kits and DNA Evidence Backlog Elimination Act. This legislation established the Debbie Smith DNA Backlog Grant Program and authorizes $755 million over a period of 5 years to address the backlog of DNA evidence in crime labs across the nation. It also provides $500 million to establish new programs to reduce other backlogs, to aid in training medical and criminal justice personnel of DNA evidence, and to encourage the employment of DNA technology to aid in identifying missing people. Title III is the Innocence Protection Act, which makes available postconviction DNA testing in the federal system. It also aids states in improving the quality of legal representation in capital cases and enhances compensation for wrongfully convicted inmates in the federal system. Title III also established the Kirk Bloodsworth Post-Conviction DNA Testing Program and authorizes $25 million over a period of 5 years to help with the cost of postconviction DNA testing.

Kirk Bloodsworth was sentenced to death in Maryland in 1985 for the 1984 rape and murder of a 9-year-old girl. His conviction was overturned in 1986 due to withheld evidence; he received a life sentence at the end of his retrial. In 1993, through the help of Centurion Ministries, DNA testing was conducted. The tests showed that Bloodsworth's DNA did not match the DNA evidence that was found at the crime scene. He was released in June 1993 and given a full pardon in 1994. In September 1993, an inmate serving time for another offense was found to be the actual offender. He was in the cell block where Bloodsworth had been confined, and the two men had routinely worked out together.

The Justice for All Act was signed into law in October 2004. The act increases the funds available to both state and local governments to help fight crimes involving DNA evidence and to help prevent convictions of innocent people, and worse, executions of innocent people. It incorporated three titles of the Advancing Justice Through DNA Technology Act, while adding one additional title. There are four separate titles to the bill. Title I is the Scott Campbell, Stephanie Roper, Wendy Preston, Louarna Gillis, and Nila Lynn Crime Victims' Rights Act. It provides for the establishment of enhanced and enforceable rights for victims of crime in the federal system and authorizes grants to assist states in establishing their own victim's rights laws. Titles II and III established the Debbie Smith DNA Backlog Grant Program. Title IV is the

Innocence Protection Act, which makes available postconviction DNA testing in the federal system.

The Justice for All Act also established increased compensation amounts for exonerated inmates. Inmates who were on death row receive $100,000 for each year of incarceration; all other exonerated inmates receive $50,000 a year for each year of incarceration. Although this provision applies only to the federal system, it urges states to enact compensation guidelines. At the moment, there are 28 states that lack any sort of compensation for exonerated inmates. Presently, the Innocence Project is focused on the states of California, Florida, Pennsylvania, and Texas. The Innocence Project wants these states to institute statutes of stronger compensation.

Looking Into the Future

Scheck, Neufeld, and Jim Dwyer believe that technological advances in the science of DNA will ultimately eliminate the need for exonerations based on DNA evidence. Already, thousands of innocent suspects—perhaps even more—have been cleared before going to trial. However, the crisis of innocent people spending years in prison is not even coming close to nearing an end. They acknowledge that there are innocent people that will stay behind bars, abandoned for the simple fact that their cases do not have biological evidence. Because these cases do not involve saliva, blood, ejaculate, or tissue, these innocent inmates will continue to be locked up. In light of this, Cardoza and Northwestern, joined by other law schools in North America, are in the process of forming a network of innocence organizations that will be equipped to handle cases of inmates who were wrongly convicted, even in the absence of DNA evidence.

Although the work of exonerating innocent people through DNA is coming to a close, the Innocence Project, along with the entire Innocence Network, does not plan to disband in the near future. However, they are looking forward to a time when their services will no longer be needed.

Nicole Hardy

See also Alliance for Justice; Wrongful Convictions

Further Readings

Buck, A. (2006, May/June). Innocence projects. *IRE Journal, 28*, 18–19.

Leahy, P. (2004). *The Justice for All Act of 2004.* Retrieved from http://leahy.senate.gov/press/200410/100904E.html

Mid-Atlantic Innocence Project. (n.d.). *Kirk Bloodsworth.* Retrieved from http://exonerate.org/case-profiles/kirk-bloodsworth

Pollack, E. (2004, July 13). *The Advancing Justice Through DNA Technology Act of 2003 (H.R. 3214): A section-by-section analysis* (Report No. RL32469). Retrieved from Open CRS (Congressional Research Service) website: http://opencrs.cdt.org/document/RL32469/2004-07-13%2000:00:00

Salemme, E. (2007, June 5). *Innocence Project marks 15th year.* Retrieved October 12, 2007, from http://www.time.com/time/nation/article/0,8599,1628477,00.html

Scheck, B., Neufeld, P., & Dwyer, J. (2000). *Actual innocence: Five days to execution and other dispatches from the wrongly convicted.* New York: Doubleday.

Websites

Centurion Ministries: http://www.centurionministries.org/index.html

Innocence Project: http://www.innocenceproject.org

IN RE GAULT

In re Gault (1967) is considered one of the most important cases in juvenile justice in the United States. *Gault* overturned procedures formalized during the 20th century that many considered paternalistic. Although the impact of *Gault* on racial discrimination in juvenile justice is unclear, it signaled a trend toward procedural safeguards similar to those available in the adult criminal justice system. All youth were at risk of being deprived of due process in juvenile justice proceedings prior to *Gault*, but minority youth had been especially victimized by the failure of states to extend the protections of the Bill of Rights to juveniles. The U.S. Supreme Court's decision in *Gault* established a number of due process rights for juveniles in delinquency proceedings, including the right to timely notice of charges, the right to counsel, and the right to confront an accuser, as well as protection against self-incrimination.

Facts of the Case

Gerald F. Gault was 15 years old at the time of his offense. Gault and a friend had been accused of making obscene phone calls to a neighbor. Gault was apprehended and questioned without his parents being given any notice from the authorities. Gault's mother was given a handwritten note from the juvenile probation officer, informing her and her husband of the delinquency hearing a week later, which she attended. However, neither Gault nor his parents received notification of the specific charges against him or the potential repercussions for Gault prior to the informal delinquency hearing. Gault was neither given nor advised of an opportunity to have a lawyer present to advise or represent him. At the hearing, the only evidence against him was hearsay evidence concerning the claims of the complaining neighbor, who did not appear, and a single prior juvenile charge of theft. In the hearing, Gault admitted to dialing the neighbor who had made the complaint but stated that he had spoken to her. Mrs. Gault's request that the neighbor be present to identify the caller was specifically denied. Gault was found to be delinquent and was sentenced to up to 6 years in the State Industrial School, which was a juvenile facility that many considered to be no less than a prison for juveniles. Had Gault been an adult, he would have faced a maximum of 60 days in jail. Because Gault was not entitled to an appeal from the delinquency hearing under the state juvenile justice system, his case challenged the law itself through a petition for habeas corpus, which is a writ inquiring into the lawfulness of the restraint of a detained person.

Decision and Reasoning of the Supreme Court

The issue before the U.S. Supreme Court on appeal was whether Gault was entitled to some of the same due process rights that adults had under the Fourteenth Amendment of the U.S. Constitution. The Court found that juveniles facing detention in juvenile justice proceedings were entitled to the rights to notice of the charges, to counsel, to be silent (i.e., against self-incrimination), to confront witnesses against him or her, to a transcript of the proceeding, and to an appeal to a higher court.

In an 8–1 opinion, the Supreme Court found that the juvenile justice system had departed far from its humanitarian roots in the beginning of the century. The idea had been that juveniles were stigmatized by treatment as adults, that the system was benign and rehabilitative, that juveniles' liberty interests were less than those of adults, and that an informal system was thus much more beneficial to juveniles. The Court found that this was not the reality of the juvenile justice system. Justice Abe Fortas, writing the opinion of the Court, looked at the adult nature of the facilities to which juveniles were sent and the number of repeat offenders. He stated that "the condition of being a boy does not justify a kangaroo court"—that is, being underage does not justify losing the protections of the Bill of Rights or the Fourteenth Amendment to the Constitution. This ruling revolutionized procedure in the juvenile justice system. The only procedural rights available to adult criminal defendants that are not available to juveniles facing detention for criminal violations are trial by jury and indictment by grand jury; there has been no significant reform movement to include either of these rights in the juvenile justice system.

Gault is considered unique because it not only reformed the law in a specific area but did so by reversing the "reforms" of the previous century.

History and Logic of the Juvenile Justice System

Common law courts considered juveniles to be either incapable of forming criminal intent, and thus legally innocent, or fully capable, in which case they were treated as adults. In the United States, this approach gradually came to be considered unjust, and segregated facilities were established for juvenile detention and correction. The child welfare doctrine of *parens patriae* ("the state as substitute parent") was used to justify what many people would now consider rehabilitative and paternalistic detention of juveniles. This practice began in the eastern United States and spread west. The Pennsylvania Supreme Court evoked and explained the philosophy of parens patriae in the 1838 case of *Ex Parte Crouse*:

> May not the natural parents, when unequal to the task of education, or unworthy of it be superseded by the *parens patriae,* or common guardian of the community? It is to be remembered that the public has a paramount interest in the virtue and knowledge of its members. . . . The [detained child] has been snatched from a course which must have ended in confirmed depravity; and not only is the restraint of her person lawful, but it would be an act of extreme cruelty to release her from it.

In 1899, Chicago established the first exclusively juvenile court, and within a few decades, the courts spread to other states. Throughout most of the 20th century, the juvenile justice system has evolved separately from the adult criminal justice system. The underlying rationale has been that juvenile delinquency should be treated differently from adult crime. Prior to *Gault,* the justifications for the lack of procedural safeguards were that delinquency proceedings were not criminal trials and that juveniles should be incarcerated in juvenile facilities, not prisons. The facts of *Gault,* however, indicate that the ideal of rehabilitating children in their formative years may have fallen short of the mark. Many believed that juvenile facilities were no better than prisons, and therefore, Gault's sentence of up to 6 years in a juvenile facility was unacceptably harsh given than an adult convicted of the same crime would have received a maximum sentence of only 60 days in jail.

Gault's Legacy

Gault stood for the idea that the juvenile justice system should treat juveniles much like adults. This idea has proven to be a double-edged sword, as the protections that the juvenile justice system offers to juveniles, apart from the adult criminal justice system, have slowly eroded. Juveniles are more and more frequently facing transfers to the adult criminal justice system, adult sentences from juvenile courts, or hybrid sentencing. The

nature of the facilities to which juveniles are committed, even strictly within the bounds of the juvenile justice system, is often analogous to those for adults. The confidential nature of the juvenile justice system has also eroded, with juvenile records, once strictly confidential, now available for more purposes once the subjects reach adulthood.

The paternalism of the juvenile justice system, for good or ill, has been slowly replaced with a focus on accountability and victim protection. *Gault* itself stood for the prospect that juveniles need to be afforded the rights of adults; however, many critics believe that an adult penal burden is also imposed on juveniles and that the juvenile justice system has itself become more punitive and less rehabilitative. One significant exception to this more punitive approach is the abolition of the juvenile death penalty by the U.S. Supreme court case of *Roper v. Simmons* (2005). *Gault* added procedural safeguards for the protection of juveniles, but its legacy has been more punitive treatment by the more formalized juvenile justice system and more transfers to the harsher and equally formalized adult criminal justice system.

Sam Swindell

See also Juvenile Crime; Juvenile Drug Courts; Juvenile Waivers to Adult Court; Youth Gangs

Further Readings

Butts, J. A., & Mitchell, O. (2000). Brick by brick: Dismantling the border between juvenile and adult justice. In *Boundary changes in criminal justice organizations* (pp. 167–213). Washington, DC: National Institute of Justice.

del Carmen, R. V., & Trulson, C. (2006). *Juvenile justice: System, process, and law.* Belmont, CA: Thomson/Wadsworth.

Roper v. Simmons, 543 U.S. 551 (2005).

INSTITUTE ON RACE AND JUSTICE

See Northeastern University Institute on Race and Justice

INSTITUTIONAL RACISM

Racism refers to a belief about the racial superiority of one group over another. Racism can be expressed in individual beliefs and actions, as well as by groups. Institutional racism is racism that is embedded in a society's institutions—for example, in the political, economic, educational, and criminal justice systems—in a subtle form that allows the dominant group to systematically exploit and dehumanize the subordinate group. Civil rights activists and political scientists are credited with introducing the concept of institutional racism. Among the functions of institutional racism is the maintenance of racist practices that create and sustain the dominant group's privileges at the expense of equal opportunities for subordinate groups. Institutional racism contributes to discriminatory systemwide norms that are embodied in institutional policies and practices. Whereas incidents of individual racism are somewhat easy to detect, institutional racism is more difficult to identify because it involves more than specific actions by individuals. This entry describes institutional racism, its history, and its impact on imprisonment and the War on Drugs.

Institutional racism consists of the policies and practices of social institutions that operate in such a way that they produce systematic and persistent differences between racial groups that contribute to social inequality. Institutional racism can occur even when no one is consciously or intentionally racist—what matters is the outcome. The key issue in institutional racism is the result, not the intent of those who are creating policies and continuing practices. Nevertheless, institutional racism is often the legacy of overt racism, whereby de facto racist practices are codified by de jure mechanisms.

Another aspect of institutionalized racism is *petit apartheid realities*. Criminologist Daniel Georges-Abeyie coined this term to refer to informal practices in the criminal justice system that discriminate against non-Whites. Examples of such practices are routine stop-and-question or stop-and-frisk practices that target minorities. Such discrimination in everyday law enforcement contributes to poor relations between the police and persons of color. Institutional racism may include not only explicitly encouraging racist behavior through institutional policies but also failing to take steps to halt such practices.

Whether the criminal justice system is racist continues to be hotly debated. Many criminal justice experts often rely on conventional wisdom that the system is racist, whereas others argue that such characterizations are a myth. William Wilbanks, in his controversial book *The Myth of a Racist Criminal Justice System* (1987), was one of the first to argue that the criminal justice system is not racist. He distinguished between individual and institutional racism and states that although individual racism occurs among police officers, attorneys, judges, and professionals in the criminal justice system, the system itself is not racist. Wilbanks confined his argument to the criminal justice system at that time and conceded that racial prejudice and discrimination had occurred in the past.

Criticism surrounding Wilbanks's book encompasses numerous issues. Wilbanks failed to recognize that the racism in the criminal justice system has become institutionalized in the same way it has in other organizational segments of the nation, such as education, politics, and the economic structure.

Historical and Contemporary Considerations

As the United States underwent the first of several waves of immigration, it was widely believed that the Irish, German, and Scandinavian immigrants were less intelligent than "real" Americans. When Irish, German, and Scandinavian immigrants settled in the United States during the 1800s, they were often viewed as less intelligent than "real" Americans; similar racist attitudes developed toward new arrivals during subsequent waves of immigration. Unemployment has always affected recent immigrants more than well-established citizens; the inability of immigrants to find work was attributed to what was perceived to be their innate laziness. Consequently, when poor, unemployed immigrants turned to street crime, perhaps in an attempt to survive harsh economic conditions, they were often viewed as a "class" of criminals. Historically, a disproportionate number of minorities and immigrants, most of them of a lower socioeconomic class, have been arrested, tried, convicted, and incarcerated.

Unlike the experience of immigrants of other ethnic groups, the experience of African American immigrants was primarily as slaves. Because the long history of slavery was maintained and nurtured by institutional racism, African Americans experienced not only individual racism but the institutional racism associated with slavery. Historically, being African American has meant having fewer legitimate opportunities in society. As a result they have had more contact with the criminal justice system than other racial groups. Following the Civil War, first- and second-generation immigrants from Europe were overrepresented in the prison population in the northern states, whereas prison inmates in the South were overwhelmingly African American. Today, African Americans—and to a lesser extent Latinos—are disproportionately represented in the prison system in all states.

According to the National Council on Crime and Delinquency, although African Americans represent only 13% of the general U.S. population, they account for 42% of all inmates held in state prisons or local jails and nearly 50% of the population on death row. Together, African Americans and Latinos comprise more than 70% of new prison admissions and more than 50% of the total prison population.

For over 20 years the federal government enforced cocaine sentencing laws that disproportionately targeted poor minorities. According to these laws, there was a mandatory minimum sentence of 5 years for possession of 5 grams of crack cocaine or 500 grams of powder cocaine. Because federal laws required a mandatory 5-year sentence for crimes involving 500 grams of powder cocaine or 5 grams of crack cocaine, about 86% of those convicted of federal crack cocaine offenses were Black; about 5% were White; thus, this sentencing disparity has a great impact on African Americans. Arguably, this sentencing disparity was a form of institutional racism. In *Kimbrough v. United States* (2007), the U.S. Supreme Court considered this disparity and ruled that the sentence of 15 years to life was unreasonable when based on sentencing disparity for crack and powder cocaine offenses.

Policy Implications

A comprehensive understanding of institutional racism in the United States must take into account the long-lasting character of racism and the fact that racism may operate, in large part, independently of the dominant group's present attitudes and behavior, with effects that outlive the initiators of racism. To be effective, structural remedies must reverse the "vicious circle" of institutional racism. For example, research on African Americans demonstrated that neighborhood segregation has led to educational disadvantage, then to occupational disadvantage, to income deficit, and even to prison. Institutional racism is considerably more intricate and entrenched than discrimination or prejudice. Remedies will require changes in the laws, in the economic structure, and in social programs if institutional racism is to be eradicated.

Kaylene A. Richards-Ekeh

See also Disproportionate Incarceration; Drug Sentencing; Drug Sentencing, Federal; Ghetto, Ethnoracial Prison; *Kimbrough v. United States*; Prison, Judicial Ghetto; Racialization of Crime; Racism; Sentencing; Sentencing Disparities, African Americans

Further Readings

Georges-Abeyie, D. E. (1990). Criminal processing of non-White minorities. In B. D. Maclean & D. Milovanovic (Eds.), *Racism, empiricism, and criminal justice*. Vancouver, BC, Canada: The Collective Press.

Goldberg, D. T. (Ed.). (1990). *Anatomy of racism*. Minneapolis: University of Minnesota Press.

Kimbrough v. United States, 552 U.S. ___ (2007).

Mann, C. R. (1993). *Unequal justice: A question of color*. Bloomington: Indiana University Press.

National Council on Crime and Delinquency. (2008). *Racial and ethnic disparities in the U.S. criminal justice system*. Prepared for the Impact Fund. Retrieved from http://steinhardt.nyu.edu/events/2008/9/16/176957

Office of the National Drug Control Policy. (2000). *Drug Policy Information Clearinghouse: Fact sheet, March 2000*. Washington, DC: U.S. Department of Justice.

Spohn, C., & Holleran, D. (2002). The effect of imprisonment on recidivism rates of felony offenders: A focus on drug offenders. *Criminology, 40*(2), 329–357.

Walker, S., Spohn, C., & DeLone, M. (2007). *The color of justice: Race, ethnicity, and crime in America* (4th ed.). Belmont, CA: Wadsworth.

Wilbanks, W. (1987). *The myth of a racist criminal justice system*. Monterey, CA: Brooks/Cole.

INTERMEDIATE SANCTIONS

Intermediate sanctions refer to punishments that fall between prison and probation. Given the disproportionate representation of people of color in prison today, the use of intermediate sanctions offers the possibility of reducing that disparity. This entry examines the range of punishments that comprise intermediate sanctions. Furthermore, an evaluation of the effectiveness of this strategy as well as directions for future research in this area are explored.

A defendant who receives a sentence involving an intermediate sanction faces a tougher and more stringent sentence than a defendant placed on probation, but that defendant avoids a harsher prison sentence. In prison, rehabilitation is virtually nonexistent, whereas a traditional probation sentence has been reprimanded as being too lenient and unstructured. Sociologist Jeffrey Ulmer found intermediate sanction sentences, which emerged during the late 1980s, involved more structure, surveillance, and treatment than did traditional probation sentences. Ulmer further observed that intermediate sanctions had become increasingly popular as they retain the "tough on crime" approach; meanwhile, this approach preserved an overcrowded and deteriorating prison system. The use of intermediate sanctions becomes particularly important when exploring the relationship between race and crime because non-Whites are disproportionately represented in America's jails and prisons.

Intermediate sanctions—also known as community corrections, alternative sanctions, and alternative punishments—can appear in a variety of forms. Some of the most popular intermediate sanctions are electronic monitoring, which can include house arrest; supervised work programs in the community; intensive probation supervision; and drug courts or substance abuse treatment. Regardless of the intermediate sanction given, the defendant remains in his or her community while adhering to the court-ordered treatment, sentence, or both. Intermediate sanctions can require intense amounts of counseling, workshops, rehabilitation programs, and time.

In addition to the cost savings of using intermediate sanctions as opposed to prison, the use of these sanctions helps reduce the stigmatization associated with incarceration. Further, it enables the defendant to maintain ties with his or her community while emphasizing rehabilitation. For example, an offender sent to drug court has an opportunity to deal with the issues that lead to continued drug use and receive various counseling and structured treatment. Drug court and substance abuse treatment centers require offenders to adhere to a strict and comprehensive plan. Numerous weekly meetings, random drug tests, and counseling sessions are just a few of the requirements to complete the program. Electronic monitoring leads to increased surveillance and can be very beneficial with people convicted of sexual offenses. Boot camps, also referred to as shock incarceration, can last many months and require defendants to follow a rigid schedule. In all of the intermediate sanctions, if the conditions assigned are not met, a prison or jail sentence usually follows.

Intermediate sanctions enable the criminal justice system to separate the serious and more dangerous criminals from the less-serious and nonviolent criminals. For the most part, the defendants who receive an intermediate sanction sentence are lower-level drug offenders, nonviolent offenders, less-serious offenders, or offenders with no prior record who committed a minor criminal offense.

The theoretical rationale for intermediate sanctions is derived from labeling, social control, and differential association theories. John Braithwaite's notion of reintegrative shaming provides a powerful foundation for the use of these sanctions. This perspective suggests a need to reduce the use of incarceration and to increasingly rely on community service. Reintegrative shaming takes into account the need to punish criminals, but it also considers the need to reduce stigma and open lines of communication within the community. If social bonds, opportunities, and socialization processes are restored, the offender is less likely to engage in criminal activity, thereby reducing the problem of recidivism. In contrast, traditional prison sentences, and the stigmatization associated with incarceration, can lead to increased criminality as well as psychological issues. Intermediate sanctions can also have a pronounced general deterrent effect, as people in the community witness the shaming and eventual reintegration of these offenders.

Evaluations of the impact of intermediate sanctions on recidivism are mixed. Similarly, there is no consensus regarding the most effective type of intermediate sanction. Some research supports intermediate sanctions in the reduction of recidivism, while other research sees little or no difference between prison and the outside sanction. Perhaps most instructive is the research of Joan Petersilia and Susan Turner. These researchers demonstrated that if intermediate sanctions focus strictly on surveillance and control, they will fail; it is imperative that the sanctions also emphasize treatment, rehabilitation, and reintegration goals for the offender.

A significant amount of research still needs to be conducted to examine the various intermediate sanctions and their potential effect on offenders and the communities involved. Future research should focus on improving probation and intermediate sanctions, while also examining offender accountability and recidivism rates. In addition, it is important for all probation departments to understand that one-size-fits-all programs will not suffice; each offender is unique with issues specific to that person. In addition, matching specific cases to a specific intermediate sanction will affect the eventual outcome of the offender.

Although intermediate sanctions are still a relatively new form of punishment being used in the criminal justice system, the method appears promising. Keeping low-level and nonviolent offenders out of prison increases their chances of staying in touch with their community and receiving treatment that would potentially decrease chances of recidivating. In addition, the preclusion of more prisoners into an already overcrowded system makes intermediate sanctions more appealing and cost-effective. Currently, the movement toward rehabilitation has been helping popularize intermediate sanctions as an effective punishment method.

Katherine Polzer

See also Drug Courts; Juvenile Drug Courts; Recidivism; Sentencing

Further Readings

Braithwaite, J. (1989). *Crime, shame, and reintegration.* Cambridge, UK: Cambridge University Press.

Dal Pra, Z. (2006). Community corrections' quest to predict violence. *Criminology & Public Policy*, 5(4), 779–784.

Maxwell, S. R., & Gray, M. K. (2000). Deterrence: Testing the effects of perceived sanctions certainty on probation violations. *Sociological Inquiry*, 70(2), 117–136.

Petersilia, J., & Turner, S. (1990). *Intensive supervision for high-risk probationers: Findings from three California experiments.* Santa Monica, CA: RAND.

Ulmer, J. (2001). Intermediate sanctions: A comparative analysis of the probability and severity of recidivism. *Sociological Inquiry*, 71(2), 164–193.

Wood, P., & May, D. (2003). Racial differences in perceptions of severity of sanctions: A comparison of prison alternatives. *Justice Quarterly*, 20(3), 605–631.

INTERRACIAL CRIME

Many sociological studies have examined how economic deprivation acts as a precipitating factor in the commission of crime across various races, and the basic theme is that poverty in a stratified society weakens institutional and social bonds. Scholars have noted that economic hardship has been especially critical in understanding the disparity occurring frequently between the crime rates of Blacks and Whites in the United States. This is particularly pronounced for Blacks, who have disproportionately higher rates of violence. Researchers have commonly assessed whether racial disparities in socioeconomic conditions influence racial differences in crime rates. They have noted that economic inequality often creates resentment and anger on the part of Blacks about what they face in competing with Whites for scarce jobs and other resources. According to criminologists, when the disadvantaged realize that they share common economic interests but are unable to get fair redistribution of resources, they become angry and frustrated; this situation can lead to committing crime against others. While this relative deprivation perspective examines the criminogenic effects of interracial inequality, other social scientists have argued that other experiences stem from economic inequality that shape group experiences independent of whether or not the individual group members experience relative deprivation. This entry reviews the research on interracial crime as well as how racial threat theory has been applied to interracial crime.

Research on Interracial Crime

Recent work that examined the association between economic inequality and crime found different measures of global inequality, interracial economic inequality, and/or intraracial inequality in assessments of the linkage. Previous research indicated that Blacks used other Blacks as a reference point for assessing themselves and that variations in race-based crime rates are best predicted by within-group, rather than between-group, economic inequality. This is best evidenced in studies that compare race-specific arrest data drawn from the FBI *Uniform Crime Reports* (UCRs) with National Crime Victimization Survey (NCVS) victimization data relating to the race of criminal offenders to determine the relative amount of crime committed by Blacks and Whites. Most robbery victims in the NCVS report their assailants to be Black, and the people arrested for robbery by police are also Black. Blacks are overrepresented in the UCR arrest data for the crimes of rape, aggravated assault, and simple assault. Some have argued that this overrepresentation is due to the fact that crimes involving Black offenders are less apt to be reported to police than are crimes involving White offenders.

Critics of the NCVS have posited that the data ignore crimes committed against businesses, government, and religious organizations, and tend to overinflate rates of crime for cities with a large nonresident population. Other studies that have used NCVS data to assess the connection between economic inequality and race-specific crime levels are also vulnerable to these criticisms. Still others indicate that although causes behind the predominantly intraracial nature of violent crime remain important for study, the proposition that Black offenders' racial hatred for Whites is what prompts high levels of interracial offending is often dismissed. Events of criminal violence motivated by racial hatred can occur in some instances. Other studies have shown that aggregated patterns demonstrate that assault offenders do not exhibit a general propensity to select victims interracially. Rather, these studies indicate that although violent offenders tend to select victims intraracially at the local level, the intraracial character of violent offending varies by crime, offender race, and locale.

Other criminologists have shown that assault is predominantly intraracial across offense and offender levels, and in some cases criminal assault is less intraracial than expected, with White offenders victimizing interracially more than random selection would expect. Recent studies have also shown that not only do Black offenders not have a propensity to select White victims for crimes of violence, but if they demonstrate a propensity, it is to select victims within their own race. That the pattern persists even when local-level segregation is taken into account makes it apparent that factors beyond residential segregation operate to produce predominantly intraracial assault offending, according to additional researchers. Hence, research studies have also shown that White and minority populations are not just segregated residentially but also segregated into different incomes, jobs, and career trajectories as well as different levels in the educational system. Here it is suggested that various factors contribute to variations in the rate of crimes that occur and exist across dimensions of race.

Theoretical Explanations of Interracial Crime

While most studies of interracial crime test the propositions derived from various theories, relatively few studies examine the association between factors derived from racial threat theory and interracial crime. Much of the research from the conflict perspective focuses on how powerful groups in society use state control to protect their position from competing subordinate groups. The racial threat perspective maintains that the maneuverings of the criminal justice system are used to control minority groups who threaten the interests of the dominant groups. Specifically, researchers have argued that as the size of the Black population grows larger, Whites increasingly view Blacks as a threat to their political and economic success. Whites then react to this threat by discriminating against Blacks so as to maintain their dominant position. Blacks will then lash out at those who are viewed as the oppressors and causes of their plight.

Racial threat is based on political competition and economic competition. In some cases, researchers have noted that Black political mobilization is related to the amount of discrimination directed at Blacks by the state and by individuals. As the political threat increases, discriminatory acts and social control efforts against Blacks intensify to pacify the perceived threat of Blacks. However, once the Black population eclipses the size of the White population, these discriminatory practices diminish because Blacks displace Whites as the majority group. Others assert that gains in Black political power serve to decrease acts of violence perpetrated by Blacks against Whites. Previous scholarship suggests that incidents of interracial violence are a reaction to the subordinate status of Blacks relative to Whites. Hence, group conflict theories generally and racial threat theory specifically have fostered several studies that evaluate whether the discriminatory treatment of Blacks is influenced by changes in factors that may be regarded as threatening the dominant position of Whites.

Zina McGee and Tyrell Connor

See also Colonial Model; Conflict Theory; Hate Crimes; Intraracial Crime; Minority Group Threat

Further Readings

D'Alessio, S. J., Stolzenberg, L., & Eitle, D. (2002). The effect of racial threat on interracial and intraracial crimes. *Social Science Research, 31,* 392–408.

Koch, L. W. (1995). Interracial rape: Examining the increasing frequency argument. *American Sociologist, 26,* 76–86.

Wilbanks, W. (1985). Is violent crime intraracial? *Crime and Delinquency, 31,* 117–128.

INTIMATE PARTNER VIOLENCE

See Domestic Violence; Domestic Violence, African Americans; Domestic Violence, Latina/o/s; Domestic Violence, Native Americans

INTRARACIAL CRIME

Intraracial crime is crime in which the victim and the offender are of the same race. It is most applicable in the context of heterogeneous societies, that is, in societies, such as the United States, where the potential victim pool is composed of more than one racial group. Of the Federal Bureau of Investigation's Part I crimes (homicide, forcible rape, assault, robbery, arson, larceny-theft, motor-vehicle theft, and burglary), most of the recorded data, in which the race of both the victim and the offender is known, centers around violent offenses, such as forcible rape, robbery, aggravated assault, and homicide. National-level arrest statistics indicate that most violent crime is intraracial. This has been shown to be especially true of homicide and assault. Fewer data are available on offender–victim race with regard to property crime, such as burglary, larceny-theft, and arson. This may be because these crimes do not require physical contact between the victim and offender; thus the race of the offender can easily go unknown. However, data that are available in which the race of both the offender and victim is known suggest that property crime is less intraracial than is violent crime.

Patterns of Intraracial Crime

Several studies have been conducted on the intraracial crime patterns among Blacks and Whites, and all have concluded that violent crime is largely intraracial, especially homicide. A classic 1958 study by Marvin Wolfgang found that, in Philadelphia, 94% of the offender–victim relationships examined involved offenders and victims of the same race. Also, a 1965 study of Houston found a similar intraracial homicide rate, approximately 86%, among Mexican Americans. Further, a study of Chicago between the years 1965 and 1973 found that intraracial homicide made up between 86% and 90% of all homicide cases. More recent studies indicate a continued trend. According to a U.S. Department of Justice report, in 2005, about 93% of Black homicide victims and 85% of White homicide victims in single victim/single offender homicides were killed by someone of their same race. National-level data regarding intraracial crime among other races are scant because many crime statistics categorize all other races as "other." However, Department of Justice data collected between 1993 and 1998 indicated that 58%

of those of "other races" were murdered by an "other race" person. Studies of victim–offender relationships for both simple and aggravated assault show that the preponderance of assault offenses is, like homicide, intraracial. National Crime Victimization Survey (NCVS) data from 2005 indicate that 67% of total assaults on White victims were at the hands of White offenders. Likewise, 69% of total assaults on Black victims were at the hands of Black offenders. A 2006 study also suggested that assault is more intraracial than interracial. Using National Incident-Based Reporting System (NIBRS) data, 27 of the largest U.S. cities that recorded NIBRS data between 2002 and 2004 were studied. Though NIBRS is not used nationwide yet, of the cities examined, it was found that White-to-White assault accounted for 47% of the cases, Black-to-Black assault accounted for 38%, Asian-to-Asian accounted for 0.25%, and Native American-to-Native American accounted for 0.14%. Due to the small representation of data, these numbers may not fully reflect the severity of assault; however, the pattern persists that much assault is intraracial.

Robbery seems to be less intraracial than assault and homicide, and more complicated to categorize due to different rates of victimization by race. Again according to 2005 NCVS data, Whites have about the same chance of robbery victimization at the hands of a Black offender as at the hands of a White offender—36% and 37%, respectively. Those of "other races" and cases where the race is unknown also engage in interracial robbery against Whites at a significant rate (26%). Thus it seems where White victims are concerned, robbery is quite interracial. Some criminologists hypothesize that Whites are often the victims of robbery because other groups perceive them as having the material possessions worth stealing (either to sell or to keep).

From the perspective of the Black victim, robbery is highly intraracial. NCVS data suggest that 87% of Black robbery victims were victimized by other Blacks; only 5% were victimized by Whites and 7% by those cases where race was unknown. Thus, whereas robbery is mostly interracial for White victims, it is mostly intraracial for Black victims. Incidentally, Blacks are incarcerated for robbery at much higher rates than other races.

Rape exhibits similar rates of victimization as robbery. Whites have a 44% chance of being raped by another White, a 36% chance of being raped by a Black, and a 22% chance of being raped by someone of "other" or unknown race. But, as was the case with robbery, rape among Black victims is largely intraracial. NCVS data estimate that in 2005, more than 90% of the rapes against Black women were by Black men.

Thus, in keeping with other findings, national-level data suggest that homicide and assault are largely intraracial. In recent years, though, it seems the nature of rape and robbery has moved more toward interracial and less toward intraracial, except when the victim is Black. Again, more data must be collected on victimization rates against other races, and particularly, with the other races separated into specific categories.

Macrostructual Opportunity Theory of Interracial and Intraracial Crime

Many of the studies that investigate the rates of intraracial crime cite macrostructural opportunity causes as an explanation for the high rates of intraracial crime. In short, this suggests that interracial violence is a function of opportunity and access. Because much of the United States is still residentially segregated, it would stand to reason that the intraracial rate of crime is high because offenders choose victims to which they have access and opportunity. Following this logic, if neighborhoods were more racially integrated, intraracial crime would decrease and interracial crime would increase. However, studies suggest that other macrostructural factors, such as income and education, may negate the effect of race on inter- and intraracial crime. That is, in neighborhoods with similar incomes and levels of education, homicide and assault are still likely to be highly intraracial. More study on this is needed.

Conclusion

National-level statistics show that most violent crime is intraracial, including homicide and assault. Although rape and robbery are less intraracial than homicide and assault, both still have significant numbers of same-race victim–offender relationships. Further, crime patterns indicate that most violent offenders do not exhibit a general propensity to select victims interracially; rather, they tend to select victims intraracially. However, as in the case of rape and robbery, this varies by crime and offender–victim race.

Phillippia Simmons

See also Interracial Crime; Social Distance; Subculture of Violence Theory; Victimization, African American; Victimization, Asian American; Victimization, Latina/o; Victimization, Native American; Victimization, White; Victimization, Youth; Violent Crime

Further Readings

Becker, S. (2007). Race and violent offender "propensity": Does the intraracial character of criminal violence persist locally? *Justice Research and Policy*, 9(2), 53–86.

Block, R. (1976). Homicide in Chicago: A nine-year study (1965–1973). *Journal of Criminal Law and Criminology*, 66(4), 496–510.

Harrell, E. (2007, August). *Black victims of violent crime* (Report No. NCJ 214258). Retrieved from Bureau of Justice Statistics: http://www.ojp.usdoj.gov/bjs/pub/pdf/bvvc.pdf

Hindelang, M. (1978). Race and involvement in common law personal crimes. *American Sociological Review*, 43(1), 93–109.

Humphrey, J., & Palmer, S. (1987). Race, sex, and criminal homicide offender-victim relationships. *Journal of Black Studies*, 18(1), 45–57.

Klaus, P., & Maston, C. (2006, December). *Criminal victimization in the United States, 2005 statistical tables, National Crime Victimization Survey* (Report No. NCJ 215244). Retrieved from Bureau of Justice Statistics: http://www.ojp.usdoj.gov/bjs/pub/pdf/cvus0502.pdf

Messner, S., & South, S. (1986). Economic depravation, opportunity structure, and robbery victimization: Intra- and interracial patterns. *Social Forces*, 64(4), 975–991.

Rennison, C. (2001, March). *Violent victimization and race, 1993–98* (Report No. NCJ 176354). Retrieved from Bureau of Justice Statistics: http://www.ojp.usdoj.gov/bjs/pub/pdf/vvr98.pdf

Silverman, R. (1975). Victim-offender relationships in face-to-face delinquent acts. *Social Problems*, 22(3), 383–393.

IQ

An intelligence quotient (IQ) is a purported measure of an individual's general intellectual ability. Over the past century there have been repeated attempts to link low intelligence with propensity to commit criminal acts and frequent claims that some supposed racial groups (in particular, Blacks) have lower intelligence than others. Critics have rejected such claims as racist pseudoscience.

History

The French psychologists Alfred Binet (1857–1911) and Theodore Simon (1872–1961) devised the first mental tests in 1905, with the aim of identifying schoolchildren who would benefit from special education programs to improve their performance. Binet and Simon attempted to identify an array of intellectual tasks that an average French child of a particular age could be expected to perform. Children who performed more than 2 years below their chronological age were identified as needing special help. The German psychologist Wilhelm Stern (1871–1938) proposed the idea of dividing mental age by chronological age (and multiplying by 100 to avoid decimals) to yield a measure of an individual's relative development, which he called an IQ. Today, IQ is generally determined by mapping relative results onto a normal distribution bell curve with 100 as the center value and a standard deviation of 15 points.

Mental testing was taken up enthusiastically in the United States and Britain, but in both countries it immediately became entangled with hereditarian, biological determinist, eugenicist, and racist ideas. For example, the American psychologist H. H. Goddard (1866–1957), who popularized Binet's tests in the United States, took IQs to represent innate intelligence, a single capacity that could be little changed by education. Goddard attributed most social ills, including crime, to low intelligence, which he linked to limited emotional control and immorality. Goddard advocated institutionalization of the "feeble minded" (whom he designated "morons") to prevent them from reproducing. Goddard's contemporary, Lewis Terman (1877–1956) of Stanford University (who created the standardized Stanford-Binet IQ tests), made the same link between low IQs and crime, arguing that although not all criminals were mentally deficient, all those significantly below average intelligence were potential criminals. Terman also argued that social classes reflected biologically inherited differences, with members of the lower classes being innately less intelligent, and that there were significant racial differences in intelligence, with American Indians, Mexicans, and Blacks all being, on average, less intelligent than Whites.

Early IQ tests were frequently administered in highly unrigorous ways in the United States, allowing results to be significantly influenced by tester prejudices, inadequate testing conditions, and culturally biased test items. In 1913, Goddard concluded that nearly 50% of immigrants from southern and eastern Europe were "feeble minded." The Harvard psychologist Robert Yerkes (1876–1956) conducted mass testing of army recruits during World War I and concluded that the average mental age of Whites was just 13, with Blacks a little over 10, and various southern and eastern European groups somewhere in between. Yerkes gave these results a hereditarian interpretation; they were used to justify class and racial prejudices and played a central role in justifying the 1924 Immigration Restriction Act, which severely limited immigration from southern and eastern Europe.

What Do IQ Tests Measure?

Mental testing has become more sophisticated since the early 20th century with, for example, removal of the most obviously culturally biased test items. Most modern tests include both verbal and nonverbal test items intended to assess a variety of abilities, including comprehension, vocabulary, arithmetic, short-term memory, and spatial visualization. But there has continued to be much controversy over exactly what IQ tests measure, with opinions varying from the blunt assertion that IQ tests measure intelligence by definition, to the view that they only measure the ability to do well at IQ tests. From the start, the tests have been calibrated to correlate with success in school, but success may be due to a variety of factors, not simply intelligence. Because there is a correlation

between scores on the different subtests (an individual who scores well on one subtest is more likely to score well on another), defenders argue that the tests measure an underlying psychological capacity, dubbed "g" to stand for general intelligence. Critics argue that g is simply a statistical artifact and that the tests function to reinforce existing social hierarchies.

One persistent difficulty for those who claim that IQ is a measure of general intelligence is that there is no clear definition of what intelligence is supposed to be, and attempts by experts to come up with such a definition have not produced a consensus. Two ideas commonly associated with intelligence by experts are ability to adapt to one's environment and ability to learn, but IQ tests are not designed to measure either of these capacities. It seems reasonable to associate some of the capacities measured by IQ tests (such as information comprehension and certain kinds of abstract reasoning and problem solving) with intelligence, but in addition to analytical skills, intelligence is generally thought to include practical and creative abilities that IQ tests ignore. The Harvard psychologist Howard Gardner (1943–) has argued that there are in fact as many as eight distinct forms of intelligence. From this perspective, IQ tests should be seen as no more than a way of assessing one kind of intelligence. If intelligence encompasses a variety of distinct capacities, it is unlikely that overall intelligence can be meaningfully ranked on a single linear scale, and even if it could be, a person's IQ score would not be that measure.

Whatever capacities IQ tests measure, the hereditarian assumption that they are largely fixed by an individual's genetic inheritance is no longer tenable. Perhaps the strongest evidence that shows that changed environment can significantly influence IQs is the so-called Flynn effect, named after the intelligence researcher James Flynn (1934–). Flynn discovered that in every country for which there are reliable records, IQ scores have been rising steadily and significantly since the first tests were devised, although periodically the average score is adjusted back to 100. For example, U.S. children with average IQ scores in the 1930s would only score around 80 on today's scale. Because there has not been enough time for significant genetic change over this period, these results indicate that IQs can be dramatically raised by changed social and environmental factors. Other researchers have noted that the analytical abilities that the tests measure are repeatedly instilled by Western-style education, indicating both that they can be improved and that the tests may still be culturally biased.

IQ and Race

Since the earliest days of mental testing, there have been repeated claims that there are genetically based differences in intelligence between racial groups. These claims were revived in the late 1960s by the Berkeley educational psychologist Arthur Jensen (1923–) and more recently by the Harvard psychologist Richard Herrnstein (1930–1994) and the journalist Charles Murray (1943–) in their highly controversial 1994 book *The Bell Curve*. Jensen pointed to the fact that IQ test scores of Whites in the United States were on average 15 points above those of Blacks and argued that this gap reflects genetic differences between the groups because there is evidence that IQ is highly heritable. Jensen relied on published studies of identical twins by the British psychologist Cyril Burt (1883–1971) to claim that the heritability of IQ is 70%, but after Burt's death it was widely concluded that his data were fraudulent. More reputable studies since that time have yielded estimates of heritability in the United States ranging from 40% to 80%. However, as Jensen's critics pointed out at the time, the heritability of a characteristic (which is a measure of the amount of variation of a trait in a population due to genetic variance) tells us nothing about the explanation for differences in the characteristic between populations. For example, even if the heritability of height in corn plants is 100% and one group of plants is taller than another, the difference between the groups may be entirely due to environmental factors. Herrnstein and Murray acknowledged this but argued that there is indirect evidence supporting the view that the Black-White IQ gap has a significant genetic basis. The year after their book was published, a task force established by the American Psychological Association rejected this conclusion.

Critics of the view that the gap is rooted in genetics have argued that race is a category with no biological significance. The Harvard geneticist Richard Lewontin (1929–), for example, has shown that there is much more genetic variation within supposed racial groups than there is between them. These critics also note that races are socially constructed, making a biological explanation for cognitive differences between them implausible. Others have pointed out that the Black–White IQ gap in the United States has narrowed significantly over the past 30 years, suggesting that if environments and educational opportunities were truly equalized, it would disappear completely. One study found that Black children adopted by White families that provided more educationally stimulating environments had IQs that were 13 points higher than Black children adopted by Black families. Another study of German children fathered by, respectively, Black and White American GIs during the post-1945 occupation, found that there was no significant difference between their IQs.

IQ and Crime

In the early 20th century, numerous studies claimed that there was a strong correlation between low IQ and crime, identifying over half of convicted criminals and juvenile delinquents as "feeble minded," but by the 1930s this research had been rejected as worthless. Since the late 1970s, more reputable studies have found a weak correlation between low IQ level and certain kinds of criminal activity—specifically those offenses typically designated as "street crime" (robbery, burglary, arson, and crimes of violence). The correlation does not seem to be fully explained by the hypothesis that criminal offenders with low IQs are simply more likely to be apprehended and convicted, since a correlation remains between IQ level and self-reported crime. But because IQ tests are designed to correlate with school performance and poor school performance is correlated with participation in street crime, a correlation between IQ and street crime is unsurprising. Critics point out, however, that existing studies ignore individuals who engage in so-called white-collar and corporate crime, which may cause more damage to society than street crime, and whose perpetrators quite likely tend to have above-average IQs.

In *The Bell Curve,* Herrnstein and Murray argue that the correlation between IQ and street crime supports shifting resources away from social programs aimed at reducing poverty and unemployment or rehabilitating criminal offenders and focusing instead on tougher punishment as the most effective strategy for reducing crime. Following a detailed analysis of the data, however, Francis Cullen (1951–) and others conclude that Herrnstein and Murray greatly inflate the importance of IQ. When other criminogenic factors are taken into account, IQ is found to have only a very small effect on criminal behavior, explaining at best less than 4% of the variation in crime rates from one decade to another. Herrnstein and Murray also make the unwarranted assumption that IQ scores cannot be significantly boosted. Even if this assumption were true, the factors with the strongest effects on crime (such as associating with other delinquents who foster antisocial behavior) are also known to be changeable through appropriate intervention, including funding for programs of the kind that Herrnstein and Murray reject.

Conclusion

Scientific debate continues over the nature of intelligence and exactly what IQ tests measure. But there is no credible evidence that differences in IQ scores between racial groups have any significant genetic basis or that IQ levels are a significant factor in the explanation of crime.

Philip Gasper

See also Biological Theories; Family and Delinquency; Violent Crime

Further Readings

Cullen, F. T., Gendreau, P., Jarjoura, G. R., & Wright, J. P. (1997). Crime and *The Bell Curve*: Lessons from intelligent criminology. *Crime & Delinquency, 43,* 387–411.

Flynn, J. R. (2007). *What is intelligence? Beyond the Flynn effect.* New York: Cambridge University Press.

Gould, S. J. (1996). *The mismeasure of man* (Rev. & expanded ed.). New York: Norton.

Herrnstein, R. J., & Murray, C. (1994). *The bell curve: Intelligence and class structure in American life.* New York: The Free Press.

Montagu, A. (Ed.). (2002). *Race and IQ* (Expanded ed.). New York: Oxford University Press.

Sternberg, R. J., Grigorenko, E. L., & Kidd, K. K. (2005). Intelligence, race, and genetics. *American Psychologist, 60,* 46–59.

Jackson, George (1941–1971)

A criminal to some and a revolutionary hero to others, George L. Jackson was born in Chicago, Illinois, on September 23, 1941. In 1956 his family moved to Los Angeles, California. In 1960, at the age of 18, George Jackson was accused of stealing $70 from a gas station in Los Angeles. Jackson was advised to plead guilty for a lighter sentence. He took the plea and received an indeterminate sentence of 1 year to life. With no definite time for his release from prison, he served 11 years in the State of California correctional system, until his death in 1971. A leader of the Black Panthers, Jackson was an eloquent advocate for prisoners. This entry examines his life and legacy.

Black Panther Party

Jackson was an active member of the Black Panther Party, the revolutionary group started in 1966 by Huey P. Newton and Bobby Seale. The Black Panther Party's mission was to obtain economic, social, and political equality for Black people. The organization was considered radical because of their willingness to take up arms to fight for their cause. Although Jackson was behind bars and never participated in the Black Panther Party's police standoff or community rallies, he was one of best-known and most celebrated leaders in the party. Other Black Panthers thought of

him as a true revolutionary and regarded his life as a symbol of power and strength.

In 1966, while being held at the Soledad Prison (California), George Jackson founded the prison gang the Black Guerrilla Family. The gang was politically driven and founded on some of the principles of Marx and Lenin. The mission of the gang was to destroy racism, maintain dignity while incarcerated, and overthrow the U.S. government. The gang remains organized in many state and federal facilities around the United States.

Because he was very vocal, George Jackson was often held in solitary confinement to stop him from organizing prisoners. Because of his leadership skills and involvement with the Black Guerrilla Family and Black Panther Party, Jackson was often isolated for 24 hours in his cell.

While in isolation, Jackson spent a great deal of his time reading and writing. He used the information he learned to fight for the oppressed behind bars. Jackson read the texts of Marx, Lenin, Trotsky, and Mao and studied the works of W. E. B. Du Bois and Frantz Fanon. He believed they spoke the language of revolution. He transformed himself into a leader and advocate for prisoners.

In his well-received 1970 book, *Soledad Brother*, Jackson chronicled his life and his internal conflicts from 1964 to 1970 through his letters. These memoirs of his experience in prison provided people with an inside view of his struggles and provided a glimpse at how difficult it is to remain strong in the system. Many readers gained insight into his loneliness, illness, and his fight for manhood through the letters. His words would incite prison advocacy and shed light on the thousands of men and women whom Jackson believed were political prisoners. His letters allowed outsiders not only to empathize with his struggles but also to sympathize with the American prisoner.

In 1970, after Black inmates were shot and the officer who shot them was found to be justified, there was an uprising in the Soledad prison. During the riot a guard was beaten to death. George Jackson and two other prisoners, John Clutchette and Fleeta Drumgo, were charged with the correction officer's murder. The trial of the Soledad Brothers, held in San Rafael, California, was followed closely by the nation and many others throughout the world.

Jackson motivated many young men inside and outside of prison walls to wage war for their dignity, including his teenage brother. On August 7, 1970, Jonathan Jackson, at the age of 17, stormed the courtroom with a machine gun in an attempt to free the Soledad Brothers. Jonathan was shot and killed in the escape vehicle. George Jackson thought of his brother as a hero whose actions were just.

On August 21, 1971, a year after the killing of his younger brother, George Jackson was shot and killed in San Quentin Prison while allegedly attempting to escape. He was found carrying a gun, but it is still under dispute whether he was actually trying to escape or whether the entire event was staged.

Jackson's Legacy

Many convicts and inmates admired Jackson for his leadership and strength. His death sparked rebellions in prisons all over the country. The most famous was the Attica uprising on September 9, 1971. Prisoners took over Attica Correctional Facility in New York and made demands that led to negotiations with the state. On September 13, 1971, negotiations were called off. In the takeover, the state police opened fire, and 29 prisoners and 10 hostages were killed.

Jackson's writings inspired many movements and revolutionary action. In 1975, the George Jackson Brigade was formed. The brigade was an armed guerrilla group that operated in the Pacific Northwest. The group was responsible for several bombings and bank robbery attempts throughout Washington State. The group was not an all-Black organization, and half of the members were women. Many were working-class citizens and ex-convicts. The George Jackson Brigade was shattered by the government. Easter Sunday, 1978, would be one of their last political actions. Many were killed or imprisoned during standoffs with the police, and others were forced to go underground.

George Jackson's determination and uprisings like the one in Attica inspired inmates around the country to stand up for their rights. Furthermore, his life and legacy forced correctional facilities to give more rights to prisoners. George Jackson's life stood as a symbol of revolutionary change.

Teresa Francis

See also Attica Prison Revolt; Black Panther Party; Political Prisoners

Further Readings

George Jackson Brigade. (1970). *The power of the people is the force of life: Political statement of the George Jackson Brigade.* Montreal, QC, Canada: Abraham Guillen Press.

George Jackson Brigade. (2003). *Creating a movement with teeth: Communiques of the George Jackson Brigade.* Montreal, QC, Canada: Abraham Guillen Press.

Jackson, G. (1970). *Soledad brother: The prison letters of George Jackson.* Chicago: Lawrence Hill Books.

Jackson, G. (1990). *Blood in my eye.* Baltimore: Black Classic Press.

Seale, B. (1970). *Seize the time.* Baltimore: Black Classic Press.

Wald, K. (1971). *Remembering the real dragon: An interview with George Jackson May 16 and June 29, 1971.* In W. Churchill & J. J. Vander Wall (Eds.), *Cages of steel: The politics of imprisonment in the United States.* Retrieved from http://historyisaweapon .com/defcon1/jacksoninterview.html

JAMAICAN POSSE

Jamaican posse is the name that is collectively used to refer to different coalitions of Jamaican nationals involved in illegal gang activities in the United States as well as other regions in the world. In the 1980s various Jamaican posse groups became increasingly and notoriously popular among law enforcement agents in the United States for their involvement in organized criminal activities. Known for their impenetrable criminal networks, sophisticated criminal techniques, and international illegal involvements, the Jamaican posses added a new dimension to the race and crime nexus in the United States. This entry presents information on the criminal enterprise of Jamaican posse groups and illustrates the impact these culturally diverse groups of immigrants have on race, crime, and ethnicity issues in the United States. Details on the origins and Jamaican roots of posse members, their formidable presence in the United States, their multiple and ingenious illegal involvements, and their eventual arrest and prosecution by law enforcement agents are presented.

Jamaican posses have been intricately linked to political parties and politically established communities in Jamaica. In fact, the names used to identify some Jamaican posse groups are names of politically segregated communities in Jamaica. Nevertheless, the direct connections and influential affiliations between U.S.-based posse groups and political parties in Jamaica have been debated. Some researchers believe that although posse members originally had strong ties to political parties in Jamaica, their political loyalties and affiliations with these parties diminished over time as they became more settled and concentrated in various parts of the United States. Conversely, others have claimed that their political and social ties to Jamaica remained strong, and profits made from drug sales and other illegal activities in the United States were used to financially support the two dominant political parties and home communities of posse members.

During the late 1970s and early 1980s, political civil unrest and escalating violence, along with dire economic hardships in Jamaican communities, led to the migration of thousands of Jamaicans to the United States. Once in the United States, the Jamaican posses created and established extensive drug and criminal networks. Posse members were at first heavily involved in the sale and distribution of marijuana, and they competed with other posse groups over the control and statewide distribution of the drug. Although each Jamaican posse had its designated leaders in different urban and suburban jurisdictions, the major posse groups were predominately

situated in Jamaican communities in Miami and New York. Two well-known and established Jamaican posse groups in the United States are the Spanglers posse and the Shower posse. Many of their early drug operations went undetected by law enforcement agents and involved minor violent incidents. In time, this changed as the Jamaican posse groups turned their attention to the sale and distribution of crack cocaine, which was not only in high demand at that time but also more profitable than marijuana.

By the mid-1980s Jamaican posses became some of the most organized and lethal drug gangs in the United States. At this time, their criminal networks and organized criminal involvements had grown exponentially and internationally to include other illegal activities, such as the production of fraudulent immigration documents, money laundering, and firearms trafficking. It is estimated that hundreds of Jamaican immigrants had joined different posses and were actively involved in the local and international drug trade in the United States, England, Jamaica, and other Caribbean countries. It is believed that the Jamaican posses were responsible for hundreds of murders, largely within immigrant communities. Posse groups were further involved in interstate and international transshipment of large quantities of high-powered guns that were used in killings in the United States and Jamaica. Jamaican posses were found to be actively operating in at least 11 cities in the United States.

Their entrance into the crack industry resulted in brutal slayings and intergroup retaliatory violence among rival drug dealers. Their involvements in the crack and powder cocaine market led to increased competition and territorial control for drug markets. Eventually, the battle over money, power, and dominance became a racially concentrated crime problem in many core communities across U.S. states where Jamaican posse groups had established their drug operations. Law enforcement investigations, studies, and reports on Jamaican posse groups have revealed that it was their callous and torturous methods of killings that distinguished Jamaican posse groups from other criminal groups in the United States. Given the criminal lifestyle of Jamaican posses, they were labeled by law enforcement agents as one of the most structured and dangerous Black criminal organizations in the United States.

Jamaican posses were viewed as a national threat and problem in the United States. It took a team of law enforcement agents and diligent work by the Bureau of Alcohol, Tobacco, Firearms and Explosives in 1987 to eradicate several Jamaican posse groups. Operation Rum Punch was a nationwide raid specifically formed to arrest, prosecute, and dismantle members of the Jamaican posse groups. This collaborative effort against the posses involved teams of federal, state, and local law enforcement from different states and agencies. The raid successfully led to the arrest of hundreds of posse members and the permanent elimination of many posse groups. Although some Jamaican posse groups remain active today, their presence and illegal involvement are minimal. Notwithstanding the fact that they are no longer a looming problem compared to what they were when they started their criminal enterprise, the presence of Jamaican posses uniquely demonstrates a different type of race and crime phenomenon in the United States because they were Jamaican immigrants who bonded to create a tight-knit criminal enterprise that engaged in crimes that were varied and extensive in nature.

Patrice K. Morris

See also Drug Dealers; Drug Trafficking; Immigrants and Crime; Organized Crime

Further Readings

Gunst, L. (1995). *Born fi' dead: A journey through the Jamaican posse underworld.* New York: Holt.

McGuire, P. (1988). Jamaican posses: A call for cooperation among law enforcement agencies. *Police Chief, 55,* 20–54.

JAPANESE INTERNMENT

When the Japanese Navy attacked Pearl Harbor on December 7, 1941, the United States entered World War II. The sudden and deliberate attack not only mobilized the U.S. military into action, but federal, state, and local authorities began the process of moving Americans of Japanese ancestry away from the West Coast and Hawai'i. This entry describes the process of Japanese internment, from the first wave of roundups to the return of Japanese Americans to their homes after the war. In addition, it briefly traces the legacy of the internment and discusses redress and reparations that occurred in the latter part of the 20th century.

Pearl Harbor's Immediate Effects

While the U.S. military mobilized for action against the forces of the Axis powers (Germany, Italy, and Japan), local authorities and the Federal Bureau of Investigation began to round up Issei (first-generation Japanese immigrant) leaders in the Japanese American communities in Hawai'i and on the mainland. In the first two days following the Pearl Harbor attack, nearly 1,300 men of Japanese ancestry were rounded up and placed in custody. These men were not held under formal charges, but family members were forbidden to see them. Most spent the war years in enemy alien internment camps run by the U.S. Department of Justice.

Two months later, on February 19, 1942, President Roosevelt signed Executive Order 9066, which allowed military authorities to exclude any group of people from any region for reasons of "military necessity." Executive Order 9066 provided the legal authority behind the mass removal of Japanese Americans from the West Coast.

To assist in the removal, the War Relocation Authority (WRA) was created in March 1942. Shortly thereafter, Congress criminalized the disobedience of military regulations. In other words, failure to abide by curfew orders and exclusion orders meant that criminal sanctions would be applied. The WRA issued exclusion orders for Japanese Americans up and down the West Coast to move out of their homes. Throughout the spring and summer of 1942, civilians of Japanese ancestry and Japanese American citizens (Nisei, or second generation) were forcibly removed from Seattle to San Diego. Most had to sell their property, vehicles, furniture, and businesses for much less than their value. Furthermore, they had few details about where they were headed and how long they would be away.

Assembly Centers and Relocation Camps

A majority of the civilians were taken to a local "assembly center" or temporary detention camp. The most famous assembly centers were racetracks in California—Santa Anita Racetrack in Arcadia and Tanforan Racetrack outside of San Francisco. Detainees cleaned out the horse stables and lived there until "relocation centers" or internment camps could be built in seven states.

A total of 10 major relocation centers housed Japanese and Japanese Americans during the war years. Throughout the summer of 1942, civilians were transferred by train or bus from the assembly centers to the desert and high country (Manzanar and Tule Lake, California; Amache, Colorado; Minidoka, Idaho; Topaz, Utah; Heart Mountain, Wyoming; Poston and Gila River, Arizona) or swampland in Rohwer and Jerome, Arkansas.

Life in the Internment Camps

Life for many in the camps was difficult. About 8,000 to 13,000 people lived in each camp. Residents could bring only a few personal belongings, usually what they could carry. The permanent camps were hastily constructed and initially offered few amenities. Temperatures were high in the summer and cold in the winter.

Barbed wire fences and guard towers with armed sentries surrounded the camps. Living facilities were organized in barracks, composed of four to six rooms. Each room (20 x 25 feet) housed one family (usually two to five people). Eating, bathing, laundry, and recreation facilities were communal. Furniture was made from construction scraps and mattresses from straw. Later, conditions improved as internees could order clothing and other amenities from mail-order catalogues.

Food was a major concern of the internees. The quantity, quality, and distribution of food were insufficient throughout the camps. Fresh meat and vegetables were rare commodities until the camps began to produce their own toward the end of the war. Health care was also a concern as there were only a handful of doctors in each camp.

Of the approximately 120,000 people under WRA control, 90,500 were transferred from assembly centers; 17,500 were taken directly from their homes; 6,000 were born to imprisoned parents; 1,700 were transferred from Immigration and Naturalization Service internment camps; 1,600 were moved after being sent from assembly centers to work crops; 1,300 were transferred from penal and medical institutions; 1,100 were taken from Hawai'i; and more than 200 mostly non-Japanese spouses entered the camps voluntarily.

Eventually, the WRA allowed internees to leave under certain conditions, especially to engage in farming, education, and permanent employment. By 1943 the WRA designated five categories of internees who could leave the camps: seasonal workers, students, those who found nonseasonal employment, armed services volunteers, and individuals thought to be "disloyal" to the United States (these "disaffected" internees were removed to segregated camps or prisons).

Japanese Americans in the Armed Forces

Despite the injustices of the internment, many Japanese Americans sought to show their loyalty to the United States by joining the military service. Unfortunately, after Pearl Harbor the U.S. War Department declared the Nisei unacceptable for military service. The Selective Service changed their classification from 1-A to 4-C ("enemy alien") and exempted them from the draft. Those who were already serving (about 6,000) were immediately dismissed. This action created difficulty for the War Department in Hawai'i, for a number of National Guardsmen were ethnic Japanese or Hawaiian Nisei. Because the military needed the manpower and were impressed by the Hawaiian Nisei's desire to prove their loyalty, by June 1942 a special Nisei Battalion of about 1,500 men—the 100th Battalion—was formed and moved to the mainland. Later that year, the 100th began fighting in Italy.

In 1943 the War Department began to organize a volunteer Japanese American unit and activated the 442nd Regimental Combat Team. Approximately 2,300 Nisei volunteered from the internment camps and joined the army. Others enlisted after they left the camps, while others from Hawai'i filled the ranks. During the war period, about 25,000 Nisei were registered and about 21,000 were inducted. Over 33,000 Japanese Americans served in the U.S. Army during World War II.

The 100th Battalion and the 442nd Regimental Combat Team fought in France and were involved in the invasion of Germany. Other units were returned to Italy during the balance of the conflict and performed important mop-up and other duties. Members of the 522nd Field Artillery were among the advance Allied troops that penetrated southern Germany and were involved in the liberation of the Dachau concentration camp outside Munich. The 442nd became one of the war's most decorated combat teams, receiving seven Presidential Distinguished Unit Citations and earning over 18,000 individual decorations, including 19 Congressional Medals of Honor, 53 Distinguished Service Crosses, 350 Silver Stars, 810 Bronze Stars, and more than 3,600 Purple Hearts.

In addition to the Japanese Americans who served as soldiers in the army, some were recruited and volunteered for a little-known unit known as the Military Intelligence Service. Prior to Pearl Harbor, a few army intelligence officers realized that if a war came, the army would need Japanese language interpreters and translators. In November, 1941, a secret language school was established at the Presidio of San Francisco to teach Japanese to carefully selected U.S. soldiers, most of whom were of Japanese ancestry. The school, called the Military Intelligence Service Language School, moved during the war, first to Camp Savage, Minnesota, then to Fort Snelling, Minnesota. After World War II, the school was reestablished at the Presidio in Monterey, California, as the Defense Language Institute.

Graduates of the school served on active duty in the Pacific theater as interpreters and helped to decode intercepted Japanese battle orders. They wrote pamphlets urging Japanese Imperial troops to surrender and were active in the battles of Iwo Jima and Okinawa, many times exposing themselves to especially hazardous duty trying to convince Japanese soldiers in caves to come out and surrender.

After the Japanese surrender in August, 1945, many Japanese American members of the Military Intelligence Service were involved in the occupation of Japan and performed valuable services in the reconstruction of Japan. By 1946, approximately 6,000 of the total 33,000 Japanese Americans who had served were associated with the Military Intelligence Service.

Returning Home

A few months before the end of World War II, internees were allowed to leave the camps. Of the 120,000 internees, less than half (about 54,000) returned to the West Coast after their incarceration. About 53,000 relocated to the interior of the United States, and nearly 5,000 moved (or were moved) to Japan. About 2,400 joined the armed forces, 1,900 died during imprisonment, and 1,300 were sent to other institutions.

Redress and Reparations for Internment

From the late 1960s to 1988, Japanese Americans sought and obtained an apology from the U.S. government for the internment and reparation payments for time served in the camps. In 1967 Edison Uno, a Nisei, began an informal campaign to educate the public and lobby legislatively for reparations of former internees. His effort, which became known as the redress movement, galvanized support among the Nisei and Sansei (third-generation Japanese Americans) communities.

The redress movement proceeded along three political channels: executive, legislative, and judicial. On the executive front, intense lobbying led to the 1976 repeal of Executive Order 9066 by President Gerald Ford. Legislatively, members of Congress from California and Hawai'i created the Commission on Wartime Relocation and Internment of Civilians, which intensively studied the reasons for the internment and its subsequent harm to U.S. citizens. Its report, *Personal Justice Denied*, showed the governmental racism that drove the removal of Japanese from the West Coast. Judicially, two lawsuits brought the internment to light. In 1983, William Hohri, with other internees, filed a class action suit accusing federal officials of conspiring to deprive Japanese Americans of their rights during the war. Known as the *Hohri* case, the suit was ultimately dismissed by the federal courts as untimely.

The second lawsuit, known as the *coram nobis* cases, reopened the *Korematsu*, *Yasui*, and *Hirabayashi* decisions of the 1940s. In the original cases three individuals were convicted of violating curfews and failing to abide by the exclusion of an area because of military necessity. In the 1980s a team of attorneys and Fred Korematsu, Min Yasui, and Gordon Hirabayashi sought to reverse their convictions through *coram nobis* proceedings. The trial courts that originally convicted them nullified their convictions 40 years later.

The confluence of executive, legislative, and judicial pressure led to the successful passage of the Civil Liberties Act of 1988. In August 1988, President Ronald Reagan signed the act into law. The Civil Liberties Act acknowledged the "fundamental injustice of the evacuation, relocation, and internment" and "apologized on behalf of the people of the United States" for those actions. Further, the act stated that the internment was "motivated largely by racial prejudice, wartime hysteria, and a failure of political leadership." Restitution in the amount of $20,000 for each surviving internee was authorized. Reparations payments along with a presidential letter of apology began in 1991 and ended in 1998.

Following the Civil Liberties Act of 1988, Japanese American organizations lobbied for and obtained a parcel of federal land on the Washington, D.C., mall near the U.S. Capitol to build a memorial to the internees and war heroes. A national fundraising campaign eventually led to the construction of the Japanese American Memorial to Patriotism During World War II. In November 2000 the memorial was officially dedicated and opened to the public. The memorial is located within three blocks of the U.S. Capitol.

Craig D. Uchida

See also Asian Americans

Further Readings

Daniels, R. (1993). *Concentration camps, North America: Japanese in the United States and Canada during World War II*. New York: Krieger.

Irons, P. (1983). *Justice at war: The story of the Japanese American internment cases*. New York: Oxford University Press.

U.S. Commission on Wartime Relocation and Internment of Civilians. (1997). *Personal justice denied: Report of the Commission on Wartime Relocation and Internment of Civilians*. Washington, DC: Government Printing Office.

Yamamoto, E. Y., Chon, M., Izumi, C., Kang, K., & Wu, F. (2001). *Race, rights, and reparations: Law and the Japanese American internment*. New York: Aspen Law & Business.

Websites

Go For Broke National Education Center: http://www.goforbroke.org

Japanese American Citizens League: http://www.jacl.org

Japanese American Veterans Association: http://www.javadc.org

National Japanese American Memorial Foundation: http://www.njamf.com

JENA 6

For years, racial tensions simmered in the small, rural Louisiana town of Jena. In August 2006 an incident there sparked marches and national discourse on the judicial system and race. This entry examines the circumstances surrounding the incident, the activism sparked by the incident, and the implications of the incident on the following youth who became known as the Jena 6: Robert Bailey, Jesse Ray Beard, Mychal Bell, Carwin Jones, Bryant Purvis, and Theo Shaw.

At Jena High School, White students generally gathered under a large shade tree, referred to as the "White tree," while African American students usually sat on the bleachers. After a Black student asked the principal at an assembly for permission to sit under the tree and the principal indicated that anyone could sit there, a few Black students did so. The next day, nooses were hung from the tree. A few days later, a protest under the tree by African American students prompted school administrators to call the student body into an assembly. District Attorney Reed Walters told the students that if further disruptive behavior occurred, it would become a criminal matter. The teenagers were arrested and remained in jail until September 2007.

Racial tensions escalated at the high school as a result of the incident with the hanging nooses. In a fight between six African American students and two White students, one of the White students, 17-year-old Justin Barker, was beaten and suffered a concussion. District Attorney Walters charged all six of the Black students with attempted second-degree murder and conspiracy. The students, who ranged in age from 15 to 17, faced up to 80 years in prison without parole. All six students were athletes; five were on Jena's high school football team.

Bell, who was 16 at the time, was the first student to go on trial. He was a football star who hoped to get an athletic scholarship to attend college. It was widely reported that he was an honor student and did not have a prior criminal record. Later, it was learned that Bell had had trouble with the judicial system and was on probation for two counts of battery and criminal damage to property. Bell was not granted bail and remained in jail for a considerable length of time before finally being released in September 2007. He was tried as an adult and convicted of aggravated battery as well as conspiracy. Although his conviction was later overturned, it was not without considerable publicity concerning the judicial system in Jena, Louisiana. On September 20, 2007, the Reverend Al Sharpton, Reverend Jesse Jackson, Martin Luther King III, radio commentator and lawyer Warren Ballentine, and many others converged on the small community to protest the charges and gross disparity in the sentencing that Bell and the other students faced. Sharpton, Jackson, and King led an estimated 20,000 protesters through the streets of Jena. Protesters came from all over the country for the march. Ki-Afi Moyo, organizer of the Dallas-based Internet community "Tx Supports Jena Six," described the protest as a rebirth of the civil rights movement. His group chartered 20 buses and brought 2,000 protesters to Jena.

The three White students involved in hanging the nooses were suspended and initially faced no charges, but after mounting criticism, they were charged with a misdemeanor. Principal Scott Windham had recommended the expulsion of the three students, but the decision was reversed by Superintendent Roy Breithaupt and the Board of Education. When asked if racism played a key role in the sentencing of Bell and the other defendants, Walters noted that no attention had been given to the victim and the serious injuries he had sustained as a result of the beating. In addition to the concussion, Barker suffered a swollen eye.

Many African American residents contend racism remains a major issue in a town that is about 85% White. Over the years, there have been other incidents both in the community of Jena and at the high school. African American residents believe that the latest injustices involving these teenagers further illuminate conditions in a community that has not moved beyond the 1960s in its racial relations. Some residents feel that the school administrators are to blame for allowing the incident with the nooses to escalate and for not handing out the appropriate discipline. They believe that by taking action against the White students, school administrators could have prevented the legal predicament that Bell and the other teenagers confronted.

Media sources called attention to the all-White jury that heard Bell's case. Two potential African American female jurors were not selected. One did not report for jury duty because she had not received her notice in the mail; the other was a sister of one of the defendants.

Though Walters repeatedly denied that the seeking to prosecute the teenagers to the fullest extent of the law was not based on their race, others suggest otherwise. African American residents reiterated that race is very much an issue and had divided the town even before the events of Jena 6. Moreover, civil rights advocates pointed out that despite Walters's reducing the charges to aggravated battery, the punishment did not fit the crime and the charges were excessive.

To get Walters to reopen the case against Bell, the Congressional Black Caucus asked the U.S. Department of Justice to look into the case. In July 2007 the caucus sent a letter to then-Governor Kathleen Blanco asking her to pardon Bell, who by this time was 17 years old. The letter, which also appeared on the Congressional Black Caucus blog, stated the following:

> This tale of two standards depicts a pattern of gross violations. First, it is unfair to punish only the African American students when all the students involved must be taught to take responsibility for their actions. Next, the charges of attempted murder and conspiracy against the African American students carry an 80-year sentence; such punishment far exceeds the offense. Additionally, the judge set outrageously high bails, ranging from $70,000 to $138,000, resulting in the juveniles being stuck in jails for months. The district attorney and the judge are abusing their power and removing the blindfold of justice.

The racial hotbed that burned for over nine months in Jena should have been contained by school and elected officials. Instead, the students were left to battle this rage without institutional support or resources.

Some residents, both African American and White, felt that the case against Bell, Bailey, Beard, Jones, Purvis, and Shaw was fair. These residents claimed that the media attention heightened racial tension in the community and that divisiveness along the color line was highly exaggerated by the media and civil rights leaders.

After Bell's release, there were concerns that he and his family, as well as the other teenagers and their families, might be targeted by White supremacists, as there had been recent threats made to the parties involved. However, no incidents were reported and after languishing in jail for well over a year, Bell was finally reunited with his family. As part of a plea agreement with Walters, who agreed to drop the conspiracy to commit battery charges against him, Bell pleaded guilty to second-degree battery as a juvenile and was sentenced to 18 months in the custody of the Office of Youth Development. He would serve the 18-month sentence concurrently with a sentence he received in another case. Additionally, he was ordered to pay court and restitution costs as well as the medical bills from Barker's visit to the emergency room, which amounted to well over $5,000. Because Bell has received the most attention, it is unclear from diverse media outlets what has happened to the other teenagers, but the consensus is that once-promising futures have essentially been ruined by the egregious charges.

The Jena 6 case has opened further scrutiny into the practices of how other African American male teenagers are being treated by the judicial system. Jena 6 has forced America to once again examine the role of race in the judicial system. Ultimately, cases such as Jena 6 point to systematic and institutional problems inherent in the judicial process that can be eradicated by acknowledging that in some jurisdictions, there are two justice systems in this country: one Black and the other White.

Yvonne Sims

See also Culture Conflict Theory; Disproportionate Arrests; Interracial Crime; Juvenile Crime

Further Readings

American Civil Liberties Union. (n.d.). *Jena Six cases* [Fact sheet]. Retrieved September 20, 2008, from http://www.aclu.org/racialjustice/racialprofiling/31880 res20070917.html

American Civil Liberties Union. (2007, November 20). *Background: Jena 6*. Retrieved from http://www.aclu .org/racialjustice/racialprofiling/31881res20070920.html

Brown, A. (2007, December 4). *Bell admits role in attack*. Retrieved from http://www.thetowntalk.com/ apps/pbcs.dll/article?AID=/99999999/NEWS/ 399990133

Color of Change. (n.d.). *Justice for the Jena 6*. Retrieved August 28, 2008, from http://colorofchange.org/jena/ message.html

Farwell, S. (2007, September 20). North Texans marching behind 6 young men in Jena. *Dallas Morning News*. Retrieved November 19, 2008, from http://www .dallasnews.com/sharedcontent/dws/dn/latestnews/ stories/092007dnmetjenasetup.3645e08.html

Fears, D. (2007, August 4). La. town fells "White tree," but tension runs deep: Black teens' case intensifies racial issues. *The Washington Post*, p. A03. Retrieved November 19, 2008, from http://www.washington post.com/wp-dyn/content/article/2007/08/03/ AR2007080302098.html

Kilpatrick, C. C. (2007, July 26). *The Congressional Black Caucus calls for blind and fair justice in Jena Six case*. Message posted to http://www.house.gov/ htbin/blog_inc?BLOG,mi13_kilpatrick,blog,999, All,Item%20not%20found,ID=070726_1016, TEMPLATE=postingdetail.shtml

John Jay College Center on Race, Crime and Justice

The Center on Race, Crime and Justice, located at John Jay College of Criminal Justice, City University of New York (CUNY), is a multidisciplinary entity created to examine the critical issues at the intersection of race/ethnicity, crime, and justice. Emerging out of the need to study the contentious nature of crime and justice in the United States and its connection to issues of race and inequality, the center's main function is to publicize, produce, and disseminate empirical research surrounding various topics related to race, crime, and justice. The center's goal is to improve the educational experiences of the students and faculty of John Jay College as well as address the concerns of surrounding communities. Embracing sophisticated research agendas, the center aims to develop sound policies that address both systemic and inadvertent bias in the criminal justice system. In the future, the center plans to collect, measure, and analyze data in the area of police use of fatal force and to establish a national database.

Through a visiting scholars program, community partnerships, and collaborative efforts within the college and across the university, center participants conduct funded research focused on major issues related to understanding crime and justice in a diverse society. The findings from these research efforts are disseminated through center-sponsored colloquia and workshops designed to help faculty incorporate discussions of racial and social justice within their course content. John Jay students at every level are encouraged to participate in the research process.

History

Under the leadership of its interim director (now director), Delores Jones-Brown, and with the support of President Jeremy Travis and Dean James Levine, the center began its strategic planning in November 2004. The Center on Race, Crime and Justice was formally established on October 11, 2005. In an effort to integrate the center into the totality of the college, a steering committee was established, bringing together faculty members across disciplines; the committee included the college president, provost, doctoral program executive officer, dean of the Office of the Advancement of Research, and chairs and/or faculty members from seven departments. Other faculty members associated with the center embrace a comprehensive approach to the study of race, crime, and justice and conduct extensive research in these areas.

The first of the center's events culminated in a 2-day planning symposium, held February 18–19, 2005, and funded by a planning grant from the Annie E. Casey Foundation, in which the steering committee received expert advice on the center's mandate and organization. Nine scholars from interdisciplinary academic fields and colleges,

community activists, and policy researchers were invited as lead scholars to present concept papers highlighting a suggested mission, focus, and activities for the center. Many grassroots organizations, not-for-profit agencies, and potential funders concerned with issues of race, crime, and justice were also present and provided valuable input in developing the center's mission and goals.

In the spring of 2007, the center welcomed its first visiting scholar, Toni Irving, Assistant Professor of English at the University of Notre Dame. Irving is working on a book titled *Disciplining Bodies: Black Female Sexuality and Citizenship From Jim Crow to the Patriot Act*. Irving's research focuses on the intersection of gender, race, class, and criminal justice and pulls from over 2,000 sexual assault cases of low-income Black women and girls ignored and not investigated in Philadelphia between 1995 and 2000.

Center Events

The center held an inaugural colloquium on December 13, 2005, in which Professors Richard Delgado and Jean Stefancic of the University of Pittsburgh School of Law presented the inaugural address titled "The Role of Critical Race Theory in Understanding Race, Crime and Justice Issues." The center celebrated the 75th anniversary of the infamous Scottsboro Alabama rape case and the 30th anniversary of the pardon of Clarence Norris, the last Scottsboro defendant, with a commemorative symposium titled "Scottsboro Then and Now: The Perpetual Struggle for Justice in the United States." The keynote address was delivered by civil rights attorney Fred Gray, Sr., of Tuskegee, Alabama.

Since its inception, the center has organized numerous faculty-led research discussions covering a range of topics, including African American women's experience with violence and violation, Black resistance to the Ku Klux Klan, African American chronology, and the historical and political implications of the use of the "N" word. Addressing the complex nature of the death penalty in the United States, the center sponsored a series of events (i.e., conferences, lectures, panels and research discussions), including "The Death Penalty in Black and White," which featured David Kaczynski and Bill Babbitt, whose personal stories shed light on the arbitrary nature of the death penalty; "Race and Death Penalty Research," which presented recent developments in quantitative research on the role of race in capital sentencing; and "A Child in the Electric Chair," highlighting the execution of 14-year-old African American George Stinney, Jr., the youngest child to be put to death in the United States under modern statutes.

The center held an "after innocence" party featuring the award-winning documentary, *After Innocence*, which chronicled the lives of men exonerated and released from prison based on DNA evidence. David Shepard, an exoneree from New Jersey featured in the film, was present to answer questions along with Alan Newton, who was exonerated after serving 22 years; Newton is currently a student at Medgar Evers College, CUNY. To highlight the injustice of the November 25, 2006, shooting of three unarmed minority males, including Sean Bell in the New York City borough of Queens, the center held an emergency forum featuring the award-winning film *Another Mother's Son* to allow students, faculty, community members, and criminal justice officials to address their concerns regarding police accountability and community relations.

Publications

The center's forthcoming publications include an anthology tentatively titled *Writings at the Intersection of Race, Crime and Justice*, which compiles original and reprinted manuscripts from John Jay faculty and a special issue of articles presented at the Scottsboro symposium to be published in the *Journal of African American Studies*. In the future, the center will continue to tackle sensitive issues that address the complex nature of race, crime, and justice in our increasingly diverse society.

An annotated listing of publications by center faculty and visiting faculty is available on the organization's website, along with a bibliography on race and crime.

Kideste M. Wilder-Bonner

See also Police Use of Force; Racialization of Crime

Further Readings

Jones-Brown, D., & Levine, J. P. (2005). *Systematic planning for a center on race, crime and justice to be established at John Jay College of Criminal Justice, City University of New York* (Annie E. Casey Foundation final progress report). New York: CUNY Research Foundation.

Websites

Center on Race, Crime and Justice: http://www.jjay.cuny .edu/centersinstitutes/racecrimejustice

JOHNSON V. CALIFORNIA

The United States currently has more than 5,000 adult prisons and jails, each with its own design features, staffing ratios, design and operational capacity, offender population, and resource level. In these facilities, administrators are responsible for maintaining order and preventing violent incidents. Risk assessment and classification are useful tools for managing inmate populations, and since 2005 they have become even more critical for prison culture as U.S. jails and prisons are no longer able to segregate inmates—based on their racial and/or ethnic background alone—for extended periods of time within the institution. According to the Commission on Safety and Abuse in America's Prisons:

> Reducing violence among prisoners depends on the decisions corrections administrators make about where to house prisoners and how to supervise them. Perhaps most important are the classification decisions managers make to ensure that housing units do not contain incompatible individuals or groups of people: informants and those they informed about, repeat and violent offenders and vulnerable potential victims, and others who might clash with violent consequences. And these classifications should not be made on the basis of race or ethnicity, or their proxies. (Gibbons & Katzenbach, 2006, p. 29)

This entry examines the U.S. Supreme Court decision in *Johnson v. California* (2005), which examined the constitutionality of segregating inmates based on race.

The *Johnson* case stemmed from the unofficial policy of the California Department of Corrections (CDC) of segregating new inmates, two per cell, for a 60-day evaluation and assessment period. In testimony before the Court, officials from the CDC asserted that the rationale behind pairing inmates in cells by race or ethnicity during the risk assessment and classification period was to offset potential violence caused by racial gangs existing within the state's correctional system. The key questions facing the Court were whether institutional security overrode the prohibition of segregating public institutions imposed by its decision in *Brown v. Board of Education* (1954) and whether this temporary housing of inmates by race or ethnicity constituted "segregation" as defined in *Brown*. Indeed, lower court testimony included confirmation that a number of states utilize the "pairing" of inmates of the same race or ethnic background for a limited duration (from hours to days) when an inmate is transferred to a new facility. However, inmate background characteristics are considered ahead of race or ethnicity in these circumstances, such as type of offense, age, and gang affiliation (if any). California's unwritten policy of segregating by race or ethnicity for as long as 60 days was unique in American corrections.

The U.S. Ninth Circuit Court of Appeals ruling was based on the traditionally recognized "institutional needs" of correctional facilities that justify restrictions on the individual rights of inmates. Broadly categorized, these institutional needs include maintenance of institutional order, maintenance of institutional security, safety of prison inmates and staff, and rehabilitation of inmates. The Ninth Circuit ruled that prisoner safety and institutional control were legitimate correctional interests, and therefore, any infringement upon the plaintiff's individual rights was superseded by the interests of the facility and did not violate the equal protection clause of the Fourteenth Amendment. Counsel for the State of California had successfully argued that the CDC's policy could be interpreted as falling under the institutional needs of order maintenance and security and therefore should not be reviewed under the standard of "strict scrutiny." Strict scrutiny is the most

stringent standard of judicial review within a hierarchy of standards that U.S. courts use to weigh asserted government interests against the constitutional rights of citizens.

Johnson's attorneys petitioned the Supreme Court arguing that the Ninth Circuit "erred in failing to apply 'strict scrutiny' and asking that the CDC be required to demonstrate that the policy is narrowly tailored to serve a compelling state interest." The Court stopped short of labeling the CDC's policy unconstitutional; rather, the case was remanded back to the Ninth Circuit for ruling under strict scrutiny guidelines.

Some observers found the Supreme Court's action in *Johnson* curious in that the Court had 30 years prior established a "balancing test" for similar lawsuits that weighed prisoners' rights claims against the legitimate needs of prisons (*Pell v. Procunier*, 1974). Some had gone as far as to say that the Supreme Court absolved itself of the challenges associated with ruling on this case by failing to invoke the balancing test itself and by remanding the case back to the Ninth Circuit. The case is also noteworthy in that the Ninth Circuit, which covers northern California, is usually seen as the most liberal U.S. Circuit Court in the nation, yet it upheld a public institution's policy of segregating individuals on the basis of race, ethnicity, or both.

The implications of *Johnson* for correctional management, both in California and nationwide, are yet to be determined. Advocates of the Supreme Court's decision in *Johnson* argue that the CDC's policy was shortsighted, even absent the temporary segregation of inmates by race. Most would agree that race or ethnicity alone is not an optimal quality by which to classify inmates, as the sort of tensions and conflicts the CDC was hoping to quell could result from numerous differences between inmates of the same race or ethnicity—CDC administrators testified to this assertion in court. Thus, from a managerial standpoint, the policy may have been flawed before it had even become a prisoners' rights case. In response, the Department of Justice developed a set of standards to be included in a performance measurement system for state correctional facilities. Standard 4 relates to the development of "offender profiles," and within this standard, demographic characteristics are but one of five "context indicators" for assessing institutional performance.

While assessments of *institutional* performance may not be at the top of the priority list for prison administrators, the criteria outlined also serve as a more useful tool for *inmate* assessment. A majority of state correctional systems use this multivariate approach to classification and risk assessment and did so prior to the *Johnson* legal proceedings. It is likely that a renewed emphasis on assessment of inmates at intake will replace the CDC's policy of race-based placement.

Don Hummer

See also Prison, Judicial Ghetto; Prison Gangs; Sentencing

Further Readings

Byrne, J. M., & Hummer, D. (2007). In search of the "tossed salad man" (and others involved in prison violence): New strategies for predicting and controlling violence in prison. *Aggression and Violent Behavior, 12,* 531–541.

Gibbons, J. J., & Katzenbach, N. de B. (2006). *Confronting confinement: A report of the Commission on Safety and Abuse in America's Prisons.* New York: Vera Institute of Justice. Retrieved from http://www.prisoncommission.org/pdfs/Confronting_Confinement.pdf

Johnson v. California, 543 U.S. 499 (2005).

Pell v. Procunier, 417 U.S. 817 (1974).

Robertson, J. E. (2006). Foreword: "Separate but equal" in prison: *Johnson v. California* and common sense racism. *Journal of Criminal Law and Criminology, 96,* 795–848.

Robinson, B. N. (2006). *Johnson v. California:* A grayer shade of *Brown. Duke Law Journal, 56,* 343–375.

Schmalleger, F., & Smykla, J. O. (2009). *Corrections in America* (4th ed.). New York: McGraw-Hill.

Taylor, J. (2004). Racial segregation of California prisons. *Loyola of Los Angeles Law Review, 37,* 139–152.

Wright, K., Brisbee J., & Hardyman, P. (2003). *Defining and measuring performance.* Washington, DC: U.S. Department of Justice.

JURY NULLIFICATION

Serving on a jury is considered to be a duty of all American citizens. Jury nullification exists when a jury ignores the facts presented in court, the legal aspects of the case, or both, and votes based on conscience, personal values and beliefs, or preconceived biases and prejudices. Through jury nullification, a jury has the power to bring about a verdict that is outside of what is expected or required by facts and law. This entry examines jury nullification by presenting it within the contexts of its history, race, ethnicity, and its future use in the criminal justice system.

History

In the initial stages of building the modern-day American criminal justice system, the concept of a "jury of peers" was introduced in the court system. This concept, still promoted today, was intended to ensure that a defendant would be judged fairly by presenting the case to a group of common citizens. These citizens are specifically not involved in the legal profession so as to be completely objective in the case at hand. The burden of proof is the responsibility of the prosecution, and the defendant is presumed innocent until proven guilty. This type of trial is and continues to be a cornerstone of the American criminal justice system.

Jury nullification was adopted by Americans and used as early as the 17th century. Its use was originally based on the common law and British antecedents that viewed the role of the jury to include judging the law and the facts. If jurors believed a conviction was unjust, they were not compelled to convict. Throughout American history, jury nullification was considered a protective device for some citizens. During the 19th century, jury members sometimes used nullification in capital punishment and fugitive slave cases in the North. In 1895 the U.S. Supreme Court ruled in *Sparf and Hansen v. United States* that nullification was acceptable. Over time jury nullification, though rarely used, has received more attention. Several cases during the 1990s, including the trials of former Mayor Marion Barry and O. J. Simpson, raised issues regarding whether or not juries composed of minority members (e.g., African American, Latina/o), would be more likely to acquit a minority defendant regardless of the facts of the case presented in court.

Race and the Jury

Citizens that serve on juries are considered to be peers of the defendant. Systematic discrimination that occurred in the early stages of the evolution of criminal justice excluded both women and minorities from jury pools. In *Strauder v. West Virginia* (1880), the Supreme Court held that excluding Blacks violated the equal protection clause of the Fourteenth Amendment, but this right was not systematically enforced until much later. In the 1940s, Congress approved of minorities serving on juries, even though it was much later when equal opportunity in jury duty actually occurred. Since the late 1960s, juries have become more representative of the communities and citizens they serve even though jury selection may not lead to equal representation if the jury pool is ethnically diverse. In some jurisdictions, minorities are still underrepresented in the jury pool and excluded during the voir dire. In others, where minorities are the majority of the population, the jury pool is predominantly minority.

Paul Butler was one of the first lawyers to identify the issue of race and jury nullification. During training for federal prosecutors in Washington, D.C., he was told that some Black jurors would not convict guilty Black defendants. For Butler, race-based jury nullification resulted from the larger issue of how race matters in the legal system. Butler offers several explanations to help understand why, in some situations, Black jurors ignore the evidence and acquit someone who is guilty. He believes that African Americans have a moral right and obligation to protest unjust laws and to be guided by what is just in cases involving nonviolent crimes.

Conclusion

The ability of juries to determine that defendants should not be punished for their acts, regardless of whether or not they broke the law, is controversial. Many argue that jury nullification has tainted the traditional jury by allowing such power to be exploited for personal or cultural use. Others argue that jury nullification is a myth and that color sensitivity and prejudice naturally occur in juries regardless of race. In spite of the controversy, nullification is not frequently used. More research is needed to better understand race and jury nullification.

Jennifer Lasswell

See also Jury Selection; O. J. Simpson Case

Further Readings

Butler, P. (1995). Racially based jury nullification: Black power in the criminal justice system. *Yale Law Journal, 105,* 677–725.

Free, M. D., Jr. (Ed.). (2003). *Racial issues in criminal justice.* Westport, CT: Praeger.

Horowitz, I. A. (1985). The effect of jury nullification instruction on verdicts and jury functioning in criminal trials. *Law and Human Behavior, 9*(1), 25–36.

Otto, C. W., Applegate, B. K., & Davis, R. K. (2007). Improving comprehension of capital sentencing instructions: Debunking juror misconceptions. *Crime and Delinquency, 53,* 502–517.

Schuetz, J., & Lilley, L. S. (Eds.). (1999). *The O. J. Simpson trials: Rhetoric, media, and the law.* Carbondale: Southern Illinois University Press.

Strauder v. West Virginia, 100 U.S. 303 (1880).

Weinstein, J. (1993). Considering jury "nullification": When may and should a jury reject the law to do justice? *American Criminal Law Review, 30*(2), 239–254.

JURY SELECTION

The jury selection process is one of the most important components in the American criminal justice system; however, it has been questioned whether court participants receive a fair trial under the present process. Juries have often not been representative of defendants' peers. Some argue that this reinforces group stereotypes and leads to biased verdicts and sentences, especially in cases involving race. This entry examines the controversy surrounding race and the jury selection process, paying particular attention to case law, racial bias, and scientific research.

The Jury Selection Process

The Sixth Amendment of the U.S. Constitution guarantees that in all criminal prosecutions, the accused is guaranteed the right to a speedy and public trial by an impartial jury in the state in which the crime was committed. The Supreme Court has held that the purpose of the Sixth Amendment is not only to guard against governmental power exercised by overzealous prosecutors and judges but also to protect litigants and defendants from jurors who are unwilling or incapable of rendering unbiased verdicts in a court of law (see *Peters v. Kiff*, 1972).

Voir dire is the process by which jurors are determined unbiased and therefore suitable to serve on a jury. During voir dire, potential jurors can be struck from selection either "for cause" or peremptorily. "For cause" challenges require proof that potential jurors cannot view the case without bias or that their biases may prevent them from making decisions based solely on the evidence presented at trial. In contrast, peremptory challenges allow counsel to eliminate potential jurors without reason.

In theory, peremptory challenges allow counsel to excuse a juror who may be biased against their clients or may not support a favorable outcome, even if the judge has rejected a "for cause" removal. In practice, the peremptory challenge has caused a great deal of controversy. Opponents of the peremptory challenge argue that the use of group stereotypes during jury selection perpetuates bias and stigmatizes certain groups during voir dire. In addition, these critics maintain that peremptory challenges are often used as a pretext to dismiss jurors because of their race, thus creating an atmosphere of suspicion and disbelief among potential jurors, members of the court, and society as a whole.

Case Law, Jury Selection, and Race

To remedy discriminatory practices that have affected defendants' right to a fair and impartial jury and to eliminate racially based exclusions in the jury selection process, the Supreme Court has delivered several important rulings. *Swain v. Alabama* (1965) held that the state's intentional denial of jury participation on the basis of race violated the rights of the defendant as guaranteed by the equal protection clause of the Fourteenth Amendment for defendants. The ruling, however, did not ensure that a particular jury would reflect the racial diversity of the community in the

jurisdiction where the trial was held. The Constitution does not guarantee defendants the right to a proportionate number of jury members of their race. In addition, the *Swain* decision determined that it was the defendants' burden to demonstrate a systematic pattern of discrimination involving the use of peremptory challenges in order to have a valid Fourteenth Amendment challenge. Some have claimed that this portion of the ruling made it difficult (or impossible) for defendants to prevail.

In *Batson v. Kentucky* (1986), the Supreme Court reaffirmed the *Swain* decision. The Court continued to stress that using peremptory challenges to excuse prospective jurors based solely on race was impermissible; however, the Court held that potential jurors were also denied equal protection under the Fourteenth Amendment if they were excluded from jury service because of their race, thus shifting the focus from the rights of defendants to the rights of potential jurors. In addition, the *Batson* Court held that the standard in *Swain* had been too restrictive. Prior to *Batson*, practices such as handing out instruction books to prosecutors advising them to eliminate minorities from the jury had been common. *Batson* established that defendants would have a claim of discrimination if there had been purposeful racial discrimination demonstrated by the prosecutorial use of peremptory challenges to remove potential jurors of the defendant's race. The Court, however, did not establish the criteria for proving purposeful racial discrimination, thereby making it difficult for lower courts to determine precisely what factors were necessary to prove that potential jurors were excluded for permissible reasons and not because of racial discrimination.

The Court extended the basic structure of *Batson* in two subsequent cases, holding that striking potential jurors on the basis of ethnicity (*Hernandez v. New York*, 1991) or gender (*J.E.B. v. Alabama*, 1994) was also prohibited. More recently, the Court reaffirmed these holdings in *Miller-El v. Dretke* (2005) and *Johnson v. California* (2005). Thus, the Court continues to emphasize that it is impermissible to exclude potential jurors based on race, ethnicity, or gender but resists establishing clear guidelines for lower courts to use in determining what constitutes an improper use of peremptory challenges.

Racial Bias and Jury Selection

Considering these rulings, one would assume that the practice of eliminating members of the jury pool based on race would be eradicated; however, doing so requires that the courts both recognize and confront racist attitudes and actions within the criminal justice community. Research suggests there is substantial racial bias within the jury selection process. The literature suggests that both the prosecution and the defense adopt parallel group stereotypes in the jury selection process as they believe they know which racial group will best serve their case. Counsel base their decisions on perceptions about the relationship between the racial composition of the jury and the outcome of the trial, despite the fact that there is little evidence that the jury's racial composition alone can predict the outcome of a trial. In reality, peremptory challenges are often based on information that is, at best, based upon weak predictions about the relationship between race and juror decisions. Nevertheless, court actors continue to use hunches and inaccurate stereotypes when selecting juries.

Critics of the jury process note that race continues to play an important role in jury selection, regardless of Supreme Court decisions. These scholars argue that racial discrimination against potential jurors remains pervasive throughout the selection process. They argue that *Batson* does more to enhance the appearance of fairness in the jury selection process than it does to ensure a racially unbiased method of seating a jury. One scholar observed that given the pervasive use of challenges to eliminate jurors based upon their race, one would expect there to be a profuse number of appeals relating to the jury selection process; however, national studies find that claims of discrimination on this ground are rare in both state and federal courts. Moreover, when these claims are raised, they are rarely successful. Thus, it appears that the practice of eliminating potential jurors because of their race is a widespread practice and that judges accept the practice. Rather than delving into whether attorneys are discriminating against potential jurors, judges are likely to accept peremptory challenges without question.

There is little motivation for judges to address the use of racial bias in the jury selection process.

Addressing the use of racial pretexts would create an extra workload for an already overburdened court system. The only remedy that the courts are willing to impose for using racial bias in peremptory challenges involves seating a new jury. Limiting courts to this remedy means that the misuse of peremptory challenges can be corrected only by a time-consuming process of selecting a new jury, if possible; this may be seen as compromising the defendant's right to a speedy trial. As a result, sanctioning attorneys for such abuses are seen as unproductive; nevertheless, sanctions could ensure that attorneys might be less inclined to misuse such challenges in the future.

Research on Jury Selection and Race

Historically, legal scholarship examining the issue of race and jury selection rarely has relied upon social science research. Attorneys are rarely trained in social science methodologies and often are unfamiliar with the basic research in the field. As a result, they may rely upon hunches, stereotypes, gut feelings, and past experiences to guide the jury selection process.

Although social science research was generally ignored in the jury selection process until the early 1970s, newer studies and jury pool consultants have advanced the state of knowledge in the field. These studies generally use attitudinal scales and assessments of background characteristics to test for relationships among variables, using mock juries or focus groups to identify significant associations that might affect the outcome of a trial. These variables then are used in the voir dire process to identify potential jurors who may provide a favorable outcome for counsel; however, research on actual or potential jurors is relatively rare.

Research on the effect of race in the jury selection process can be categorized into four general methodologies: (1) archival analyses of actual verdict outcomes, (2) mock jury experiments that simulate the jury process, (3) surveys about perceptions of the jury process, and (4) interviews and surveys of jurors and potential jurors. These varying methodologies have produced mixed results. Most existing research, however, suggests that minority defendants are viewed in a more negative light than are White defendants. Research on mock juries and archival studies support this conclusion. Likewise, research on attitudes toward the judicial system and jury selection provides evidence that many African Americans view the system as biased and unfair. African Americans also are more likely to support the idea that juries need to be racially representative to ensure fair outcomes. Finally, research on potential jurors finds that African Americans report more bias in the justice system. Ironically, they also do not believe they are more likely to be excused from jury service because of their race, despite the fact that they appear to be disproportionately excused by prosecutors. Other important factors besides race, however, also appear to affect these views, including age, income, and general perceptions of system fairness.

Although there has been a recent increase in the research conducted on the connection between racial bias and the jury selection process, many believe that additional research in this area is needed. Mock jury studies provide important information in the area, but these studies are merely substitutes for research on actual jurors. With the limited number of studies on juror perceptions, conclusive evidence on the subject and solutions to the problems cannot be obtained. Additional research should focus on increasing sample sizes, response rates, and participation by minorities. In addition, studies need to be more representative of the general population. Current studies overrepresent Whites, higher-income individuals, and those who have actually shown up for jury service. These studies also underrepresent minorities, especially those who are not of African American descent.

Although the Supreme Court has held that excluding potential jurors on the basis of race is impermissible, and critics have argued that race plays an undeniable role in peremptory strikes, empirical examination of the issue remains limited. Not only is more research needed, but research also needs to address the issues in a more complex way. The criminal justice system is a complex organism that has many branches. If we are to gain a better understanding of perceptions of racial bias in the system, it is imperative that we begin to reject the notion that these views can be assessed by examining a single encounter with one aspect of this complex system.

Tammy S. Garland, Helen Eigenberg,
and Karen McGuffee

See also Batson v. Kentucky; Jury Nullification; *Norris v. Alabama*

Further Readings

Bader, C. G. (1996). *Batson* meets the First Amendment: Prohibiting peremptory challenges that violate a prospective juror's speech and association rights. *Hofstra Law Review, 24,* 567–621.

Baldus, D. C., Woodworth, G., Zuckerman, D., Weiner, N. A., & Broffitt, B. (2001). The use of peremptory challenges in capital murder trails: A legal and empirical analysis. *University of Pennsylvania Journal of Constitutional Law, 3,* 4–170.

Batson v. Kentucky, 476 U.S. 79 (1986).

Charlow, R. (1997). Tolerating deception and discrimination after *Batson. Stanton Law Review, 50,* 9–64.

Hafemeiser, T. L. (2000). Supreme Court examines impact of errors in detecting bias during jury selection. *Violence and Victims, 15*(2), 209–224.

Hurwitz, J., & Peffley, M. (2005). Explaining the great racial divide: Perceptions of fairness in the U.S. criminal justice system. *Journal of Politics, 67,* 762–783.

Levine, J. P. (2000). The impact of racial demography on jury verdicts in routine adjudication. In M. Markowitz & D. Jones-Brown (Eds.), *The system in Black and White: Exploring the connections between race, crime and justice* (pp. 153–170). Westport, CT: Praeger.

McGuffee, K., Garland, T. S., & Eigenberg, H. (2007). Is jury selection fair? Perceptions of race and the jury selection process. *Critical Journal of Crime, Law and Society 20*(4), 445–468.

Ogletree, C. (1994). Just say no! A proposal to eliminate racially discriminatory uses of peremptory challenges. *American Criminal Law Review, 31*(4), 1099–1151.

Rose, M. R. (1999). The peremptory challenge accused of race or gender discrimination? Some data from one county. *Law and Human Behavior, 23*(6), 695–702.

Rose, M. R. (2003). Symposium: III. The jury in practice: A voir dire of voir dire: Listening to jurors' views regarding the peremptory challenge. *Chicago-Kent Law Review, 78,* 1061.

JUVENILE CRIME

Children in American society have, historically, been regarded as innocent beings who are still at a relatively early stage of their development and are behaviorally, cognitively, and emotionally immature. Society is keen to impute to children all of the characteristics that are believed to represent the vulnerable nature of childhood—goodness, inexperience, and blamelessness; consequently, when children violate the law, social sensibilities are offended. It is inconceivable that one so young could commit so horrendous an act as robbery, rape, or murder. Yet juveniles (as the law regards those who have not yet reached the age of majority in a given jurisdiction) commit crimes varying from the more trivial (such as truancy or petty vandalism) to the gravest (such as arson or homicide), and the law has established mechanisms to deal with those eventualities. This entry examines the types of behaviors that constitute juvenile crime, as well as the characteristics of juveniles who are most frequently arrested for their unlawful actions, and concludes with a brief overview of possible explanations for juvenile crime. It is noteworthy that a significant proportion of these juveniles are individuals of color, and accordingly, criminologists continually strive to explore the relationship between race and formal processing by the justice system.

Defining Juvenile Crime

Generally, the definition of juvenile crime comprises three elements: age, behavior, and adjudication. In other words, to be described as a juvenile delinquent, an individual must be of a certain age, have behaved or acted in a way that has been designated as unlawful, and have been formally processed and given the label of a juvenile criminal or delinquent.

Age

Depending on the particular jurisdiction, the *age* criterion may vary. State statutes prescribe the upper and lower limits of the jurisdiction of the juvenile court, thereby signifying the age at which a juvenile can first be held legally culpable for his or her actions (the age of responsibility) as well as the age at which a juvenile is automatically excluded from juvenile court jurisdiction. Children younger than the age of responsibility are presumed to be incapable of forming *mens rea* (criminal intent) and consequently are ineligible to be prosecuted for their actions. Any individual who

has attained the age of responsibility but who is younger than the age of majority as dictated by state statute may be regarded as a juvenile.

Conduct

The second element in juvenile crime pertains to the wrongfulness of the *conduct* involved; in other words, whether or not the action that has been committed constitutes a crime. The same behaviors that are considered unlawful or criminal if engaged in by adults are likewise regarded as unlawful or criminal if engaged in by juveniles. Additionally, juveniles are precluded from engaging in certain behaviors that are permissible if engaged in by adults, such as truancy, drinking, smoking, running away from home, having undesirable companions, and being disobedient to parents and teachers. These behaviors are called status offenses and are considered to serve as an early warning system of potential risk; a juvenile who drinks, smokes, skips school, and runs away from home is believed to demonstrate by his or her actions that something is amiss at home or at school and that, if left untreated, further problematic behavior may ensue. Action is believed to be warranted, then, in the juvenile's best interest as well as in the interest of public order and safety.

Adjudication

Finally, unlawful behavior by young people is not officially classified as juvenile crime until it has been formally ascribed that label through the process of *adjudication*. Since 1899, a juvenile justice system has existed to handle the formal processing of young offenders who are presumed, by virtue of their actions, to require some measure of court intervention. The creation of the juvenile court in Cook County, Illinois, at the end of the 19th century was the culmination of the widespread efforts of a group of social reformers who called themselves the Child Savers. These middle-class philanthropists and activists, many of them women, viewed children's lawbreaking behavior as the byproduct of poor parenting and exposure to corruptive influences, and they believed that a special paternalistic body should be put in place to ensure that children were shown the error of their ways and set back on the path to righteous action.

Thus the juvenile court, as initially conceived, was designed to function along the lines of the doctrine of *parens patriae*, where the State would assume quasi-parental status in determining how best to treat a particular child and prevent future recidivism. The aim of the juvenile justice system as it was first created was to provide individualized treatment and care for young offenders instead of subjecting them to the punishment that invariably would be doled out if they were treated as adults. In recent years, some criminologists have argued that crime prevention and deterrence measures aimed at juvenile offenders have become increasingly punitive and that the original philosophy of the creators of the juvenile court has been gradually eroded. Indeed, the actions of some juveniles are seen as so egregious that it is believed the juvenile court system as initially conceived is ill equipped to address them appropriately, and consequently, the juvenile court system has in place a variety of mechanisms whereby particular practitioners (namely, judges, prosecutors, or even legislators) can waive jurisdiction over specific groups of individuals on the basis of certain aggravating factors; these individuals, then, would be tried as adults in the criminal justice system. Regardless of the specific system in which adjudication takes place, it is only following formal processing that the wrongful behavior of a young person can officially be called "juvenile crime."

Statistics on Juvenile Crime in the United States

Despite media reports that persistently convey the impression that juvenile crime rates continue to increase and that the American public is currently faced with a new breed of juvenile superpredators, the likes of which have never previously been seen, statistical data actually reveal that the reverse is true. According to *Juvenile Offenders and Victims: 2006 National Report,* published by the Office of Juvenile Justice and Delinquency Prevention (OJJDP), the arrest rate for violent juvenile crime has declined consistently over the past 10 years and continues to do so to the extent that it currently stands at its lowest since at least the 1970s. Likewise, downward trends in the commission of property crimes by juveniles suggest that juveniles generally are committing fewer

delinquent and criminal acts than in previous years, with the exception of weapons law violations and drug offenses.

Not all juveniles commit crimes at the same levels of frequency and severity. Juvenile crime is overwhelmingly a male phenomenon, with the majority of offenses being committed by boys. Until relatively recently, the presumption was that girls are simply uninvolved (or at least involved to a lesser degree) in such activities as gang behavior and bullying, but criminologists now recognize that girls simply commit these crimes in different ways than boys do. For example, while boys tend to bully utilizing direct, aggressive means (such as kicking, punching, hitting, stealing, and so on), girls resort to more indirect, insidious methods (such as spreading malicious gossip, ostracizing individuals, proposing dangerous dares, and others). As a result, girls' behavior is less likely to be identified by teachers and school administrators as bullying, and fewer recorded instances of their actions are likely to follow. Nonetheless, despite these challenges in identifying and recording violent acts by girls, the OJJDP has reported that while juvenile violence overall has been decreasing, the proportion of female violent crime arrestees has increased, particularly for assault.

Similarly, juveniles who commit crimes are not equally likely to be arrested for their unlawful conduct; minority juveniles are disproportionately likely to be arrested and formally processed. The OJJDP estimates that the rate of arrest of African American juveniles in 2004 for violent crime was more than 4 times the rate of arrest for White juveniles and for Native American juveniles and almost 10 times greater than the rate of arrest for Asian American juveniles. This disparity, however startling, has declined since the 1980s, at which time African American juveniles were arrested for violent crime at more than 6 times the rate of arrest for White juveniles. Arrests for property crimes in 2004 also revealed a disparity among racial and ethnic groups, albeit somewhat lower. African American juveniles were arrested for property crimes at 2 times the rate of White juveniles and Native American juveniles and 4 times the rate of Asian American juveniles. Debates continue to transpire among criminologists as to whether this differential rate of arrest of juveniles for the commission of both violent and property crimes is due to institutional racism within the criminal and juvenile justice systems or to the increased criminality or delinquency among members of minority groups who are statistically more likely to be faced with a multitude of social problems such as poverty, unemployment, and poor educational opportunities.

Explaining Juvenile Crime

Explanatory factors to account for juvenile crime range from those focusing on the individual—such as a child's genetic makeup, neurological deficits, personality disorders, subconscious psychological conflict, and even biochemical agents that may be ingested through diet or environmental pollutants—to those focusing on the social environment. Sociological theories of juvenile crime may fall into one of two categories: those based on social structure and those based on social process. First, theories of *social structure* posit that individuals may engage in criminal behavior as a result of the social strain caused by economic disparities or other inequities that are the by-product of the social and political system. Those children who grow up in impoverished, rundown housing and who are judged by their teachers according to middle-class values and experiences may find that they never quite measure up. In retaliation, and in an attempt to rebel against the sense of frustration and dejection that they may experience, they may reject those middle-class norms and standards and become instead everything that those who espouse middle-class ideals seem to revile. They may, in a sense, deliberately become drug dealers or thieves to flout the middle-class ideology that they feel has let them down.

Other sociological perspectives focus less on the individual's place in the social structure and more on the importance of relationships, or *social process*. These approaches examine the role that various agents, such as the family, the school, the church, the peer group, and to some extent the media, play in the socialization process as an individual learns the cultural norms and mores of a given society. The family is the primary agent of socialization. Parents dictate not only the rules by which a child must live but also the child's exposure to other agents of socialization. For example, parents determine what kind of school a child will attend and may further affect the choice of school by where they opt to live. This decision will ultimately impact the kind of education that a child receives and the extent to which he or she identifies with academics. In short, the home environment may be the most influential factor in shaping the kind of individual a child grows up to be, as the family is a force that can either inhibit or promote delinquency. Those children who are raised in homes that are nurturing, warm, and loving are likely to feel connected and to become positively attached, clear-headed, future-oriented individuals; conversely, those children reared in environments characterized by strife, conflict, and constant bickering are more predisposed to becoming anxiously attached, impulsive, and exhibiting low self-control.

One of the areas of greatest debate centers around the link between broken homes (those family environments in which one parent is permanently absent) and criminality, the main premise being that if a child's development is disrupted through abandonment, divorce, separation, or death, then that disruption is likely to result in cognitive, affective, or psychological problems. Moreover, there is some concern that with only one parent present (and probably obligated to work), the amount of time a child spends unsupervised may lead to problematic behavior. The counterargument to this position suggests that, first, homes with parents who are abusive or argumentative may provide a far more dangerous environment to a developing child than those homes where a parent is absent; and, second, that in many instances, older siblings, after-school care providers, or other appropriate adults may provide the necessary alternative supervision to keep a child out of trouble.

Leanne Owen

See also Female Juvenile Delinquents; Juvenile Waivers to Adult Court; Myth of a Racist Criminal Justice System; Sentencing; Violent Juvenile Offenders; W. Haywood Burns Institute for Juvenile Justice Fairness and Equity; Youth Gangs; Youth Gangs, Prevention of

Further Readings

Huizinga, D., & Elliott, D. S. (1987). Juvenile offenders: Prevalence, offender incidence, and arrest rates by race. *Crime and Delinquency, 33,* 206–233.

Muncie, J. (2004). *Youth and crime*. Thousand Oaks, CA: Sage.

O'Mahony, D. (2000). Young people, crime, and criminal justice: Patterns and prospects for the future. *Youth and Society, 32*, 60–80.

Snyder, H. N. (2006). *Juvenile arrests 2004*. Retrieved from Office of Juvenile Justice and Delinquency Prevention: http://www.ojjdp.ncjrs.gov/publications/PubAbstract.asp?pubi=236114

Snyder, H. N., & Sickmund, M. (2006). *Juvenile offenders and victims: 2006 national report*. Retrieved from Office of Juvenile Justice and Delinquency Prevention: http://ojjdp.ncjrs.org/ojstatbb/nr2006/index.html

JUVENILE DRUG COURTS

Juveniles and adults have historically been treated differently in the criminal justice system. On the basis of the notion that juveniles are more amenable to treatment, alternative forms of corrections and sanctions for young offenders have been developed over time. Juvenile drug courts are just one of many examples of alternative ways in which *some* juveniles under the age of 18 are handled in the criminal justice system. This entry presents a summary of the history, organization, and effectiveness of juvenile drug courts, as well as an examination of racial and ethnic cleavages in these courts.

History

Juvenile drug courts came into existence in response to a rise in the number of juvenile drug arrests clogging the judicial system in the 1990s. This was also occurring in the midst of the rise in court systems that were developed to handle special cases. Some examples of boutique court systems include gun control courts, adult drug courts, domestic violence courts, and mental health courts.

Juvenile drug courts provide a departure from the traditional juvenile justice systems insofar as they looked at arrests as a sign of a larger problem in need of intervention and treatment. That is, drug offenses were seen as less of a criminal issue and more of a symptom of a larger drug use problem. Buttressed against this change in perspective

regarding drug arrests, juvenile drug courts also redefined the role of the judge, lawyer, and accused, thus creating a cooperative environment that tries to pool key players in community services together with those in the justice system in order to rehabilitate rather than punish the offender.

Juvenile drug courts were originally developed to provide services to young drug users in a way that brought together individuals from myriad social service programs. These individuals, prosecutors, defense attorneys, judges, drug treatment providers, and social workers, work together to establish the best course of action for young offenders.

Organization

Previous scholarship has indicated that there are five principles that differentiate juvenile drug courts from other judicial systems. First, juvenile drug courts provide immediate intervention. As compared to other systems of justice that are habitually slow to process and apply sanctions, drug courts are supposed to be expedient and thus try to provide services as soon as possible to the offender. Second, they are nonadversarial in nature. Rather than organized like a traditional trial where the prosecution and defense present their case, this nonadversarial approach is more holistic in nature and includes the participation of treatment providers. Third, they require a certain amount of judicial involvement that goes beyond simple decision making to active participation in the determination of what is best for the accused. As part of the nonadversarial approach, judges can ask questions and play a central part of managing the case. Fourth, juvenile drug courts also incorporate treatment programs into the judicial system that have structure and well-defined organizational objectives. Finally, these court systems include lawyers, caseworkers, judges, treatment providers, and others into the sentencing phase.

Even though these principles are used by scholars to differentiate between juvenile drug courts and other systems of justice, extensive research has uncovered the fact that no juvenile court system is exactly like the next. Each state has its own system, and each county has its own way of implementing programs and handling offenders. Accordingly, there is significant variation in the kinds of program available, treatment facilities used, and resources put into curtailing juvenile drug use and crime.

Effectiveness

Given the growth in popularity of juvenile drug courts, much research has been conducted to evaluate whether participation in drug court programs reduces recidivism and drug use among juveniles. The results of these studies have demonstrated mixed findings, and theoretical explanations for the varied results are also inconclusive. Most of the scholarship in this area is divided into three camps. There are those who say drug treatments issued by juvenile drug courts are effective at reducing future arrests and subsequent drug use. A second camp of scholars suggests that these programs do not work but rather cast a net so broadly that they actually increase the likelihood of juveniles testing positive for minor drug infractions and criminal events. In the final camp are scholars who believe that these programs neither help nor hurt juveniles and are no more effective in reducing recidivism and drug use than preexisting programs or doing nothing at all.

Racial and Ethnic Cleavages

The impact of drug courts and treatment programs is highly suspect to many scholars who study the intersection of race and crime. Their research has continually found that the impact of such programs exacerbated preexisting cleavages among Whites and ethnic/racial minorities. Youth who are from poor, less-educated, and minority heritages are less likely to be diverted into drug court programs, receive adequate services, and succeed in these programs. The data suggest that ethnic minorities are less likely to complete the programs they are sent to and more likely to test positive for harder drugs than are their White counterparts. There is no conclusive evidence that this can be fully attributed to differences in drug-using behavior. In general, scholarship that has looked specifically at the effectiveness of drug courts has been inconclusive.

Jennifer Christian

See also Drug Courts; Drug Treatment; Drug Use by Juveniles; Juvenile Crime; Juvenile Waivers to Adult Court

Further Readings

Rodriguez, N., & Webb, V. J. (2004). Multiple measures of juvenile drug court effectiveness: Results of a quasi-experimental design. *Crime & Delinquency, 50,* 292–314.

Sampson, R. J., & Laub, J. H. (1993). Structural variations in juvenile court processing: Inequality, the underclass, and social control. *Law & Society Review, 27,* 285–311.

Sloan, J. J., III, & Smykla, J. O. (2003). Juvenile drug courts: Understanding the importance of dimensional variability. *Criminal Justice Policy Review, 14,* 339–360.

JUVENILE WAIVERS TO ADULT COURT

Juvenile waiver is a process that permits transfer of jurisdiction over juveniles to the adult court system. A waiver system for serious violent and/ or habitual juvenile offenders has been created by legislative initiatives in all 50 states and the District of Columbia. Juvenile waivers are sometimes referred to as either transfers or certifications and are based on the assumption that some crimes by juveniles are so serious that they warrant criminal prosecution. However, juvenile waivers represent a departure from the original goals of the juvenile justice system, which focused on protecting and rehabilitating youth offenders. Critics of juvenile waivers also argue that they have had a dramatic impact on increasing the rate of disproportionate confinement of minority youth. This entry first reviews the development of the American juvenile justice system and juvenile waivers. It then describes the "get tough" philosophy toward juvenile offenders that emerged during the latter part of the 20th century. Lastly, the entry presents types of waivers and examines race and the impact of juvenile waivers on minorities, especially African American youth.

Development of the American Juvenile Justice System

The American juvenile justice system grew out of the efforts of early reformers, who emphasized the welfare of children and recognized the diminished mental capacity of children relative to adults and involvement in criminal or delinquent activity. Following the English, early reformers accepted the common law practice that prevented any child under the age of 7 from being found criminally liable. Children between the ages of 7 and 14 enjoyed similar protection from criminal liability unless proven to the contrary. Reformers advocated for moral and educational training of children and the elimination of arbitrary forms of punishment. To salvage the lives of juveniles and ensure the tranquility of society, early American reformers also adopted the concept of *parens patriae* (i.e., the State as the ultimate parent), age classifications for delinquent juveniles, youth institutions, and apprenticeship programs.

Early efforts to save children fostered the creation of the first house of refuge in New York City in 1825. A primary aim of the houses of refuge was to provide facilities for children only. Despite the noble origins, it was not long before institutions began housing nonoffending and offending juveniles, without due process of law, until their 21st birthday. During the 19th century, African American youth were not afforded the same opportunities for rehabilitation. Segregation and limited resources were common. At the time, it was common practice for youth to be placed in the homes of (White) families as a form of punishment and rehabilitation; African American youth were harder to place than were White youth. Before and after the Civil War, African American youth continued to be treated as adults and did not receive more lenient treatment until after the creation of the first juvenile court in the United States in Cook County, Illinois, in 1899.

By 1925, all but two states had passed laws establishing juvenile courts. By this time, child savers who were concerned with the well-being of American youth were instrumental in creating juvenile facilities. Although most juveniles were treated like adults prior to the reform efforts in the 19th century, the importance of separating them from adults in facilities and courts was recognized and accepted in the 20th century. Since the creation of juvenile courts, they have retained the right to waive juvenile offenders to adult court and did so. One criticism of the juvenile court movement was the failure to recognize juveniles' rights to due process during juvenile hearings. To remedy this, the U.S. Supreme Court established due process rights for juvenile delinquents during the 1960s. Cases such as *Kent v. United States* (1966), *In re Gault* (1967), *In re Winship* (1970), *McKeiver v. Pennsylvania* (1971), and *Breed v. Jones* (1975) established constitutional rights, including, but not limited to, the right to counsel, freedom from self-incrimination and double jeopardy, the right to cross-examine witnesses, and the right to due process. *Kent v. United States* and *Breed v. Jones* provided due process guarantees during waiver proceedings.

It was during the mid-1980s that the use of waivers increased as a result of several factors, including rising rates of delinquency, juvenile arrests for violent crimes, and acceptance of the prevailing "nothing works" doctrine that diminished the importance of rehabilitative approaches.

Emergence of a "Get Tough" Philosophy Toward Juvenile Crime

The "get tough" approach to juvenile offending resulted in setbacks for the juvenile justice system and the youth it seeks to salvage. Advocates of rehabilitation argue that getting tough on crime by waiving and sentencing juveniles to adult correctional systems is an illogical approach by justice officials and legislatures. They criticize the get tough philosophy embodied in juvenile waivers and adult imprisonment policies for failing to take into account research suggesting that inferior socioeconomic conditions are causal factors of juvenile crime and delinquency. In spite of opposition, waivers have emerged as an important tool in efforts to prevent and control juvenile delinquency.

Some support for the impact of the get tough movement on juvenile waivers is found in the reported data on waivers. According to the Office of Juvenile Justice and Delinquency Prevention, the number of waivers steadily increased between the mid-1980s and mid-1990s and then began to decrease, a reflection of decreases in reported juvenile crime between 1994 and 2004. Fewer cases were waived in 2001 and 2002 compared to 1985. With the exception of the years 1989 through 1991, when drug offense cases were waived more often, between 1985 and 2002 most cases that were waived were for person offenses.

The get tough movement assumed that treating juveniles like adults would deter juvenile crime. Even though there are few recent national studies, the available research on the effect of waivers on deterrence and recidivism is mixed. Some recent studies report limited general and specific deterrence and increases in recidivism for juveniles waived when compared to juveniles adjudicated in juvenile courts.

Types of Juvenile Waivers

Juvenile waivers may take one of three forms: judicial, prosecutorial, or legislative. With a judicial waiver, the juvenile court judge is the primary decision maker as to whether the juvenile is deemed appropriate for adult prosecution. The judicial waiver takes place in the form of a hearing. The prosecutor requests that the juvenile court judge waive the court's jurisdiction over the youth's violation and transfer the matter to adult court for criminal prosecution. The decision of the judge is typically based on what is referred to as a "goodness of fit" test. This test routinely considers several factors that include, but are not limited to, the juvenile's age, prior offenses, amenability to future treatment, family status, past treatment failures, present offense seriousness, and the need for public safety. The three criteria bearing most weight in the decision are age, present offense seriousness, and amenability to future treatment. A youth's assessment regarding amenability to future treatment is normally determined by primary factors that include psychological testing, the availability of alternative dispositions, and the time available for treatment or sanctions. Despite established criteria, states vary in the flexibility afforded judges in determining judicial waiver. Some states grant complete discretion to the judge, whereas other states either outline circumstances under which judicial waivers are mandatory or establish presumptions in favor of judicial waivers. This type of waiver was the initial primary method of transfer for most states.

A prosecutorial waiver is another type of juvenile waiver. This type of juvenile waiver, also referred to as direct file or concurrent jurisdiction, grants discretion to the prosecuting attorney as to whether the juvenile will be charged in adult court or granted disposition in juvenile court. As is done with the judicial waiver, the prosecutor (in some states) typically takes into account factors such as the seriousness of the offense, past criminal record, and amenability to treatment. The prosecutorial waiver has been deemed an executive function paralleling decision making involved in other charging pronouncements. Unlike a judicial waiver, a prosecutorial waiver is not subjected to the constitutional criteria of due process for juveniles as established in *Kent*. The prosecutor's decision to charge a juvenile as an adult can be reversed only by a criminal court judge. In reversing a prosecutorial waiver, the criminal court judge must feel that the juvenile and the public's interest will be better served in juvenile court. The practice of a criminal court judge sending a case back to juvenile court under these criteria is referred to as decertification, or a reverse waiver.

The third type of waiver is the legislative provision waiver. This type of waiver, adopted by state legislatures, sought to hold juveniles more accountable by removing waiver decisions from judges and prosecutors. These legislative waivers also drastically curtail the jurisdictional boundaries of the juvenile court through legislative amendments. The legislative waiver or statutory exclusion automatically places youth meeting the established criteria, typically by offense, into the adult system at the time of arrest. The juvenile court has no jurisdictional oversight.

Legislative waivers have strong public support primarily because they tend to be more uniform in their application and seek to incarcerate violent juveniles. It is worth noting that these types of waivers typically have minimum age and offense requirements (typically, violent offenses and some felonies). Despite the option of allowing cases to be decertified by the juvenile court, most legislative waivers and amendments have adopted the policy of "once an adult, always an adult." With the present ideological climate toward juvenile offending, this type of waiver has grown in utility and furthered the transition of viewing juveniles like adults.

The increased use of juvenile waivers and concern about their impact have resulted in the enactment and growth of reverse waivers. Reverse waivers, which exist in over 20 states, are forms of legislation that allow criminal courts to remand cases of juveniles to juvenile courts based on the type of offense, the amenability of the juvenile, or both. Typically, reverse waivers allow for individual reviews of juvenile cases waived to adult courts. Also, reverse waivers simultaneously identify a range of cases appropriate for criminal prosecution. In some states with reverse waivers, the criminal court judge may impose a juvenile disposition in lieu of a criminal disposition. Generally, reverse waivers use the "best interest" criteria like that of the juvenile court.

Race and Juvenile Waivers

The unprecedented use of juvenile waivers today is indicative of a shift in public opinion and the law toward holding juveniles more accountable for criminal violations. High-profile violent juvenile crimes and the news media's sensationalization of them have dramatically affected the landscape of juvenile justice. Juveniles are increasingly viewed as rational young adults rather than adolescents. The decision to waive or transfer a juvenile to juvenile court is still rare even though more juveniles are waived than in the past. During the past 2 decades, Black youth were more likely to be waived than were White youth. Some of the disparity is due to the disproportionate arrest of Black youth for person offenses that are more likely to result in waivers.

The 2006 report of the Office of Juvenile Justice and Delinquency Prevention, titled *Juvenile Offenders and Victims: 2006 National Report*, states that an estimated 96,655 juveniles were in residential placement facilities in 2003, and approximately 59,000 were minorities. Opponents of juvenile waivers believe they have increased the rate of disproportional confinement for African American youth in juvenile and adult facilities.

Conclusion

It may seem logical to some that the adult correctional system should seek to provide as much special assistance as needed for youthful inmates because of the likelihood of their experiencing difficult adjustments to the adult correctional environment. Opponents of juvenile waivers will continue to highlight the potential dangers and marginal resources available for youthful inmates. Contrarily, proponents and policymakers will contend that removing violent, repeat juveniles from the general population is necessary.

Willie M. Brooks, Jr., and Tonya Y. Willingham

See also Child Savers; Disproportionate Minority Contact and Confinement; Houses of Refuge; *In re Gault*

Further Readings

Breed v. Jones, 421 U.S. 519, 533, 95 S.Ct. 1779, 1787, 44 L.Ed.2d 346 (1975).

Finley, M., & Schindler, M. (1999). Punitive juvenile justice policies and the impact on minority youth. *Federal Probation, 63*(2), 11–15.

In re Gault, 387 U.S. 1, 19–21, 26–28, 87 S.Ct. 1428, 1439–1440, 1442–1444, 18 L.Ed.2d 527 (1967).

In re Winship, 397 U.S. 358, 90 S.Ct. 1068, 25 L.Ed.2d 368 (1970).

Kent v. United States, 385 U.S. 541, 86 S.Ct. 1045, 16 L. Ed.2d 84 (1966).

McKeiver v. Pennsylvania, 403 U.S. 528, 547, 91 S.Ct. 1976, 1987, 29 L.Ed.2d 647 (1971).

Snyder, H. N., & Sickmund, M. (2006). *Juvenile offenders and victims: 2006 national report.* Retrieved from Office of Juvenile Justice and Delinquency Prevention: http://ojjdp.ncjrs.org/ojstatbb/nr2006/index.html

Ziedenberg, Z., & Schiraldi, V. (1998). Risk juveniles face when incarcerated with adults. *Reclaiming Children and Youth, 7*(2), 83–86.

KENNEDY V. LOUISIANA

The case of *Kennedy v. Louisiana,* decided by the U.S. Supreme Court on June 25, 2008, has again brought the death penalty to the forefront of the legal debate in the United States concerning the Eighth Amendment's prohibition against cruel and unusual punishment. Although the Court did not discuss race in its decision, the fact that the defendant was African American does make the case significant with respect to race and the death penalty. This entry presents a review of several death penalty decisions, the facts and decision in *Kennedy v. Louisiana,* and the significance of the decision.

Capital punishment has a checkered history in the United States, where, in contrast to most developed nations in the West, the death penalty is still upheld as a legitimate punishment for certain criminal acts. In *Furman v. Georgia* (1972), the U.S. Supreme Court recognized that the death penalty was applied in a haphazard and discriminatory manner, noting that its arbitrary application indicated racial bias against Black defendants. The decision in *Furman* invalidated many existing capital punishment statutes. In 1976, however, the Court held in *Gregg v. Georgia* that the death penalty in and of itself did not amount to cruel and unusual punishment and thus did not violate the Eighth Amendment.

However, the U.S. Supreme Court has recognized some limitations on the application of the death penalty. It is unconstitutional to execute juveniles—minors under the age of 18—under the Court's ruling in *Roper v. Simmons* (2005). In *Atkins v. Virginia* (2002), the Court held that it is unconstitutional to execute those who are mentally retarded (2002). Under the Court's decision in *Coker v. Georgia* (1977), it is unconstitutional to execute those who have been convicted of the rape of an adult. In *Kennedy v. Louisiana,* the Court ruled that it is a violation of the Eighth Amendment's prohibition of cruel and unusual punishment to impose the death penalty for the rape of a child when the crime did not result, and was not intended to result, in the death of the child. Thus, the imposition of the death penalty in the case of Patrick Kennedy was found to be unconstitutional.

As indicated in, among others, *Furman v. Georgia,* the fact that significantly more African American persons have been sentenced to death for similar crimes for which Whites had not been so sentenced was a basis for declaring the death penalty unconstitutional. Thus, *Kennedy* can be seen as a further step in establishing criteria for the use of capital punishment that help prevent the arbitrary application of the death penalty prohibited by *Furman.*

The Facts

The essential facts of the case are as follows: In 1998, Patrick Kennedy raped his 8-year-old stepdaughter, causing severe injuries that required emergency surgery. The defendant attempted to blame the rape on some neighborhood boys, but the defense was rejected by the jury. He was found guilty of aggravated rape and was sentenced to death, as allowed by the laws of Louisiana. The conviction was affirmed by the Louisiana Supreme Court. Kennedy appealed to the U.S. Supreme Court, which accepted certiorari.

The Supreme Court's Decision

The Court's decision was limited in its scope. It focused on the facts of the case and whether it is constitutionally permissible to apply the death penalty to a person who has raped a juvenile, when the juvenile has not died. In *Kennedy v. Louisiana*, the Court ruled that an application of the death penalty in such circumstances is prohibited by the Eighth Amendment. However, the scope of the legal principle that the death penalty is not appropriate where a person has not committed homicide has yet to be fully tested.

Significance of the Ruling

Kennedy had been convicted and sentenced to death before the trial court, and his appeal to the Louisiana Supreme Court had been denied. Not until his appeal to the U.S. Supreme Court was the imposition of the death penalty reversed. This procedural history clearly shows that there are still problems with the imposition of the death penalty.

The decision did not explicitly recognize that the defendant was African American. However, this factor cannot be ignored, especially considering the extensive history of disproportionate application of the death penalty to racial minorities in the United States. It is undisputed that, as a general rule, African Americans have been more severely punished for crimes than Caucasians who have committed the same crimes, including the crime of rape.

Although the decision in *Kennedy v. Louisiana* applies to all persons, regardless of race or other minority status, the fact that Kennedy is African American does suggest that African Americans are starting to make inroads into the racial discrimination that has for so long marred the American criminal justice system.

William C. Plouffe, Jr.

See also Coker v. Georgia; Death Penalty; *Furman v. Georgia*; *Gregg v. Georgia*; Martinsville Seven; *Roper v. Simmons*

Further Readings

Atkins v. Virginia, 536 U.S. 304 (2002).

Coker v. Georgia, 433 U.S. 584 (1977).

Del Carmen, R. V., et al. (2005). *The death penalty: Constitutional issues, commentaries and case briefs.* New York: Anderson/Mathew Bender/LexisNexis.

Furman v. Georgia, 408 U.S. 238 (1972).

Gregg v. Georgia, 428 U.S. 153 (1976).

Hood, R. (1989). *The death penalty.* New York: Oxford University Press.

Kennedy v. Louisiana, 554 U.S. ___ (2008).

Kleck, G. (1981). Racial discrimination in criminal sentencing. *American Sociological Review, 46,* 783.

Roper v. Simmons, 543 U.S. 551 (2005).

KIMBROUGH V. UNITED STATES

In *Kimbrough v. United States* (2007), the U.S. Supreme Court addressed the long-standing sentencing disparity between crack and powder cocaine. Federal drug laws in the latter half of the 1980s set penalties for crack cocaine sales and possession that were significantly more punitive than those for powdered cocaine. These laws were widely regarded as racist because they disproportionately affected African Americans, who were more likely to be sentenced for crack cocaine possession and sales than were non–African Americans. The *Kimbrough* Court decided whether judges could sentence people for crack cocaine violations outside the ranges prescribed in federal sentencing guidelines.

The Omnibus Anti-Drug Abuse Act of 1986 established mandatory prison sentences for violations of heroin and cocaine statutes and created marked sentencing disparities for the sale of crack and powder cocaine. The Omnibus Anti-Drug Abuse Act of 1988 also created sentencing disparities for the simple possession of crack and powder cocaine. The crack/powder cocaine sentencing disparity rested on the assumptions that crack cocaine was more harmful to users than powder cocaine and that crack users and dealers were more likely to be violent than users and dealers of other drugs. This sentencing disparity was commonly referred to as the "100-to-1 ratio" because according to federal laws, a conviction for possessing or selling 5 grams of crack cocaine—the weight of two pennies—carried the same penalty of 5 years imprisonment as a conviction for possessing or selling 500 grams of powder cocaine—a little more than 1 pound.

In the mid-1980s, a gram of powder cocaine could be purchased for $100, while a vial of crack cocaine could be purchased for as little as $5. Hence, crack cocaine became popular with drug users in poor urban areas—largely African American—and was inextricably linked with pernicious, stereotypic images of violent inner-city African American youth. The 100-to-1 sentencing disparity predominantly affected small-time, local drug sellers in African American communities instead of the major drug traffickers who sold the powdered cocaine that was converted into crack in those neighborhoods. Because of the federal sentencing disparity, crack cocaine sellers could spend more time in prison than the wholesale cocaine distributors who supplied the drug. Although nearly two thirds of crack cocaine users were Latina/o or White, African Americans constituted nearly 85% of the people who were convicted for selling or possessing crack cocaine and who were sentenced to lengthy prison terms.

On April 10, 1995, the U.S. Sentencing Commission proposed amendments to the federal sentencing guidelines that would reduce the sentencing disparity between crack and powder cocaine. Speaking on behalf of the Department of Justice, Attorney General Janet Reno was vehemently opposed to the reduction. The Clinton administration was successful in its opposition to the amendments, and for the first time in history, Congress rejected the Sentencing Commission's recommendations. In the late 1990s, the Senate thwarted both the Sentencing Commission's subsequent efforts to reduce the crack/powder cocaine ratio from 100-to-1, to 5-to-1, as well as the Clinton administration's efforts to reduce the ratio to 10-to-1, which reflected a change in the president's position on the issue.

A Sentencing Commission Report in 2007 further criticized the crack/powder cocaine disparity. Specifically, the commission noted that crack and powder cocaine were comparable in terms of their deleterious effects on users. Moreover, the commission reported that the predicted epidemic of crack cocaine use among youth never materialized, and that the trafficking of crack cocaine was associated with less violence than the trafficking of powder cocaine. The Sentencing Commission voted in December 2007 to reduce the prison terms of people sentenced under the 100-to-1 guidelines and to apply more relaxed sentencing guidelines retroactively to 1,600 federal inmates convicted of selling crack cocaine.

Kimbrough was argued before the U.S. Supreme Court on October 2, 2007, and decided on December 10, 2007. The basic questions in the case involved how much authority district court judges have in departing from federal sentencing guidelines; whether district court judges may consider the Sentencing Commission's arguments against the 100-to-1 sentencing disparity in their sentencing decisions; and how a district court judge can balance the imperatives of federal drug laws with the Sentencing Commission's objections against those laws.

Derrick Kimbrough, a veteran of the Gulf War, had been arrested in Norfolk, Virginia, and was charged (among other crimes) with the possession and intent to distribute crack and powder cocaine. Although he had no previous arrests, and despite his honorable military record, Kimbrough was sentenced in district court to 19 years in prison— the lengthy sentence being attributable mostly to the involvement of crack cocaine in the case. Kimbrough's defense attorney urged the judge to reduce the sentence to 15 years, noting that the defendant had more powder than crack cocaine in his possession. The district court judge agreed, and sentenced Kimbrough to 15 years in prison. The government appealed the case.

The U.S. Court of Appeals for the Fourth Circuit determined that the district court had erred by imposing a sentence outside the sentencing guidelines due to the court's discomfort with the sentencing disparity between crack and powder cocaine. The Fourth Circuit overturned the district court's ruling and restored Kimbrough's original prison sentence of 19 years, claiming that the lower court's ruling was unreasonable because it was predicated on the court's disagreement with the crack/powder cocaine sentencing disparity.

In *Kimbrough,* the U.S. Supreme Court overturned the appellate court's decision and ruled that federal judges may impose prison terms for crack cocaine convictions that deviate from the sentencing guidelines and fall below the lower range of the mandatory minimum prison sentence for such crimes. In a vote of 7–2, the majority ruled that federal judges should impose prison terms that are fair, responsive to the particular circumstances of a case, and unbounded by onerous sentencing guidelines. In the majority's opinion, written by Justice Ruth Bader Ginsburg, judges are obliged to avoid unwarranted sentencing disparities and should view sentencing guidelines as advisory instead of peremptory.

Arthur J. Lurigio

See also Crack Babies; Crack Epidemic; Crack Mothers; Drug Dealers; Drug Sentencing; Drug Sentencing, Federal; Drug Trafficking; Drug Use

Further Readings

American Civil Liberties Union. (2002). *Interested persons memo on crack/powder cocaine sentencing policy.* Retrieved from http://www.aclu.org/drugpolicy/sentencing/10662leg20020521.html

Kimbrough v. United States, 552 U.S. ___ (2007).

Lavoie, D. (2008). *Crack-vs.-powder disparity is questioned.* Retrieved from http://www.usatoday.com/news/nation/2007-12-24-2050621119_x.htm

Mears, B. (2007). *Justices: Judges can slash crack sentences.* Retrieved from http://www.cnn.com/2007/US/law/12/10/scotus.crack.cocaine/index.html

KING, RODNEY (1965–)

Rodney Glen King is an African American male who made national headlines after four White Los Angeles Police Department (LAPD) officers were unknowingly videotaped using excessive force against him. The videotape was aired by every major television network across America and only affirmed for many what minorities have argued for years: the criminal justice system in America is biased and unjust at all levels when dealing with minorities. This entry describes the horrors of the Rodney King beating and the aftermath of those events, to assist in raising the awareness of the level of mistreatment and discrimination of minorities in the criminal justice system.

King was born April 2, 1965, in Sacramento, California. He was the second of five children and a high school dropout with minimal literacy skills. King fathered two children early in life and later was married to Crystal Waters, who also had two children of her own. King, a laborer, found routine work as a construction worker and at the time of the 1991 beating was working construction at Dodger stadium.

On March 3, 1991, King fell into the national spotlight when, while on parole for a robbery of a convenience store, he led the California Highway Patrol on a chase in excess of 110 miles per hour. After King exited the freeway and drove approximately 8 miles into a Los Angeles neighborhood, the Los Angeles Police Department joined the California Highway Patrol in their pursuit. Four of the 11 responding officers from the Los Angeles Police Department (Officer Laurence Powell, Officer Timothy Wind, Officer Theodore Briseno, and Sergeant Stacey Koon), while using excessive force, beating, and kicking King, were unknowingly videotaped by a citizen onlooker, George Holliday.

The initial moments of the incident were not captured on video and involved King being ordered to step out of his vehicle and instructed by the officers to lie down on the ground on his stomach. When King refused to comply with the orders given by the officers, they tried to physically force King down to the ground, but he resisted and became combative. The officers retreated, and Sergeant Koon fired 50,000-volt Taser darts into King in an attempt to stun and subdue him.

The videotape then begins, showing King rising from the ground and charging toward Officer Powell. California Highway Patrol Officer Melanie Singer testified that she observed Officer Powell strike King "with a power swing . . . across the top of his cheekbone, splitting the face from the top of his ear to his chin," causing him to fall to the ground. King attempted to rise but was repeatedly struck by Powell and Wind with their metal batons.

During the beating, Officer Powell struck King in his chest, and King rolled over and did not move for about 10 seconds. The officer then reached for his handcuffs, and Officer Briseno placed his foot on King's upper back-neck region (the only use of force by Briseno). King collapsed onto the ground, at which time Officers Powell and Wind began to kick and strike King with their metal batons for approximately 19 more seconds. When King finally put his hands behind his back, the officers handcuffed him. Throughout the ordeal King was struck a total of 56 times, which caused him to suffer multiple skull fractures, a shattered eye socket and cheekbone, broken teeth, a concussion, kidney injuries, permanent brain damage, facial nerve damage that left his face partially paralyzed, injuries to both knees, and a broken leg, which left him with a permanent limp. After the beating, King was hogtied and dragged to the side of the road, where he was left without any medical assistance from the officers.

Comments made by Officer Powell after the arrest heightened the severity of the incident. After Officer Powell called for an ambulance, he sent a message over a police communications network that said, "I haven't beaten anyone this bad in a long time."

On March 14, 1991, all three officers and the sergeant were indicted for "assault by force likely to produce great bodily injury" and with "assault under color of authority." The defense was able to successfully file for a change of venue, away from Los Angeles County, where they argued they could not receive a fair trial, to Ventura County, which is much more affluent and has a smaller proportion of African American residents. On April 29, 1992, Officers Briseno and Wind and Sergeant Koon were acquitted of all charges by a jury of 10 Whites, one Latino, and one Asian. The jury was unable to reach a verdict on one charge against Officer Powell. A retrial was ordered on the charge and resulted in a hung jury.

Upon hearing the verdict, African Americans in south central Los Angeles rioted for three days, attacking citizens, looting, and burning businesses throughout the city. When the rioting was over, more than 50 people had been killed (mostly Koreans and Latinos), more than 2,000 injured, and more than 7,000 arrested. There were more than 7,000 fire responses, more than 3,100 damaged businesses, and more than $1 billion in property damage. On May 1, 1992, the third day of the riots, King appeared before several television news

cameras and pleaded to the people for peace, asking, "People, I just want to say, you know, can we all get along?"

On August 4, 1992, the four officers were indicted by a federal grand jury under 18 U.S.C. § 242, charging them with violating King's constitutional rights. The three officers were charged with "willfully and intentionally using unreasonable force," and Sergeant Koon was charged with "willfully permitting and failing to take action to stop the unlawful assault." Officers Wind and Briseno were acquitted of all charges; Officer Powell and Sergeant Koon were found guilty and sentenced to 2½ years in prison.

King was later awarded $3.8 million in a federal civil case against Los Angeles. He used some of the money to start a hip hop music label and moved to Fontana, California. King has since filed for bankruptcy and has been in trouble with the law on numerous occasions for various criminal acts, including, but not limited to, being arrested for DUI (driving under the influence) twice, hit and run driving, indecent exposure, using PCP, crashing his Ford Expedition into a house while high on PCP, and punching his girlfriend in the stomach.

Georgen Guerrero

See also Los Angeles Race Riots of 1992; Police Use of Force; Race Relations; Race Riots; Racial Conflict

Further Readings

Cannon, L. (1999). *Official negligence: How Rodney King and the riots changed Los Angeles and the LAPD.* New York: Basic Books.

Koon, S. (1992). *Presumed guilty: The tragedy of the Rodney King affair.* Washington, DC: Regnery.

Ku Klux Klan

The Ku Klux Klan (KKK) is the most infamous racist organization to exist in the United States, in addition to being the first terrorist group to operate in America. With an ideology borne of White supremacy, this organization has often used violence and acts of intimidation, such as cross burnings and lynching, to harass those social or ethnic groups they deem inferior to the "White, Christian race." For more than a century, the KKK has engaged in a campaign of racist violence and intimidation throughout the United States.

History

Founding

The Klan was formed during the Reconstruction era in May 1866, during which time the Northern states attempted to resolve those political, economic, and social issues that arose in the process of reinstating the Southern states into the Union. In response, veteran Confederate soldiers banded together in Pulaski, Tennessee, with the goal of maintaining the racist ideology of the South, and over the course of the next year they traveled throughout the Southern United States spreading their philosophies and using violent tactics against Black Americans, sympathetic Whites, and Southern Republicans (members of the party that had recently freed the slaves). The attackers, considered White supremacists because they believed that the White race is dominant to all others, derived the name of the group from the Greek word *kyklos,* meaning "circle," and the Scottish Gaelic term *clann,* meaning "family." In 1867, a significant group of local Klans met in Nashville, Tennessee, in an effort to build a nationwide hierarchical organization that would designate members at county, state, and national positions. The first Grand Wizard, or national leader, of the group was Nathan Bedford Forrest, a highly decorated general during the Civil War and former slave owner. While some other leaders of the organization at the state or county levels acquired titles such as "Imperial Wizard," or "Exalted Cyclops," the Klan never reached a state of formal organizational structure that was able to unite and coordinate multigroup efforts.

Early Years

During the next 5 years, the Klan played an important role in restoring White Democratic control in Georgia, Tennessee, and North Carolina. At this time, the organization's goal was to lead the Confederate Democrats back into power and to restore White supremacy in the South through peaceful, political means. Although they advocated violence only in the attempt to disarm Black Union soldiers who were given firearms during the war, leaders of the Klan also alleged that many unaffiliated individuals, acting under their own volition, were using violent means to achieve the same goal, wearing commonplace masks, white cardboard hats, and white sheets to disguise themselves in order to escape recognition and thus penalty for their actions. Most of these violent acts included the lynching or assault of Blacks, whipping of White Unionists, or the burning of Black homes, churches, and schools.

The Klan slowly started its decline in 1870 after Forrest, realizing the increasingly violent, nonpolitical agenda of the rest of the organization, called for its disbandment. In 1871, President Ulysses S. Grant signed the Ku Klux Klan Act, introduced to enforce the civil rights provisions in the U.S. Constitution. This legislation allowed federal authorities to have jurisdiction over the Klan members, an area typically reserved for state militias; hundreds of members were charged and brought to trial. As its members were being fined and imprisoned, and the national leader stepped down, the Klan began to disappear from public view. Before they completely vanished, the Klan was held responsible for the Colfax massacre on April 13, 1873, in Colfax, Louisiana. More than 100 Black people were shot or beaten to death at the local courthouse for attempting to find safety after being targeted by local Whites following a contested election in which a Unionist supporter was elected into office.

First Revival

There was a resurgence of the Klan in the beginning of the 20th century with the 1915 release of the film *The Birth of a Nation,* which glorified the original organization. Also during this time, Leo Frank was lynched by the Knights of Mary Phagan, a subgroup of the Klan later credited with bringing about its revival. Frank was a Jewish man in Atlanta, Georgia, who was accused of raping and murdering a young White girl; after being sentenced to life in prison, he was kidnapped from jail and hung. The story was sensationalized by the media, and the events surrounding the case were exaggerated. Much of the public became outraged by the implications of the events, and support for a new Klan emerged. The new Klan focused not only on African Americans but also on immigrants, Catholics, and Jews, deriving its ideology from both White supremacy and Christian fundamentalism. In November 1922, the Klan elected Hiram W. Evans as the new Imperial Wizard. Under Evans's leadership, the Klan grew rapidly, and members were quickly elected into positions of political power. In the 1920s, Klan members held positions as state officials in Texas, Oklahoma, Oregon, Indiana, and Maine. By 1925, membership reached 4 million. During the next 20 years, the Klan was involved in various political and violent acts of intimidation against those they deemed a danger to either the Constitution or to White, Christian ideals. However, due to successful prosecution efforts by local and federal governments, sex scandals, and a large amount of unpaid taxes, this first revival of the Klan had slowly disintegrated by 1944.

Second Revival

The second revival of the Klan took place when individual groups banded together to resist the civil rights movement in the late 1950s. This movement was directed specifically at Black Americans involved in the movement and their White sympathizers. Numerous violent acts, including shootings, bombings, and lynchings, were rampant in the Klan's efforts to sweep away opposition. Medgar Evers and Vernon Dahmer, Sr., both leaders for the National Association for the Advancement of Colored People (NAACP), were assassinated, as was Viola Liuzzo, a White sympathizer who was transporting civil rights marchers at the time of her death. Numerous other civil rights workers were attacked and harassed, beaten, or killed. At this time, violent means were more popular than ever. Firebombs were used to burn churches, houses, and vehicles. This continued throughout the next 10 years, when Klan efforts came to be directed at affirmative action and desegregation efforts such as busing. In 1971, 10 busses used for transporting Black students to segregated schools were destroyed by bombs. Also, during this time, in 1974, David Duke surfaced as a future leader within the organization.

Duke created the Louisiana-based group, Knights of the Ku Klux Klan, in 1974. In marketing himself to the rest of the White supremacist world, he represented a new image for the Klan: clean-cut, intelligent, and professional. The Klan flourished under his leadership, and Duke urged members to run for political office. Women were beginning to be treated as equals in the organization, and Catholics were encouraged to join. Duke organized the largest Klan rally held in nearly 2 decades in 1976 in Walker, Louisiana. Duke left the KKK in 1980, after a scandal in which he was accused of attempting to sell his subgroup to another Klan leader. He went on to form the National Association for the Advancement of White People (NAAWP) and became a Louisiana state representative in 1989.

The Klan became more decentralized in the 1980s as a result of legal attacks brought on by the Southern Poverty Law Center (SPLC), founded by Morris Dees and Joe Levin in 1971. In 1981, one of these attacks targeted the United Klans of America (UKA), located in Tuscaloosa, Alabama. During the civil rights movement, this subgroup of the Klan, led by Imperial Wizard Robert Shelton, was the largest in the organization, claiming tens of thousands of members. Membership slowly decreased during the late 1970s and 1980s, when the UKA found itself involved in a civil suit with the SPLC over the hanging of a Black teenager, Michael Donald, in 1981. After the SPLC won the suit, in 1987, the UKA collapsed under the ensuing monetary penalty awarded to Donald's family. The family gained possession of the United Klans' 7,200-square-foot national headquarters in Tuscaloosa and were awarded a $7 million settlement. This was one of several successful attempts by both civil rights organizations and the government in targeting the Ku Klux Klan and other White supremacist groups.

Klan Atrocities Against Civil Rights Workers

On June 21, 1964, three civil rights workers, James Chaney, a 21-year-old Black man from Mississippi; Andrew Goodman, a 20-year-old Jewish student from New York; and Michael Schwerner, a 24-year-old Jewish social worker from New York, had disappeared in Mississippi after being involved in efforts to register Blacks to vote. Their bodies were found on August 4, 1964, outside of Philadelphia, Mississippi. Chaney had been beaten and shot, while Goodman and Schwerner had both been shot in the heart. E. G. Barnett and Edgar Ray Killen were implicated for the murders in 1967 but were set free due to a deadlocked jury. Due to strong media coverage and public outrage, nearly 40 years later, on June 21, 2005, Killen was convicted of three counts of manslaughter and sent to prison. Additionally, James Ford Seale, a former Klan member, was convicted on June 14, 2007, for kidnapping and conspiracy in the commission of the murders of Charles Eddie Moore and Henry Hezekiah Dee, both civil rights workers, on May 2, 1964, in Mississippi. These successful prosecutions, in addition to the civil suits initiated by the SPLC, have served to severely weaken the structure and functionality of the Klan.

The Disintegration of the Klan's Organizational Structure

In addition to forcing several Klan chapters to disintegrate, these convictions of Klan members affected the structure of the organization as a whole. The differing groups slowly began to become decentralized and act independently of one another. For this reason, in the beginning of the 21st century, the Klan is widely distributed throughout the country. Separate factions of the KKK are located around the world but are much more prevalent in the United States. The largest "umbrella" chapters in the United States are the Imperial Klans of America (headquartered in Dawson Springs, Kentucky), headed by Imperial Wizard Ron Edwards, and the Knights of the White Kamelia (east Texas), led by Imperial Wizard James Roesch. Each group has its own headquarters and network structure, although Klan leadership has continually been weakening.

In July 2006, Jeff Berry, former Imperial Wizard, was assaulted by his son, Anthony Berry, and Fred Wilson, both members of the KKK, after becoming involved in an argument at a Klan gathering in which the two assailants wished to invigorate the Klan in Indiana. In January 2007, Gordon Young, the former leader of the World Knights' North Carolina-based faction of the Ku Klux Klan, was accused and convicted of child molestation. Finally, on March 29, 2007, Joseph Bednarsky, leader of the Confederate Knights of the Ku Klux Klan, resigned from his position as Imperial Wizard, stating that infighting and a lack of progress were the reasons for his decision.

Despite these incidents, the Anti-Defamation League reported that there may be more than 100 different chapters of Klan organizations in the United States, and it has been estimated that there may currently be more than 5,000 members of the Klan, a significant decrease in number from the past under the leadership of both Hiram Evans and David Duke. However, there may be a third revival of the Klan in the works, as the political and social controversy surrounding the illegal immigration movement increases in the United States.

The Modern Klan

America has recently seen a resurgence in the number of individuals joining White supremacist groups in an effort to combat illegal immigration, an issue that is quickly spreading fear among those hate groups that strive to keep Whites in power. These growing chapters are engaging in numerous protests around the country, alongside other anti–illegal immigration groups such as the Minuteman organization, in order to garner public support for their cause as well as recruit more members. There have been recent reports of the Klan engaging in vandalism, cross burning, and leafleting incidents, in order either to intimidate those people whose property is being targeted or to gain the attention of locals with the aim of garnering further support. The current organization, staying true to its White supremacist heritage, also engages in occasional assaults of those individuals traditionally targeted by the Klan.

In 1998, in Jasper, Texas, James Byrd, Jr., a Black man, was beaten and then dragged behind a truck for 3 miles, killing him. The three assailants, including John William King, a known member of the Confederate Knights of America, were convicted of the murder and sentenced to either life in prison or the death penalty. More recently, on June 30, 2006, Jarred Hensley and Andrew Watkins, both members of the Imperial Klans of America, physically assaulted a young Hispanic man while shouting racial slurs at the Meade County Fairgrounds in Brandenburg, Kentucky. Both Klansmen were arrested and charged with assault and public intoxication, indicted on hate crime charges, and sentenced to 3 years in prison on February 22, 2007.

Additionally, different chapters of the organization have created and maintained group Websites, using these venues to facilitate communication opportunities between members or associates from other groups. There are frequent overlaps of members from other organizations who hold the same or similar racist or neo-Nazi philosophies, such as the National Socialist Movement, Aryan Nations, American Nazi Party, or the American White Nationalist Party. These Websites provide a place for the group to post meeting times and places as well as allow the Klan to sell various paraphernalia. This is one of the main funding sources for the chapters: selling shirts, hats, flags, CDs, and other materials. Other sources include membership dues and donations through group Websites, rallies and protests, and organized group events. Different chapters of the Klan also produce publications, including *Klan Kourage, White Patriot, The Torch, White Beret,* and *The Klansmen,* which allow the groups to disseminate their racist message and ideology to those who subscribe.

The Ku Klux Klan, while still espousing White supremacist and fundamentalist Christian ideologies, has changed drastically since the beginning of the movement more than a century and a half ago. The Klan has become wholly decentralized, and membership is informal and often changing, although members continue to engage in violent and threatening actions against Blacks, Jews, and other minorities. While the United States has seen the rise and fall of significant Klan movements, the group's recent anti–illegal immigration stance has seen an increase in recruitment and propaganda use, which could potentially indicate a fourth revival.

Megan L. Gray and Michael T. Coates

See also African Americans; Anti-Semitism; *Birth of a Nation, The*; Byrd, James, Jr.; Hate Crimes; Ku Klux Klan Act; Lynching; Minutemen; Southern Poverty Law Center; White Gangs; White Supremacists

Further Readings

Anti-Defamation League. (2008). *About the Ku Klux Klan.* Retrieved from http://www.adl.org

Builta, J. A. (1996). *Extremist groups: An international compilation of terrorist organizations, violent political groups, and issue-oriented militant movements.* Chicago: University of Illinois at Chicago, Office of International Criminal Justice.

George, J., & Wilcox, L. (1992). *Nazis, Communists, Klansmen, and others on the fringe: Political extremism in America.* Buffalo, NY: Prometheus.

Southern Poverty Law Center. (n.d.). *Active U.S. hate groups in 2006: Ku Klux Klan.* Retrieved October 10, 2008, from http://www.splcenter.org

KU KLUX KLAN ACT

The Ku Klux Klan Act of 1871 (also known as the Civil Rights Act) was one of three laws passed as part of the U.S. government's attempts to "reconstruct" the Southern states following the Civil War. The act itself, as indicated by the name, was directed at the Ku Klux Klan. The Ku Klux Klan was a series of loosely affiliated gangs who used violence to impose their agenda on the state governments established following the Civil War by killing freed slaves and those supporting them. The act, aiming particularly at conspiracies, made it a federal offense to deny a person his or her civil rights. With the new legislation, federal law enforcement vigorously prosecuted Klan members. Five years later, the U.S. Supreme Court invalidated portions of the law, contributing to its subsequent disuse. Although only used for a short time, the Ku Klux Klan Act of 1871 served as the model for more lasting civil rights laws and established precedent for federal intervention into crime problems states could or would not address.

Following the Civil War, the federal government had to decide how to handle the former Confederate states. Although the Union had won the war, the former Confederate states did not abandon their beliefs about slavery and their distaste for equality with freed slaves. In some parts of the South, organized resistance arose to Republican officeholders, who had supported emancipation of the slaves and supported equality between African Americans and the former slave owners. The resistance consisted of White, former slave-holding Democrats who sought to keep the freed slaves from exercising their newfound voting rights. To keep the freed slaves from voting, these organized groups resorted to violence and intimidation. One particular group, the Ku Klux Klan, was exceptionally violent.

The Republican state governments proved unable to control the violence and sought assistance from the federal government. The Army could not intervene because of legal restrictions. As a result, Congress adopted three "Enforcement Acts" so that federal law enforcement could intervene in the situation. These acts were derived from the enforcement clauses of the Fourteenth and Fifteenth Amendments, passed following the Civil War's conclusion. Each succeeding act provided more enforcement power for the federal government. The first act, passed in May 1870, criminalized interference with voting rights. The second act, passed in February 1871, provided for federal supervision of voter registration and elections. The third act, passed in May 1871 and named the Ku Klux Klan Act, criminalized conspiracy to prevent people from holding office, serving on juries, enjoying equal protection of the law, and voting. It also permitted use of the army to enforce the law, suspension of the writ of habeas corpus in counties in a state of insurrection, and removal of Klan members from both petit and grand juries.

Enforcement by the Department of Justice began immediately. President Ulysses Grant sent the military to the various Southern states, particularly nine counties in South Carolina where the violence was most prevalent. The military both protected freed slaves and Radical Republicans and investigated the Ku Klux Klan. The information obtained from locals about the Klan served as the basis for mass arrests and indictments. Attorney General Amos Akerman coordinated the federal efforts with assistance from the local U.S. attorneys and U.S. marshals. In the years following the enactment of the Ku Klux Klan Act, there were more than 3,000 indictments filed across the South, with the most coming from South Carolina and northern Mississippi. Ultimately, because of the flood of cases that entered the system, most cases were dismissed. Of the 600 cases tried, more than 67% were convicted at trial. Sentences for those convicted varied widely from small fines to 5 years in prison.

Despite, or perhaps because of, its widespread use, the law generated a great deal of controversy. Democrats and Liberal Republicans opposed its use on racial and constitutional grounds. Democrats strongly opposed any hints of equality between the freed slaves and their former owners.

They engaged in further violence, often abusing, assaulting, and murdering prosecutors, marshals, and witnesses. Liberal Republicans sought a more moderate approach to Reconstruction through a general amnesty for former Confederates. For their part, Liberal Republicans decried the infringement upon states' rights brought about by the acts and their enforcement. They viewed the act as the federal government invading the states' police power. They supported their argument by citing the indictments filed by the prosecutors that highlighted state crimes such as burglary, robbery, and murder. The prosecutors argued these acts were merely the acts demonstrating the conspiracy.

Ultimately, the U.S. Supreme Court would have to decide the issue. They did so in 1876 but could have done so much sooner. Within the Grant administration, Attorney General Akerman was the driving force behind the act's enforcement. He was removed and replaced by George Williams, who lacked the interest his predecessor displayed for civil rights prosecutions. As a result, Williams took steps to prevent early cases from reaching the U.S. Supreme Court, limited future prosecutions to the most serious abuses, and eventually terminated prosecutions once the Supreme Court could hear a case. Upon hearing the case, the Supreme Court found much of the Ku Klux Klan Act of 1871 unconstitutional.

Overall, the Ku Klux Klan Act aided the government by scattering the Ku Klux Klan members, but it did not eliminate the violence and opposition to freed slaves voting. However, the statute's long-term impact proved greater. In the 20th century, the law served as the basis for the Civil Rights Acts of 1957 and 1960. It also provided a precedent for federal intervention when states could or would not remedy a crime problem. This precedent set the stage for future federal criminal law. Finally, those supporting the act first developed the legal arguments that would eventually succeed in making the Bill of Rights apply to the several states through the Fourteenth Amendment.

Scott Ingram

See also Ku Klux Klan; Racial Conflict; Victim and
   Witness Intimidation

Further Readings

Cresswell, S. (1987). Enforcing the enforcement acts: The Department of Justice in northern Mississippi, 1870–1890. *The Journal of Southern History, 53*(3), 421–440.

McPherson, J. M. (1982). *Ordeal by fire: The Civil War and Reconstruction*. New York: Knopf.

Swinney, E. (1962). Enforcing the 15th Amendment. *The Journal of Southern History, 28*(2), 202–218.

Williams, L. F. (1996). *The great South Carolina Ku Klux Klan trials, 1871–1872*. Athens: University of Georgia Press.

LABELING THEORY

Labeling theory is a criminological theory stemming out of a sociological perspective known as "symbolic interactionism," a school of thought based on the ideas of George Herbert Mead, John Dewey, W. I. Thomas, Charles Horton Cooley, and Herbert Blumer. The first as well as one of the most prominent labeling theorists was Howard Becker (1963). Two questions became popular with criminologists during the mid-1960s: What makes some acts and some people deviant or criminal? During this time, scholars tried to shift the focus of criminology toward the effects of individuals in power responding to behavior in society in a negative way; they became known as "labeling theorists" or "social reaction theorists."

Blumer (1969) emphasized the way that meaning arises in social interaction through communication, using language and symbols. The focus of this perspective is the interaction between individuals in society, which is the basis for meanings within that society. These theorists suggested that powerful individuals and the state create crime by labeling some behaviors as inappropriate. The focus of these theorists is on the reactions of members in society to crime and deviance, separating them from other scholars of the time. These theorists shaped their argument around the notion that, even though some criminological efforts to reduce crime are meant to help the offender (such as rehabilitation efforts), they may move offenders closer to lives of crime because of the label they assign the individuals engaging in the behavior. As members in society begin to treat these individuals on the basis of their labels, the individual begins to accept this label him- or herself. In other words, an individual engages in a behavior that is deemed by others as inappropriate, others label that person to be deviant, and eventually the individual internalizes and accepts this label. This notion of social reaction, reaction or response by others to the behavior or individual, is central to labeling theory. Critical to this theory is the understanding that the negative reaction of others to a particular behavior is what causes that behavior to be labeled as "criminal" or "deviant." Furthermore, it is the negative reaction of others to an individual engaged in a particular behavior that causes that individual to be labeled as "criminal," "deviant," or "not normal." According to the literature, several reactions to deviance have been identified, including *collective rule making, organizational processing*, and *reaction to reaction*.

Becker defined deviance as a "social creation in which social groups create deviance by making the rules whose infraction constitutes deviance, and by applying those rules to particular people and labeling them as outsiders." Becker grouped behavior into four categories: falsely accused, conforming, pure deviant, and secret deviant. *Falsely accused* represents those individuals who have engaged in obedient behavior but have been perceived as deviant; therefore, they would be falsely labeled as deviant.

Conforming represents those individuals who have engaged in obedient behavior that has been viewed as obedient behavior (not been perceived as deviant). *Pure deviant* represents those individuals who have engaged in rule breaking or deviant behavior that has been recognized as such; therefore, they would be labeled as deviant by society. *Secret deviant* represents those individuals that have engaged in rule breaking or deviant behavior but have not been perceived as deviant by society; therefore, they have not been labeled as deviant.

According to sociologists like Émile Durkheim, George Herbert Mead, and Kai T. Erikson, deviance is functional to society and keeps stability by defining boundaries. In 1966, Erikson expanded labeling theory to include the functions of deviance, illustrating how societal reactions to deviance stigmatize the offender and separate him or her from the rest of society. The results of this stigmatization is a self-fulfilling prophecy in which the offender comes to view him- or herself in the same ways society does.

Key Concepts: Primary and Secondary Deviance

Primary deviance refers to initial acts of deviance by an individual that have only minor consequences for that individual's status or relationships in society. The notion behind this concept is that the majority of people violate laws or commit deviant acts in their lifetime; however, these acts are not serious enough and do not result in the individual being classified as a criminal by society or by themselves, as it is viewed as "normal" to engage in these types of behaviors. Speeding would be a good example of an act that is technically criminal but does not result in labeling as such. Furthermore, many would view recreational marijuana use as another example. *Secondary deviance*, however, is deviance that occurs as a response to society's reaction of the individual engaging in the behavior as deviant. This type of deviance, unlike primary deviance, has major implications for a person's status and relationships in society and is a direct result of the internalization of the deviant label. This pathway from primary deviance to secondary deviance or acceptance as normal is illustrated as follows:

primary deviance → others label act as deviant → actor internalizes deviant label → secondary deviance

Theoretical Contributions

There are three major theoretical directions to labeling theory, including Bruce Link's modified labeling theory, John Braithwaite's reintegrative shaming, and Ross L. Matsueda and Karen Heimer's differential social control.

Link's Modified Labeling Theory

Link's modified labeling theory (2001) expanded the original framework of labeling theory to include a five-stage process of labeling. The stages of his model include the extent to which people believe that mental patients will be devalued and discriminated against by other members of the community, the time period by which people are officially labeled by treatment agencies, when the patient responds to labeling through secrecy, withdrawal, or education, the negative consequences to this individual's life that were brought about as a result of labeling, and the final stage of vulnerability to future deviance as a result of the effects of labeling.

Braithwaite's Reintegrative Shaming Theory

The theory of reintegrative shaming, by John Braithwaite (1989), examines the difference between stigmatization of the individual and reintegrative shaming, or encouragement to stop the behavior without labeling and stigmatizing the individual in society. This theory essentially posits that reintegrative shaming will reduce crime, unlike stigmatization, which, according to labeling theory, essentially increases it by encouraging future deviance. The framework behind this theory is that individuals, after committing an act deemed as criminal or delinquent, will be shamed by society for that act and then reaccepted back into society without a permanent label of "not normal," "deviant," or "criminal." Furthermore, a second concept of this theory is the notion of *restorative justice,* or making amends for wrong actions with those who were affected by the behavior. The argument driving this theory is the notion that reintegrative shaming demonstrates that a behavior is wrong without hurting the individual accused of that behavior. Rather, society encourages the individual to make up for what he or she has done, show remorse for the choice of behavior, and learn from the mistake. Under this theory, society teaches its members and then readily accepts them back into the group without permanent labels or stigmas attached. Essentially, society forgives.

Matsueda and Heimer's Differential Social Control Theory

Matsueda and Heimer's theory (1992) returns to a symbolic interactionist perspective, arguing that a symbolic interactionist theory of delinquency provides a theory of self- and social control that explains all components, including labeling, secondary deviance, and primary deviance. This theory relies on the concept of *role taking,* a concept that illustrates how individuals reflect on their behavior, how they are able to put themselves in the shoes of others in order to view the situation or behavior from the other's standpoint, and how they evaluate alternative actions that would be more acceptable and not seem as inappropriate in the eyes of others. Heimer and Matsueda expanded this notion to include the term *differential social control*, which emphasizes that social control through role taking can take a conventional direction or a criminal direction because the acceptable courses of actions by peers may not necessarily be conventional or nondeviant courses of action.

Recent Directions in Labeling Theory

Several articles published in the past few years have examined the effects of labeling in adolescents. This literature further examines the concept of stigma and the role that power plays in labeling an individual. This literature further examines the problems associated with labeling and stigmatizing individuals, including status loss, stereotyping, and discrimination. Also more recently examined have been measures for perceived labeling. This literature suggests that

adolescents who perceive more deviant labels than positive ones for themselves are more likely to engage in delinquency.

Criticisms of Labeling Theory

There are many criticisms that have been raised about traditional labeling theory. Labeling theory prospered throughout the 1960s, bringing about policy changes such as deinstitutionalization of the mentally ill and juvenile diversion programs; however, it came under attack in the mid-1970s as a result of criticism by conflict theorists and positivists for ignoring the concept of deviance; these theorists believed that deviance does exist and that secondary deviance was a useless concept for sociologists. This criticism has survived and continues to haunt labeling theorists today because of the recent empirical evidence on the theory. Two main hypotheses have been identified through these empirical tests, including the status characteristics hypothesis and the secondary deviance hypothesis. *The status characteristics hypothesis* explains how individual attributes affect the choice of who is and who is not labeled, and the *secondary deviance hypothesis* argues that negative labels cause future deviance.

Labeling theory predicts that labeling will vary by status characteristics even when controlling for previous deviant behavior. The criticism, however, stems from the fact that labeling theory does not require that status characteristics are the most important determinant of labeling.

Secondary deviance implies a long, causal chain of events, including negative labels, objective and perceived opportunities, and deviant self-images. It is important to keep in mind, however, that some groups may be more vulnerable than others to these events. The literature in this area has not provided support for or contradicted labeling theory, as it simply focuses on future deviance without thoroughly examining the process. Most research conducted on labeling theory appears to simply take for granted that this process is a given; however, it is problematic to assume it as such without proper empirical support. This is a key point that ties this theory back into literature on race and crime; some individuals are more

vulnerable to the label and therefore more susceptible to the problems that occur as a result of
being stigmatized.

Sherry Lynn Skaggs

See also At-Risk Youth; Focal Concerns Theory, Labeling;
    Juvenile Crime; Recidivism; Restorative Justice

Further Readings

Adams, M. S., Robertson, C. T., Gray-Ray, P., & Ray,
    M. C. (2003). Labeling and delinquency. *Adolescence,
    38,* 149.

Becker, H. (1963). *Outsiders.* New York: The Free Press.

Blumer, H. (1969). *Symbolic interactionism: Perspective
    and method.* Berkeley: University of California Press.

Braithwaite, J. (1989). *Crime, shame, and reintegration.*
    Cambridge, UK: Cambridge University Press.

Link, B. G., & Phelan, J. C. (2001). Conceptualizing
    stigma. *Annual Review of Sociology, 27,* 363–385.

Matsueda, R. L. (1992). Reflected appraisals, parental
    labeling, and delinquency: Specifying a symbolic
    interactionist theory. *American Journal of Sociology,
    97,* 1577–1611.

Matsueda, R. L., & Heimer, K. (1987). Race, family
    structure and delinquency: A test of differential
    association and social control theories. *American
    Sociological Review, 52,* 826–840.

Paternoster, R., & Bachman, R. (2001). *Explaining
    criminals and crime.* Los Angeles: Roxbury.

Tannenbaum, F. (1938). *Crime and the community.*
    Boston: Ginn.

Vold, G., Bernard, T., & Snipes, J. (2002). *Theoretical
    criminology* (5th ed.). New York: Oxford University
    Press.

LATINA/O CRIMINOLOGY

The incorporation of Latinas and Latinos in
criminological research is important because the
Latina/o population is now the second largest
group in the United States. It is also important to
include Latinos since there are considerable race
and ethnic disparities in violence across the
nation. For example, Latinos were 3 times *more*
likely than non-Latina/o Whites to be a victim
of homicide but almost 3 times *less* likely than

Blacks to be killed. National crime victimization
surveys indicate that Latinos and Blacks were victims of robbery at similarly high rates, but,
Latinos were victims of aggravated assault at a
level in line with Whites and Blacks. These differences are a reminder that criminological research
on racial and ethnic variations in crime must
incorporate Latinos and consider variations within
Latina/o groups in order to fully understand
group differences in criminal and delinquent
behavior. This entry outlines the contours of
Latina/o violent crime and serious delinquent
behavior research.

National Victimization Survey

The primary source of survey-based crime data
in the United States is the National Crime
Victimization Survey (NCVS), a nationally representative study of person and household victimization administered by the U.S. Census Bureau.
Unlike the *Uniform Crime Reports* (UCR), which
is regarded as the primary source of official crime
data in the United States, the NCVS records the
race (White, Black, or Other) and Hispanic origin
of the victim (Hispanic or non-Hispanic). The
incorporation of ethnicity in the NCVS permits
estimates of both racial and ethnic differences in
crime or criminal victimization and makes this
survey probably the leading source of Hispanic or
Latina/o crime across the United States.

Other researchers have noted that racial and
ethnic disparities are usually not as heightened in
the NCVS as they are in official police crime statistics; that is probably the case for most types of
serious criminal victimization. For example,
Latinos are more likely to be victims of robbery
than are non-Hispanics, and the Black robbery
victim rate is in line with that of Hispanics.
Victimization differences between Latinos and
other racial/ethnic group members for other types
of violent crime are usually minor, but Latinos are
more likely to be victims of aggravated assault
than are Whites.

Information regarding gender disparities in
Latina/o crime is scarce, and violent crime research
on Latinas is in even shorter supply, but the NCVS
has demonstrated that some gender differences
in violence exist. There are obvious disparities

between Latina/o male and female victimization, but those differences vary by type of violence and even the relationship between victim and offender. For example, Latino male youth encounter significantly higher risks of stranger violence than do Latina youth. This finding is not surprising, given traditionally high levels of violence among young males in violent crime studies. In contrast, levels of non-stranger violence were similar among Latino and Latina youth. This interesting finding is probably linked to protective factors at home or some other influence not included in the survey. This area requires more research and should attract more attention in the future.

The NCVS has also collected race and ethnicity information since at least 1993, allowing the examination of changes over time in violent crime victimization. The overall violent victimization rate among Latinos has declined dramatically, with the rate going down almost 55% between 1993 and 2005. This decline, however, was consistent across all racial and ethnic groups, thus Latinos appear equally likely to have experienced similar declines in violent crime victimization as other racial/ethnic group members. This finding is important because it counters beliefs by immigrant opponents in the popular media who contend that immigrants have "contributed" to crime rates in their local areas. Latinos, legality aside, as a whole have long had the same levels of violent crime as Whites and Blacks, and violent crime victimization has declined among all groups, even in an era of intense immigration.

National Self-Report Surveys

A few national studies gather self-report of delinquency, risk, and health-related behaviors, but most of these studies have traditionally focused on Black or White delinquency. One exception is the National Longitudinal Study of Adolescent Health (Add Health), a study that initially explored the causes of health-related behaviors in a nationally representative sample of adolescents. Unlike most of the other national surveys, the Add Health asks the respondents to provide detailed information on Latina/o background—Mexican, Mexican American, Cuban, Puerto Rican, Central American,

and Other Latino (heavily South American)—which provides a unique opportunity to examine the range of groups that comprise the Latina/o population.

For most of the self-reported behaviors, Latina/o group variations are relatively minor, but in the cases where differences exist there are some interesting findings that should be examined by criminologists in the future. Respondents who identify themselves as Chicano or Puerto Rican are usually more likely than Mexican, Cuban, Central American, or Other Latinos to have seen a shooting or stabbing, had a knife or gun pulled on them, or gotten into a physical fight. In two of those self-reported behaviors, the percentages were highest among Chicano respondents, and in the other, Chicano and Puerto Rican youths had equal proportions (27%) exposed to viewing a shooting or stabbing.

On two other items, Chicano respondents had much higher proportions of violent activity than all other Latino groups. For example, nearly one third of Chicano respondents reported being jumped or assaulted, a level twice that of Mexicans, Puerto Ricans, Other Latinos, Central Americans and almost three times that of Cubans. Although relatively low, about 14% of surveyed Chicano youths reported having pulled a knife or a gun on someone, a level at least twice that of Other Latino respondents. For most of the remaining behaviors, all six groups are nearly equally exposed to low levels (less than 10%) of being shot, stabbed, or shooting or stabbing someone.

As a whole, the comparison of racial/ethnic differences across various national data sources illustrates that the primary difference in violent crime victimization among Blacks, Whites, and Latinos appears sizeable in the case of robbery and modest on other types of violent crime. When focusing on Latina/o youth, within Latina/o group disparities are greater for some types of violent activities, at least for Chicanos and to a lesser extent for Puerto Ricans, when compared to Cubans, Mexicans, Central Americans, and Other Latinos. Perhaps the most important outcome of this analysis is that while reliable Latina/o crime data are rare, the existing sources confirm that including Latinos and distinct Latina/o groups is important to the study of racial and ethnic disparities in crime.

City- and Community-Level Studies

Much of the recent research on race/ethnicity and crime has been conducted at the aggregate level with official crime data. Unfortunately, this literature has until very recently rarely considered the level of Latina/o crime or compared Latinos to other ethnic minority groups, largely due to official crime data limitations. This omission in part has led some researchers to revisit the long tradition of research on communities and crime, a tradition in criminology that dates back to the founding of American criminology.

Most of the handful of early ethnicity and crime studies focused on European immigrants in Chicago. A notable exception to this pattern is *Mexican Labor in the United States, Volume II*. In this study, Paul S. Taylor describes the criminal justice experiences of persons of Mexican origin in Chicago. By linking arrest statistics (felonies and misdemeanors) to local population sizes, he was able to compare White and Mexican criminal activities. While Mexicans were arrested at a percentage 2 to 3 times their population size, most of the arrests were not related to violence but were for property and alcohol-related offenses, a finding linked to the high number of single males in the population. This is important to highlight because patterns of criminal involvement were shaped by the age and sex distributions of the immigrant population, not the inherent criminality of immigrant Latinos.

Researchers now compare and contrast the characteristics of Black, White, and Latina/o homicides or control for social and economic determinants of crime thought to shape racial/ethnic disparities across neighborhoods. This is important because there is a strong relationship among economic disadvantage, affluence, and violent crime, and this connection has received a great deal of attention given the racial/ethnic differences and the strength of the association between crime and socioeconomic context at the community level. To a large extent, this notion is rooted in the claim by Robert Sampson and William J. Wilson that the sources of violent crime are rooted in structural differences across communities, which helps explain the racial/ethnic differences in violence. This thesis has become known as the "racial invariance" in the fundamental causes of violent crime. Still, the racial invariance thesis has rarely been applied to ethnicity and crime. While other conceptual or theoretical overviews on Latina/o crime and delinquency exist, attention is directed to macrolevel approaches, since this is where the bulk of Latina/o violence research is located.

Latinos and Immigration

In general, researchers have evaluated whether the structural conditions relevant for Black and White violence also apply to Latinos. Using homicide or violent crime data gathered directly from police departments and linked to census tracts that are widely used as proxies for communities, some criminologists have analyzed Latino-specific homicide either alone or in comparison with models for native-born Blacks and Whites, and sometimes immigrant Haitians, Jamaicans, or Latina/o subpopulations, for example, Mariel Cubans. These criminologists note that Latinos usually follow the same familiar pattern as Blacks and Whites in terms of the all-encompassing effect of concentrated disadvantage, even though some predictors of Latina/o homicide are to some extent distinct.

One issue influencing Latinos much more so than Whites or Blacks is the impact of immigration on crime in general and Latina/o violence specifically. For example, some scholars have written about the "Latino Paradox" wherein Latinos, especially immigrants, show lower levels of criminal behavior on certain indicators, including violence, than do Blacks, and in some cases Whites, despite their higher levels of disadvantage. Thus, Latinos have high levels of poverty but lower levels of homicide or violence than expected, given the power of economic disadvantage (or deprivation). The impact of recent immigration and the role of immigrant concentration appear to construct a different story with respect to violence than the impact of deprivation on African Americans appearing in the race and crime literature.

Criminologists have also been at the forefront of researchers debunking the popular notion that higher levels of immigration lead to increased violence and challenge the belief that more immigrants mean more homicide. In fact, higher levels of immigration generally have no effect on violence, contrary to expectations dating back to the turn of the past century that an influx of immigrants disrupts communities, creates neighborhood instability, and contributes to violent crime. Instead, studies support the finding that extreme disadvantage matters more for violence across racial, ethnic, and even immigrant groups than the presumed deleterious impact of immigration on violence proffered by immigrant opponents. Future researchers should pay closer attention to potential variations across and within groups of various immigrant and ethnic variations, especially among Latina/o groups.

Research Directions

There are a number of important questions that should be addressed in the future. More data collection is necessary to answer questions on Latina/o violence. For example, more data should be collected on the country of origin to help us better understand complex neighborhood dynamics. As immigrant Latinos move into older Latina/o areas, should we expect more or less crime in places like Miami, where Cubans are replaced by Colombians or Nicaraguans? Or, does Latina/o violence rise in cities like Los Angeles and Houston, where a dominant population of Mexican origin (native and foreign born alike) resides when Salvadorans and other Latina/o group members move in? It is also possible that, as disadvantaged as conditions in U.S. barrios may be, immigrant Latinos may use their sending countries, with even worse economic and political conditions, as reference points when assessing their position relative to others, thus canceling out possible inequality effects.

It is also important to note that violence is shaped by gender, and the case of Latinas has been ignored in the social science literature. Research should explore a variety of issues: little is known about the extent or sources of Latina victimization or offending; about whether Latina violence is shaped by interpersonal relations at home, work, school, or in the streets; and about whether immigrant status matters when Latinas report crime. Future studies moving beyond quantitative studies should help us understand why Latinos are less crime-prone than expected in various settings and fill in the gap in the Latina violence literature.

Given the growth in the number of Latinos and the corresponding increase in ethnic diversity across the country, it is important to not only ask more questions about Latina/o violence and delinquency but to answer them with more serious cutting-edge research studies on violence that cross theoretical and methodological approaches, academic disciplines, and data sources. This entry describes many studies focusing on Latinos that serve as starting points for future research, but much more work remains to help assess the powerful protective role of immigration in Latina/o communities and provide more meaningful context to explanations of ethnicity and crime.

Ramiro Martinez, Jr.

See also Immigrants and Crime; Latina/o/s; Media Portrayals of Latina/o/s; Victimization, Latina/o

Further Readings

Martinez, R., Jr. (1996). Latinos and lethal violence: The impact of poverty and inequality. *Social Problems, 43*, 131–146.

Martinez, R., Jr. (2002). Latino homicide: Immigration, violence and community. New York: Routledge.

Peterson, R. D., & Krivo, L. J. (2005). Macrostructural analyses of race, ethnicity, and violent crime: Recent lessons and new directions for research. *Annual Review of Sociology, 31*, 331–356.

Taylor, P. S. (1970). *Mexican labor in the United States* (Vol. 2). New York: Arno Press and New York Times. (Originally published in 1932)

LATINA/O/S

Latina/o Americans constitute the fastest-growing pan-ethnic population group in the United States. These self-identified or otherwise identified Latina/o Americans have originated from, or are descendants from, a Spanish-speaking country and share, in some way, a colonial experience from Spain. Although they are homogenous in this sense, they are heterogeneous and diverse in national origin, generational status, geographic residence, Spanish-language capacity, and phenotypic features, as well as other socioeconomic factors. Because the growth of the Latina/o American population in the United States has outpaced other pan-ethnic groups in the general population, and the increasing numbers of Latina/o Americans in the incarcerated population, their immigration in sheer numbers and increasing diversity have caused social scientists, researchers, policymakers, and laypeople to recognize their impact on the criminal justice system. This entry provides a brief historical account of the Latina/o American population; explores the issue of their identities and categorization; outlines their pan-ethnic and inter-ethnic demographic characteristics; focuses on their involvement in the U.S. criminal justice system—particularly issues surrounding re-arrest, reincarceration, imprisonment, and release; and offers recommendations for future research on this population.

Historical Context

The arrival of the Spanish in North America in the early 16th century marks the time when Latina/o Americans (defined as Spanish-speaking people or descendants of Spanish-speaking people) first inhabited what is now the continental United States. Since that time, Canada, Mexico, and the United States formed, and boundaries between them have been drawn and redrawn. Migration patterns have fluctuated, definitions and prosecutions of immigrant crimes have changed, and political power and economic conditions have become intertwined, all of which have affected Latina/o Americans. For people of Mexican descent—the largest Latina/o American population—many of those now living in the American Southwest that was a part of Mexico prior to the mid-19th century, before the U.S.–Mexican War and the subsequent Treaty of Guadalupe Hidalgo. This group was promised certain rights but did not necessarily receive them.

Enumerating Latina/o Americans, mainly Mexicans, during this time was difficult and was based on inaccurate methodological techniques. Part of the problem that arose and continues is that Latina/o Americans have been identified as a racial group instead of an ethnic group. U.S. intervention in Spanish-speaking countries during the past two centuries has contributed greatly to the influx of and current characteristics of Latina/o Americans currently residing in the United States.

Identities and Categorization

Individuals who would be considered Latina/o American, as specified by the U.S. Census Bureau, come from countries where Spanish is spoken. Other opinions have included those of scholars of Latina/o American studies, who have debated how individuals should be classified as Latina/o American; the general agreement is that those who come from Spanish-speaking places or speak Spanish would be classified as Latina/o American (another suggested term is "Hispanic," although this term generates much less agreement). Under this classification, specific groups who would be considered Latina/o American are from Mexico, the Caribbean (e.g., Puerto Rico), and Central and South American countries (e.g., El Salvador and Venezuela, respectively). The U.S. Census Bureau allows individuals who are Latina/o American to identify as such or as another related pan-ethnic identifier and then to indicate their specific national origin.

Another categorical issue is how to classify this population—as citizens, naturalized citizens, resident "aliens," and/or illegal (undocumented) immigrants. In the most recent decennial census, Latina/o Americans were given the option of identifying themselves not according to their legal identity but rather as belonging to more than one race—which is important to note, because they can belong to any of the constructed racial groups.

The U.S. Census Bureau first began to collect data on immigration in 1860, inquiring about country of origin to identify immigrants, particularly from Mexico. Between 1880 and 1970, the bureau asked questions regarding national origin and information about respondents' parents. From the early part of the 20th century through 1970 (excluding 1950), the U.S. Census concentrated on enumerating immigrants and their children, but individuals were identified and categorized according to the language they spoke at home as children.

In 1930, the U.S. Census Bureau experimented with the term *Mexican* as a race, but because this was difficult to measure, the label was discarded. As an alternative, in the 1950 Census, Spanish surnames were used to identify the Latina/o American population, but this approach was restricted to certain states, and the surnames did not comprehensively include all of those who identified as Latina/o-Hispanic; or it excluded those who were not descendants of people from other "non-Latina/o" countries. Still, this approach was used until 1980. The U.S. Census Bureau first asked about Hispanic and/or Spanish origin in 1970, listing ethnic and national origin identifiers.

In 1977, the Office of Management and Budget issued Directive 15. This was an influential change in how Latina/o Americans were counted, both in the general population and in the incarcerated population, as Latina/o Americans were required to be included in the national data collection efforts (this was reaffirmed in 1997 by the Interagency Committee for the Review of Racial and Ethnic Standards). However, it was not until the 1980s that criminal justice data on Latina/o Americans was compiled at the federal level.

In 2000, more inclusive categories are included under the Hispanic or Latino race category, and ethnic groups are more easily identified within the category (Mexican, Puerto Rican, Cuban, Other Hispanic, or Latino); in the census, 15% of Latinos identified themselves as such, as opposed to nation-specific ethnic identities. This represented a 200% increase from 1990; in 2000, approximately 10 million individuals identified themselves as "other Hispanic" or "Latino"—again, not by nation-specific origin. In the 21st century, Latinos are expected to be twice as likely to identify as "mixed heritage" than to state a single identity.

Characteristics of the Latina/o American Population

The Latina/o American population now numbers more than 44 million (nearly 15% of the U.S. population), according to nationally projected estimates by the U.S. Census Bureau. Between 2005 and 2006, the Latina/o American population had the largest growth rate (3.4%) of any racial and/or ethnic group. In addition, the population figures for this group increased from just over 22 million in 1990 to slightly more than 35 million in 2000. This 58% increase contrasts with a 13.2% increase for the total U.S. population.

The Latina/o American growth rate of 4.7% between 1990 and 2000 has been attributed mostly to the high birth rates and the increased influx of immigrants, the majority of whom originated in Mexico. During that time, more than half of the Latina/o American population had roots in Mexico (more than two thirds), followed by Puerto Ricans (nearly 10%), Central Americans (approximately 7%), other Latina/o Americans (nearly 7%), South Americans (nearly 6%), Cubans (nearly 4%), Dominicans (nearly 3%), and Spanish (1%).

In terms of demographic indicators, the Latina/o American population has increased to varying degrees in every state. There has been a noticeable migration of Latina/o Americans to cities in the central, midwestern, and southern areas of the United States. The majority (approximately 80%) of this population resides in just nine states: California (30%), Texas (19%), Florida (8%), New York (7%), Illinois (4%), Arizona (4%), New Jersey (3%), Colorado (2%), and New Mexico (2%). Of the states with the highest percentage of Latina/o Americans, New Mexico topped the list at 43%, followed by Texas and California, each at 35%, and Arizona at 28%.

A significant portion of the population of Latina/o Americans consists of those who are foreign born, as well as the undocumented population. According to recent figures, 40% (15 million) of Latina/o Americans in the United States were foreign born, and among them, most (52.1%) came to the United States between 1990 and 2002. Slightly more than a fourth entered in the 1980s, and a little more than a fifth entered the country before 1980.

As for noncitizens, approximately 25% of Latino Americans in the United States can claim that designation. More than 11 million Latinos—regardless of citizenship status—reside in the United States. Of these, an estimated 6 million, or 57%, are from Mexico, and an estimated 80% to 85% of the immigrant population consists of undocumented Mexicans. Of the undocumented immigrants, more than 83% are older than 18 years of age.

Incarceration and Imprisonment

At the end of 2005, more than 1.5 million adults in the United States were under the jurisdiction of either federal or state correctional authorities—including federal and state prisons, territorial prisons, local jails, Bureau of Immigration and Customs Enforcement (previously the Immigration Naturalization Service), military facilities, jails on Native American land, and juvenile detention facilities. By the end of the same year, approximately 2.3 million had been incarcerated.

Also, it is estimated that more than 5.5 million adults had served time in prison by the end of 2001, and of these individuals, about 1 million were Latina/o Americans. This represented an increase from 102,000 in 1974. Among all Latina/o Americans, the rate of having been incarcerated was 7.7%, and in 2001, 17% of Latino males had a chance of going to prison. Moreover, a projected 1 in 6 Latino American males will go to prison if the current rates of incarceration continue.

In addition, at the end of 2005, the nearly 300,000 Latina/o Americans who were incarcerated represented 20% of the inmate population. This represented an increase of 16% since 1995—the largest increase of any incarcerated racial or ethnic group. An estimated 279,000 of these Latina/o Americans were serving a prison sentence longer than a year. Further, between 1994 and 1997, more than 40% of Latina/o Americans were reconvicted. As for Latina Americans, nearly 16,000 were incarcerated in 2005, a rate of 76 per 100,000 based on those who were likely to be in prison at the end of 2005. In terms of offenses that resulted in incarceration, 2005 data show that for property offenses, 17% of those convicted were Latina/o American, and of the total population incarcerated for drug-related offenses, 23% consisted of Latinos.

A significant aspect of the criminal justice system concerns the sentencing of individuals who are found guilty or who plead guilty. After analyzing the Bureau of Justice Statistics State Court Processing Statistics biannually through the 1990s (through 1996), researchers Demuth and Steffensmeier found that Latina/o Americans received prison sentences corresponding more to African Americans' than to White individuals'. Latina/o Americans, however, have been overrepresented for robbery and drug trafficking violations that result in imprisonment. In regard to decisions regarding length of sentence, those researchers found no evidence of racial and/or ethnic differences.

In addition, in their analysis of individuals processed before trial in large urban court systems, Demuth and Steffensmeier found that 33% of Latina/o Americans were able to meet the financial requirements of bail, compared to 47% of African Americans and 58% of Whites who were able to do so. In analyzing those who were incarcerated before trial, 51% of Latina/o Americans were incarcerated, compared to 42% of African Americans and 32% of Whites.

Latina/o American households are more likely to be victimized by one or more crimes than are either African Americans or White Americans; however, because the National Crime Victimization Survey does not allow for reports of Latina/o Americans as perpetrators, interethnic and intraethnic crimes against Latina/o Americans are unknown in the national context. Notwithstanding this methodological problem, violent crimes committed against Latina/o Americans decreased by 56% between 1993 and 2000 (more than 690,000 instances of violent crime); Latina/o Americans were as likely as African Americans and Whites to be victimized.

A majority of incarcerated and imprisoned individuals eventually are released. In a landmark study of prisoner reentry—including re-arrest, reconviction, and reincarceration—of more than 250,000 individuals, released prisoners were tracked for 3 years after their release in 1994. More than two thirds of former inmates who were released were re-arrested for a new offense, and this arrest was almost always for a felony or a "serious" misdemeanor. Fewer than half of those arrested were reconvicted for a crime they had not committed in the past, and just over a fourth were resentenced for a new crime. In terms of re-arrests, similar to the overall inmate cohort released, more than two thirds of Latina/o Americans were re-arrested for a felony or serious misdemeanor, and more than 40% were reconvicted. Approximately half returned to prison eventually, with or without a new sentence; this figure was similar to all prisoners in this study as well. What emerged from this study and was argued by the researchers was that the longer prisoners were incarcerated, the more likely the former inmates were to recommit a new crime after release.

Directions for Future Research

Latina/o Americans are a diverse and heterogeneous population. They have experienced varied conditions that, for one reason or another, have led some, either as citizens or as noncitizens, to come into contact with the U.S. criminal justice system. Often, demographic and population counts in crime-and-justice-related research have glossed over the interethnic and intraethnic differences and similarities among the many Latina/o American subgroups. The issues explored in this entry warrant further exploration and research to include Latina/o American subgroups. Further, the examination of generational and immigration status and its interaction with community and familial effects has been limited within the context of crime and the criminal justice system as applied to Latina/o Americans.

Recommendations for effectively researching and understanding Latina/o Americans' social, familial, and community experiences include a few pertinent pursuits. Merely extrapolating a compilation of statistics for the larger Latina/o American groups is not enough. Research and study should be expanded to include other subgroups as well. In addition, many research studies have focused on Latinos who are single-ethnic individuals. Bi-ethnic and multiethnic Latina/o Americans must be included in various types of research. Also, nonimmigrant and immigrant Latina/o Americans comprise groups whose experiences living in the United States often are markedly different from other Latina/o American groups, based primarily on legal, and—to a lesser although important extent—to linguistic capacity. Such differentiation should be communicated, outlined, and investigated, as the criminal justice system responds in different ways to these different groups.

Finally, less emphasis should be placed on differentiating Latina/o Americans from other racial and ethnic groups, as this decision results in making broad generalizations without providing unique, clear, substantive insights into the specific group. The recommendations in this brief summary are necessary to advance serious inquiry into understanding Latina/o Americans in a way that produces or contributes to clear, logical, thoughtful clinical and policy interventions.

Damian J. Martinez

See also Domestic Violence, Latina/o/s; Latina/o Criminology; Latino Gangs; Media Portrayals of Latina/o/s; National Council of La Raza; Victimization, Latina/o

Further Readings

Bonczar, T. P. (2003). *Prevalence of imprisonment in the U.S. population, 1974–2001* (No. NCJ 197976). Washington, DC: Bureau of Justice Statistics.

Chapa, J. (2000). Hispanic/Latino ethnicity and identifiers. In M. J. Anderson (Ed.), *Encyclopedia of the U.S. Census* (pp. 243–246). Washington, DC: Congressional Quarterly Press.

Demuth, S., & Steffensmeier, D. (2004). Ethnicity effects on sentence outcomes in large urban courts: Comparisons among White, black, and Hispanic defendants. *Social Science Quarterly, 85*(4), 994–1011.

Guzmán, B. (2001). *The Hispanic population* (No. C2KBR/01-3). Washington, DC: U.S. Government Printing Office.

Harrison, P. M., & Beck, A. J. (2006). *Prisoners in 2005* (No. NCJ 215092). Washington, DC: Bureau of Justice Statistics.

Langan, P. A., & Levin, D. J. (2002). *Recidivism of prisoners released in 1994* (No. NCJ 193427). Washington, DC: Bureau of Justice Statistics.

Martinez, D. J. (2004). Hispanics incarcerated in state correctional facilities: Variations in inmate characteristics across Hispanic subgroups. *Journal of Ethnicity in Criminal Justice, 2*(1/2), 119–131.

Mirandé, A. (1990). *Gringo justice.* Notre Dame, IN: University of Notre Dame Press.

Reynoso, C. (2004). Hispanics and the criminal justice system. In P. S. J. Cafferty & D. W. Engstrom (Eds.), *Hispanics in the United States: An agenda for the twenty-first century* (pp. 277–315). New Brunswick, NJ: Transaction.

LATINO GANGS

Latino gang is a broad term that can apply to groups that have ties to Cuba, Colombia, South America, Mexico, Puerto Rico, and the Dominican Republic. Some of these gangs have become a major problem for law enforcement in the United States. The gangs participate in a wide range of criminal activity, including assault, auto theft, robbery, drug trafficking, and homicide. Latino gangs often have distinct ways of dressing (or displaying colors) and communicating (with symbols, graffiti, and tattoos); observe a strict code of silence when dealing with law enforcement; and have an intergenerational membership. The Latino gang culture exemplifies male machismo. Although women often play secondary roles, there are a few gangs in which women take a more prominent role. Latino gangs are quite effective at defending their geographical territories by using violence that is quite frequently lethal. The entry provides an overview of several Latino gangs that pose a serious threat to their communities: the Mexican Mafia, La Nuestra Familia, Latin Kings, and MS-13.

Mexican Mafia

La Eme, or the Mexican Mafia, was formed in east Los Angeles in the early 1950s. Originally composed of several smaller gangs dating back as early as the 1920s, the Mexican Mafia began as a protection service primarily in the California prison community. By the late 1960s, the Mexican Mafia controlled the majority of illegal activities inside the correctional institutions. As the gang's size and influence increased, so did its brutality. The primary customers of the gang's criminal enterprise were White and African American, but any non-gang member within the system could easily find himself a target of violence. With ruthlessness being key to their success, gang members do not hesitate to eliminate any who get in the way, including rivals or members. Their primary criminal activities inside prison include gambling, drug dealing, and male prostitution rings. Outside of prison in California, La Eme controls gang activity in east Los Angeles as well as other southern California territories and manages most of the drug dealing in these areas. Armed robberies are another major source of income, and any rivals who attempt to move in on the Mexican Mafia's territory face a quick and brutal end. Currently, this gang's presence can be felt in correctional facilities across the United States.

Of all the Mexican gangs, members of the Mexican Mafia are arrested at the highest rate. Theorists explain the arrest disparity in a few different ways. One explanation places responsibility on the extensive crime networks that put more people on the streets doing illegal acts and thus increase the likelihood of contact with law enforcement. Additionally, prison is like home to many members of the gang; they can cope on the inside, whereas they may lack survival skills for mainstream society.

Considered a highly organized and well-established gang by law enforcement, the Mexican Mafia's success can be explained by its leadership system. At the top, the godfather or president wields the most power, and below that position is an underboss or vice president responsible for managing the gang's activities. Within each prison is a regional general, who leads the lieutenants and sergeants in their roles as supervisors to the soldiers and workers. A similar structure comprises the street side of the organizations, and the prison and street leaders are interchangeable, depending on who is in prison and who is on the street at any given time. Historically, a member released from prison could leave the gang; however, disassociation is no longer accepted. Currently, anyone who attempts to defect is killed. Once a member is released from prison, he is expected to make contact with other members on the outside and continue illicit operations or pay with his life.

The Mexican Mafia is represented by the Mexican flag or by the flag's colors—red, green, and white. Other symbols include MM, M, EME, a single black handprint, or the number 13, which stands for the 13th letter of the alphabet (M). They are very closely allied with the Surenos and with MS-13.

La Nuestra Familia

Established in 1958, La Nuestra Familia is the rival gang of the Mexican Mafia. Translated into English, their name means "Our Family." The gang consists of Mexican Americans from the Los Angeles area. Unlike La Eme, La Nuestra Familia is involved with many Chinese gangs, such as the Wah Ching and Chung Ching Yee. Through these alliances, La Nuestra Familia participates in both the trafficking and sale of heroin. Throughout the 1980s, La Nuestra Familia experienced a great decline in power because of membership loss and inefficient management. As its members deserted in large numbers, leaders promised reform but did not implement successful strategies to maintain dominance in the crime world. Its primary rival, the Mexican Mafia, was gaining influence and taking over former La Nuestra Familia's territory. Concomitantly, law enforcement increased its crime control efforts, arresting and charging many leaders under the Racketeer Influenced Corrupt Organization (RICO) laws, which ultimately weakened the organization.

The family made money through other criminal activities, including burglary, robbery, and larceny. While not as violent and brutal as its rival, La Nuestra Familia will not hesitate to protect its assets or operation through the use of violence. La Nuestra Familia's drug ring extends to both the streets and prison.

Military rank structure applies to this gang as well. Generals command inside the correctional system as well as outside and use captains as overseers. Captains are in charge of lieutenants who directly command the soldiers, the lowest rank in the system. Mobility is possible, as opportunities for advancement are present. If a member shows outstanding executive abilities or performs three killings, he is eligible for promotion.

Symbols for La Nuestra Familia include NF, LNF, and the number 14, which stands for the 14th letter of the alphabet, N. They are closely allied with the Nortenos and have an uneasy working relationship with Black Guerilla Family (they have common enemies).

Almighty Latin King and Queen Nation

The Almighty Latin King and Queen Nation (ALKQN) is a gang who closely resemble the Chinese street gangs of New York; their original purpose was to protect the residents of their neighborhoods from unprovoked attacks from competitors or other ethnic groups. First appearing in Chicago about 50 years ago, the Latin Kings were fierce protectors of Hispanic culture and, consequently, their territory. They also had a significant presence in Illinois prisons, where ethnic stratification forced Latino inmates together. Most ALKQN members were in the prison system when they joined. Their presence has recently expanded to the streets as many members released from prison continue their participation in crime. Their primary income derives from street-level drug trafficking, but they are also involved in extortion and arms trafficking. Recruitment takes place both in prison and in Latina/o neighborhoods, where gang members appeal to young Latinos by stressing Latin pride and heritage. ALKQN maintain a dominant presence in Illinois, Connecticut, and New York. Although the overwhelming majority of their membership is Latino, a small percentage is African American as well as White.

Departing from other gang structures, the Latin Kings designate members' positions by age. "Pee Wee" members are newly recruited members between 10 and 12 years of age. "Juniors" are between the ages of 12 and 14, and "Homeboys" are between the ages of 16 and 20. Females, who are required to follow all of the same codes as the males, are considered part of the Almighty Latin Queen Nation, and play supporting roles to Kings' criminal activities and act as sex partners to the male members. However, the Kings and Queens don't adhere to strict gender norms; many females occupy important leadership roles and follow the same code as males. For members who do not follow the codes, serious consequences await. A disobedient gang member can expect beatings, torture, or murder as possible punishment, but offenders are given a trial and able to defend themselves; if they cannot be present, they may submit their defenses in writing.

The Almighty Latin King and Queen Nation has a very complex and highly organized leadership system and is seen by experts as one of the largest and most structured gangs in the United States. The Council Committee sits at the top of the leadership pyramid and has a Crown Chairman with complete control over the gang; his second in command is the Executive Crown. The Prime Minister of Defense directs all security issues, and the Crown Treasurer manages the gang's financial matters. The Crown Secretariat is in charge of all administrative duties. The second level of leadership is the Supreme Chapter. The Supreme First Crown runs his region, with the Supreme Second Crown as his second in charge. His commands are considered law and must be followed. The Supreme Warlord Nation maintains order in the gang and imposes punishments among members who fail to comply with the guidelines. His primary muscle is the Supreme Crown of Arms, who upgrades the gang's weapons arsenal. The Regional Chapter is the lowest level of organization. The First Crown and Second Crown share control of a specific area. The Minister of Defense maintains records of possible threats to the gang and ongoing conflicts. His primary assistant is the Crown of Arms. The Crown Advisor is similar to a historian; he maintains records of the gang's procedures and past. Finally, the Crown Prince is responsible for all field operations, ensuring that everyone participates and performs his or her tasks correctly. ALKQN earns its reputation of possessing a thorough organizational structure.

The Latin Kings favor the colors black and gold. Black symbolizes death, while gold symbolizes life. To show respect, many gang members will wear black beads to represent deceased ALKQN members. The primary symbol for the ALKQN is a five-point golden crown. Each point on the crown stands for one of the characteristics of love, respect, honor, sacrifice, and obedience. Gang members attribute their problems to White, upperclass society and their perpetuation of inequality within society and government.

MS-13

Established in Los Angeles in the early 1980s, Mara Salvatrucha, or MS-13, has quickly become one of the most dangerous Latina/o gangs in America. With a civil war raging in El Salvador, people being hunted by death squads needed a way out of the danger. They found asylum in the United States, but given the prevalence of Latina/o gangs in California, the Salvadorans quickly became rivals for territory with the local Mexican gangs. In order to survive, they created their own organization, using Latin heritage as a hook for recruiting purposes. While MS-13 was originally formed for protection of displaced immigrants, the group rapidly transformed into a violent criminal organization. As the 12-year-long civil war raged in El Salvador, Salvadorans continued to move to Los Angeles and also to Washington, D.C. Many of the Salvadorans maintained ties to their resistance groups in El Salvador, including the Farabundo Marti National Liberation Front (in Spanish, the *Frente Farabundo Martí para la Liberación Nacional*) and La Mara, a violent street gang in El Salvador. Members of these groups are hard-core, highly trained guerillas, capable of using many different types of explosives and booby traps.

MS-13 exists in at least 42 American states and most of Central America. Law enforcement officials remain unclear about the specific leadership system in MS-13, including the existence of a central council. According to the Federal Bureau of Investigation, MS-13 is a loosely structured street gang and not a highly organized criminal enterprise. In the United States, arrests of MS-13 members have taken place in Georgia, West Virginia, Iowa, Illinois, New York, New Jersey, Alaska, North Carolina, Florida, Virginia, Texas, California, Washington, D.C., and many other cities and states; they cover a large territory despite their reputation of being less orderly than other gangs. MS-13 members can be found in the prison systems of New York, Virginia, Maryland, Guatemala, and El Salvador.

In El Salvador, MS-13's reputation is that of a dangerous and brutal paramilitary group. They are responsible for countless beheadings and grenade attacks throughout Central American countries. Initiation, not surprisingly, is quite brutal. While many MS-13 cliques have a traditional brutal jumping-in process, more hard-core cliques require a potential member to commit a violent offense, such as a rape, murder, or beating. Females seeking initiation have an additional option of being "sexed in" by having sex with six of the strongest members of that clique. However, females can also be jumped in with some women and show even more violent behavior than their male counterparts. Once the member has been initiated, death is the only way out of the gang. Deserters are brutally killed, reflecting the influence of past Latin American warfare on the group. This ritual may act as a deterrent to other members. Gang members often dismember victims with a machete and frequently behead them. Rape, drug dealing, people smuggling, assault, prostitution, kidnapping, home invasions, and vandalism are frequently used intimidation tactics.

Criminal activity in MS-13 is quite extensive. Because of their guerilla ties in Central America, MS-13 has easy access to military-grade arms like grenades and automatic weapons, positioning MS-13 in the crime world as a major illegal arms distributor. Auto theft is another profitable criminal enterprise in the network. Members steal cars in the United States and ship them back to El Salvador and South America. An estimated 80% of vehicles owned in El Salvador were stolen in the United States.

Law enforcement use multiple strategies to apprehend MS-13 members and stop their activities. By arresting and deporting members, the police can reduce the MS-13 presence, but neither of these approaches is very effective in ending the MS-13 reign. MS-13 has such a large hold on prison culture that many members consider it a privilege to be incarcerated, and there is a 60% incarceration rate for gang members. Deportation is ineffective as well, because it sends MS-13 leadership back to the host country to recruit even more members. However, deportation is more feared by MS-13 members than prison. Once they are deported, they become priority targets for Sombra Negra, or Black Shadow. The El Salvadorian government denies Sombra Negra's existence, but it is identified by others as a death squad administering vigilante justice to high-profile criminals and gang members. Rumors suggest Sombra Negra is made up of military personnel and police officers.

While the MS-13 fear Sombra Negra, they do not fear the police in Central American countries. When police make an important arrest in the gang, MS-13 retaliate against them using brutal tactics and traps. Not easily intimidated, law enforcement officers are frequently assaulted, and several federal agents have been killed in their work against MS-13. To help combat this powerful gang, the FBI created an MS-13 National Gang Task Force in 2004.

Members of MS-13 prominently display and even flaunt their membership. Representing colors include blue and white, which are taken from the Salvadorian flag. Members are usually heavily tattooed, with ink covering most of their bodies, including the face. A typical hand signal is three fingers spread apart and pointing, so that it resembles an "M." Rivalries include the 18th Street Gang, the Brown Pride Gang, Salvadorians With Pride (SWP-18), La 18, 42nd Street Little Criminals, the Surenos, and the Latin Kings.

Catherine E. Burton and
Daniel P. Stevens

See also Mara Salvatrucha (MS-13); Prison Gangs; Subculture of Violence Theory

Further Readings

Brotherton, D., & Barrios, L. (2004). *The almighty Latin king and queen nation.* New York: Columbia University Press.

Federal Bureau of Investigation. (2006, April). A close-up of MS-13: FBI executive visits El Salvador. *National Gang Threat Assessment 2005.* Washington, DC: Department of Justice. Retrieved from http://www.fbi.gov/page2/april06/burrus041906.htm

Federal Bureau of Investigation. (2008, January). The MS-13 threat: A national assessment. *Headline Archives (Violent Gang Website).* Washington, DC: Department of Justice. Retrieved from http://www.fbi.gov/page2/jan08/ms13_011408.html

Grennan, S., & Britz, M. (2006). *Organized crime: A worldwide perspective.* Upper Saddle River, NJ: Prentice Hall.

Grennan, S., Britz, M., Rush, J, & Barker, T. (2000). *Gangs: An international approach.* Upper Saddle River, NJ: Prentice Hall.

Knox, G. W. (2000). *An introduction to gangs.* Chicago: New Chicago School Press.

Swecker, C. (2005, April). Statement before the subcommittee on the western hemisphere international relations. *Congressional testimony 2005.* Washington, DC: Department of Justice. Retrieved from http://www.fbi.gov/congress/congress05/swecker042005.htm

LatinoJustice PRLDEF

LatinoJustice PRLDEF (formerly the Puerto Rican Legal Defense and Education Fund) is an organization that supports the Latina/o community to create an equal society among all. LatinoJustice PRLDEF creates opportunities for Latinos by using the legal system, education, policy, support, and sponsorship. LatinoJustice PRLDEF wants these citizens to garner success at work, school, and home and to fulfill their dreams. This entry reviews the history of LatinoJustice PRLDEF, the details of the first case litigated by the organization, a more recent illustration of LatinoJustice PRLDEF litigation, and some closing thoughts on the organization and its role in society.

History of LatinoJustice PRLDEF

After World War II, Puerto Ricans began migrating to the United States in an effort to attain a better life. These immigrants endured many hardships, including trouble finding employment and not receiving the proper education at school. Another issue was the fact that they were widely viewed as illegal immigrants when in fact they were legal U.S. citizens. On March 12, 1917, President Woodrow Wilson approved the Jones-Shafroth Act, thereby cementing Puerto Ricans' place in the United States. The act separated the executive, legislative, and judicial branches of the Puerto Rican government, empowered individuals with civil rights, and implemented an elected bicameral legislature; that is, the legislature is divided into two houses: the upper, which is the Senate, and the lower, known as the House of Representatives. The governor of Puerto Rico and the president of the United States retain the right to veto acts passed by the legislature. Moreover, the U.S. Congress has the power to halt any action taken by the legislature. Lastly, the United States maintains control over all mail services, defense, immigration, fiscal and economic matters, and all other basic governmental affairs. This law was passed 19 years after the Spanish ceded Puerto Rico to the United States upon the conclusion of the Spanish-American War in 1898.

Victor Marrero, Cesar Perales, and Jorge Batista, all lawyers, were the founding fathers of PRLDEF. This program was established in 1972 in an unremarkable building on Second Avenue in New York City to give legal support to the Puerto Rican community. Soon afterward, this new organization was approached by Aspira, a youth development group, with their first legal case. The importance of LatinoJustice PRLDEF is that it helps provide Latinos an opportunity to succeed with their education, employment, and voting and to ensure that Latinos have a voice in American democracy.

LatinoJustice PRLDEF's First Case

In 1972 the youth development group Aspira approached PRLDEF to request help with a case against the New York City Board of Education.

Aspira is a national nonprofit group committed to leadership development and education of the Puerto Rican community. The name Aspira is derived from the Spanish word *aspirar*, or *aspire* in English. In that year there were approximately 1,130,000 registered immigrant students in the United States. Out of that total, 27% (nearly 260,000) were Puerto Rican students who lived in New York. The problem was that few teachers were bilingual and could not help the children who were not proficient in English to get the proper education. Instead of addressing the issue, the board of education ignored it, and those children did not receive the proper education. These children were identified as limited English proficiency (LEP) students.

A consent decree was issued that put into operation a program that would transition the students from Spanish speaking to English speaking over a period of time while also allowing the students to learn the current curriculum. Essentially it was a start to the current English as a Second Language programs now in service at schools with non–English-speaking students. Although the case *Aspira v. the Board of Education of the City of New York* was won and a new program was put into service, all was not well. There was still the issue of actually implementing the verdict at educational institutions. The result came 4 years after the board and Aspira had arrived at an agreement. LEP students were offered a way to receive the same education as the other students, while also participating in a program designed to teach them the English language.

After 10 years, a review was conducted and the results implied that although the courts had played a major role in changing the face of education and its approach to the LEP students, large numbers of non–English-speaking students at all grade levels still were not receiving a proper education. The immigrant students were being left behind in all the basic educational necessities. In most of the cases, the students spoke little or no English but were forced to attend classes where all the texts, subjects, and instruction were provided only in English. Consequently they were failing math, English, science, and social studies. The problem stemmed from the inability to monitor and enforce the decree at schools and from not following up on schools that did adhere to the decree in order to distinguish the educational benefits for the students who did participate. The solution to this seemingly insurmountable problem was actually quite simple. It required the active participation of the students' parents to keep applying pressure to the faculty and for politicians at the local and state levels to implement policies that address language issues at school.

Recent Case Handled by LatinoJustice PRLDEF

In the small town of Mamaroneck, New York, a number of day laborers had been accustomed to making the trek from home, and some from other villages, to a local park. All of these 200 or so men, mostly immigrants who could not speak English, came to this location daily, and had done so for years past, where contractors and various other employment providers would come to hire the workers. For most of these men, this was their only source of income. In the spring of 2006, the village mayor ordered the village's police department to close down the hiring site.

On April 27, 2006, a couple of weeks after the hiring site in the village closed down, representatives of PRLDEF and of the village of Mamaroneck entered the courtroom as participants in a lawsuit filed by six of the day laborers. During the hearing it emerged that police officers had set up checkpoints for contractors and various other individuals looking for laborers while other officers were aggressively ticketing any of the men who tried to approach the original site to look for work. In some instances the officers had followed laborers around in a police cruiser with lights flashing and would ticket anyone who approached them. Later, police had begun following the day laborers even when they were not in the park. The mayor stated that these actions were taken to protect the people and in order to keep the park clean. Some specific reasons for initiating a ban on laborers gathering at the park were given, but the accusations were found to be without merit. In fact crime had not risen and the laborers were not trashing the park. Finally, it emerged that only Latinos had been targeted during this operation.

After the first court date, when matters did not proceed in the village's favor, the mayor approached the laborers, and the parties began negotiating to settle the matter out of court. Without acknowledging any wrongdoing on the part of the village, the mayor met with six of the immigrants to discuss how to improve the relations between laborers and police while also creating a safe and secure environment for all local residents. Subsequently, the village allowed the laborers to resume gathering at or near the original location, where many continued working for the contractors as before. On June 11, 2007, the two sides came to a settlement. Mamaroneck police officers have been prohibited from discrimination against day laborers or misconduct toward them. The village also agreed to pay $550,000 for the day laborers' legal fees. To ensure that the village follows the order, a court-appointed monitor was assigned.

Conclusion

LatinoJustice PRLDEF is intended to help Latinos secure the benefits to which they are entitled as citizens. LatinoJustice PRLDEF works to ensure that LEP students in the U.S. educational system will receive the proper education. In the *Aspira v. Board of Education of the City of New York* (1972) decision, the court ruled in favor of the immigrants and simply ordered that no educational facility will deter a student from receiving suitable education on the basis of an inability to use the English language. In 2002 in Connecticut, PRLDEF filed an unfair labor suit against Beauty Enterprises when that company tried to impose an English-only mandate within the company, thus discriminating against its Latina/o employees only. PRLDEF was also responsible for helping diversify the New York Police Department (NYPD). In 1972 the NYPD was dominated by White officers. Now all races are participating in keeping the streets of the city safe, and many Latina/o officers patrol as well as have higher-ranking positions on the NYPD. Cesar Perales is still involved with the PRDLEF to this day.

Abraham Castillo

See also NAACP Legal Defense Fund; National Association for the Advancement of Colored People (NAACP); Universal Negro Improvement Association; W. Haywood Burns Institute for Juvenile Justice Fairness and Equity

Further Readings

Lambert, B. (2005, December 17). L.I. is ordered to give notice of house raids. *The New York Times*. Retrieved from http://www.nytimes.com/2005/12/17/nyregion/17brookhaven.html

O'Connor, A. (2006, May 20). Mamaroneck seeks to settle lawsuit filed by laborers. *The New York Times*. Retrieved from http://www.nytimes.com/2006/05/20/nyregion/20westchester.html

Santiago, I. (1986, November). The education of Hispanic Americans: A challenge for the future. *American Journal of Education*, 995(1), 149–199.

U.S. Census Bureau. (2004, March). *Global population profile: 2002* (International Population Report No. WP/02). Retrieved from http://www.census.gov/prod/2004pubs/wp-02.pdf

Websites

LatinoJustice PRLDEF: http://www.prldef.org

LEAGUE OF UNITED LATIN AMERICAN CITIZENS

The League of United Latin American Citizens (LULAC) was formed on February 17, 1929, in Corpus Christi, Texas. It is the oldest and largest Hispanic advocacy group in the United States. Its roots and reason for existing, however, go back nearly 100 years prior to its inception. LULAC has played an important role in justice for Mexican Americans. This entry describes the history, mission, role of LULAC in addressing racial discrimination faced by Mexican Americans, and its future.

Beginnings

In the early 1800s, Mexico held claim to a large portion of what is now the modern United States of America. In 1835, the residents of the Mexican province of Texas revolted against the government of Mexico, beginning the Texas War of Independence. After more than a year of fighting battles, including the famous battle of the Alamo, Mexican President Santa Anna signed the Treaty of Velasco in 1836, ceding what is now the state of Texas.

The newly emerging Republic of Texas continued to deal with border disputes with Mexico and in 1845 decided to join the United States. This action led in 1846 to the U.S.–Mexican War, which after 2 years culminated in Mexico's defeat and the subsequent annexation of land previously held by Mexico. This land today constitutes the states of California, Arizona, New Mexico, Nevada, and Utah.

With literally the stroke of a pen, 77,000 Mexicans became U.S. citizens. These Mexican American citizens suffered a great deal of discrimination for generations. Relegated to second-class citizen status, Mexican Americans were denied basic civil rights, their land was often taken from them, and they were segregated from mainstream American society. Like the Blacks in the South, Mexican Americans were forced to use "Mexican only" water fountains and were not served in White restaurants.

The emergence of LULAC was more of a progression than a revolution. Several Mexican American organizations were already in existence prior to LULAC. The most influential of these groups were the Knights of America, the Order of the Sons of America, and the newly formed League of Latin American Citizens. Ben Garza, a Corpus Christi businessman and a leader in the Order of the Sons of America, called for the uniting of all Mexican American organizations. Bringing together the leaders of these groups, Garza proposed a merger, and on February 17, 1929, in Corpus Christi, Texas, Ben Garza was installed as the chair of the unified organization now known as the League of United Latin American Citizens; its motto is "All for One, One for All."

Mission

The official mission statement of LULAC is to "advance the economic condition, educational attainment, political influence, health and civil rights of the Hispanic population in the United States." Mandated by the leadership of LULAC, these goals were to be attained by adopting cultural patterns and attitudes of American society. This process of assimilation served two purposes. First, it portrayed a group who believed in the "American way"—that education and hard work are valued and will be compensated both economically and civilly. Second, it diffused fear that LULAC was a fringe group promoting an "un-American" agenda. To emphasize that it was indeed an American organization with corresponding values, LULAC adopted the American flag as its official flag and "America the Beautiful" as the official song. LULAC members were also encouraged to learn the English language as well as to obtain citizenship.

Today LULAC has more than 115,000 members spread across 700 councils in the United States and Puerto Rico. LULAC continues to be an effective advocate at the local level as well as a national political powerhouse. In keeping with its mission statement, LULAC operates 48 employment centers offering job placement as well as job skills training. Operating 16 regional education centers throughout the United States, LULAC provides educational services as well as financial assistance and counseling to more than 18,000 students a year. LULAC, through community partnerships and corporate sponsors, also awards $1 million a year in scholarships.

Politics

The founders of LULAC recognized the racial discrimination faced by Mexican Americans. Leaders of LULAC truly believed that by assimilating into the culture of America and embracing American values, Mexican Americans could overcome racial bias. Its deliberate manner of dealing with racial, economic, and civil rights issues faced by Mexican Americans through the legal system has set LULAC apart from other, perhaps more confrontational, Hispanic advocacy groups and has contributed to its success over the past 75 years. Adhering to this policy, LULAC has brought forth and won many important legal battles, benefiting not only Mexican Americans but all minority classes.

Probably the most important piece of litigation brought forth by LULAC is the 1946 case *Mendez v. Westminster*. Gonzalo and Felicitas Mendez sued the Westminster School District of Orange County, California, when their children were denied enrollment at the Main Street School. The basis for the denial was that Mexicans were inferior and needed separate schools because of their lack of English proficiency. The Mendezes won,

and the case was upheld by the Ninth Federal District Court. As a direct result of the *Mendez* case, California on June 14, 1947, passed the Anderson Bill, repealing all California school codes mandating segregation. The bill was signed into law by then-California Governor Earl Warren, who would later, as a Supreme Court Justice, write the majority opinion in the *Brown v. Board of Education* decision.

Another landmark case, *Hernandez v. Texas*, was brought forth by LULAC in 1954 and was eventually decided in the U.S. Supreme Court. This case involved the systematic exclusion of Mexican Americans from juries in Jackson County, Texas. The decision won the right of Mexican Americans to serve on juries and was once again written by Justice Earl Warren, who stated in his majority opinion that members of a class cannot be systematically excluded; juries should be selected from all qualified persons regardless of national origin or descent.

Programs

In keeping with the spirit of working hard and being self-sufficient, LULAC does not rely solely on the courts or the political winds of change to advance its mission. Rather, LULAC continues to develop and nurture new ideas. Many of these ideas have become national programs that further its mission of advancing the economic condition, educational attainment, political influence, and health and civil rights of the Hispanic population. These programs are discussed next.

American GI Forum

Facilitated by LULAC, the GI Forum was formed by Dr. Hector P. Garcia, a returning World War II veteran in 1946. The organization's main goals were to fight against discrimination of all veterans, regardless of race, color, sex, age or national origin. With a decidedly Mexican American bent due to its roots in Deep South Texas, the GI Forum has fought issues ranging from the failure of the Veteran's Administration to deliver benefits to military veterans to ensuring that convicted murderers receive their due process rights guaranteed under the Constitution.

Mexican American Legal Defense and Educational Fund

Founded in 1968 by Pete Tijerina, LULAC's civil rights chairman for the state of Texas at that time, the Mexican American Legal Defense and Educational Fund's (MALDEF) mission is to foster sound public policies, laws, and programs to safeguard the civil rights of the 45 million Latinos living in the United States and to empower the Latina/o community to fully participate in our society. Not only does MALDEF provide financial assistance for legal defense for Mexican Americans, it also provides scholarship money to Hispanic law students.

SER: Jobs for Progress

SER is an acronym for "Service, Employment and Redevelopment," and in Spanish, *ser* means "to be." Formed in 1965, SER is recognized by the U.S. Department of Labor as the premier community-based organization serving the employment needs of the Hispanic community. SER provides a multitude of services not only to Hispanics but to anyone in need of employment education assistance or job placement. Funded by the U.S. Department of Labor as well as corporations such as The Home Depot, SER has provided service to more than 1 million people since its inception.

Robert Irving

See also Immigration Legislation; Jury Selection; Latina/o/s; Media Portrayals of Latina/o/s

Further Readings

Allsup, C. (1982). *American G. I. Forum: Origins and evolution.* Austin: University of Texas Press.

Hernandez v. Texas, 347 U.S. 475 (1954). Certiorari to the court of criminal appeals of Texas.

Kanellos, N. (1993). *The Hispanic-American Almanac: A reference work on Hispanics in the United States.* Detroit, MI: Gale.

League of United Latin American Citizens. (n.d.). *"All for One—One for All"—History of LULAC.* Retrieved September 3, 2008, from http://www.lulac.org/about/history.html

Lee, R. (2008). *The Mexican-American War.* Retrieved http://www.historyguy.com

Marquez, B. (1989, June). The politics of race and assimilation: The League of United Latin American Citizens 1929–40. *The Western Political Quarterly, 42*(2), 355–375.

Meier, M. S., & Gutierrez, M. (2000). *Encyclopedia of the Mexican American civil rights movement.* Westport, CT: Greenwood.

Meier, M. S., & Rivera, F. (1981). *Dictionary of Mexican American history.* Westport, CT: Greenwood.

Mendez v. Westminster School Dist. of Orange County, 64 F.Supp. 544 (D.C. Cal. 1946).

Nevaer, L. E., & Ekstein, V. P. (2007). *HR and the new Hispanic workforce: A comprehensive guide to cultivating and leveraging employee success.* Mountain View, CA: Davies-Black.

Websites

Mexican American Legal Defense and Educational Fund: http://www.MALDEF.org

LOS ANGELES RACE RIOT OF 1965

In 1965, the city of Los Angeles endured one of the worst riots in its history. Although the riot was prompted by a single incident, the predominantly Black area known as Watts was characterized by a widespread perception and feelings of racial isolation, grievance, and discrimination. These racial issues, prevalent throughout the United States at that time, sparked several riots in cities across the country. In Los Angeles, however, the riots reached such great proportions that law enforcement was stymied as to how to respond. This entry examines the root causes of the riot, including the building tensions within the Black community and the incident that seemingly prompted the violent rioting, which ensued for 6 straight days. This entry also explores the findings and policy proposals of the California Governor's Commission submitted in the aftermath of the riot as well as criticism of some of the points made in that report.

Racial Tensions in the Summer of 1965

In the summer of 1964, riots broke out in at least seven major cities around the United States. Fueled by racial tensions, many of participants in these riots were similar in their ethnic makeup to the Watts area of Los Angeles. Unlike Los Angeles, however, many of these riots were more easily contained and law enforcement was able to get them quickly under control. Although the specific causes of the riots are not known, several factors may have contributed to the buildup of racial tensions in the area.

Since World War II, many of the large cities had witnessed a displacement of populations. Black populations began to fill the central city areas, while White populations began moving into the suburban areas. The increasing density of Blacks in these areas created a variety of social, economic, and law enforcement problems that likely established the foundation for the Los Angeles Riot of 1965, also known as the "Watts Riots."

Blacks who moved into the larger cities were hoping for more opportunities than their ancestors had had in the rural communities from which they came. However, what they found was that they lacked the education, skills and training needed for success in a modern city. Due to the displacement of Whites to the suburbs, pockets of Black communities began to experience social and economic isolation. The high density of Blacks in these areas made employment difficult to find, social programs were insufficient, and law enforcement was tenuous at best. Paramount to these issues was the ever-present feeling of resentment that Blacks had toward their situation. Lack of education and employment created a sense of failure, which contributed to a continuously disintegrating social fabric within the Black communities. All of these issues would continue to add to the buildup of resentment; ultimately one incident would be enough to spark the violent protest that would become a 6-day riot.

The Riot

On August 11, 1965, a California Highway Patrolman made a routine stop on a car that was being driven recklessly. The stop occurred in a Black neighborhood near the area of Los Angeles known as Watts. Two brothers were in the car: Marquette Frye (driver) and Ronald Frye (passenger). Marquette appeared intoxicated and was asked to exit the car and take a standard field sobriety test. Upon failing the sobriety test, Marquette Frye was placed under arrest, and Ronald Frye went to his nearby home to get his mother so she could claim the car. The patrolman radioed to have the car towed. Both the tow truck and Ronald and Mrs. Frye arrived back at the scene at the same time. At this point, approximately 250 spectators had gathered. Marquette Frye, who was still under arrest, had a mild altercation with his mother and then began to shout into the crowd that the officers would have to kill him before he would be taken to jail. With this incitement, the crowd became hostile and began to harass the patrolmen at the scene. As several other highway patrolmen arrived to assist, the Frye brothers began to fight with the officers. All three Fryes were placed under arrest. By then, the crowd had grown to more than 1,000 people.

As tensions continued to escalate, the officers arrested two more people at the scene. When the officers drove away, the mob threw rocks at their car. As word of this incident spread, many false and distorted stories began to circulate throughout the neighborhood. It was believed that the police mistreated the Fryes and that the police may have beaten and arrested a pregnant woman. Within an hour of the incident, the mob began to throw rocks, pull motorists out of their cars, vandalize buildings, and loot stores.

Initially, it appeared that the incident was confined to that one night. Los Angeles Police Department (LAPD) met with leaders of the Black community the next day to persuade them to calm the crowds. However, this meeting turned into a forum to discuss the grievances of the Black communities. LAPD intended to remove White police officers from the troubled area and replace them with Black police officers, an untried method of crowd and riot control. Before this new method could be implemented, rioting broke out again. On Friday morning, August 13, about 1,000 National Guardsmen were requested, but they were not deployed until late that evening. Until this point, the rioting was contained inside the Watts area. As Friday evening progressed, the rioting had spread to surrounding areas of southeast Los Angeles. The rioting was so widespread by the end of Friday evening that a curfew was established for subsequent nights. Any unauthorized persons on the streets after 8:00 p.m. would be arrested. Control of the situation was not regained until late Saturday. The rioting continued sporadically for the next few days.

The statistics taken after the riots reported that 34 people were killed, including two law enforcement officers, and more than 1,000 people were injured. The estimated property damages exceeded $40 million, with more than 600 buildings damaged by fire or looting. More than 3,000 people were arrested, including juveniles. Of the 2,000 adult felony cases filed, more than 800 were found guilty.

The Governor's Commission

As the LAPD and the National Guard contained the majority of the rioting, Los Angeles started to return to normal. The curfew was lifted when the looting stopped, and the focus began to shift on the reasons the rioting occurred. The California governor at the time, Edmund Brown, asked for a commission to be formed to seek an immediate explanation for the riots. The commission, headed by John McCone (and subsequently known as the "McCone Commission") consisted of notable representatives from all levels of government, law enforcement, and the local communities. The goal of the commission was to provide an objective viewpoint on the root causes of the Los Angeles riots.

The McCone Commission took 100 days before publishing their final report. The 90-page report consisted of an extensive background on the social and economic conditions of Los Angeles, specifically regarding Black and other minority communities. The report not only highlighted several key areas that may have significantly contributed to the pervasive discontent but also provided several recommendations on how to address these areas. One conclusion was that there was no single root cause for why these riots occurred. Rather, the commission reported that the riots were a symptom of the larger social, psychological, and economic picture of the minority communities in Los Angeles in the 1960s.

The commission recommended several major changes. One of these recommendations involved revamping police tactics and involvement within the communities to improve police–community relations. These improved relations would allow the communication lines to be more open between communities and law enforcement. Another change recommended was to minimize the social isolation Black communities feel. This could be accomplished by integrating community programs between the suburban White communities and the central district Black communities. A third change recommended by the McCone Commission was to provide more social programs targeting minority youth in order to prevent the discontent and frustration caused by poor education and limited employment opportunities. Ultimately, the McCone Commission called for improved leadership in government administration, law enforcement, businesses, schools, and the communities.

Criticisms of the McCone Commission Report

Although the McCone Commission accomplished its goal of promptly delivering a detailed report of the Los Angeles Riots of 1965, it has been criticized as being hastily written and only scratching the surface of the deeper problems manifested during the riots. Critics argue that the McCone Commission was established to appease the public and make it appear that something was being done to prevent future rioting. Therefore, critics say many of the conclusions drawn in the McCone Commission report are vague, ambiguous, and abstract. Additionally, the theories proposed apply only to specific facets of the riots but not to the social situation as a whole. One criticism of the McCone Commission report is that it marginalized the riots by stating that they were unwarranted and not directly connected to the general discontent felt by the minority communities. Another criticism is that the commission failed to understand the true plight of the minority communities and stereotyped many of the social perceptions incorrectly.

The Los Angeles Riots of 1965 had been difficult to predict as well as difficult to stifle. Whether the riots occurred because of one incident or because of a series of events creating widespread racial discontent, it is certain the riots terrorized Los Angeles for 6 days. The McCone Commission proffered several policy changes that could be effective; however, solving the root problems of racial discontent would continue to pose problems. Los Angeles would experience more riots throughout the next 30 years.

Jennifer Lasswell

See also Los Angeles Race Riots of 1992; Race Relations; Race Riots; Zoot Suit Riots

Further Readings

Baldassare, M. (Ed.). (1994). *The Los Angeles riots: Lessons for the urban future.* Boulder, CO: Westview.

Fogelson, R. M. (Ed.). (1969). *Mass violence in America: The Los Angeles riots.* New York: Arno Press and the New York Times.

Jacobs, P. (1967). *Prelude to riot: A view of urban America from the bottom.* New York: Random House.

Menninger, W. W. (1970). Violence and the urban crisis. *Crime & Delinquency, 16,* 229–237.

Los Angeles Race Riots of 1992

The connection between race and crime is clear in the Los Angeles Riots of 1992. The message sent by the acquittal of four White officers accused of assaulting and using excessive force on a Black man struck a chord across the country. In the years following the civil rights movement and the Watts Riots in the 1960s, Los Angeles had remained highly segregated, with poverty and economic inequalities concentrated within the African American population. The acquittal of the White officers was the proverbial last straw for many Los Angelenos, igniting riots across the city in protest to the inequalities and prejudice felt by many African Americans. Lasting 5 days, the riots resulted in death and injuries among rioters and innocent bystanders, as well as property damage. The riots live on in infamy for those who survived in Los Angeles and those who watched the gruesome scenes unfold on television. Many researchers have compiled studies on how the Los Angeles Riots of 1992 affected the country, ushering in a tide of awareness of the inequalities inherent in American life as well as issues within the criminal justice system.

The Beginning

Shortly after midnight on March 3, 1991, Rodney King was driving down Interstate 210, the Foothill Freeway in Los Angeles. Police officers Tim and Melanie Singer, members of the California Highway Patrol, signaled King's speeding car to pull over, beginning a 7.8-mile pursuit. King's Hyundai Excel was clocked at speeds of 110 to 115 mph while on the freeway and about 85 mph on residential streets. As King led police through the streets of Los Angeles, the Los Angeles Police Department (LAPD) joined pursuit. In total, there were about 15 LAPD officers, including an LAPD helicopter. When King finally heeded orders to stop near Hansen Dam Park, he ignored commands to step out of the vehicle. Officers on the scene described his behavior as erratic; he seemed drunk or under the influence of phencyclidine (PCP). Tasers were readied for action, as King's behavior alarmed Sergeant Stacey Koon. Officers Theodore Briseno, Laurence Powell, Timothy Wind, and Rolando Solano attempted to restrain King, grabbing his arms and legs. Throwing the officers off, King was again ordered to lie on the ground. The Taser was fired as King ignored commands. Unaffected by the Tasings, King appeared to lunge toward officers; they were ordered to hit King with their batons. Throughout the beating, Officers Powell, Briseno, and Wind and Sergeant Koon struck King multiple times with batons and kicked him. King suffered multiple skull fractures, a fractured fibula, brain damage, kidney damage, contusions, bruises, and abrasions. In his own words, he felt like "a crushed can." King was arrested and taken to jail; the report did not refer to the beating explicitly but simply stated that force had been used to make the arrest.

In an apartment across the street, George Holliday had been awakened by the noise of sirens and the hovering LAPD helicopter. As he watched the events unfold from his apartment, he recorded the scene with his video camera. Holliday held onto the tape until March 4, when he delivered it to a local television station, KTLA. As the video was broadcast on television, word of the incident quickly spread across the nation.

The Trial

Many Los Angeles residents and citizens across the country were outraged at the behavior of the LAPD. The videotape provided evidence that the police assaulted a man for no apparent reason. Attention shifted to the police; Koon, Powell, Wind, and Briseno were charged with assault with a deadly weapon and using excessive force. The charges against King were dropped. As the investigation into the behavior of the officers began, it was broadcast from opening statement to verdict across television and radio.

Before the trial began, a request for a change of venue was made due to the extensive media coverage of the incident in Los Angeles County. From March 1991 until the end of the riots, Holliday's videotape was aired 246 times on the three major news networks: ABC, NBC, and CBS. It was presumed that a large proportion of those drawn for jury duty in Los Angeles had already heard of the case and seen the videotape. The trial was moved to Simi Valley in nearby Ventura County. On April 29, 1992, at 3:00 p.m., the jury brought back not guilty verdicts on all charges except for a charge of excessive force against Officer Powell. That charge was later dismissed. All four were later tried in federal court on charges of violating King's civil rights; Powell and Koon were convicted and sentenced to 30 months in prison.

Critics cite several reasons for the acquittals in the criminal trial. Rather than the police, it seemed to be King who was on trial. Continual reference to the trial as the "Rodney King Trial" and the prosecutor's opening statement, which included more than a half-hour focused on the laws that King had broken (driving while intoxicated and evading officers while on probation), added speculation about the verdict. The jury itself, selected in Ventura County, a predominately White area, may not have been representative of King's peers. The videotape, often cited as clear-cut evidence of the use of excessive force, was cited as a reason for the verdict. An additional portion of the tape, left out by the media, was revealed to the jury; it showed what appeared to be King lunging at police. These few seconds were said to have been justification for the actions of the LAPD officers.

Reaction

After the verdict was announced, anger and outrage were common responses as news spread across the Los Angeles area. Crowds began to gather in south central Los Angeles to discuss the verdict. Many were outraged that what appeared to be blatant assault was not seen as excessive force in the eyes of the law. King had been severely beaten by four LAPD officers, and in the crowds' eyes, the criminal justice system had not delivered justice. Growing more enraged, the crowds developed into mobs of rioters. The first incidents of looting were reported around 4:15 p.m. on Florence Boulevard and Normandie Avenue. Motorists were assaulted and pulled from their cars. A large percentage of the rioters were young males who engaged in looting, assault, arson, and even murder.

As the riots escalated, police officers who were posted in south central Los Angeles were ordered to stand down. Essentially, the LAPD abandoned certain areas of the city to prevent harm to themselves, in effect allowing the riots to continue. The riots continued through the night as fires were set and property destroyed. Though the Justice Department announced that it would be continuing investigation into the Rodney King incident, rioters were not quelled; the riots now symbolized more than retaliation. The governor of California, Pete Wilson, declared a state of emergency, and by May 1 the National Guard, the Army, and the Marines were called in to help calm the riots. Their orders were simple: Fire when fired upon.

During the riots some particularly gruesome incidents occurred. On top of the looting, fires, and gun shots that rang through the city of Los Angeles, there were reports of personal violence against White individuals. Reginald Denny, a White truck driver, was pulled from his truck at an intersection on Normandie Avenue. He had assumed that the cargo in his truck—sand—would be of no value or interest to looters. Denny's memory of the events are not very clear, but a news helicopter overhead filmed the entire event. Rioters threw rocks through the windshield of Denny's truck before dragging him to the ground, kicking him and beating him with a barrage of blows using various items, including a slab of concrete. When Denny lost consciousness, the rioters abandoned

Denny's body and left looters to clean out his pockets. His body was rescued by an African American man, and he was treated by paramedics. The video of Denny's beating was shown on television—a message to all viewers about the conditions in Los Angeles. It appeared that the Black community was retaliating for Rodney King's beating—if four White men could beat a Black man and get away with it, Black men could do the same to a White man. Los Angeles had resorted to an-eye-for-an-eye justice. Throughout the city, citizens of Asian and Hispanic ethnicities were also beaten by rioters.

A large portion of the rioting took place in the areas of south central Los Angeles and Koreatown but extended well beyond these areas. Stores targeted were most likely to be owned by Korean Americans, not Caucasians. As the LAPD became overwhelmed with the chaos that ensued, many civilians took it upon themselves to defend their families, property, and stores. Pictures from the riots often show Korean Americans firing back against the rioters and looters attempting to take items from their stores. While this action on the part of Korean Americans may have seemed like a natural course of events as self-defense, it only added to the violence already rampant on the streets.

The riots were declared over when Los Angeles Mayor Tom Bradley lifted the dusk-until-dawn curfew on the city. By the time the National Guard left on May 8, there were reports of more than $1 billion worth of damage to the area. Of the 51 persons who died, 26 were African American, 14 were Latino, 9 were White (non-Hispanic), and 2 were Asian. The races and ethnicities of some who died in fires could not be determined. Injuries reportedly totaled 2,383, and more than 5,000 individuals had been arrested.

While the Rodney King incident may seem to have been the catalyst for the riots, other precipitating factors existed in Los Angeles. Living conditions in Los Angeles, especially in south central where much of the riots were concentrated, were less than ideal. One major factor cited is the changing population. While south central Los Angeles had been a predominantly African American area, the Hispanic population was increasing in 1992. Shifting power in the area was also a point of contention, as the two groups competed and racial prejudices and conflicts developed. Tensions frequently rose between the longtime residents (African Americans) and the new kids on the block (Hispanic Americans). In addition to the racial and ethnic conflict, the poverty in the area has also been cited as a catalyst for the riots. Aside from high rates of unemployment in the area of south central, Los Angeles was poor in general. Many businesses, banks, and other institutions, including the local government, had moved out. Racial tensions in general between residents of south central and the LAPD were already high before the Rodney King beating. It had long been suggested that the LAPD engaged in racial profiling: targeting racial or ethnic minorities, such as African Americans.

After the riots, many hoped that the conditions in Los Angeles would improve. Sadly, that hope would not quickly be realized. Many business owners struggled to rebuild their sources of income in the wake of the riots. Rioters served jail time, and those injured struggled to pay their medical bills. Many African Americans moved out of south central, making way for an influx of Hispanic Americans. Though the riots shed light on the plight of those living in Los Angeles, specifically poor African Americans, for many people changes in the area were gradual. The riots affected individuals across the country, highlighting the inequalities and magnifying instances of racial prejudice not only in Los Angeles but everywhere.

Kristin Lavin

See also Intraracial Crime; King, Rodney; Police Use of Force; Race Riots

Further Readings

Baldassare, M. (Ed.). (1994). *The Los Angeles Riots: Lessons for the urban future.* Boulder, CO: Westview.

Cannon, L. (1997). *Official negligence: How Rodney King and the riots changed Los Angeles and the LAPD.* New York: Random House.

Gooding-Williams, R. (Ed.). (1993). *Reading Rodney King/Reading urban uprising.* New York: Routledge.

Olzak, S., Shanahan, S., & McEneaney, E. (1996). Poverty, segregation, and race riots: 1960 to 1993. *American Sociological Review, 61,* 590–613.

Tervalon, J. (2002). *Geography of rage: Remembering the Los Angeles riots of 1992.* Los Angeles: Really Great Books.

LYNCHING

Lynching involves mob violence that is done under the guise of vigilante justice. It has played an extraordinarily important role in American history. For example, from the end of the Civil War in 1865 through the middle of the 20th century, African Americans were subjected to horrific lynchings, often sanctioned by the state, that were aimed at keeping them in their "proper place" in the political, economic, social, cultural, and legal order. "Nigger hunts" and "coon barbecues" were carefully calculated to achieve a common end: limiting the rights of free Blacks, forcing them into submission, and returning them to their pre–Civil War slave status. It should be noted that lynching also occurred in the western United States, with Latinos, Native Americans, and Asian Americans being the targets of the violence. This entry focuses primarily on lynching targeted at African Americans in the southern United States.

The Mechanics of Lynching

Each lynching was wholly unique. They were generally spontaneous events—a response to a local crisis, rumored or real—that escalated into a deadly drama. Lynch mobs were often made up of a collection of local rabble and respected upper-class citizens who added moral authority and legitimacy to the lynching process. Some lynch mobs consisted of only two, three, or four "righteous" citizens; others were composed of hundreds, even thousands, of participants and curious onlookers, including women and children. Some mobs held informal trials; others dispensed with any semblance of legal formality.

Moreover, they did not always kill their victims. Whipping, beating, branding, and tarring and feathering were sometimes used for lesser offenses, especially before the 1880s. But serious crimes, especially attacks on White women by "savage Black beasts," warranted a more dramatic and bloody response, one that would serve as an example and deterrent to other "disrespectful niggers." Hanging, burning, and a variety of barbaric tortures—for example, cutting off fingers, toes, or ears—were common. Rapists were frequently castrated. The sexual organ was a prized souvenir.

The 1899 execution of Sam Hose in Georgia reflects the elaborate rituals and bloody carnival of fury that surrounded many Black lynchings. Hose, a farm hand charged with killing his employer and then ravishing his wife, was captured by a lynch mob on April 23, 1899. A crowd of more than 3,000 spectators—some coming aboard a special excursion train from Atlanta, arriving after church services—assembled to witness the ritual. Hose was stripped, chained to a tree, surrounded with logs, and doused with kerosene. His face was skinned and his fingers, ears, and genitals cut off. Then, the fire was lit. After death, his bones were broken and sold as souvenirs, along with his extremities and body parts. Hose's knuckles were put in a jar and placed on display in a grocery store. Mob members were proud of their work. They traveled to the state capitol to present the governor with a souvenir from their work. He declined.

Spectacles of Hose-like public savagery were common. Jesse Washington was dragged from a Waco, Texas, courtroom on May 8, 1916, minutes after a jury convicted him of raping a White woman. Washington was kicked, beaten, stabbed, doused with oil, and suspended from a tree limb. His fingers, toes, ears, and penis were cut off. Then, he was set on fire. A man on horseback dragged his charred corpse through the streets.

The 1934 Florida lynching of Claude Neal was equally brutal. Neal, a farm worker accused of killing a White woman, was abducted by a mob, which then took 2 days to plan the execution. The Associated Press followed the case closely, providing announcements of when, where, and how the lynching was to take place. A crowd of more than 7,000 spectators from 11 states gathered to witness the event. Newspapers provided graphic first-hand accounts: Neal's penis and testicles were cut off; he was poked with hot irons, cut with a knife, and strung up. After several hours, he died. His body was tied to a truck and dragged to the home of the victim's mother, where the orgy of violence continued. Neal's ravaged remains were then put on display in the courthouse.

Women were not exempt from mob violence. In May 1918, Mary Turner threatened to pursue legal action against Georgia mob members who had lynched her husband. She paid for her insolence. A large crowd, including women and children, assembled to witness Mary Turner receive southern justice. Mary, who was 8 months pregnant, was stripped, hung by her ankles, doused with gasoline, and set on fire. Before the flames engulfed her, a mob member pulled out a knife and slit open her stomach. As soon as the baby fell to the ground, its head was smashed under a boot heel.

Lynching: The Body Count

The body count is staggering. Although estimates vary, Walter White (1929) uncovered 4,951 lynchings in the United States between 1882 and 1927. Predictably, most of this violence was racially driven: 3,513 Blacks and 1,438 Whites. Ninety-two females were also killed: 76 Blacks and 16 Whites. Seventy-four percent of these lynchings occurred in 10 southern states:

Mississippi:	561 (517 Blacks, 44 Whites)
Georgia:	549 (510 Blacks, 39 Whites)
Texas:	534 (370 Blacks, 164 Whites)
Louisiana:	409 (347 Blacks, 62 Whites)
Alabama:	356 (304 Blacks, 52 Whites)
Arkansas:	313 (244 Blacks, 69 Whites)
Florida:	275 (247 Blacks, 28 Whites),
Tennessee:	268 (213 Blacks, 55 Whites)
Kentucky:	253 (154 Blacks, 79 Whites)
South Carolina:	174 (165 Blacks, 9 Whites)

Several states—New Hampshire, Vermont, Rhode Island, Delaware—had no lynchings. Western lynch mobs were formed primarily to deal with White criminals: thieves, cattle rustlers, rapists, and murderers. In fact, several western states and territories—Arizona (31), Idaho (21), and Nevada (6) lynched only Whites. Lynching was primarily a late 19th-century phenomenon. Mob violence peaked in 1892, with 253 recorded lynchings in the United States and the next highest numbers being 211 in 1884 and 200 in 1893. According to White (1929), lynchings steadily declined in the 20th century: 1890–1900 recorded 1,665; 1900–1910 saw 921; 1910–1920 saw 840, 1920–1927 saw 304.

These statistics do not, however, reflect the full body count. Some lynchings were recorded as murders, with no indication of the dynamics of death. Moreover, some victims were disposed of without a trace, leaving their families to say that their loved ones had "disappeared" or "gone missing." Newspaper coverage, which served as a foundation for lynching tallies, was erratic, especially when it became a relatively common occurrence (i.e., "hardly newsworthy"). Sheriffs and police officials, especially in the South, sometimes recorded lynchings as "justifiable homicide" or "suicide."

Attacks on Blacks committed during riots were not recorded. In the 1863 New York Draft Riot, for example, an unknown number of Blacks, some hung from telegraph poles and lamp posts, were killed by White rioters. Blacks were also murdered with impunity in riots in New Orleans (1900), Atlanta, Georgia (1906), Springfield, Illinois (1908), East St. Louis, Illinois, (1917), and Chicago, Illinois (1919). Lynchings were also an integral component of "clearances." Blacks were given a choice: Leave the area and abandon your homes and possessions, or face death. Some clearances were aimed at driving out individuals or families. Others involved mass clearances—for example, Wilmington, North Carolina (1898), and Rosewood, Florida (1923)—that drove virtually every Black resident out of town.

Although most accounts of lynching in the United States have focused on violence against African Americans in the South, Gonzales-Day uncovered 350 instances in California between 1850 and 1935. Most of these victims were Latinos, Native Americans, and Asian Americans, with the greatest number being Latino.

Terrorizing Black America: Lynching and Social Control

The unpredictable nature of White mobs terrorized African Americans. African American males knew that a charge of rape, assault, or remotely improper behavior directed at a White woman was tantamount to a death sentence, especially in the South. But Blacks were also lynched for a range of other "socially unacceptable" acts: stealing a chicken, stealing a shoe, making an insulting remark, saying hello, bumping into a girl, jostling a horse, being involved in a buggy collision, refusing to remove a military uniform, testifying for a Negro, writing an improper note, refusing to dance on a White's command, trying to pass as a White man, refusing to move, being boastful, committing slander, accruing personal debt, discussing a lynching, public drunkenness, disorderly conduct, failing to yield the sidewalk, refusing to take off a hat to a White person, resisting assault by a White person, improper laughing, and finally, displaying a sarcastic grin.

Black Americans were fully aware that education, personal achievement, and social status would not protect them from mob violence. James Weldon Johnson, executive director of the National Association for the Advancement of Colored People (NAACP), was nearly lynched in Florida in 1901 for sitting on a park bench with a White woman. Walter White, Weldon's successor as the NAACP's executive director, was nearly lynched during the 1906 Atlanta race riot when he was just 12 years old and on several other occasions when he was working as an undercover NAACP investigator. In 1946, a group of armed Black World War II veterans rescued a lawyer who had just won a case in Tennessee involving two Black defendants. Spared from the hangman's noose, Thurgood Marshall went on to become the nation's first Black Supreme Court Justice.

Black Americans also knew that they could not rely on the criminal justice system to protect them from lynching. Sympathetic sheriffs aided mobs by failing to adequately protect their prisoners and by revealing transportation routes and arranging abductions. In some instances, they directly coordinated and openly participated in the execution. Despite the fact that mob members did not wear masks and often posed for photos—even lynching postcards, which were legally sent through the mail—investigations rarely resulted in arrests. If an arrest was made, prosecutors dropped the charges. Judges who might be facing reelection did not want to anger voters. Jurors were often ardent racists or did not want to face the wrath of the community by convicting their White neighbors.

On a larger contextual scale, the U.S. Supreme Court provided indirect cover for lynching by issuing a series of rulings that reinforced the sanctity of states' rights. Federal investigators and courts were blocked from intervening in lynching cases

until the middle of the 20th century. Put simply, bigots—sometimes members of the Ku Klux Klan—were in charge of southern justice.

"Nigger hunts" received direct and indirect support from a number of sources. Some southern governors, senators, and congressmen openly endorsed lynching. Ben Tillman, South Carolina's governor and later a U.S. senator, maintained that Blacks were related to baboons and that slavery was the best thing that ever happened to the African race. In a 1903 speech on the Senate floor, Tillman proudly described his role in stuffing ballot boxes, disenfranchising Blacks, and participating in lynch mobs. A number of conservative Protestant evangelical ministers were also avid racists, preaching that lynching was a necessary evil, especially when the cursed children of Ham assaulted White women.

"Scientific evolutionary theories" provided indirect justification for lynching by supporting notions of Negro inferiority. In 1890, Daniel Brinton, professor of archaeology at the University of Pennsylvania, declared that Blacks were located somewhere between orangutans and European Whites on the evolutionary scale. Louis Agassiz, chairman of the anthropology department at Harvard University, maintained that Africans were a separate and inferior species. Late 19th- and early 20th-century Social Darwinists were firmly convinced that the quality of American racial stock was being diluted by immigrants and Blacks. Eugenicists called for protective measures: immigration restriction, miscegenation laws, as well as laws permitting the sterilization of criminals and mental defectives. For eugenical extremists, lynching was a form of race control: God-approved social engineering.

Antilynching Campaigns

Lynching did not go unchallenged. Ida Wells-Barnett, a Black journalist who was enraged by an 1892 Tennessee lynching, was the nation's foremost antilynching campaigner, writing books and newspaper articles and giving speeches across the United States and in Europe. Frederick Douglass, William Monroe Trotter, W. E. B. Du Bois, Walter White, and dozens of other Black civil rights leaders also campaigned against lynching. Black and White organizations—the National Association of

Colored Women, National Association for the Advancement of Colored People, British Anti-Lynching Committee, Association of Southern Women for the Prevention of Lynching—launched national and international campaigns aimed at exposing the horrors of lynching.

Courageous White governors, senators, and congressmen battled southern bigots, vainly trying to pass antilynching legislation: Dyer Act, Wagner-Costigan Bill, Gavagan Bill. Liberal academicians—sociologists, psychologists, and biologists—provided scathing critiques of studies that argued that Blacks were biologically, mentally, and morally inferior. Conservative southern Protestant ministers eventually joined Catholic and Jewish religious leaders in denouncing racism and lynching. Southern newspapers, responding to public pressure and rising standards of journalism, increasingly called for an end to "nigger hunts." In the 1950s and 1960s, the U.S. Supreme Court issued a series of rulings that expanded due process rights for Black citizens and dismantled the racist shield of states' rights. The Federal Bureau of Investigation conducted lynching investigations. Collectively considered, Hose-like lynching carnivals became morally, politically, and legally risky.

Declining southern support for lynching was, however, largely a function of economics. Northern and European business interests became increasingly reluctant to invest in a part of the country that engaged in crass barbarity. A low point: the Nazis mocked Americans for preaching equality, democracy, and justice and then tolerating, if not supporting, lynching. But southern businessmen and farmers had more immediate concerns.

Lynching, the sharecropping system, Jim Crow laws, political disenfranchisement, discrimination in housing, health care, recreation, and education made life in the South intolerable for Blacks. During World War I and World War II, millions of southern Blacks migrated to the North to work in factories and seek a better life. The loss of servants, sharecroppers, factory workers, and skilled artisans created severe labor shortages that alarmed southerners, including the Ku Klux Klan. Simply stated, lynching was bad for business.

National responses to two mid-20th-century lynchings reflected this new mind-set. In November 1933, Governor James Rolph of California created an international sensation by openly supporting a lynching. After hearing that two suspected murderers were going to be abducted by a San Jose mob, Rolph declined an invitation to an out-of-state governor's convention, fearing that his lieutenant governor, who would be acting governor, would thwart the lynching. According to plan, the mob stormed the jail and hung the suspected murderers. Rolph sparked an international debate by openly commending the mob. Rolph's decision was hailed by a number of groups, including the editors of the *Harvard Crimson*. But many other prominent religious, media, and legal organizations denounced the governor, calling him a national disgrace.

The August 1955 murder of 14-year-old Emmett Till in Mississippi, who was killed for whistling at a White woman in a convenience store, was another pivotal event in the history of American lynching and race relations. Till's deformed and bloated body was displayed in an open casket. The nation, with the exception of ardent racists, was shamed and enraged. The age of bloody state-sanctioned orgies of violence was at an end.

The efforts of antilynching crusaders did not, however, end racism or racist killings. By the late 1940s and 1950s, the age of public sadistic spectacles—burning bodies, taking souvenirs, posing for pictures, circulating lynching postcards—was clearly over. Racially motivated killings were increasingly carried out by individuals or small groups of men who committed their acts in secrecy, shunning publicity. Numerous unsuccessful attempts have been made to pass federal legislation outlawing lynching, although it would now fall under the definition of a hate crime. In 2005, an antilynching resolution was passed by the Senate apologizing to victims of lynching for the Senate's historical and consistent failure to outlaw lynching.

Lynching is not merely a historical curiosity. Black Americans who grew up in the South under Jim Crow in the 1950s and 1960s still remember riding in the backs of buses, being prohibited from entering restaurants, drinking out of "colored only" water fountains, and being forced to attend segregated schools. For them, the threat of lynching and "underground lynching" was real. "Nigger hunts" and "coon barbecues" provide a troubling reminder that the United States has a long history of racial oppression and state-sanctioned savage cruelty. The 1998 murder of James Byrd, who was chained to a pickup truck and dragged to death on a rural Texas road by three White men, was a demonstration of the continued existence of racial brutality.

Alexander W. Pisciotta

See also African Americans; Black Codes; Du Bois, W. E. B.; Dyer Bill; Hate Crimes; Ku Klux Klan; Ku Klux Klan Act; Race Riots; Till, Emmett; Tulsa, Oklahoma, Race Riot of 1921; Wells-Barnett, Ida B.

Further Readings

Allen, J., Als, H., Lewis, J., & Litwack, L. F. (2004). *Without sanctuary: Lynching photography in America.* Santa Fe, NM: Twin Palms.

Ayres, E. L. (1984). *Vengeance and justice: Crime and punishment in the 19th-century American South.* New York: Oxford University Press.

Dray, P. (2002). *At the hands of persons unknown: The lynching of Black America.* New York: Modern Library.

Gonzales-Day, K. (2006). *Lynching in the West: 1850–1935.* Durham, NC: Duke University Press.

Litwack, L. F. (1998). *Trouble in mind: Black southerners in the age of Jim Crow.* New York: Vintage Books.

Patterson, O. (1998). *Rituals of blood: Consequences of slavery in two American centuries.* New York: Basic Civitas Books.

Royster, J. J. (Ed.). (1997). *Southern horrors and other writings: The anti-lynching campaign of Ida B. Wells, 1892–1900.* Boston: Bedford Books.

White, W. (1929). *Rope and faggot: A biography of Judge Lynch.* New York: Knopf.